The Australian

Wine
Annual
2008

The Definitive Guide to Australian Wine

Your complete guide to drinking pleasure
with nearly 10,000 wines rated

- ■ Alphabetical, indexed and easy to follow
- ■ Tasting notes for every new release
- ■ Australia's best under-$20 wines
- ■ Labels for all wines in full colour

Published and designed in Australia.

Jeremy Oliver
565 Burwood Rd Hawthorn, Victoria, 3122 Australia
Tel: 61 3 9819 4400   Fax: 61 3 9819 5322

Printed by	KHL Printing Co Pte Ltd, Singapore
Design and Layout by	Artifishal Studios, Melbourne, Victoria, Australia
Distributed to book retailers in Australia by	Macmillan Publishing Services Free call 1800 684 459 Free fax 1800 241 310
Distributed to wine retailers in Australia by	Fine Wine Partners Tel: 1300 668 712 Fax: 1300 668 512

Copyright © Jeremy Oliver 2007

ISBN 978-0-9581032-9-9

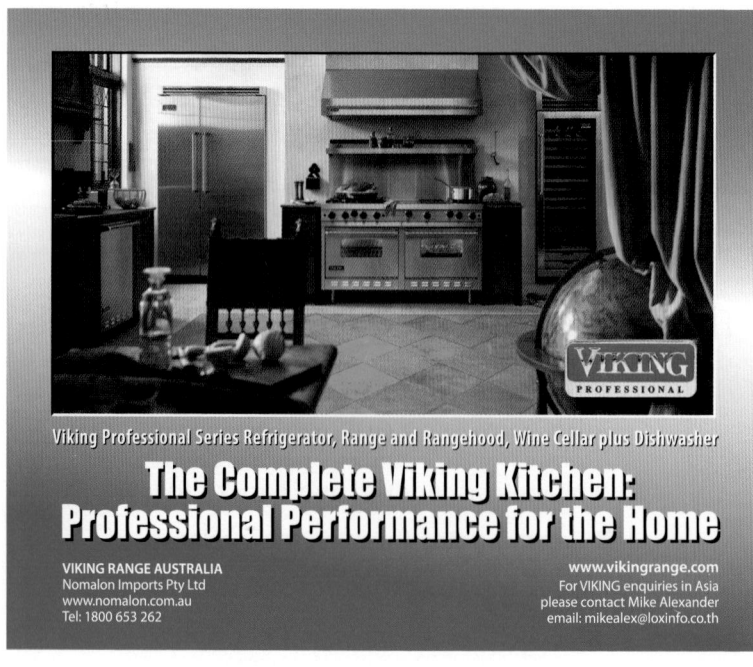

Contents

Introduction

It has been a tumultuous year for Australian wine. Twelve months ago there was a surplus of wine in this country, which a large proportion of the industry was attempting to deal with by making it ever more accessible and affordable.

The tables have turned, for today Australia is actually bordering on a wine deficit. The over-supply has gone up in smoke. Against a surplus of around 460 million litres, the vintage was deficient by approximately 350 million litres. So even while export growth was on par for a correction in about 18 months, it has virtually happened overnight.

Furthermore, despite plentiful rainfalls in the southeast corner of the continent, it remains extremely unlikely that there will be much other than maintenance allocations of water for vine irrigation in the Murray-Darling basin, which produces around 65% of Australian wine. In other words, while there is less concern that vines will die from severe moisture stress, it is unlikely that the 2008 vintage will exceed the small harvest of 2007.

That outcome will further tilt in the balance between demand and supply, so wine prices must increase. Furthermore and crucially, the wine industry has finally realised that Australia is not the logical source of the world's cheapest wine and that the ultra-cheap market should always have been left to competitors with lower costs and cheaper land.

The short 2007 harvest indirectly increased costs, as wineries paid between 15–20% more for fruit and processing costs increased by around 33%. Most costs associated with winemaking are fixed, so in a small season the only savings that can be made are in power usage and to some extent in new oak.

These are the short-term reasons why Australian wine must become more expensive, something it can do and still remain extremely competitive. The long-term reasons have more to do with the sort of wine industry Australia wants to have, which is in my view some distance from what it has today.

The wine industry has to be viable. It is not in the interests of anyone who supports Australian wine, from the growers to the consumers, for it not to be a profitable source of business. But the current reality is a sobering one. If the wine industry cannot increase the value of its net business (domestic and export) from $26 billion to $30 billion over the next five years, its future is under a cloud. By and large, the industry will not have produced a sufficient return to be economically sustainable. Starkly, if it continues doing business as it currently is, it will trade itself into oblivion.

The value of the domestic Australian wine industry has fallen by $200 million in wholesale value from 2002/2003 to 2005/2006. The average wholesale price per litre has fallen from $5.21 per litre to $4.44 per litre in the same period. I regularly taste wine that in any other time would be considered too good for its price-point.

If the industry as we know it is to survive, growers and makers need not only to meet costs, but also to make profits. Today much of the wine industry is publicly listed, and its shareholders expect returns. Too many small family-owned wineries are just hanging in there, saved only from receivership by the Federal Government's increase in Wine Equalisation Tax rebate.

Hopefully, the changing circumstances will hasten the demise of many of the cleanskin sales operations and the various discount clearance centres that have emerged as a temporary by-product of the over-supply and the difficulties faced by many small producers in getting their wines into traditional retail outlets. Walking into them is akin to visiting a palliative care centre for dying wine brands.

Australia needs to make wine of more value and lustre, at higher price-points. As the massively increasing sales of imported wine to this country illustrate, there has been a significant improvement in the wines of other countries across wine worlds old and new. The realisation is dawning that there is more wine made on this planet than there are people to drink it. With more choices available than ever before, only those of genuine quality will last the distance.

Australia has what it takes to rise to the challenge and meet its targets; to become sustainable and then profitable in the process. However, it's going to take a lot of re-evaluation of brands, sites, wines and vineyards to do so. Heart can be taken from the fact that much of the wine presently available for $25 and under more than stacks up against its international competition on a quality basis. But much doesn't. Some companies have considerably more to do than others to raise their game to the new level demanded.

Directions to 2025

To the wine industry's credit, it recognised these issues and did something positive and tangible about them. It created a taskforce chaired by Kevin McLintock, Deputy Chairman of McWilliam's Wines and one of the industry's great modern visionaries and agent provocateurs, with a view to upgrading the market and economic intelligence behind the industry's original *Strategy 2025*, which is today an 11 year-old document. Their job was to set Australian wine with a new target and furnish it with the tools to get there.

The outcome is *Directions to 2025* — which for the sake of journalistic integrity I now declare I had a hand in drafting — a comprehensive suite of deeply considered goals and rationale. It helps individual wineries benchmark their performance, provides market intelligence, competitor analysis, web-based marketing and promotional tools and, most importantly, with a brand new communications strategy.

The key recurrent themes behind *Directions* are profitability and sustainability. Crucially, the industry recognises that its long-term profitability is closely linked with its ability to manage and conserve its environment.

The launch of *Directions* was timed to coincide with a period of research and consultation as the industry prepares to rationalise its industry bodies, to align more closely its various research activities and to take a more proactive stance in its relationship with government. One of the early steps in this process was to appoint David Clarke, chairman of Macquarie Bank, as chairman of the Winemakers Federation of Australia. His role, clearly, is to make things happen.

I applaud *Directions* and the intentions behind it. The wine industry has done as much as possible to place its destiny in its own hands. I expect it to be emulated around the world to at least the broad extent of its predecessor.

Australia's new wine communications strategy

Instead of the notional and rather meaningless 'Wine Brand Australia' message which did little other than to promote the bottom tier of its wine, Australian wine will be promoted on the strength of four discrete and eminently marketable personalities.

'Brand Champions' are exactly what they sound like, the mainstream international brands like [yellowtail], Jacob's Creek and Rosemount. 'Generation Next' encompasses wines that by some means or other express innovation or experimentation through their varietal mix, package, means of making, or whatever. It emphasises Australia's dynamic and occasionally iconoclastic attitude towards wine, as well as the country's lack of restrictive AOC-style control.

'Regional Heroes' represent Australia's well-established and successful combinations of region and variety, such as Eden Valley riesling, Hunter semillon, Margaret River chardonnay and Coonawarra cabernet. It makes perfect sense to up sell this category to existing buyers of Brand Champions, for it's easy to identify the added quality these wines represent. 'Landmark Australia' are the benchmark, iconic wines, such as the Perfect 1s (as well as many of the 2-ranking wines) in this book, identified as being amongst the best of their kind in Australia — or for that matter, anywhere.

The concept is uniquely Australian in that it is flexible, easily understood, and anything but an attempt at a classification or appellation scheme. It empowers Australians to encourage retailers to stock, and consumers to buy, our higher-value wines — by alerting them of their existence, and with its powerful inherent message to 'drink up' to better wines.

I have helped introduce this strategy into several Asian markets, and I have seen its effectiveness at first hand. If it succeeds, as I expect it will, Australian wine will have a new problem on its hands — to create more wine of genuinely international quality. This is, of course, precisely the problem it wants to have.

Australian wine has long needed a circuit breaker. This country's best wines don't have the overseas profile they actually deserve, largely because they don't comprise enough critical mass to command attention. Out top tier is still way too thin. Look at the wines that regularly appear amongst my finalists for Wine of the Year, or look at the remarkably small number of 'Perfect 1' rating wines in this book. I'd love to give out more, but…

Winemakers and growers are at present too nervous to shoot for the stars. To do so would be very expensive, the resultant wines would demand very high prices, and the wineries would have difficulty selling them because their unknown icon wines would lack the necessary prestige and track record.

You don't without good reason suddenly attempt to dethrone the wines of Bordeaux with an unheralded but super-expensive Yarra Valley cabernet. But you can tackle the most expensive Hermitage with a shiraz from Barossa or McLaren Vale, because those Australian regions are now as well recognised for shiraz as anywhere else on earth. The challenge is to give the length and breadth of top-level Australian wine the same opportunity as was famously but fortuitously given to warm-climate South Australian shiraz.

Australian wine needs more drinkers around the world to demand more from it than its very successful Brand Champions, and it also needs more of its winemakers to let go of their shackles and let the excellence of their best sites be expressed in their wines. *Directions to 2025* could perhaps be the trigger for both.

Acknowledgements

This book would not have been created without the dedicated assistance provided by a number of people. Thanks to Toby Hines, Stephen O'Connor, Robyn Heald and Frank Ameneiro of Artifishal Studios. Special thanks also to Michael Wollan, a champion in the making. Sincere thanks also to Cath Willock and Neil McLeish, as well as my father, Rodney Oliver. Thanks again to my wife, Jennifer, and son, Benjamin. Ben, next year I promise the book deadline won't be on your birthday!

Jeremy Oliver, July 2007.

How to use this book

Finding the wine or winery

It is dead easy to find the wine you're after in The Australian Wine Annual. Each winery or brand of wine is presented in alphabetic order. Under the winery heading, each of its wines or labels is then listed alphabetically. To find the tasting note and ratings for Rosemount Estate Roxburgh Chardonnay, for example, simply search for the start of Rosemount Estate's entries, which begin on page 234 then turn alphabetically through the pages to the Roxburgh Chardonnay, which appears on page 235. This year I have also experimented with a full index at the back of the book for quick scanning.

Winery information

Wherever possible, the actual address of each winery is listed in this book — not its head office or marketing office — plus its region, telephone number, fax number and web site and e-mail address if appropriate. On those occasions where the entries refer to a vineyard whose wines are made elsewhere, the address usually supplied is for the vineyard itself. So, if you're thinking of visiting a vineyard and wish to be sure whether or not it is open for public inspection, I suggest you telephone the company using the number provided.

Each winery included is accompanied by a listing of its winemaker, viticulturist and chief executive, plus brief details concerning any recent changes of ownership or direction, key wines and recent developments of interest.

The Wine Ranking

The Australian Wine Annual provides the only Australian classification of nearly all major Australian wine brands determined on the most important aspect of all: quality. Unlike the very worthwhile Langton's Classification of Distinguished Australian Wine, which presents a more limited overview of the super-premium market and which is largely based on resale price and performance at auction, the Wine Rankings in this book are not influenced in any way by price or other secondary factors. Being a secondary market, the auction market is usually slow to respond to the emergence of new quality wines, while in some cases, for example the plethora of so-called 'cult' shirazes from the Barossa and McLaren Vale, it can produce excessive prices grossly disproportionate to genuine wine quality.

The Wine Ranking is your easiest and most convenient guide to wine quality. This book allocates to the best wines in Australia a Wine Ranking from 1 to 5, based on the scores they constantly receive in my tastings, which are printed adjacent to each entry. Unless I have good reason to do otherwise, such as opening a bottle spoiled for some reason, the scores printed in this edition relate to the most recent occasion on which I have tasted each wine. Any wine to be allocated a Wine Ranking at all must have scored consistently well in my tastings. So, even if its Ranking is a lowly 5, the wine might still represent excellent value for money.

To provide a rough basis for comparison, a Wine Ranking of 1 is broadly equivalent to a Grand Cru classification in France. Several wines included in this book are not given Wine Rankings, since the minimum requirement for a ranking of 5 is still pretty steep.

At the head of the next page is a rough guide to the way Wine Rankings relate to scores out of 100, and how they compare to different medal standards used in the Australian wine show system.

Wine Ranking	Regular Score in Jeremy Oliver's Tastings	Approximate Medal Equivalent
RATING ❶	96+	Top gold medal
RATING ❷	94–95	Regular gold medal
RATING ❸	92–93	Top silver medal
RATING ❹	90–91	Regular silver medal
RATING ❺	87–89	Top bronze medal

See the flap on the inside front cover for further information.

As far as this book is concerned, if a brand of wine improves over time, so will its Wine Ranking. Similarly, if its standard declines, so will its ranking. Since Wine Rankings are largely a reflection of each label's performance over the last four years, they are unlikely to change immediately as a result of a single especially poor or exceptionally good year.

Reassessing back vintages

While I taste thousands of current and forthcoming releases each year, I also taste hundreds of back vintages. I have the classic wine writer's cellar, comprising single bottles of many wines, which I open regularly. If a wine is drinking significantly differently to the details I have previously published, I update them. Throughout the year. I also attend a large number of tastings that give me the chance to refresh my views on entire verticals of wines. These are invaluable, since they tend to even out the changes in wine fashion, viticulture and winemaking techniques that inevitably occur over time.

I believe it is important for critics to re-evaluate wine, and to be prepared to alter scores if necessary. There are so many variables that can affect the way even the most professional taster can perceive a wine from one tasting to the next that it is ludicrous for anyone to expect a wine to attract precisely the same score, time and again.

Current Price Range

With all the wines listed, I have allocated a price range within which you can usually (but not always) expect to find their latest releases.

When to drink each wine

To the right hand side of the wine listings is a column that features the suggested drinking range for every vintage of each wine included, within which I would expect each wine to reach its peak. If a '+' sign appears after a range of years, it is quite possible that well-cellared bottles may happily endure after the later year of the specified range.

These drinking windows are my estimations alone, since it's apparent that different people enjoy their wines at different stages of development. Some of us prefer the primary flavours of young wine, while others would rather the virtually decayed qualities of extremely old bottles. However, it's a day-to-day tragedy how few top Australian cellaring wines of all types and persuasions are actually opened at, or even close to, their prime.

For quick and easy reference, a broad indication of each vintage's maturity is provided with a simple colour background. The chart inside the front cover explains how the colours indicate whether a wine is drinking at its best now, will improve further if left alone, or if it is likely to be past its best.

Best Australian Wines Under $20

There has never been a better time to buy Australian wine under $20. Each of these wines has achieved a score of 90-plus, and in my estimation qualifies for at least Silver Medal status. These wines are listed here because their usual retail price is under $20, so this list does not take into account the walk-in specials, or 'loss-leaders' deployed by the large chains to attract you to shop in their stores. On any given day, some amazing wine or other is being sold somewhere for well below its genuine value.

As usual, riesling is the strongest variety by some margin. While the prices of the better rieslings have increased, there is still plenty of spectacular value with this variety for around $15, and even below.

Cabernets and Blends

Lake Breeze Cabernet Sauvignon 2004	93
Peter Lehmann Barossa Cabernet Sauvignon 2004	92
Woodlands Cabernet Merlot 2005	91
Devil's Lair Fifth Leg Red 2005	90
Grant Burge Cameron Vale Cabernet Sauvignon 2004	90
Wynns Cabernet Shiraz Merlot 2005	90

Chardonnay

Barwang Chardonnay 2005	91
Lillydale Chardonnay 2006	90
Orlando St Hilary Chardonnay 2005	90
Richmond Grove French Cask Chardonnay 2006	90
Westend 3 Bridges Chardonnay 2004	90

Riesling

The Wilson Vineyard DJW Riesling 2006	94
Alkoomi Riesling 2006	93
Jim Barry Watervale Riesling 2006	93
Bethany Eden Valley Riesling 2006	92
Delatite Riesling 2006	92
Leasingham Magnus Riesling 2006	92
McWilliams Clare Valley Riesling 2005	92
Wellington FGR Riesling 2005	92
3drops Riesling 2005	91
Feathertop Riesling 2005	91
Heggies Riesling 2006	91
Helm Wines Riesling 2005	91
Pewsey Vale Riesling 2006	91
Plantagenet Riesling 2006	91
Richmond Grove Watervale Riesling 2006	91
Bethany Riesling 2006	90
Brown Brothers Victoria Riesling 2006	90
Dal Zotto Riesling 2006	90
Domain Day Riesling 2006	90
Jacob's Creek Reserve Riesling 2005	90
Leasingham Bin 7 Riesling 2006	90
Leo Buring Eden Valley Riesling 2006	90
Peter Lehmann Eden Valley Riesling 2006	90
Pikes Traditionale Riesling 2006	90
Rockford Hand Picked Riesling 2004	90

Sauvignon Blanc

Amberley Sauvignon Blanc 2005	93
Grant Burge Kraft Sauvignon Blanc 2005	92
Smithbrook Sauvignon Blanc 2006	92
d'Arenberg The Broken Fishplate Sauvignon Blanc 2005	91
Redgate Reserve Sauvignon Blanc 2005	91
Rosily Sauvignon Blanc 2006	91

Semillon and Blends

Voyager Sauvignon Blanc Semillon 2006	93
Redgate Sauvignon Blanc Semillon 2006	91
Allandale Semillon 2005	90
Bethany Semillon 2004	90
Brokenwood Semillon 2006	90
Grant Burge Zerk Semillon Viognier 2006	90
Houghton Crofters Semillon Sauvignon Blanc 2005	90
Rosabrook Semillon Sauvignon Blanc 2005	90
St Hallett Semillon 2004	90

Shiraz and Blends

Lake Breeze Beernoota Shiraz Cabernet 2004	94
Morris Shiraz 2004	91
Angoves Vineyard Select Shiraz 2004	90
Coriole Redstone Shiraz 2004	90
Huntington Shiraz 2002	90
Metala Shiraz Cabernet 2004	90
Omrah Shiraz 2005	90
Peter Lehmann Barossa Shiraz 2004	90
Richmond Grove Limited Release Barossa Shiraz 2002	90
St Hallett Faith Shiraz 2005	90
Wynns Shiraz 2005	90

Other Reds

Bleasdale Malbec 2003	90
Heartland Dolcetto Lagrein 2005	90
Yalumba Bush Vine Grenache 2005	90

Other Whites

Lillydale Estate Gewurztraminer 2005	93
Gramp's Botrytis Semillon 2004	91
Domain Day Garganega 2006	90
Skillogalee Gewurztraminer 2005	90

Current Trends in Australian Wine

Forgive me this year if I don't spend much space dealing with the two biggest trends in Australian wine: sweet confectionary sauvignon blanc and equally sweet and confectionary rosé, some of which fizz a bit. By which, incidentally, I do not mean quality sparkling rosé. Other books deal in more depth with such wines.

So now, if I haven't lost your attention, let's consider the trends evident in quality Australian wine.

The Alternative Approach

There is an obvious move towards organic and biodynamic activity, although there is not yet a widespread understanding of these terms. And let's be clear that we're talking only about viticulture, for the term 'organic winemaking' is really little more than a con.

Will organic or biodynamic principles make a better wine? In some parts, where rain and disease are a regular hazard, it's conceivable that they might lead to a diminution of fruit quality. In more usual circumstances, however, they will result in better soil, more microbial activity, and superior vine health and nutrition.

It's still too early to correlate precisely better wine with this viticultural approach, even though I often observe the differences in soil health and texture that repeat themselves when people have changed from an old-fashioned and relatively thoughtless approach to viticulture to biodynamics. Would the same have occurred without going the whole hog, by just taking a more fastidious approach to viticulture with conventional modern means? Maybe yes, maybe no. Impossible, in many cases, to say.

Just because a vigneron has adopted biodynamics or an organic philosophy in the vineyard, there is no empirical reason for them to make better wine than their neighbour who might not. There are simply too many other variables involved, such as trellising, improved canopy management and air drainage, soil drainage and seasonal variation, to name a few. In a decade's time, we will be much better placed to understand the effects of organic and biodynamic philosophies in vineyards good, bad and ordinary.

However, much of what is being carried out under these banners is in pursuit of fewer chemicals, a genuine love and respect for land, a sense of guardianship for future generations, and a conviction that quality will ultimately come from a process that cares for the soil and nurtures the vine. In itself, that is a very good thing.

Only the crass and the incompetent will seize upon these philosophies purely to gain a marketing advantage. Sadly, many already have.

Chardonnay reinvented

There is no subtle or polite way to make this next point. If you are one of the many wine drinkers who go out of their way to shun chardonnay on the basis that it is fat, flabby, over-oaked or else just simply unfashionable, then you've got it all wrong.

Modern Australian chardonnay, season of course permitting, is a very different beast to that which your criticisms might have been more correctly applied several years ago. The market has spoken and the makers have reacted. Australian chardonnay been redrafted. It has never been better, fresher or tighter. Rejoice in that, for someone has actually listened to your comments. Deny this change and you're in danger of becoming a drinking dinosaur. Don't say you weren't warned!

Cabernet sauvignon

Finally, some of us want to drink something other than shiraz. Some of us might not actually be aware that prior to the resurgence of shiraz in the mid 1990s, Australia's most fashionable red wine was cabernet. Recently, cabernet has been made as ripe and oaky as much of our shiraz, as certain a move as possible to discourage people from drinking it.

Cabernet has been around Australia for more than 160 years, and does especially well in Margaret River, Coonawarra and the Yarra Valley. Even the Barossa, the heartbeat of modern shiraz, can deliver exceptional cabernet in cooler seasons. In Penfolds Block 42, planted during the mid 1880s, Australia has the oldest producing cabernet sauvignon vineyard in the world.

A steadily expanding band of Australian winemakers is genuinely excelling with cabernet, and some of the better expressions are high-profile enough to have reclaimed a lot of attention. The cabernets from Cullen, Moss Wood, Mount Mary, Penfolds and Woodlands are inspiring other makers to emulate their styles and standards. Larger companies are beginning to pursue cabernets that actually taste the way they should — without over-ripeness, but with an underlying structure and with an elegance and sense of finesse that is rare in shiraz. The market is perhaps beginning to realise that mature cabernet from top sites and top vintages can be every bit as delicious and intriguing as the younger shirazes and pinots they are presently enjoying. Even more so, perhaps.

New, different, and first-class!

It's taken a few years, but there are now at least three Australian sangioveses, three nebbiolos, four tempranillos and about twenty other red wines of recently-introduced parentage that are now absolutely mandatory tasting for anyone who reckons they're serious about Australian wine. Small numbers to be sure, but that's a massive improvement on what I might have suggested just two years ago.

For several years, I remained convinced that it was their novelty factor that gave so much press to wines from new varieties. I haven't changed on that, but being a hard, but hopefully also fair critic, I recognise that the best of these wines have now staked their claim on merit as well. That's why there's a steadily increasing number given coverage in this book. They demand to be here.

Tall Poppy Sommeliers

It's been a long time since I heard an Australian sommelier talk up an Australian wine. In fact, it's almost become the height of fashion within our sommelier community to talk up any wine that isn't Australian. Like many a wine enthusiast, I have been captivated and delighted by many of the new and different tastes and textures offered by contemporary offerings from places like Spain, Italy and southern France. I enjoy enthusing about some such wines, and frequently do. But it's not like football. With wine, you can support all the good teams, including the local ones.

I am the first to agree that we should move freely from wine style to wine region to wine country, even if only because they're there. It's a treat that there are so many top-level imported wines — at a range of prices — in Australia today. They expand our comprehension about wine, find their own niches in our own lifestyles, and keep our own winemakers honest. Ever felt the only wine you could drink on any given evening was a Chianti Classico from a decent maker and vintage? Or a bone-dry Austrian riesling? But that shouldn't mean that the following day you might want most in the world a Beechworth shiraz, a Yarra Valley pinot, a Margaret River cabernet or an Eden Valley riesling.

It's lamentable and inexcusable, in my view, to read time and again that Sommelier X from restaurant Y can only trot out a fairly predictable list of European wines when asked for his or her favourite recommendations. Our top wine producers can stand up in any company, and we have an emergent breed of energetic young maker and grower that will turn the wine world on its head. It's high time they were given more support by their own constituency.

The Top Tens...

People are always asking wine writers for their 'best of' lists. These questions typically draw a blank from me, for I'm always nervous about missing something out. So here are some predetermined lists of Top Tens, with a special emphasis on the most important wine varieties made in Australia today. I have tasted each of these wines within the last twelve months and, to the best of my knowledge they are all still currently available at the time of publication of this book.

The Top Ten Bargain Ranges

- Angoves Long Row
- Deakin Estate
- Jacob's Creek (especially the Reserve range)
- Hardy's Oomoo
- Leasingham Magnus
- Lindemans Bin Series
- McWilliams Hanwood
- Rosemount Diamond Series
- Wyndham Estate Bin Series
- Yalumba Y

The Top Ten Chardonnays

1. Bindi Quartz 2005 — 97
   (Macedon Ranges)
2. Pierro 2005 — 97
   (Margaret River)
3. Penfolds Yattarna 2004 — 96
   (Henty)
4. Woodlands Chloe Reserve 2006 — 96
   (Margaret River)
5. Coldstream Hills Reserve 2005 — 96
   (Yarra Valley)
6. Petaluma Tiers 2005 — 96
   (Adelaide Hills)
7. Moss Wood 2005 — 96
   (Margaret River)
8. Hardys Eileen Hardy 2004 — 95
   (Tasmania, Tumbarumba, Yarra Valley)
9. Mount Mary 2006 — 95
   (Yarra Valley)
10. Yalumba FDW7C 2005 — 95
    (Adelaide Hills)

The Top Ten Rieslings

1. Leasingham Classic Clare 2005 — 96
   (Clare Valley)
2. Jacob's Creek Steingarten 2005 — 96
   (Eden Valley)
3. Frankland Estate Isolation — 95
   Ridge 2006 (Frankland River)
4. Granite Hills 2005 — 95
   (Macedon Ranges)
5. Tim Adams Reserve 2006 — 95
   (Clare Valley)
6. Pewsey Vale The Contours 2001 — 95
   (Eden Valley)

7. Grosset Polish Hill 2006 — 95
   (Clare Valley)
8. Seppelt Drumborg 2006 — 95
   (Henty)
9. Capel Vale Whispering Hill 2007 — 95
   (Great Southern)
10. Heggies Reserve 2001 — 95
    (Eden Valley)

The Top Ten Cabernets and Blends

1. Cullen Diana Madeline 2005 — 97
   (Margaret River)
2. Woodlands Margaret
   Cabernet Merlot 2005 — 97
   (Margaret River)
3. Penfolds Bin 707 2004 — 97
   (Barossa Valley, McLaren Vale, Coonawarra)
4. Petaluma Coonawarra 2004 — 97
   (Coonawarra)
5. Mount Mary Quinet 2005 — 96
   (Yarra Valley)
6. Woodlands 2005 — 96
   (Margaret River)
7. Wynns Coonawarra Estate John
   Riddoch 2004 — 96
   (Coonawarra)
8. Voyager Estate
   Cabernet Sauvignon Merlot 2003 — 96
   (Margaret River)
9. Hardys Thomas Hardy 2004 — 96
   (Margaret River)
10. Wantirna Estate Hannah
    Cabernet Franc Merlot 2005 — 96
    (Yarra Valley)

The Top Ten Pinot Noirs

1. Bindi Block 5 2005 — 97
   (Macedon Ranges)
2. Coldstream Hills Reserve 2005 — 96
   (Yarra Valley)
3. Main Ridge Estate Half Acre 2005 — 96
   (Mornington Peninsula)
4. Bass Phillip Reserve 2005 — 96
   (South Gippsland)
5. Moondarra Samba Side 2005 — 95
   (Gippsland)
6. Yeringberg 2005 — 95
   (Yarra Valley)

7. Epis 2005 (Macedon Ranges)	95
8. Yarra Yering 2005 (Yarra Valley)	95
9. Bay of Fires 2005 (Tasmania)	95
10. Kooyong Haven 2004 (Mornington Peninsula)	95

The Top Ten Dry Semillons

1. Thomas Braemore 2006 (Lower Hunter Valley)	94
2. Moss Wood 2006 (Margaret River)	94
3. Mount Pleasant Lovedale 2006 (Lower Hunter Valley)	93
4. Thomas OC 2006 (Lower Hunter Valley)	93
5. Capercaillie The Creel 2006 (Lower Hunter Valley)	93
6. Henschke Louis 2006 (Eden Valley)	93
7. Killerby 2006 (Geographe)	93
9. Tyrrell's Single Vineyard HVD 2001 (Lower Hunter Valley)	92
9. Rockford Local Growers 2004 (Barossa Valley)	92
10. Briar Ridge Karl Stockhausen 2006 (Lower Hunter Valley)	92

The Top Ten Shiraz

1. Henschke Hill of Grace 2002 (Eden Valley)	97
2. Penfolds Grange 2002 (South Australia)	97
3. Oliver's Taranga HJ Reserve 2002 (McLaren Vale)	97
4. Primo Estate Joseph Angel Gully 2004 (McLaren Vale)	96

5. Wynns Coonawarra Estate Michael 2004 (Coonawarra)	96
6. Langmeil The Freedom 2004 (Barossa Valley)	96
7. Penfolds RWT 2004 (Barossa Valley)	96
8. Hardys Eileen Hardy 2004 (McLaren Vale predom.)	96
9. Giaconda Warner Vineyard 2005 (Beechworth)	96
10. Peter Lehmann Stonewell 2002 (Barossa Valley)	96

The Top Ten Wines from New Varieties

1. Castagna Un Segreto Sangiovese Syrah 2005 (Beechworth)	96
2. Primo Estate Joseph Nebbiolo 2005 (McLaren Vale)	95
3. Tim Adams Reserve Tempranillo 2005 (Clare Valley)	94
4. Pizzini Coronamento Nebbiolo 2002 (King Valley)	94
5. Freeman Rondinella Corvina 2003 (Hilltops)	93
6. Dal Zotto Arneis 2006 (King Valley)	93
7. Pizzini Nebbiolo 2002 (King Valley)	93
8. Primo Estate Il Briccone Shiraz Sangiovese 2005 (McLaren Vale)	91
9. Dal Zotto Prosecco 2005 (King Valley)	91
10. Domain Day Garganega 2006 (Barossa)	90

The Top Ten Tips for Wine Investment

- ■ Stick with established brands, large and small.
- ■ Avoid poor or ordinary vintages like they're carrying a communicable disease.
- ■ If you buy in dozens, unopened boxes are best.
- ■ The market, especially the overseas component, is spending big on older vintages of top labels and good years.
- ■ Just because a currently available wine may be expensive, it doesn't mean that it is any good, and that it will appreciate in value.
- ■ Shiraz is still king, locally and overseas.
- ■ Magnums cost more than they should in Australia, but they do appreciate more quickly.
- ■ Check the track record of the agent or auction house, plus the selling and buying commissions applicable.
- ■ Buy at or before release if you can, for the lowest possible price.
- ■ Check on provenance whenever and wherever you can.

Australia's Perfect 1s

Of the thousands of table wines made in Australia today, I have allocated the highest possible wine ranking of 1 to a mere 18. These are the benchmarks, the Grand Cru standards, the wines against which all others can be measured. As a group, they are continually improving, but together they define the highest limits of contemporary Australian wine.

Each has its particular stamp. Each certainly reflects vintage variation from year to year, usually without compromising the special qualities associated with the label.

Bass Phillip Reserve Pinot Noir

Australia's best and longest-living pinot noir, made in Gippsland, by Phillip Jones, is a frustratingly rare, full orchestra wine capable of stunning evolution and expression of briary, meaty complexity and layered structure.

Clarendon Hills Astralis Syrah

Sourced from ancient vines near Clarendon, Roman Bratasiuk's ultimate red has performed exceptionally well in recent years, rising to extraordinary levels of strength and finesse. A powerful statement at the more sumptuous end of the shiraz spectrum.

Clonakilla Shiraz Viognier

Tim Kirk is succeeding in his ambition of creating an exotically perfumed, deeply scented and powerfully flavoured shiraz-viognier blend in a style faithful to the best from the northern Rhône Valley. Poles apart from mainstream Australian shiraz, this savoury, firm and fine-grained red has spawned a generation of imitators.

Cullen Diana Madeline

An essay in concentration, elegance and refinement, this blend of cabernet sauvignon and merlot is not without power and presence. The piercing intensity, refined structure and enormous potential of Vanya Cullen's premier wine leaves little to the imagination.

Giaconda Chardonnay

My pick as Australia's finest chardonnay, this is extraordinarily well structured, meaty, savoury and complete. Expressing a heritage more Burgundian than Australian, it is made by Rick Kinzbrunner at Beechworth in Victoria.

Giaconda Shiraz

Over its relatively short lifetime, this deeply flavoured but very savoury, spicy and meaty shiraz has evolved more significantly in power and weight, building more muscle and oak with the passing vintages. Importantly, they maintain their balance and finesse.

Grosset Polish Hill

A modern icon in Australian wine, Jeffrey Grosset's standout Clare Valley Riesling stretches the limits of what this most traditional of Australian varieties is able to achieve.

Henschke Hill of Grace

In a country full of spectacular single-vineyard shiraz wines, Steven Henschke's signature wine from this individual Eden Valley vineyard marries firmness with velvet-like fineness; vitality with longevity.

Jacob's Creek Steingarten Riesling

This apogee of the great riesling vineyard resources and experience within Orlando Wyndham (now Pernod Ricard Pacific) marries exceptional fruit intensity and fragrance with mouth-watering minerality and tight acidity.

Leeuwin Estate Art Series Chardonnay

At the forefront of Australian chardonnay since its first vintage in 1980, this luscious and long-living Margaret River wine has been for many palates the real 'white Grange'.

Leo Buring Leonay Eden Valley Riesling

A classic and traditional Australian label, whose most recent releases — erratic as their appearances may have been — have invariably proved spectacular. The cellaring potential of these wines is simply legendary.

Mount Mary Cabernet 'Quintet'

An inspiration by John Middleton in Victoria's Yarra Valley, this is the nearest Australian wine to a premier Bordeaux red and a global standard in its own right. Recent vintages have been downright brilliant.

Penfolds Bin 707 Cabernet Sauvignon

Penfolds' most eloquent expression of cabernet sauvignon. This multi-regional blend, matured in new American oak, represents the pick of Penfolds' entire South Australian cabernet crop.

Penfolds Grange

Australia's definitive red wine has been a model of style and consistency since 1951. Based on Barossa shiraz, it incorporates contributions from other regions and small amounts of cabernet sauvignon.

Pierro Chardonnay

Once the role model for so many of Australia's more opulent and hedonistically proportioned chardonnays, this stunning expression of Margaret River chardonnay by Mike Peterkin is now becoming more elegant and mineral.

Seppelt St Peters Shiraz

A definitive Great Western shiraz from the Grampians region of western Victoria. Arthur O'Connor and his team are unashamedly seeking Grand Cru status for this wine, sourced from the low-yielding St Peters, Imperial and Police vineyards.

Wendouree Shiraz

A fastidiously maintained ancient dryland vineyard in Clare is at the heart of this great wine. The past ten years have seen the development of more fruit sweetness in new releases without compromising the legendary structure and longevity of this wine.

Wolf Blass Platinum Label Shiraz

Proof positive that Australia's largest winemakers are working as hard as ever to make the country's leading wine. Sourced from a collection of small vineyards in the Eden Valley, Barossa floor and Adelaide Hills, this is consistently complex and musky, delivering intensely pure and vibrant shiraz flavour.

Jeremy Oliver's Wine of the Year

This edition marks the eighth naming of Jeremy Oliver's Wine of the Year, drawn from the ten best current-release Australian wines I have tasted throughout the previous year.

In sequence, the previous winners have been Rosemount Estate's 1996 Mountain Blue Shiraz Cabernet Sauvignon, Cullen's 1998 Cabernet Sauvignon Merlot 1998, Hardy's Eileen Hardy Shiraz 1998, Mount Mary Quintet 2000, Lake's Folly's Cabernet Blend 2001, Wolf Blass Platinum Label Shiraz 2001, Leeuwin Estate's Art Series Chardonnay 2002 and Balnaves' The Tally Reserve Cabernet Sauvignon 2004.

While quality clearly remains paramount in making this award, the winning wine must be commercially available around or shortly after the time of publication and represent some special characteristic of individuality, innovation, maturity or longevity. Wines selected must make a positive statement about style, terroir and winemaking direction.

Here are the finalists for Jeremy Oliver's 2007 Wine of the Year, including the winner itself.

Wine of the Year

Henschke Hill of Grace 2002 (97)

Here is an unforgettable, seamless, long, fine-grained and sumptuous wine that simply builds on the palate, and a most worthy winner of this title. From one of the greatest and most professionally managed of Australia's old vineyards comes this textbook wine. After a cold and wintry spring that provided a very poor fruit set, Eden Valley experienced a late, cool and very low-yielding vintage in 2002. In the face of these difficulties comes this profoundly flavoured and velvet-smooth shiraz, a wine that defines both the rare and special nature of Eden Valley shiraz, as well as Hill of Grace's own particular stamp of uniqueness.

The eight-hectare Hill of Grace vineyard is four kilometres northwest from the Henschke cellars. Taking its name from the adjacent Lutheran church of Gnadenberg, itself named after a region in Silesia, its principal grape is shiraz, although it hosts small plantings of riesling, semillon and mataro (mourvèdre). The oldest vines, the 'Grandfathers', which were planted in the 1860s, still typically crop around a healthy 2.5 tonnes per acre. They form the basis of an ongoing forty-year clonal selection program which viticulturist Prue Henschke commenced in 1986, whose object is to continue the vineyard's special lineage as older vines die and ultimately need replacing.

Over recent years, I have received a great deal of comment, most of it very negative and ill-informed, about my views and ratings for recent Henschke releases. Some time ago I wrote that as soon as this highly respected small maker began making reds of its customary high standards again, I'd be the first to let people know. That time came with the release of its 2002 reds, of which this wine is the crowning achievement. The company has clearly worked very hard to overcome the issues that had a profoundly negative effect on its wine quality, and for this they have nothing less than my complete admiration and respect.

Finalists

Bindi Block 5 Pinot Noir 2005 (97)

Now with mature vines at his disposal, and what was for him a textbook season, Michael Dhillon continues to turn the popular conceptions of Australian pinot noir on their head. Our best pinot can be ethereal, apparently fragile, but in reality sumptuously and profoundly flavoured and structured; this wine says it all. It will take a lot of climate change before this vineyard is adversely affected.

Bindi Quartz Chardonnay 2005 (97)

It's an extraordinary effort for a small vineyard to have two wines in this list. From the best and most quartz-affected section of Bindi's heat trap-like site near Gisborne comes this uniquely sumptuous and mineral chardonnay whose layers of fruit and texture provide a mirror-like reflection of the wine's low-cropped, mean-soiled and volcanic origins. The first time I tasted this wine I just knew it was something special.

Cullen Diana Madeline 2005 (97)

Wow! One of the stars of a tasting of Australia's finest cabernet that I recently staged in Tokyo, this glorious young cabernet marries the typically layered Cullen richness, fruit ripeness and glorious oak handling with a natural extract of the best tannin I have seen from Margaret River. If you never thought Australia would achieve the extract and structure of the finest Bordeaux, you'd better buy this.

Jacob's Creek Centenary Hill Shiraz 2002 (97)

This smooth, seamless and deeply layered individual vineyard shiraz is a more elegant southern Barossa style, all about cracked pepper, cloves and deep, penetrative flavours of liqueur red cherries and blackberries. Planted in 1921 and owned by the Koch family, first cousins of the same Gramps who established Orlando, the vineyard is about a kilometre north of the Jacob's Creek winery.

Pierro Chardonnay 2005 (97)

Mike Peterkin continues to stamp class and longevity all over his finest wine. While the earlier vintages of Pierro Chardonnay were notable for their impressive richness and concentration, Peterkin has successfully sought a finer, purer expression of fruit which he has deftly married with oak and underpinned by a superbly textured chassis of chalky minerality. A classic.

Penfolds Bin 707
Cabernet Sauvignon 2004 (97)

Being an unashamed fan of Bin 707 since my university days, it's a delight to see it again in top form. Powerful, penetrative fruit is artfully married with great oak and a robust and dependable extract of pliant tannin in this seamless, superbly balanced long-term benchmark. It's a wonder, given that there was a Block 42 Cabernet Sauvignon made from this year, that Penfolds was able to make this wine this good.

Penfolds Grange 2002 (97)

After the catastrophe of 2000 and a good, honest wine in 2001, Grange returns to centre stage. One of its finest vintages comes from this unusually cool season, which has delivered a Grange of exceptional elegance, restraint, finesse and smoothness. It does all this without any compromise to its depth of flavour, or to what its drinkers will immediately identify as 'Grange character'.

Petaluma Coonawarra 2004 (97)

Reminiscent of the brilliantly elegant and long-living 1991 vintage, this is Petaluma Coonawarra at its finest, as a recent vertical tasting of this exceptional wine confirmed. With the passage of time, the wines under this label have moved away from a retentive and even formulaic construction to a more natural and effortlessly balanced expression of what its vineyards deliver. The great 2004 vintage has certainly come up trumps.

Woodlands Margaret
Cabernet Merlot 2005 (97)

If it's a Woodlands red from 2004 or 2005, buy it. Already steeped in luscious dark cherry, berry and plum-like fruit, this is a complex and supremely elegant blend whose combination of richness, chalky tannins and near-perfect balance ensures the expected longevity of dead-serious cabernet. Woodlands has been one of the great revelations of the past three years.

Cellaring Wine

If you're going to cellar wine...

Keep your wine upside down. While some scientists suggest that the partial pressure of water between the wine's surface and the cork in an upright bottle is enough to keep the cork sufficiently moist, I'm not prepared to take the risk. If corks dry out, air gets in. This is ruinous. An added advantage of the growing number of both red and white wines packaged with screwcap seals for longevity and to guard against cork taint is that you can actually cellar them upright without concern. I have been amazed at the ability of both whites and reds to mature with these seals.

Keep your wine in the dark. Ultra-violet light can penetrate most glass bottles to some degree (especially the clear ones) and oxidise the wine inside. This is why so many cellars are dimly lit. If you haven't the space for a dark cellar, keep your bottles in their boxes or else behind a heavy curtain.

Keep your wine still and undisturbed. Regular vibrations accelerate the ageing process with wine. Furthermore, there's no need to turn your bottles every morning, as some people regularly do. This habit began when English gentlemen needed an unobtrusive means of checking that their household staff hadn't secreted any away from their premises, so they actually did this to count their stock.

Temperature should be both constant and low. There is debate about the ideal cellaring temperature. In my experience, if wine is cellared above 18 degrees Celsius it ages too quickly. If it is cellared at around 10–12 degrees, it ages very slowly, perhaps too slowly for some of us. Around 14 degrees is probably ideal, which means that in most parts of Australia, you will need some temperature control. Most importantly, changes in temperature from day to night and from season to season must be avoided if wine is to be kept for even a few months. So keep wine well away from windows and external walls, unless they're very thick.

Think about humidity. If a cellar is too humid then labels and racks may go mouldy. It's unlikely that the wines themselves will be adversely affected, but it's not worth the risk with rare and expensive wines. If there's not enough humidity in the cellar, the outward ends of wine corks may shrink and reduce their ability to impart a seal. This can considerably shorten a wine's longevity. If there's too much humidity, a small fan can help to keep air moving.

If there's not enough, a bowl of water, or even water tipped onto a gravel floor, can help.

To make the most of your cellar...

Start by keeping good records. Bookkeeping is essential unless you can readily remember the quantity, name and age of every wine you own. There's nothing worse than finding a good wine left beyond its peak, so a record-keeping system is crucial. Do it on the computer. There are several cellar management systems available to choose from. Use one that enables you to customise its logic to suit your own cellar. There's another big advantage if your cellar is computerised: you don't have to worry about the bin size or having to construct single bottle slots. All you do is search for a wine by name in your database and its location will automatically appear. Furthermore, in the unfortunate event of fire or flood, your records will at least give you a sporting chance when you make an insurance claim for your cellar contents.

Think about your buying and drinking habits. If you regularly buy wine by the dozen, you'll need bins for twelve bottles, bins for half-dozens and perhaps single bottle slots. That way you can put a new dozen straight into the system, move it along when you're half way through, and then insert the remaining bottles into their own slots. If you're designing a cellar this way, keep between 40–50% for single bottles.

Try to buy by the dozen. Most of us miss wine at its peak by purchasing a small amount and drinking it too soon. With a dozen bottles it has more of a chance and besides, some of us can only summon sufficient resistance with the sight of an unopened box. But if you've bought a dozen, don't rest on your laurels for a decade or more without taking a peep at the wine. Sometimes it's possible to wait too long. Sample a bottle about four years before the wine is expected to peak and then, all being well, about two years before. Your expectations will then be confirmed, or you should alter your approach towards the wine in question. Then, once you expect the time is near, try a bottle every six months or so. That way you should not only have enjoyed watching the wine develop, but have about six or seven bottles left to experience at their best.

So if your dream home wasn't built with a cellar...

Think about a temperature and humidity-controlled wine cabinet. Then you won't have a worry in the world about the health of your wine or your ability to access it. Some of these units are particularly impressive. Factors you might take into account if considering this option include your ability to change temperature settings, the ease of access to the wines inside, possible temperature zoning within the unit to provide different compartments for 'drink now' wines, whether or not fresh air circulates throughout the unit, that the inside of the unit is dark, that it is lockable, that any glass doors are UV-treated, and that the degree of vibration caused by motor units is minimal.

Find yourself a commercial cellaring facility. When choosing which cellaring facility to go with, ask about the temperature and humidity issues, find out about their data keeping facilities, how much and on what basis you will be charged, the security against theft, flood and fire and what sort of pick-up and delivery service you're offered. Will you be told when a wine is nearing its peak? Will you have the ability to buy from and trade with other customers? Some of these operations are equipped with professional standard tasting rooms and commercial kitchens and even offer club-style memberships to their customers, including newsletters, tastings and dinners. Other leading operations of this kind are networked over the entire country, so you can keep wine in different cities, depending on where you bought it.

Seasonal Variation and Quality

It's clear just by glancing through this book that the same grape varieties from the same vineyard invariably produce very different wines from year to year. Traditionally, vintage variation in Australia has been considered merely a fraction of that encountered in most European wine regions of any quality, but the last five years have proven it to be a very significant variable that demands consideration when buying wine.

Even if all other variables were consistent from year to year, which they certainly are not, weather provides the greatest single influence in wine quality and style from season to season. Weather can influence wine in an infinite number of ways, from determining whether conditions at flowering are favourable or not, all the way through to whether final ripening and harvest occur in the warmth of sunshine or through the midst of damaging rains. If viticulturists were to turn pagan, it would be to a god of weather that they would build their first shrine.

Weather-influenced variation is nearly always more pronounced and more frequent in the cooler, more marginal viticultural regions. While Australia is principally a warm to hot wine producing nation, a significant proportion of the country's premium wine now comes from cooler regions in the southwestern and southeastern corners of the continent. The spectrum of diverse weather encountered in these regions far exceeds that of the traditional Australian wine growing areas like the Barossa Valley, McLaren Vale, central Victoria and the Clare Valley. Paradoxically, the best years in cool climates are typically the warmer seasons that accelerate the ripening period, creating a finer acid balance, superior sugar levels, flavours and better-defined colours.

Variety by variety, this is how Australia's premium wine grapes are affected by seasonal conditions:

White wines

Chardonnay

Cool years cause chardonnay and most white varieties to accumulate higher levels of mineral acids, resulting in lean, tight wines with potential longevity, provided they have sufficient intensity of fruit. Cool year chardonnays can display greenish, herbal and green cashew flavours, and can resemble grapefruit and other citrus fruit, especially lemon. Warmer year wines become richer and rounder, with fruit flavours more suggestive of apple, pear, quince and cumquat. In hot seasons, chardonnays become flabbier, faster-maturing wines with flavours of peach, green olive, melon and tobacco.

Riesling

Although riesling does not need to ripen to the sugar levels necessary for a premium chardonnay, cool-season riesling tends to be lean and tight with hard steely acids, possibly lacking in length and persistence of flavour. Better rieslings from superior years have succulent youthful primary fruit flavours of lime juice, ripe pears and apples, with musky, citrus rind undertones. Significantly broader and less complex than wines from better seasons, warmer year rieslings tend to mature faster, occasionally becoming broad and fat on the palate after a short time.

Sauvignon Blanc

Cool season sauvignon blancs tend to be hard-edged wines with steely acids, with over-exaggerated and undesirable herbaceous flavours suggestive of asparagus and 'cat pee', a description for which I have yet to find a polite alternative even half as succinct.

The warmer the season the riper the fruit becomes and the less grassy and vegetal the aroma. The downside is often a reduction in the intensity of the wine's primary fruit flavours. Expect sweet blackcurrants, gooseberries and passionfruit from sauvignon blancs in good seasons, with at least a light capsicum note. Warmer seasons create broader, occasionally oily and less grassy wines, with more emphasis on passionfruit, lychee and tropical fruit flavours.

Semillon

Semillon tends to react to cooler seasons by creating very tight, lean wines with more obvious grassy influences, but perhaps lacking in primary fruit character. On occasions, these rather one-dimensional young wines can develop stunning flavours in the bottle over many years, as classically unwooded Hunter semillon proves time and again. The best cellaring examples need length on the palate and an absence of green characters while young.

Red wines

Cabernet Sauvignon

A late-ripening grape variety which reacts very poorly to cool, late seasons, cabernet sauvignon has traditionally and wisely been blended with varieties like merlot (in Bordeaux) and shiraz (commonly, until recently in Australia). Cool season cabernet sauvignon makes the classic doughnut wine: intense cassis/raspberry fruit at the front of the palate with greenish, extractive tannin at the back and a hole in the middle. Under-ripe cabernet sauvignon reveals less colour and a thin, bitter finish. Its tannins are often greenish and under-ripe, tasting sappy or metallic, while its flavour can be dominated by greenish snow pea influences more suggestive of cool-climate sauvignon blanc.

Warmer seasons create much better cabernet, with genuinely ripe cassis/plum flavours, a superior middle palate and fine-grained, fully ripened tannins, although a slight capsicum note can still be evident. In really hot years, the wines tend to become jammy and porty, suggestive of stewed, dehydrated prune and currant-like fruit flavours and lacking in any real definition and fineness of tannin.

Pinot Noir

Pinot noir does not react well to very cool seasons, becoming herbal and leafy, with a brackish, greenish palate and simple sweet raspberry confection fruit. Warmer seasons produce the more sought-after primary characters of sweet cherries and plums, fine-grained tannins and spicy, fleshy middle palate. Too warm a season and the wine turns out to be undefined, simple and fast maturing, often with unbalanced and hard-edged tannins.

Shiraz

Thin and often quite greenish — but rarely to the same extent as cabernet sauvignon — cool-season shiraz often acquires leafy white pepper characters, with spicy, herby influences plus metallic, sappy and green-edged tannins. Provided there's sufficient fruit, which may not be the case in cool seasons, it can still be a worthwhile wine, although not one likely to mature for long in the bottle. Warmer years create shiraz with characteristic richness and sweetness, with riper plum, cassis and chocolate flavours and fully-ripened tannins. Hot year shiraz is often typified by earthy flavours suggestive of bitumen and leather, with dehydrated prune juice and meaty characters.

2007 Australian Vintage Report

Occurring at the likely coincidence of the height of a once-in-a-century drought and the ongoing process of climate change, the 2007 vintage was unprecedented in several ways. It was extraordinarily early, was affected by an incredible range of severe climatic effects, and it was dramatically small, falling by an estimated 25% to 1.42 million tonnes. Science tells us that we should expect an increasing number of climatic catastrophes as the planet warms up, but the sequence faced by the wine and grape growing industries prior to the 2007 vintage was nothing short of Biblical in its impact and diversity.

The drought and global warming effects led to an unusually early budburst, which in many southerly or higher altitude regions occurred under cloudless skies and freezing nights. Under these conditions, the impact of repetitive frost incidences was unprecedented. Across several regions, some of which received up to thirteen separate major frosts, not only primary but secondary buds were damaged. So crops were extremely low, and there remain ongoing concerns not only regarding the 2008 harvest but also of vine health beyond.

Many Australian vineyards are 'protected' by overhead 'frost-free' irrigation systems, but these are of course only serviceable when there is a supply of water. In many cases over the 2006/2007 season, growers were unable to use their defence systems.

The hot, dry windy conditions also helped to promote one of Australia's earliest and worst bushfire seasons. While only a small percentage of vineyards in bushfire-prone regions like Victoria's King Valley were actually burned out, bushfire smoke entirely covered many wine regions in the country's southeast for an extended period during the ripening process, including much of the state of Victoria. Smoke taint is not readily identifiable in wine until the fermentation is finished, and because many makers are not experienced in either identifying or dealing with the issue, its impact is not yet fully accounted for in the crop statistics.

Then, just prior to the harvest of smaller than anticipated crops, regions like McLaren Vale received significant and abrupt rainfalls, the effect of which was not to aid but to damage the fruit. Fruit splitting was rife in several warmer regions, causing further losses. Afterwards, the final ripening around Australia tended to occur in hot, dry conditions that in many cases led to fruit stress and uneven ripening.

Ultimately, red grapes were greatly more affected than white, being down on 2006 levels by 35% and 14% respectively. While shiraz and cabernet sauvignon were both down by 36%, chardonnay was only down by 8%.

There has perhaps never been a more patchy vintage from a quality perspective.

As ever, fruit and wine quality will depend on whether or not vineyards were able to coincide the ripening of sugar, flavour and tannins. In many warmer regions, sugar levels ripened well in advance of flavour, creating more wines with meaty, stewed characters and well as herbaceous, under-ripe influences as well as green-edged tannins. Because of the extreme earliness of the season, as well its exceptional heat, this phenomenon would also have repeated across cooler regions.

Despite these valid misgivings, I should observe that I have been pleasantly surprised by the small number of 2007 releases I have tasted prior to the completion of this book, in mid-July.

New South Wales

While the Hunter Valley produced some exceptional semillons with bright luminous green colours, it could also be a good year for the riper expressions of its shiraz. This region managed to escape smoke taint entirely in 2007. Cowra's yields were down, but semillon and other whites were of good quality. Mudgee struggled to produce its best quality. Orange did not perform quite as well in the warmer season, with sound enough chardonnay but ordinary sauvignon blanc.

While yields were well down in Griffith, its reds are bright and intense. Whites were less impressive, but rains in May helped growers produce good botrytis-affected late harvest whites. The outcome for regions like Hilltops, Gundagai and Tumbarumba was very much a vineyard-by-vineyard issue, largely depending on the water availability for each site.

South Australia

Drought, heat and frost were the major influences on grape quality in South Australia — and whether indeed some vineyards were or were not harvested. Warm sites in warm regions like Clare, the Barossa and McLaren Vale were subject to accelerated sugar ripening, and are less likely to produce wine of typical standard. The interval between veraison and harvest was unusually short in many cases. However, Clare and Eden Valley rieslings are better than those from 2006. The Riverlands produced good fruit brightness and intensity.

However later, cooler sites in these areas, and cooler districts like Eden Valley, the Adelaide Hills, the Fleurieu Peninsula and Langhorne Creek fared significantly better, Langhorne Creek in fact having an exceptionally good season. The Coonawarra vineyards that were not wiped out by frost produced excellent whites and medium-bodied reds, Padthaway had a reasonable vintage, while Robe's was excellent.

Tasmania

A frost-reduced crop which reduced yields by around 40% produced some good results from a very early vintage. In most cases, pinot fared best with some high-standard wines, while riesling and chardonnay were of sound quality. Even ripeness was not aided by primary and secondary crops being harvested together.

Victoria

Victoria's vintage was uniformly early and small, but quality has surprised by being acceptable to good, with some genuine highlights where growers were not frosted and had adequate water. Smoke taint might yet prove a major ongoing issue for wineries in the Yarra Valley, the Strathbogies and the King Valley, especially with red wines. Frost was also a major issue with the Yarra Valley, Geelong, central Victoria, the Strathbogies, King Valley and Rutherglen.

The Yarra and Mornington Peninsula can anticipate some fine pinot noir, while across the state it was very tough for cabernet and sauvignon, which were generally harvested below genuine ripeness.

Western Australia

Only 15–17% down on volume, 2007 was a dry, warm but high-quality vintage in the west. While some Swan Valley, Perth Hills and Gingin crops were affected by sunburn, these regions should produce some good dry whites. Geographe harvested ripe reds and some good whites, while Margaret River's reds should be of comparable standard to the excellent 2004s. The region will also deliver some very herbal sauvignon blanc, some ripe and juicy semillon and some flavoursome chardonnay.

Pemberton experienced a fine white vintage, especially for sauvignon blanc. From a very dry season, Frankland River's reds will be ripe and firm, while the rieslings should be sound. Mount Barker produced encouraging chardonnay and excellent reds from shiraz and cabernet sauvignon.

Alkoomi

RMB 234, Wingebellup Road, Frankland WA 6396. Tel: (08) 9855 2229. Fax: (08) 9855 2284.
Website: www.alkoomiwines.com.au Email: info@alkoomiwines.com.au

Region: **Frankland River** Winemaker: **Michael Staniford** Viticulturist: **Wayne Lange** Chief Executive: **Merv Lange**

Alkoomi is one of the oldest and most important vineyards of the Great Southern region. Located in the northern Frankland River subregion, it has developed a strong reputation for the strength, luscious ripeness and longevity of its reds. With the 2006 vintage as a leading example, Alkoomi is also a leading light in the region's finer, musky and perfumed expression of riesling, which with the Blackbutt 2004, is the pick of its current releases.

BLACKBUTT CABERNET BLEND

RATING **3**

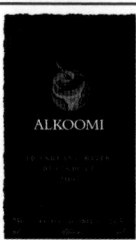

Frankland River		$30–$49
Current vintage: 2004		92

A polished, smooth and elegant cabernet blend of Alkoomi's typically unctuous and dark-fruited style. Its confiture-like fragrance of blackberries, dark plums and cassis reveals herbal undertones of crushed vine leaves and cedary oak. Silky and refined, the palate's deep fruit flavours and dusty, lightly smoky vanilla oak are coated by fine tannins. Tightly focused, it finishes with a tangy note of dark olives.

2004	92	2012	2026
2002	92	2010	2014+
2001	93	2013	2021
1999	88	2004	2007
1998	92	2006	2010+

CABERNET SAUVIGNON

RATING **5**

Frankland River		$20–$29
Current vintage: 2005		86

A well handled but slightly under-ripened short-term cabernet whose meaty, earthy and green-edged aromas of dark plums and cassis overlie creamy cedary oak. Supported by firm and gritty tannin, it begins with vibrant fruit but becomes more lean and dilute towards the finish.

2005	86	2010	2013
2004	89	2012	2016
2003	84	2005	2008+
2002	86	2007	2010
2001	89	2009	2013
1999	92	2011	2019
1998	92	2010	2018
1996	81	2001	2004
1995	82	2003	2007
1994	89	2002	2006
1993	88	1998	2001
1992	88	1997	2000
1991	89	2003	2011
1990	90	2002	2010
1989	88	2001	2009
1988	87	2000	2005

CHARDONNAY

RATING **5**

Frankland River		$20–$29
Current vintage: 2005		86

Likely to develop quickly, this marmalade-like chardonnay is dominated to some extent by a big, buttery malolactic fermentation. Its toasty, honeyed aromas of lime juice and melon overlie smoky, bacony undertones. Finished with austere acidity, it's broad and quite phenolic, lacking a little brightness and revealing sweetcorn-like undertones.

2005	86	2007	2010
2004	89	2006	2009
2003	86	2005	2008
2002	93	2007	2010
2001	89	2003	2006+
2000	88	2002	2005
1998	87	2000	2003
1997	92	2002	2005
1996	88	1998	2001

JARRAH SHIRAZ

RATING **3**

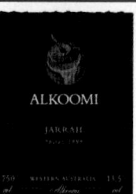

Frankland River		$30–$49
Current vintage: 2003		89

Dark, spicy, deeply flavoured and brooding, this leathery and rustic shiraz presents meaty flavours of blackberries, mulberries and plums with cedary oak over musky and rather reductive undertones. It's long, linear, fine and quite restrained, marrying sweet berry fruit with pencil shavings-like oak, but appears to have been slightly over-protected from oxygen, of which it could perhaps have seen more.

2003	89	2011	2015+
2002	92	2010	2014+
2001	89	2006	2009
2000	86	2005	2008
1999	93	2007	2011+

RIESLING

RATING 3

Frankland River $12–$19
Current vintage: 2006   **93**

Taut, lean and refreshing, this pristine, musky and penetrating young riesling unfolds a floral and limey perfume underpinned by minerals, pear and apple. It's long and finely crafted, with piercing fresh fruit all along its brightly lit palate, before a clean and zesty finish.

2006	93	2011	2014+
2005	86	2007	2010
2004	90	2009	2012+
2003	93	2011	2015+
2002	89	2004	2007
2001	93	2009	2013
1999	88	2001	2004+
1998	90	2006	2010
1997	91	2005	2009
1996	91	2004	2008
1995	91	2000	2003+
1994	94	2002	2006
1993	87	1998	2001

SAUVIGNON BLANC

RATING 5

Frankland River $20–$29
Current vintage: 2006   **92**

Tight and well defined, this shapely young sauvignon blanc has a lightly herbal fragrance of gooseberries, cassis, violets and minerals. Its vibrant, tangy palate is long and finely sculpted, delivering a pleasingly complex expression of varietal flavour and earthy complexity punctuated by crisp and refreshing acids.

2006	92	2007	2008+
2005	82	2005	2006+
2004	89	2005	2006
2003	87	2003	2004
2002	82	2003	2004
2001	89	2002	2003
2000	93	2001	2002
1999	87	2001	2004
1998	88	2000	2003
1997	90	1998	1999

SHIRAZ VIOGNIER (Shiraz pre 2002)

RATING 4

Frankland River $20–$29
Current vintage: 2005   **88**

An honest and flavoursome, if slightly unevenly ripened wine whose slightly jammy, peppery and currant-like aromas offer some pleasing fruit sweetness, lift and spice. Initially deep, smooth and juicy, the palate becomes slightly angular and awkward at the finish, lacking a little generosity and richness.

2005	88	2007	2010+
2004	91	2009	2012
2003	91	2008	2011+
2002	91	2007	2010+
2001	87	2003	2006+
2000	81	2002	2005
1999	89	2007	2011
1998	86	2003	2006
1997	87	1999	2002

All Saints Estate

All Saints Road, Wahgunyah Vic 3687. Tel: (02) 6035 2222. Fax: (02) 6035 2200.
Website: www.allsaintswine.com.au Email: wine@allsaintswine.com.au

Region: **Rutherglen** Winemaker: **Dan Crane** Viticulturist: **Tjomas Lefebvre** Chief Executive: **Eliza Brown**

All Saints Estate is one of the grand original properties of the Rutherglen region, today owned by the family of Peter Brown, one of the Brown Brothers of Milawa fame. Peter died tragically and prematurely in November, 2005 and his children, Eliza, Angela and Nicholas Brown have taken on the management of the company. The 2004 Family Cellar Reserve Shiraz is the finest red I have tasted from All Saints for several years, and bodes well for the family as they streamline the business.

FAMILY CELLAR RESERVE SHIRAZ (formerly Carlyle)

RATING 4

Rutherglen $50–$99
Current vintage: 2004   **91**

Fragrant and spicy, this smooth and surprisingly elegant shiraz delivers a peppery expression of red and black berries, cherries and plums underpinned by firmish, but fine and pliant tannins. Backed by earthy nuances of cloves, cinnamon and licorice, its restrained and creamy palate builds in weight intensity towards its persistent and brightly flavoured finish. A charming regional classic.

2004	91	2009	2012+
1999	83	2001	2004
1998	77	2000	2003
1997	91	2005	2009
1996	89	1998	2001
1995	86	2000	2003
1994	91	2004	2008

SHIRAZ

RATING 5

Rutherglen	$20–$29
Current vintage: 2004	**87**

Meaty, rather cooked and very oaky, this rustic shiraz has a very ripe and porty aroma backed by cinnamon, cloves, white pepper and spirity nuances of alcohol. Firm, slightly raw and blocky, its palate of sweet, jammy blackberry fruit culminates in a dusty, earthy finish. It needs time to settle.

2004	87	2009	2012
2003	80	2005	2008
2002	85	2007	2010
2000	87	2005	2008
1999	88	2004	2007
1998	87	2003	2006
1997	88	2002	2005
1996	87	1998	2001
1994	92	2002	2006+
1993	90	2001	2005
1992	88	2000	2004
1989	88	1997	2003

Amberley

Thornton Road, Yallingup WA 6282. Tel: (08) 9366 3900. Fax: (08) 9321 6281.
Website: www.amberleyestate.com.au Email: pauld@amberley-estate.com.au
Region: **Margaret River** Winemaker: **Paul Dunnewyk** Viticulturist: **Phil Smith** Chief Executive: **Eddie Price**

Now part of The Hardy Wine Company, Amberley looks set to realise its undoubted potential. The stylish First Selection Cabernet Sauvignon has been joined by the savoury and rather showy 2004 Shiraz, which suggests Amberley's reds will benefit from the cut and polish associated with its new parent and its Houghton stablemate. Sadly, the Sauvignon Blanc did not perform as well in the cloudy 2006 vintage.

FIRST SELECTION CABERNET SAUVIGNON
(formerly Reserve)

RATING 3

Margaret River	$30–$49
Current vintage: 2001	**93**

A finely balanced and very youthful-appearing wine for the long term. Framed by firm, loose-knit tannin, its lively but restrained flavours of cassis, dark cherries, blackberries and boysenberries are tightly knit with dusty, cedary oak and kept fresh and vibrant by clean acidity. Its violet bouquet and earthy, meaty, lightly herbal undertones add plenty of interest to its juicy expression of fruit, while it finishes with exceptional length and focus.

2001	93	2009	2013+
2000	92	2008	2012+
1997	87	2005	2009
1996	88	2008	2016
1995	91	2007	2015
1993	85	2001	2005
1992	87	2000	2004+

FIRST SELECTION CHARDONNAY

RATING 5

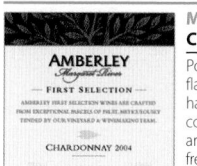

Margaret River	$20–$29
Current vintage: 2004	**90**

Polished, round and generous, this sumptuously flavoured, smooth and creamy chardonnay easily handles a healthy measure of winemaker-induced complexity. Its reserved peach/grapefruit aromas are backed by creamy, nutty leesy influences and fresh vanilla oak, while its substantial palate of juicy, tangy fruit culminates in a warm, slightly spirity and savoury finish.

2004	90	2006	2009
2003	87	2005	2008
2002	81	2003	2004
2001	87	2003	2006

FIRST SELECTION SHIRAZ

RATING 5

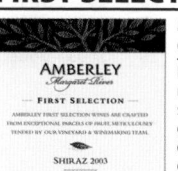

Margaret River	$20–$29
Current vintage: 2004	**91**

Rather a showy shiraz, whose smoky bouquet of mocha, cassis, blackberries and dark plums reveals spicy, peppery and meaty undertones. Slightly exaggerated and caricature-like, its smooth, sweet-fruited, elegant and oaky palate bursts with juicy flavours of dark berries and plums. It's framed by tight-knit, fine-grained tannins, finishing long and savoury with more than a hint of reductive complexity.

2004	91	2012	2016
2003	88	2008	2011+
2002	88	2004	2007+
2001	82	2003	2006
2000	86	2002	2005+
1999	88	2004	2007
1998	81	2000	2003
1997	89	2002	2005

SAUVIGNON BLANC

Margaret River	$12–$19	2006	80	2006	2007
Current vintage: 2006	**80**	2005	93	2006	2007+
		2004	83	2004	2005
		2002	89	2003	2004
		2001	85	2002	2003+
		2000	82	2001	2002

Oily and vegetative, sweaty and flabby, this rather cabbagey white wine is ageing quickly.

Angove's

Bookmark Avenue, Renmark SA 5341. Tel: (08) 8580 3100. Fax: (08) 8580 3155.
Website: www.angoves.com.au Email: angoves@angoves.com.au
Regions: **Various** Winemakers: **Warwick Billings, Tony Ingle** Viticulturist: **Nick Bakkum**
Chief Executive: **John Angove**

One of Australia's largest family-owned wine producers, Angove's is also emerging as one of our quiet achievers. I am particularly impressed with its winemaking attitude, which is to attempt to create the most elegant and balanced wine possible, regardless of the ultimate price of the finished product. The results are seen in the freshness and perhaps unexpected finesse of the Vineyard Select range, as well as the sheer value for money found under the Long Row label.

VINEYARD SELECT RIESLING

Clare Valley	$12–$19	2006	87	2008	2011
Current vintage: 2006	**87**	2005	86	2010	2013
		2004	88	2009	2012
		2003	83	2004	2005+
		2002	75	2003	2004

Very fruity, dry and generous, this floral and slightly confectionary riesling has a citrusy fragrance and a tangy, juicy palate of lemon tart-like fruit that finishes long and lean. There's a hint of bathpowdery texture and a refreshingly clean and acidic finish.

VINEYARD SELECT CABERNET SAUVIGNON

Coonawarra	$12–$19	2005	88	2010	2013+
Current vintage: 2005	**88**	2004	89	2009	2012
		2003	87	2005	2008+
		2002	85	2004	2007+
		2001	88	2006	2009+

Fine, supple and stylish, this juicy young cabernet marries dark cherry, plum and blackberry flavours with sweet cedar/vanilla/mocha oak, and lightly herbal undertones. Framed by a dusty, fine-grained extract, it's just slightly cooked and currant-like, but finishes with length and texture.

VINEYARD SELECT SHIRAZ

McLaren Vale	$12–$19	2005	88	2007	2010+
Current vintage: 2005	**88**	2004	90	2009	2012
		2003	88	2008	2011
		2001	86	2003	2006

Very approachable and open, this fragrant, peppery shiraz offers restrained blackberry, dark plum and redcurrant flavours backed by lightly smoky chocolate/vanilla oak, with undertones of cloves, cinnamon and treacle. It's elegant and vibrant, with a pleasing length of fruit framed by fine tannins.

Annie's Lane

Quelltaler Estate, Quelltaler Road, Watervale SA 5452. Tel: (08) 8843 0003. Fax: (08) 8843 0096.
Website: www.annieslane.com.au Email: cellardoor@annieslane.com.au

Region: **Clare Valley** Winemaker: **Mark Robertson** Viticulturist: **Peter Pawelski** Chief Executive: **Jamie Odell**

While the 'reserve' level Copper Trail wines show exactly what this label is capable of, I can't help the feeling that Annie's Lane is suffering as a lesser priority within the expansive Foster's wine portfolio. Recent releases have lacked the intensity, freshness and polish typically associated with the brand, which is often sold around the trade at prices I find hard to believe are sustainable. Sadly, it appears a makeover is in order.

CABERNET MERLOT   RATING 5

Clare Valley $20–$29
Current vintage: 2005   87

Fractionally hollow, made from fruit whose tannins lacked complete ripeness, this is an honest enough red with intense, briary aromas of slightly minty and herbal small dark berries and plums backed by vanilla/chocolate oak. Framed by firmish tannins, it's forward and minty, with intense flavours of berries that thin out a little towards the finish.

2005	87	2007	2010+
2002	91	2010	2014
2001	85	2003	2006
2000	87	2002	2005
1999	86	2001	2004
1998	90	2003	2006
1997	87	2002	2005
1996	82	1998	2001
1995	94	2003	2007

COPPER TRAIL RIESLING   RATING 3

Clare Valley $20–$29
Current vintage: 2005   91

Delicate aromas of lime juice, lemon rind and chalky, powdery mineral influences overlie a floral, rose garden-like perfume. Fine and juicy, its effortlessly smooth expression of delicate citrus and mineral character culminates in a lingering and silky finish whose lively core of fruit and refreshing acidity help to conceal a hint of sweetness.

2005	91	2010	2013+
2004	92	2009	2012+
2003	94	2008	2011
2002	95	2010	2014+

COPPER TRAIL SHIRAZ (formerly The Contour)   RATING 3

Clare Valley $50–$99
Current vintage: 2000   88

A typical 2000 vintage wine whose meaty mulberry, cassis and plum-like fruit presents some under- and over-ripe influences. Laced with herbal and spicy notes of cinnamon and cloves, it's given sweetness and length through some fine-grained cedar/vanilla oak, before finishing slightly green-edged and sappy.

2000	88	2002	2005+
1999	92	2007	2011
1998	93	2006	2010
1997	93	2005	2009
1996	95	2004	2008+
1995	90	2003	2007

RIESLING   RATING 5

Clare Valley $12–$19
Current vintage: 2006   87

Clean, flavoursome and with a hint of sweetness, this lively young riesling has a slightly candied, lemon tart-like aroma lifted by hints of flowers and minerals. It's a little sweet and sugary, with a moderate length of citrusy fruit and bathpowdery complexity, and finishes with refreshing acidity.

2006	87	2008	2011
2005	87	2007	2010+
2004	86	2004	2005+
2003	89	2005	2008
2002	93	2007	2010+
2001	89	2006	2009
2000	89	2002	2005
1999	81	2000	2001
1998	94	2003	2006+
1997	90	2005	2009

SEMILLON   RATING 5

Clare Valley $12–$19
Current vintage: 2005   87

Clean and refreshing, this simple and austere semillon has a dusty, creamy nose of green melon and butter with grassy undertones, which gradually reveals floral suggestions and hints of sweet oak. There's a chalkiness beneath its melon/lemon fruit and restrained vanilla oak, while it finishes with tangy, citrusy acids.

2005	87	2006	2007+
2004	90	2006	2009
2003	89	2005	2008
2002	88	2004	2007+
2001	88	2003	2006
2000	82	2001	2002
1999	87	2004	2007
1998	91	2000	2003
1997	87	1999	2002
1996	93	2004	2008

SHIRAZ

Clare Valley	$12–$19
Current vintage: 2005	**85**

A pretty little quaff, with a juicy aroma of black and red berries, vanilla oak and dusty spices. While it's soft and approachable, with some lively raspberry and plum flavour, it thins out towards the finish.

2005	85	2007	2010
2003	89	2011	2015+
2002	82	2004	2007
2001	90	2006	2009
2000	88	2002	2005+
1999	86	2001	2004
1998	90	2003	2006
1997	89	2002	2005
1996	90	2001	2004
1995	88	2000	2003

Armstrong

Military Road, Armstrong Vic 3377. Tel: (08) 8277 6073. Fax: (08) 8277 6035. Email: armvyd@bigpond.net.au

Regions: **Grampians, Great Western** Winemaker: **Tony Royal** Viticulturist: **Geoff Morley** Chief Executive: **Tony Royal**

Armstrong is the pet project of experienced winemaker Tony Royal, a long-time senior winemaker for Seppelt. The Shiraz and Shiraz Viognier often reveal a herbal thread, but as the vineyard gains maturity, they are becoming longer, finer, more elegant and complete, acquiring the typical longevity of Great Western shiraz.

SHIRAZ

Great Western	$30–$49
Current vintage: 2002	**89**

A minty perfume of violets, cassis and dark plums is tightly integrated with lightly smoky scents of fine-grained vanilla oak, with meaty undertones of cloves, cinnamon and menthol. Long, smooth and structured, the palate delivers intense cassis and dark plum flavours framed by a slightly drying extract of firm, but fine-grained tannins. It finishes long and savoury, with nuances of menthol, but doesn't quite appear to be able to shake an underlying herbal thread.

2002	89	2010	2014
2001	93	2009	2013
2000	93	2008	2012
1999	89	2007	2011
1998	83	2000	2003
1996	88	2001	2004+

Arundel

Arundel Road, Keilor Vic 3036. Tel: (03) 9335 3422. Fax: (03) 9335 4912.
Website: www.arundel.com.au Email: bianca@arundel.com.au

Region: **Sunbury** Winemaker: **Bianca Hayes** Viticulturist: **Mark Hayes** Chief Executive: **Bianca Hayes**

A tiny vineyard near Keilor, Victoria, Arundel is proving that its early promise was no fluke. While its Viognier still requires some fine-tuning, its Shiraz is usually a spicy, peppery, fine-grained and savoury Rhône-inspired wine delivering dark, briary and penetrative fruit. Similar to many other 2005 shirazes, the Arundel wine shows some signs of raisin-like fruit stress, but has retained good quality in a difficult season.

SHIRAZ

Sunbury	$30–$49
Current vintage: 2005	**88**

Slightly cooked and meaty, with smoky, gamey undertones, this dark-fruited shiraz combines flavours of plums, blackberries, raisins and currants with sweet vanilla oak and a smooth, powdery extract. It's rich and juicy, then slightly soft-centred, but finishes with lingering savoury qualities and flavours of spicy plums and berries.

2005	88	2010	2013
2004	91	2009	2012
2003	90	2008	2011+
2002	90	2007	2010+
2001	92	2009	2013
2000	93	2005	2008+
1999	89	2001	2004+
1997	77	1998	1999

Baileys of Glenrowan

RMB 4160 Taminick Gap Road, Glenrowan Vic 3675. Tel: (03) 5766 2392. Fax: (03) 5766 2596.
Website: www.baileysofglenrowan.com.au Email: paul.dahlenburg@beringerblass.com.au

Region: **NE Victoria** Winemaker: **Paul Dahlenburg** Viticulturist: **Paul Dahlenburg** Chief Executive: **Jamie Odell**

Baileys is a fine example of how a small and relatively idiosyncratic brand of rustic red wines and luscious fortifieds can thrive and prosper in a multinational environment. Located in the picturesque northeast corner of Victoria, it produces a trio of shirazes, the elder two of which are named according to the age of their vineyards. The common thread is their richness, ripeness and meaty, spicy expression of varietal flavour. Typically firm, often closed in their youth, they open up to reveal generous depth and flavour. In sporting parlance, they're fighting above their weight.

1904 BLOCK SHIRAZ

RATING **3**

NE Victoria	$30–$49
Current vintage: 2004	**94**

A sumptuous, long and varietal shiraz whose deeply spicy, meaty and plummy aromas of small dark berries, cloves and cinnamon are backed by earthy, rustic nuances and hints of white pepper. Its deeply fruited palate of sweet, dark plums and berries overlies a tight, firm spine of powdery tannins, finishing long and persistent, with lingering sweet fruit and leathery undertones.

2004	94	2016	2024
2003	90	2015	2023
2000	90	2005	2008
1999	93	2011	2019+
1998	91	2010	2018

1920s BLOCK SHIRAZ

RATING **4**

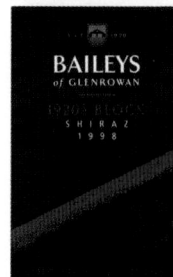

NE Victoria	$20–$29
Current vintage: 2005	**93**

A natural, stable and well-made wine with a future. Its smoky fragrance of sweet blackberries, cassis and violets is backed by spicy nuances of cloves, cinnamon and nutmeg, with a whiff of rosemary. Sumptuous and deeply concentrated, its thick, full-bodied palate backs its evenly ripened fruit with a firm spine of chalky tannin and meaty, mineral undertones. Rustic but well crafted, with a touch of attitude.

2005	93	2017	2025+
2003	91	2015	2023
2001	87	2003	2006
2000	92	2005	2008+
1999	91	2011	2019
1998	89	2006	2010+
1997	87	2002	2005
1996	88	2001	2004
1995	86	2000	2003
1994	93	2006	2014
1993	87	1998	2001
1992	90	2000	2004
1991	94	2003	2011

SHIRAZ

RATING **5**

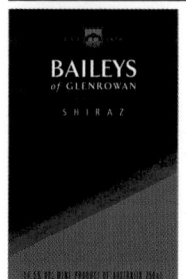

NE Victoria	$12–$19
Current vintage: 2005	**89**

Framed by firm, pliant tannins and backed by slightly toasty oak, this full to medium-bodied shiraz marries ripe, juicy flavours of dark plums, cassis and raspberries with toasty cedar/vanilla oak and meaty, peppery undertones. Youthful, sweet-fruited and vibrant, with a heady, spicy perfume, it should develop over the medium term.

2005	89	2010	2013+
2004	89	2012	2016+
2003	90	2008	2011
2002	91	2010	2014+
2000	89	2005	2008
1999	87	2004	2007

Balgownie Estate

Hermitage Road, Maiden Gully Vic 3551. Tel: (03) 5449 6222. Fax: (03) 5449 6506.
Website: www.balgownieestate.com.au Email: info@balgownieestate.com.au
Region: **Bendigo** Winemaker: **Tobias Ansted** Viticulturist: **John Monteath** Chief Executive: **Des Forrester**
Balgownie has come a long way from its early times as a small individual domaine near Bendigo. The brand today also encompasses a significant hotel, restaurant and resort development in the Yarra Valley, where it also owns some promising vineyards. The 2005 season provided a difficult challenge for the Bendigo site, but Balgownie has managed to retain its exceptional recent consistency, which now sees it as a modern benchmark.

CABERNET SAUVIGNON

RATING 3

Bendigo	$30–$49
Current vintage: 2005	94

A fine piece of winemaking has developed a powerful, assertive but carefully balanced red for the long haul. Scented with cassis, violets, plums and well-knit cedar/vanilla oak, its sumptuous palate is coated with a drying, chalky astringency. There's just a hint of currant and meatiness beneath its richly ripened dark berry and plum-like fruit, which simply soaks up its substantial oak treatment.

2005	94	2017	2025
2004	93	2016	2024
2003	93	2015	2023
2002	93	2014	2022+
2001	89	2013	2021
2000	90	2012	2020
1999	89	2004	2007
1998	87	2006	2010+
1997	86	2005	2009
1996	90	2008	2016
1995	88	2007	2015
1994	87	2002	2006
1993	88	2005	2013
1992	93	2004	2012
1991	88	2011	2021
1990	95	2010	2020

SHIRAZ

RATING 3

Bendigo	$30–$49
Current vintage: 2005	90

Firm and drying, this ripe, meaty and smoky shiraz delivers a ripe, slightly jammy expression of vibrant plum and blackberry fruit without the presence of overcooked characters. Laced with minty and herbal undertones, its briary fruit aromas are underpinned by nuances of smoked meats and mocha-like oak. Enlivened by refreshing acidity, its richly fruited palate finishes with suggestions of chocolate and vanilla.

2005	90	2013	2017
2004	91	2012	2016+
2003	95	2011	2015+
2002	94	2010	2014+
2001	92	2009	2013
2000	89	2005	2008
1999	89	2004	2007
1998	89	2003	2006+
1997	93	2009	2017
1996	93	2004	2008+
1995	94	2007	2015
1994	90	2002	2006
1993	93	2005	2013
1990	94	2002	2010

Balnaves

Main Road, Coonawarra SA 5263. Tel: (08) 8737 2946. Fax: (08) 8737 2945.
Website: www.balnaves.com.au Email: kirsty.balnaves@balnaves.com.au
Region: **Coonawarra** Winemaker: **Peter Bissell** Viticulturist: **Peter Balnaves** Chief Executive: **Doug Balnaves**
Given its recent form and its respected attention to detail, it's hardly surprising that Balnaves has made such a good fist of the 2005 vintage, which was variable at least in the Coonawarra region. Balnaves' 2005 collection are typically wild and briary, with some of the meaty ripeness associated with the season, but largely retain the finesse and balance the company has recent delivered consistently. Most impressive is their cellaring potential.

CABERNET SAUVIGNON MERLOT

RATING 4

Coonawarra	$20–$29
Current vintage: 2005	89

Impressively made, but fractionally cooked and stewed, this slightly dehydrated cabernet blend has a deep, briary and minty perfume of dark plums, cassis and blackberries backed by slightly smoky, grainy new oak and meaty undertones of currants and prunes. Deep and dark-fruited, but lacking great brightness through the palate, its robust and powerful prune and currant-like fruit is still closed and withdrawn.

2005	89	2010	2013+
2004	95	2016	2024
2002	87	2007	2010+
2001	90	2009	2013
2000	88	2002	2005+
1998	93	2006	2010

CABERNET SAUVIGNON

Coonawarra	$30–$49
Current vintage: 2005	**91**

Deeply flavoured, dark-fruited and brooding. Scented with blackberries, cassis, Christmas cake and mocha/dark chocolate oak, it's backed by dusty herbal notes and a hint of meatiness, with faint undertones of cedar, cigarboxes and treacle. Plush and smooth, its powerfully ripened black fruits are underpinned by powdery tannins, finishing firm and drying. Marginally too cooked for a higher rating.

2005	91	2013	2017
2004	95	2016	2024
2002	91	2010	2014+
2001	88	2006	2009
2000	86	2002	2005
1999	89	2007	2011
1998	92	2006	2010+
1997	87	2002	2005
1996	90	2004	2008+

CHARDONNAY

Coonawarra	$20–$29
Current vintage: 2005	**90**

Smooth and creamy, this long, evenly balanced and elegant chardonnay marries a slightly funky and leesy expression of white peach, stonefruit and melon with slightly meaty undertones and vanilla oak. It's backed by suggestions of cloves and cinnamon, with a savoury wheat biscuit-like quality. It finishes long and smooth, with soft acidity.

2005	90	2007	2010+
2004	87	2006	2009
2003	91	2005	2008
2002	88	2004	2007
2001	83	2006	2009+
1999	86	2000	2001+

SHIRAZ

Coonawarra	$20–$29
Current vintage: 2005	**92**

Dark, peppery and palate-staining flavours of dark berries, plums and cassis are matched with lightly smoky, fine-grained cedar/vanilla oak, backed by smooth, supple tannins. Medium to full in weight, it's lifted with a musky clove and cinnamon-like perfume, while its long, vibrant and slightly jammy palate finishes with sour-edged red fruits flavours and an attractive meatiness.

2005	92	2013	2017
2004	95	2012	2016+
2002	87	2007	2010
2001	90	2003	2006
1999	89	2001	2004+

THE BLEND

Coonawarra	$20–$29
Current vintage: 2005	**90**

A balanced, modern and stylish red with an unusually prevalent presence of mint and eucalypt characters for the Coonawarra region. Scented with violets, cassis and cedar/vanilla oak, it's firm and powdery, with an excellent length of primary dark berry/dark cherry flavour supported by chalky tannin. It finishes with lingering dark fruits and a suggestion of menthol.

2005	90	2010	2013+
2004	93	2012	2016+
2002	86	2004	2007+
2001	86	2006	2009
2000	86	2002	2005+

THE TALLY RESERVE CABERNET SAUVIGNON

Coonawarra	$50–$99
Current vintage: 2005	**94**

A powerful and savoury cabernet whose deep, dark, rather closed and tight-fisted aromas of black fruits, dark chocolate and dried herbs reveal a meaty aspect. Its long and finely honed palate marries deep, bright and dark-fruited cabernet flavour with assertive but balanced smoky and cedary oak and a frame of fine, firm and powdery tannin. It finishes very long indeed, with slightly herbal undertones of mint and menthol, plus a marginally baked note at the back of the palate. A very good wine indeed despite a slight rawness, that just lacks the even ripeness and regal structure of the 2004 vintage.

2005	94	2013	2017+
2004	97	2024	2034
2001	96	2013	2021
2000	91	2008	2012+
1998	93	2010	2018

A B C D E F G H I J K L M N O P Q R S T U V W X Y Z

Bannockburn

1750 Midland Highway, Bannockburn Vic 3331. Tel: (03) 5281 1363. Fax: (03) 5281 1349.
Website: www.bannockburnvineyards.com Email: info@bannockburnvineyards.com

Region: **Geelong** Winemaker: **Michael Glover** Viticulturist: **Lucas Grigsby** Chief Executive: **Phillip Harrison**

Bannockburn must be looking forward to the release of its 2006 wines, the first entirely made under the new regime headed by Michael Glover. While there has not been a release of Serré or SRH for a year or two, the 2005 Bannockburn table wines have clearly suffered at the hands of the ongoing drought and the resultant moisture stress, which has seriously affected the Geelong region.

CHARDONNAY

RATING **3**

Geelong	$50–$99
Current vintage: 2005	**87**

A luscious, marmalade-like chardonnay whose flavours of citrus fruits, melon and sweetcorn reveal undertones of wheatmeal. It's lightly floral and spirity, with a concentrated, juicy palate whose luscious citrus peel-like fruit is smooth and candied, finishing with a slightly cloying, barley sugar-like note.

Year	Rating		
2005	87	2007	2010
2004	88	2006	2009
2003	93	2008	2011+
2002	94	2007	2010+
2001	88	2006	2009+
2000	90	2002	2005+
1999	94	2004	2007
1998	93	2006	2010
1997	94	2002	2005+
1996	95	2001	2004
1995	96	1997	2000
1994	95	2002	2006
1993	96	2001	2005
1992	94	2000	2004

PINOT NOIR

RATING **4**

Geelong	$50–$99
Current vintage: 2005	**80**

Simple, meaty, vegetal and browning. Its rather cooked, raisined and currant-like fruit lacks much in the way of perfume, becoming meaty and syrupy on the palate. It's initially smooth and luscious, but loses brightness and freshness before finishing with drying, metallic tannins and raw acids. Very rustic and farmyard-like.

Year	Rating		
2005	80	2007	2010
2004	88	2006	2009+
2003	86	2005	2008
2002	91	2007	2010+
2001	90	2006	2009
2000	91	2005	2008
1999	94	2007	2011
1998	94	2003	2006
1997	94	2005	2009
1996	93	2004	2008+
1995	93	2003	2007+
1994	94	2002	2006+
1993	88	1998	2001+
1992	96	2004	2012

SERRÉ (Pinot Noir)

RATING **2**

Geelong	$50–$99
Current vintage: 2003	**92**

Wild, meaty and floral, this heady, earthy and early-maturing pinot presents a rustic fragrance suggestive of violets, smoked meats and briar. Smooth and juicy, it's deeply and lavishly flavoured, presenting a long and luscious palate of cherries, plums and cassis backed by savoury and earthy complexity. Framed by tight, fine-grained tannins, it's polished and supple. Its underlying brett-derived influences might be contributing to some tightening of palate length.

Year	Rating		
2003	92	2005	2008
2000	88	2005	2008
1999	96	2007	2011+
1998	96	2006	2010+
1997	95	2005	2009
1996	92	2004	2008+
1995	95	2003	2007
1994	96	2006	2014
1993	93	2001	2005
1991	72	1993	1996
1990	88	1998	2002+

SHIRAZ

2005	80	2007	2010
2004	89	2009	2012
2003	89	2008	2011+
2002	88	2004	2007+
2001	95	2009	2013+
2000	96	2012	2020
1999	89	2001	2004+
1998	95	2006	2010
1997	95	2009	2017
1996	93	2004	2008
1995	87	2000	2003
1994	95	2002	2006
1993	90	1998	2001
1992	95	2000	2004
1991	94	1999	2003+
1990	90	1998	2002

Geelong $50–$99
Current vintage: 2005   80

Dusty, earthy and browning, with floral, herbal aromas of lightly meaty fruit backed by sweet cedary oak and suggestions of capsicum. Rather baked flavours of redcurrants and plums are backed by raw oak, finishing with powerful notes of dried herbs and licorice. Lacking great length of fruit, it might also be starting to dry up. In all likelihood, made from very stressed vines.

SRH (Chardonnay)

RATING 2

2000	95	2005	2008+
1999	95	2004	2007
1995	94	1997	2000
1994	93	1996	1999
1993	97	1998	2001

Geelong $50–$99
Current vintage: 2000   95

Revelling in its customary palate fatness, toasty oak and savoury qualities, this steadily maturing and genuinely complex chardonnay backs its slightly edgy and oxidative expression of floral, nutty, melon-like and citrusy fruit with appealingly smoky, nougat-like undertones. Supported by smart, spicy new cooperage, it's chewy and viscous, but finishes long and waxy, with lingering fruit and matchstick-like oak.

Baptista

139 High Street, Nagambie Vic 3608. Tel: (03) 5794 2514. Fax: (03) 5794 1776.
Website: www.dromanaestate.com.au Email: DTW1@bigpond.com

Region: **Heathcote** Winemaker: **David Traeger** Viticulturist: **David Traeger** Chief Executive: **David Traeger**
Winemaker David Traeger has redeveloped one of Victoria's oldest shiraz vineyards, from which he crafts this rare and not inexpensive wine. Typically, the releases to date have aged fairly quickly with respect to their flavour profile and their brightness, while retaining a firm underlying structure of fine tannin.

SHIRAZ

RATING 4

2001	89	2013	2021
2000	91	2008	2012+
1999	92	2011	2019
1998	90	2006	2010+
1997	88	2005	2009+

Heathcote $50–$99
Current vintage: 2001   89

Very firm and fine-grained, this spicy, minty and earthy shiraz frames its meaty expression of dark plums, berries, licorice and cloves with a pliant but powerful chassis of drying tannin. While its rustic flavour profile and browning colour are beginning to show genuine development, its structure looks set for a longer term. It finishes with nuances of menthol and steadily opening layers of fruit.

2008 THE AUSTRALIAN WINE ANNUAL   35
www.jeremyoliver.com

Barossa Valley Estate

Seppeltsfield Road, Marananga SA 5355. Tel: (08) 8562 3599. Fax: (08) 8562 4255.
Website: www.bve.com.au Email: sales@bve.com.au

Region: **Barossa Valley** Winemaker: **Stuart Bourne** Viticulturist: **Kirsty Waller** General Manager: **Christine Hahn**

With the exception of the gamey and leathery E & E Black Pepper Shiraz, this winery struggled to maintain freshness and brightness in its 2003 reds. The 2004 edition of this wine is surprisingly cooked and jammy, lacking its typical shape and texture. As usual, the Ebenezer wines are very approachable, and incorporate the underlying structure required for future cellaring.

E&E BLACK PEPPER SHIRAZ

RATING

	Barossa Valley	$50–$99
	Current vintage: 2004	**88**

Slightly cooked and jammy, lacking its typical precision and focus, this very approachable and confiture-like shiraz reveals plenty of blackberry, raspberry and blackcurrant-like fruit combined with vanilla/coconut/dark chocolate oak. Long and smooth, with a plush core of flavour, it's backed by suggestions of mint and menthol and framed by well-knit and fine-grained tannin.

2004	88	2009	2012
2003	90	2011	2015
2002	94	2010	2014+
2001	94	2013	2021
2000	87	2002	2005+
1999	91	2004	2007+
1998	96	2010	2018
1997	90	2005	2009
1996	96	2004	2008+
1995	93	2007	2015
1994	93	2002	2006
1993	93	2001	2005
1992	91	2000	2004
1991	95	2003	2011

E&E SPARKLING SHIRAZ

RATING

	Barossa Valley	$50–$99
	Current vintage: 2003	**88**

Meaty, gamey and developed, this rustic and earthy sparkling shiraz has a slightly baked expression of dark plum, prune and currant-like fruit with undertones of polished leather and raisins. It's smooth and polished, generously flavoured, but lacks great length of fruit. A fair effort from a hot vintage.

2003	88	2008	2011
2002	92	2010	2014+
2001	90	2006	2009
1999	88	2007	2011+
1998	95	2006	2010
1996	93	2001	2004+
1995	91	2000	2003
1994	94	1999	2002+

EBENEZER CABERNET SAUVIGNON (Merlot)

RATING

	Barossa Valley	$20–$29
	Current vintage: 2003	**84**

The makers of this slightly porty, developed and earthy cabernet perhaps tried to compensate for its meaty, rather vegetal expression of red fruit and its slightly hollow mid palate with an astringent cut of rather raw and gritty tannin. It lacks the depth and richness of fruit for its substantial extract.

2003	84	2008	2011
2002	89	2010	2014
2001	86	2003	2006+
2000	85	2002	2005
1999	90	2004	2007
1998	87	2003	2006
1997	80	1999	2002
1996	91	2001	2004

EBENEZER SHIRAZ

RATING

	Barossa Valley	$20–$29
	Current vintage: 2004	**88**

Just slightly overcooked, with some green-edged fruit beneath its evolved and leathery expression of blackberries, dark plums and raisins. It's backed by older, lightly smoky vanilla oak and underpinned by fine, dusty tannins. Initially intense and vibrant, it has a smooth and moderately long palate.

2004	88	2006	2009+
2003	85	2005	2008+
2002	87	2004	2007+
2001	87	2006	2009
2000	83	2002	2005+
1999	88	2004	2007
1998	90	2003	2006
1997	88	2002	2005
1996	88	2001	2004
1995	92	2000	2003
1994	91	1999	2002
1993	86	1998	2001

Barwang

Barwang Road, Young NSW 2190. Tel: (02) 6382 3594. Fax: (02) 6382 3594.
Website: www.mcwilliams.com.au   Email: mcwines@mcwilliams.com.au

Region: **Hilltops** Winemaker: **Jim Brayne** Viticulturist: **Murray Pulleine** Chief Executive: **George Wahby**

Barwang is an individual vineyard site that has become the flag-bearer for the emerging Hilltops region of New South Wales. While recent releases have been affected by the ongoing drought which has caused a distinctly evident level of fruit stress, the Barwang label has established a reliable reputation for its mineral, grainy Chardonnay and long-living, deeply flavoured and robust red wines. Its elegant 2005 Merlot is especially encouraging.

CABERNET SAUVIGNON

RATING **4**

Hilltops $20–$29
Current vintage: 2003   91

A sumptuously ripened, concentrated and robust cabernet whose rich and minty expression of briary cassis, dark plum and blackberry-like fruit, and sweet mocha/vanilla oak are framed by firm, chalky tannins. While it reveals some pleasing herbal undertones, it's almost but not quite overcooked, retaining plenty of fruit brightness and intensity.

2003	91	2011	2015
2002	88	2010	2014
2001	92	2009	2013
2000	91	2012	2020
1999	90	2004	2007
1998	90	2006	2010+
1997	94	2005	2009+
1996	87	2001	2004
1995	89	2003	2007
1994	90	2002	2006
1993	91	2001	2005
1992	90	2000	2004
1991	95	1999	2003

CHARDONNAY

RATING **5**

Hilltops $12–$19
Current vintage: 2005   91

Delicate, grainy, wheatmeal aromas are accompanied by nuances of peach, quince and apple plus a hint of lanolin. Fine, taut and savoury, its long and elegant palate delivers a restrained expression of nutty fruit flavours before a tightly focused, lingering and mineral finish. Attractively reserved and lean.

2005	91	2007	2010+
2004	84	2005	2006
2002	87	2004	2007
2001	87	2003	2006
2000	90	2002	2005
1999	87	2001	2004
1998	94	2003	2006
1997	90	2002	2005
1996	92	2001	2004
1995	88	1997	2000
1994	91	1996	1999
1993	89	1995	1998

MERLOT

RATING **5**

Hilltops $20–$29
Current vintage: 2005   91

Polished and stylish, with a sweet, earthy perfume of cherries, plums and dried herbs backed by sweet chocolate/vanilla oak. Smooth and cedary, if just a little oaky, its vibrant berry/cherry fruit knits tightly with firmish, bony tannin, finishing with fresh acidity and lingering nuances of chocolate and dark cherry.

2005	91	2010	2013+
2002	91	2010	2014
2001	84	2006	2009+
2000	87	2002	2005+

SHIRAZ

RATING **4**

Hilltops $20–$29
Current vintage: 2003   86

A deeply flavoured and firmly structured shiraz whose powerfully spiced, meaty fruit profile of under-ripe and over-ripe flavour does suggest some stress in the vineyard prior to harvest. Spicy clove and cinnamon-like aromas of raisined fruit are lifted by cedary oak, while the palate is rather raw and sappy, with a metallic extract of drying tannin.

2003	86	2008	2011
2002	88	2007	2010+
2001	93	2009	2013
2000	89	2005	2008+
1999	88	2004	2007
1998	94	2006	2010
1997	94	2005	2009
1996	87	1998	2001
1995	93	2003	2005
1994	92	1999	2002
1993	94	1998	2001
1992	89	2000	2004

Bass Phillip

Tosch's Road, Leongatha South Vic 3953. Tel: (03) 5664 3341. Fax: (03) 5664 3209.
Email: bpwines@tpg.com.au

Region: **South Gippsland** Winemaker: **Phillip Jones** Viticulturist: **Phillip Jones** Chief Executive: **Phillip Jones**

The hot, dry 2005 vintage has helped fashion a series of brooding, bruising pinot from Bass Phillip's home block. While the Estate Pinot Noir was relatively easy to understand when tasting, since it presents a more restrained and supple expression of Bass Phillip's occasionally full orchestra style, the bottles tasted of Premium and Reserve provided some of the more interesting and challenging moments in the preparation of this book. Both are massively concentrated and, at this time, extremely oaky. They should have the depth and richness of fruit to develop into complex, if typically rustic Bass Phillip wines.

CROWN PRINCE PINOT NOIR

RATING **3**

South Gippsland $50–$99
Current vintage: 2003 82

Slightly cooked, stewy and varnishy, with over-ripened fruit partnered by raw oak. Very forward, lacking length and structure, delivering a thick, cloying and syrupy expression of fruit.

2003	82	2005	2008
2001	93	2003	2006+
2000	91	2005	2008
1999	93	2001	2004

ESTATE PINOT NOIR

RATING **3**

South Gippsland $50–$99
Current vintage: 2005 93

Deep-fruited and slightly hazy, this profound and meaty Estate pinot does require some cellaring. Its oaky bouquet of cherries and red plums overlies complex suggestions of undergrowth, duck fat and herbal tones. Sumptuous and deeply weighted, it's long and firm, with layers of fruit and structure backed by sweet cedar/vanilla oak.

2005	93	2010	2013+
2004	91	2009	2012
2003	83	2005	2008+
2002	93	2010	2014+
2001	95	2006	2009
2000	89	2005	2008
1999	94	2004	2007
1998	92	2003	2006
1997	93	2002	2005

PREMIUM PINOT NOIR

RATING **2**

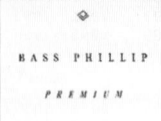

South Gippsland $100–$199
Current vintage: 2005 91

A bruising, slightly varnishy, sour-edged and brooding pinot with all the skeleton and fruit intensity, but not yet the flesh and the balance. It's briary and meaty, with layers of black and red berries, currants and dark chocolate oak framed by firm, drying tannins. An extremely difficult wine to evaluate so early in its youth, but one I would certainly wait for.

2005	91	2013	2017
2004	95	2009	2012+
2003	95	2011	2015+
2002	93	2014	2022+
2001	93	2009	2013
2000	87	2005	2008
1999	96	2007	2011
1998	88	2003	2006
1997	96	2009	2017
1996	90	2004	2008
1995	88	2003	2007
1994	96	2002	2006+
1993	95	1998	2001+

RESERVE PINOT NOIR

RATING **1**

South Gippsland $200+
Current vintage: 2005 96

Typically hazy and lightly browning, this presently raw-edged and blocky but actually well composed cellar style of pinot is heady, wild and concentrated, with a powerful presence of black cherry, black-berry and plum-like fruit. It's deep and musky, with scents of cloves, cinnamon, undergrowth and duck fat backed by dark chocolate/vanilla oak. Luscious and sumptuous, it finishes with great length and intensity. All it needs is time, and plenty of it!

2005	96	2013	2017+
2004	97	2012	2016+
2003	96	2015	2023
2001	96	2013	2021
2000	87	2002	2005
1999	83	2001	2004+
1998	93	2003	2006+
1997	97	2009	2017+
1996	95	2004	2008+
1995	93	2003	2007+
1994	93	2002	2006
1991	95	2003	2011
1989	95	2001	2009

VILLAGE PINOT NOIR

RATING **4**

| | | South Gippsland | $30–$49 |
| | | Current vintage: 2004 | 90 |

Slightly unpolished, this delicious young pinot has a heady, perfumed bouquet of rose garden fragrances, raspberries and sweet red cherries over subtle suggestions of caramel and spearmint. Round and sumptuous, its juicy and slightly confectionary expression of pristine pinot flavour is long and luscious, supported by fine and supple tannins. It finishes with characteristically soft acids.

2004	90	2006	2009+
2003	95	2008	2011
2001	92	2003	2006
1999	89	2001	2004

Batista Estate

Franklin Road, Middlesex WA 6258. Tel: (08) 9772 3530. Fax: (08) 9772 3530.
Region: **Manjimup** Winemaker: **Bob Peruch** Chief Executive: **Bob Peruch**
Batista is one of the leading small vineyards in the Pemberton/Manjimup/Warren Valley region, whose Pinot Noir and Shiraz are deeply flavoured, herbal and spicy. The 2005 Pinot Noir is extremely rustic and wild.

PINOT NOIR

RATING **5**

| | | Pemberton | $30–$49 |
| | | Current vintage: 2005 | 77 |

Meaty, wild and browning, this gamey, rather horsey young pinot would appear to have a significant presence of brettanomyces taint. Rich, savoury and quite powerful, it finishes rather drying and Bandaid-like.

2005	77	2007	2010
2002	86	2004	2007
2000	89	2002	2005
1999	86	2001	2004
1998	89	2003	2006
1997	87	2002	2005

Battle of Bosworth

Gaffney Road, Willunga SA 5171. Tel: (08) 8556 2441. Fax: (08) 8556 4881.
Website: www.battleofbosworth.com.au Email: bosworth@edgehill-vineyards.com.au
Region: **McLaren Vale** Winemaker: **Joch Bosworth** Viticulturist: **Joch Bosworth**
Chief Executives: **Louise Hemsley-Smith & Joch Bosworth**
The Bosworth family has been growing grapes in McLaren Vale since the 1840s, while this generation has been involved since the early 1970s. They earn their place in this book because of their evident determination to make top-level wine, as shown by the dramatic improvement in their reds since 2004.

CABERNET SAUVIGNON

RATING **5**

| | | McLaren Vale | $20–$29 |
| | | Current vintage: 2005 | 89 |

Backed by meaty and herbal nuances, this well-ripened cabernet presents juicy flavours of dark plums and cassis backed by creamy cedar/vanilla oak, with a faint vegetal background. It's long, smooth and sumptuous, with a firm frame of drying tannins and a lingering, but fractionally hot and spirity finish.

2005	89	2010	2013
2004	90	2009	2012+
2003	80	2005	2008
2002	79	2004	2007

SHIRAZ

RATING **5**

| | | McLaren Vale | $20–$29 |
| | | Current vintage: 2005 | 90 |

A fine wine indeed from this vintage whose bright, piercing and sour-edged flavours of dark plums and blackberries are tightly knit with sweet vanilla/cedar oak and undertones of white pepper, cloves, sage and cinnamon. Pleasingly long, smooth and vibrant, it's penetrative, sour-edged and supported by pliant but crunchy tannins.

2005	90	2010	2013
2004	90	2012	2016
2003	82	2008	2011
2002	80	2004	2007

Best's

Best's Road, Great Western Vic 3377. Tel: (03) 5356 2250. Fax: (03) 5356 2430.
Website: www.bestswines.com Email: info@bestswines.com

Regions: **Grampians, Great Western** Winemakers: **Viv Thomson, Adam Wadewitz**
Viticulturist: **Ben Thomson** Chief Executive: **Viv Thomson**

An icon in Australian wine, Best's is an historic winery in western Victoria whose shirazes rate among Australia's finest. The 2004 Thomson Family Reserve is rather more robust and powerful than most in recent years, and like the dark and brooding Bin O, should cellar well for the long term. The Bin 1 Shiraz, made from 'younger' vines, has produced two fine, savoury and peppery releases in 2004 and 2005. The other pick of current releases is another elegant and supple Cabernet Sauvignon, a delightful medium-bodied cellaring prospect.

BIN NO O SHIRAZ

RATING **3**

Grampians, Great Western	**$50–$99**	2004	93	2016	2024

Current vintage: 2004   93

Very closed, musky and brooding, this deeply layered, dark and savoury shiraz has a strength and depth that belies its comparative elegance and tightness. It's deep, dark and ethereal, encapsulating powerful, densely packed dark meaty fruits that slowly emerge with scents of black pepper and a suggestion of mint. Underpinned by an iron-like rod of tannin, it's long-term wine with a huge future.

2004	93	2016	2024
2003	87	2011	2015
2002	87	2010	2012
2001	92	2009	2013+
2000	93	2008	2012
1998	95	2010	2018+
1997	90	2005	2009
1996	95	2004	2008
1995	95	2007	2015
1994	88	2006	2014+
1993	86	1998	2001
1992	95	2004	2012
1991	91	1999	2003

CABERNET SAUVIGNON

RATING **4**

Grampians, Great Western   **$20–$29**

Quite a supple, elegant and charming cabernet whose sweet, perfumed expression of raspberry, cherry and cassis-like fruit reveals undertones of tightly knit vanilla oak and suggestions of forest floor. Long, succulent and finely crafted, with lingering fruit sweetness and a pleasing balance with fine tannins and restrained oak, it finishes with length of fruit and fresh acidity.

2005	90	2013	2017
2001	91	2009	2013+
2000	87	2005	2008
1999	91	2011	2019
1998	91	2010	2018
1997	90	2005	2009+
1996	88	1998	2001
1995	90	2007	2015
1993	87	2001	2005
1992	90	2004	2012
1991	90	1999	2003+
1990	92	1998	2002
1989	82	1991	1994

Current vintage: 2005   90

CHARDONNAY

RATING **5**

Grampians, Great Western $20–$29

Current vintage: 2005   89

Just a fraction candied, this elegant and shapely young chardonnay has a smoky, lightly funky, creamy and meaty expression of tangy quince, cumquat, melon and lemon-like fruit neatly tied together by tight, taut acidity. It's complex and elegant, with well-handled vanilla oak and plenty of length. It finishes with a cooked hint of skinsy character.

2005	89	2007	2010+
2003	87	2005	2008
2001	92	2006	2009
2000	84	2002	2005
1998	86	2003	2006
1997	88	2002	2005
1996	89	1998	2001
1995	93	2003	2007
1994	94	2006	2014

PINOT MEUNIER

RATING **5**

Grampians, Great Western   **$50–$99**

Current vintage: 2003   87

It retains plenty of fruit, but this slightly cooked and meaty pinot meunier is beginning to show its age. Backed by sweet cedar/vanilla oak, its gamey flavours of raspberries, cherry and plums overlie suggestions of cloves and cinnamon. Supple and fine-grained, with a firm, bony grip, it finishes slightly raw-edged, with lingering currant-like flavours.

2003	87	2008	2011
2002	87	2007	2010+
2001	87	2003	2006
1999	90	2004	2007
1998	89	2003	2006
1997	87	2005	2009
1996	90	2004	2008
1995	88	2003	2007
1994	89	2002	2006

PINOT NOIR

RATING **5**

Grampians, Great Western $20–$29
Current vintage: 2004   87

Charmingly regional and minty, but rather a simple, fruit-driven pinot that lacks genuine silkiness and perfume. It offers a light floral fragrance, and its confectionary expression of cherries, raspberries and plums overlies earthy and meaty qualities, with hints of clove and under-brush. Smooth and elegant, it finishes with moderate length and a fine, powdery grip.

2004	87	2009	2012
2001	88	2003	2006+
2000	87	2005	2008
1999	87	2001	2004
1998	89	2000	2003+
1997	77	1998	1999
1996	89	2001	2004

RIESLING

RATING **4**

Great Western $20–$29
Current vintage: 2007   89

Ripe and juicy, with slightly confectionary lemon rind, lime juice, pear and apple-like fruit. Its lifted floral aromas precede a smooth, tangy and intensely flavoured palate of pleasing freshness and crispness, but with a lightly candied aspect that might reduce its longevity. It finishes long, fresh and racy, with clean acids and a lingering presence of powdery phenolics.

2007	89	2012	2015
2006	93	2014	2018
2005	91	2013	2017
2004	90	2009	2012+
2003	92	2011	2015
2002	93	2010	2014
2001	88	2003	2006+
2000	88	2005	2008
1999	93	2007	2011
1998	88	2003	2006
1997	82	1999	2002
1996	89	1998	2001
1995	94	2003	2007
1994	94	2006	2014
1993	83	1995	1998

THOMSON FAMILY SHIRAZ

RATING **2**

Grampians, Great Western $50–$99
Current vintage: 2004   95

Rich, powerful and assertive, and just within the bounds of genuine ripeness. Deep, dark and spicy, its meaty, leathery and briary expression of intense red and black berry fruits is backed by dusty clove and vanilla-like oak. Framed by a firm and palate-coating extract of drying tannin, it finishes long and persistent, nutty and savoury. Slightly raw, it's an unashamed cellar style that needs time to reach its ultimate balance and integration.

2004	95	2024	2034
2001	93	2013	2021
1998	93	2006	2010
1997	94	2005	2009+
1996	97	2008	2016
1995	96	2007	2015+
1994	93	2004	2012
1992	96	2004	2012

Bethany

Bethany Road, Bethany via Tanunda SA 5352. Tel: (08) 8563 2086. Fax: (08) 8563 0046.
Website: www.bethany.com.au Email: bethany@bethany.com.au
Region: **Barossa Valley** Winemakers: **Geoff & Robert Schrapel, Colin Slater**
Viticulturists: **Geoff & Robert Schrapel** Chief Executives: **Geoff & Robert Schrapel**

It's exciting to see that with the GR Reserve Shiraz from 2004 and its two Rieslings from 2006, Bethany is re-emerging as a maker of serious Barossa wine. There has been little doubt concerning the quality of the vineyard available to the company, and what seems to be a renewed commitment to viticulture and winemaking is paying off. The wines show a more even length of ripeness and intensity, plus a bit more polish and finesse.

CABERNET MERLOT

Barossa Valley $12–$19
Current vintage: 2004   80

Simple, stewy aromas of plums, cranberries and currants with greenish, stressed undertones precede a forward and rather lifeless palate of prunes and currants that is loosely framed by green and metallic edges.

2004	80	2006	2009
2002	82	2004	2007
2001	82	2003	2006
2000	88	2002	2005+
1999	82	2001	2004
1998	87	2003	2006
1997	81	1999	2002
1996	84	1998	2001
1995	87	1997	2000
1994	90	2002	2006
1993	82	1995	1998

EDEN VALLEY RIESLING

Eden Valley $12–$19
Current vintage: 2006   92

A delicate limey, mineral and slightly funky riesling whose smoky, earthy bouquet precedes a long and juicy palate whose citrusy fruit overlies a powdery backbone. It finishes shapely and focused, with suggestions of minerality and wet slate. Very interesting and approachable.

2006	92	2011	2014+
2003	90	2008	2011
2002	82	2004	2007
2001	89	2006	2009
2000	82	2001	2002
1999	88	2001	2004
1998	84	2000	2003
1997	83	1998	1999
1996	90	2001	2004+
1995	87	2000	2003+

GR RESERVE RED

Barossa Valley $50–$99
Current vintage: 2004   93

Finely crafted, elegant and restrained, this supple, silky-smooth shiraz marries pristine, vibrant and juicy small berry and plum-like fruit with spicy, dark chocolate-like oak and fine-grained dusty tannins. It's tightly integrated, finely balanced and permeated by nuances of cloves, cinnamon and white pepper, before finishing long and savoury.

2004	93	2016	2024
1999	82	2001	2004
1998	82	2003	2006+
1997	77	1999	2002
1996	90	2001	2004
1995	86	2000	2003
1994	92	1999	2002+
1992	90	1997	2000

RIESLING

Barossa Valley, Eden Valley $12–$19
Current vintage: 2006   90

Smooth, generous and approachable, this beautifully shaped young riesling has a delicate floral perfume of pear and lemon drops with faint undertones of bathpowder. Finishing with well-defined crispness and definition, its vibrant expression of lemon, lime and apple flavour has plenty of length and brightness.

2006	90	2011	2014
2005	88	2007	2010+
2004	91	2006	2009
2003	87	2004	2005+
2002	89	2004	2007+
2001	87	2003	2006
2000	87	2001	2002+
1999	89	2001	2004
1998	88	2000	2003
1997	81	1999	2002
1996	90	2001	2004
1995	87	2000	2003

SELECT LATE HARVEST RIESLING

Barossa Valley $20–$29
Current vintage: 2006   88

Generous and juicy, fresh and fruity, with slightly spicy and spiky flavours of Packham pear, apple and lime juice and a lingering palate of medium sweetness and lusciousness. With lemon sherbet-like and powdery texture, it finishes with refreshing acids and a hint of spiciness.

2006	88	2007	2008
2005	86	2007	2010
2004	86	2005	2006+
2003	89	2004	2005+
2002	87	2003	2004+
1999	90	2001	2004
1998	89	2000	2003+
1997	90	1999	2002
1996	91	2001	2004
1995	87	1997	2000

SEMILLON

Barossa Valley $12–$19
Current vintage: 2004   90

A tangy and varietal semillon whose fresh, fruit-driven aroma of melon, lemon, hints of quince and cumquat overlies a light background of toasty vanilla oak. Round, soft and generous, its lightly oaked palate of smooth, juicy fruit is as approachable as it is fresh and lively. It finishes with a faint hint of ashtray-like oak.

2004	90	2006	2009+
2003	88	2005	2008
2002	89	2004	2007
2001	86	2003	2006
2000	88	2002	2005
1999	89	2001	2004
1998	89	2000	2003

Bindi

343 Melton Road, Gisborne Vic 3437. Tel: (03) 5428 2564. Fax: (03) 5428 2564.
Email: mdhillone@bigpond.net.au

Region: **Macedon Ranges** Winemakers: **Michael Dhillon, Stuart Anderson** Viticulturist: **Michael Dhillon**
Chief Executive: **Michael Dhillon**

Led by the Quartz Chardonnay and the Block 5 Pinot Noir, both of which are on the cusp of a '1' ranking in this guide, Bindi continues to refine its art. Its wines marry a hedonistic perfume with palate intensity, but most importantly a definition and structure rare in New World wine. With increasing vine age now providing more underlying richness and complexity, its low-cropped wines are entering a new phase of excellence.

BLOCK 5 PINOT NOIR

RATING **2**

Macedon Ranges	$50–$99
Current vintage: 2005	**97**

An exceptional pinot of exemplary perfume, length, structure and intensity. Enhanced by sweet new oak, its ethereal bouquet unfolds aromas of brooding black and red cherries, musky spices, red berries, cloves and cinnamon. Silky and supple yet powerfully flavoured, it's steeped in flavours of cherries, plums, chocolate and briar, with an assertive but pliant underswell of tannins that leave an impression of hidden power and strength.

2005	97	2013	2017+
2004	96	2012	2016
2003	97	2011	2015
2002	89	2004	2007
2001	94	2006	2009+
2000	87	2002	2005+
1998	92	2003	2006
1997	96	2005	2009

COMPOSITION CHARDONNAY (formerly Chardonnay)

RATING **2**

Macedon Ranges	$30–$49
Current vintage: 2006	**91**

Pleasingly generous and succulent, but also tightly focused, long and slatey, this savoury young chardonnay reveals lively flavours of melon, nectarine and citrus fruit over nuances of funkiness, cloves and dusty vanilla oak. With some initial roundness and juiciness, it finishes with pleasing length and persistence of lemon zest and quince-like fruit.

2006	91	2008	2011+
2005	94	2010	2013
2004	91	2006	2009
2003	95	2008	2011+
2002	95	2007	2010+
2001	89	2003	2006+
2000	87	2002	2005+
1999	86	2001	2004
1998	88	2003	2006
1997	93	2002	2005
1996	87	1998	2001
1995	93	2000	2003
1994	95	2002	2006

ORIGINAL VINEYARD PINOT NOIR

RATING **3**

Macedon Ranges	$50–$99
Current vintage: 2005	**92**

Brambly, slightly herbal aromas of maraschino cherries, raspberries and cranberries precede a smooth, elegant palate whose stylish expression of mouthfilling small fruits conceals a light herbaceousness that might diminish or become more tobaccoey. It's underpinned by fine, silky tannins and is likely to build quite handsomely.

2005	92	2010	2013
2004	95	2009	2012
2003	95	2008	2011
2002	90	2007	2010
2001	90	2006	2009
2000	87	2005	2008
1999	86	2001	2004
1998	91	2003	2006
1997	95	2002	2005
1996	95	2004	2008
1995	94	2000	2003
1994	94	2002	2006

QUARTZ CHARDONNAY

RATING **2**

Macedon Ranges	$50–$99
Current vintage: 2005	**97**

A sophisticated, taut and stylish chardonnay with excellent length and balance. Its restrained and slightly oaky bouquet opens to reveal layers of citrus, melon and pineapple over wheatmeal and floral nuances. Its smooth, measured palate seamlessly marries restrained but piercingly intense flavours of melon, pineapple and grapefruit with spicy vanilla oak, before a lingering austere and mineral finish of chiselled acidity.

2005	97	2010	2013+
2004	95	2009	2012
2003	97	2011	2015
2002	97	2007	2010+
2001	93	2006	2009
2000	93	2005	2008+
1999	90	2001	2004+
1998	95	2003	2006+
1995	95	2000	2003

Blackjack

Calder Highway, Harcourt Vic 3453. Tel: (03) 5474 2355. Fax: (03) 5474 2355.
Website: www.blackjackwines.com.au Email: sales@blackjackwines.com.au
Region: **Bendigo** Winemakers: **Ian McKenzie, Ken Pollock** Viticulturist: **Ian McKenzie**
Chief Executive: **Ian McKenzie**

Blackjack is an established Bendigo red wine maker with a solid track record that dates back to the early 1990s.
Its 2005 Block 6 is its finest yet, with a dimension of suppleness and smoothness that contrasts with the more
confiture-like property of the 'standard' edition. The Cabernet Merlot from the same year is finely structured
and layered, with deliciously intense flavour.

BLOCK 6 SHIRAZ

RATING **4**

Bendigo $30–$49
Current vintage: 2005 91

A modern, spotless shiraz whose deep, dark and
spicy perfume of blackberries, cassis and sweet
new dark chocolate/vanilla oak reveals undertones
of cloves, cinnamon and black pepper. Smooth
and sumptuous, its pristine, vibrant dark fruit flavours
are backed by mocha-like oak, suggestions of mint
and menthol and a light minerality. Framed by
silky, fine-grained tannins, it's long, juicy and
persistent.

2005	91	2013	2017
2004	89	2009	2012
2003	88	2008	2011
2002	91	2007	2010

CABERNET MERLOT

RATING **5**

Bendigo $20–$29
Current vintage: 2005 89

Rather simple at present, this fine effort from a
hot year should flesh out well in the bottle. Its meaty,
earthy flavours of plums, blackberries and currants
and slightly overt vanilla/cedar/dark chocolate
oak reveal minty, iodide-like undertones. It's
smooth but assertively structured, with layers of
persistent black-fruited flavour and assertive oak
finishing with length and polish.

2005	89	2013	2017+
2004	90	2012	2016
2003	85	2005	2008+
2002	89	2007	2010
2001	90	2009	2013+
2000	89	2005	2008+
1999	83	2001	2004
1998	89	2003	2006
1997	90	2005	2009
1996	87	2001	2004
1995	85	1997	2000

SHIRAZ

RATING **5**

Bendigo $30–$49
Current vintage: 2005 88

Smoky aromas of dark chocolate, dark plums, blackberries and cedary oak precede a sweetly oaked
and slightly jammy, juicy palate. Backed by sweet
coconut ice-like oak, its approachable palate of
confiture-like raspberry, cassis and blackberry flavour
is framed by smooth, silky tannins, finishing long
and minty. It would rate more highly if not for a
medicinal oak-derived aspect.

2005	88	2010	2013+
2004	88	2006	2009+
2003	87	2005	2008
2002	87	2004	2007+
2001	92	2006	2009+
2000	90	2002	2005+
1999	88	2004	2007
1998	89	2003	2006+
1997	90	2002	2005
1996	90	2001	2004
1995	82	1997	2000

Bleasdale

Wellington Road, Langhorne Creek SA 5255. Tel: (08) 8537 3001. Fax: (08) 8537 3224.
Website: www.bleasdale.com.au Email: bleasdale@bleasdale.com.au

Region: **Langhorne Creek** Winemakers: **Michael Potts, Renae Hirsch** Viticulturist: **Robert Potts**
Chief Executive: **David Foreman**

Bleasdale is a stalwart of Langhorne Creek, whose wines are typically ripe, generous, approachable and relatively long-living. They're also among the most affordable of their kind. The 2004 Frank Potts blend is a finely crafted, silky and balanced wine, while the Mulberry Tree Cabernet Sauvignon from the same vintage is easy to enjoy. Some wines still reflect the vine stress that has affected the Langhorne Creek region.

BREMERVIEW SHIRAZ

RATING **5**

Langhorne Creek	$12–$19
Current vintage: 2004	**87**

Rather simple and unsophisticated, this fresh and juicy young shiraz is more of an honest quaffer. It's quite evolved, with a meaty, leathery bouquet that just lacks a little brightness. Full to medium in weight, its smooth and vibrant expression of small black and red berry flavours and smoky coconut oak is framed by soft, pliant tannins. The palate is much more interesting than the nose, but shows signs of drying out.

2004	87	2006	2009
2003	85	2008	2011
2002	87	2007	2010+
2001	89	2003	2006+
2000	90	2008	2012
1999	89	2004	2007
1998	87	2003	2006
1997	92	2005	2009
1996	89	2001	2004
1995	90	2000	2003
1993	82	1995	1998
1992	88	2000	2004

FRANK POTTS CABERNET BLEND

RATING **4**

Langhorne Creek	$20–$29
Current vintage: 2004	**91**

Lightly floral aromas of violets, blackberries, cranberries and sweet red plums are backed by cedar/vanilla oak, with underlying herbal complexity. Long, fine and supple, the smooth and polished palate of vibrant, surprisingly generous and brightly lit small berry fruit is backed by silky tannin and sweet cedar/vanilla oak. Its natural balance and stability will assist its likely longevity.

2004	91	2016	2024
2003	90	2011	2015
2002	89	2010	2014+
2001	89	2009	2013
2000	89	2005	2008+
1999	93	2007	2011
1998	90	2003	2006+
1997	90	2005	2009
1996	92	2004	2008+
1995	92	2003	2007
1994	87	1999	2002

MALBEC

RATING **5**

Langhorne Creek	$12–$19
Current vintage: 2003	**90**

A sound, firm and well-balanced malbec with a sweet, earthy and slightly confectionary aroma of cassis and raspberries that reveals floral undertones of mint and violets. Smooth and generous, it's pleasingly bright and spicy, with lingering flavours of ripe berry fruit framed by a drying and fine-grained astringency plus light oak influences.

2003	90	2011	2015
2002	82	2004	2007
2001	90	2006	2009
2000	89	2005	2008
1999	87	2004	2007
1998	88	2000	2003
1997	85	1998	2001
1996	84	1998	2001
1994	88	1999	2003
1992	82	1997	2000

MULBERRY TREE CABERNET SAUVIGNON

RATING **5**

Langhorne Creek	$12–$19
Current vintage: 2004	**88**

Sweet and fragrant, fresh and floral, with sweet red and black berry aromas over earthy, gamey complexity, this vibrant, juicy and forward young cabernet delivers bright cassis, mulberry, plum and raspberry flavour in an uncomplicated, pliant fashion that is ready to enjoy.

2004	88	2009	2012
2003	87	2005	2008+
2002	87	2010	2014
2001	87	2006	2009
2000	87	2005	2008
1999	90	2004	2007
1998	88	2003	2006
1997	88	2002	2005+
1996	89	2004	2008
1995	82	1997	2000
1993	87	2001	2005
1992	89	2000	2004

Blue Pyrenees

Vinoca Road, Avoca Vic 3467. Tel: (03) 5465 3202. Fax: (03) 5465 3529.
Website: www.bluepyrenees.com.au Email: info@bluepyrenees.com.au
Region: **Pyrenees** Winemaker: **Andrew Koerner** Chief Executive: **John B. Ellis**

While its table wines have been affected by recent hot and dry vintages, there is still plenty of evidence that Andrew Koerner is turning around one of the largest quality wine operations in central Victoria. The very fine Chardonnays and the Shiraz Viognier from 2004 are ample proof of that. Blue Pyrenees is blessed with exceptional infrastructure and vineyard resources.

CABERNET SAUVIGNON

RATING **5**

Pyrenees $12–$19
Current vintage: 2004 89

An honest, vibrant, minty and violet-like cabernet with pleasing length, tightness and elegance. Its fragrance of blackberries, dark plums, plain chocolate and dark olives precedes a long and dusty palate whose bright, minty berry/plum flavours knit tightly with polished oak and tannin.

2004	89	2009	2012+
2003	82	2005	2008
2002	81	2007	2010
2001	88	2003	2006+
2000	83	2002	2005
1999	89	2001	2004

CHARDONNAY

RATING **4**

Pyrenees $12–$19
Current vintage: 2005 87

Moderately intense and lightly toasty, with nutty/vanilla oak and creamy, buttery influences beneath its melon and peach-like fruit. Smooth and generous, with a pleasing length of fruit before a fresh, but fractionally sweet finish.

2005	87	2007	2010
2004	90	2005	2006+
2003	90	2005	2008
2002	84	2003	2004
2001	82	2002	2003
2000	87	2002	2005

ESTATE RESERVE CHARDONNAY

RATING **3**

Pyrenees $30–$49
Current vintage: 2004 95

Pleasing indeed to see this important Victorian winery back in top form. This spotless and tightly crafted chardonnay reveals a complex floral perfume whose white peach and honeydew melon aromas are supported by fine-grained, spicy oak. Long and silky, its tightly focused palate boasts a pristine core of vibrant nutty fruit punctuated by refreshing but unusually soft acids.

2004	95	2006	2009+
2001	95	2006	2009
2000	86	2001	2002+
1999	93	2004	2007
1998	88	2000	2003
1997	93	2002	2005
1996	91	2001	2004+
1995	88	1997	2000
1994	89	1999	2002

ESTATE RESERVE (Cabernet Blend)

RATING **5**

Pyrenees $30–$49
Current vintage: 2002 86

A rustic, old-fashioned central Victorian red whose minty expression of plums and small berries is backed by eucalypt and menthol-like undertones. A little dull and meaty on the nose, it reveals more fruit sweetness on the palate, where structure and firm, drying tannins are also evident. With lingering nuances of leather and chocolate, it's a little too lean and hard-edged.

2002	86	2007	2010+
2001	87	2009	2013+
2000	84	2005	2008
1999	93	2007	2011+
1998	93	2010	2018
1997	89	2005	2009
1996	93	2008	2016
1995	93	2003	2007
1994	95	2002	2006+
1993	94	2001	2005
1992	92	2000	2004

RESERVE SHIRAZ VIOGNIER

RATING **4**

Pyrenees	$30–$49
Current vintage: 2004	91

Stylish, fine-grained and elegant, this willowy, shiraz-dominant blend supports its minty, peppery expression of cassis, blackberries and blueberries with dusty, drying tannins. It's scented with violets, musk, cinnamon and cloves, with a whiff of peppermint and sweet cedar/chocolate/vanilla oak. Just slightly confectionary, it's artfully balanced, delivering a full length of spicy fruit finished with a pleasing grip and fresh acidity.

2004	91	2012	2016
2003	89	2008	2011+
2002	81	2004	2007

SHIRAZ

RATING **5**

Pyrenees	$12–$19
Current vintage: 2004	83

Slightly browning, with a minty, meaty and toothpaste-like expression of blackberry jam, menthol and dark chocolate over nuances of dried herbs. Rather dominated by mintiness, and lacking genuine mid-palate freshness and fruit.

2004	83	2006	2009+
2003	86	2005	2008+
2002	85	2004	2007
2001	90	2006	2009
2000	90	2002	2005+
1999	82	2001	2004

Bowen Estate

Riddoch Highway, Coonawarra SA 5263. Tel: (08) 8737 2229. Fax: (08) 8737 2173.
Website: www.coonawarra.org/wineries/bowen/ Email: bowen@bowenestate.com.au
Region: **Coonawarra** Winemakers: **Doug Bowen, Emma Bowen** Viticulturist: **Doug Bowen**
Chief Executive: **Joy Bowen**

2005 has seen some riper, slightly meatier reds from this well-established family winery. Bowen Estate, which was established in the early 1970s, is today a significant presence in Coonawarra, with the second generation deeply involved in its winemaking. While it is principally a red specialist, its Chardonnay shows more interest and savoury complexity than ever before.

CABERNET SAUVIGNON

RATING **3**

Coonawarra	$30–$49
Current vintage: 2005	92

Handsomely backed by dark, toasty, smoky oak, this sumptuous and cedary cabernet carries its 15% alcohol surprisingly well. Scented with dark plums, berries and cedar, with underlying meaty complexity, it's smooth, even and juicy. Fractionally warm, with a plush, pristine expression of concentrated cassis/dark berry flavour and lightly roasted French oak, it's framed by firm, smooth tannin.

2005	92	2013	2017+
2004	95	2016	2024+
2003	90	2011	2015
2002	92	2010	2014
2001	94	2006	2009+
2000	90	2005	2008
1999	82	2001	2004
1998	95	2010	2018
1997	87	2005	2009
1996	88	2008	2016+
1995	77	1997	2000
1994	90	2002	2006
1993	84	1998	2001
1992	93	2000	2004+

CHARDONNAY

RATING **5**

Coonawarra	$20–$29
Current vintage: 2005	89

A maturing, balanced, shorter-term chardonnay whose buttery bouquet of peach, nectarine and sweet vanilla and clove-like oak has a background of wheatmeal and nutmeg. Long, taut and tangy, its nutty, mealy palate of quince, lemon and cumquat-like fruity finishes with light undertones of cheesy and meaty complexity.

2005	89	2007	2010
2004	89	2006	2009
2003	89	2005	2008
2001	86	2002	2003
2000	77	2002	2005
1999	89	2001	2004

SHIRAZ

RATING 2

Coonawarra	$30–$49
Current vintage: 2005	**92**

Dusty aromas of sweet juicy small black and red berries, smoky vanilla French oak, white pepper, cloves and cinnamon precede a firm, pliant palate of length and richness. Backed by smooth, creamy oak, it is plush, fractionally meaty and currant-like, but has enough deep and bright, vibrant fruit for sound medium-term cellaring.

2005	92	2010	2013+
2004	94	2012	2016+
2003	93	2011	2015
2002	95	2014	2020
2001	95	2009	2013+
2000	94	2008	2012+
1999	81	2001	2004
1998	93	2010	2018
1997	88	2005	2009
1996	88	2001	2004
1995	90	2003	2007
1994	93	2002	2006
1993	94	2001	2005
1992	95	2000	2004
1991	94	1996	1999

Brand's

Main Road, Coonawarra SA 5263. Tel: (08) 8736 3260. Fax: (08) 8736 3208.
Website: www.mcwilliams.com.au Email: brands_office@mcwilliams.com.au
Region: **Coonawarra** Winemaker: **Peter Weinberg** Viticulturist: **Trent Brand** Chief Executive: **George Wahby**

Brand's is the Coonawarra base for the McWilliam family. Its wines are typically fine, full to medium in weight, smooth and elegant. The 2005 Cabernet Sauvignon, a wine that exemplifies Coonawarra elegance and charm, is what they're all about.

CABERNET SAUVIGNON

RATING 4

Coonawarra	$20–$29
Current vintage: 2005	**91**

A finely balanced and structured young cabernet whose intense, slightly minty flavours of cassis, dark plums, blackberries and mulberries are supported by vanilla oak and a fine-grained, rather silky backbone of sandpapery tannin. Ripe and juicy, it's long, stylish and backed by suggestions of dried herbs and a hint of menthol.

2005	91	2010	2013+
2004	90	2009	2012+
2003	82	2005	2008+
2002	84	2004	2007
2001	91	2006	2009+
2000	91	2002	2005+
1999	91	2004	2007+
1998	92	2006	2010
1997	90	2002	2005
1996	82	1998	2001
1995	87	2000	2003
1994	91	1999	2002

CHARDONNAY

RATING 5

Coonawarra	$12–$19
Current vintage: 2006	**85**

Simple and honest, with ripe and rather confectionary-like flavours of lemon, melon and peach backed by modest smoky and slightly vanilla oak. It's meaty and funky, with some charcuterie-like complexity, finishes a little short, with an under-ripe suggestion of sweetcorn.

2006	85	2008	2011
2005	87	2006	2007+
2004	88	2005	2006+
2003	88	2004	2005+
2002	83	2003	2004
2001	87	2002	2003+

MERLOT

RATING 4

Coonawarra	$20–$29
Current vintage: 2004	**90**

Smooth, effortless, pretty and easy-drinking, this supple young merlot marries pleasingly sour-edged dark cherry and plum-like fruit with sweet, creamy and chocolatey oak. Its spicy, floral perfume of sweet varietal fruit and cedary oak precedes a restrained palate whose juicy flavours and fine tannins finish with bright, clean acids.

2004	90	2009	2012
2003	90	2008	2011
2002	84	2004	2007+
2001	93	2006	2009
2000	90	2002	2005+
1999	90	2001	2004
1997	90	1999	2002

PATRON'S RESERVE (Cabernet Sauvignon Shiraz Merlot)

RATING **3**

Coonawarra	$50–$99
Current vintage: 2002	**86**

Full to medium in weight, with some pleasing fruit brightness and intensity, this moderately firm but slightly sappy red lacks genuine ripeness and balance. There's a herbal thread beneath its slightly dull aromas of plums, berries and cedar/vanilla oak, while it finishes rather greenish, with some modest fruit intensity and length.

2002	86	2007	2010+
2001	90	2009	2013
2000	92	2008	2012
1999	95	2007	2011+
1998	94	2006	2010+
1997	88	2002	2005+
1996	95	2004	2008+
1991	92	1999	2003+
1990	85	1995	1998

SHIRAZ

RATING **5**

Coonawarra	$20–$29
Current vintage: 2003	**88**

Leathery and lightly meaty aromas of red cherries, raspberries, fresh plums and sweet vanilla oak are backed by spicy nuances of cloves and cinnamon. Medium to full in weight, it's moderately fleshy, with a lively flavours of red berries and plums framed by slightly sappy and metallic tannins. Pleasing for the shorter term.

2003	88	2005	2008
2002	86	2004	2007
2001	92	2006	2009+
2000	87	2002	2005+
1999	89	2001	2004
1998	90	2000	2003+
1997	91	2002	2005
1996	89	1998	2001
1995	86	1997	2000
1994	82	1996	1999

STENTIFORD'S RESERVE OLD VINES SHIRAZ

RATING **2**

Coonawarra	$50–$99
Current vintage: 2002	**87**

Dusty, herbal and minty aromas of jammy plums and berries are backed by meaty, leathery undertones. Initially forward and juicy, it presents some fruit attractive sweetness and depth, but lacks conviction. It finishes with slightly raw and metallic tannins and green-edged fruit.

2002	87	2007	2010
2000	89	2005	2008+
1999	95	2007	2011+
1998	96	2010	2018
1997	94	2005	2009
1996	95	2004	2008
1995	91	2003	2007
1991	87	1996	1999
1990	86	1992	1995+
1988	87	1996	2000
1987	79	1992	1995
1986	91	1994	1998+
1985	92	1997	2005

Bremerton

Strathalbyn Road, Langhorne Creek SA 5255. Tel: (08) 8537 3093. Fax: (08) 8537 3109.
Website: www.bremerton.com.au Email: info@bremerton.com.au

Region: **Langhorne Creek** Winemaker: **Rebecca Willson** Viticulturist: **Tom Keelan** Chief Executive: **Craig Willson**
A family affair at Langhorne Creek, Bremerton has struggled a little to maintain the freshness and brightness of its red wines due to some very challenging seasons. These are typically quite assertive wines, with layers of rich, minty fruit supported by assertive and grainy oak. It will be interesting to see how the Willsons have handled the 2004 and 2005 vintages, which should have made red winemaking rather more satisfying.

OLD ADAM SHIRAZ

RATING **5**

Langhorne Creek	$30–$49
Current vintage: 2002	**87**

Sweet, slightly medicinal and menthol-like aromas of cassis, plums and restrained vanilla oak present a rather chemical note. The palate, however, has depth and richness of dark berry/plum fruit framed by a firm grip of drying tannins and supported by toasty vanilla oak. There's a hint of rawness and saltiness, but it's solid and firm, with lingering mint/menthol characters.

2002	87	2007	2010
2001	89	2006	2009
1999	86	2001	2004+
1998	88	2000	2003
1997	83	2002	2005
1996	90	2001	2004

RESERVE CABERNET SAUVIGNON (formerly Walter's)

RATING 5

Langhorne Creek	$30–$49
Current vintage: 2002	**82**

Earthy, meaty, browning and vegetal, this rather raw and drying cabernet presents rather a modest depth of berry/plum flavour that tends to be dominated by firm, grippy tannins and vegetal undertones.

2002	82	2007	2010
2001	89	2009	2013+
2000	86	2002	2005
1999	88	2004	2007
1998	90	2006	2010
1997	86	1999	2002
1996	89	2004	2008

SELKIRK SHIRAZ

RATING 5

Langhorne Creek	$20–$29
Current vintage: 2003	**87**

A competent, modern and oaky wine from a tough vintage. Its slightly cooked and jammy aromas of black and red berries, plums and mocha/chocolate oak overlie meaty, pruney influences. Smooth and persistent, it's moderately long and juicy, with some pleasing fruit sweetness, but reveals more raisined and currant-like flavours towards its slightly dehydrated and salty finish.

2003	87	2005	2008
2002	87	2004	2007+
2000	92	2005	2008+
1999	86	2001	2004
1998	85	2000	2003
1997	80	1999	2002
1996	89	2004	2008

VERDELHO

RATING 5

Langhorne Creek	$20–$29
Current vintage: 2006	**82**

Up-front, forward and rather oily, this lightly herbal and spicy verdelho has a juicy, candied expression of banana and melon-like tropical fruit. Initially round and luscious but lacking genuine length, it finishes with a light mineral note.

2006	82	2006	2007
2005	88	2006	2007
2004	87	2004	2005+
2003	87	2003	2004+
2002	88	2003	2004+

Brian Barry

Juds Hill Vineyard, Clare SA 5453. Tel: (08) 8363 6211. Fax: (08) 8362 0498.
Website: www.brianbarrywines.com Email: brianbarrywines@optusnet.com.au
Region: **Clare Valley** Winemakers: **Brian Barry, Judson Barry** Viticulturist: **Brian Barry** Chief Executive: **Brian Barry**
Brian Barry is a long-established and traditional maker of regional Clare Valley wines, with a particular focus on its Juds Hill Riesling. It is also presently developing a new 'icon' level label for its best blocks of riesling and red varieties.

JUDS HILL VINEYARD CABERNET BLEND

RATING 4

Clare Valley	$20–$29
Current vintage: 2004	**86**

Rich, flavoursome but rather cooked cabernet whose meaty and slightly tarry aromas of blackcurrants, currants, plums and raisins are backed by herbal, minty undertones. Its forward and treacle-like palate is thick and chewy, but doesn't offer any great length.

2004	86	2009	2012+
2002	89	2010	2014+
2000	93	2008	2012
1999	91	2007	2011
1997	81	1999	2002
1996	89	2008	2016
1995	88	2007	2015
1994	87	2006	2014
1993	83	1995	1998

JUDS HILL VINEYARD RIESLING

RATING 4

Clare Valley $20–$29
Current vintage: 2005 86

Spicy, spiky and slightly oxidative and varnishy aromas of lemon blossom and apricots have a rather syrupy aspect. Its juicy, but rather candied flavours of apple and pear overlie a minerally backbone. It improves significantly with breathing, but remains a little too sweet and spiky.

2005	86	2010	2013
2004	89	2006	2009+
2003	88	2005	2008+
2002	90	2007	2010+
2001	94	2009	2013+
2000	86	2002	2005
1999	80	1999	2000
1998	94	2003	2006+
1997	80	1998	1999
1996	93	2001	2004+
1995	93	2003	2007
1994	95	2002	2006

Briar Ridge

593 Mount View Road, Mount View NSW 2325. Tel: (02) 4990 3670. Fax: (02) 4990 7802.
Website: www.briarridge.com.au Email: indulge@briarridge.com.au
Region: **Lower Hunter Valley** Winemakers: **Mark Woods, Karl Stockhausen** Viticulturist: **Robert Thomson**
Chief Executive: **John Davis**

Briar Ridge is one of my favourite small Hunter makers. Its wines are very true to the region's long-held traditions of elegance and complexity. The 2006 Semillon is a classic example of the sort of wine Karl Stockhausen was making at Lindemans almost a lifetime ago, while the 2005 Shiraz is rustic, meaty and very regional.

KARL STOCKHAUSEN SEMILLON

RATING 3

Lower Hunter Valley $20–$29
Current vintage: 2006 92

A fine, old-fashioned Lindemans style of Hunter semillon, made by a Lindemans legend of yesteryear. With a dusty, chalky and talc-like aroma of lemon zest and melon and a trim, lean and focused palate finishing with freshness and austerity, it's very true to type and likely to age slowly.

2006	92	2014	2018
2005	90	2010	2013+
2003	82	2005	2008
2002	93	2010	2014

KARL STOCKHAUSEN SHIRAZ

RATING 3

Lower Hunter Valley $20–$29
Current vintage: 2005 93

Rustic and regional, this meaty, moderately firm and leathery shiraz has a slightly minty bouquet of blackberries, dark plums, cedar/vanilla oak and a whiff of menthol. Medium to full-bodied, it's smooth and polished, with plush, vibrant dark fruit flavour that becomes more evolved, funky and savoury towards the finish. Framed by slightly chalky, fine-grained tannin, it will become even more expressive and possibly even feral with time in the bottle.

2005	93	2013	2017
2002	90	2007	2010+
2001	89	2003	2006
2000	85	2005	2008
1999	95	2007	2011
1998	95	2006	2010+
1997	94	2005	2009
1996	84	2001	2004
1995	92	2007	2015
1994	88	1999	2002
1993	93	2001	2005

ROCK PILE CHARDONNAY

RATING 5

Lower Hunter Valley $20–$29
Current vintage: 2005 90

Elegant and quite complex, with lightly honeyed and spicy aromas of melon and butter overlying restrained dusty vanilla/matchstick oak. Soft and forward, its generous but reserved palate reveals spicy clove and cinnamon-like influences, finishing with suggestions of charcuterie.

2005	90	2007	2010+
2004	88	2006	2009
2003	76	2003	2004
2002	87	2004	2007
2001	90	2003	2006+
2000	87	2002	2005
1999	82	2001	2004
1998	90	2000	2003+
1997	88	1999	2002
1996	93	2001	2004

Bridgewater Mill

Mount Barker Road, Bridgewater SA 5155. Tel: (08) 8339 9200. Fax: (08) 8339 9299.
Website: www.bridgewatermill.com.au Email: bridgewatermill@petaluma.com.au
Region: **Adelaide Hills** Winemaker: **Andrew Hardy** Viticulturist: **Mike Harms** Chief Executive: **Anthony Roberts**
Its owners have finally returned Bridgewater Mill, whose home is a delightful sparkling wine cellar and restaurant high in the Adelaide Hills, to again being a label for freshly flavoured and varietal wines from its region. The 2006 Sauvignon blanc is rather a disappointment, since it began as a rather credible second label for Petaluma.

CHARDONNAY   RATING 5

	Adelaide Hills	$20–$29	2005	87	2007	2010
	Current vintage: 2005	**87**	2004	92	2006	2009+
			2002	83	2003	2004+
	A floral, lemon-scented bouquet of peaches,		2001	81	2002	2003
	creamy and butter/vanilla oak reveals delicate bath		2000	88	2002	2005
	salt-like undertones. Initially smooth and juicy, with		1999	87	2001	2004

concentrated flavours of lemon, peach and melon, it then becomes rather more angular, finishing with green-edged suggestions of cashews and a faint lingering sourness.

MILLSTONE SHIRAZ   RATING 4

	Various, SA	$20–$29	2001	91	2006	2009
	Current vintage: 2001	**91**	2000	89	2002	2005+
			1997	86	2002	2005
	A very good shiraz from this challengingly hot vintage,		1996	90	2001	2004
	whose deeply spiced and earthy bouquet of		1995	88	2000	2003
	dark chocolate, plums and blackberries reveals some		1994	91	1999	2002
	pleasingly meaty undertones. Medium to full in		1993	92	2001	2005
	weight, it's smooth and savoury, presenting a delight-		1992	93	1997	2000
	fully sour-edged expression of plum and cherry		1991	88	1996	1999

flavour beneath leathery and chocolate-like qualities. Pleasingly evolved in a Rhône-like fashion.

SAUVIGNON BLANC   RATING 5

	Adelaide Hills	$12–$19	2006	82	2006	2007
	Current vintage: 2006	**82**	2005	88	2005	2006
			2004	87	2004	2005+
	Fresh, delicate and herbal, with a rather closed and		2003	87	2003	2004
	slightly confectionary aroma of peach, lemon and		2002	89	2002	2003

melon. Rather broad and generous, with melon-like fruit that lacks intensity, focus and genuine varietal appeal, it's clean, sound but not particularly enticing.

Brokenwood

McDonalds Road, Pokolbin NSW 2320. Tel: (02) 4998 7559. Fax: (02) 4998 7893.
Website: www.brokenwood.com.au Email: sales@brokenwood.com.au
Regions: **Various** Winemaker: **Peter-James Charteris** Viticulturist: **Keith Barry** Chief Executive: **Iain Riggs**
While the Hunter Valley remains the epicentre of Brokenwood's activity, its viticulture has spread significantly, into Beechworth, Bathurst, Orange, McLaren Vale and the King Valley. The newer wines are typically well-made expressions of their varieties, but I firmly believe that the magic behind the label remains Hunter-based. A notable exception is the 2004 Cabernet blend, which combines an unlikely but delicious array of fruit.

CABERNET BLEND   RATING 4

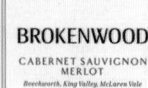

	Beechworth, King Valley,		2004	92	2012	2016+
	McLaren Vale	$20–$29	2003	83	2005	2008
	Current vintage: 2004	**92**	2002	91	2007	2010+
			2000	89	2005	2008
	Finely crafted and harmonious, with restrained		1999	90	2004	2007+
	but lively flavours of small red berries, redcurrants,		1997	90	2000	2005
	blackberries and dark plums tightly knit with		1996	87	2004	2008
	cedar/vanilla oak and a fine, crunchy spine of bony		1994	90	2002	2006
	tannins. It's floral and perfumed, with undertones		1992	93	2000	2004
	of dried herbs and a creamy cushion of dark		1991	93	1996	1999
	chocolate flavour. Supple and restrained, it's		1990	92	1995	1998

delightfully balanced and harmonious.

GRAVEYARD VINEYARD (Shiraz)

RATING **2**

Lower Hunter Valley $50–$99
Current vintage: 2005 95

Slightly meaty and musky, with ethereal aromas of dark berries, plums and violets backed by sweet, fine-grained oak. Long, fine and elegant, with a lingering and palate-staining core of cassis, blackberries and dark plums, it's tightly matched with sweet vanilla, cedar and dark chocolate oak. A slightly more powerful expression of Hunter shiraz, with underlying firmness and plenty of spicy regional quality.

2005	95	2017	2025
2004	95	2016	2024
2003	92	2015	2023
2002	93	2014	2022
2001	86	2006	2009
2000	97	2012	2020
1999	94	2011	2019
1998	95	2010	2018
1997	86	2002	2005+
1996	89	2004	2008+
1995	91	2003	2007
1994	88	2006	2014
1993	84	1998	2001+
1991	94	2003	2011+
1990	89	2002	2010
1989	87	1997	2001
1988	91	2000	2008

ILR RESERVE SEMILLON

RATING **3**

Lower Hunter Valley $30–$49
Current vintage: 2001 91

Meaty and rather savoury, this maturing semillon reveals toasty, honeyed and buttery nuances beneath its generous slightly confectionary melon-like fruit. Comparatively mature for its age, it's scented with dried flowers and lemon sherbet, while its richly flavoured, soft and moderately long palate lacks really tight definition.

2002	96	2012	2022
2001	91	2009	2013
2000	88	2005	2008+
1999	95	2007	2011+
1998	87	2003	2006+
1997	92	2005	2009
1996	90	2004	2008
1995	87	2000	2003
1994	93	2006	2014
1993	91	2001	2005

RAYNER VINEYARD SHIRAZ

RATING **3**

McLaren Vale $50–$99
Current vintage: 2004 88

A meaty, tarry McLaren Vale shiraz with an almost brooding expression of dark fruit. There's a jammy regional aspect about its impressively concentrated aromas, which are backed by restrained cedar/vanilla oak and nuances of dark olives. Forward and juicy, it does dry out a little towards its slightly cooked and dead-fruited finish, which just lacks the freshness and brightness for a higher rating and later drinking window.

2004	88	2009	2012
2003	93	2011	2015+
2002	94	2010	2014+
2001	93	2009	2013
2000	91	2005	2008
1999	89	2001	2004+
1996	93	2004	2008

SEMILLON

RATING **4**

Lower Hunter Valley $12–$19
Current vintage: 2006 90

Long, taut and refreshing, this lightly herbal semillon marries delicate, slightly candied melon and lemon flavours with a tea tin-like spiciness. Of medium intensity, it's fine and restrained but also surprisingly juicy and concentrated, culminating in a typically tight, dry and acidic finish. More traditional and regional than previous vintages, which have been more grassy and aromatic.

2006	90	2011	2014
2005	90	2007	2010
2004	91	2005	2006+
2003	86	2004	2005+
2002	90	2004	2007
2001	91	2002	2003
2000	91	2001	2004+
1998	95	2003	2006+
1997	91	2002	2005
1995	94	2003	2007
1994	93	2002	2006
1993	88	2001	2005
1992	87	2000	2004

SHIRAZ

BROKENWOOD
SHIRAZ
McLaren Vale, Padthaway Beechworth
750ml   WINE OF AUSTRALIA   14.5% VOL

Lower Hunter Valley	$30–$49
Current vintage: 2004	**93**

A very fine, medium-weight and deeply flavoured Hunter shiraz made along classically elegant and fragrant lines. Its spicy black pepper perfume of piercing small dark berry fruit and cedary oak reveals complex suggestions of leather, undergrowth and smoked meats. Elegant, smooth and savoury, it's long, smooth and fine-grained, with a lingering finishing of intense, spicy small berry fruit and earthy undertones.

2004	93	2012	2016
2003	82	2005	2008
2001	92	2006	2009
2000	87	2002	2005
1998	90	2003	2006
1996	88	2001	2004

Brown Brothers

239 Milawa-Bobinawarrah Road, Milawa Vic 3678. Tel: (03) 5720 5500. Fax: (03) 5720 5511
Website: www.brownbrothers.com.au Email: bbmv@brownbrothers.com.au

Region: **NE Victoria** Winemakers: **Wendy Cameron, Hamish Seabrook, Marc Scalzo, Joel Tilbrook, Cate Looney** Viticulturist: **Mark Walpole** Chief Executive: **Ross Brown**

Brown Brothers occupies a unique place in Australian wine, largely because it has continually shown a determination to make table wines out of virtually every variety grown commercially in this country. While there have been some steady improvements with its Italian varieties, I think Brown Brothers deserves most credit for the consistency and quality of the Patricia Pinot Chardonnay Brut, its lively Victoria Riesling and its traditionally robust and long-living blend of Cabernet, Shiraz and Mondeuse.

CABERNET SHIRAZ MONDEUSE BLEND

AGED WINE RELEASE

NE Victoria	$20–$29
Current vintage: 2005	**93**

Powerfully fruited, firm, astringent and assertively oaked, with lightly raisined and meaty flavours of blackberries and dark plums backed by nuances of baked earth and polished leather. Its dark chocolate, cedar and vanilla oak is almost overdone, but its chalky extract will help to ensure its customary longevity.

2005	93	2025	2035
1998	90	2010	2018+
1997	90	2009	2017+
1996	91	2008	2016
1995	87	2007	2015
1992	92	2004	2012
1990	91	2002	2010
1989	90	2001	2009
1988	90	2000	2005
1987	90	1999	2004
1986	91	2006	2016
1985	91	2015	2025
1984	85	1992	1996
1983	91	2003	2013
1982	90	1994	1999
1981	90	1993	1998
1980	94	2010	2020

KING VALLEY BARBERA

BARBERA

King Valley	$12–$19
Current vintage: 2005	**89**

An intensely flavoured, savoury and peppery expression of this variety, with a slightly cordial-like aroma of raspberries, cherries, plums and sweet vanilla oak, backed by a whiff of violets. Smooth and supple, its juicy palate supports its spicy flavours of redcurrants, cherries and plums with fine-grained, firm and pliant tannins, finishing savoury and persistent, with lingering fruit and fresh acidity.

2005	89	2010	2013
2002	87	2004	2007
2001	91	2003	2006
1999	87	2001	2004+
1998	81	1999	2000
1997	85	1998	1999
1996	88	1998	2001

PATRICIA NOBLE RIESLING

RATING 3

King Valley — $30–$49
Current vintage: 2002 — 93

A luscious, intensely flavoured and pristine dessert wine that avoids the cloying nature of so many of its kind. Its honeyed aromas of tinned tropical fruits, pear and apricot reveal complex undertones of pastry. Slightly buttery, very ripe and concentrated, the palate delivers an elegant, smooth and juicy expression of stonefruits, honeycomb and tropical flavours before finishing fresh and clean with zesty lemony acidity.

2002	93	2007	2010+
2000	93	2005	2008+
1999	89	2004	2007
1998	89	2003	2006
1997	85	1998	1999
1996	81	1998	2001
1994	82	1999	2002
1993	92	1998	2001

PATRICIA PINOT CHARDONNAY BRUT

RATING 2

King Valley — $30–$49
Current vintage: 2001 — 93

Evolved, toasty and honeyed, with underlying meaty, aldehydic undertones, this smooth, generous, round and chewy sparkling wine reveals floral aromas, suggestions of grilled nuts and creamy flavours of peach and melon. Punctuated by clean, refreshing acidity, it's long and focused, with length and persistence.

2001	93	2006	2009
2000	95	2005	2008+
1999	90	2004	2007+
1998	94	2003	2006+
1997	88	2002	2005
1996	90	2001	2004
1995	95	2000	2003+
1994	89	1999	2002
1993	79	1995	1998

VICTORIA CABERNET SAUVIGNON

RATING 5

Victoria — $12–$19
Current vintage: 2004 — 84

Fine and supple, smooth and fine-grained, with a floral, violet-like perfume of cassis, raspberries and older vanilla oak. Framed by slightly raw and muddy tannins, its smooth palate of blackberry, blueberry and plum flavours lacks much depth and emphasis.

2004	84	2006	2009+
2003	86	2008	2011
2002	87	2007	2010
2001	89	2006	2009+
2000	82	2002	2005
1999	82	2001	2004
1998	85	2000	2003
1997	88	2002	2005
1996	90	2001	2004
1994	89	2002	2006
1993	90	2005	2013

VICTORIA CHARDONNAY

RATING 5

Victoria — $12–$19
Current vintage: 2005 — 83

Dull, flat and simple, with a juicy, clean and slightly green-edged expression of juicy melon, lemon and cashew-like fruit and light vanilla oak. It's unassuming, with an olive oil-like viscosity.

2005	83	2006	2007
2004	87	2006	2009
2003	85	2004	2005
2001	83	2002	2003+
2000	89	2002	2005
1999	80	2000	2001
1998	82	2000	2003
1997	88	1999	2002

VICTORIA RIESLING

RATING 5

Victoria — $12–$19
Current vintage: 2006 — 90

A stylish young riesling whose floral, slightly candied aromas of lime juice and apple reveal undertones of bathpowder and mineral salts. Generous and juicy, its stylish palate of tangy lime, lemon and apple-like fruit is tightly wound around a powdery spine of fine mineral phenolics, finishing fresh and tangy with citrusy acids.

2006	90	2011	2014+
2005	90	2010	2013+
2004	87	2006	2009
2003	87	2004	2005+
2002	90	2004	2007
2001	80	2001	2002
2000	84	2002	2005
1999	87	2001	2004
1997	87	1999	2002
1996	86	1998	2001
1995	85	2000	2003

Burge Family

Barossa Valley Way, Lyndoch SA 5351. Tel: (08) 8524 4644. Fax: (08) 8524 4444.
Website: www.burgefamily.com.au Email: draycott@burgefamily.com.au

Region: **Barossa Valley** Winemaker: **Rick Burge** Viticulturist: **Rick Burge** Chief Executive: **Rick Burge**

Rick Burge has crafted an elegant, complex and rustic collection of 2005 reds with the common thread of approachability and fine, powdery tannin. Perhaps the finest is the Olive Hill red blend, which is already drinking deliciously well as an old-fashioned Australian 'burgundy' style.

DRAYCOTT SHIRAZ
RATING **3**

Barossa Valley $30–$49
Current vintage: 2005 89

Deep, meaty, gamey and slightly pruney aromas of spicy Barossa shiraz precede a palate of full to medium weight whose ripe, forward and jammy flavours of red berries, cassis and red plums thin out marginally towards a lean and slightly drying finish. Underpinned by fine, powdery tannins, it lacks a little freshness and length.

2005	89	2010	2013
2004	95	2016	2024+
2003	80	2005	2008
2001	93	2009	2013
2000	88	2005	2008
1999	95	2007	2011

OLD VINES GARNACHA
RATING **4**

Barossa Valley $20–$29
Current vintage: 2005 89

Meaty, savoury and drying but not excessively over-cooked, this generous, juicy and smoky grenache has a spicy bouquet of plums and redcurrants over suggestions of smoked meats. Forward and deeply flavoured, with a fine, powdery undercarriage, it finishes with lingering nuances of licorice and cloves.

2005	89	2010	2013
2004	88	2006	2009+
2003	90	2008	2011+
2001	92	2006	2009+
2000	92	2005	2008
1999	90	2003	2006+

OLIVE HILL SEMILLON
RATING **4**

Barossa Valley $12–$19
Current vintage: 2006 89

A sumptuous Barossa semillon whose toasty American oaked bouquet of juicy melon and lemon juice, coconut and vanilla precedes a smooth, generous and buttery palate of length and viscosity. Its oak is presently a little raw and toasty, but should settle with time, as it softens and integrates.

2006	89	2008	2011
2005	90	2007	2010
2004	81	2004	2005
2002	90	2004	2007
2001	87	2002	2003
2000	86	2001	2002
1999	90	2004	2007

OLIVE HILL SHIRAZ MOURVÈDRE GRENACHE
RATING **3**

Barossa Valley $30–$49
Current vintage: 2005 90

Charming and rustic, with a slightly meaty and spicy fragrance of dark berries cherries and plums over complex smoky, earthy nuances. Ripe and juicy, its smooth and vibrant palate reveals undertones of currant and redcurrant, but delivers a pleasing length of flavour underpinned by fine, supple tannins and finished with soft acidity.

2005	90	2010	2013
2004	92	2009	2012+
2003	91	2011	2015+
2002	93	2007	2010+
2001	94	2006	2009+
2000	87	2002	2005
1999	94	2007	2011
1998	89	2000	2003

By Farr

101 Kelly Lane, Bannockburn, Vic, 3331 Tel: (03) 5281 1733. Fax: (03) 5281 1433.
Website: www.byfarr.com.au Email: kalvos@datafast.net.au
Region: **Geelong** Winemakers: **Gary Farr, Nick Farr** Viticulturist: **Gary Farr** Chief Executive: **Gary Farr**

Led by its sumptuous Chardonnay, its spicy and very Rhône-like Shiraz and its deeply layered and ethereal reserve level 'Sangreal' Pinot Noir, By Farr has turned out an excellent collection of 2005 wines. They share substantial depth, texture and savoury finish, and reflect Farr's willingness to do things his own way.

CHARDONNAY RATING 3

Geelong	$50–$99
Current vintage: 2005	**95**

Chardonnay with attitude. Beautifully shaped, sumptuous and creamy, it's smooth, seamless and utterly hedonistic. Backed by meaty, creamy and mineral undertones, its luscious expression of grapefruit, lemon and melon-like flavour has a juiciness and a youthful fatness, but ties together neatly around some refreshing but very finely integrated acidity. Complete, balanced and persistent.

2005	95	2010	2013
2004	95	2009	2012
2003	87	2005	2008
2002	93	2007	2010
2001	87	2003	2006
2000	91	2005	2008
1999	91	2004	2007

PINOT NOIR RATING 3

Geelong	$50–$99
Current vintage: 2005	**93**

Likely to evolve into a delicious and charming pinot in typical dusty, red-fruited Farr style, this heady, floral and perfumed young wine has a pure core of vibrant cherry and raspberry flavour lifted by a floral rose petal perfume, fresh spices and dusty nuances of forest floor. It's lightly herbal and stalky, with pleasing length and juiciness over a powdery undercarriage of fine tannins.

2005	93	2010	2013
2004	95	2009	2012
2003	88	2005	2008
2002	82	2004	2007
2001	89	2006	2009
2000	87	2002	2005
1999	94	2004	2007+

SHIRAZ RATING 3

Geelong	$30–$49
Current vintage: 2005	**95**

Smoky, savoury, meaty and Rhône-like, this smooth, supple and spicy shiraz is steeped in flavours of liqueur plums, cherries and blackberries, with undertones of black pepper, suede leather, dark chocolates and briar. Framed by long, fine-grained tannins and backed by assertive cedary oak, it's gamey and spicy, with a deeply layered palate finishing with lingering fruit and musky, underbrush-like complexity.

2005	95	2010	2013+
2004	93	2009	2012+
2003	86	2005	2008
2002	86	2004	2007+
2001	91	2006	2009+
2000	89	2005	2008
1999	94	2004	2007+

VIOGNIER RATING 4

Geelong	$30–$49
Current vintage: 2005	**89**

Heady and perfumed, floral and spicy, this slightly raisined but lusciously flavoured and spotlessly presented viognier is scented with spicy suggestions of apricot blossom and tangerine. Long and generous, its plush and juicy palate avoids the blousiness of so many richly flavoured viogniers, but can't quite conceal a slightly skinsy aspect. It finishes with refreshing acidity.

2005	89	2007	2010+
2004	92	2006	2009
2003	88	2005	2008
2002	87	2004	2007
2001	93	2003	2006
2000	89	2002	2005
1999	87	2001	2004

Campbells

Murray Valley Highway, Rutherglen Vic 3685. Tel: (02) 6032 9458. Fax: (02) 6032 9870.
Website: www.campbellswines.com.au Email: wine@campbellswines.com.au
Region: **Rutherglen** Winemaker: **Colin Campbell** Viticulturist: **Malcolm Campbell**
Chief Executives: **Colin & Malcolm Campbell**

Campbells is a long-established family winery in Rutherglen, best known for its richly flavoured, but soft and smooth duo of Bobbie Burns Shiraz and The Barkly Durif. 2004 has possibly produced the best-ever Bobbie Burns, a wine that delivers plenty of rich, rustic Rutherglen fruit with charming elegance and a touch of polish. Like many others in its region, Campbells has a well-deserved reputation for fortified wine, muscat and tokay especially. Its style is rich, soft, sweet and generous, with a distinctive lightness and elegance.

BOBBIE BURNS SHIRAZ

RATING **4**

Rutherglen	$20–$29
Current vintage: 2004	**94**

A classical Rutherglen shiraz whose vibrant minty aromas of cassis, dark cherries, mulberries and licorice overlie floral nuances and suggestions of turned earth. Full to medium in weight, it's deeply flavoured but fine and supple, delivering a spicy and richly fruited palate framed by silky-fine tannins. It finishes long and meaty, with earthy, tarry undertones.

2004	94	2016	2024
2003	91	2011	2015
2002	87	2007	2010
2001	90	2006	2009
2000	90	2008	2012
1999	89	2004	2007
1998	90	2006	2010
1997	89	2002	2005+
1996	90	2008	2016
1995	93	2003	2007+
1994	91	2002	2006+
1993	88	2001	2005+
1992	92	2000	2004+

CHARDONNAY

RATING **5**

Rutherglen	$12–$19
Current vintage: 2006	**84**

Lightly toasted peachy and nutty aromas backed by vanilla oak precede a juicy, generous, soft and approachable palate whose simple, fresh flavours border on cloying, but finish with clean acids.

2006	84	2007	2008+
2005	77	2005	2006
2004	87	2005	2006
2002	87	2003	2004+
2001	86	2002	2003
2000	86	2002	2005
1999	83	2001	2004
1998	87	1999	2000

RIESLING

RATING **5**

Rutherglen	$12–$19
Current vintage: 2006	**88**

Lightly dusty aromas of lime juice and fresh apple precede a juicy, clean and refreshing palate whose moderate length of bright pear, apple and peach-like flavour finishes crisp and dry.

2006	88	2008	2011
2005	88	2010	2013+
2004	87	2006	2009
2003	79	2004	2005
2002	86	2003	2004+
2001	87	2006	2009
2000	87	2005	2008
1999	87	2004	2007
1998	86	2003	2006
1997	83	2002	2005
1996	88	2001	2004

THE BARKLY DURIF

RATING **4**

Rutherglen	$30–$49
Current vintage: 2003	**89**

Closed and rather introverted, with meaty, briary plum, blackberry, redcurrant flavours and smoky, gamey undertones, this robust but finely balanced and structured durif is marginally cooked and jammy. Framed by assertive but well integrated tannin, it becomes more generously flavoured, rustic and slightly raisined with breathing.

2003	89	2011	2015
2002	89	2010	2014+
2001	90	2006	2009
1998	89	2003	2006
1997	89	2002	2005
1996	91	2001	2004+
1995	89	2000	2003
1994	93	2002	2006
1993	88	2001	2005
1992	94	2000	2004+
1991	90	1999	2003
1990	91	2002	2010

Cannibal Creek

260 Tynong North Road, Tynong North Vic 3813. Tel: (03) 5942 8380. Fax: (08) 5942 8202.
Website: www.cannibalcreek.com.au Email: wine@cannibalcreek.com.au

Region: **Gippsland** Winemaker: **Patrick Hardiker** Viticulturist: **Patrick Hardiker**
Chief Executives: **Patrick, Kirsten & Kath Hardiker**

There isn't a lot of Australian varietal sauvignon blanc of international standard, but Cannibal Creek makes a wine of intense passionfruit and gooseberry flavour that is usually supported by a fine, powdery and mineral backbone of tightly knit phenolics. It's one of the few Australian makers whose sauvignon blancs can rival the best from Marlborough in New Zealand.

SAUVIGNON BLANC   RATING 3

Gippsland $20–$29
Current vintage: 2006   **93**

Tightly focused, with a lightly grassy fragrance of gooseberries and mineral undertones. Mouthfilling and juicy, its long, powdery palate of lingering citrus, ripe peach and gooseberry flavour finish with refreshing acids and a tangy, briney aspect. Excellent sculpted shape and flavour.

2006	93	2007	2008+
2005	93	2005	2006+
2004	92	2004	2005+
2003	91	2003	2004+

Cape Mentelle

Wallcliffe Road, Margaret River WA 6285. Tel: (08) 9757 0888. Fax: (08) 9757 3233.
Website: www.capementelle.com.au Email: info@capementelle.com.au

Region: **Margaret River** Winemaker: **Robert Mann** Viticulturist: **Steve Meckiff** Chief Executive: **Tony Jordan**

Cape Mentelle has crowned its excellent 2004 red vintage with a stellar edition of its flagship Cabernet Sauvignon, while its 2005 whites — the Wallcliffe blend especially — appear to have performed to a similarly high level. 2004 also saw the first edition of a very fine, savoury and sour-edged Wallcliffe Shiraz, a polished and luxuriant wine that should cellar very well.

CABERNET MERLOT 'TRINDERS'   RATING 5

Margaret River $20–$29
Current vintage: 2005   **89**

An honest and regional cabernet blend with a little polish. Ripe, juicy and slightly confectionary, its aroma of red and black berries, plums and cedar/mocha oak is backed by lightly herbal, tobaccoey undertones. Its forward, flavoursome palate delivers a meaty expression of berry/plum flavour underpinned by firmish, loose-knit tannin and finished with fresh acids.

2005	89	2010	2013
2004	91	2012	2016
2003	89	2005	2008+
2002	86	2004	2007
2001	91	2006	2009
2000	86	2005	2008
1999	82	2001	2004
1998	86	2000	2003
1997	83	1999	2002+
1996	90	2004	2008
1995	90	2003	2007
1994	90	1999	2002

CABERNET SAUVIGNON   RATING 3

Margaret River $50–$99
Current vintage: 2004   **96**

Aristocratic, firm and artfully balanced, with a lightly herbal and violet-like scent of briary fruit and classy new oak. Its deep flavours of small berries, dark cherries, plums and cassis overlie nuances of dried herbs, undergrowth, charcuterie-like complexity and toasty, cedary dark chocolate oak. Long and vibrant, its pristine palate is supported by firm, grainy and powdery tannins, before finishing with persistent and slightly meaty dark fruit.

2004	96	2016	2024+
2003	88	2011	2015
2002	87	2010	2014
2001	95	2013	2021+
2000	93	2008	2012+
1999	93	2007	2011+
1998	93	2010	2018
1996	92	2004	2008+
1995	88	2003	2007
1994	93	2014	2024
1993	94	2005	2013
1992	94	2004	2012
1991	96	2003	2011
1990	94	1998	2002
1989	94	1997	2001
1988	92	2000	2008
1987	94	2007	2017
1986	91	1998	2006
1985	90	1993	1997

CHARDONNAY

RATING 3

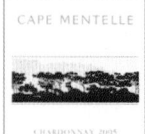

Margaret River $30–$49
Current vintage: 2006 **95**

A chardonnay of great purity and complexity whose floral fragrance of fresh melon, grapefruit and lime juice is backed by floral yeast-like influences, nuances of wheatmeal and measured vanilla/lemony oak. Its long, elegant palate marries pristine chardonnay fruit with fresh vanilla oak and a tangy, almost mineral acidity. Fresh, long and vibrant, it has a delightful shape and tightness, easily balancing its funky complexity with brightness and polish.

2006	95	2011	2014
2005	93	2010	2013
2004	87	2006	2009
2003	91	2005	2008+
2002	90	2004	2007+
2001	93	2003	2006
2000	93	2005	2008
1999	95	2004	2007+
1998	95	2003	2006+
1997	90	2002	2005
1996	95	2001	2004
1995	96	2003	2007
1994	94	2002	2006

SAUVIGNON BLANC SEMILLON

RATING 3

Margaret River $20–$29
Current vintage: 2006 **82**

Rather simple, lean and lacking its customary presence of fruit, this lightly grassy young blend has a light tropical fruit aroma and a clean palate without much by way of concentration.

2006	82	2006	2007
2005	94	2006	2007+
2004	93	2004	2005+
2003	94	2004	2005+
2002	90	2002	2003+
2001	87	2001	2002
2000	88	2001	2002
1999	88	1999	2000
1998	95	2000	2003

SHIRAZ

RATING 3

Margaret River $30–$49
Current vintage: 2005 **90**

A rather exaggerated shiraz whose heady, smoky and briary aromas of cassis, raspberries, plums and red cherries are backed by suggestions of mint, menthol and tomato stalk. Full to medium in weight, it's very smooth and polished, with intense flavours of cassis, blueberries and raspberries supported by tightly knit cedar/vanilla oak and framed by firmish, fine-grained tannins. Well made, but too tomatoey and regional for a higher rating.

2005	90	2013	2017
2004	96	2012	2016+
2003	91	2011	2015
2002	92	2010	2014+
2001	94	2009	2013+
2000	90	2005	2008+
1999	93	2007	2011
1998	93	2010	2018
1997	94	2009	2017
1996	93	2004	2008+
1995	92	2007	2015
1994	95	2006	2014
1993	89	2001	2005
1992	95	2004	2012+

WALLCLIFFE SAUVIGNON BLANC SEMILLON

RATING 2

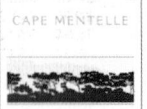

Margaret River $30–$49
Current vintage: 2005 **95**

Very generous, but tight, stylish and shapely, this smoky and lightly herbaceous blend effortlessly integrates its piercingly fresh flavours of melon and gooseberries with toasty vanilla oak and refreshing acidity. There's a hint of minerality and mealiness beneath its lightly grassy and well-oaked aromas, while its long, smooth palate finishes with a hint of citrus and nettle-like herbaceousness.

2005	95	2010	2013
2004	95	2006	2009+
2003	93	2005	2008+
2002	93	2004	2007+
2001	95	2003	2006
2000	87	2001	2002
1999	88	2001	2004

ZINFANDEL

RATING 3

Margaret River $30–$49
Current vintage: 2004 **92**

A very elegant, fine and modern zinfandel whose meaty expression of jujube-like blackberry, blueberry and tomato-like fruit is framed by a smooth and fine-grained cut of moderately astringent tannin. It's spicy, floral and confiture-like, with a vibrant palate tightly knit with assertive cedar/vanilla oak, finishing with flavours of dark berries and ripe tomato. I'd prefer a drier and more savoury finish.

2004	92	2012	2016+
2003	94	2011	2015+
2002	94	2010	2014+
2001	87	2009	2013
2000	92	2008	2012
1999	93	2007	2011
1998	95	2006	2010+
1997	94	2005	2009+
1996	97	2001	2004
1995	94	2003	2007
1994	89	2002	2006

Capel Vale

Lot 5 Stirling Estate, Mallokup Road, Capel WA 6271. Tel: (08) 9727 1986. Fax: (08) 9727 1904.
Website: www.capelvale.com   Email: winery@capelvale.com

Regions: **Geographe, Mount Barker, Pemberton, Margaret River** Winemakers: **Rebecca Catlin, Larry Cherubino** Viticulturists: **Neil Delroy, Steve Partridge** Chief Executive: **Peter Pratten**

Capel Vale appears to be moving back into the mainstream of more stylish and contemporary winemaking, as its beautifully focused 2007 Whispering Hill Riesling and finely crafted 2005 Cabernet Sauvignon suggest. This relatively small winery business has established itself in most Western Australian regions, where it owns or has access to some fine mature vineyards. Its future looks encouraging.

CABERNET SAUVIGNON

RATING **5**

Various, WA	$20–$29
Current vintage: 2005	**90**

Just a little too leafy for a higher score, this tightly crafted and rather stylish cabernet marries intense cassis, dark cherry and plum-like flavour with fresh cedar/vanilla oak and fine, powdery tannin. It's scented with violets and underbrush, and there's a herbal thread beneath the long and elegant palate.

2005	90	2010	2013+
2002	88	2010	2014
2001	88	2003	2006
2000	86	2005	2008
1999	84	2000	2001+
1998	81	2000	2003
1997	81	1999	2002
1996	87	1998	2001
1995	93	2003	2007
1994	92	2002	2006

RIESLING

RATING **5**

Mount Barker	$12–$19
Current vintage: 2004	**86**

A perfume of pear, apple, white peach and tangerine precedes a smooth, juicy and generously flavoured palate whose pear/apple flavours finish with green-edged metallic acids and a notion of tinned tropical fruit. Good length and intensity.

2004	86	2006	2009+
2003	90	2008	2011
2002	91	2007	2010
2001	84	2002	2003+
2000	87	2005	2008
1999	77	2000	2001
1998	87	2000	2003
1997	80	1997	1998
1996	87	2001	2004
1995	89	2003	2007
1994	90	1999	2002
1993	94	2001	2005
1992	87	1997	2000

WHISPERING HILL RIESLING

RATING **3**

Great Southern	$20–$29
Current vintage: 2007	**95**

An alluringly floral perfume of pear, apple and musky spices precedes a long, juicy palate whose pristine limey flavours overlie a bracing, tightly knit spine of nervy acidity. It's beautifully focused, with genuine depth of fruit over complex suggestions of wet slate and minerals.

2007	95	2015	2019+
2004	94	2012	2016
2003	87	2005	2008
2002	86	2004	2007
2001	86	2003	2006
2000	92	2008	2012
1998	87	2000	2003+
1997	93	2002	2005
1996	94	2004	2008

Capercaillie

Londons Road, Lovedale, NSW 2325. Tel: (02) 4990 2904. Fax: (02) 4991 1886.
Website: www.capercailliewine.com.au
Region: **Hunter Valley** Winemakers: **Alasdair Sutherland, Daniel Binet** Viticulturist: **Alasdair Sutherland**
Chief Executives: **Alasdair & Patricia Sutherland**

There's an appealing eccentricity about Capercaillie that I thoroughly enjoy. While Alasdair Sutherland is not afraid to blend from fruit all over New South Wales and South Australia with his locally-sourced Hunter crop, it's in his purebred Hunter varietals that I find most interest and intrigue. These are individual interpretations of a well-established regional theme, and they can be totally delicious.

CEILIDH SHIRAZ
RATING 5

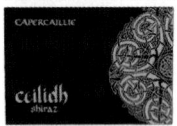

McLaren Vale, Hunter Valley $30–$49
Current vintage: 2005 86

Meaty, rather spirity and porty aromas of currant-like fruit, dark chocolates and raisins with undertones of menthol precede a rather cooked and stewy palate that relies on some decent American oak to lift its sweetness and brightness.

2005	86	2010	2013
2003	88	2008	2011+
2001	94	2009	2013
2000	82	2002	2005

CREEL SEMILLON
RATING 4

Lower Hunter Valley $20–$29
Current vintage: 2005 92

Finely crafted, elegant and generously flavoured, this is a tight, shapely semillon whose lightly floral and sherbet-like aromas of apple, lime and melon precede a long, supple and mineral palate. Underpinned by chalky phenolics, its clean fruit and crisp, refreshing acid finishes with length and clarity.

2005	92	2013	2017
2002	90	2010	2014
2001	91	2011	2015
1999	93	2011	2019

CUILLIN CHARDONNAY
RATING 5

Lower Hunter Valley $20–$29
Current vintage: 2006 87

Likely to age rather quickly, with a smoky, toasty and buttery aroma of lemon, quince and vanilla backed by suggestions of lanolin and vanilla oak. Ripe and generous, it's slightly oily and forward, with juicy flavours of quince, pineapple and melon finishing slightly short with some awkward oak and angular acidity. It should settle down over the short term.

2006	87	2008	2011
2005	89	2007	2010
2004	86	2005	2006
2003	82	2004	2005+

THE CLAN (Cabernet Blend)
RATING 5

Hilltops, McLaren Vale, Mudgee $20–$29
Current vintage: 2005 88

Firm and savoury, this is a medium-term red of some interest and strength. Its complex, meaty bouquet of blackcurrants, plums, dark cherries and restrained cedar/vanilla oak has an appealing floral lift. Its fine-grained, astringent palate frames dark, plummy fruit around chalky tannins, finishing with suggestions of mint and menthol.

2005	88	2013	2017
2004	90	2012	2016+
2002	81	2004	2007
2001	90	2009	2013

THE GHILLIE SHIRAZ
RATING 3

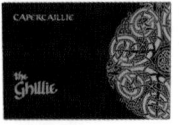

Lower Hunter Valley $30–$49
Current vintage: 2005 87

Slightly under-ripened and over-oaked, with a spicy, reductive and smoky background beneath its intense aromas of dark cherries and plums. Full to medium in weight, it's meaty and green-edged, with a moderately rich expression of dark plums, olives and cassis supported by fractionally metallic tannins.

2005	87	2007	2010+
2003	95	2015	2023
2002	95	2014	2022+
2000	90	2008	2012+

Carramar Estate

Wakley Road, Yenda NSW 2681. Tel: (02) 6961 3000. Fax: (02) 6961 3099.
Website: www.casellawines.com Email: info@casellawines.com
Region: **Riverina** Winemakers: **Alan Kennett, Phillip Casella** Viticulturist: **Marcello Casella**
Chief Executive: **John Casella**

Carramar Estate is owned by the Casella family, owners of the [yellow tail] wine phenomenon. Its leading wine is this typical Griffith-grown late harvest semillon, which John Casella prefers to craft in a finer, more elegant and less syrupy style than many local expressions of this genre. The latest vintage is easily the best released under this label. Funny, really, to consider that a wine like this can indeed come from a complex like that!

BOTRYTIS SEMILLON

RATING 5

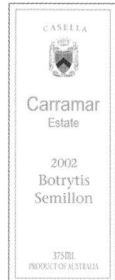

Riverina	$20–$29 (375 ml)
Current vintage: 2006	**94**

A beautifully balanced, luscious and even dessert wine with a floral, honeysuckle-like bouquet backed with hints of brioche. Long, smooth and pristine, with sweet apricot, pear, peach and melon-like fruit finished by superbly vibrant and refreshing acids, if finishes with wonderful persistence and undertones of custard pie. Should develop very well indeed.

2006	94	2008	2011+
2002	90	2004	2007
2000	89	2002	2005
1999	92	2004	2007
1998	86	2000	2003
1997	83	1998	1999

Cassegrain

764 Fernbank Creek Road, Port Macquarie NSW 2444. Tel: (02) 6582 8377. Fax: (02) 6582 8378.
Website: www.cassegrainwines.com.au Email: info@cassegrainwines.com.au
Region: **Hastings River** Winemaker: **John Cassegrain** Viticulturist: **John Cassegrain**
Chief Executive: **John Cassegrain**

Cassegrain has embraced the hybrid French variety chambourcin as a cornerstone of its identity, a decision I admire more for its bravery than its wisdom. Its best wine, the Fromenteau Vineyard Chardonnay, is a complex and heavily richly textured example of this variety with genuine character, and the smoky and rather funky 2005 vintage is again reminiscent of the wines under this label of a decade ago. The straight Shiraz from the Northen Slopes is rather an individual style — meaty, rustic and sinewy, but with layers of fruit and earth.

FROMENTEAU RESERVE CHARDONNAY

RATING 4

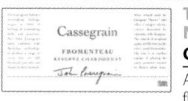

Tumbarumba, Northern Slopes	$20–$29
Current vintage: 2005	**91**

A tight, brooding chardonnay that needs time to flesh out. Its lightly smoky, meaty and funky aromas of peach, quince and melon-like fruit overlie lightly toasty, creamy and lightly reductive complexity. Richly textured, its long and deeply fruited palate of melon, quince and pineapple fruit extends towards a lightly powdery finish of lemony acidity.

2005	91	2010	2013
2004	91	2006	2009
2003	89	2005	2008
2002	93	2004	2007+
2001	89	2003	2006
2000	91	2002	2005+
1998	80	1999	2000
1996	88	1998	2001
1995	91	2000	2003
1993	88	1998	2001
1991	94	1996	1999

RESERVE CHAMBOURCIN

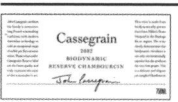

Hastings River	$20–$29
Current vintage: 2002	**81**

Meaty, earthy, herbal aromas of plums, raspberries and cherries, before a lean, green-edged palate whose light small berry fruit is underpinned by sweet vanilla oak but wrapped in searing, steely acidity.

2002	81	2004	2007
2001	79	2003	2006
2000	82	2002	2005
1998	87	2003	2008
1997	79	1999	2002
1996	87	1998	2001
1995	83	1997	2000

RESERVE SHIRAZ

Northern Slopes, Cowra $20–$29
Current vintage: 2004   87

A leathery, meaty shiraz already showing plenty of developed character. Rather old-fashioned, its tiring expression of plums and small berries slowly emerges over its firm chassis of chalky, drying tannins. Backed by herbal undertones, it's gamey and peppery, but does come to show genuine elegance, restraint and lingering savoury qualities with aeration.

2004	87	2006	2009
2003	91	2011	2015+
2001	84	2006	2009
2000	88	2005	2008

SEMILLON

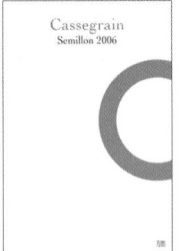

Hunter Valley,
Hastings River $12–$19
Current vintage: 2006   84

Fine, supple, but slightly out of focus, with lightly dull, confectionary and tropical aromas of green melon and sherbet-like undertones, which just lack a little brightness. It's slightly soapy and green-edged, with a fleshy viscosity at its heart, but then finishes rather lean, with limey acids and lingering herbaceous suggestions of snow peas.

2006	84	2006	2011
2005	83	2006	2007
2004	89	2006	2009+
2003	87	2005	2008
2002	87	2004	2007
2001	89	2003	2006+
2000	85	2001	2002
1998	88	2000	2003
1997	87	2002	2005
1996	88	2001	2004
1993	90	2001	2005
1992	87	1997	2000

Castagna

Ressom Lane, Beechworth Vic 3747. Tel: (03) 5728 2888. Fax: (03) 5728 2898.
Website: www.castagna.com.au Email: castagna@enigma.com.au
Region: **Beechworth** Winemaker: **Julian Castagna** Viticulturist: **Julian Castagna**
Chief Executive: **Julian Castagna**
Castagna is one of Beechworth's emergent clan of high-quality and high-elevation small vineyards. In 2005 it did not make its typically excellent La Chiave Sangiovese, since Julian Castagna opted instead to create his first 'Super Beechworth' a 60:40 blend of sangiovese and shiraz called Un Segreto. It's musky, spicy, smoky and savoury, laden with deep dark fruits. Castagna's intent is to make the three wines each year, vintage permitting.

GENESIS SYRAH

Beechworth $50–$99
Current vintage: 2005   95

Sporting more overt ripeness than previous vintages, but retaining that all-important length of vibrant fruit flavour, it manages to avoid over-cooked influences. Its heady, spicy aromas of black pepper, dark plums, cassis and blackberries integrated neatly with mocha-like oak and meaty, forest floor undertones. Dark and briary, it's firm, fine-grained and powdery, delivering an excellent length of sour-edged fruit and a hint of minerality that culminates in a long, savoury finish.

2005	95	2013	2017+
2004	95	2009	2012+
2002	95	2010	2014+
2001	91	2003	2006+
2000	90	2002	2005
1999	95	2006	2007

LA CHIAVE SANGIOVESE

Beechworth $50–$99
Current vintage: 2004   95

Closed and brooding, this tight-fisted sangiovese reveals a dusty and slightly minty fragrance of sour cherries, plums, chocolate and meaty, forest floor-like undertones. Its typically sour-edged dark fruit knits with a firmish spine of astringent tannins, finishing long, with nuances of nicotine.

2004	95	2009	2012+
2002	95	2007	2010
2001	87	2002	2003+

Castle Rock Estate

Porongorup Road, Porongorup WA 6324. Tel: (08) 9853 1035. Fax: (08) 9853 1010.
Website: www.castlerockestate.com.au Email: diletti@castlerockestate.com.au

Region: **Porongorup** Winemaker: **Robert Diletti** Viticulturist: **Angelo Diletti** Chief Executive: **Angelo Diletti**

This small cool-climate estate in the Porongorups continues to perform well with the variety that has proven to be the bête noir of nearly all Western Australian growers to have attempted it: pinot noir. The 2005 vintage is typically fine, dusty and delicate, with what can riskily be described as 'Burgundian' characters. Either way, it's charming and intriguing, like several of its recent predecessors

CABERNET SAUVIGNON MERLOT

RATING **5**

Porongorup $20–$29
Current vintage: 2001 89

Elegant, fine-grained and supple, this restrained and lightly herbal blend reveals cedary aromas of sweet red berries, violets and dark plums. Framed by fine, powdery tannins, its reserved palate of vibrant small berry fruits and cedar/dark chocolate oak finishes with length and style, but a faintly greenish acidity.

2001	89	2006	2009+
2000	72	2002	2005
1999	81	2001	2004
1998	88	2003	2006+
1997	87	2002	2005
1996	84	2001	2004

PINOT NOIR

RATING **5**

Great Southern $20–$29
Current vintage: 2005 90

Tightly crafted, lean and rather introverted, this fine, supple and fragrant young pinot marries reserved flavours of maraschino cherries and plums with savoury undertones of smoked bacon, dried herbs and cedary oak. Long and finely balanced, it should flesh out well.

2005	90	2010	2013
2004	88	2006	2009
2003	90	2005	2008
2002	86	2004	2007
2001	90	2003	2006
2000	84	2001	2002
1999	84	2000	2001
1998	88	2000	2003

RIESLING

RATING **4**

Great Southern $12–$19
Current vintage: 2006 89

Slightly herbal and angular, this delicate and distinctive riesling has a perfume of pear and citrus blossom, with a long and very chalky palate whose lime/apple fruit is cut by a snap of intense mineral acidity. Presently a little awkward, but with plenty of fruit and brightness, it should settle down.

2006	89	2011	2014
2005	84	2007	2010
2004	93	2009	2012
2003	94	2008	2011+
2002	90	2007	2010+
2001	86	2006	2009
2000	89	2008	2012
1999	80	2000	2001
1998	93	2006	2010
1997	88	2002	2005

Chandon

Green Point Maroondah Highway, Coldstream Vic 3770. Tel: (03) 9738 9200. Fax: (03) 9738 9201.
Website: www.chandon.com.au Email: info@domainechandon.com.au
Region: **Southern Australia** Winemakers: **Tony Jordan, Matt Steel, John Harris, Glenn Thompson**
Viticulturist: **Bernie Wood** Managing Director: **Tony Jordan**

With its opening in the mid 1980s, Domaine Chandon not only reinvented Australia's approach and attitude towards sparkling wine, but it single-handedly created a market for cool climate-grown wines from classic Champagne varieties. Today it stands alone for the depth and breadth of its range. A vertical tasting late in 2006 of selected old vintages confirms the ability of the best Chandon wines to cellar surprisingly well.

GREEN POINT CUVÉE (formerly Prestige Cuvée) RATING 2

Southern Australia $30–$49
Current vintage: 1995 91

A developed mushroomy, toasty, buttery and honeyed fragrance of floral fruit and hay-like aromas. Rich, chewy and toasty, it's smooth and mature, with an assertive and creamy palate still revealing small berry fruit flavours.

1995	91	2000	2003
1994	95	1999	2002
1993	95	1998	2001+
1992	95	1997	2000
1989	95	1997	2001+

TASMANIAN CUVÉE RATING 3

Tasmania $30–$49
Current vintage: 2004 87

Toasty and herbaceous, with a presence of melon and tropical fruits backed by creamy, butterscotch-like notes and green-edged flavours and acids. It reveals plenty of yeast-derived complexity and texture, but finishes rather herbal and angular, with lingering tropical undertones.

2004	87	2006	2009+
2003	93	2005	2008+
2002	95	2007	2010
1998	91	2003	2006
1995	94	2000	2003
1992	89	1997	2000

VINTAGE BLANC DE BLANCS RATING 2

Southern Australia $30–$49
Current vintage: 2004 93

Rather forward and ripe, perhaps lacking the elegance of the ZD of the same vintage, this is a lightly herbal, toasty and honeyed sparkling chardonnay with a fine bead and some development. Its ripe flavours of melon, peach and nectarine reveal nutty, creamy and pastry-like undertones, culminating in a lingering citrusy finish bound by refreshing acidity.

2004	93	2006	2009
2003	94	2005	2008+
2002	94	2004	2007+
2000	85	2002	2005
1999	89	2004	2007
1998	95	2003	2006
1997	94	2002	2005
1996	91	1998	2001
1995	95	2000	2003
1993	95	1998	2001+
1992	93	1997	2000

VINTAGE BLANC DE NOIRS RATING 2

Southern Australia $30–$49
Current vintage: 1999 93

A maturing and complex wine whose lightly meaty and creamy, earthy bouquet still reveals nuances of raspberry confection. Its generous and deeply textured palate delivers gamey, toasty flavour that finishes long and savoury, with a lingering pastry-like aspect. An authentic blanc de noirs style.

1999	93	2004	2007
1997	95	2002	2005+
1996	89	2001	2004
1994	95	1999	2002
1993	94	1998	2001
1992	95	1997	2000

VINTAGE BRUT

RATING 2

Southern Australia	$30–$49
Current vintage: 2004	**91**

Perfumed and floral, with nutty, creamy and leesy complexity beneath its peach, melon and grapefruit-like flavour, this creamy, smooth and crackly young wine has a fluffy texture and a fine bead. It finishes without exceptional length, but with crisp, refreshing acids and lingering nutty, savoury and oatmeal-like complexity.

2004	91	2009	2012
2003	94	2008	2011
2002	96	2007	2010
2001	95	2003	2006+
1999	94	2004	2007
1998	89	2003	2006+
1997	95	2002	2005
1996	87	1998	2001+
1995	96	2000	2003+
1994	94	1999	2002
1993	93	1998	2001

VINTAGE BRUT ROSÉ

RATING 3

Southern Australia	$30–$49
Current vintage: 2004	**93**

A fine, dry and savoury rosé with a delightful colour and creamy, slightly meaty and savoury expression of vibrant raspberry and cherry fruit. It's long and lightly chalky, with a creamy, crackly effervescence and a fine length of fruit that finishes crisp and tangy, with lively and refreshing acidity. Elegant and finely crafted.

2004	93	2006	2009+
2003	94	2005	2008+
2001	88	2003	2006+
1999	87	2001	2004+
1998	94	2003	2006
1997	95	2002	2005
1996	93	2001	2004
1995	91	2000	2003
1994	94	1996	1999

ZD CHARDONNAY

RATING 3

Southern Australia	$30–$49
Current vintage: 2004	**94**

Long, creamy and very complex, this stylish and easy-drinking sparkling wine has a nutty, doughy and pastry-like bouquet whose white peach and nectarine-like fruit is backed by a slight meatiness. Generous, round and creamy, with a deliciously creamy bead, it's elegant and tightly focused, delivering a lingering core of slightly tropical and stonefruit flavour finishing with a nutty dryness.

2004	94	2006	2009+
2003	91	2005	2008+
2002	95	2004	2007+
2001	92	2006	2009
2000	88	2005	2008

Chapel Hill

Chapel Hill Road, McLaren Vale SA 5171. Tel: (08) 8323 8429. Fax: (08) 8323 9245.
Website: www.chapelhillwine.com.au Email: winery@chapelhillwine.com.au

Region: **McLaren Vale** Winemakers: **Michael Fragos, Bryn Richards** Viticulturist: **Danny Higgins**
Chief Executive: **Jim Humphrys**

Chapel Hill continues its process of evolution. Recent times have seen the departure of Pam Dunsford, one of the leading professionals in South Australian wine, but the arrival in the hot seat of Jim Humphrys, who brings plenty of experience from his Hardys days. Michael Fragos has taken more control in the winery, and has already stamped his personality on the 2005 Shiraz, a luscious red that gives some lustre to a tough vintage.

CABERNET SAUVIGNON

RATING 5

McLaren Vale, Coonawarra	$30–$49
Current vintage: 2005	**89**

Rich and meaty, its dark, concentrated aromas of plums, cherries and blackcurrant are backed by sweet cedar/vanilla oak and undertones of dried herbs. Smooth and sumptuous, it's rich and ripe, with a long, creamy palate of dark plum and berry flavours integrated with firm, powdery tannins. There's a hint of mint and eucalypt, with lingering undertones of mocha and coffee grounds-like oak. It has avoided over-ripe flavours and should develop over the short to medium term.

2005	89	2010	2013+
2002	86	2004	2007+
2001	88	2006	2009+
2000	87	2005	2008
1999	88	2001	2004
1998	83	2003	2006
1997	93	2005	2009
1996	93	2004	2008+
1995	89	2000	2003
1994	92	2002	2006
1993	93	2001	2005
1992	92	1997	2000

McLAREN VALE SHIRAZ

RATING 4

McLaren Vale	$30–$49
Current vintage: 2005	**90**

A deep, dark, meaty and slightly jammy aroma of ripe shiraz fruit with currant and prune-like undertones reveals a faint spirity aspect. It's substantial and densely packed, but smooth and sumptuous, with black, spicy fruit over nuances of currants and dark olives. Long, firm and fine-grained, finishing with a bright acidity, it's a lavishly oaked exercise in restrained power.

2005	90	2013	2017
2002	87	2007	2010
2001	89	2009	2013
2000	86	2003	2005+
1999	90	2004	2007
1998	92	2006	2010+
1997	94	2005	2009
1996	94	2001	2004+
1995	92	2000	2003
1994	93	1999	2002
1993	94	2001	2005
1992	93	2000	2004
1991	94	1999	2003
1990	91	2002	2010

UNWOODED CHARDONNAY

RATING 5

Padthaway, South Australia	$12–$19
Current vintage: 2006	**88**

Fresh and tightly focused, this vibrant, tangy and lemony chardonnay has a slightly buttery aroma of peach, nectarine and cashew. Its taut and focused palate borders on excessively acidic, but retains plenty of freshness and leanness.

2006	88	2008	2011
2005	88	2006	2007
2003	89	2004	2005
2002	90	2003	2004
2001	82	2002	2003
2000	86	2001	2002

VERDELHO

RATING 5

McLaren Vale	$12–$19
Current vintage: 2006	**87**

Fragrant aromas of lemon, lime and apple with mineral undertones precede a bright, clear, palate whose tangy expression of pristine varietal fruit is punctuated by a biting cut of sharp acidity. Very refreshing, but at a cost to the tooth enamel!

2006	87	2008	2011
2005	83	2005	2006+
2004	87	2005	2006
2003	86	2003	2004+
2002	87	2003	2004
2001	89	2002	2003+
2000	84	2001	2002
1999	86	2000	2001
1998	91	2000	2003

Charles Melton

Krondorf Road, Tanunda SA 5352. Tel: (08) 8563 3606. Fax: (08) 8563 3422.
Website: www.charlesmeltonwines.com.au Email: cmw@charlesmeltonwines.com.au
Region: **Barossa Valley** Winemaker: **Graeme Melton** Viticulturist: **Peter Wills** Chief Executive: **Graeme Melton**

Charles Melton bounced back into top gear with the fabulous 2004 vintage, especially with its two benchmarks, the Nine Popes and Shiraz. While there's a little stress evident in the Cabernet Sauvignon, these wines are sumptuous but not over-ripened, with a brightness that has been less evident in recent vintages, most of which have been hot and difficult.

CABERNET SAUVIGNON (Cabernet Shiraz in 2000)

RATING 5

Barossa Valley	$30–$49
Current vintage: 2004	**88**

Made from fractionally stressed and dehydrated fruit, this is a full, richer Barossa cabernet that just lacks the intensity of vibrant fruit required for a higher rating. Its meaty, currant-like aromas of dark plums and prunes are lifted by sweet oak. Full to medium in weight, it's initially forward and sumptuous, with a generous complement of juicy, rather jammy and slightly baked fruit. However, this does fall a fraction hollow and short.

2004	88	2009	2012+
2003	87	2008	2011
2002	86	2007	2010
2001	87	2006	2009
2000	87	2002	2005
1999	82	2001	2004
1998	93	2003	2006+
1996	87	2001	2004
1993	87	2001	2005

NINE POPES

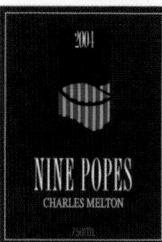

Barossa Valley	$30–$49
Current vintage: 2004	**93**

Smooth, soft and approachable, this very fruit-driven, concentrated and deeply ripened blend is significantly less funky and evolved than many other expressions of this style. Floral and perfumed, its heady, spicy and confiture-like aromas of blackberries, blueberries and dark plums overlie spicy nuances of cloves, cinnamon and licorice. Bursting with vibrant small berry flavour and supported by fine, powdery tannins, it's long and unusually shapely, deliciously fresh and persistent. It finishes with faint earthy, currant-like notes.

2004	93	2009	2012
2003	90	2008	2011
2002	92	2010	2014
2001	88	2003	2006+
2000	86	2002	2005
1999	89	2004	2007
1998	92	2006	2010
1997	88	1999	2002
1996	95	2004	2008
1995	94	2003	2007+
1994	89	1999	2002
1993	87	2001	2005
1990	92	1998	2002

BAROSSA SHIRAZ

Barossa Valley	$30–$49
Current vintage: 2004	**93**

A sumptuous, ripe and very approachable Barossa shiraz whose delicious sour-edged and slightly jammy expression of blackberry, mulberry and blueberry fruit is backed by a sweet complement of coconut ice-like oak, some deliciously smoky complexity and framed by a smooth, silky cut of fine tannin. Perfumed and floral, scented with white pepper, it finishes long and quite savoury, with a fresh acidity.

2004	93	2009	2012+
2003	89	2008	2011
2002	88	2004	2007+
2001	85	2003	2006
2000	88	2005	2008
1999	90	2004	2007+
1998	95	2003	2006
1997	89	2005	2009
1995	94	2003	2007
1990	92	1998	2002+

Chateau Reynella

Reynell Road, Reynella SA 5161. Tel: (08) 8392 2222. Fax: (08) 8392 2202.

Region: **McLaren Vale** Winemaker: **Paul Lapsley** Viticulturist: **Brenton Baker** Chief Executive: **John Grant**

Chateau Reynella has traditionally made the expression of Australian 'Vintage Port' against which others are compared. As the exceptional 1998 vintage illustrates, it has nothing to do with the Portuguese style, but is a typically ripe, jammy and astringent wine, usually fortified with fabulous spirit, that can develop in the bottle for decades. The Cabernet Sauvignon and Shiraz are found under the 'Reynell' entry.

VINTAGE PORT

McLaren Vale	$30–$49
Current vintage: 1998	**97**

About as good as it gets for traditional Australian vintage port. A heady, spicy and deeply concentrated aroma of briary cassis, plums and violets overlies a tarry, treacle-like background and chocolate/vanilla oak. Warm, ripe and spirity, its velvet-smooth and sumptuous palate reveals layers of dark plum and berry fruit before finishing long and savoury with a firm spine of powdery tannins. Excellent balance and integration.

1998	97	2018	2028
1997	90	2009	2017
1996	93	2008	2016
1994	96	2014	2024
1993	94	2013	2023
1990	95	2010	2020
1987	96	2007	2017
1983	93	2003	2013
1982	90	2002	2012
1981	93	2001	2009
1980	90	2000	2005

A
B
C
D
E
F
G
H
I
J
K
L
M
N
O
P
Q
R
S
T
U
V
W
X
Y
Z

Chestnut Grove

Chestnut Grove Road, Manjimup WA 6258. Tel: (08) 9758 5999. Fax: (08) 9758 5988.
Website: www.chestnutgrove.com.au Email: winery@chestnutgrove.com.au
Region: **Manjimup** Winemaker: **Jarrad Olsen** Viticulturist: **Southern Viticultural Services**
Chief Executive: **Mike Calneggia**
While it produces a full range of table wines, Chestnut Grove has been most successful on the show circuit with its rather oaky, tomatoey and very herbaceous Merlot. Whether it's known as Pemberton, Manjimup or the Warren Valley, this region appears to have a strong affinity for this variety.

MERLOT

RATING **5**

Pemberton	$30–$49
Current vintage: 2004	**87**

Elegant, stylish and finely balanced, with deep flavours of cassis, mulberries, dark plums and blackberries supported by retrained dusty, cedary oak and minty undertones of dried herbs. Its violet-like perfume is fragrant and heady, while its long, smooth palate is framed by fine, powdery tannin. Destined to cellar superbly.

2004	87	2009	2012
2003	86	2005	2008+
2002	87	2004	2007
2001	88	2003	2006+
2000	87	2002	2005
1999	89	2001	2004
1998	75	1999	2000
1997	81	1998	1999

Chestnut Hill

1280 Pakenham Road, Mount Burnett Vic 3781. Tel: (03) 5942 7314. Fax: (03) 5942 7314.
Website: www.chestnuthillvineyard.com.au Email: sales@chestnuthillvineyard.com.au
Region: **Mount Burnett** Winemaker: **Charlie Javor** Viticulturist: **Ivka Javor** Chief Executive: **Charlie Javor**
Also capable of some eye-catching chardonnay, Chestnut Hill is one of Australia's better makers of sauvignon blanc. The vineyard's style is dry, sculpted and mineral, with plenty of texture and briney finish. They're about as far away from the popular ideal of sweaty, grassy, sweet and oily sauvignon blanc as you can get, which is one of the reasons I like them so much! Keep an eye out for this little-known vineyard; its time is near.

SAUVIGNON BLANC

RATING **3**

Mount Burnett	$20–$29
Current vintage: 2006	**93**

Very fragrant, with a scent of gooseberries, passionfruit and dried herbs over slatey mineral nuances. Juicy and vibrant, with tangy lemony and lightly tropical fruit, it finishes long and austere, with a lick of bathpowdery texture and sculpted mineral acids.

2006	93	2008	2011
2005	93	2006	2007+
2004	92	2006	2009
2003	92	2004	2005+

Clairault

Caves Road, Willyabrup WA 6280. Tel: (08) 9755 6225. Fax: (08) 9755 6229.
Website: www.clairaultwines.com.au Email: clairault@clairaultwines.com.au
Region: **Margaret River** Winemaker: **Will Shields** Chief Executive: **Bill Martin**

With its 2002 Estate Cabernet Sauvignon, made in anything but a great year for Margaret River cabernet, Clairault has created its best red since since the 1998 edition of the same wine. I view this as a strong sign that Clairault is heading back to the quality standards of the 1980s and mid 1990s, when it was one of the region's finer makers. The 2006 Semillon Sauvignon Blanc blend is delightfully mineral and shapely.

ESTATE CABERNET SAUVIGNON
(formerly 'Reserve', also 'The Clairault')

RATING **5**

	Margaret River	$50–$99
	Current vintage: 2002	91

A fine and quite stylish Margaret River cabernet whose typically dark-fruited qualities and smart new oak combine smoothly with a fine-grained tannic backbone. Its briary and slightly meaty aromas of cassis and dark plums are backed by suggestions of dried herbs and slightly gamey undertones of chocolate/mocha oak. Long and lively, its palate sumptuously delivers dark berry, dark cherry and plum-like fruit ably supported by dark chocolate/vanilla oak. The slight green edges about the wine's acidity should soften with time.

2002	91	2010	2014
2001	89	2006	2009+
2000	86	2005	2008+
1999	81	2001	2004+
1998	92	2006	2010+
1997	81	2002	2005
1996	87	2001	2004+
1995	94	2003	2007
1994	94	2006	2014
1993	88	2001	2005
1991	95	2003	2011
1990	93	2002	2010
1989	91	1997	2001
1988	91	1996	2000
1987	87	1995	1999
1986	93	1998	2006

SAUVIGNON BLANC

RATING **5**

	Margaret River	$20–$29
	Current vintage: 2006	89

Smooth, generous and juicy, with aromas of passionfruit, cassis and gooseberries backed by hints of nettle, asparagus and a suggestion of sweatiness. It's long and sappy, with a lightly grassy and intensely fruity palate culminating in a clean finish of lively acidity.

2006	89	2007	2008
2005	86	2006	2007+
2004	87	2005	2006
2003	87	2004	2005
2002	85	2003	2004

SEMILLON SAUVIGNON BLANC

RATING **5**

2006	90	2008	2011
2005	83	2006	2007+
2003	86	2004	2005
2002	86	2002	2003
2001	92	2006	2009
2000	88	2002	2005

	Margaret River	$20–$29
	Current vintage: 2006	90

Semillon adds brightness and minerality to this lightly herbaceous blend whose lightly sweaty and lemony scents of candied citrus rind, passionfruit and fresh gooseberries reveal a lively hint of musk stick. Long, fresh and brightly flavoured, with fresh melon and citrus fruit, it's tangy and juicy, with a lingering finish of fresh mineral acidity.

Clarendon Hills

Lot 11 Brookman Road, Blewitt Springs SA 5171. Tel: (08) 8364 1484. Fax: (08) 8383 0544.
Website: www.clarendonhills.com.au Email: clarendonhills@bigpond.com

Region: **McLaren Vale** Winemaker: **Roman Bratasiuk** Viticulturists: **Various** Chief Executive: **Roman Bratasiuk**

Roman Bratasiuk should be pretty happy with his 2005 collection. Yes, as a group they reveal significantly more over-ripe influence than the stellar 2004 vintage, but that is the case pretty well all over South Australia. Importantly for me, the leading combinations of vineyard and variety under this welter of red wine labels actually performed really well, with terrific length of fruit, excellent structure and layers of flavour. These wines are well ahead of most of their imitators, whose makers are seemingly content to offer soupy fruit and sweet oak without much heed to structure or integrity.

ASTRALIS SYRAH

RATING **1**

McLaren Vale		$200+
Current vintage: 2005		**95**

Dark and peppery, black and spicy, this deeply flavoured, assertive and brooding young shiraz marries lashings of toasty, bacony new oak with layers of blackcurrant, dark plum and blackberry flavour. Coated with very firm but finely polished tannin, it's sumptuous and concentrated, delivering its thick, juicy dark and marginally raisined fruit over faint suggestions of mint and menthol.

2005	95	2010	2013+
2004	97	2016	2024
2003	97	2015	2023+
2002	93	2010	2014+
1999	96	2011	2019
1998	93	2010	2018
1997	93	2009	2017
1996	95	2008	2016
1995	96	2007	2015
1994	94	2006	2014

BLEWITT SPRINGS GRENACHE

RATING **3**

McLaren Vale		$50–$99
Current vintage: 2005		**90**

Warm and spirity, this richly ripened grenache delivers a sumptuous measure of explosive redcurrant, raspberry and blueberry flavour with meaty, earthy undertones. Underpinned by fine but firm tannins, it's long and luscious, before finishing dry and savoury with lingering, confectionary suggestions of red berries and fennel.

2005	90	2010	2013+
2004	95	2009	2012+
2003	92	2008	2011
2002	88	2004	2007+
1999	87	2001	2004+
1998	92	2003	2006
1997	90	2002	2005
1995	95	2003	2007+
1994	91	2002	2006

BROOKMAN MERLOT

RATING **5**

McLaren Vale		$50–$99
Current vintage: 2005		**87**

Intense flavours of blackberries, plums and currants combine with charry, smoky and bacony new oak to help conceal its greenish undertones of capsicum and asparagus. Sappy and slightly medicinal, its awkward, rather stodgy palate of fruitcake-like berries and raisins begins with richness and intensity, but finishes quite flat, hard-edged and under-ripe.

2005	87	2010	2013
2004	82	2006	2009
2003	85	2005	2008+
2002	87	2010	2014+
2001	88	2013	2021
1998	87	2003	2006

BROOKMAN SYRAH

RATING **3**

McLaren Vale		$50–$99
Current vintage: 2005		**94**

Deep, brooding and dark-fruited, this powerful and deeply layered shiraz complements its slightly jujube-like flavours of black and red berries with charry oak plus nuances of smoked meats, cloves, nutmeg and white pepper. It's briary and perfumed, with ethereal suggestions of sarsaparilla over meaty and leathery undertones. Long, smooth and seamless, it's framed by firm, pliant tannins, finishing peppery and savoury.

2005	94	2013	2017
2004	96	2012	2016
2003	87	2005	2008+
2002	90	2007	2010+
1999	89	2004	2007
1998	87	2003	2006
1997	87	2005	2009

CLARENDON GRENACHE

RATING 3

CLARENDON HILLS	McLaren Vale	$50–$99
GRENACHE	**Current vintage: 2005**	**94**

Powerful and slightly raw-edged, this rustic and dark-fruited grenache is firm and powdery, strong and savoury. With a heady, meaty bouquet and a sumptuous palate steeped in layers of earthy, brambly flavours of blueberries, dark plum and aniseed, it's long, smooth and easily soaks up its assertive smoky oak. Packed with terrific depth and richness, this is tantamount to grenache on steroids.

2005	94	2013	2017
2004	93	2009	2012+
2003	94	2008	2011+
2002	89	2004	2007+
2001	89	2006	2009
1999	89	2001	2004+
1998	92	2003	2006
1997	80	1999	2002
1996	85	2004	2008

HICKINBOTHAM SYRAH

RATING 3

CLARENDON HILLS	McLaren Vale	$100–$199
SYRAH	**Current vintage: 2004**	**92**

Profoundly assertive and searingly concentrated, this sumptuous shiraz builds a massive presence on the palate but never loses its silkiness and charm. Rather closed, its dark and meaty aromas of berries and plums are cloaked by oaky influences of mocha and vanilla. Its rich, dark-fruited palate is coated by firm but velvet-like tannins and creamy oak. Backed by suggestions of mint, menthol and black olives, its impact lasts and lasts.

2004	92	2009	2012
2003	95	2011	2015
2002	95	2010	2014+
2001	83	2006	2009
1999	88	2004	2007
1998	91	2003	2006

LIANDRA SYRAH

RATING 5

CLARENDON HILLS	McLaren Vale	$50–$99
SYRAH	**Current vintage: 2005**	**89**

A massive, deeply concentrated shiraz with a slightly baked expression of blackberries, plums, raisins and currants over spirity, rather brandied suggestions of spice cake and bitumen. Wild and briary, it's backed by excellent dusty vanilla oak, presenting a smooth, seamless palate that breaks up fractionally at the finish. Very well handled in the cellar, but slightly overcooked in the vineyard.

2005	89	2010	2013+
2004	87	2006	2009+
2003	88	2005	2008+
2002	88	2010	2014
2001	89	2006	2009
1999	95	2007	2011
1998	91	2003	2006
1997	93	2005	2009+

MORITZ SYRAH

RATING 5

CLARENDON HILLS	McLaren Vale	$50–$99
SYRAH	**Current vintage: 2005**	**83**

Slightly dirty and quite jammy, with briary, black jujube-like fruit, smoky oak and rather a gritty extract. Lacking freshness and brightness, it's forward and then hollow, finishing hot, stale and licorice-like, lacking finesse or an even ripeness.

2005	83	2010	2013
2004	90	2009	2012
2003	91	2008	2011
2002	88	2007	2010
2001	84	2003	2006+
1999	89	2004	2007+

PIGGOTT RANGE SYRAH

RATING 3

CLARENDON HILLS	McLaren Vale	$200+
SYRAH	**Current vintage: 2005**	**92**

Big, black and brooding, this palate-staining, wild and briary shiraz is packed with intense plum and blackberry fruit backed with smoky, bacony and vanilla oak, cloves and pepper, with undertones of eucalypt and menthol. Framed by firm, dusty tannins, it's long and assertive, with layers of fruit, oak and structure.

2005	92	2013	2017
2004	92	2012	2016
2003	97	2015	2023
2002	89	2010	2014+
1999	94	2007	2011
1998	90	2003	2006+
1997	88	2002	2005+

Clayfield

25 Wilde Lane, Moyston Vic 3377. Tel: (03) 5354 2689. Fax: (03) 5354 2679.
Website: www.clayfieldwines.com Email:clayfieldwines@netconnect.com.au

Region: **Grampians** Winemaker: **Simon Clayfield** Viticulturist: **Simon Clayfield** Chief Executive: **Simon Clayfield**

Simon Clayfield is an experienced and talented maker of Victorian red wines, and under his own label he crafts classically elegant and exotically spiced Shiraz of considerable finesse and longevity. The 2005 vintage does not appear to have lived up to the standard he has set for several years, lacking the winemaking polish this label usually stands for. This happens. Making small batches of wine is fraught with danger.

SHIRAZ

RATING **2**

Grampians	$30–$49
Current vintage: 2005	87

Very ripe and meaty for this important small label, this sumptuously fruited and sour-edged shiraz is just a little developed and oxidative, lacking in genuine brightness and freshness. Black and meaty, its licorice-like aromas of plums, currants, cassis and cloves precede a long, firmish and peppery palate. There's an oxidised aspect to some otherwise intense flavours of blackberries, dark plums and cherries, while it finishes with lively acidity.

2005	87	2010	2013+
2004	95	2016	2024
2003	89	2008	2011
2002	95	2014	2022
2001	95	2009	2013+
2000	87	2005	2008

Clonakilla

Crisps Lane off Murrumbateman Road, Murrumbateman NSW 2582. Tel: (02) 6227 5877.
Fax: (02) 6227 5871. Website: www.clonakilla.com.au Email: wine@clonakilla.com.au

Region: **Canberra** Winemaker: **Tim Kirk** Viticulturist: **Michael Lahiff** Chief Executive: **John Kirk**

Clonakilla is a small producer in the Canberra wine region that has pioneered the Côte-Rôtie-styled expression of shiraz and viognier blend in Australia. The exceptionally early 2006 vintage has delivered a lighter Shiraz Viognier, but one with some finesse, while the Viognier is simply superb. The 2007 Riesling is another fine and chalky expression of this under-rated wine.

BALINDERRY CABERNET BLEND

RATING **4**

Canberra	$30–$49
Current vintage: 2006	89

Long and savoury, this slightly minty and rather stylish young cabernet blend has a sweet, violet-like perfume of blackcurrant, blackberries and cedar/vanilla oak before a smooth, fine-grained palate. Underpinned by fine, bony tannins, it's dark-fruited and cedary, with just a little hollowness in mid-palate.

2006	89	2011	2014
2005	91	2013	2017
2004	90	2009	2012+
2003	86	2008	2011+
2002	90	2007	2010
2001	93	2009	2013+
2000	93	2008	2012+
1999	91	2007	2011
1998	93	2003	2006+
1997	88	2005	2009+
1996	84	1998	2001
1995	88	2003	2007
1994	92	2002	2006

HILLTOPS SHIRAZ

RATING **4**

Hilltops	$20–$29
Current vintage: 2006	88

A very well handled wine from a slightly cooked and meaty expression of redcurrant, berry, plum and raisin-like fruit that retains a spicy, peppery perfume. Framed by a firmish, fine-grained and drying extract, it's backed by herbal nuances and steadily reveals more depth of minty fruit.

2006	88	2008	2011+
2005	92	2010	2013+
2004	89	2006	2009
2003	87	2005	2008
2002	87	2004	2007
2001	92	2003	2006+
2000	91	2002	2005+

RIESLING

Canberra	$20–$29
Current vintage: 2007	**93**

Scented with lime and lavender, this shapely, mineral and tightly focused riesling complements its fresh but slightly oily flavours of pristine citrusy fruit with a fine-grained, chalky undercarriage. It's long, tangy and finely sculpted, with vibrant, crystal-clear fruit.

2007	93	2012	2015
2006	88	2008	2011
2005	93	2013	2017+
2004	91	2006	2009+
2003	88	2005	2008+
2002	93	2004	2007+
2001	88	2003	2006+
2000	92	2008	2012
1999	95	2004	2007+
1998	94	2003	2006+
1997	93	2005	2009
1996	94	2001	2004
1995	92	2003	2007

SHIRAZ VIOGNIER

RATING **1**

Canberra	$50–$99
Current vintage: 2006	**90**

Fresh and vibrant, medium to full in body, this supple and willowy blend combines slightly raisined flavours of blackberries, red cherries, cloves and cinnamon with nuances of marzipan and a meaty aspect. Scented with a floral perfume, it's smooth and polished, with rather a delicate, fine structure and a savoury finish. Lacks the depth and structure of the best vintages of this wine.

2006	90	2008	2011
2005	96	2013	2017
2004	97	2012	2016+
2003	96	2011	2015+
2002	96	2010	2014
2001	97	2009	2013+
2000	90	2005	2008+
1999	89	2003	2007
1998	96	2010	2018
1997	95	2009	2017
1996	90	2001	2004+
1995	89	2003	2007+
1994	93	2002	2006+
1993	89	1998	2001+
1992	89	1997	2000

VIOGNIER

RATING **3**

Canberra	$50–$99
Current vintage: 2006	**94**

A complex, musky, spicy and perfumed viognier whose sumptuous, fruit-driven palate culminates in a finely shaped finish of exceptional persistence and smoothness. Scented with lemon blossom and apricot, it's creamy and nutty, with undertones of melon and acacia. Very elegant and seamless, with a persistent core of fruit and a refreshing, but soft acidity.

2006	94	2008	2011
2005	95	2007	2010
2004	84	2005	2006
2003	94	2004	2005+
2002	95	2004	2007
2001	92	2003	2006
2000	93	2002	2005
1999	92	2000	2003

Clover Hill

60 Clover Hill Road, Lebrina Tas 7254. Tel: (03) 6395 6114. Fax: (03) 6395 6257.
Website: www.taltarni.com.au Email: info@taltarni.com.au

Region: **Pipers River** Winemakers: **Leigh Clarnette, Loïc Le Calvez, Louella McPhan**
Viticulturist: **Kym Ludvigsen** Chief Executive: **Adam Torpy**

Clover Hill is a Taltarni-owned operation in northern Tasmania that specialises in sparkling wine. As the 2003 vintage reveals, its wines are typically fragrant, creamy and crisply defined, with a fruit profile often slightly herbaceous and tropical. The 2001 and 2002 releases are excellent.

VINTAGE

RATING **3**

Pipers River	$30–$49
Current vintage: 2003	**89**

Toasty and herbal, slightly heavy and lacking its typical freshness, this remains a pretty stylish and textured sparkling wine whose fresh melon, white peach and lightly tropical flavour builds on the palate. It's chewy and crackly, with nutty, meaty and leesy complexity, finishing with dryness, austerity and bakery yeast-like flavour.

2003	89	2005	2008+
2002	93	2004	2007
2001	94	2006	2009
2000	87	2005	2008
1999	94	2004	2007+
1998	87	2000	2003+
1997	82	1999	2002
1996	92	2001	2004
1995	91	1997	2000
1994	94	1999	2002

Coldstream Hills

31 Maddens Lane, Coldstream Vic 3770. Tel: (03) 5964 9388. Fax: (03) 5964 9389.
Website: www.coldstreamhills.com.au

Region: **Yarra Valley** Winemaker: **Andrew Fleming** Viticulturist: **Richard Shenfield** Chief Executive: **Jamie Odell**

Coldstream Hills certainly enjoyed its best ever vintage in 2005, in which Andrew Fleming and his team crafted an artful series of wines across the range. Most impressive are the stunning Reserve releases of Pinot Noir and Chardonnay, which really show the benefit of mature vines planted on high-quality sites, as well as a patient and sensible approach towards vinification. More recent vintages have certainly been more difficult, but at least this Fosters-owned brand has the luxury of deciding what fruit to accept, and what to reject.

CHARDONNAY
RATING 4

Yarra Valley $20–$29
Current vintage: 2006 87

Slightly developed for its age, this lightly candied young chardonnay has a creamy, peachy and tropical aroma with undertones of banana, grapefruit and fresh cashew/vanilla oak. Forward and juicy, its tangy melon-like fruit finishes with moderate length and freshness.

2006	87	2007	2008+
2005	90	2007	2010
2004	90	2005	2006+
2003	90	2004	2005+
2001	92	2003	2006
2000	88	2002	2005
1999	87	2001	2004
1998	90	2000	2003
1997	92	1999	2002
1996	91	1998	2001

MERLOT
RATING 4

Yarra Valley $20–$29
Current vintage: 2005 93

Briary, meaty aromas of dark cherries, blackberries and lightly smoky/mocha oak precede a generous, ripe and juicy palate built around a firm structure of drying, papery tannins. It's gamey and varietally correct, with pleasing length and balance. A trifle sinewy today, it should flesh out in future.

2005	93	2010	2013+
2004	86	2006	2009
2003	91	2005	2008
2001	89	2003	2006+
2000	83	2002	2005
1997	89	1999	2002

PINOT NOIR
RATING 4

Yarra Valley $20–$29
Current vintage: 2006 90

Firm and astringent, this rather powerful and sumptuous pinot delivers a wild, heady bouquet of deep black cherry and plum aromas over sweet chocolate/mocha oak and some slightly cooked and stewed elements. Dark flavours of blueberries, cherries and cassis stain its sumptuous, drying palate.

2006	90	2008	2011
2005	93	2007	2010+
2003	90	2005	2008+
2002	86	2003	2004
2001	90	2003	2006
2000	91	2002	2005+
1999	93	2001	2004
1998	86	1999	2000
1997	91	2002	2005
1996	92	1998	2001

RESERVE CABERNET SAUVIGNON
RATING 4

Yarra Valley $30–$49
Current vintage: 2003 89

A fine, supple, smooth and elegant cabernet whose vibrant violet-like tones of cassis, mulberries and dark plums reveal just a little too much herbaceous character for a higher rating. It's fragrant, heady and handsomely oaked, with an assertive but integrated background of cedar, dark chocolate and vanilla influences before finishing just a fraction green and sappy.

2003	89	2011	2015
2001	93	2009	2013+
2000	95	2008	2012+
1998	82	2000	2003
1997	84	2002	2005
1995	90	2000	2003
1994	91	2002	2006
1993	93	1998	2002
1992	96	2004	2012+
1991	93	1999	2003

RESERVE CHARDONNAY

RATING 2

Yarra Valley $30–$49
Current vintage: 2005 96

A high-class chardonnay whose complex and slightly smoky bouquet of melon, grapefruit and minerals has a lifted floral quality and a hint of sweetcorn. Effortlessly smooth and refined, it's generous and slightly fatty in texture, tightly marrying pristine chardonnay fruit with harmonious wine-making artefact. Finishing with refreshing mineral acids, it leaves a lingering impression of fruit and zest.

2005	96	2010	2013+
2004	95	2009	2012+
2003	94	2008	2011
2002	93	2007	2010
2000	90	2002	2005
1999	90	2001	2004+
1998	94	2003	2006
1997	90	2002	2005
1996	88	2001	2004
1995	94	2000	2003
1994	95	1999	2002
1993	90	1995	1998
1992	96	2000	2004

RESERVE MERLOT

RATING 3

Yarra Valley $30–$49
Current vintage: 2000 93

Very smart merlot with strength, ripeness and structure. There's some tobaccoey and herbal complexity behind its varietally correct expression of dark cherries, mulberries and plums, while its assertive vanilla and mocha oak is tightly integrated. It has perfume, length and finish, with pleasing balance and texture.

2000	93	2005	2008
1998	92	2003	2006
1997	87	2002	2005+

RESERVE PINOT NOIR

RATING 2

Yarra Valley $50–$99
Current vintage: 2005 96

Perhaps the finest Coldstream Hills pinot yet made, with an unbelievably floral, perfumed, smoky and fragrant bouquet of intense raspberry, cherry-like fruit backed by nuances of cassis and sweet chocolate/mocha/vanilla oak. Silky-smooth, it is long and even, presenting a spotless array of pristine berry/cherry fruit tightly knit with sweet oak and framed by fine, supple tannins. Finishing with vibrant acidity, it has plenty of length and persistence. Top-class.

2005	96	2010	2013+
2004	95	2009	2012+
2002	89	2004	2007+
2000	93	2005	2008+
1998	95	2006	2010+
1997	96	2005	2009
1996	93	2001	2004+
1995	90	1997	2000
1994	93	2012	2014
1993	88	1995	1998
1992	95	2004	2012

Coombe Farm

11 St Huberts Road, Coldstream Vic 3770. Tel: (03) 9739 1131. Fax: (03) 9739 1154.
Website: www.coombefarm.com.au Email: info@coombefarm.com.au

Region: **Yarra Valley** Winemaker: **Chris Bolden** Viticulturist: **Xavier Mende** Chief Executive: **Scott Benton**

Coombe Farm is an emerging Yarra Valley producer with high quality aspirations. Its first releases have been pretty impressive, with tightly focused and finely honed Chardonnay partnered by supple, sappy but deeply flavoured and savoury Pinot Noir. Given their quality, they are exceptionally affordable.

CHARDONNAY

RATING 3

Yarra Valley $20–$29
Current vintage: 2006 93

Tightly defined, with brightly flavoured peach, grapefruit and sweet, buttery vanilla oak neatly tied in by an almost brittle, crystalline acidity. It's initially rather closed and dusty, with toasty undertones, but opens up on the palate, becoming luscious and creamy, building more weight and generosity towards the finish. Delightful focus and brightness.

2006	93	2008	2011
2005	88	2007	2010
2004	90	2006	2009
2003	95	2005	2008+

PINOT NOIR

| Yarra Valley | $20–$29 |
| Current vintage: 2006 | 91 |

Rather chewy and powerful, this is a sleeper of a pinot, with spicy and floral scents of maraschino and black cherries backed by restrained oak and meaty, mineral suggestions. Dusted with nuances of cloves and cinnamon, it's smooth and vibrant, with intense berry/cherry fruit overlying chewy, fine-grained tannins. It has the structure and the depth, so it's just a matter of waiting for the charm to arrive.

2006	91	2008	2011+
2004	89	2006	2009
2003	87	2004	2005

Coriole

Chaffeys Road, McLaren Vale SA 5171. Tel: (08) 8323 8305. Fax: (08) 8323 9136.
Website: www.coriole.com Email: info@coriole.com
Region: **McLaren Vale** Winemakers: **Matthew Broomhead, Simon Whitehas** Viticulturist: **Rachel Steer**
Chief Executive: **Mark Lloyd**

Like most McLaren Vale makers, Coriole produced rather meatier, chewier reds in 2005 than it did in 2004, a vintage of exceptional charm, brightness and elegance. As a result, the 2005s are likely to be less long-living. Coriole has however managed to retain its particular flair, with a series of relatively complex, more natural and less exaggerated wines than the pumped-up efforts of many of its neighbours.

CHENIN BLANC

| McLaren Vale | $12–$19 |
| Current vintage: 2006 | 87 |

A typically fruity and confectionary chenin blanc with lightly grassy aromas of stonefruit and lemon. Soft and juicy, its mouthfilling palate of fresh tropical and peachy flavour finishes with pleasing length and smooth acids.

2006	87	2007	2008+
2005	88	2006	2007
2003	89	2004	2005+
2002	87	2003	2004+
2001	87	2002	2003

LLOYD RESERVE SHIRAZ

| McLaren Vale | $50–$99 |
| Current vintage: 2005 | 91 |

Rich and meaty, this thick, juicy shiraz has a heady bouquet of violets, cassis, dark plums and spicy, dusty vanilla oak with smoky, menthol-like undertones. Handsomely crafted, it's powerful but measured, delivering a deeply flavoured, luscious and slightly jammy expression of blackberries, dark plums and sweet oak framed by firm, drying powdery tannin. Very Australian and lacking its typical elegance, but a fine effort from this vintage.

2005	91	2013	2017+
2004	96	2016	2024
2002	89	2007	2010+
2001	94	2013	2021
2000	87	2005	2008+
1999	94	2007	2011+
1998	96	2010	2018+
1997	90	2005	2009
1996	95	2008	2016
1995	95	2007	2015
1994	94	2006	2012
1993	89	2001	2005
1992	95	2004	2012
1991	94	2003	2011+
1990	91	2002	2010
1989	93	2001	2009

MARY KATHLEEN RESERVE CABERNET MERLOT

| McLaren Vale | $30–$49 |
| Current vintage: 2004 | 90 |

Sumptuously flavoured, this finely balanced, smooth and juicy cabernet blend reveals an earthy, slightly meaty bouquet of restrained blackberry, plum and cedar. Supported by firm, fine and drying tannin, its long and cedary palate of intense berry, plum and redcurrant fruit is tightly knit with sweet vanilla/cedar oak.

2004	90	2012	2016
2003	93	2011	2015+
2002	90	2010	2014
2001	91	2013	2021
2000	88	2005	2008
1999	92	2011	2019
1998	93	2010	2018
1997	89	2005	2009
1996	93	2004	2008+
1995	90	2003	2007
1994	89	2002	2006

REDSTONE SHIRAZ (formerly Shiraz Cabernet)

RATING **4**

McLaren Vale	$20–$29
Current vintage: 2004	90

Scented with white pepper, cloves and cinnamon, this vibrant, slightly jammy and juicy young shiraz delivers intense and slightly sour-edged flavours of dark plums, berries and dark chocolate, finishing with lingering notes of blackberry confiture. Medium to full-bodied, it's smooth and savoury, with lingering meaty qualities and a firmish, slightly grippy finish. It contains 10% cabernet.

2004	90	2009	2012
2003	89	2011	2015
2002	89	2007	2010
2001	91	2006	2009
2000	91	2005	2008+
1999	87	2004	2007
1998	89	2003	2006+
1997	87	2002	2005
1996	87	2004	2008
1995	89	2001	2004
1994	91	2002	2006
1993	86	1998	2001
1992	89	2000	2004

SANGIOVESE

RATING **4**

McLaren Vale	$20–$29
Current vintage: 2005	89

Ripe and juicy, but varietally correct, this fine, drying and savoury sangiovese has a spicy, earthy and leathery aroma of red cherries, baked earth and briar. Smooth and fine-grained, with a chassis of powdery tannin, its sweet flavours of cherries, blackberries, raspberries and blueberries finish long and dusty.

2005	89	2007	2010+
2004	92	2009	2012+
2003	91	2008	2011
2002	89	2004	2007+
2001	87	2003	2006+
1999	88	2004	2007
1998	86	2000	2003
1997	90	2002	2005
1996	90	2001	2004
1995	90	2003	2007
1994	89	1999	2002
1993	88	2001	2005
1992	84	1997	2000

SEMILLON (formerly Lalla Rookh Semillon)

RATING **5**

McLaren Vale	$20–$29
Current vintage: 2005	89

A lively, fresh and tangy semillon whose lightly herbal aromas of honeydew melon precede a long and almost creamy palate whose pristine sherbet-like fruit has a powdery, chalky undercarriage of fine phenolics. It finishes pleasingly clean, crisp and taut.

2005	89	2007	2010+
2002	88	2004	2007+
2001	90	2006	2009
2000	89	2002	2005
1999	88	2001	2004+
1998	94	2003	2006
1997	91	2002	2005
1996	89	2001	2004
1995	90	1997	2000

SHIRAZ

RATING **3**

McLaren Vale	$20–$29
Current vintage: 2005	89

Firm and polished, this long, vibrantly fruited and handsomely oaked shiraz reveals meaty and minty aspects, but avoids over-ripeness. Its rather confiture-like expression of berries and plums overlies fruitcake and currant-like aspects. Framed by drying, powdery tannins, it delivers a long, smooth palate whose juicy fruit is backed by creamy vanilla oak and suggestions of menthol.

2005	89	2010	2013+
2004	92	2009	2012+
2002	93	2007	2010+
2001	92	2006	2009+
2000	86	2002	2005+
1999	89	2004	2007
1998	89	2006	2010
1997	89	2002	2005
1996	92	2001	2004
1995	93	2002	2007
1994	89	2002	2006
1993	91	2001	2005
1992	93	1997	2000

Craiglee

Sunbury Road, Sunbury Vic 3429. Tel: (03) 9744 4489. Fax: (03) 9744 4489.
Website: www.craiglee.com.au Email: patatcraiglee@hotmail.com

Region: **Sunbury** Winemaker: **Patrick Carmody** Viticulturist: **Patrick Carmody** Chief Executive: **Patrick Carmody**

In late 2006 Pat Carmody staged a remarkable tasting of all Craiglee Shirazes, dating back to 1980. The tasting underlined that Craiglee is an exceptional site for growing savoury, spicy and fine-grained shiraz, but like any other vineyard, it struggles to maintain elegance and brightness in its wine when heavily stressed by drought. It also revealed the extent to which climate change and water scarcity had played their roles in influencing this wine. Most importantly, it confirmed how well Craiglee's Shiraz is able to cellar.

CHARDONNAY

RATING **5**

Sunbury	$20–$29
Current vintage: 2006	**87**

Rather broad and smoky, this viscous, oily chardonnay partners its peach, melon and green olive-like fruit with slightly raw-edged notes of cashew, vanilla and buttery oak. It should age fairly quickly.

2006	87	2008	2011
2005	90	2010	2013
2004	89	2006	2009
2003	88	2005	2008+
2002	93	2007	2010+
2001	89	2003	2006+
2000	90	2008	2012
1999	90	2001	2004
1998	80	1999	2000
1997	90	2002	2005
1996	89	2004	2008
1995	91	2000	2003
1994	93	2002	2006

SHIRAZ

RATING **2**

Sunbury	$30–$49
Current vintage: 2005	**91**

A finely crafted, stylish and savoury shiraz of medium depth and weight with a floral, spicy perfume of cloves and cinnamon. Framed by fine, drying tannins, its supple and minty palate of sweet blackberry, cassis and mulberry flavour and dusty, herbal undertones knits tightly with chocolate oak, finishing with lingering dark fruit and regional influences of mint and menthol.

2005	91	2013	2017+
2004	93	2012	2016
2003	92	2011	2015
2002	94	2010	2014
2001	93	2009	2013
2000	95	2012	2020
1999	92	2007	2011+
1998	93	2006	2010+
1997	93	2009	2017+
1996	94	2008	2016
1995	86	2003	2007
1994	92	2006	2014
1993	89	2001	2005+
1992	95	2004	2012
1991	95	2003	2011
1990	93	2002	2010
1989	89	1997	2003

Crawford River

741 Upper Hotspur Road, Condah Vic 3303. Tel: (03) 5578 2267. Fax: (03) 5578 2240.
Email: crawfordriver@h140.aone.net.au

Region: **Henty** Winemaker: **John Thomson** Viticulturist: **John Thomson** Chief Executive: **John Thomson**

Located in the pastoral country of western Victoria, Crawford River's most popular wine is perhaps its rather accentuated, estery and spicy Riesling. Recent red releases have clearly been affected by the severe drought that has clearly hampered the vineyard's ability to produce fruit of genuine physiological ripeness.

CABERNET MERLOT

RATING **5**

Henty	$30–$49
Current vintage: 2004	**81**

Rather tiring and browning, meaty and herbal, with a mint/menthol presence beneath its stewed flavours of berries and plums. It has received some classy cedar/vanilla oak, but remains lean and hollow, lacking fruit depth and richness. Drying out, it's clearly made from stressed fruit.

2004	81	2006	2009
2003	81	2005	2008+
2002	87	2007	2010
2001	89	2006	2009
1999	89	2004	2007

CABERNET SAUVIGNON

Henty $30–$49
Current vintage: 2003 80

Dull and woolly, with green-edged fruit backed by meaty, leathery and menthol-like flavours. Lean and green, it finishes rather metallic. Undoubtedly the reflection of stressed fruit.

2003	80	2005	2008
2001	93	2009	2013+
2000	89	2005	2008
1999	95	2007	2011+
1997	90	2005	2009
1996	95	2004	2008+
1995	93	2003	2007+
1992	89	2000	2004
1991	95	1999	2003+
1990	89	1995	1998
1989	88	1994	1997

RIESLING

Henty $20–$29
Current vintage: 2006 90

Heady and floral, with aromas of apricots, tropical fruits and lime juice backed by a confectionary aspect, with lemon sherbet and bathpowder-like undertones. Remarkably concentrated, richly fruited and assertive, this juicy and explosive young riesling has the mouthfeel of a dessert wine, but finishes with only a hint of residual sweetness.

2006	90	2011	2014
2005	89	2010	2013+
2004	90	2009	2012+
2003	90	2005	2008+
2001	94	2006	2009
2000	87	2002	2005
1999	92	2004	2007
1995	91	2003	2007+
1994	94	2002	2006
1993	95	2001	2005
1992	94	1997	2000
1991	90	1996	1999
1990	93	1999	2002

SAUVIGNON BLANC SEMILLON BLEND

Henty $20–$29
Current vintage: 2006 90

Tightly crafted and sculpted, with underlying chalkiness and a racy acidity, this lightly dusty, nutty and herbaceous blend reveals a fresh, racy presence of gooseberries, melon and passionfruit. It's long, tangy and intensely flavoured.

2006	90	2007	2008+
2005	87	2006	2007
2004	89	2006	2009+
2003	90	2004	2005+
2002	82	2002	2003
2001	93	2003	2006
2000	89	2002	2005+

Cullen

Caves Road, Willyabrup WA 6284. Tel: (08) 9755 5277. Fax: (08) 9755 5550.
Website: www.cullenwines.com.au Email: enquiries@cullenwines.com.au
Region: **Margaret River** Winemakers: **Vanya Cullen, Trevor Kent** Viticulturist: **Michael Sleegers**
Managing Director: **Vanya Cullen**

With the release of what might yet prove to be the finest Cullen red yet, Vanya Cullen's focus on a biodynamic approach to viticulture is paying dividends with deeper flavours and a finer but more profound grade of natural tannin than ever before. In 2006 she also chose not to blend together the Sauvignon Blanc Semillons from the Cullen and Mangan vineyards, releasing them as separate wines. She attributes much of their minerality and accent on texture on biodynamics and a natural ferment, and expects the wines to age more slowly. From 2006, but not before, the ratings for this wine in this book will reflect the Cullen Vineyard blend.

CHARDONNAY

Margaret River $50–$99
Current vintage: 2005 93

Still a little youthful and angular, this substantial and searingly intense chardonnay should settle down nicely. Slightly spirity and oaky, its intense aromas of lime juice and ruby grapefruit are backed by nuances of cloves and wheatmeal. Its sumptuous, smooth and even palate of piercing, tangy mango, melon and grapefruit flavour and assertive new oak is punctuated by rather a bracing cut of acidity. Long and dry, it simply needs time.

2005	93	2010	2013
2004	88	2006	2009
2003	83	2005	2008
2002	96	2007	2010+
2001	95	2006	2009+
2000	94	2005	2008
1999	95	2004	2007
1998	94	2000	2003
1997	96	2002	2005+
1996	95	2001	2004+
1995	94	2000	2003
1994	95	2002	2006

CULLEN VYD SAUVIGNON BLANC SEMILLON

RATING 2

Margaret River	$30–$49
Current vintage: 2006	**95**

Exploring the limits of this regional style, this funky, briney and slatey white blend reveals rather a meaty, pungent bouquet whose aromas of gooseberry and honeysuckle are backed by toasty oak and reductive, earthy elements. Punchy and savoury, its rich, chewy palate delivers plenty of intense fruit before finishing tightly with refreshing mineral acids. Unusually wild and complex

2005	95	2010	2013
2004	90	2006	2009
2003	89	2005	2008
2002	96	2004	2007+
2001	96	2006	2009
2000	95	2002	2005+
1999	96	2007	2011
1998	91	2000	2003
1997	94	2005	2009
1995	91	2000	2003
1994	93	1996	1999
1993	95	1998	2001

DIANA MADELINE (Cabernet Sauvignon Merlot)

RATING 1

Margaret River	$50–$99
Current vintage: 2005	**97**

Wow! Elegance meets structure, meets sophistication. Scented with violets and sweet cedary new oak, its perfume of small red and black berries, dark cherries reveals complex earthy undertones with a hint of gravel. Full to medium in body but steeped with vibrant flavours of dark berries, and cherries, its seductively smooth but opulent palate revels in its marriage of fruit, oak and firm, Graves-like chalky tannin. Exceptionally long and perfectly harmonious, it's both polished and powerful, with a brilliant future.

2005	97	2025	2035
2004	97	2024	2034
2003	95	2015	2023
2002	95	2014	2022
2001	97	2013	2021+
2000	97	2012	2020+
1999	97	2019	2029
1998	96	2010	2018+
1997	93	2009	2017
1996	95	2008	2016
1995	96	2015	2025
1994	95	2006	2014
1993	94	2005	2013+
1992	94	2004	2012+
1991	89	2003	2011
1990	90	2002	2010
1989	95	2001	2009

MANGAN (Malbec, Petit Verdot blend)

RATING 3

Margaret River	$30–$49
Current vintage: 2005	**92**

Vibrant spicy, meaty and lightly peppery aromas of dark cherries and plums are handsomely backed by assertive but balanced cedar/vanilla oak, backed by hits of mint and typical regional earthy undertones. Intense, mouthfilling black fruits are supported by a firmish and astringent rod of drying but loose-knit tannin, finishing long and savoury. It's firmer and slightly more raw than previous Mangans, but should cellar well as more of a serious wine.

2005	92	2010	2013+
2004	92	2009	2012
2003	88	2005	2008
2002	93	2007	2010
2001	89	2004	2007

Curlewis

55 Navarre Road, Curlewis Vic 3222. Tel: (03) 5250 4567. Fax: (03) 5250 4567.
Website: www.curlewiswinery.com.au Email: curlewis@datafast.net.au

Region: **Bellarine Peninsula** Winemaker: **Rainer Breit**
Viticulturists: **Rainer Breit, Wendy Oliver** Chief Executives: **Rainer Breit, Wendy Oliver**

Curlewis is presently riding high on a crest of popularity. Its owners fell in love with the more funky and wild expressions of Burgundy, then wanted to make similar wines in Australia. While their wines are unquestionably of the more adventurous and savoury style that evolves complexity rather quickly, there is an evident trend to capture and focus more emphasis on brightness of fruit.

CHARDONNAY

RATING 4

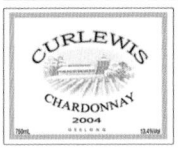

		Bellarine Peninsula	$30–$49
		Current vintage: 2005	**92**

Evolved and technically quite awkward, this is a red wine drinker's chardonnay steeped in richness, flavour and complexity. Smoky, toasty and rather funky, its nutty and almost aldehydic bouquet reveals meaty, cheesy evolution. Smooth and savoury, with sumptuous flavours of melon, citrus and butterscotch over a chalky texture, it finishes with lemon sherbet-like and very slightly green-edged acids. You'll either love it or hate it.

2005	92	2007	2010
2004	89	2006	2009
2003	95	2005	2008+
2002	83	2003	2004+
2001	90	2003	2006+

PINOT NOIR

		Bellarine Peninsula	$30–$49
		Current vintage: 2004	**82**

Browning, with greenish, metallic aspects beneath its floral and gamey expression of cherries and plums. It's spicy and sappy, with some pretty souredged cherry/berry fruit becoming quite lean towards the finish.

2004	82	2006	2009
2003	86	2005	2008
2002	87	2004	2007
2001	89	2006	2009
2000	86	2002	2005

RESERVE PINOT NOIR

RATING 5

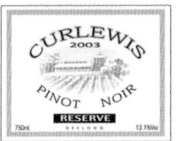

		Bellarine Peninsula	$50–$99
		Current vintage: 2004	**88**

A developing and slightly awkward effort at a more complex and savoury pinot noir. Slightly browning, with some spiky and green-edged acids and flavours beneath its meaty, gamey expression of cherries and small berries, it's supported by a genuine spine of fine tannins. There's a slight bitterness at the finish, but it should develop further interest and character with more time in the bottle.

2004	88	2009	2012
2003	89	2006	2009
2002	82	2004	2007
2001	82	2003	2006
2000	80	2002	2005+
1998	77	2000	2003

d'Arenberg

Osborn Road, McLaren Vale SA 5171. Tel: (08) 8329 4888. Fax: (08) 8323 8423.
Website: www.darenberg.com.au Email: winery@darenberg.com.au
Regions: **McLaren Vale, Fleurieu Peninsula, Adelaide Hills** Winemakers: **Chester Osborn, Phillip Dean**
Viticulturists: **Chester Osborn, Giulio Dimasi** Managing Director: **d'Arry Osborn**
Faced with a very different set of vintage conditions in 2005, Chester Osborn's team made a good fist of the
extreme heat. It's only natural — in a very literal sense — that the d'Arenberg reds from this season are rather
more cooked and lack the natural balance and ripeness of the 2004s, but they still offer plenty of regional
character and charm. Like most interested onlookers, I am keen to discover what new left-of-centre blends
are currently knocking around the corners of the Chester Osborn brain.

D'ARRY'S ORIGINAL SHIRAZ GRENACHE   RATING 4

McLaren Vale $12–$19
Current vintage: 2005 84

Cooked and jammy, this meaty, briary and dark-fruited grenache has a spirity scent of dark plums, blackberries and baked earth. Initially rich and forward, it becomes quite awkward and hollow by mid-palate, falling away before a thin and rather flat finish that lacks brightness and fruit.

2005	84	2007	2010
2004	92	2016	2024+
2003	87	2008	2011+
2002	90	2010	2014+
2001	87	2006	2009
2000	90	2005	2008+
1999	89	2004	2007+
1998	90	2006	2010+
1997	89	2002	2005+
1996	89	2004	2008
1995	92	2003	2007
1994	92	2002	2006
1993	89	2001	2005
1992	91	2000	2004
1991	88	1999	2003
1990	91	1998	2002
1989	87	1997	2001
1988	93	2000	2008

THE BROKEN FISHPLATE SAUVIGNON BLANC   RATING 5

McLaren Vale $12–$19
Current vintage: 2006 87

A broader, rather confectionary sauvignon blanc whose lightly grassy, tropical aromas of passionfruit and melon precede a rich and juicy palate. It's very generous, with a hint of capsicum and a little spirity warmth, but finishes clean and a little austere.

2006	87	2006	2007
2005	91	2006	2007+
2004	85	2004	2005
2003	86	2003	2004+
2002	90	2003	2004

THE COPPERMINE ROAD CABERNET SAUVIGNON   RATING 3

McLaren Vale $50–$99
Current vintage: 2005 89

A deep, rich and profoundly fruited cabernet whose dark, brooding aromas of cassis, dark plums and dark chocolate are backed by a hint of menthol. It's firm and robust, with deep, powerful flavours of dark fruits, minerals and chocolate oak framed by drying, astringent and ironstone-like tannins. It's just a fraction raw-edged and jammy, but not overcooked.

2005	89	2017	2025
2004	93	2016	2024+
2003	93	2015	2023
2002	93	2014	2022
2001	93	2009	2013+
2000	93	2012	2020
1999	89	2007	2011+
1998	94	2010	2018+
1997	90	2005	2009+
1996	89	2008	2016

THE CUSTODIAN GRENACHE   RATING 4

McLaren Vale $20–$29
Current vintage: 2005 87

Slightly overcooked, this well-polished grenache reveals deep, dark, rather closed and meaty aromas of ripe plums and currants with a spirity background. Its forward, intense and jammy flavours of raspberries and redcurrants thins out marginally towards a lean and angular finish of pleasing acidity.

2005	87	2007	2010+
2004	90	2006	2009+
2002	92	2010	2014+
2001	89	2009	2013
2000	92	2005	2008+
1999	91	2004	2007+
1998	87	2003	2006
1997	92	2002	2005
1996	91	2004	2008
1995	93	2003	2007

THE DEAD ARM SHIRAZ

RATING **3**

McLaren Vale			$50–$99	
Current vintage: 2005			90	

Pungent and powerful, this rich and very ripe shiraz is presently slightly raw-edged, but should become more polished with time. Its briary, meaty aromas of blackberry, currant and plum-like fruit are backed by sweet cedary oak. Framed by firm, dusty tannins and supported by carefully handled oak, its substantial and persistent palate delivers a powerful after-burn of fruit richness. Will cellar well for a 2005.

2005	90	2013	2017
2004	96	2016	2024+
2003	92	2015	2023
2002	94	2010	2014
2001	93	2013	2021+
2000	93	2012	2020
1999	89	2007	2011
1998	93	2010	2018
1997	92	2005	2009
1996	95	2008	2016
1995	95	2007	2015
1994	93	2006	2014

THE DERELICT VINEYARD GRENACHE

RATING **4**

McLaren Vale			$30–$49	
Current vintage: 2004			95	

Rustic and ethereal, wild and spicy, with earthy, briary aromas of dark plums, blackberries, blueberries and charcuterie meats preceding a firm, deeply flavoured and beautifully structured palate of palate-staining intensity and explosive brightness. It's long and seamless, with a firm, drying undercarriage of tight-knit tannins. One of the best Australian grenaches I have ever tasted.

2004	95	2012	2016+
2003	89	2008	2011+
2002	87	2007	2010

THE DRY DAM RIESLING

RATING **5**

McLaren Vale			$12–$19	
Current vintage: 2006			87	

Sweaty, reductive aromas eventually blow away to reveal a scent of fresh lime and a long, tangy and austere palate that finishes with refreshing acidity. Sadly bottled without adequate care to ensure a minimum of unbound sulphide, which of course its screw cap will only exacerbate. Contrary to the views of many English critics, this is not the fault of the seal, but of the finishing of the wine.

2006	87	2008	2011
2005	87	2010	2013
2004	87	2006	2009
2003	90	2008	2011+
2002	90	2007	2010
2001	87	2003	2006
2000	87	2005	2008
1999	92	2004	2007
1997	87	2002	2005

THE FOOTBOLT SHIRAZ

RATING **5**

McLaren Vale			$20–$29	
Current vintage: 2005			87	

A rich, forward, hot year wine that lacks typical intensity and focus. Its dark, jammy and rather cooked aromas of redcurrants and raisins overlie modest influences of cedar/chocolate oak. Its thick, drying palate begins with sumptuous dark fruits, becomes rather hollow, then finishes firm and raw-edged with slightly metallic acids.

2005	87	2010	2013
2004	90	2012	2016+
2003	85	2005	2008+
2001	87	2003	2006+
2000	87	2002	2005+
1999	89	2004	2007+
1998	90	2006	2010
1997	87	2002	2005+
1996	90	2004	2008
1995	90	2003	2007
1994	91	2006	2014
1993	90	2001	2005
1992	90	2004	2012

THE GALVO GARAGE CABERNET BLEND

RATING **4**

McLaren Vale, Adel. Hills			$30–$49	
Current vintage: 2004			91	

Tightly balanced, finely polished and presented, this smooth and pliant red marries piercing and penetrating blackberry and plum-like flavour with newish mocha/dark chocolate oak and firm, powdery tannin. Its minty small berry/cherry aromas reveal undertones of eucalypt, menthol and a faint meatiness, while its sumptuous palate is long, even and finely balanced.

2004	91	2016	2024
2003	90	2008	2011+
2002	90	2010	2014
2001	90	2009	2013

THE HIGH TRELLIS CABERNET SAUVIGNON

McLaren Vale	$20–$29
Current vintage: 2005	**86**

High-toned, ultra-ripe and slightly caramelised aromas of berries and plums, mint and menthol precede a slightly awkward palate whose depth of meaty, dark olive-like fruit is backed by a modest grip of papery tannin. Slightly overcooked, finishing with nuances of dark olives, menthol and blackberry confiture.

2005	86	2010	2013+
2004	89	2009	2012+
2003	89	2011	2015
2002	89	2007	2010+
2001	85	2006	2009
2000	87	2005	2008
1999	87	2004	2007
1998	93	2006	2010
1997	88	2002	2005+
1995	92	2003	2007
1994	88	1999	2002
1993	87	2001	2005

THE IRONSTONE PRESSINGS (Grenache Shiraz Mourvèdre)

McLaren Vale	$50–$99
Current vintage: 2005	**90**

Slightly spicy and rather jammy, its currant-like aromas of plums and berries precede a surprisingly fresh and vibrant palate. Framed by carefully integrated smooth, silky tannins, its rather closed expression of confection-like blueberry, blackberry and raspberry flavour reveals suggestions of plums and currants, finishing with brightness and freshness. A very good effort from this vintage.

2005	90	2010	2013+
2004	95	2016	2024+
2003	91	2011	2015+
2002	94	2014	2022+
2001	92	2013	2021
2000	89	2005	2008
1999	89	2007	2011
1998	89	2010	2018
1997	91	2005	2009
1996	94	2008	2016
1995	93	2007	2015
1994	89	2006	2014
1993	91	2005	2013
1992	95	2000	2004
1991	91	2003	2011
1990	90	2002	2010

THE LAST DITCH VIOGNIER

McLaren Vale, Adelaide Hills	$12–$19
Current vintage: 2006	**88**

A savoury, supple and charming wine whose vibrant, dusty aromas of tangerine, cloves and cinnamon sport something of a funky edge. Its smooth and unusually restrained palate of spicy, citrusy flavour finishes with moderate length and freshness, but with just a hint of metallic greenness.

2006	88	2007	2008+
2005	88	2006	2007+
2004	87	2005	2006
2003	82	2004	2005
2002	87	2003	2004+
2001	89	2003	2006

THE LAUGHING MAGPIE (Shiraz Viognier)

McLaren Vale	$20–$29
Current vintage: 2005	**85**

Meaty, rather evolved, earthy and spicy aromas of red and black berries are lifted by a viognier's floral qualities but still lack genuine intensity. Simple and forward, its warm, slightly soupy palate lacks genuine length of fruit, finishing cooked and stale but lifted to a degree by some pleasing oak.

2005	85	2007	2010
2004	92	2009	2012+
2003	90	2005	2008+
2002	92	2007	2010+
2001	90	2006	2009
2000	87	2005	2008

THE NOBLE RIESLING

McLaren Vale $20–$29 (375 ml)
Current vintage: 2006   **86**

Already a burnished amber appearance, with candied, crème caramel and barley sugar-like flavours of citrus, pear and apple, it's rather short, cloying and simple, lacking much by way of noble rot.

Year	Score	Drink	Drink
2006	86	2007	2008
2003	84	2004	2005
2002	88	2004	2007+
2001	86	2003	2006
2000	88	2002	2005+
1999	88	2001	2004+
1998	84	2000	2003
1997	90	2002	2005
1996	87	1998	2001
1995	90	2000	2003
1994	93	2002	2006
1993	89	1995	1998

THE OLIVE GROVE CHARDONNAY

McLaren Vale, Adel. Hills $12–$19
Current vintage: 2006   **81**

Backed by reductive, cheesy and sweetcorn-like undertones, its meaty, melon-like aromas have a confectionary aspect. Thick and cloying, its forward, juicy palate becomes more oily and syrupy, with overcooked and lifeless fruit tending towards excessive fatness and flabbiness.

Year	Score	Drink	Drink
2006	81	2007	2008
2005	88	2007	2010
2004	88	2005	2006+
2003	87	2005	2008
2002	90	2004	2007
2001	81	2002	2003
2000	88	2002	2005
1999	92	2001	2004+
1998	92	2003	2006
1997	88	1999	2002

THE TWENTYEIGHT ROAD MOURVÈDRE

McLaren Vale $30–$49
Current vintage: 2005   **87**

Firm, lean and slightly herbal, this shorter-term red wine has a meaty, rustic bouquet of red and black berries, sweet leather and dark chocolate. Its palate begins with intense flavours of berries and plums, becoming meatier as it dries out a little towards an astringent, almost chalky finish.

Year	Score	Drink	Drink
2005	87	2010	2013+
2004	91	2012	2016+
2002	90	2010	2024+
2001	93	2009	2013+
2000	87	2005	2008
1999	88	2007	2011
1998	89	2003	2006+
1997	87	2002	2005
1996	92	2004	2008+
1995	89	2003	2007

VINTAGE DECLARED FORTIFIED SHIRAZ
(formerly Vintage Port)

McLaren Vale $30–$49
Current vintage: 2004   **94**

Deep, dark and spicy aromas of dark plums, currants and cassis overlie nuances of licorice, cloves and cinnamon, with a very clean and aromatic lift of spirit. Very clean, restrained and fine-grained, its savoury and spicy palate is partially reminiscent of the Portuguese expression of vintage port. Its tannins are tight and powdery, its lingering finish slightly meaty and spicy.

Year	Score	Drink	Drink
2004	94	2016	2024
2003	93	2015	2023+
2002	93	2014	2022+
2001	94	2013	2021+
2000	95	2020	2030+
1999	90	2011	2019+
1998	93	2010	2018
1997	93	2005	2009+
1995	94	2007	2015
1993	93	2005	2013
1987	94	2007	2017
1978	90	1998	2008
1976	93	1996	2006
1975	93	1995	2005
2004	89	2009	2012
2003	87	2005	2008+
2001	89	2009	2013
2000	83	2005	2008
1999	84	2004	2007+
1998	87	2003	2006
1997	87	2002	2005
1996	91	2004	2008+
1995	92	2003	2007+
1994	89	2006	2014
1993	84	2001	2005
1992	88	2000	2004

A B C D E F G H I J K L M N O P Q R S T U V W X Y Z

Dal Zotto

Main Road, Whitfield, King Valley Vic 3733. Tel: (03) 5729 8321. Fax: (03) 5729 8490.
Website: www.dalzotto.com.au Email: christian@dalzotto.com.au

Region: **King Valley** Winemakers: **Michael Dal Zotto, Otto Dal Zotto** Viticulturist: **Otto Dal Zotto**
Chief Executives: **Otto & Elena Dal Zotto**

This excellent new addition to this guide offers tremendous value for money with its deeply flavoured and
naturally balanced wines, most of which have the ability to cellar for a considerable time. They're made in an
uncomplicated way that leaves them unaffected by overt or excessive artefact. The delicious and savoury
Prosecco is rightly gathering a strong cult following.

CABERNET MERLOT

RATING 4

King Valley	$20–$29
Current vintage: 2002	90

2002	90	2014	2022
2001	86	2009	2013
1998	93	2010	2018+

Pleasingly complex and finely balanced, this earthy and slightly meaty cabernet blend has a maturing bouquet of small black and red berries backed by cedar/vanilla oak. Smooth and supple, with deep flavours of small berries and plums underpinned by a grainy and slightly raw-edged undercarriage of unpolished tannin, it simply needs more time to develop further character and harmony.

MERLOT

RATING 4

King Valley	$20–$29
Current vintage: 2002	89

2002	89	2010	2014
2001	90	2009	2013+
2000	90	2008	2012+

Earthy and slightly meaty with a leathery bouquet of black cherries, dark plums, cedar and dried herbs, with undertones of mint, menthol and iodide. Fleshy and juicy, it's deep fruit is framed by drying, savoury and mouth-coating tannin, finishing with lingering fruit and undertones of herbs and vanilla oak. Give it more time.

PROSECCO

RATING 4

King Valley	$30–$49
Current vintage: 2006	90

2006	90	2008	2011
2005	91	2007	2008
2004	89	2005	2006+

Dusty and refreshing with a lively expression of lemon zest, apple and pear, this savoury and lightly toasty young wine has a bubbly effervescence before a long, lingering finish of pristine fruit and soft acidity. It's deliciously dry and persistent.

RIESLING

RATING 4

King Valley	$12–$19
Current vintage: 2006	90

2006	90	2011	2014+
2005	93	2013	2017
2004	91	2012	2016

Tight, focused and citrusy, with a penetrative floral perfume and a long, lingering palate. Its tangy flavours of apple and pear, lime juice and lemon rind overlie suggestions of peach and minerals, while it's underpinned by a fine chalkiness. It finishes with pleasing shape and refreshing acidity.

Dalwhinnie

448 Taltarni Road, Moonambel Vic 3478. Tel: (03) 5467 2388. Fax: (03) 5467 2237.
Website: www.dalwhinnie.com.au Email: dalwines@iinet.net.au

Region: **Pyrenees** Winemaker: **David Jones** Viticulturist: **David Jones** Chief Executive: **David Jones**

Dalwhinnie is a small vineyard that has a healthy reputation for its deeply layered and intensely flavoured Shiraz and its occasionally superlative Cabernet. While its current releases include another spicy and savoury edition of its flagship Eagle Series Shiraz from 2004, the 2005 vintage was clearly affected by extreme levels of drought-related stress. Similarly, the 2004 vintages is the pick of the new South West Rocks Shiraz.

CHARDONNAY

RATING **3**

Pyrenees	$30–$49
Current vintage: 2004	**93**

A long, smooth, austere and minerally chardonnay whose delicate aromas of citrus fruit, honeydew melon, guava and wheatmeal overlie dusty nuances of vanilla oak and lifted floral scents. Seamless, savoury and nutty, it's a generous but restrained marriage of lime and melon fruit with fresh vanilla oak and lees-derived complexity punctuated by slightly sour-edged and steely acids.

2004	93	2009	2012
2003	92	2005	2008
2002	89	2004	2007+
2001	93	2006	2009
2000	92	2002	2005+
1999	87	2001	2004
1998	94	2003	2006
1997	94	2002	2005
1996	92	2001	2004
1995	94	2000	2003
1994	94	2002	2006
1993	95	1998	2001
1992	93	2000	2004

EAGLE SERIES SHIRAZ

RATING **2**

Pyrenees	$100–$199
Current vintage: 2004	**94**

Lacking the exceptional length of fruit for true greatness, this remains a fine expression of controlled power, strength and balance in a savoury and meaty expression of Victorian shiraz. Its musky, spicy and briary aromas of dark berries, plums and cassis overlie charcuterie-like reductive influences. Richly fruited and finely balanced, it's robust, bony and likely to develop plenty of complexity over time.

2004	94	2016	2024
2001	86	2003	2006
2000	95	2012	2020
1998	93	2003	2006
1997	97	2005	2009
1992	94	2000	2004
1986	93	1998	2006

MOONAMBEL CABERNET

RATING **3**

Pyrenees	$30–$49
Current vintage: 2005	**83**

Honest and regional, but from a hot, fruit-stressed year, this rather cooked and minty cabernet reveals jammy, currant-like aromas of red berries and menthol. Lacking genuine fruit brightness, its hollow palate relies on creamy vanilla oak for sweetness. Framed by drying, powdery tannins, it finishes tinny and dehydrated.

2005	83	2010	2013+
2004	97	2016	2024+
2003	90	2011	2015
2002	92	2014	2022
2000	91	2012	2020
1999	93	2011	2019
1998	94	2010	2018
1997	92	2009	2017
1996	86	2004	2008
1995	93	2003	2007+
1994	90	2002	2006
1993	85	2001	2005+
1992	94	2004	2012+
1991	92	2003	2011
1990	88	2002	2010
1989	91	1997	2001
1988	89	1996	2000+
1987	82	1992	1995
1986	93	1998	2006
1985	86	1990	1993
1984	80	1989	1992
1983	87	1995	2003

MOONAMBEL SHIRAZ

RATING

Pyrenees	$50–$99		
Current vintage: 2005	**88**		

Meaty, chocolatey aromas of dark plums and black pepper precede a relatively light palate for this vineyard, whose rather pretty expression of cassis and raspberry flavours knits well with sweet oak and slightly gritty tannins that smooth out towards the finish. It does culminate with rather cooked and dehydrated characters plus some metallic elements, and appears to have been made from slightly riper fruit than its alcoholic strength of 14.3% would indicate.

2005	88	2010	2013
2004	97	2012	2016+
2003	89	2008	2011+
2002	90	2007	2010+
2001	94	2009	2013+
2000	95	2008	2012+
1999	94	2007	2011+
1998	95	2006	2010
1997	94	2005	2009
1996	95	2004	2008
1995	92	2003	2007
1994	93	2002	2006
1993	87	2001	2005
1992	97	2004	2012
1991	95	1999	2003+
1990	93	2002	2010
1989	82	1994	1997
1988	89	2000	2008

De Bortoli

De Bortoli Road, Bilbul NSW 2680. Tel: (02) 6966 0100. Fax: (02) 6966 0199.
Website: www.debortoli.com.au Email: reception_bilbul@debortoli.com.au
Region: **Riverina** Winemakers: **Darren De Bortoli, Julie Mortlock** Viticulturist: **Kevin De Bortoli**
Chief Executive: **Darren De Bortoli**

De Bortoli created the genre of late-harvest semillon in Australia with the first vintage of what was then labelled 'Semillon Sauterne' in 1982. Since then the wine has been renamed 'Noble One', and has become virtually mandatory on Australian wine lists. The 2005 release is a sumptuous, concentrated but earlier-maturing style.

NOBLE ONE

RATING

Riverina	$20–$29 (375 ml)		
Current vintage: 2005	**90**		

Forward and candied, with typically luscious and marmalade-like flavours of cumquat and apricot, melon and lemon rind over suggestions of toast and toffee, it's luscious, rich and concentrated. Sweet and syrupy, backed by a lick of fine, powdery texture, it finishes with refreshing acids and smoky undertones. Rather developed; a shorter-term style.

2005	90	2007	2010+
2004	89	2006	2009+
2003	92	2005	2008+
2002	96	2010	2014
2001	90	2003	2006
2000	93	2005	2008
1999	93	2004	2007
1998	95	2010	2018
1997	89	2002	2005
1996	95	2004	2008
1995	95	2003	2007
1994	96	2002	2006

De Bortoli Yarra Valley

Pinnacle Lane, Dixon's Creek Vic 3775. Tel: (03) 5965 2271. Fax: (03) 5965 2442.
Website: www.debortoli.com.au Email: Yarra_Cellar_Door@debortoli.com.au
Region: **Yarra Valley** Winemakers: **Stephen Webber, David Slingsby-Smith, Bill Downie, Sarah Fagan, Paul Bridgeman** Viticulturist: **Stuart Proud** Chief Executive: **Darren De Bortoli**

De Bortoli is one of the Yarra Valley's largest winemakers, and while recent vintage are not quite up to the brand's established standard, given the scale of its operations it does an excellent job in delivering consistently flavoursome wines of quality and distinction. While De Bortoli's team has never been afraid to administer a decent measure of newish oak to its riper and richer reds, I am more concerned that recent vintages might be taking the notion of low-interventionist winemaking that little step too far.

CABERNET SAUVIGNON

RATING

Yarra Valley	$30–$49		
Current vintage: 2003	**87**		

An ageing, slightly meaty and cedary cabernet whose delicate, slightly cigarboxy bouquet of dark berries and plums has a background of undergrowth and green olives. Moderately firm and slightly green-edged, its earthy expression of blackberries and plums is framed by firm and powdery tannins. It's a little gritty and could use more intensity, polish and finesse.

2003	87	2008	2011
2001	85	2003	2006+
2000	92	2008	2012
1999	89	2004	2007
1998	90	2003	2006
1997	92	2005	2009
1996	91	2001	2004
1995	95	2007	2015
1994	89	1999	2002

CHARDONNAY

RATING **5**

Yarra Valley	$30–$49
Current vintage: 2006	**88**

An elegant and complex young chardonnay whose smoky, rather reductive aromas of melon and citrus fruit reveal nutty, creamy undertones and suggestions of apricot blossom. Smooth and creamy, with well-knit citrus/melon fruit and nutty oak, it finishes with length, freshness and just a hint of sweetness.

2006	88	2008	2011
2005	88	2007	2010
2004	86	2006	2009
2003	89	2005	2008
2002	94	2007	2010
2001	89	2003	2006
2000	93	2002	2005+
1999	93	2004	2007
1998	93	2003	2006
1997	90	1999	2002+
1996	94	2001	2004+

PINOT NOIR

RATING **5**

Yarra Valley	$20–$29
Current vintage: 2005	**86**

Rather a caricature-like pinot whose slightly stewed aromas of plums and cherries struggle against some very assertive and planky oak. Smoky, hard-edged and raw, the palate reveals modest cherry-like fruit rather overwhelmed by its smoky oak, finishing a little thin and simple.

2005	86	2007	2010
2004	86	2006	2009
2003	83	2005	2008
2002	89	2004	2007+
2001	85	2002	2003+
2000	87	2002	2005
1999	89	2001	2004
1998	89	2000	2003
1997	94	2002	2005
1996	95	2001	2004

SHIRAZ VIOGNIER

RATING **5**

Yarra Valley	$20–$29
Current vintage: 2005	**90**

Viognier-lifted, with a spicy floral bouquet of intense small black and red berries and stonefruit, it's smooth, juicy and vibrant. Very polished, with a sumptuous palate of intense forward fruit qualities that border on the confectionary, it's a pleasingly delicious quaffer.

2005	90	2007	2010
2004	88	2006	2009+
2003	87	2005	2008+

Deakin Estate

Kulkyne Way, Iraak via Red Cliffs Vic 3496. Tel: (03) 5029 1666. Fax: (03) 5024 3316.
Website: www.deakinestate.com.au Email: deakin@wingara.com.au

Region: **Murray Darling** Winemaker: **Phil Spillman** Viticulturist: **Craig Thornton**
Chief Executive: **David Yunghanns**

While the Sauvignon Blanc and Merlot are typically vibrant and juicy, the other Deakin Estate wines reviewed this year lack their customary freshness and quality. Deakin Estate remains, however, a terrific source of great drinking at a very affordable price.

CABERNET SAUVIGNON

RATING **5**

Murray Darling	$5–$11
Current vintage: 2005	**81**

Cooked and currant-like, with some presence of red plum and small berry flavour, but essentially over-ripened and lacking genuine depth of fruit sweetness. Quite firm, it becomes hollow, then dull to finish.

2005	81	2006	2007+
2004	87	2006	2009
2003	87	2005	2008+
2002	87	2004	2007
2001	84	2002	2003
2000	86	2001	2002
1999	81	2000	2001

MERLOT

Murray Darling	$5–$11
Current vintage: 2004	88

This nicely balanced wine of genuine varietal character reveals meaty, earthy aromas of dark plums and cherries over nuances of leather. Moderately firm, long and powdery, its pleasingly long and vibrant palate of dark and deeply ripened fruit is framed by fine tannins, supported by sweet vanilla oak and finished by refreshing acidity.

2004	88	2006	2009
2003	82	2004	2005
2002	87	2003	2004
2001	88	2002	2003+
2000	84	2001	2002
1999	87	2000	2001+

SAUVIGNON BLANC   RATING 5

Murray Darling	$5–$11
Current vintage: 2006	88

Great value at its price, this long, varietal and refreshing sauvignon blanc has a lively and lightly grassy aroma of fresh gooseberries, lemon and melon. Its vibrant palate of lightly herbal passionfruit and gooseberry flavours culminates in a refreshingly crisp and acidic finish. Batting above its average.

2006	88	2007	2008
2005	88	2005	2006
2004	87	2004	2005
2003	83	2003	2004
2002	84	2002	2003
2001	87	2001	2002

SHIRAZ

Murray Darling	$5–$11
Current vintage: 2005	86

Lightly smoky aromas of violets, blackberries, cassis and white pepper precede a generous and juicy palate whose rich, ripe red and black fruit flavours are backed by sweet toasty vanilla oak. Framed by firmish, pliant tannin, it's moderately long and balanced, finishing with clean acids and no hint of overcooked flavour.

2005	86	2007	2010
2004	80	2005	2006+
2003	87	2005	2008
2002	86	2004	2007
2001	86	2002	2003+
2000	87	2001	2002
1999	82	2000	2001
1998	83	1999	2000

Delatite

Corner Stoney's & Pollard Roads, Mansfield Vic 3722. Tel: (03) 5775 2922. Fax: (03) 5775 2911.
Website: www.delatitewinery.com.au Email: info@delatitewinery.com.au
Region: **Mansfield** Winemakers: **Jane Donat, David Ritchie** Viticulturist: **Andrew Storrie**
Chief Executive: **David Ritchie**

While it produces a wide range of different wines from an impressively broad range of varieties, Delatite's best wines are its perfumed and mineral Rieslings, occasionally deeply floral Dead Man's Hill Gewürztraminer and refreshing Demelza sparkling wine. Artfully made, the 2006 whites share a sculpted, tightly focused nature and the promise of longevity.

DEAD MAN'S HILL GEWÜRZTRAMINER   RATING 5

Mansfield	$20–$29
Current vintage: 2006	92

A more adventurous style than usual under this label, with a smoky, slightly confectionary perfume of rose oil and lychees. Finely crafted and restrained, it brings a slightly meaty and rather savoury edge to its attractive varietal flavours. Long and smooth, it finishes with a trace of sweetness and a hint of spirity warmth.

2006	92	2011	2014
2005	88	2007	2010+
2004	85	2006	2009
2003	89	2005	2008+
2002	87	2003	2004+
2001	94	2006	2009
2000	91	2005	2008
1999	87	2001	2004
1998	88	2000	2003
1997	89	1999	2002
1996	91	2004	2008
1995	87	2000	2003
1994	93	1999	2002
1992	91	2000	2004+

DEMELZA

RATING 3

Mansfield $30–$49
Current vintage: 2002   **88**

Toasty, floral, buttery and creamy aromas are backed by nuances of honey, citrus and wheatmeal. Rather broad, thick and cloying, with crackly, creamy yeast-derived influences, its simple, buttery and rather herbal palate lacks its customary freshness and charm.

2002	88	2004	2007+
2001	92	2006	2009
2000	87	2002	2005
1996	93	2001	2004+
94–95	93	1999	2002+
1991	84	1996	1999
87–88	87	1995	1997

RIESLING

RATING 3

Mansfield $12–$19
Current vintage: 2006   **92**

Tight and mineral and floral, with intense flavours of lime juice, pear and apple over a powdery spine of fine phenolics, this is a typically steely and sculpted Delatite riesling with austerity and length. It finishes with lingering citrusy fruit, refreshing acids and undertones of schisty minerality.

2006	92	2014	2018
2005	91	2010	2013+
2004	93	2012	2016
2003	89	2005	2008+
2002	92	2007	2010+
2001	90	2006	2009
2000	91	2005	2008+
1999	92	2007	2011
1998	94	2006	2010
1997	88	2005	2009
1996	93	2004	2008
1995	93	2000	2003
1994	94	2002	2005
1993	95	2001	2005
1992	95	2000	2004

SAUVIGNON BLANC

RATING 5

Mansfield $20–$29
Current vintage: 2005   **75**

Flat, stale, herbal and sweet; possibly the result of a stuck ferment.

2005	75	2005	2006
2004	86	2005	2006
2003	91	2003	2004+
2002	87	2002	2003
2001	89	2002	2003+

VS LIMITED EDITION RIESLING

RATING 3

Mansfield $12–$19
Current vintage: 2004   **92**

A delicate floral perfume with lime and mineral undertones heralds a tight, long and moderately phenolic and chalky palate whose pristine fresh lemon rind and lime juice flavours culminate in a taut and racy finish of just slightly exaggerated minerality.

2004	92	2012	2016
2001	95	2009	2013
1999	95	2007	2011+

Devil's Lair

Rocky Road, via Margaret River WA 6285. Tel: (08) 9757 7573. Fax: (08) 9757 7533.
Website: www.devils-lair.com

Region: **Margaret River** Winemaker: **Stuart Pym** Viticulturist: **Simon Robertson** Chief Executive: **Jamie Odell**

The excellent 2004 season helped Devil's Lair fashion a really elegant flagship red with plenty of Margaret River's distinctive dark cherry regional character. While the 2006 Fifth Leg white is a little disappointing, it was a difficult season for the region's more southerly vineyards. The 2005 Chardonnay is taut and racy.

CHARDONNAY — RATING 3

Margaret River $30–$49
Current vintage: 2005 92

Fragrant, measured and well made, this intense and vibrant chardonnay is long, supple and dusty. Its fresh aromas of white peach, melon and grapefruit overlie buttery suggestions of creamy vanilla oak and wheatmeal. Brightly lit with fresh melon, tropical and grapefruit flavour, it's backed by lightly toasted oak and finishes with a lively, bracing cut of lemon zest-like acidity.

2005	92	2010	2013
2004	87	2006	2009
2003	94	2005	2008
2002	90	2004	2007+
2001	91	2003	2005+
2000	95	2005	2008
1999	95	2004	2007
1998	89	2000	2003+
1997	95	2002	2005

FIFTH LEG RED — RATING 5

Margaret River $12–$19
Current vintage: 2005 90

A delicious young and early-drinking red packed with genuinely ripe but not overcooked flavours of dark berries, cherries and plums. Its bouquet has a floral aspect, with undertones of dark chocolate/cedar oak and nuances of dried herbs. Medium to full in weight, its fruit-driven palate is framed by very fine, dusty tannins. It finishes long and lingering with fresh dark fruit and lively acidity.

2005	90	2007	2010
2004	89	2006	2009
2003	83	2004	2005+
2002	89	2004	2007
2001	89	2003	2006+
2000	90	2002	2005+
1999	92	2001	2004
1997	80	1998	1999
1996	90	1998	2001

FIFTH LEG WHITE — RATING 5

Margaret River $12–$19
Current vintage: 2006 82

Light, tropical and herbal aromas precede a forward, juicy, warm and spirity palate whose simple flavours lack much length and intensity.

2006	82	2006	2007
2005	88	2006	2007
2004	88	2005	2006
2003	82	2003	2004+
2002	89	2003	2004

MARGARET RIVER CABERNET (Cabernet Merlot) — RATING 5

Margaret River $50–$99
Current vintage: 2004 92

A finely focused, elegant and tightly balanced cabernet blend with typical regional dark cherry and earthy undertones. Its sweet fragrance of violets and small berries is handsomely backed by dusty, cedary vanilla oak, while its smooth and creamy palate of intense mulberry and cassis-like fruit has a powdery chassis of drying tannin.

2004	92	2012	2016+
2003	87	2008	2011+
2002	84	2007	2010
2001	84	2006	2009
2000	89	2008	2012+
1999	93	2007	2011
1998	95	2010	2018
1997	89	2002	2005+
1996	95	2004	2008
1995	94	2003	2007
1994	93	2002	2006
1993	94	2001	2005
1992	93	2004	2012
1991	91	1999	2003

Diamond Valley

PO Box 4255, Croydon Hills Vic 3136. Tel: (03) 9722 0840. Fax: (03) 9722 2373.
Website: www.diamondvalley.com.au Email: enq@diamondvalley.com.au

Region: **Yarra Valley** Winemaker: **James Lance** Viticulturist: **David Lance** Chief Executive: **Graeme Rathbone**

Graeme Rathbone has altered the winemaking philosophy at Diamond Valley by replacing the single-vineyard Estate label with a new Reserve label in which fruit from the original Diamond Valley site is blended with grapes from a second Yarra vineyard, Candlebark Ridge. The white Reserve label also now includes a Shiraz. The blue labelled Yarra Valley wines are still sourced from various sites in the Yarra Valley region.

RESERVE CHARDONNAY (formerly Estate)   RATING 3

Yarra Valley	$30–$49
Current vintage: 2005	93

Stylish and fruit-driven, with bright, juicy grapefruit, melon, cumquat and peach-like fruit backed by complex nuances of smoked bacon, matchstick, cream and butterscotch. Backed by well-integrated smoky oak, it's long and racy, finishing tight and refreshing.

2005	93	2007	2010+
2004	88	2006	2009
2003	93	2005	2008+
2002	94	2007	2010
2001	87	2003	2006
2000	92	2005	2008
1999	88	2001	2004
1998	89	2000	2003
1997	88	1999	2002
1996	87	1998	2001
1995	92	2000	2003
1994	93	2002	2006

RESERVE PINOT NOIR (formerly Estate)   RATING 4

Yarra Valley	$50–$99
Current vintage: 2005	89

Herbal and slightly sappy, this fine, smooth and silky pinot reveals some ethereal, perfumed and sweetly oaked cherry/berry varietal flavour backed by suggestions of cinnamon and pepper. It's elegant and stylish, but finishes marginally short, with slightly green-edged and metallic tannins.

2005	89	2007	2010+
2004	88	2006	2009+
2003	90	2005	2008
2002	93	2007	2010
2001	90	2003	2006+
1999	93	2007	2011
1998	94	2003	2006
1997	96	2002	2005+
1996	89	2001	2004
1995	90	2000	2003
1994	88	1996	1999

YARRA VALLEY CABERNET MERLOT   RATING 5

Yarra Valley	$20–$29
Current vintage: 2003	81

Ageing and rather herbaceous, with a slightly jammy expression of green-edged berry and cherry fruit backed by sweet cedary oak, it's medium-bodied and slightly short, finishing with suggestions of bell pepper and a firmish grip of tannin that appears rather excessive for its weight of fruit.

2003	81	2005	2008
2002	90	2004	2007+
2001	82	2003	2006
2000	87	2002	2005
1999	87	2001	2004+

YARRA VALLEY CHARDONNAY   RATING 4

Yarra Valley	$20–$29
Current vintage: 2005	87

Lightly oaked, with a buttery expression of creamy peach and melon flavour delivering a smooth, juicy palate finished by fresh, lemony acids. Elegant, but slightly angular.

2005	87	2006	2007+
2004	89	2006	2009
2003	90	2005	2008
2002	90	2003	2004+
2000	90	2002	2005
1999	90	2001	2004

YARRA VALLEY PINOT NOIR

RATING **5**

Yarra Valley	$20–$29
Current vintage: 2005	86

Meaty and green-edged, with moderately intense flavours of red cherries and plums backed by sweet cedar/vanilla oak and earthy, lightly toasty undertones. Supported by fine, smooth tannins, it's initially promising on the palate but thins out towards a slightly dilute finish.

2005	86	2007	2010
2004	86	2006	2009
2003	90	2005	2008
2002	89	2004	2007
2001	89	2003	2006
2000	89	2002	2005
1999	90	2001	2004
1998	90	2000	2003
1997	94	1998	2001
1996	91	1998	2001
1994	85	1996	1999

Domaine A

105 Tea Tree Road, Campania Tas 7026. Tel: (03) 6260 4174. Fax: (03) 6260 4390.
Website: www.domaine-a.com.au Email: althaus@domaine-a.com.au

Region: **Coal River Valley** Winemaker: **Peter Althaus** Viticulturist: **Peter Althaus** Chief Executive: **Peter Althaus**

Domaine A is the label for the small volumes of handcrafted wines Peter Althaus bottles from his Stoney Vineyard in the Coal River Valley. Perhaps extraordinarily for a Tasmanian vineyard, its most consistent performer is its Cabernet Sauvignon, which in years like 1991, 1994, 1995, 1998, 2000 and 2001 has acquired the depth of flavour and structure one might expect from a good Bordeaux growth. The Pinot Noir can also be excellent, while the Lady A Fumé Blanc is a very distinctive wood-aged expression of sauvignon blanc.

CABERNET SAUVIGNON

RATING **3**

Coal River Valley	$50–$99
Current vintage: 2001	94

A long, firm and cedary cabernet likely to become deeper, more profound and bold before it becomes finer and more elegant with longer cellaring. It opens with a dusty fragrance of cedar, mulberries and ripe black and red berries before revealing nuances of mint, dried herbs and chocolate/vanilla oak. Firm, tight and powdery, its slightly sour-edged palate of dark berry/plum flavours, fine-grained oak and meaty, lightly reductive complexity finishes with mineral undertones.

2001	94	2013	2021
2000	96	2012	2020+
1999	90	2007	2011+
1998	93	2010	2018
1997	87	2005	2009
1995	94	2007	2015
1994	93	2006	2014
1993	89	2005	2013
1992	90	2004	2012
1991	95	2003	2011
1990	87	1995	1998

LADY A FUMÉ BLANC

RATING **3**

Coal River Valley	$50–$99
Current vintage: 2004	93

An extraordinarily concentrated sauvignon blanc of almost exaggerated intensity and tightness. Powerful scents of tropical fruits, gooseberries and lychees overlie toasty nuances of vanilla oak, lively cut grass aromas and hints of mineral. Packed with fruit, it's long, juicy and zesty, with a taut finish of steely austerity and a lingering briney aspect. It needs time to settle, but should mature with interest!

2004	93	2009	2012+
2003	91	2008	2011+
2002	94	2007	2010
2001	82	2003	2006

PINOT NOIR

RATING **3**

Coal River Valley	$50–$99
Current vintage: 2003	90

An assertive, powerful and slightly hard-edged pinot whose spicy clove and cinnamon-like fragrance of cherries, red plums and sweet cedar/vanilla oak is backed by nuances of mint and menthol. Its firm, polished palate of sour-edged cherry, currant and plum flavours is framed by fine, drying tannins. Backed by smoky oak and minty undertones of forest floor, it should become brighter and more elegant with time.

2003	90	2008	2001+
2001	92	2009	2013
2000	92	2005	2008+
1999	89	2004	2007
1998	95	2003	2006+
1997	94	2005	2009
1995	89	1997	2000
1994	95	1999	2002+
1992	94	1997	2000+

Dominique Portet

870 Maroondah Highway, Coldstream Vic 3770. Tel: (03) 5962 5760. Fax: (03) 5962 4938.
Website: www.dominiqueportet.com.au Email: dominique@dominiqueportet.com.au
Regions: **Yarra Valley, Heathcote** Winemakers: **Dominique Portet, Scott Baker**
Chief Executive: **Dominique Portet**

Dominique Portet is the highly experienced and affable French winemaker whose long association with Taltarni introduced him to thousands of Australian wine drinkers. Now, having gone out on his own, he is based on the Maroondah Highway, where he makes a number of regional wines from the Yarra Valley and Heathcote. While Portet's natural inclination is to make reds of finesse and polish, recent Heathcote vintages have been too hot to avoid cooked and soupy characters.

CABERNET SAUVIGNON

RATING **5**

Heathcote (or Yarra Valley)	$30–$49
Current vintage: 2004	89

Sweet-fruited, smooth and elegant, this honest and flavoursome cabernet has a juicy aroma of blackberries, red berries and fragrant cedar/dark chocolate and vanilla oak influences. Long and even, its fine-grained palate of vibrant berry fruit is framed by dusty, silky tannins, finishing with a pleasing length of flavour.

2004	89	2009	2012
2002	86	2004	2007+
2001	90	2006	2009+
2000	88	2005	2008

HEATHCOTE SHIRAZ

RATING **5**

Heathcote	$30–$49
Current vintage: 2004	77

Meaty, cooked and dull, with a spicy and rather flat aroma of dehydrated fruit. It offers some fruit towards the front of the palate but dries out, lacking length, freshness and intensity.

2004	77	2006	2009+
2003	83	2005	2008
2002	89	2004	2007+
2001	82	2003	2006
2000	89	2005	2008

SAUVIGNON BLANC

RATING **4**

Yarra Valley	$20–$29
Current vintage: 2006	86

Very oaky and showing some spirity warmth, this smooth and approachable sauvignon blanc presents juicy flavours of gooseberries and melon backed by a light grassiness and some slightly over-assertive nutty/vanilla oak. It's initially punchy and fruity, but lacks genuine length and intensity.

2006	86	2006	2007
2005	93	2005	2006
2004	91	2004	2005+
2003	90	2003	2004+
2002	81	2002	2003
2000	87	2000	2000

Dromana Estate

555 Old Mooroduc Road, Tuerong Vic 3933. Tel: (03) 5974 4400. Fax: (03) 5974 1155.
Website: www.dromanaestate.com.au Email: info@dromanaestate.com.au
Region: **Mornington Peninsula** Winemaker: **Rollo Crittenden** Viticulturist: **Rollo Crittenden**
Chief Executive: **Richard Green**
Now part of a publicly listed company and based in a new winery, Dromana Estate was one of the first producers on Victoria's Mornington Peninsula. Its wines are sound and competent, but lack the pace-setting flair that helped to launch the brand. The punchy 2004 Reserve Pinot Noir is the best under this label for several years.

CABERNET MERLOT

RATING **4**

| Mornington Peninsula | $20–$29 |
| Current vintage: 2004 | 80 |

Light, rather simple flavours of cassis, mulberries and raspberries overlie restrained cedar/vanilla oak and rather a leafy, greenish aspect. Forward and green-edged, it's under-ripe and hollow.

2004	80	2006	2009
2003	89	2008	2011
2002	81	2004	2007
2001	93	2009	2013
2000	93	2008	2012+
1999	92	2007	2011
1998	90	2006	2010
1997	92	2005	2009
1996	83	1998	2001+

CHARDONNAY

RATING **5**

| Mornington Peninsula | $20–$29 |
| Current vintage: 2004 | 86 |

Dusty, rather oxidative aromas of citrus fruit, slightly raw and toasty oak and wheatmeal precede a forward, slightly syrupy and candied palate of peach, nectarine and barley sugar-like flavour that finishes a little flat and cloying.

2004	86	2006	2009
2003	92	2005	2008
2002	89	2004	2007
2001	89	2003	2006
2000	82	2001	2002
1999	93	2001	2004

PINOT NOIR

RATING **5**

| Mornington Peninsula | $20–$29 |
| Current vintage: 2004 | 87 |

Long, savoury and fine-grained, with spicy, cinnamon-like aromas of sweet red cherries and raspberries over lightly meaty and herbal nuances. An attractive and slightly layered palate with underlying meaty aspects finishes with good length and a dusty, fine-grained structure.

2004	87	2006	2009
2003	82	2005	2008
2002	89	2004	2007
2001	85	2002	2003+
2000	90	2005	2008
1999	87	2001	2004
1998	88	1999	2000
1997	91	2002	2005
1996	93	2001	2004

RESERVE CHARDONNAY

RATING **4**

| Mornington Peninsula | $30–$49 |
| 2004 | 89 |

Slightly brassy and forward, with round, juicy flavours of peach, melon and nectarine perhaps a shade too generously complemented by sweet, toasty and buttery vanilla oak. It's slightly hot and spirity, with undertones of honey, dried flowers and wheatmeal, finishing rather savoury, with lingering nuances of smoke and bacon.

2004	89	2006	2009
2002	92	2004	2007+
2001	91	2003	2006+
2000	90	2002	2005
1998	91	2003	2006
1997	95	2002	2005
1996	91	2001	2004
1995	92	1997	2000
1994	94	1996	1999

RESERVE PINOT NOIR

RATING **4**

| Mornington Peninsula | $30–$49 |
| Current vintage: 2004 | 92 |

Heady, floral and bacony, with a slightly stalky and earthy bouquet of fresh cherries, berries and plums. Richly flavoured and rather substantial, its concentrated palate of intense maraschino cherry and redcurrant fruit is long and slightly sappy, with a slight jamminess and some youthful green edges. It should settle with time into a delicious and punchy pinot.

2004	92	2009	2012+
2002	88	2004	2007
2001	89	2003	2006
2000	85	2002	2005
1998	91	2000	2003+
1997	95	2002	2005+
1996	94	2001	2005+
1995	93	2000	2003+

Elderton

3–5 Tanunda Road, Nuriootpa SA 5355. Tel: (08) 8568 7878. Fax: (08) 8568 7879.
Website: www.eldertonwines.com.au Email: elderton@eldertonwines.com.au

Region: **Barossa Valley** Winemaker: **Richard Langford** Viticulturist: **David Young**
Chief Executive: **Lorraine Ashmead**

Elderton is a very successful Barossa wine producer with significant export markets. Perhaps its experience with riper, richer styles led it to fashion a very approachable, if somewhat oaky and uncomplicated Command Shiraz from the very hot 2003 vintage. I also have a a soft spot for the meaty and smoky Shiraz 2004. Its wines are steadily returning to the pristine richness and intensity that helped the brand become immediately popular.

ASHMEAD CABERNET SAUVIGNON   RATING 5

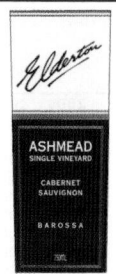

Barossa Valley	$50–$99
Current vintage: 2002	**93**

A deeply accentuated, heady and minty aroma of dark olives and plums, cassis and menthol, backed by nuances of graphite and iodide. Medium to full in weight, it's concentrated but surprisingly elegant and polished, even finely crafted and restrained. It easily carries its chocolate/vanilla oak, while there's just a hint of currant about its brambly fruit. Framed by firmish, but velvet-smooth tannins.

2002	93	2010	2014+
2000	88	2002	2005+
1999	89	2007	2011+
1998	89	2006	2010

CABERNET SAUVIGNON   RATING 5

Barossa Valley	$20–$29
Current vintage: 2004	**85**

An up-front, juicy and generous short-term cabernet whose sweet, jammy aromas of red-currants, raspberries and cassis are backed by sweet vanilla oak and dusty, leafy undertones. Smooth, generous and fine-grained, it's very approachable and forward, but finishes rather flat and dull.

2004	85	2006	2009
2003	82	2005	2008
2002	91	2007	2010+
2001	86	2003	2006
2000	89	2005	2008
1999	87	2004	2007
1998	91	2003	2006
1997	87	1999	2002+
1996	89	2001	2004
1995	88	2000	2003
1994	93	1999	2002
1993	91	1998	2001
1992	88	1997	2000
1991	91	1996	1999

COMMAND SHIRAZ   RATING 3

Barossa Valley	$50–$99
Current vintage: 2003	**92**

Elderton shows its experience with ripe fruit with a very good wine from a hot and difficult vintage. Dark, inky iodide-like aromas of dark plums, cassis and slightly varnishy oak precede a smooth and luxuriant palate. Intense, if rather uncompli-cated dark fruit flavours are given plenty of sweet coconut ice and vanilla oak, finishing with cigarboxy undertones and a hint of currant.

2003	92	2011	2015
2002	93	2014	2022
2001	89	2009	2013
2000	93	2008	2012+
1999	90	2004	2007
1998	89	2006	2010
1997	83	2002	2005
1996	89	2004	2008
1995	91	2003	2007
1994	94	2002	2006
1993	89	2001	2005
1992	95	2000	2004+
1990	92	1995	1998
1988	87	1996	2000
1987	94	1999	2004

CSM CABERNET SAUVIGNON SHIRAZ MERLOT

RATING **5**

Barossa Valley $30–$49
Current vintage: 2001 83

Rather clumsy and both over-and under-ripe, with jammy, cooked aromas of stressed fruit backed by greenish suggestions of mint and menthol. Simultaneously herbal and meaty, with a slightly metallic grip of sappy tannin, the palate relies on its oak for sweetness. It's built with a firm spine of gritty tannin, but lacks sufficient fruit for it to be genuinely balanced.

2001	83	2006	2009
2000	86	2002	2005
1999	90	2004	2007+
1998	86	2003	2006
1997	88	1999	2002
1996	87	2001	2004
1995	88	1998	2001
1994	90	1999	2002

SHIRAZ

RATING **5**

Barossa Valley $20–$29
Current vintage: 2004 90

Meaty, ripe and mouthfilling, this smooth and pliant shiraz has a floral aroma of raspberries, blackberries and cassis backed by assertive and lightly toasty vanilla oak, with undertones of cloves, cinnamon and white pepper. Round and generous, its juicy, vibrant palate of slightly jammy and sour-edged fruit is tightly knit with smoky savoury oak and framed by firm but gentle tannins.

2004	90	2009	2012
2003	88	2005	2008+
2002	89	2004	2007+
2001	89	2003	2006+
2000	90	2005	2008
1999	83	2001	2004
1998	90	2003	2006
1997	87	1999	2002
1996	87	1998	2003+
1995	90	2000	2003
1994	89	1999	2002
1993	90	1995	1998
1992	88	2000	2004
1991	90	1999	2003

Epis

812 Black Forest Drive, Woodend Vic 3442. Tel: (03) 5427 1204. Fax: (03) 5427 1204
Email: domaineepis@iprimus.com.au
Region: **Macedon Ranges** Winemaker: **Stuart Anderson** Viticulturist: **Alec Epis** Chief Executive: **Alec Epis**

Epis is a small Macedon Ranges wine producer that specialises in Pinot Noir and Chardonnay from its estate block near Woodend, as well as a steadily improving Cabernet Sauvignon Merlot blend from a mature vineyard near Kyneton initially developed by central Victorian wine pioneer, Laurie Williams. Proprietor Alec Epis attributes much of the wines' quality to some pretty fastidious and extremely low-cropping viticulture which, incidentally, he is responsible for. Global warming hasn't hurt, either!

CHARDONNAY

RATING **2**

Macedon Ranges $30–$49
Current vintage: 2005 95

Marrying intense, complex fruit qualities with structure and minerality, it presents a zesty, slatey fragrance of grapefruit, peaches, tangerine and lime backed by lightly creamy suggestions of grilled nuts, wheatmeal and lemon rind. Long and austere, it's tightly focused and shapely, delivering juicy citrus flavours, sweet and buttery oak plus a lingering dry and savoury finish of refreshing mineral acidity.

2005	95	2007	2010+
2004	95	2009	2012+
2003	95	2008	2011
2001	96	2006	2009+
2000	95	2005	2008+
1998	95	2003	2006+

EPIS & WILLIAMS CABERNET MERLOT

RATING  **2**

Macedon Ranges	$30–$49
Current vintage: 2005	95

A stylish, polished young blend of cabernet with 10% merlot, whose briary flavours of blackberries, cassis, dark plums and mulberries overlie nuances of dark cherries, cloves and dried herbs. Backed by smooth, dusty oak and framed by a structure of fine-grained, powdery tannin that builds steadily in the mouth, it's long and juicy, before finishing with suggestions of dark chocolate and dried herbs. It should build considerably in the bottle.

2005	95	2013	2017
2004	95	2012	2016
2003	93	2011	2015+
2002	89	2007	2010+
2001	94	2013	2021
2000	95	2008	2012+
1999	93	2007	2011+

PINOT NOIR

RATING **2**

Macedon Ranges	$30–$49
Current vintage: 2005	95

Sumptuous and succulent, with a heady, perfumed rose garden-like aroma and layers of spicy small berry/cherry fruit over suggestions of undergrowth and restrained oak. Initially smooth and silky, its vibrant and surprisingly powerful depth of pristine red and black cherry flavour builds in the mouth, unearthing a lingering core of fruit. Supported by genuinely firm but smooth-edged tannins, it finishes with refreshing acidity. Likely to build considerably in the bottle.

2005	95	2010	2013+
2004	95	2006	2009+
2003	96	2008	2011
2001	96	2006	2009+
2000	93	2005	2008+
1998	94	2003	2006+

Evans & Tate

Corner Caves & Metricup Roads, Willyabrup WA 6280. Tel: (08) 9755 6244. Fax: (08) 9755 4362.
Website: www.evansandtate.com.au Email: et@evansandtate.com.au

Region: **Margaret River** Winemaker: **Richard Rowe** Viticulturist: **Murray Edmonds**
Chief Executive: **Martin Johnson**

At time of writing, fate could see Evans & Tate linked with a group associated through ownership with Lake's Folly, Millbrook and Deep Woods, or tied up by the owners of Ferngrove. Either way, it is managing in what must be difficult circumstances to produce competent, if not spectacular wine. Given the status of the brand, and the residual affection for it, one hopes for a swift and productive resolution.

GNANGARA SHIRAZ

Western Australia	$12–$19
Current vintage: 2005	81

Lightly browning, this rather jammy, cooked and smoky shiraz has some moderately intense forward plum and small berry flavour, but becomes more green-edged, stewy and thin towards its finish of slightly sour acidity.

2005	81	2006	2007
2004	77	2005	2006
2003	88	2008	2011
2002	82	2003	2004
2000	87	2002	2005
1999	80	2000	2000
1998	88	2000	2003+
1997	80	1999	2002
1996	89	1998	2001

MARGARET RIVER CLASSIC

RATING **5**

Margaret River	$12–$19
Current vintage: 2006	87

Clean, approachable and moderately intense, this lightly herbal wine presents juicy passionfruit and tropical flavours and smoky, capsicum-like undertones finished by a lively, zesty acidity.

2006	87	2006	2007+
2005	88	2005	2006+
2004	88	2004	2005
2003	86	2003	2003

MARGARET RIVER SAUVIGNON BLANC SEMILLON RATING 4

Margaret River	$20–$29
Current vintage: 2006	**90**

A typically intense, tangy and lightly grassy Margaret River blend whose juicy, tropical flavours of gooseberries, melon and passionfruit overlie a fresh herbaceousness and a lightly chalky undercarriage. It finishes with plenty of length, clean and refreshing.

2006	90	2007	2008+
2005	88	2006	2007
2004	90	2005	2006
2003	88	2003	2006+
2002	89	2003	2004+

MARGARET RIVER SHIRAZ

RATING 5

Margaret River	$20–$29
Current vintage: 2004	**81**

A browning, minty and menthol-like shiraz whose moderately intense flavours of red plums and berries have a meaty, cooked aspect. It's hard-edged and hollow, raw and drying, lacking its usual richness and fruit.

2004	81	2006	2009
2003	84	2005	2008+
2002	87	2004	2007+
2001	90	2006	2009
2000	90	2005	2008
1999	90	2004	2007
1998	91	2003	2006+
1997	89	2005	2009
1996	96	2004	2008
1995	92	2007	2015
1994	94	2002	2006
1993	86	2001	2005
1992	93	2000	2004
1991	93	1999	2003

Farr Rising

101 Kelly Lane, Bannockburn, Vic 3331. Tel: (03) 5281 1733. Fax: (03) 5281 1433.
Website: www.byfarr.com.au Email: kalvos@datafast.net.au
Region: **Geelong** Winemaker: **Nick Farr** Viticulturist: **Nick Farr** Chief Executive: **Gary Farr**

Nick Farr is the son of Gary Farr, the winemaker who made his reputation at Bannockburn in Victoria. He makes wine at his parents' By Farr winery alongside his father, but has the necessary strength of character to do things his own way. The new releases are approachable and savoury, with a point of difference.

CHARDONNAY

RATING 4

Geelong	$30–$49
Current vintage: 2005	**91**

Complex and heavily worked, this shapely, finely structured and impressively textured chardonnay is still all about its fruit. Backed by sweet buttery and vanilla oak, its intense grapefruit, white peach, nectarine and quince-like flavours are backed by creamy leesy qualities, fine powdery phenolics, and suggestions of butterscotch. It finishes with lingering hints of lemon sherbet and refreshing acidity.

2005	91	2007	2010+
2004	90	2006	2009+
2003	87	2004	2005+
2002	91	2004	2007
2001	89	2003	2006+

PINOT NOIR

RATING 4

Geelong	$30–$49
Current vintage: 2005	**92**

With a sour-edged expression of dark cherry, redcurrant and dark plum-like flavour supported by fine, bony tannins, this is a complex, approachable and finely crafted wine. Musky and meaty, with a smoky, floral perfume and undertones of smoked meats and briar, it's medium to full in weight, with lingering suggestions of charcuterie and savoury spices. It finishes with vibrant intensity.

2005	92	2010	2013
2004	93	2006	2009+
2003	90	2008	2011
2002	85	2004	2007
2001	85	2003	2006

Feathertop

6619 Great Alpine Road, Porepunkah Vic 3740. Tel: (03) 5756 2356. Fax: (03) 5756 2610.
Website: www.boynton.com.au Email: boynton@boynton.com.au

Region: **Alpine Valleys** Winemaker: **Kel Boynton** Viticulturist: **Kel Boynton** Chief Executive: **Kel Boynton**

Kel Boynton has long been a champion of alpine-grown Victorian wine, although he would be the first to concede that to a greater extent than most Australian grape-growers, he is at the mercy of a challenging climate. Wines like the delicious 2005 Riesling rather eloquently show the quality he is consistently trying to achieve.

CABERNET SAUVIGNON

RATING **5**

FEATHERTOP

Alpine Valleys	$20–$29
Current vintage: 2004	89

Elegant, floral and savoury, this fine-grained and loose-knit cabernet marries small dark berry and plum-like fruit with cedar, vanilla and dark chocolate oak influences. It's dusty and restrained, with a lingering core of dark fruit.

2004	89	2009	2012
2003	83	2005	2008
2002	87	2007	2010
2000	82	2002	2005+
1998	89	2003	2006
1997	91	2005	2009
1996	86	2005	2009
1995	75	1997	2000
1994	94	2002	2006
1993	93	2001	2005+
1992	92	2000	2004
1991	87	1996	1999
1990	95	1998	2002

RIESLING

RATING **4**

FEATHERTOP

Alpine Valleys	$12–$19
Current vintage: 2005	91

Fresh aromas of apple, pear and tropical fruits precede a juicy palate that becomes long, tight and slightly chalky. Its lingering expression of tangy fruit finishes clean and refreshing, with a light sweetness similar to the German halbtrocken style. Should flesh out and develop well.

2005	91	2010	2013
2002	87	2004	2007
2001	90	2006	2009
2000	86	2002	2005
1998	85	2000	2003

Ferngrove

Ferngrove Road, Frankland River WA 6396. Tel: (08) 9363 1300. Fax: (08) 9363 1333.
Website: www.ferngrove.com.au Email: info@ferngrove.com.au

Region: **Frankland River** Winemaker: **Kim Horton** Viticulturist: **Chris Zur** Chief Executive: **Anthony Wilkes**

From its very affordable 'Symbols' range of varietal wines to the flagship 'The Stirlings' blend of cabernet sauvignon with shiraz, Ferngrove's hallmark is its presentation of bright, focused varietal qualities, which it typically delivers with a combination of elegance and structure. This edition introduces 'The Stirlings', a wine which has the unusual distinction of regularly appealing to the show judges as well as having the necessary elegance and focus to cellar well, and for a substantial period.

COSSACK RIESLING

RATING **4**

FERNGROVE
FRANKLAND RIVER

WESTERN AUSTRALIA
2006
COSSACK
RIESLING
750ml

Frankland River	$20–$29
Current vintage: 2006	91

Fragrant aromas of apple and pear drops are backed by lightly spicy, mineral undertones. Long, fine and juicy, its smooth and almost slippery palate of vibrant, tangy citrus fruits finishes crisp and clear, with lingering mineral influences. Very supple and elegant, this is a riesling of attractive brightness and freshness.

2006	91	2011	2014+
2005	93	2013	2017
2004	90	2009	2012+
2003	90	2005	2008
2002	94	2007	2010+
2001	86	2003	2006

THE STIRLINGS CABERNET SHIRAZ

RATING 3

Frankland River $30–$49
Current vintage: 2004 94

Silky-smooth and elegant, with intense blackberry, blueberry and cassis-like fruit tightly partnered with assertive sweet oak and fine, supple tannin. Brightly lit and seamless, with a spicy, peppery perfume of violets, white pepper and cinnamon backed by sweet oak and suggestions of mint and menthol, it builds on the palate to a crescendo of vibrant dark plum and cherry fruit.

2004	94	2012	2016
2003	94	2015	2017+
2001	93	2013	2021

Fox Creek

Malpas Road, McLaren Vale SA 5171. Tel: (08) 8556 2403. Fax: (08) 8556 2104.
Website: www.foxcreekwines.com Email: sales@foxcreekwines.com
Region: **McLaren Vale** Winemakers: **Chris Dix, Scott Zrna** Viticulturist: **Nick Wiltshire**
Chief Executives: **Jim & Helen Watts**

As you might expect, the better Fox Creek wines fared more successfully in the challenging conditions provided by 2005, the meaty and velvet-like Reserve Shiraz especially. Several of the wines are simply not up to their usual standard, but this is entirely understandable and acceptable given the circumstances. Enthusiasts of this very professional wine outfit should stick with it.

DUET CABERNET MERLOT

RATING 5

McLaren Vale $20–$29
Current vintage: 2005 87

A firm, drying but earlier-drinking red whose minty expression of dark berries, plums and vanilla oak overlies meaty, currant-like influences. Firm and earthy, it dries out a little towards a slightly raw and drying finish. Quite good length, but needs more depth of fruit.

2005	87	2007	2010
2004	88	2009	2012
2003	87	2003	2006+
2002	88	2004	2007
2001	87	2005	2008

JSM SHIRAZ CABERNET FRANC

RATING 5

McLaren Vale $20–$29
Current vintage: 2005 88

Flavoursome and approachable, with a dark, smoky, meaty and slightly baked and gamey bouquet of dark plums and berries supported by dusty cedar/vanilla oak. Its intense and moderately long expression of small black and red berries and plums is framed by a fine-grained, supple and loose-knit extract with just a slight metallic edge. Honest and not overcooked.

2005	88	2007	2010+
2004	89	2006	2009+
2003	87	2008	2011
2002	88	2004	2007+
2001	91	2003	2006+
2000	90	2002	2005+
1999	89	2001	2004
1998	89	2003	2006
1997	87	1999	2002
1996	84	1998	2001+

RESERVE CABERNET SAUVIGNON

RATING 4

McLaren Vale $30–$49
Current vintage: 2005 89

Backed by assertive vanilla oak, this ripe and very slightly cooked cabernet marries deep, plum and cassis-like fruit with sweet vanilla/dark chocolate oak and suggestions of currants and prunes. Underpinned by a firm, fine-grained astringency and with genuine depth of bright fruit, it just begins to break up at the finish.

2005	89	2013	2017
2004	90	2012	2016+
2002	92	2010	2014+
2001	92	2009	2013+
2000	90	2005	2008
1999	90	2004	2007+
1998	89	2006	2010
1997	90	2005	2009+
1996	92	2004	2008+
1995	88	2000	2003

RESERVE MERLOT

RATING 4

McLaren Vale	$30–$49
Current vintage: 2005	**85**

2005	85	2007	2010+
2001	92	2006	2009
2000	90	2005	2008+
1999	88	2001	2004
1998	87	2003	2006+
1997	87	2002	2005+

Overcooked and gritty, this very ripe but rather tough and charmless merlot relies on sweet vanilla/mocha oak to enliven its fruitcake-like expression of raisins, currants and plums. Initially quite meaty, it's lean and tough-edged to finish.

RESERVE SHIRAZ

RATING 2

McLaren Vale	$50–$99
Current vintage: 2005	**90**

2005	90	2010	2013+
2004	95	2016	2024
2002	93	2010	2014+
2001	96	2013	2021
2000	88	2005	2008
1999	95	2007	2011+
1998	90	2003	2006+
1997	88	2002	2005+
1996	95	2008	2016
1995	89	1997	2002
1994	94	2006	2014

Rich, ripe and meaty, this smooth and very pliant young shiraz has a spicy bouquet of juicy cassis, blackberries and currants amply supported by sweet vanilla/chocolate oak. Its deep, unctuous and slightly jammy palate of vibrant blackberry, redcurrant and plum-like flavour and mocha-like oak overlies a refined cut of velvet tannin. Just lacks genuine finesse and brightness.

SHORT ROW SHIRAZ

RATING 3

McLaren Vale	$20–$29
Current vintage: 2005	**82**

2005	82	2007	2010
2004	93	2009	2012
2003	93	2008	2011
2002	88	2004	2007
2001	91	2003	2006+
2000	87	2002	2005
1999	90	2001	2004

A fast-fading casualty of the vintage, with a ripe, jammy and almost confectionary expression of blackberries, blackcurrants and dark plums backed by cloves and cinnamon that relies on its sweet vanilla oak for palate length.

VERDELHO

RATING 5

South Australia	$12–$19
Current vintage: 2006	**85**

2006	85	2007	2008
2005	89	2007	2010
2004	88	2005	2006+
2003	90	2004	2005+
2002	86	2003	2004
2001	86	2002	2003+
2000	82	2001	2002

Punctuated by fresh, citrusy acids, its candied, lemon drop-like fruit is forward and juicy, lacking a little definition. Backed by a light chalkiness, it reveals a slight minerality.

Frankland Estate

Frankland Road, Frankland WA 6396. Tel: (08) 9855 1544. Fax: (08) 9855 1549.
Website: www.franklandestate.com.au Email: info@franklandestate.com.au
Region: **Frankland River** Winemakers: **Barrie Smith, Judi Cullam** Viticulturist: **Elizabeth Smith**
Chief Executives: **Barrie Smith, Judi Cullam**

With its best collection of Rieslings since 2001 and some evidence that its red wines are gaining some polish,
Frankland Estate is kicking goals. The 2006 Rieslings comprise a sumptuous, perfumed example from the Cooladerra
Vineyard, a penetrative and sculpted Poison Hill Vineyard release and a smoky, limey and schisty effort from
the Isolation Ridge Vineyard, the best wine I have ever tasted from this maker.

COOLADERRA VINEYARD RIESLING   RATING 3

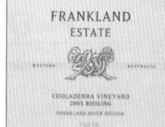

Frankland River $20–$29
Current vintage: 2006   90

An Alsatian-styled riesling whose pungent, almost
oily and meaty bouquet of musky, citrus blossom
and stonefruit aromas precede a rich, sumptuous
and marginally sweet palate. A juicy, almost
crunchy expression of citrus fruit overlies a fine-
grained chalky spine, finishing savoury and fractionally short, with tangy mineral influences.

2006	90	2008	2011
2005	93	2010	2013
2004	93	2006	2009
2002	94	2007	2010+
2001	94	2006	2009+

ISOLATION RIDGE VYD CABERNET SAUVIGNON   RATING 5

Frankland River $20–$29
Current vintage: 2004   87

Firm and heavily worked, with meaty, menthol and
herbal aspects, this rustic and smoky cabernet
delivers a pinot-ish fragrance of gamey, earthy
qualities and a rather a dried-out palate whose
currant-like fruit suggests a considerable hang
time. While it hasn't great fruit brightness, its savoury
suggestions of charcuterie and its astringent
structure have a certain appeal.

2004	87	2012	2016
2003	86	2008	2011+
2002	87	2007	2010
2001	83	2006	2009
1998	84	2003	2006
1997	89	2002	2005
1996	91	2008	2016
1995	87	2007	2015
1994	87	1999	2002
1993	91	2005	2013
1992	88	1997	2000
1991	88	1996	1999

ISOLATION RIDGE VINEYARD RIESLING   RATING 3

Frankland River $20–$29
Current vintage: 2006   95

An austere, schisty and tightly focused riesling whose
alluringly juicy and sumptuous palate is tightly
chiselled around a bracing acidity. It's scented with
spicy, lightly reductive aromas of lime and
minerals, while its deeply concentrated palate of
stonefruit, mango and citrus finishes with a trace
of sugar and lingering smoky undertones.

2006	95	2011	2014+
2005	86	2007	2010
2004	93	2009	2012
2003	93	2008	2011+
2002	89	2004	2007
2001	95	2006	2009+
2000	93	2005	2008
1999	85	2001	2004
1998	93	2006	2010
1997	88	2002	2005
1996	91	2001	2004
1995	91	2000	2003
1994	88	1999	2002
1993	87	1995	1998
1992	89	1997	2000
1991	90	1993	1996

POISON HILL VINEYARD RIESLING   RATING 3

Frankland River $20–$29
Current vintage: 2006   94

Taut, sculpted and pleasingly textured with a mineral,
chalky palate punctuated by a rather brittle
acidity, it's scented with lifted floral qualities, white
peach and suggestions of apricot. There's an attractively handled reductive aspect beneath its lean
and shapely palate, whose piercing lime juice, lemon
and stonefruit flavours finish with a hint of
residual sugar.

2006	94	2011	2014+
2005	88	2007	2010
2004	86	2005	2006
2002	93	2007	2010
2001	95	2006	2009+

Freycinet Vineyard

15919 Tasman Highway, Bicheno Tas 7215. Tel: (03) 6257 8574. Fax: (03) 6257 8454.
Website: www.freycinetvineyard.com.au Email: freycinetwines@tassie.net.au
Region: **East Coast Tasmania** Winemaker: **Claudio Radenti** Viticulturists: **Claudio Radenti & Lindy Bull**
Chief Executive: **Geoff Bull**

Its heat-trap vineyard on Tasmania's temperate east coast provides Freycinet with a fine climate for the ripening of wine grapes, with special preference to chardonnay, pinot noir and riesling. The red Bordeaux varieties do well occasionally, but generally require a very warm and late vintage. A highlight of the current releases is the stunningly tight, fragrant and focused Chardonnay from 2006.

CABERNET MERLOT   RATING 5

East Coast Tasmania	$30–$49
Current vintage: 2004	**89**

Restrained, elegant and regional, this firm but fine-grained cabernet blend has a dusty, herbal bouquet of sweet but slightly stewed plums, cherries, redcurrants and blackberries supported by cedar/vanilla oak. Its supple, minty palate of fresh berry/plum fruit and cedar/vanilla oak finishes with nuances of dried herbs.

2004	89	2012	2016
2003	86	2008	2011
2002	81	2004	2007
2001	88	2006	2009
2000	95	2012	2020
1999	89	2005	2007+
1998	93	2006	2010+
1997	87	2002	2005
1995	87	2000	2003
1994	94	2002	2006

CHARDONNAY   RATING 3

East Coast Tasmania	$30–$49
Current vintage: 2006	**95**

Pristine, fresh and vibrant, this beautifully handled chardonnay reveals a delicate perfume of grapefruit, white peach and tightly knit nutty vanilla oak backed by a genuinely floral fragrance. Long and seamless, its vibrant palate of sumptuous melon, mango and pawpaw-like fruit and restrained oak finish with refreshing, focused acidity.

2006	95	2011	2014
2005	93	2010	2013+
2004	88	2006	2009
2003	96	2005	2008+
2002	87	2004	2007
2001	88	2003	2006
2000	87	2002	2005
1999	93	2004	2007
1998	90	2000	2003+
1997	87	1999	2002
1996	89	1998	2001
1995	95	2003	2007

PINOT NOIR   RATING 3

East Coast Tasmania	$50–$99
Current vintage: 2005	**92**

A very good pinot from a hot year whose heady, musky aromas of rose petals, cherries, briar and cinnamon-like spice reveal slightly meaty undertones. Smooth and even, it's pleasingly sappy and supple, with lively berry/cherry fruit over a firmish and assertive spine of fine tannin, finishing with slightly cooked and currant-like influences and a hint of menthol.

2005	92	2010	2013
2004	90	2009	2012
2003	94	2008	2011+
2002	90	2004	2007+
2001	95	2006	2009+
2000	92	2005	2008
1999	93	2004	2007+
1998	95	2006	2010
1997	93	2005	2009
1996	89	2001	2004
1995	93	2000	2003+
1994	95	1999	2002+

RIESLING   RATING 2

East Coast Tasmania	$20–$29
Current vintage: 2006	**94**

A long-term and finely structured riesling whose penetrative citrusy fruit overlies a powdery chassis of chalky phenolics. Its punchy fragrance of lime juice, lemon rind and mineral undertones precedes a vibrant, brightly lit, refreshing and balanced palate of excellent length and definition.

2006	94	2014	2018+
2005	93	2010	2013+
2004	94	2009	2012+
2003	95	2011	2015+
2002	93	2007	2010
2001	88	2003	2006+
2000	95	2005	2008
1999	92	2004	2007
1998	94	2006	2010

Gapsted Wines

Great Alpine Road, Gapsted Vic 3737. Tel: (03) 5751 1383. Fax: (03) 5751 1368.
website: www.gapstedwines.com.au Email: admin@gapstedwines.com.au
Regions: **King Valley, Alpine Valleys** Winemakers: **Shayne Cunningham & Michael Cope-Williams**
Viticulturist: **John Cavedon** Chief Executive: **Shayne Cunningham**

Gapsted is the brand owned by a contract wine producer in northern Victoria, the Victorian Alps Wine Company, whose wines feature the canopy system chosen to maximise sunlight penetration and fruit exposure in this chilly segment of the viticultural world. The company has made a feature of relatively new varieties for the Australian scene, such as barbera, petit manseng, saperavi and tempranillo. In my view its best wines still come from the more traditional varieties, cabernet sauvignon especially. The 2002 release is another polished example.

BALLERINA CANOPY CABERNET SAUVIGNON

RATING 4

King Valley	$20–$29
Current vintage: 2002	91

Framed by fine, loose-knit firm tannins and backed by cedar/vanilla oak, this elegant and handsomely crafted cabernet has a fresh perfume of violets, cassis and dark plums backed by undertones of dried herbs, chocolate and vanilla. Medium to full in weight, it's brightly lit, delivering an intense and pristine expression of lightly herbal cool climate flavours of cassis, mulberry and dark plums.

2002	91	2010	2014+
2001	88	2006	2009+
2000	92	2008	2012+
1999	87	2007	2011
1998	90	2006	2010+

BALLERINA CANOPY MERLOT

RATING 5

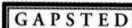

King Valley, Alpine Valleys	$20–$29
Current vintage: 2002	88

A pretty varietal merlot whose herbal, tobaccoey aromas of red cherries, plums and restrained cedar/vanilla oak precede a soft, plump and juicy palate of cherry/plum flavours backed by restrained vanilla oak and framed by fine-grained, powdery tannins. There's a faint herbaceousness that is likely to become more cigarboxy in time.

2002	88	2007	2010
2001	89	2006	2009
2000	87	2005	2008
1999	90	2007	2011

Gembrook Hill

2850 Launching Place Road, Gembrook Vic 3783. Tel: (03) 5968 1622. Fax: (03) 5968 1699.
Website: www.gembrookhill.com.au Email: enquiries@gembrookhill.com.au
Region: **Yarra Valley** Winemaker: **Timo Mayer** Viticulturist: **Ian Marks** Chief Executive: **Ian Marks**

Gembrook Hill is a genuinely cool-climate and high altitude Yarra Valley vineyard that is steadily coming of age. Its Sauvignon Blanc can be spectacular; its Chardonnay long and mineral. The vineyard's cooler and later-ripening site is perhaps the reason why its 2005 wines lack their customary intensity and freshness.

CHARDONNAY

RATING 5

Yarra Valley	$30–$49
Current vintage: 2005	86

Fragrant, spicy estery and lemony aromas with undertones of minerals precede a fine, smooth and creamy palate whose developed qualities of buttery, creamy and slightly meaty complexity tend to overshadow its forward, peachy primary fruit. Fine and smooth, it's just a little dilute at the finish.

2005	86	2007	2010
2004	87	2006	2009+
2003	87	2005	2008
2002	84	2004	2007
2001	95	2006	2009
2000	92	2005	2008
1997	86	1999	2002
1995	91	2000	2003
1994	89	1999	2002
1993	92	1998	2001

PINOT NOIR

RATING **4**

Yarra Valley $30–$49
Current vintage: 2005 88

Scents of rose petals, raspberries and cherries are backed by earthy, herbal and currant-like undertones with a herbal, under-ripe aspect. Initially supple and smooth, then a little dilute at the finish, its forward flavours of raspberries, redcurrants and cherries appear to become more stressed down the palate, finishing with greener influences and a slight rawness. It should build a little in the bottle, but is for the medium term at best.

2005	88	2007	2010+
2004	88	2006	2009
2003	91	2008	2011
2002	87	2007	2010
2001	93	2003	2006+
2000	94	2005	2008
1998	91	2003	2006
1997	89	1999	2002

SAUVIGNON BLANC

RATING **4**

Yarra Valley $30–$49
Current vintage: 2005 87

Slightly spicy, almost spiky aromas of tropical fruits, asparagus and capsicum precede a juicy and forward palate that becomes quite slatey and mineral towards the finish, but just a little thin and powdery. It's a fair attempt at a more sophisticated and structured sauvignon blanc, with possibly a slightly stressed ferment. Perhaps it just needs more time for its mid palate fruit to flesh out.

2005	87	2007	2010
2004	87	2005	2006+
2003	93	2005	2008
2002	93	2004	2007
2001	90	2003	2006
2000	90	2002	2005
1999	86	2000	2001
1998	94	2000	2003

Geoff Weaver

2 Gilpin Lane, Mitcham SA 5062. Tel: (08) 8272 2105. Fax: (08) 8271 0177.
Website: www.geoffweaver.com.au Email: weaver@adelaide.on.net

Region: **Lenswood** Winemaker: **Geoff Weaver** Viticulturist: **Geoff Weaver** Chief Executive: **Geoff Weaver**

Geoff Weaver has long been a champion of Adelaide Hills riesling, and his 2005 release marries some delightful elements of perfume flavour and texture. With Tim Knappstein and the Henschkes, Weaver was one of the first to plant a significant vineyard at Lenswood, in former apple-growing country. With the passage of time, more of Weaver's energy is directed towards his whites, which now include the impressively steely and briny Ferus Sauvignon Blanc (94/100, drink 2007-2010+).

CHARDONNAY

RATING **4**

Adelaide Hills $30–$49
Current vintage: 2005 87

Nutty and spicy, with apple, pear, grapefruit and melon flavours subdued to an extent by some assertive, buttery and sawdust-like oak. It's a little cloying to begin with, then becoming rather flat and lacking brightness.

2005	87	2007	2010
2001	93	2003	2006+
2000	86	2002	2005
1999	84	2001	2004
1998	88	2003	2006
1997	94	2002	2005+
1996	92	1998	2001
1995	94	2000	2003+
1994	90	1999	2002

RIESLING

RATING **3**

Adelaide Hills $20–$29
Current vintage: 2005 93

Delicate floral aromas of lime juice and minerals precede a fine, supple, clear and stylish palate that delivers a lingering core of juicy citrus fruit culminating in a chalky, dry and slatey finish of some austerity. There's plenty of concentrated flavour and some admirable elegance and refinement.

2005	93	2013	2017
2004	91	2009	2012+
2003	93	2008	2011+
2001	91	2006	2009+
2000	93	2008	2012+
1999	92	2007	2011
1998	93	2003	2006
1997	94	2005	2009
1996	87	1998	2001
1995	92	2003	2007
1994	77	1995	1996

SAUVIGNON BLANC

RATING 4

Adelaide Hills	$20–$29
Current vintage: 2006	**87**

Spicy, herbal and rather sweaty aromas of goose-berries and lychees reveal a capsicum and asparagus-like vegetal aspect. Forward and juicy, it become more lean and slightly thin towards the finish, leaving a lingering powdery impression on the palate. It might yet flesh out further.

2006	87	2006	2007
2005	93	2007	2010
2004	91	2005	2006+
2003	89	2004	2005+
2002	94	2003	2004+
2001	87	2001	2002
2000	87	2001	2002
1999	84	2000	2001
1998	94	2000	2003

Giaconda

Corner Wangaratta & McClay Roads, Beechworth Vic 3747. Tel: (03) 5727 0246. Fax: (03) 5727 0246.
Website: www.giaconda.com.au Email: sales@giaconda.com.au

Region: **Beechworth** Winemaker: **Rick Kinzbrunner** Viticulturist: **Rick Kinzbrunner**
Chief Executive: **Rick Kinzbrunner**

This edition welcomes another Giaconda wine to the '1' ranking — the Warner Vineyard Shiraz. Ever since the first release of this wine I have been waiting for this time, since it was clear that Rick Kinzbrunner's determination to do something pretty special with shiraz was matched by the quality of the site. I watched with fascination over a four-day period as a bottle of the 2005 Shiraz gradually became less closed and introverted, and finally began to realise its incredible depth of fruit and character. This wine is the best of the vintage, although the Chardonnay is typically complex, powerful and savoury.

AEOLIA ROUSSANNE

RATING 2

Beechworth	$50–$99
Current vintage: 2006	**90**

Slightly cooked and toasty aromas of barley sugar, honeysuckle and musk precede a rounded, supple and creamy palate whose toasty, candied expression of spicy fruit and honeyed development finish soft and smooth, with lingering notes of rose water. It's moderately long and very complex, pretty and delicate, but lacks its customary freshness and intensity.

2006	90	2007	2008+
2005	93	2007	2010
2004	94	2006	2009+
2003	94	2005	2008
2002	92	2004	2007
2001	94	2003	2006
2000	95	2002	2005+

CABERNET SAUVIGNON

RATING 3

Beechworth	$50–$99
Current vintage: 2005	**87**

Dusty, herbal and briary aromas of cassis, black-berries, red berries and dark plums knit tightly with cedar/vanilla oak. Already rather herbal and likely to become more vegetal, its palate of sweet mulberries and plums is handsomely cloaked in fine, polished tannin and smooth vanilla oak, but despite its elegance and style has too much green-edged flavour for a higher rating.

2005	87	2013	2017
2004	95	2016	2024+
2003	80	2005	2008
2002	95	2014	2022
2001	90	2006	2009+
1999	96	2011	2019
1998	93	2006	2010
1997	92	2005	2009
1996	90	2004	2008+
1995	94	2003	2007
1994	87	1999	2002+
1993	83	1995	1998
1992	87	1997	2000+
1991	93	2003	2011
1990	93	2002	2010

CHARDONNAY

RATING **1**

Beechworth $100–$199
Current vintage: 2005   95

A typically complex but possibly quite evolved chardonnay with a very developed colour and a smoky, mineral and reductive bouquet of charcuterie, matchstick, honeydew melon and lime. It's unctuous and richly fruited, with deep, lingering flavours of grapefruit, melon and cumquat backed by suggestions of smoked ham and bacon, finishing long and tangy, with lime juice and lemony acids.

2005	95	2010	2013
2004	93	2009	2012
2002	97	2007	2010+
2001	91	2003	2006
2000	94	2005	2008
1999	94	2001	2004+
1998	97	2006	2010
1997	92	2002	2005
1996	98	2001	2004+
1995	96	2000	2004+
1994	95	2002	2006
1993	94	1998	2001+
1992	96	2000	2004+
1991	95	1999	2003
1990	95	1998	2002
1989	91	1994	1997+

NANTUA LES DEUX (Chardonnay Roussanne)

RATING **4**

Beechworth $50–$99
Current vintage: 2006   87

Early-drinking, with brassy, cooked and candied aromas of peach, melon and lemon peel backed by sweet buttery vanilla oak and smoky leesy complexity. Ripe, juicy and forward, its rather broad and brassy palate of lemon tart, melon and confectionary fruit finishes with moderate length and soft acidity.

2006	87	2007	2008+
2005	89	2007	2010
2004	91	2006	2009
2002	88	2003	2004+
2000	91	2002	2005

NANTUA VINEYARD PINOT NOIR

RATING **3**

Beechworth $50–$99
Current vintage: 2005   91

Very funky and evolved, this artfully made but supple and restrained pinot slowly unfolds its floral perfume of sweet berries, cherries and plums with stony, undergrowth-like undertones. Smooth and lightly herbal, its pristine palate of small cherry/berry fruit is long and juicy, with an underswell of slightly riper stewed fruit characters, assertive new oak and funky, meaty nuances. It finishes savoury, and would rate higher if not for some persistent herbaceous undertones.

2005	91	2010	2013
2004	94	2012	2016
2002	95	2010	2014
2001	88	2003	2006
2000	86	2002	2005
1999	84	2001	2004
1998	89	2003	2006
1997	86	1999	2002
1996	83	1998	2001
1995	77	1996	1997
1994	82	1996	1999
1993	86	1995	1998
1992	93	2000	2004+
1991	94	1996	1999
1990	87	1995	1998
1989	97	2001	2009

WARNER VINEYARD SHIRAZ

RATING **1**

Beechworth $100–$199
Current vintage: 2005   96

A massively proportioned shiraz by the standards of this vineyard, and one whose meaty ripeness and treatment with bruising, charry oak simply demands time in the cellar. It opens with exaggerated slowness to reveal deep, brooding, briary and brambly fruit and smoky, charcuterie-like undertones. Closed down to the point of lacking personality at present, it ultimately reveals deep, spicy, seamless qualities and a superb, long-term structure. Don't be misled by its raw smokiness if you open it too early — simply wait a day or three.

2005	96	2013	2017+
2004	96	2012	2016+
2002	98	2014	2022
2001	95	2009	2013
2000	93	2008	2012
1999	96	2007	2011
1998	88	2000	2003+

A B C D E F G H I J K L M N O P Q R S T U V W X Y Z

Giant Steps

336-364 maroondah Highway, Healesville Vic 3777. Tel: (03) 5962 6111. Fax: (03) 5962 6199.
Website: www.giant-steps.com.au Email: mail@giant-steps.com.au
Region: **Yarra Valley** Winemaker: **Steve Flamsteed** Viticulturist: **Maris Feldgen** Chief Executive: **Phil Sexton**

Phil Sexton, founder of the Devil's Lair vineyard and winery in Margaret River and an experienced operator in the small brewery and hospitality industry, has set up camp in a very major way at Healesville in the Yarra Valley, with the spectacular Innocent Bystander winery and hospitality centre. The Giant Steps wines are thoroughly professional in their handling, but at this stage are seeking more of a wow factor.

SEXTON VINEYARD CHARDONNAY

RATING

Yarra Valley	$20–$29	2005	89	2007	2010
Current vintage: 2005	89	2004	92	2006	2009
		2003	87	2005	2008
		2002	86	2003	2004+

Slightly introverted, but appealingly approachable and complex, this warm and juicy chardonnay has a toasty, buttery bouquet of quince, cumquat, peach and melon knit tightly with creamy vanilla oak and backed by nutty, mealy suggestions. Long, smooth and generous, its slightly souredged fruit ties neatly with sweet oak and refreshing lemony acids, finishing with lingering fruit, and just a hint of spirit and sweetcorn.

SEXTON VINEYARD PINOT NOIR

RATING

Yarra Valley	$20–$29	2005	87	2007	2010+
Current vintage: 2005	87	2004	90	2006	2009+
		2003	86	2005	2008
		2002	87	2003	2004+

Rather closed and lacking brightness, this firm, drying and powdery pinot marries a herbal and slightly green-edged expression of plum and cherry fruit with restrained oak and earthy, meaty undertones. It appears to lack confidence.

Glaetzer

34 Barossa Valley Way, Tanunda SA 5352. Tel: (08) 8563 0288. Fax: (08) 8563 0218.
Website: www.glaetzer.com Email: admin@glaetzer.com
Region: **Barossa Valley** Winemakers: **Colin & Ben Glaetzer** Chief Executive: **Colin Glaetzer**

One of Australia's busiest and most demanded contract winemakers, Ben Glaetzer is the winemaking inspiration behind this series of Barossa reds. His style is rich and generous, with as much winemaking-derived complexity as his fruit can handle. Importantly, while the wines have the balance and structure to cellar well, they are typically ready to enjoy in their youth.

AMON-RA SHIRAZ

RATING

Barossa Valley	$100–$200	2005	91	2010	2013
Current vintage: 2005	91	2004	94	2012	2016
		2003	95	2011	2015+
		2002	96	2014	2022+

Typically ripe and sumptuous, this slightly meaty and raisined shiraz opens with a confiture-like aroma of sweet red and black berries backed by smoky cedar/vanilla oak. Plush and luxuriant, it reveals deep flavours of plums and berries but is unable to conceal some overcooked and dehydrated influences of currant-like fruit suggestive of extended hang time. Framed by firm, fine tannins and artfully supported by new oak, it lacks the genuine length of intense fruit of the top vintages.

BISHOP SHIRAZ

RATING **4**

2005	91	2010	2013+
2004	91	2006	2009
2002	89	2004	2007+
2001	90	2006	2009
1999	88	2004	2007

Barossa Valley $30–$49
Current vintage: 2005 91

Slightly warm and spirity aromas of violets, sweet red berries and blackberries precede a smooth, supple and evenly measured palate whose deep, juicy and mouthfilling flavours of dark berries and plums finish with just a hint of hotness and sourness. Of moderate richness, it's backed by chocolate-like oak, it finishes savoury and slightly mineral with suggestions of black olives. Very good focus and length, but slightly cooked.

SHIRAZ

RATING **5**

2004	93	2012	2016+
2002	89	2010	2014
2001	89	2009	2013
1999	86	2001	2004+
1998	91	2010	2018
1997	88	1999	2002

Barossa Valley $50–$99
Current vintage: 2004 93

Smooth, polished and artfully balanced, with a spicy and floral fragrance of violets, white pepper and cloves beneath pristine aromas of cassis, plums and blackberries. Restrained cedar/vanilla oak also underpins its silky palate of deep blackberry, dark plum and blueberry flavours, along with nuances of dark olives and minerals.

Goundrey

Langton, Muir Highway, Mount Barker WA 6324. Tel: (08) 9892 1777. Fax: (08) 9851 1997.
Website: www.goundreywines.com.au Email: info@goundreywines.com.au
Regions: **Great Southern, Mount Barker** Winemakers: **David Martin, Stephen Craig, Mick Perkins**
Viticulturists: **Cate Finlay, Rob Hayes** Chief Executive: **Rich Hanen**

Changing ownership yet again, this time into the Hardy Wine Company stable through mutual new owner Constellation Brands, Goundrey is a reliable maker of elegant and flavoursome regional styles from the Great Southern. Its present Reserve range is strong, with a particular highlight in the smoky, dark-fruited and savoury 2005 Reserve Shiraz.

RESERVE CABERNET SAUVIGNON

RATING **4**

2004	90	2012	2016
2003	91	2011	2015
2002	87	2004	2007+
1998	78	2000	2003
1997	80	1999	2002
1996	90	2002	2008
1995	90	2003	2007
1993	87	2001	2005
1992	85	1997	2000
1991	93	2003	2011
1990	85	1998	2002

Great Southern $20–$29
Current vintage: 2004 90

Smooth and polished, with nothing out of place, this elegant and harmonious cabernet supports its intense but moderately rich palate of dark berries and plums with supple, fine-grained tannins. Handsomely cloaked in smoky dark chocolate/cedary oak, it reveals faint nuances of dried herbs before finishing firm and focused.

RESERVE CHARDONNAY

RATING **5**

2004	90	2006	2009+
2003	85	2005	2008
2002	91	2004	2007
2001	86	2003	2006
1999	81	2000	2001
1998	85	2000	2003
1997	88	1999	2002
1995	87	1997	2000

Mount Barker $20–$29
Current vintage: 2004 90

Tightly crafted in a juicy, fruity style, this pleasingly bright and fluffy chardonnay has a lightly tropical and herbal bouquet backed by nuances of butter and sweet corn. Its fresh, restrained and creamy palate of peach and nectarine flavour marries with toffee-like malolactic notes before a clean and lingering finish of soft acids. Should flesh out nicely.

RESERVE RIESLING

Mount Barker	$20–$29
Current vintage: 2005	**91**

Smoky, slightly reductive aromas of lime juice and minerals are lifted by a complex floral perfume. Long, taut and lean, its crystalline expression of vibrant citrusy fruit and reductive complexity overlies a chalky mineral texture and a crackly, almost brittle acidity at the finish. It's fresh, clean and racy.

2005	91	2010	2013+
2004	87	2006	2009
2003	93	2008	2011
2002	84	2002	2004
2000	84	2005	2008
1999	82	2001	2004
1998	88	2000	2003
1997	90	2002	2005
1996	93	2004	2008
1995	87	2003	2007
1994	94	2002	2006
1993	95	1998	2001

RESERVE SHIRAZ

Great Southern	$20–$29
Current vintage: 2005	**92**

Meaty, spicy, smoky and gamey, with plenty of character and complexity. It reveals a slightly autumnal, peppery and herbal aspect, with undertones of licorice, nutmeg and even venison-like character. Its deep, briary core of persistent dark plum and berry flavour is framed by chalky, but pliant tannin, finishing with accompanying meaty and oaky influences.

2005	92	2010	2013+
2002	90	2007	2010
2001	82	2003	2006
2000	85	2002	2005+
1999	90	2004	2007
1998	80	2000	2003
1997	83	1999	2002
1996	81	1997	1998
1994	93	2002	2006
1993	91	2001	2005
1992	94	2000	2004

Gramp's

Barossa Valley Way, Rowland Flat SA 5352. Tel: (08) 8521 3111. Fax: (08) 8521 3100.
Website: www.gramps.com.au
Region: **Barossa Valley** Winemakers: **Don Young, Hylton McLean, Nick Bruer** Viticulturist: **Joy Dick**
Chief Executive: **Laurent Lacassgne**
The logic behind the labelling of Pernod Ricard's best dessert wine, a semillon from Griffith, under its Barossa-based Gramp's label still eludes me, but the 2004 release continues its consistent run of restrained and elegant vintages made without excessive sweetness or fatness. The pick of the Barossa wine is the richly flavoured and robustly constructed Cabernet Merlot from 2004, which brings with it some genuine ability to age.

BOTRYTIS SEMILLON

Griffith	$12–$19 (375 ml)
Current vintage: 2004	**91**

Complex, honeyed and toasty, with fresh, sweet and luscious expression of apricot, lemon and melon flavour over suggestions of vanilla oak, brioche and crème caramel. It's long and smooth, restrained and finely balanced, with a refreshing finish of vibrant acidity and no suggestion of cloying. Great value.

2004	91	2008	2012
2003	90	2005	2008+
2002	91	2004	2007+
2001	88	2003	2006
1999	90	2001	2004+
1998	83	1999	2000
1997	89	1999	2002
1996	89	1998	2001
1994	82	1995	1996

CABERNET MERLOT

Barossa Valley	$12–$19
Current vintage: 2004	**89**

A powerful, sumptuous Barossa blend whose sweet, juicy and slightly jammy flavours of blackberries, red plums and cassis are knit with cedar/vanilla oak and backed by hints of mint and menthol, it's heady and floral, but dark and profoundly fruited on the palate. Framed by firm, drying tannins, it's long and ripe, finishing with sweet flavours of plums and oak.

2004	89	2012	2016
2003	88	2008	2011
2002	82	2004	2007
2001	82	2002	2005
1999	86	2001	2004
1998	88	2003	2006
1997	89	2002	2005
1996	86	1998	2001
1995	85	1997	2000
1994	82	1999	2002
1993	75	1995	1998

CHARDONNAY

Barossa Valley $12–$19
Current vintage: 2005 85

Rather candied, simple and hot, with a rich, toasty and honeyed expression of buttery melon, fig and cumquat backed by creamy vanilla oak. It's forward and moderately fleshy, but lacks length and freshness.

2005	85	2006	2007+
2003	85	2004	2005
2002	89	2004	2007
2001	80	2002	2003
2000	87	2001	2002
1999	87	2001	2004
1998	82	1999	2000

GRENACHE   RATING 5

Barossa Valley $12–$19
Current vintage: 2005 88

Meaty, rather porty and raisined aromas of baked plums, currants and licorice precede a slightly cooked but soft and approachable palate of spicy redcurrant, dark plum and pruney flavour. Velvet-smooth, with plenty of forward brightness and intensity, it's also evolved and gamey, finishing wrapped in firm, fine tannins with length of flavour.

2005	88	2007	2010+
2004	88	2006	2009+
2002	86	2004	2007
1999	89	2004	2007
1998	87	2000	2003+
1997	88	1999	2002

Granite Hills

1481 Burke & Wills Track, Baynton Vic 3444. Tel: (03) 5423 7264. Fax: (03) 5423 7288.
Website: www.granitehills.com.au Email: knights@granitehills.com.au
Region: **Macedon Ranges** Winemakers: **Llew Knight, Ian Gunter**
Chief Executives: **Gordon, Heather & Llew Knight**
One of the most extraordinary vertical tastings over the past year was the staging of Llew Knight's Riesling and Shiraz. Perhaps it's the warmer run of seasons, given the extremely cool nature of the site, but each of these wines has performed especially well over the last five years. The other message was the exceptional longevity of these styles, which I admit to having under-estimated. The intensity, balance, freshness and complexity of some of the older wines was remarkable indeed.

CABERNET SAUVIGNON   RATING 5

Macedon Ranges $20–$29
Current vintage: 2001 82

Earthy, herbal and meaty, cedary aromas precede an up-front palate of green-edged small red berries, finishing lean and sappy.

2001	82	2003	2006
2000	77	2002	2005
1999	94	2007	2011+
1998	90	2006	2010
1997	86	2002	2005
1996	84	2001	2004
1995	89	2003	2007
1992	86	1997	2000
1991	87	2003	2011
1989	86	1991	1994
1988	82	1996	2000

CHARDONNAY   RATING 5

Macedon Ranges $20–$29
Current vintage: 2004 87

A charming, brightly flavoured and early-drinking chardonnay with a fresh, tropical aroma of melon and peaches backed by light vanilla and cashew-like oak. Smooth and supple, it's bright and forward, with attractive if uncomplicated primary fruit finishing a little greenish with slightly tinny acids.

2004	87	2006	2009
2003	88	2005	2008
2002	88	2003	2006
2001	82	2002	2003
2000	87	2002	2005
1999	85	2000	2001
1998	86	2000	2003
1997	83	1999	2002
1996	90	2001	2004
1995	93	2003	2007
1994	83	1996	1999
1993	92	1998	2001

RIESLING

RATING **3**

Macedon Ranges	$20–$29
Current vintage: 2006	**94**

Massively concentrated and powerful by riesling standards, with remarkable length, balance and longevity. Its musky, floral perfume of lime juice and lemon overlies hints of candy and a light spiciness. Searingly intense, its long, austere palate of pristine lime juice and lemon sherbet-like fruit is underpinned by a taut and assertive spine of tingling acidity. It finishes very dry indeed.

2006	94	2014	2018
2005	95	2017	2025
2004	92	2012	2016
2003	91	2008	2011+
2002	90	2010	2014
2001	84	2006	2009
2000	86	2005	2008+
1999	89	2007	2011
1998	95	2010	2018
1997	92	2005	2009
1996	94	2004	2008+
1995	88	2000	2003+
1994	95	2006	2014
1993	86	1998	2001
1992	92	2004	2012+

SHIRAZ

RATING **3**

Macedon Ranges	$20–$29
Current vintage: 2003	**88**

Wild, meaty aromas of plums, berries and currants with sweet undertones of vanilla/chocolate oak are backed by spicy hints of black pepper. Initially rich, smooth and sumptuous, with juicy, rather jammy fruit, it then thins out a little, finishing slightly cooked.

2005	95	2017	2025
2004	94	2012	2016+
2003	88	2011	2015
2002	93	2010	2014
2001	89	2009	2013+
2000	85	2005	2008
1999	93	2007	2011+
1998	91	2010	2018
1997	89	2005	2009+
1996	81	2001	2004

Grant Burge

Barossa Valley Way, Jacob's Creek, Tanunda SA 5352. Tel: (08) 8563 3700. Fax: (08) 8563 2807.
Website: www.grantburgewines.com.au Email: admin@grantburgewines.com.au
Region: **Barossa Valley** Winemaker: **Grant Burge** Viticulturist: **Toby Mifflin** Chief Executive: **Grant Burge**
This significant family-owned wine company has developed several tiers of wine, plus a number of special run labels along the lines of big company limited releases. Typically consistent and flavoursome, its steadily expanding folio of red wines reveals a slightly old-fashioned Australian approach. I am particularly impressed by the 2004 Filsell Shiraz, with its smooth Lyndoch-based red berry flavours and elegance, but also with its handsome structure.

BAROSSA VINES SHIRAZ

Barossa Valley	$12–$19
Current vintage: 2005	**86**

Ripe, smooth, sweet and juicy, with blackberries, plums and sweet vanilla oak backed by nuances of game meats and menthol. It's slightly hollow, cooked and raisined, but has an approachable frame of smooth tannins.

2005	86	2007	2010
2004	86	2006	2009
2003	86	2005	2008
2002	87	2003	2004+
2001	86	2003	2006
2000	82	2001	2002
1999	88	2001	2004
1998	85	1999	2000

CAMERON VALE CABERNET SAUVIGNON

RATING **5**

Barossa Valley	$12–$19
Current vintage: 2004	**90**

A deep, palate-staining cabernet whose fresh, minty aromas of cassis, dark plums, violets and cedar/vanilla oak precede a juicy but still rather closed and youthful palate that just hints at its latent depth of vibrant, dark-fruited flavour. Finely balanced and framed by firmish, drying tannin, it's surprisingly elegant and measured. Give it time.

2004	90	2012	2016
2003	82	2008	2011
2002	87	2007	2010
2001	89	2006	2009
2000	82	2002	2005
1999	82	2001	2004
1998	88	2006	2010
1997	87	2002	2005
1996	91	2004	2008
1995	91	2003	2007
1994	89	2002	2006
1993	88	2001	2005

FILSELL SHIRAZ

RATING 3

Barossa Valley $20–$29
Current vintage: 2004 94

A typically elegant and sweetly fruited Lyndoch shiraz whose wild, heady and alluring perfume of small dark fruits, musk, cloves and black pepper overlie meaty nuances of dark olives and dark chocolate/vanilla oak. On one hand, it is sumptuous and richly fruited, with deep flavours of plums, black-berries and cassis; on the other, it's elegant and approachable, supported by firmish but pliant tannin.

2004	94	2012	2016+
2003	94	2011	2015+
2002	90	2010	2014+
2001	86	2003	2006+
2000	93	2008	2012
1999	88	2001	2004+
1998	94	2006	2010
1997	88	2002	2005
1996	95	2004	2008+
1995	91	2000	2003
1994	95	2002	2006+
1993	82	1998	2001
1992	90	2000	2004
1991	93	2003	2011

KRAFT SAUVIGNON BLANC

RATING 5

**Barossa Valley,
Adelaide Hills** $12–$19
Current vintage: 2006 85

Rather candied and likely to become quite broad rather quickly, this lightly grassy and confectionary wine delivers ripe flavours of gooseberries, melon and passionfruit, but lacks genuine mid-palate fruit sweetness and depth. It finishes with a light sweetness and soft acidity.

2006	85	2007	2008
2005	92	2005	2006+
2003	81	2003	2004
2002	89	2002	2003+
2001	83	2001	2002
2000	87	2001	2002
1999	84	2000	2000
1998	90	1999	2000

MESHACH

RATING 2

Barossa Valley $50–$99
Current vintage: 2002 95

An elegant Meshach, but no shrinking violet, either. Very intense and assertively oaked, with dark plums, blackcurrants and dark chocolate backed by toasty aromas of vanilla, coconut ice, cedar and cigarboxes, it's also perfumed and floral. Surprisingly fine, elegant and seamless, its palate is saturated with jammy black and red berry flavours and supported by fine, firm tannins of genuine strength. It finishes long and savoury, with lingering sug-gestions of licorice, cloves and minerals.

2002	95	2014	2022
2001	88	2009	2013
2000	93	2008	2012+
1999	96	2007	2011+
1998	97	2010	2018+
1996	93	2008	2016
1995	96	2007	2015
1994	95	2006	2014
1993	93	2001	2005
1992	93	2000	2004
1991	95	2003	2011
1990	93	1998	2002+

MIAMBA SHIRAZ

RATING 5

Barossa Valley $12–$19
Current vintage: 2005 82

Simple, slightly raw and angular, with sweet, jammy red and black berry flavours and sweet oak backed by nuances of cedar and cinnamon. Forward and juicy, it depends rather too much on its vanilla oak for length and sweetness on the palate. Honest enough, but lacking genuine balance.

2005	82	2007	2010
2004	89	2009	2012
2003	91	2005	2008+
2002	84	2004	2007
2001	87	2003	2006
2000	88	2002	2005+
1999	89	2001	2004+

MSJ RESERVE CABERNET SHIRAZ BLEND

RATING 3

Barossa Valley $50–$99
Current vintage: 1999 87

Meaty and aged, this rustic, earthy and oaky Barossa blend does reveal some pleasing spicy and floral perfume, as well as some fineness and subtlety. The palate, however, is just too hollow, lean and lacking freshness for a higher rating.

1999	87	2007	2011
1998	91	2006	2010
1996	93	2004	2008+
1994	95	2006	2014

A B C D E F G H I J K L M N O P Q R S T U V W X Y Z

SHADRACH CABERNET SAUVIGNON

Barossa Valley   **$50–$99**
Current vintage: 2001   **88**

Generous and concentrated, but rather old-fashioned and lacking finesse, this rather blocky and sinewy cabernet reveals a ripe, jammy and slightly meaty bouquet. Earthy aromas of dark plums, cassis and sweet chocolate/mocha/vanilla oak overlie nuances of currant and raisins. Initially intense, but lacking genuine mid-palate depth and presence, it dries out towards an astringent, slightly sappy and mineral finish.

2001	88	2009	2013
2000	82	2005	2008
1999	87	2004	2007
1998	93	2006	2010+
1996	92	2008	2016
1994	93	2006	2014
1993	90	2013	2023

SUMMERS CHARDONNAY

Eden Valley, Adelaide Hills   **$12–$19**
Current vintage: 2005   **87**

An early-drinking chardonnay whose light, peachy aromas are backed by sweet buttery vanilla oak and nuances of wheatmeal. Round and generous, with bright stonefruit flavours, toasty oak and soft acids, it's well composed but finishes just a fraction thin.

2005	87	2007	2010
2004	87	2005	2006
2003	87	2004	2005
2002	88	2002	2004+
2001	80	2002	2003
2000	88	2002	2005
1999	87	2001	2004

THE HOLY TRINITY (Grenache Shiraz Mourvèdre)

Barossa Valley   **$30–$49**
Current vintage: 2002   **88**

A rather old-fashioned and sweet-fruited red blend whose floral and slight confectionary aromas of cranberries and plums reveal earthy, spicy undertones and suggestions of mint and menthol. Smooth and supple, its vibrant expression of spicy blueberry and plum-like fruit is framed by tight, fine and powdery tannin. Restrained and savoury, it's just beginning to age and dry out.

2002	88	2007	2010
2001	85	2003	2006+
2000	87	2002	2005
1999	92	2004	2007
1998	90	2000	2003+
1997	89	1999	2002
1996	89	1998	2001
1995	86	1997	2000

THORN RIESLING

Eden Valley   **$12–$19**
Current vintage: 2006   **88**

A generous, flavoursome if slightly broader riesling with candied, citrusy aromas and a smooth and approachable palate finished by fresh, soft acids. For the short term.

2006	88	2007	2008
2005	88	2007	2010+
2004	93	2009	2012+
2002	90	2007	2010
2001	91	2006	2009+
2000	87	2002	2005+
1999	88	2001	2004+
1998	93	2003	2006
1997	87	1999	2002

ZERK SEMILLON VIOGNIER (formerly Semillon)

Barossa Valley   **$12–$19**
Current vintage: 2006   **90**

Scented with musky nuances of apricot blossom and zesty lemon, this round, smooth and richly textured white blend delivers plenty of tangy citrus and stonefruit flavour. It finishes with lingering flavour and refreshing acids. Viognier cheerfully dominates this blend, semillon delivering the length and focus.

2006	90	2007	2008+
2005	89	2006	2007+
2004	86	2005	2006
2002	92	2003	2004+
2001	84	2002	2003
2000	87	2001	2002
1999	92	2001	2004+
1998	88	2000	2003
1997	87	2002	2005

Green Point

Green Point Maroondah Highway, Coldstream Vic 3770. Tel: (03) 9738 9200. Fax: (03) 9738 9201.
Website: www.greenpointwines.com.au

Regions: **Yarra Valley, Various** Winemakers: **Tony Jordan, Matt Steel, John Harris, Glenn Thompson**
Viticulturist: **Bernie Wood** Managing Director: **Tony Jordan**

Green Point is the label by which Domaine Chandon's Australian sparkling wines are sold in overseas markets, as well as the company's brand of still table wines sold in Australia. Its range is now sourced exclusively from Victoria. 2005 will go down as the vintage in which Green Point mastered chardonnay. Its two wines are finely crafted, vibrant and generous, each finishing with refreshingly tight and crisp acidity.

RESERVE CHARDONNAY
RATING 5

Yarra Valley $30–$49
Current vintage: 2005 95

Smoky, meaty and reductive, with a nectarine and white peach fragrance backed by fresh vanilla and lemony oak and funky hints of smoked bacon. Initially round and juicy, its generous, sumptuous palate is finely sculpted by a trim, taut acidity and backed by mealy, waxy and lanolin-like complexity. It's long, lean and vibrant, and should easily develop into the finest white yet under this label.

2005	95	2010	2013
2004	89	2006	2009
2003	88	2005	2008+
2002	89	2007	2010
2001	88	2003	2006
2000	87	2002	2005

RESERVE PINOT NOIR
RATING 5

Yarra Valley $20–$29
Current vintage: 2004 87

A stylish, firm and assertively structured pinot with a comparatively simple expression of confection-like raspberries, red cherries and berries. While it's lifted by sweet vanilla oak and spicy scents of clove and cinnamon, its smooth-centred palate remains slightly thin. It finishes with pleasing acidity, but without great length of fruit.

2004	87	2006	2009
2003	82	2005	2008
2002	90	2004	2007
2001	87	2003	2006
2000	89	2005	2008

RESERVE SHIRAZ
RATING 4

Victoria $20–$29
Current vintage: 2005 90

Spicy and lightly peppery aromas of dark cherries, cassis and dark plums are backed by sweet chocolate/vanilla oak and charcuterie-like reductive undertones. Medium to full in weight, it's generous and juicy, with a pleasing length of vibrant dark cherry/berry fruit before a lingering and slightly smoky, savoury finish.

2005	90	2010	2013
2004	90	2009	2012
2003	85	2005	2008

YARRA VALLEY CHARDONNAY
RATING 5

Yarra Valley $20–$29
Current vintage: 2005 91

Elegant and finely balanced, this floral, tightly focused and restrained young chardonnay reveals a pleasing juiciness before finishing long, fine and savoury. Scented with lemon, white peach, vanilla oak and a light spiciness, it's supple and generous, with lingering flavour and a crisp, refreshing finish. Great balance.

2005	91	2007	2010+
2004	89	2006	2009
2003	90	2005	2008
2002	87	2004	2007
2001	84	2003	2006
2000	86	2000	2003
1999	81	2000	2001
1998	83	2000	2003
1996	82	1996	1997
1995	93	2000	2003
1994	92	1999	2002
1993	89	1998	2001

Grey Sands

6 Kerrisons Road, Glengarry Tas 7275. Tel: (03) 6396 1167. Fax: (03) 6396 1153.
Website: www.greysands.com.au Email: info@greysands.com.au
Region: **Tamar Valley** Winemakers: **Fran Austin, Andrew Pirie** Viticulturist: **Bob Richter**
Chief Executive: **Bob Richter**

Grey Sands is a 2.5 hectare close-spaced vineyard planted exclusively to pinot gris and merlot. Its Pinot Gris is a ripe and sumptuous style given full malolactic fermentation and four months of lees contact to develop texture and complexity. The 2005 vintage is typically smoky and complex, long and savoury. The vineyard is open to visitors by appointment.

PINOT GRIS

	Tamar Valley	$30–$49
	Current vintage: 2005	**94**

A smooth, generous and intensely fruited pinot gris whose musky perfume of rose oil, pear and apple-like fruit is backed by nutty undertones. It's chalky and powdery, with some smoky, charcuterie-like reductive complexity beneath its pristine, juicy flavours. It finishes long and savoury, with lingering citrus notes and soft acids. Lovely balance and varietal purity.

2005	94	2007	2010
2004	93	2005	2006+
2003	80	2003	2004
2001	81	2002	2003
2000	94	2002	2005

Grosset

King Street, Auburn SA 5451. Tel: (08) 8849 2175. Fax: (08) 8849 2292.
Website: www.grosset.com.au Email: info@grosset.com.au
Region: **Clare Valley** Winemaker: **Jeffrey Grosset** Viticulturist: **Jeffrey Grosset** Chief Executive: **Jeffrey Grosset**

Top vineyards can still make terrific wine in tough vintages, which is precisely what Jeff Grosset has been able to achieve with the Polish Hill and Watervale wines, although neither is as long-living a wine as usual. While Grosset attracts considerable attention for its riesling, it also produces an very fine, supple and finely balanced Piccadilly (chardonnay), whose very creditable 2005 vintage has an excellent powdery texture.

GAIA (Cabernet blend)

	Clare Valley	$50–$99
	Current vintage: 2004	**90**

Vibrant aromas of small black and red berries, cedar/vanilla oak are lifted by scents of flowers and a slight meatiness, while there's a hint of herbaceousness underneath. Smooth and juicy, its substantial palate of ripe fruit flavours, newish oak and firm, pliant tannins overlies some genuine minerality as well as regional suggestions of mint and eucalypt. Modern and stylish, it's just a fraction overcooked for a higher score.

2004	90	2012	2016+
2003	93	2011	2015+
2002	90	2014	2022+
2001	94	2013	2021
2000	91	2008	2012+
1999	90	2007	2011
1998	95	2010	2018
1996	91	2004	2008
1995	93	2007	2015
1994	94	2006	2014
1993	94	2005	2013
1992	95	2004	2012
1991	88	1996	1999
1990	89	2002	2010

PICCADILLY (Chardonnay)

	Adelaide Hills	$30–$49
	Current vintage: 2005	**93**

A little firmer than usual, this dry and savoury chardonnay retains its typical intensity and depth of flavour. Backed by sweet butter/vanilla oak, with light mineral-like undertones, its fresh aromas of white peach and melon reveal a suggestion of wheatmeal. Smooth and creamy, its generous and silky palate of ripe peach/melon fruit is underpinned by a finely powdered chassis, culminating in a lingering finish of persistent flavour and fine extract.

2005	93	2010	2013
2004	95	2009	2012
2003	96	2008	2011
2002	95	2007	2010
2001	94	2006	2009
2000	95	2005	2008
1999	95	2004	2007+
1998	90	2003	2006
1997	94	2002	2005
1996	95	2001	2004
1995	94	2000	2003
1994	94	2002	2006

PINOT NOIR

GROSSET

Adelaide Hills $50–$99
Current vintage: 2005 91

A rich, deeply fruited and brooding pinot whose ripe, slightly stewy presence of maraschino cherries and plums overlies meaty, charcuterie-like undertones backed by cloves, cinnamon and a hint of rhubarb. Underpinned by firm, drying but fine-grained tannins, it's fairly closed but deeply layered, finishing with an impression of hidden strength. It retains elements of style and finesse.

2005	91	2020	2013
2004	91	2009	2012
2003	93	2005	2008+
2002	92	2007	2010+
2001	88	2003	2006
2000	82	2002	2005
1998	93	2003	2006
1997	95	2002	2005+
1996	94	2004	2008
1995	91	1997	2000
1994	93	1999	2002
1993	90	1998	2001

POLISH HILL

GROSSET

Clare Valley $30–$49
Current vintage: 2006 95

A shapely and finely presented Polish Hill that will develop beautifully in the bottle, but perhaps for not as long as its more classic vintages. Scented with minerally notes of lime and talcum powder, its floral perfume remains delicate and rather closed. Long and supple, its smooth and stylish palate of intensely concentrated lime juice, lemon rind, pawpaw and white peach flavours belies the earliness of the season, culminating in a tightly sculpted finish of musky fruit and citrusy acids.

2006	95	2011	2014+
2005	98	2017	2025
2004	95	2012	2016+
2003	96	2015	2023
2002	97	2014	2022
2001	96	2009	2013+
2000	95	2008	2012
1999	95	2007	2011+
1998	92	2006	2010
1997	97	2009	2017+
1996	94	2004	2008
1995	93	2003	2007+
1994	95	2006	2014
1993	90	2001	2005
1992	93	2004	2012

SEMILLON SAUVIGNON BLANC

Clare Valley, Adelaide Hills $20–$29
Current vintage: 2006 88

Lightly herbal and fractionally sweaty, with restrained aromas of gooseberries, white peach and melon backed by nutty, leesy undertones. Lean, taut and forward, its palate has plenty of length and presence of fruit but finishes slightly hot and sweet. Wrapped in clean acids, it's sound and flavoursome, but lacks genuine cut and shape.

2006	88	2007	2008+
2005	90	2007	2010+
2004	89	2004	2005+
2003	92	2004	2005+
2002	90	2004	2007
2001	92	2006	2009
2000	91	2002	2005
1999	90	2004	2007
1998	93	2003	2006
1997	90	1998	1999
1996	93	1998	2001
1995	94	1997	2000
1994	94	1999	2003
1993	94	2001	2005

WATERVALE RIESLING

Clare Valley $30–$49
Current vintage: 2006 94

An earlier-maturing riesling whose pronounced and musky floral perfume reveals lemon cordial-like fruit and lime juice over dusty suggestions of bathpowder. It's a textural wine, whose smooth expression of assertive tropical, citrus and stone-fruit flavours overlies a chalky spine before finishing with pleasing length and tangy, lemony acids.

2006	94	2011	2014
2005	96	2013	2017+
2004	93	2009	2012+
2003	95	2008	2011+
2002	96	2010	2014+
2001	95	2009	2013
2000	95	2008	2012+
1999	95	2004	2007+
1998	90	2003	2006+
1997	95	2002	2005+
1996	94	2001	2004+
1995	92	2000	2003
1994	94	2002	2006
1993	90	1998	2001
1992	90	1997	2000
1991	96	2003	2011
1990	94	2002	2010

Gulf Station

Pinnacle Lane, Dixon's Creek Vic 3775. Tel: (03) 5965 2271. Fax: (03) 5965 2442.
Website: www.debortoli.com.au Email: dbw@debortoli.com.au
Region: **Yarra Valley** Winemakers: **Stephen Webber, David Slingsby-Smith** Viticulturist: **Philip Lobley**
Chief Executive: **Darren De Bortoli**

Gulf Station is a De Bortoli label that offers affordable and sometimes upmarket drinking from Yarra Valley vineyards. Its easy-drinking Chardonnay and floral Riesling are typically fresh and vibrant, while I am less convinced by the rather reductive Shiraz Viognier.

CHARDONNAY
RATING 5

Yarra Valley	$12–$19				
Current vintage: 2006	87	2006	87	2007	2008+
		2005	80	2006	2007
Simple and fruity, but clean and refreshing with		2004	87	2005	2006
lively peach and melon fruit over suggestions of		2003	89	2004	2005+
wheatmeal, vanilla and a hint of sweetcorn. With		2002	89	2003	2004+
a lingering presence of fruit and oak, it's finished		2001	81	2002	2003
with pleasing balance and a tangy acidity.					

RIESLING

Yarra Valley	$12–$19				
Current vintage: 2006	82	2006	82	2007	2008
		2005	77	2006	2007
Musky, traminer-like scents of apple, pear and lime		2004	87	2006	2009
precede a broad, rather coarse and simple palate		2003	81	2003	2004
that lacks finesse and intensity.		2002	87	2002	2003
		2001	77	2001	2002
		2000	82	2001	2002
		1999	80	2000	2001
		1998	91	2003	2006
		1997	87	2002	2005

SHIRAZ VIOGNIER (formerly Shiraz)
RATING 5

Yarra Valley	$12–$19				
Current vintage: 2005	83	2005	83	2007	2010
		2003	88	2005	2008+
Rather awkward and reductive, with meaty,		2002	89	2004	2007
smoky undertones beneath its flavours of dark		2001	87	2006	2009
plums, berries and cherries and a restrained lift		2000	88	2001	2002+
of viognier. Slightly stewy, with a rather thin palate,		1999	83	2001	2004
it finishes with a raw, drying extract. Lacks bright-		1998	83	2000	2003
ness.		1996	92	2008	2016

Hanging Rock

88 Jim Road, Newham Vic 3442. Tel: (03) 5427 0542. Fax: (03) 5427 0310.
Website: www.hangingrock.com.au Email: hrw@hangingrock.com.au
Region: **Macedon Ranges** Winemaker: **John Ellis** Viticulturist: **John Ellis** Chief Executive: **John Ellis**

Hanging Rock creates a wide range of inexpensive wines under its Rock label, but I am more interested in its steadily expanding top tier of slightly idiosyncratic wines sourced from a number of regions, with a developing focus on Heathcote. The current releases of Heathcote Shiraz and The Jim Jim Sauvignon Blanc tend to lack their customary intensity, but the sparkling Macedon is typically wild and evolved.

HEATHCOTE SHIRAZ
RATING 4

Heathcote	$50–$99				
Current vintage: 2004	88	2004	88	2012	2016
		2003	91	2015	2023
Tight, closed, peppery and spicy, with restrained		2002	93	2010	2014+
aromas of black and red berry/plum fruit,		2001	89	2006	2009
chocolate/cedar oak and a hint of iron filings. Its		2000	91	2008	2012+
lean and partially stressed palate slowly builds in		1999	93	2011	2019
intensity towards the finish, but finishes quite savoury,		1998	93	2010	2018
with an assertive presence of American oak.		1997	90	2005	2009
		1992	95	2012	2022
		1991	95	2003	2011+
		1990	95	2002	2010+
		1989	89	1997	2001+
		1988	91	2000	2008

MACEDON

RATING 4

Macedon Ranges	$30–$49
Current vintage: Cuvée XI	**86**

A deliberately extreme expression of sparking style fashioned in an overtly oxidative and aldehydic style. Its very evolved, toasty, honeyed and buttery bouquet is very fragrant and meaty, while its palate is richly textured, chewy and rather stale, finishing with a lingering suggestion of apple cider. I admire the style and the ambitions behind it, but believe this wine has gone too far.

Cuvée XI	86	2005	2008
Cuvée X	86	2004	2007
Cuvée IX	87	2003	2005
Cuvée VIII	91	2002	2006+
Cuvée VII	94	2000	2003
Cuvée VI	88	1999	2002
Cuvée V	87	1997	2000
Cuvée IV	94	1996	1999
Cuvée III	91	1995	1999

THE JIM JIM SAUVIGNON BLANC

RATING 5

Macedon Ranges	$20–$29
Current vintage: 2006	**88**

Herbal and dusty, with light gooseberry aromas and a refreshing, forward and fruity palate that lacks great length and presence. It's clean and varietal, but could use more punch and intensity.

2006	88	2007	2008
2005	88	2006	2007
2004	94	2005	2006+
2003	88	2004	2005
2002	87	2003	2003
2001	90	2003	2006
2000	87	2001	2002
1999	86	2000	2001
1998	90	2000	2003

Hardys

Reynell Road, Reynella SA 5161. Tel: (08) 8392 2222. Fax: (08) 8392 2202.
Website: www.hardywines.com.au Email: corporate@hardywines.com.au

Regions: **South Australia, Tasmania, Victoria** Winemakers: **Peter Dawson** (chief), **Paul Lapsley** (red), **Tom Newton** (white), **Ed Carr** (sparkling) Viticulturist: **Brenton Baker** Chief Executive: **John Grant**

Part of one of the world's largest wine companies in Constellation Wines, The Hardy Wine Company still produces a number of apparently disparate but usually terrific wines under its original name. The flagship Eileen Hardy wines have again delivered handsomely, especially the classic and brooding 2004 Shiraz. Although it is strictly now a Bay of Fires wine, I have listed the Arras sparkling wine here for a final year. The 2001 release is spectacular.

ARRAS SPARKLING CHARDONNAY PINOT NOIR

RATING 2

Tasmania	$50–$99
Current vintage: 2001	**96**

Perfumed and floral, with fresh aromas of white peach, meaty cracked yeast and grilled nuts before a luxuriantly long, creamy and sumptuous palate. Its lingering palate of pristine and explosive stonefruit, citrus and melon-like flavour is creamy and crackly, with a tight, fine mousse and refreshingly dry and tangy lemon sherbet-like finish of crisp acidity and a sour cherry note. Charmingly evolved, complex and complete.

2001	96	2009	2013
2000	94	2005	2008
1999	95	2007	2011
1998	94	2003	2006+
1997	90	1999	2002
1995	95	2003	2007

EILEEN HARDY CHARDONNAY

RATING 2

Tasmania, Yarra Valley, Tumbarumba, Adelaide Hills	$50–$99
Current vintage: 2005	**94**

A more powerful, sumptuous and assertive wine than the taut and finely crafted 2004 edition. Slightly juicy aromas of peach/melon fruit are backed by lightly smoky and spicy nuances of fine-grained and clove-like oak, with undertones of dried herbs and appealing reductive complexity. There's almost a sour-edged and drying aspect about its long palate whose slightly phenolic texture is enhanced by its pleasingly funky qualities.

2005	94	2010	2013
2004	93	2009	2012
2003	95	2008	2011+
2002	94	2007	2010
2001	95	2006	2009+
2000	95	2005	2008
1999	96	2004	2007+
1998	94	2003	2006
1997	92	1999	2002
1996	95	2001	2004+
1995	93	2000	2003
1994	91	1996	1999
1993	90	1998	2001
1992	85	1997	2000
1991	93	1996	1999+

EILEEN HARDY SHIRAZ

RATING **2**

McLaren Vale $50–$99
Current vintage: 2004 96

A long-term McLaren Vale classic, with a deep, dark and spicy perfume of blackberries, cassis and smoked oyster-like oak overlying nuances of ginger and sage. Deep, dark and brooding, its sumptuous palate of profoundly intense fruit is neatly backed by a silky-smooth cut of tannin, finishing with a slightly salty tang of mineral. It should flesh out superbly over time.

2004	96	2016	2024
2002	95	2014	2022
2001	95	2013	2021
2000	93	2008	2012+
1999	96	2011	2019
1998	97	2010	2018
1997	93	2005	2009
1996	96	2016	2026
1995	95	2003	2007
1994	95	2006	2014
1993	89	2001	2005
1992	90	2000	2004
1991	92	1999	2003
1990	93	2002	2010+
1989	90	1997	2001
1988	93	2000	2008+
1987	91	1995	1999

NOTTAGE HILL CABERNET SHIRAZ

South Australia $5–$11
Current vintage: 2006 85

Pretty, forward and juicy, with lively flavours of plum, red and black berries and sweet cedar/vanilla oak, it's supple and earthy, marginally short and framed by fine, dusty tannins.

2006	85	2007	2008
2005	88	2007	2010
2004	86	2006	2009
2003	87	2005	2008
2002	81	2003	2004+
2001	78	2002	2003
2000	80	2001	2002
1999	80	2000	2001

THOMAS HARDY CABERNET SAUVIGNON

RATING **3**

Margaret River, Coonawarra $50–$99
Current vintage: 2001 92

Floral aromas of sweet red cherries, raspberries and violets overlie cedar/vanilla oak and undertones of dried herbs and dark olives. Full to medium in weight, it's firm and fine-grained, with a vibrant length of restrained small black and red berry flavours, over chalky tannins and dusty, fine-grained chocolate-like oak. Elegant and harmonious, it finishes with a slightly greenish aspect.

2004	96	2016	2024+
2001	92	2009	2013+
2000	89	2008	2012+
1999	93	2011	2019
1996	94	2008	2016
1995	92	2003	2007+
1994	94	2006	2012
1993	90	2001	2005
1992	93	2000	2004
1991	94	2003	2011
1990	95	2002	2010
1989	94	2001	2009

Heartland Wines

34 Barossa Valley Way, Tanunda SA 5352. Tel: (08) 8563 0288. Fax: (08) 8431 4355.
Website: www.heartlandwines.com.au Email: admin@heartlandwines.com.au
Regions: **Langhorne Creek, Limestone Coast** Winemaker: **Ben Glaetzer** Viticulturist: **Geoff Hardy**
Chief Executive: **Grant Tilbrook**
Heartland Wines sources its fruit from mature vineyards at Langhorne Creek and the Limestone Coast. Made under the guidance of one of its partners, Ben Glaetzer, it releases an interesting and eclectic series of wines deliberately made to be ready for early enjoyment, such as the innovative blends of Dolcetto Lagrein and Viognier Pinot Gris (up-front and refreshing).

DIRECTOR'S CUT SHIRAZ

RATING **4**

Langhorne Creek,
Limestone Coast $30–$49
Current vintage: 2005 90

This slightly minty and sour-edged shiraz appreciates all the time you can give it in a decanter. Ripe and juicy, with a confiture-like aroma of brambly dark cherries and plums with undertones of chocolate mint, it reveals a smooth, refined palate of medium to full weight. Backed by toasty oak, its lingering flavours and slightly warm palate are framed by tight-knit but chalky tannins.

2005	90	2010	2013
2004	90	2012	2016
2003	85	2008	2011+
2002	87	2010	2014

DOLCETTO LAGREIN

RATING **4**

Langhorne Creek,	$20–$29	2006	84	2007	2008+
Current vintage: 2006	84	2005	90	2007	2010+
		2004	91	2006	2009

Powdery and drying, with a modest depth of earthy, spicy flavours of dark and briary cherries and plums, this leaner medium-weight blend finishes savoury, with suggestions of currants and dried herbs. It lacks great depth, impact and length.

Heathcote Estate

Drummonds Lane, Heathcote Vic 3523. Tel: (03) 5433 2107. Fax: (03) 5433 2152.
Website: www.heathcoteestate.com Email: info@heathcoteestate.com
Region: **Heathcote** Winemakers: **Tod Dexter, Larry McKenna** Chief Executive: **Louis Bialkower**

Louis Bialkower, the founder of Yarra Ridge, and Robert Kirby have combined to create this ambitious new brand whose home is nearly 40 hectares of vineyard adjacent to Jasper Hill. It's largely planted to shiraz, with a small area of grenache, which also appears in the finished wine. The wines are made by a very experienced duo in Tod Dexter (formerly Stonier) and Larry McKenna (formerly Martinborough Vineyard).

SHIRAZ

RATING **3**

Heathcote	$30–$49	2005	89	2010	2013+
Current vintage: 2005	89	2004	93	2012	2016+
		2003	92	2011	2015
		2002	89	2007	2010

Firm, brooding and chalky, this polished, spicy but rather cooked shiraz combines flavours of plums, blackberries, raisins and currants with mocha/coffee grounds-like oak and spicy cinnamon/clove influences. It's ripe and forward, with a measured level of alcohol that is not excessive, but does need time to integrate.

Heathcote Winery

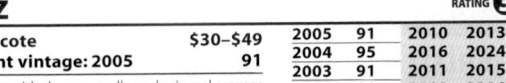

183 High Street, Heathcote Vic 3523. Tel: (03) 5433 2595. Fax: (03) 5433 3081.
Website: www.heathcotewinery.com.au Email: winemaker@heathcotewinery.com.au
Region: **Heathcote** Winemaker: **Rachel Brooker** Viticulturist: **Brett Winslow** Chief Executive: **Steve Wilkins**

Heathcote Winery is a shiraz and viognier specialist with more experience than most Australian wineries in the art of using viognier to add complexity and lift to shiraz without making it patently obvious that you have done so. The Curagee Shiraz from 2004 is a classic example of this — a firm and floral wine with classic mineral undertones. While the Mail Coach Shiraz is typically elegant and balanced, the 2005 vintage has been seriously affected by the ongoing drought.

CURAGEE SHIRAZ

RATING **3**

Heathcote	$30–$49	2005	91	2010	2013+
Current vintage: 2005	91	2004	95	2016	2024
		2003	91	2011	2015
		2002	91	2010	2014
		2001	95	2009	2013
		1999	87	2004	2007+
		1998	95	2006	2010+
		1997	94	2005	2009

Very ripe, with deep, gravelly and mineral aromas of dark plums and berries over suggestions of mint and menthol. Meaty, ripe and briary, its concentrated, dark-fruited palate reveals funky, reductive undertones and sweet vanilla/cedar oak, but finishes with length and brightness. Very smooth and polished, despite a handsome level of alcohol.

MAIL COACH SHIRAZ

RATING 4

Heathcote	$20–$29
Current vintage: 2005	**81**

Rather exaggerated, cooked and medicinal, with smoky, Bovril-like and meaty flavours of currants and raisins with undertones of mint and menthol. Rather cherry brandy-like, raw and over-extracted. Out of balance and porty.

2005	81	2010	2013
2004	90	2009	2012+
2003	86	2011	2015
2002	89	2010	2014
2001	91	2006	2009+
2000	93	2008	2012
1999	92	2007	2011
1998	93	2006	2010+
1997	93	2002	2005+
1995	85	1997	2000
1994	91	1999	2002

MAIL COACH VIOGNIER (formerly Curagee Viognier)

RATING 5

Heathcote	$20–$29
Current vintage: 2006	**87**

Developed and toasty, likely to age quite quickly, this round, generous and spirity young viognier has a lightly spicy fragrance of lemon, cloves and cinnamon, with a hint of apricot blossom. Toasty and forward, it presents a pleasing length and juicy presence of spicy, apricot-like fruit, finishing with a slight hotness. Likely to become quite brassy.

2006	87	2007	2008
2005	87	2006	2007+
2004	87	2005	2006+
2003	86	2004	2005
2002	86	2003	2004+
2001	88	2003	2006
2000	91	2002	2005
1998	89	2000	2003

Heggies Vineyard

Heggies Range Road, Eden Valley SA 5235. Tel: (08) 8561 3200. Fax: (08) 8561 3393.
Website: www.heggiesvineyard.com Email: info@heggiesvineyard.com
Region: **Eden Valley** Winemaker: **Peter Gambetta** Viticulturist: **Robin Nettelbeck**
Chief Executive: **Robert Hill Smith**

While the new Heggies releases include a spectacular Viognier, it also features a new I Block Reserve Chardonnay sourced from a parcel within the vineyard planted to four different Bernard clones. The first release of this wine, from 2005, has produced a sumptuous, smooth and seamless wine of great class (94/100, drink 2007–2010+), while the 'standard' wine is very good, but slightly broad and flabby by comparison. There is also a classy new 2001 Reserve Riesling (95/100, drink 2009-2013+), which is about half-way to maturity.

CHARDONNAY

RATING 4

Eden Valley	$20–$29
Current vintage: 2005	**90**

Restrained and lightly buttery aromas of grapefruit, quince and melon overlie sweet vanilla oak and lightly spicy, mineral influences. Smooth and creamy, with undertones of charcuterie and leesy complexity, its ripe and slightly spirity palate of melon and grapefruit just becomes a fraction broad and flabby before finishing with refreshing acids. Would rate higher if slightly tighter.

2005	90	2007	2010
2004	92	2006	2009
2003	90	2005	2008
2002	93	2004	2007
2001	90	2003	2006
2000	85	2002	2005
1998	89	2000	2003+
1997	87	1999	2002
1996	87	1998	2001
1995	91	2000	2003

MERLOT (formerly Cabernet Blend)

RATING 5

Eden Valley	$20–$29
Current vintage: 2005	**83**

Framed by firmish, powdery tannins and supported by plenty of assertive vanilla oak, this rather meaty and herbaceous merlot lacks genuine length and ripeness, finishing rather dilute and lacking in intensity. Its cherry/plum fruit overlies evident herbaceous and menthol characters.

2005	83	2007	2010
2002	89	2007	2010+
2001	93	2008	2013
2000	87	2002	2005+
1999	88	2001	2004+
1998	89	2003	2006
1996	90	2001	2004
1995	90	2000	2003+
1994	93	2002	2006
1993	94	2001	2005
1992	87	2000	2004
1991	88	1996	1999
1990	91	1998	2002

RIESLING

Eden Valley	$12–$19
Current vintage: 2006	**91**

Gentle and generous, supple and restrained, this brightly scented and floral young riesling has a slightly funky perfume of citrus and wet stone aromas. Smooth and seamless, its long, creamy expression of delicate pear, apple and lime juice flavour has a real juicy quality. It finishes with fresh, gentle acids.

2006	91	2011	2014
2005	95	2013	2017
2004	93	2009	2012+
2003	92	2008	2011+
2002	92	2010	2024+
2001	90	2006	2009
2000	90	2005	2008+
1999	95	2007	2011
1998	96	2006	2010+
1997	89	2002	2005
1996	88	2003	2007
1995	94	2003	2007

VIOGNIER

RATING 3

Eden Valley	$20–$29
Current vintage: 2005	**95**

An excellent viognier whose pungent, floral aromas of rose oil and apricot blossom overlie complex undertones of smoked meats, spice and creamy, leesy influences. Nutty and slightly meaty, its brightly fruited palate reveals complex, vibrant fruit characters, retaining plenty of intensity and freshness before finishing long and savoury. It's very classy indeed, with terrific underlying firmness and structure.

2005	95	2007	2010
2004	92	2005	2006+
2003	89	2004	2005+
2002	94	2004	2007
2001	90	2002	2003+
2000	89	2002	2005
1999	82	2001	2004
1998	93	2000	2003
1997	92	1999	2002
1996	86	1997	1998

Henschke

Henschke Road, Keyneton SA 5353. Tel: (08) 8564 8223. Fax: (08) 8564 8294.
Website: www.henschke.com.au Email: info@henschke.com.au
Region: **Eden Valley** Winemaker: **Stephen Henschke** Viticulturist: **Prue Henschke**
Chief Executive: **Stephen Henschke**

Henschke is a small and iconic Australian winery in Eden Valley with access to several landmark old vine vineyards in the Eden Valley itself, plus some steep but relatively modern plantings at Lenswood in the Adelaide Hills. The ongoing release of the company's premier red wines from the watershed 2002 vintage has continued with excellent wines from not only the superlative 2004 season, but more importantly, perhaps, from the ultra-challenging 2003.

ABBOTTS PRAYER

RATING 4

Adelaide Hills	$50–$99
Current vintage: 2002	**86**

Dusty, sweet and perfumed aromas of mulberries, cassis and violets reveal undertones of capsicum and tomato stalk. Its green-edged palate lacks a genuine core and length of fruit, culminating in a sappy, slippery finish of underripe tannins and acids.

2002	86	2004	2007+
2001	90	2009	2013
2000	85	2002	2005
1999	92	2011	2019
1998	82	2000	2003
1997	87	2005	2009
1996	94	2004	2008+
1995	94	2003	2007
1994	95	2006	2014
1993	94	2005	2013
1992	92	2000	2004
1991	93	2003	2011
1990	96	2002	2010

CRANES EDEN VALLEY CHARDONNAY

RATING 5

Eden Valley	$30–$49
Current vintage: 2006	**88**

Vibrant, floral and slightly confectionary aromas of white peach and citrus blossom overlie some smart clove/vanilla/cinnamon-like oak. Fine and elegant, dusty and savoury, it's long, vibrant and pleasingly restrained, finishing with fresh acids and tightly knit oak. Honest, clean and refreshing, but just lacking genuine distinction.

2006	88	2008	2011
2002	87	2004	2007
2000	82	2002	2005
1999	82	2000	2001
1998	92	2003	2006
1997	90	2002	2005
1996	93	2001	2004
1995	90	1997	2000
1994	93	1999	2002
1993	91	1995	1998
1992	92	1997	2000
1991	94	1996	1999

Lenswood $30–$49
Current vintage: 2005 87

Slightly cooked and brassy, this rather old-fashioned chardonnay reveals creamy, lightly smoky and quite floral aromas of fresh lemon and melon. It's smooth and forward, rather candied and funky, with plenty of sweet and slightly toasty oak to support its modest fruit. It finishes with clean acidity.

2005	87	2008	2009
2004	92	2006	2009
2002	87	2004	2007
2000	87	2002	2005
1999	84	2001	2004
1998	94	2003	2006+
1997	87	2002	2005
1996	94	2001	2004
1995	90	1997	2000
1994	94	1999	2003

CYRIL HENSCHKE CABERNET SAUVIGNON

RATING 3

Eden Valley $100–$200
Current vintage: 2003 93

A very good red from a difficult season. Lightly smoky and cedary, its vibrant bouquet of cassis, mulberries, dark plums and cigarboxes overlies nuances of violets, dark chocolate, mint and baked earth. Plush, smooth and sumptuous, its intense expression of fruit has a slightly cooked and currant-like aspect, but finishes with pleasing freshness. Surprisingly elegant, it's supported by supple, fine-grained tannins.

2003	93	2015	2023
2002	96	2014	2022
2001	88	2009	2013
2000	88	2005	2008
1999	81	2004	2007
1997	88	2005	2009
1996	95	2008	2016+
1995	91	2003	2007
1994	89	2002	2006+
1993	87	2001	2005
1992	94	2004	2012
1991	95	2003	2011
1990	95	2002	2010
1989	91	2001	2009
1988	96	1996	2000
1987	87	1992	1995
1986	92	1998	2003
1985	93	1997	2002
1984	95	1992	1996
1983	90	1995	2000
1982	87	1987	1990
1981	94	1993	1998

EUPHONIUM KEYNETON ESTATE

RATING 3

Eden Valley $30–$49
Current vintage: 2004 94

An intense, elegant and measured red that takes time to open in the glass. Its minty, violet-like perfume of redcurrant, cassis, plums and fresh cedar/vanilla oak overlies a suggestion of dark chocolate and a slightly herbal hint of white pepper. Long, smooth and tightly knit, its vibrant palate of spicy berry and plum-like flavour overlies a dusty, fine-grained spine. It finishes savoury and slightly mineral with a persistent core of fruit.

2004	94	2016	2024
2002	95	2014	2022+
2001	86	2006	2009
1999	86	2004	2007
1998	92	2006	2010
1997	87	2002	2005
1996	93	2004	2008+
1994	93	2002	2006
1993	94	2005	2013
1992	93	1997	2000
1991	95	2003	2011
1990	88	1995	1998
1989	87	1994	1997
1988	93	1996	2000
1987	85	1992	1995
1986	94	1998	2003

GILES PINOT NOIR

RATING 5

Lenswood $30–$49
Current vintage: 2004 88

Slightly jammy and confectionary aromas of wild berries, plums and sweet vanilla oak reveal reductive and meaty undertones. Supple and sappy, its juicy Beaune-like palate reveals some pure berry/cherry fruit, but lacks genuine length and follow-through, finishing quite oaky and porty, with creamy, mouth-coating tannins.

2004	88	2006	2009+
2003	87	2005	2008
2002	82	2004	2007
2001	87	2003	2006+
1999	89	2004	2007
1998	84	2003	2006+
1997	90	2002	2005
1996	90	2001	2004
1994	89	1999	2002

Lenswood $20–$29
Current vintage: 2005   93

Lightly sweet and surprisingly broad and generous for this region, this slightly reductive and mineral riesling has a toasty fragrance of lime juice and candied citrus peel. Very concentrated and lemony, its palate reveals length, balance and harmony, with rich, generous citrus flavour becoming rather crunchy at the finish.

2005	93	2010	2013+
2004	90	2006	2009
2002	87	2004	2007
2001	82	2003	2006
2000	87	2002	2005+
1999	90	2001	2004
1998	93	2003	2006+
1997	94	2005	2009
1996	95	2004	2008
1995	93	2003	2007
1994	93	2002	2006
1993	94	1998	2001

HENRY'S SEVEN (Shiraz, Grenache, Viognier)   RATING 4

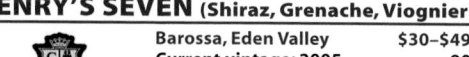

Barossa, Eden Valley $30–$49
Current vintage: 2005   90

Slightly jammy but right on the style button, this spicy, floral and vibrant young blend marries spicy, briary flavours of blueberries, cassis, dark plums and blackberries with cedary oak and nuances of clove, cinnamon and undergrowth. It's smooth and elegant, with a fine length of deep, dark fruit supported by silky tannins and finishing savoury, but with a hint of oaky sweetness.

2005	90	2007	2010
2004	93	2009	2012
2003	91	2005	2008
2002	89	2004	2007+
2001	90	2003	2006

HILL OF GRACE   RATING 1

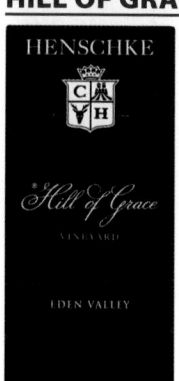

Eden Valley $200+
Current vintage: 2002   97

A near-perfect Eden Valley shiraz whose deep scents of violets, cassis, cherries, mulberries and ripe plums overlie sweet cedar/vanilla/coconut ice-like oak, pepper, musky spice and nuances of undergrowth. It's supremely smooth and unctuous, presenting an intense, long and vibrant core of dark berry/plum fruit with a slightly wild and briary aspect. Underpinned by classically fine and powdery tannin, it finishes with lingering fruit and licorice-like influences. Artfully balanced and integrated.

2002	97	2022	2032+
2001	91	2009	2013+
1999	90	2011	2019
1998	96	2018	2028
1997	95	2017	2027
1996	97	2008	2016+
1995	93	2015	2025
1994	93	2002	2006+
1993	91	2013	2023
1992	95	2012	2022
1991	95	2011	2021
1990	94	2002	2010+
1989	87	1994	1997
1988	96	2008	2018
1987	88	1999	2007+
1986	97	2006	2016
1985	91	2005	2015
1984	88	1996	2004
1983	84	1991	1995
1982	89	1994	2002
1981	84	1986	1989
1980	89	1992	2000
1979	90	1991	1999
1978	95	1998	2008
1977	90	1989	1997+
1976	94	1996	2006
1975	87	1983	1987
1973	95	1993	2003
1972	94	1992	2002

JOHANN'S GARDEN (Grenache, Shiraz & Mourvèdre)

RATING **3**

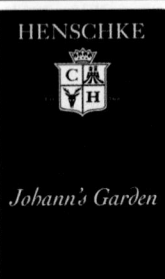

Barossa Valley $30–$49
Current vintage: 2005 **94**

Stylish and Rhôney, this vibrant wine combines deliciously intense fruit with complexity, shape and savoury quality. Its ethereal, floral perfume reveals a plummy aspect of grenache, with undertones of dark berries. It's sumptuous, ripe and juicy, with intense, mouthfilling fruit finely integrated with a powdery spine of dusty, crunchy tannin.

2005	94	2010	2013
2004	91	2006	2009+
2003	95	2008	2011+
2002	90	2004	2007+
2001	93	2006	2009

JULIUS RIESLING

RATING **3**

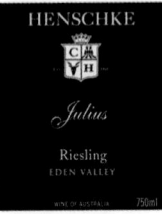

Eden Valley $20–$29
Current vintage: 2006 **93**

A very pretty medium to long term riesling with some stylish elements of austerity and racy acidity. Scented with a musky perfume of fresh lemon rind and lime juice, it presents a long and lingering palate whose refreshing citrus flavours are underpinned by a drying chalkiness. There's plenty of juicy richness and pleasing concentration of flavour, all of which is neatly balanced by a racy acidity.

2006	93	2011	2014+
2005	93	2013	2017+
2004	93	2009	2012+
2003	90	2008	2011
2002	94	2010	2014
2001	88	2009	2013
2000	84	2002	2005
1999	93	2004	2007
1998	91	2006	2010
1997	94	2005	2009
1996	94	2004	2008
1995	91	1997	2000
1994	95	2006	2014
1993	95	2000	2005
1992	94	2000	2004
1991	95	1999	2003
1990	95	1995	1998
1989	87	1994	1997
1988	88	1993	1996
1987	94	1999	2007
1986	90	1991	1994

LOUIS EDEN VALLEY SEMILLON

RATING **4**

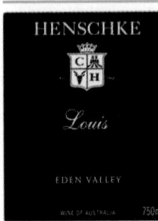

Eden Valley $20–$29
Current vintage: 2006 **93**

Delicate, floral aromas of apple, melon and lemon with a light lift of grassiness and lemon blossom precede an elegant, smooth and creamy palate. Lightly oaked, with a toasty expression of fresh fruit and soft acids, it's very approachable and fluffy, finishing with lingering flavour and a refreshing tightness.

2006	93	2011	2014+
2005	90	2010	2013
2002	90	2007	2010
2000	87	2002	2005
1999	83	2001	2004
1998	88	2003	2006
1997	90	2002	2005
1996	86	1998	2003
1995	94	2000	2003
1994	93	2002	2006
1993	95	1998	2001

MOUNT EDELSTONE

RATING **2**

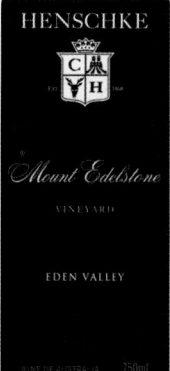

Eden Valley	$50–$99
Current vintage: 2004	**95**

Very smooth, concentrated and stylish, this is a sweet, luscious shiraz of full to medium weight. Its musky, peppery perfume of blackcurrants, plums, licorice, cloves and cinnamon is backed by a lightly smoky, coconut crème-like oak. It's long, dark and sumptuous, with a peppery palate saturated with small berry fruits and framed by firm, pliant tannins. It finishes with lingering dark-stained fruit and sweet oak.

2004	95	2016	2024
2003	95	2015	2023+
2002	97	2014	2022+
2001	92	2009	2013
2000	82	2002	2005+
1999	92	2007	2011
1998	88	2000	2003+
1997	87	2005	2009
1996	90	2004	2008
1995	93	2007	2015
1994	92	2002	2006
1993	95	2005	2013
1992	94	2004	2012
1991	95	2003	2011
1990	95	2002	2010
1989	89	1997	2003
1988	94	2000	2005
1987	87	1995	2001
1986	93	1998	2003
1985	87	2005	2015
1984	88	1996	2001
1983	90	1995	2000
1982	90	1994	1999

Hewitson

66 London Road, Mile End SA 5031. Tel: (08) 8443 6466. Fax: (08) 8443 6866.
Website: www.hewitson.com.au Email: dean@hewitson.com.au

Regions: **Barossa Valley, Fleurieu Peninsula** Winemaker: **Dean Hewitson** Chief Executive: **Dean Hewitson**

Dean Hewitson appears to be enjoying himself thoroughly at his self-appointed task of making small parcels of distinctive wine from ancient vineyards. His wines reflect not only a technical stability and correctness, but a level of artisanship rare in Australian wine. Typically full-flavoured, firm and tightly structured, his savoury and earthy reds combine deep, complex and concentrated fruit quality with rusticity and flair. The Mad Hatter from 2005 is a terrific effort.

EDEN VALLEY RIESLING

RATING **4**

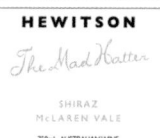

Eden Valley	$20–$29
Current vintage: 2006	**88**

Pleasingly open and flavoursome, but perhaps lacking a little mid-palate intensity, this fragrant young riesling reveals a limey, zesty and floral perfume with mineral undertones. Slightly soapy, its juicy and slightly oily palate delivers attractive citrusy riesling flavour, finishing with tangy acidity.

2006	88	2008	2011
2005	92	2010	2013+
2004	90	2009	2012
2003	91	2008	2011
2002	88	2004	2007
1998	90	2003	2006

THE MAD HATTER SHIRAZ (formerly l'Oizeau)

RATING **3**

McLaren Vale	$30–$49
Current vintage: 2005	**92**

A very good shiraz from this unpleasantly hot vintage. Its deep, nearly baked aromas of black-berries and dark plums overlie slightly meaty, currant-like nuances, while there's just a hint of varnish. Sumptuous and juicy, its spicy, full-bodied palate is supported by fine, chalky tannin and packed with searingly intense and almost gamey cassis, raspberry and cherry-like fruit. It finishes with length and freshness, retaining pleasing fruit sweetness.

2005	92	2010	2013+
2004	90	2012	2016+
2002	93	2010	2014+
2001	88	2003	2006+
2000	93	2008	2012+
1999	86	2004	2007
1997	87	1999	2002
1996	86	2001	2004

MISS HARRY (Grenache Shiraz Mourvèdre)

RATING **4**

HEWITSON

Miss Harry

DRY GROWN & ANCIENT
BAROSSA VALLEY

750ML AUSTRALIAN WINE

Barossa Valley $20–$29
Current vintage: 2006   91

Fresh and juicy, then dry and savoury, this spicy, ripe and plummy young blend has a slightly meaty aroma of faintly baked dark plum and berry fruit over earthy, floral undertones. Smooth and vibrant, its generous cherry, plum and blackberry flavours are framed by pliant, silky tannins and deliver plenty of fruit sweetness before a fresh, lingering finish of licorice, cloves and dark cherries.

2006	91	2008	2011+
2005	91	2007	2010
2004	90	2005	2006+
2003	90	2004	2005+
2002	91	2003	2004+
2001	90	2003	2006

NED & HENRY'S SHIRAZ

RATING **4**

HEWITSON

Ned & Henry's

SHIRAZ
BAROSSA VALLEY

750ml AUSTRALIAN WINE

Barossa Valley $30–$49
Current vintage: 2006   89

A well composed and varietal shiraz that neatly balances its regional intensity and ripeness with a firmish, pliant structure. Scented with violets and white pepper, its aromas of cassis, raspberries and dark plums reveal a slight meatiness. Backed by smooth, vanilla oak, its long, juicy and bacony expression of plum and small berry fruit finishes slightly meaty and cooked, but with a hint of mineral and dark olive.

2006	89	2011	2014+
2005	89	2007	2010
2004	90	2007	2009
2002	90	2004	2007+

OLD GARDEN MOURVÈDRE

RATING **4**

HEWITSON

Old Garden

MOURVÈDRE
BAROSSA VALLEY

750ML AUSTRALIAN WINE

Barossa Valley $30–$49
Current vintage: 2005   81

Lacking genuine ripeness and rather reliant on mocha/vanilla oak for length and sweetness, this early-drinking red has a dark, meaty and smoky aroma of plums, raisins and dark berries that lacks genuine punch and intensity. There's an initial burst of small berry and dark cherry/plum fruit on the palate, but it finishes thin and herbal.

2005	81	2007	2010
2004	87	2006	2009
2003	91	2005	2008+
2002	92	2010	2014+
2001	91	2009	2013
2000	95	2012	2020

Hill Smith Estate

Flaxmans Valley Road, Eden Valley SA 5235. Tel: (08) 8561 3200. Fax: (08) 8561 3393.
Website: www.hillsmithestate.com Email: info@hillsmithestate.com

Region: **Eden Valley** Winemaker: **Kevin Glastonbury** Viticulturist: **Robin Nettelbeck**
Chief Executive: **Robert Hill Smith**

Hill Smith Estate is a mature Eden Valley vineyard linked through ownership to the Yalumba winery. Its typically grassy Sauvignon Blanc — its sole remaining wine — is usually refreshing and tightly defined.

SAUVIGNON BLANC

RATING **5**

Eden Valley $20–$29
Current vintage: 2006   87

Attractively varietal, with a lightly grassy, smoky and asparagus-like aroma of delicate gooseberry, passionfruit and melon backed by suggestions of minerals and nettles. Lively and fresh, but fractionally hollow in mid-palate, it's a clean, herbaceous and refreshing expression of sauvignon blanc.

2006	87	2007	2008
2005	90	2006	2007
2004	89	2005	2006+
2003	90	2004	2005+
2002	88	2003	2004
2001	81	2001	2002
2000	81	2001	2002
1999	92	2000	2001

Hollick

Corner Ravenswood Lane & Riddoch Highway, Coonawarra SA 5263. Tel: (08) 8737 2318.
Fax: (08) 8737 2952. Website: www.hollick.com Email: admin@hollick.com

Region: **Coonawarra** Winemakers: **Ian Hollick, Matt Caldersmith** Viticulturist: **Ian Hollick**
Chief Executive: **Ian Hollick**

The good news for Hollick fans is that the company has turned the corner with its red wines. Its 2005 reds represent a substantial improvement in richness of fruit, polish and structure. This family-owned wine company, found in the heart of the Coonawarra region, should now be able to realise the full potential of its mature and well-sited vineyard.

CABERNET SAUVIGNON   RATING **4**

Coonawarra	$20–$29
Current vintage: 2005	**91**

Fine and elegant, this charming cabernet has a sweet floral perfume of violets, blackcurrants, plums and dried herbs, with undertones of mint and cedary oak. It's very slightly meaty, with a smooth, polished palate of vibrant, if uncomplicated flavours of fresh berry/cherry/plum-like fruit framed by powdery tannins and backed by dark chocolate/cedary oak.

2005	91	2013	2017
2004	88	2009	2012
2003	86	2005	2008+
2002	90	2007	2010+

RAVENSWOOD (Cabernet Sauvignon)   RATING **5**

Coonawarra	$50–$99
Current vintage: 2002	**88**

Quite deep and developed, this rather old-fashioned and herbal style has an autumnal, oaky bouquet of small berries, plums and cedar/vanilla oak. It has a bright and lingering core of sweet and initially juicy blackberry and cassis-like flavour, and while it's backed by sweet newish oak, it does finish with distinctly green-edged notes.

2002	88	2007	2010
2001	84	2006	2009
2000	89	2005	2008
1999	84	2004	2007
1998	94	2006	2010+
1996	87	2001	2004
1994	89	2002	2006+
1993	92	2001	2005
1992	93	2000	2004
1991	95	2003	2011
1990	94	2002	2010
1989	92	2001	2009
1988	93	2000	2005

RESERVE CHARDONNAY   RATING **5**

Coonawarra	$20–$29
Current vintage: 2005	**88**

Lively and slightly angular, this intense young wine has a citrus, melon and banana-like flavour backed by slightly raw vanilla oak. It's juicy and generous, with creamy, buttery undertones and a tangy, lemony and mineral finish. There's a little funkiness, but it's really rather uncomplicated, clean and refreshing.

2005	88	2007	2010
2004	80	2004	2005
2003	87	2005	2008
2002	89	2003	2004+

RIESLING   RATING **5**

Coonawarra	$12–$19
Current vintage: 2004	**87**

An early-drinking riesling whose honeyed aromas of pear, peaches and lemon detergent precede a juicy, forward palate of generous lime/lemon and apricot-like flavours. It finishes with some tightness, but with a metallic hint of green acidity.

2004	87	2005	2006+
2003	87	2005	2008
2002	85	2003	2004
2001	86	2003	2006
2000	87	2002	2005

SHIRAZ CABERNET SAUVIGNON

RATING **5**

| Coonawarra | $20–$29 |
| Current vintage: 2005 | 89 |

Honest and flavoursome, with just a little style, it has a peppery, spicy aroma of cassis, blackberries and lightly smoky vanilla oak lifted by a whiff of clove and cinnamon. Long, smooth and measured, its vibrant, juicy flavours of dark cherries and plums are sweetly oaked, finishing with fine tannins and a hint of licorice.

2005	89	2010	2013
2004	86	2006	2009
2002	84	2004	2007
2001	83	2003	2006
2000	90	2001	2002
1998	90	2000	2003+
1997	82	1999	2002

WILGHA SHIRAZ

RATING **5**

| Coonawarra | $30–$49 |
| Current vintage: 2005 | 90 |

A delicious, youthful wine with flavour, balance and structure. Peppery, violet-like aromas of blackberries, smoked bacon and cedar precede a smooth, elegant and sumptuous palate of vibrant blackberry, cassis and blueberry flavours framed by fine, powdery tannins. It finishes long and spicy, with refreshing acids.

2005	90	2010	2013+
2003	89	2008	2011
2002	83	2004	2007
2000	87	2002	2005
1999	88	2001	2004+
1998	81	2000	2003

Houghton

Dale Road, Middle Swan WA 6056. Tel: (08) 9274 5100. Fax: (08) 9250 3872.
Website: www.houghton-wines.com.au
Regions: **Various WA** Winemakers: **Robert Bowen, Ross Pamment, Simon Osicka** Viticulturist: **Ron Page**
Chief Executive: **John Grant**
Houghton is the major WA-based label and winemaking facility for The Hardy Wine Company. As such, it has the ability to source fruit from all over the State's various wine regions, including a number of special parcels that ultimately appear in the steadily increasing number of high-end labels such as the Gladstones Shiraz and Cabernet Sauvignon, as well as the Jack Mann cabernet blend, its leading wine.

CROFTERS CABERNET MERLOT

RATING **5**

Great Southern,	
Margaret River	$20–$29
Current vintage: 2004	90

Likely to become quite classy, this elegant and finely crafted cabernet blend matches blackberry and dark cherry-like fruit with cedar/vanilla oak and dusty undertones of dried herbs and menthol. Long and firm, with a powdery chassis of chalky tannin beneath its slightly closed and herbal palate, it's likely to fill out, finding more richness and balance.

2004	90	2012	2016
2003	86	2008	2011
2002	86	2007	2010
2001	87	2006	2009
2000	90	2008	2012+
1999	87	2007	2011
1998	88	2003	2006

FRANKLAND RIVER SHIRAZ

RATING **5**

| Frankland River | $20–$29 |
| Current vintage: 2003 | 86 |

This rather firm, unfinished and old-fashioned shiraz has very ripe, jammy and lightly spicy aromas of plums and blackcurrants backed by chocolate/mocha oak. Its porty, leathery and chocolate-like flavour is overwhelmed by an excessively raw and astringent coating of tannin. Lacks length and brightness.

2003	86	2008	2011
2002	88	2007	2010
2001	87	2006	2009+
2000	89	2008	2012
1999	90	2004	2007

GLADSTONES SHIRAZ

RATING **3**

Frankland River $50–$99
Current vintage: 2003 89

A rustic and meaty shiraz whose deep flavours of red and black berries are perhaps overwhelmed by an even more assertive extract and oakiness. Its smoky, charcuterie-like aromas of raspberries, dark cherries and cassis reveal undertones of dried herbs, while its deep, robust palate is framed by slightly blocky and raw-edged tannins. It finishes with gamey and tomato-like undertones.

2003	89	2008	2011
2002	90	2010	2014+
2001	88	2009	2013+
2000	95	2012	2020
1999	96	2007	2011+

JACK MANN RED

RATING **2**

Various WA,
mainly Great Southern $50–$99
Current vintage: 2001 94

A deep, closed, brooding and rather old-fashioned wine with dark, minty aromas of cassis, plums and violets tightly knit with sweet vanilla and cedary oak. It's long, very firm and tight-fisted, with a dark, powerful core of concentrated fruit firmly wrapped around an astringent spine of drying, powdery tannin. Give it plenty of time to breath if you're thinking of opening it before it's really ready.

2004	97	2016	2024+
2003	91	2015	2023
2002	95	2014	2022+
2001	94	2011	2021+
2000	86	2008	2012+
1999	93	2011	2019
1998	96	2018	2028
1996	91	2008	2016
1995	93	2007	2015+
1994	95	2006	2014+

MARGARET RIVER CABERNET SAUVIGNON

RATING **4**

Margaret River $20–$29
Current vintage: 2002 88

Rather overpowering, mouth-coating tannins grip this slightly heavy-handed and juicy expression of blackberry, cherry and plum-like fruit. Its cedary bouquet reveals dusty, herbal and slightly cheesy undertones, while the firm and tightly-knit palate opens with richness and depth, but lacks great length and penetration.

2002	88	2007	2010+
2001	92	2009	2013
2000	90	2005	2008+
1999	85	2001	2004+

PEMBERTON CHARDONNAY

RATING **4**

Pemberton $20–$29
Current vintage: 2005 88

A competent chardonnay that is almost a great deal better. Its smoky aromas of grapefruit, pineapple and melon are backed by vanilla and matchstick-like oak, with undertones of butterscotch and lemon zest. Generous and juicy, it marries brightly lit fruit with malolactic undertones, assertive but measured oak and refreshing acidity. The only drawback is a slightly acrid and smoky presence that emerges after the finish.

2005	88	2007	2010
2004	90	2006	2009
2003	93	2005	2008+
2002	91	2004	2007+
2001	92	2003	2006

PEMBERTON SAUVIGNON BLANC

RATING **4**

Pemberton $20–$29
Current vintage: 2006 88

Fresh aromas of gooseberries and citrus fruit with herbal undertones precede a broad, rather generous palate of juicy forward flavours and some minerality. It finishes with some briny notes, but lacks genuine length.

2006	88	2006	2007+
2005	90	2006	2007+
2004	93	2005	2006+
2003	91	2003	2004+
2002	93	2003	2004+
2001	85	2002	2003

A B C D E F G **H** I J K L M N O P Q R S T U V W X Y Z

WHITE CLASSIC (formerly White Burgundy)

RATING 5

HOUGHTON

2006 VINTAGE
White Classic
The Original White Burgundy from Western Australia

Western Australia	$12–$19
Current vintage: 2006	**87**

Tropical, passionfruit-like and lightly grassy aromas precede a juicy, vibrant and early-drinking palate whose attractive bright fruit finishes with clean acids and a faint lingering sweetness.

2006	87	2006	2007
2005	86	2005	2006
2004	86	2005	2006
2003	87	2003	2004+
2002	82	2002	2003
2001	87	2002	2003+
2000	77	2001	2002
1999	87	2001	2004
1998	87	2000	2003

Howard Park

Lot 377, Scotsdale Road, Denmark WA 6333. Tel: (08) 9848 2345. Fax: (08) 9848 2064.
Miamup Road, Cowaramup, WA, 6284 Tel: (08) 9756 5200. Fax: (08) 9756 5222.
Website: www.howardparkwines.com.au Email:hpw@hpw.com.au.

Regions: **Great Southern, Margaret River** Winemakers: **Tony Davis, Andy Browing, Matt Burton**
Viticulturist: **David Botting** Chief Executive: **Jeff Burch**

Howard Park now has a change in winemaking regime. Its best reds in recent years have not been its most expensive, but the Margaret River reds sold under its Leston label. Furthermore, while I have been critical of its white wines over the years, the last two vintages of Riesling and Chardonnay have been massively improved, the Chardonnay in particular. The only weakness at present appears to be with its Great Southern red fruit, which traditionally has provided the core of its flagship cabernet blend.

CABERNET SAUVIGNON MERLOT

RATING 4

HOWARD PARK

CABERNET SAUVIGNON
WESTERN AUSTRALIA

Great Southern, Margaret River	$50–$99
Current vintage: 2003	**88**

Closed, earthy and angular, this browning and slightly vegetal cabernet blend marries currant-like flavours of plums and blackberries with aggressive, cedary oak and rather a raw and drying astringency. Its under-ripe and over-cooked, with a meaty listlessness and a lack of genuine brightness. It should become a little more charming over the medium term.

2003	88	2011	2015
2002	88	2007	2010+
2001	89	2009	2013+
2000	90	2005	2008+
1999	92	2004	2007+
1998	83	2003	2006
1997	86	2002	2005+
1996	96	2008	2016
1995	83	2000	2003
1994	96	2014	2024
1993	92	2001	2005+
1992	97	2004	2012+
1991	93	2003	2011
1990	95	2002	2010+
1989	95	2001	2009
1988	96	2008	2018
1987	90	1995	1999+
1986	95	2006	2016

CHARDONNAY

RATING 3

HOWARD PARK

WESTERN AUSTRALIA
CHARDONNAY

Great Southern	$30–$49
Current vintage: 2005	**94**

Measured, fine and elegant, with delicate citrusy and tropical fruits tightly knit with nutty vanilla oak and creamy, leesy complexity. Lightly spicy, it's smooth and silky, with a fluffy palate of stonefruit, pear and apple leading towards a savoury finish of citrusy acids. Handsomely oaked, but carefully so.

2005	94	2010	2013+
2004	95	2009	2012
2003	89	2005	2008
2002	87	2004	2007
2001	86	2006	2009
2000	89	2002	2005
1999	90	2001	2004
1998	90	2000	2003
1997	87	1999	2002
1996	91	1998	2001
1995	94	2000	2003
1994	94	1999	2002
1993	93	1998	2001

LESTON CABERNET SAUVIGNON

RATING 3

| Margaret River | $30–$49 |
| Current vintage: 2004 | 93 |

Elegant, stylish and tightly crafted, this balanced and firmish cabernet has an intense bouquet of slightly meaty and gamey dark plum, blackberry and cassis-like aromas overlying sweet cedary oak and nuances of mint, mineral and dried herbs. Long, supple and deeply flavoured, its handsomely oaked and sumptuous palate is intermeshed with a firm spine of drying, bony tannins.

2004	93	2012	2016+
2003	93	2011	2015+
2002	89	2007	2010+
2001	90	2006	2009
2000	89	2005	2008+

LESTON SHIRAZ

RATING 4

| Margaret River | $30–$49 |
| Current vintage: 2004 | 92 |

A violet-like perfume of cassis, raspberries, redcurrant and sweet cedar/vanilla oak is backed by spicy, licorice-like undertones. Fine, polished and elegant, its smooth, willowy and spotless palate of medium to full weight bursts with intense flavours of red and black berries with nuances of dark plums and tomato stalk. It finishes savoury, with a fine coating of tight-knit tannins.

2004	92	2009	2012
2003	89	2008	2011
2002	88	2004	2007+
2001	88	2003	2006+
2000	91	2005	2008
1999	87	2001	2004

RIESLING

RATING 3

| Great Southern | $20–$29 |
| Current vintage: 2006 | 93 |

Howard Park has long been associated with complex and long-living riesling from WA's Great Southern region, ever since the first stellar wine of John Wade's from 1986. A heady, musky and floral traminer-like perfume of fresh apple, pear and lime precedes a long, fine and supple palate whose racy, brightly lit fruit is neatly wrapped in a taut, refreshing cut of citrusy acidity. Very elegant, precisely sculpted and vibrant, without any of the sweet-sour acidity that has been a feature of some recent vintages.

2006	93	2014	2018
2005	93	2010	2013+
2004	87	2006	2009
2003	95	2011	2015
2002	84	2004	2007+
2001	88	2006	2009
2000	87	2008	2012
1999	86	2001	2004+
1998	92	2003	2006
1997	94	2005	2009+
1996	93	2004	2008
1995	94	2000	2003+
1994	92	2002	2006
1993	95	2001	2005
1992	95	2004	2012
1991	94	2003	2011

SCOTSDALE CABERNET SAUVIGNON

RATING 5

| Great Southern | $30–$49 |
| Current vintage: 2004 | 81 |

Hollow, thin and green, with a polished cut of sweet vanilla and cedary oak that fails to compensate for the greenish and under-ripe small red berry flavours that are framed by a sappy extract of metallic tannin.

2004	81	2006	2009
2003	86	2008	2011
2001	93	2006	2009+
2000	82	2002	2005
1999	87	2001	2004

SCOTSDALE SHIRAZ

RATING 5

Great Southern	$30–$49
Current vintage: 2004	86

Rather simple, cooked and oaky, with herbal undertones. Ground coffee and mocha oak tends to dominate meaty aromas of prune and currant-like fruit, while the palate is excessively reliant on its sweet oak for brightness and length. Meaty and dehydrated, it falls away towards a flat and sappy finish of lingering herbal influences.

2004	86	2006	2009
2003	89	2005	2008
2002	93	2007	2010
2001	88	2003	2006+
2000	91	2002	2005+

Huntington Estate

Cassilis Road, Mudgee NSW 2850. Tel: (02) 6373 3825. Fax: (02) 6373 3730. Email: huntwine@hwy.com.au

Region: **Mudgee** Winemaker: **Tim Stevens** Viticulturist: **Tim Stevens** Chief Executive: **Syzan Martin**

Now owned by Tim and Connie Stevens of nearby Abercorn, Huntington Estate makes ripe, firm and rustic red wines that offer both value and character. Its Special Reserve releases offer an extra degree of intensity, evolution and structure, and receive additional time in newer oak. 2002 was the best Huntington red vintage for several years, while the cabernets from 2003 are rustic and charming, but rather meaty.

CABERNET SAUVIGNON

RATING 5

Mudgee	$12–$19
Current vintage: 2003	89

Generous, ripe and flavoursome, this older style cabernet has a juicy, sweet aroma of blackberries, cassis and dark plums over light cedar/vanilla oak, with dusty herbal undertones. Smooth and dark-fruited, its vibrant palate of small berries, plums and cedary oak is coated with firm, grainy tannin. Long and just slightly raw-edged in its comparative youth, it's a charming rustic style.

2003	89	2011	2015+
2002	90	2010	2014+
2001	87	2009	2013
1999	89	2007	2011+
1998	88	2006	2010
1997	85	2002	2005+
1995	88	2003	2007
1994	88	2002	2006
1993	89	2001	2005
1992	93	2004	2012
1991	90	1996	1999

RESERVE CABERNET SAUVIGNON

RATING 4

Mudgee	$20–$29
Current vintage: 2003	88

Rustic, meaty and leathery, this youngish, slightly raw and aggressive cabernet simply needs time to dampen down. Its earthy and slightly baked aromas of dark plums and blackberries precede a robust, powdery and grippy palate whose almost currant-like fruit is backed by a faint herbal aspect.

2003	88	2011	2015+
2002	91	2014	2022
2001	93	2013	2021
1999	92	2011	2019
1997	87	2005	2009
1994	80	2002	2006

RESERVE SHIRAZ

RATING 5

Mudgee	$20–$29
Current vintage: 2002	89

An oaky and spirity Mudgee red that needs time. Its assertively wooded and slightly meaty aromas of blackberry and redcurrant confiture reveal nuances of polished leather and clove-like spiciness. Firm and sinewy, its deeply fruited palate of black and red berries is presently overawed by its rather raw and angular oak, but should have what it takes to come together.

2002	89	2010	2014+
2001	87	2006	2009
1999	86	2004	2007

SEMILLON

Mudgee $12–$19
Current vintage: 2006 86

Clean and forward this juicy, early-drinking semillon has a fresh, lime juice and melon-like aroma backed by lightly herbal hints of green olives. Its fresh but slightly candied palate of lemon and melon flavour lacks great length, finishing spicy and slightly attenuated with citrusy acids. Should flesh out a little.

2006	86	2007	2008+
2005	89	2007	2010+
2004	82	2005	2006
2003	83	2005	2008
2002	87	2004	2007
2000	90	2002	2005
1999	84	2001	2004
1998	86	2000	2003
1997	90	2002	2005
1996	93	2001	2004
1995	92	2000	2003

SHIRAZ

Mudgee $12–$19
Current vintage: 2002 90

An oaky and spirity Mudgee red that needs time. Its assertively wooded and slightly meaty aromas of blackberry and redcurrant confiture reveal nuances of polished leather and clove-like spiciness. Firm and sinewy, its deeply fruited palate of black and red berries is presently over-awed by its rather raw and angular oak, but should have what it takes to come together.

2002	90	2010	2014+
2001	84	2003	2006+
1999	87	2004	2007+
1998	81	2003	2006
1997	90	2005	2009
1995	89	2003	2007+
1994	86	1999	2002
1993	95	2005	2013
1992	89	1997	2000
1991	91	1999	2003

'i'

RMB 555 Old Moorooduc Road, Tuerong Vic 3933. Tel: (03) 5974 4400. Fax: (03) 5974 1155.
Website: www.dromanaestate.com.au Email: info@dromanaestate.com.au

Regions: **Alpine Valleys, Mornington Peninsula** Winemaker: **Rollo Crittenden** Viticulturist: **Rollo Crittenden**
Chief Executive: **Richard Green**

Made by Dromana Estate, this range of Italian-inspired wines pioneered varieties like arneis and dolcetto (when made in an Italian fashion) in Australia. It was also one of the first Australian makers of nebbiolo, barbera and sangiovese. While the intention remains, it appears that the fire is not burning with the same intensity as before, which has helped a few other makers surpass its more recent efforts.

ARNEIS

King Valley,
Mornington Peninsula $20–$29
Current vintage: 2005 83

Honeyed, estery and herbaceous, with spicy, rather spiky pear-like aromas backed by candied suggestions of barley sugar. Awkward and slightly sweet, it's juicy and generous, with a broad palate of pear and apple notes that finishes rather green-edged.

2005	83	2006	2007+
2004	87	2006	2009
2003	90	2003	2004
2002	77	2002	2003
2001	89	2003	2006
2000	89	2001	2002+
1999	86	2000	2001

BARBERA

Alpine Valleys $20–$29
Current vintage: 2002 80

Cooked, meaty and varnishy, revealing under-and over-ripe sweet and moderately intense flavours of black and red berries with greenish, herbaceous undertones. Medium in weight, its spicy palate lacks length and structure, finishing with a varnishy and tomatoey aspect.

2002	80	2004	2007
2001	89	2003	2006
2000	89	2001	2002+
1999	86	2000	2001
1998	84	2000	2003
1997	89	2002	2005
1996	89	1998	2001+
1995	90	2000	2003

NEBBIOLO

RATING **5**

NEBBIOLO

2001   750ml

Alpine Valleys $20–$29
Current vintage: 2002   89

Presently raw-edged and varnishy, this powerful, drying and earthy wine delivers a meaty, slighted stewy expression of plums and black cherries with tarry undertones. It's substantial and concentrated, and should come together with bottle-age.

2002	89	2010	2014+
2001	83	2006	2009
2000	88	2005	2008
1999	89	2007	2011
1998	93	2003	2006+
1997	91	2002	2005+
1996	88	2004	2008
1995	89	2002	2007
1994	87	2002	2006
1993	83	1998	2001

SANGIOVESE

RATING **4**

GARRY CRITTENDEN

SANGIOVESE

2003   750ml

Alpine Valleys $20–$29
Current vintage: 2004   87

Fresh, slightly leafy and dusty aromas of raspberries and cherries are lifted by floral undertones. Supple, smooth and vibrant, it's forward and juicy, but with modestly intense red berry/cherry flavour backed by fine, chalky tannins. It finishes clean and savoury, with a slightly herbal edge.

2004	87	2006	2009
2003	87	2004	2005+
2002	84	2004	2007
2001	90	2003	2006
2000	89	2001	2002
1999	94	2004	2007
1998	93	2000	2003+
1997	89	1999	2002
1996	90	2001	2004

Irvine Wines

Roeslers Road, Eden Valley SA 5235. Tel: (08) 8564 1046. Fax: (08) 8546 1314.
Website www.irvinewines.com.au Email: merlotbiz@irvinewines.com.au

Region: **Eden Valley** Winemakers: **James & Joanne Irvine** Viticulturist: **James Irvine** Chief Executive: **James Irvine**

James Irvine has achieved an international reputation for his robust and extensively oak-matured Grand Merlot. Made in a traditional Australian fashion, it has made a habit of collecting major international awards. He has recently introduced The Baroness, a merlot-based wine whose first two releases have also contained cabernet sauvignon and cabernet franc. Making the matter slightly confusing, these wines are also multi-vintage blends encompassing a range between 1998 and 2001. Regrettably, a series of unfortunate incidents will delay the release of the next Grand Merlot.

GRAND MERLOT

RATING **4**

Eden Valley $50–$99
Current vintage: 2002   87

A smooth and carefully handled merlot whose slightly jammy expression of blackcurrant, dark plum and mulberry flavour can't quite conceal an underlying thread of herbaceousness. There's a meaty and vegetal aspect about its violet-like perfume, while its plump and succulent palate of vibrant fruit and restrained cedar/chocolate oak finishes with a disappointing note of capsicum and green bean.

2002	87	2007	2010+
1999	90	2007	2011
1998	91	2003	2006+
1997	87	2005	2009
1996	89	2004	2008
1995	92	2003	2007
1994	95	2006	2014
1993	95	2005	2013
1992	89	2000	2004
1991	94	1999	2003
1990	93	2002	2010

Jacob's Creek

Barossa Valley Way, Rowland Flat SA 5352. Tel: (08) 8521 3111. Fax: (08) 8521 3100.
Website www.jacobscreek.com.au

Region: **Southern Australia** Winemakers: **Philip Laffer, Bernard Hickin, Susan Mickan**
Viticulturist: **Joy Dick** Chief Executive: **Laurent Lacassgne**

Today the Jacob's Creek label encompasses a number of wines that were previously sold under the Orlando banner. Of these, the Centenary Hill Shiraz and Johann Shiraz Cabernet from 2002 are simply outstanding. I am constantly impressed by the value for money represented by all these wines, especially the Reserve level wines, which deliver plenty of bang for their buck. The St Hugo Cabernet Sauvignon produced a classic in 2004, and a recent vertical tasting underlined the longevity and quality of this popular wine.

CENTENARY HILL SHIRAZ   RATING 2

Barossa Valley $30–$49
Current vintage: 2002   97

A truly exceptional Barossa shiraz whose superlative expression of vibrant fruit integrates tightly with excellent oak and fine, bony tannins. Its violet-like perfume of cassis, plums and raspberries is unusually floral and heady, revealing superbly measured walnut and cedar-like oak. Long, fine and elegant, it offers classic Barossa intensity and spiciness, with cloves, cinnamon and white pepper highlighting its lingering core of pristine liqueur cherry fruit. Finishing long and savoury, it's an essay in intensity, balance and harmony.

2002	97	2022	2032
1999	95	2011	2019
1998	88	2006	2010
1997	90	2009	2017
1996	94	2008	2016
1995	94	2003	2007
1994	96	2006	2014+

CHARDONNAY

Southern Australia $5–$11
Current vintage: 2006   86

Candied and citrusy, with undertones of sweet vanilla oak, tropical fruit and sweetcorn, it's smooth and vibrant, with pleasing intensity and brightness. Clean and refreshing but fractionally short, its melon and citrusy palate is backed by cashew/vanilla oak.

2006	86	2006	2007+
2005	86	2005	2006+
2004	89	2005	2006+
2003	86	2004	2005
2002	82	2002	2003
2001	82	2001	2002

JOHANN SHIRAZ CABERNET (formerly Limited Release)   RATING 2

Southern Australia $50–$99
Current vintage: 2002   95

Sumptuous and bruising, it's packed with meaty, black and briary fruit amply balanced by sweet, toasty cedar/vanilla oak and firm, presently rather blocky tannins. Dense and deeply layered, with thick, concentrated and profoundly ripened fruit, assertive oak and a robust, drying astringency. Bordering overcooked, it's actually finely balanced although it is years away from being ready to drink.

2002	95	2014	2022+
2001	95	2013	2021+
2000	93	2012	2020
1999	96	2011	2019+
1998	96	2010	2018
1997	86	1999	2002
1996	94	2008	2016
1994	88	1999	2002

MERLOT   RATING 5

Southern Australia $5–$11
Current vintage: 2004   87

A genuinely varietal merlot with a spicy perfume of vibrant dark plums, cherries and currants over earthy undertones of riverland fruit. Its smooth, measured and even palate delivers a lively expression of earthy and rather minty flavour before a firm and savoury finish.

2004	87	2005	2006+
2003	88	2005	2008
2002	81	2003	2004
2001	82	2002	2003+

REEVES POINT CHARDONNAY
(formerly Limited Release)

RATING 3

Padthaway $30–$49
Current vintage: 2004   94

A vibrant and tightly focused chardonnay of elegance and complexity. Zesty, floral aromas of grapefruit, melon and lime juice are backed by very restrained and dusty vanilla oak. Long and silky, its generously fruited palate seamlessly integrates with fresh oak and crisp acids, with a persistent core of intense flavour. Excellent balance and potential.

2004	94	2009	2012
2003	94	2005	2008+
2002	86	2004	2007
2001	90	2003	2006+
2000	88	2002	2005
1999	82	2000	2001
1998	86	1999	2000
1996	88	1997	1998

RESERVE CABERNET SAUVIGNON

RATING 5

Southern Australia $12–$19
Current vintage: 2004   82

Rather overcooked and under-fruited for its surprisingly hard-edged extract. Raisined and jammy, it does deliver some up-front plum and blackberry-like flavour backed by vanilla and cedary oak, but becomes slightly hollow, exposing the rawness of its tannin.

2004	82	2006	2009
2002	84	2004	2007
2001	86	2003	2006
2000	89	2005	2008
1999	87	2001	2004+
1998	87	2000	2003

RESERVE CHARDONNAY

RATING 5

Southern Australia $12–$19
Current vintage: 2005   88

Smooth, tightly integrated and elegant, with a restrained bouquet of grapefruit, melon and vanilla oak before a juicy, tangy palate of lemon, melon and green olive flavour, finishing with refreshing acids and a lingering core of citrusy fruit.

2005	88	2007	2010
2003	88	2005	2008
2002	90	2004	2007
2001	88	2003	2006
2000	87	2002	2005
1999	88	2001	2004

RESERVE RIESLING

RATING 3

Southern Australia $12–$19
Current vintage: 2006   88

A fresh, vibrant and slightly confectionary riesling whose floral aromas of lime, lemon juice and bathpowder precede a forward and generous, if rather simple and slightly cloying palate. Moderately long, it finishes with clean, crisp acidity.

2006	88	2008	2011
2005	90	2010	2013+
2004	93	2009	2012+
2003	93	2008	2011+
2002	92	2007	2010
2001	88	2003	2006

RESERVE SHIRAZ

RATING **4**

Southern Australia	**$12–$19**
Current vintage: 2004	**89**

An especially minty shiraz whose intense and juicy expression of cassis and blackberries has a tangy sourness. Supported by lightly toasty vanilla oak and framed by firm, powdery tannin, it's long and pliant, finishing with lingering berry fruit and suggestions of menthol.

2004	89	2009	2012
2003	90	2008	2011+
2002	93	2007	2010+
2001	89	2006	2009
2000	87	2002	2005+
1999	89	2001	2004+
1998	87	2000	2003

RIESLING

RATING **5**

Southern Australia	**$5–$11**
Current vintage: 2006	**87**

Generous and uncomplicated, this tangy and mouthfilling young riesling has a pungent and slightly skinsy aroma of lime and apple, with a juicy, clean and refreshing palate of vibrant varietal flavour.

2006	87	2008	2011
2005	88	2007	2010+
2004	89	2005	2006+
2003	89	2005	2008+
2002	86	2003	2004+
2001	89	2003	2006
2000	88	2005	2008
1999	89	2001	2004
1998	86	1999	2000
1997	88	1999	2002
1996	89	2001	2004

SHIRAZ CABERNET

RATING **5**

Various	**$12–$19**
Current vintage: 2005	**87**

Slightly meaty and stewy aromas of very ripe black and red berries, dark plums and earthy undertones reveal a cinnamon-like spiciness. Long, fine-grained and savoury, it's an honest but well composed fusion of ripe fruit with firmish but pliant tannin and typical muddy riverland undertones.

2005	87	2010	2013+
2004	90	2009	2012+
2003	87	2008	2011
2002	90	2010	2014
2001	87	2006	2009
2000	86	2002	2005+
1999	90	2007	2011+
1998	89	2003	2007+
1997	82	1999	2002
1996	85	1998	2001+

ST HUGO CABERNET SAUVIGNON

RATING **3**

Coonawarra	**$30–$49**
Current vintage: 2005	**92**

Vibrant, intense and minty, with violet-like aromas of cassis and sweet chocolate/vanilla/cedar oak backed by nuances of mocha and menthol. Delightfully fresh and punchy, its moderately rich palate of cassis, blackberry, mulberry and plum-like fruit is yet to flesh out fully and integrate with a firm but balanced extract of drying, chalky tannins. Long and persistent, it's finished with a fresh acidity.

2005	92	2013	2017+
2004	95	2016	2024+
2003	92	2015	2023
2002	90	2010	2014
2001	93	2013	2021
2000	88	2005	2008+
1999	95	2019	2029+
1998	95	2010	2018+
1997	87	2005	2009
1996	94	2008	2016
1994	95	2006	2014+
1993	91	2001	2005
1992	88	1997	2000
1991	95	2003	2011
1990	94	2002	2010
1989	94	1997	2001
1988	91	1996	2000
1987	89	1995	1999
1986	90	1994	1998
1985	92	1990	1993

A B C D E F G H I J K L M N O P Q R S T U V W X Y Z

STEINGARTEN RIESLING

Eden Valley $20–$29
Current vintage: 2005 **96**

Heady and floral, its schisty and slightly smoky fragrance of fresh lime juice, pear and apple is backed by a hint of lemon rind and a bathpowder-like minerality. Initially round, luscious and very concentrated, it's a juicy, sumptuous mouthful of citrus and white peach-like riesling, with a long, sculpted finish framed by tight, lemony acids. Very focused and perfectly ripened, it's another classic release under this label.

2005	96	2013	2017
2003	98	2015	2023+
2002	97	2014	2022
2001	96	2009	2013+
2000	95	2008	2012+
1999	94	2007	2011
1998	95	2010	2018
1997	95	2005	2009
1996	96	2008	2016
1995	91	2000	2003
1994	96	1999	2002+
1992	93	2004	2012
1991	96	2003	2011
1990	95	1998	2002+
1989	88	1991	1994
1988	90	1993	1996
1987	90	1999	2004
1979	94	1987	1991+

Jansz

1216B Pipers Brook Road, Pipers Brook Tas 4254. Tel: (03) 6382 7066. Fax: (03) 6382 7088.
Website: www.jansztas.com Email: info@jansztas.com

Region: **Pipers River** Winemaker: **Natalie Fryar** Viticulturist: **Robin Nettelbeck** Chief Executive: **Robert Hill Smith**
Owned by S. Smith & Son of Yalumba fame, Jansz is a cutting-edge Australian sparkling label able to source exceptional cool-climate fruit from northern Tasmania. With its new interactive wine visitor centre in Pipers Brook and a developing track record of fine, tightly sculpted and beautifully presented sparkling wines, Jansz is going to take some beating. However, I must admit to a trace of disappointment that the Late Disgorged effort from 1997 has developed just too much tropical and herbaceous influence to live up to the expectations developed by the outstanding 'standard' wine from the same vintage.

VINTAGE CUVÉE (formerly Brut Cuvée)

Pipers River $30–$49
Current vintage: 2002 **90**

Generous and shapely, with a creamy, crackly bead, it's lightly toasty and buttery, with white peach, apple, pear, paw paw and tropical melon flavour lifted by suggestions of dried flowers, roasted nuts and bakery yeasts. It finishes savoury and biscuity, with herbal nuances beneath its fresh tropical flavours and lively acidity.

2002	90	2007	2010
2001	86	2006	2009
2000	91	2005	2008
1999	93	2007	2011+
1997	95	2005	2009+
1996	89	2001	2004+
1995	87	2000	2003
1994	95	2002	2006
1993	86	1998	2001
1992	94	1997	2000+
1991	89	1996	1999+
1990	95	1998	2002

LATE DISGORGED CUVÉE

Northern Tasmania $30–$49
Current vintage: 1997 **90**

Fragrant and tropical, with faintly angular and estery aromas of pineapple, citrus fruits and creamy leesy undertones, it's long, fine and savoury. There's a hint of sweetness about its creamy and slightly herbaceous palate of citrusy fruit and bakery yeast, while it finishes with some greenish edges. Given its age and treatment, it's very much driven by primary fruit.

1997	90	2005	2009
1996	87	2001	2004
1995	90	2003	2007
1992	95	2000	2004

Jasper Hill

Drummonds Lane, Heathcote Vic 3523. Tel: (03) 5433 2528. Fax: (03) 5433 3143.
Website: www.jasperhill.com Email: info@jasperhill.com.au

Region: **Heathcote** Winemaker: **Ron Laughton** Viticulturist: **Ron Laughton** Chief Executive: **Ron Laughton**

Jasper Hill is a dryland vineyard, so several recent seasons — which have witnessed the death of many large trees on the property — have naturally been more difficult from the perspective of making balanced and brightly-fruited wine. The 2005 Emily's Paddock shows evidence of stress, but the smoky, bony and rather funky Georgia's Paddock from the same vintage has come out comparatively unscathed. Again, Jasper Hill has made a delicious Riesling; the 2006 edition is finely sculpted and mineral.

EMILY'S PADDOCK SHIRAZ CABERNET FRANC   RATING **3**

Heathcote	$100–$199
Current vintage: 2005	86

Stressed, meaty and herbal, with a light, mint/menthol-like aroma of red berries, plums and stewy, mineral-like undertones. Tight, firm and drying, it's meaty and rustic, delivering a lean, almost hollow palate framed by drying tannin. There are pleasing savoury, earthy and mineral qualities, but the wine lacks the essential component of ripe fruit.

2005	86	2010	2013+
2004	90	2012	2016
2003	90	2011	2015+
2002	88	2010	2014
2001	95	2013	2021+
2000	93	2008	2012+
1999	86	2004	2007
1998	90	2006	2010+
1997	94	2009	2017
1996	89	2000	2008
1995	87	2000	2003
1994	88	2002	2006
1993	93	2001	2005+
1992	87	2012	2022
1991	96	2003	2011
1990	94	2002	2010

GEORGIA'S PADDOCK NEBBIOLO   RATING **3**

Heathcote	$50–$99
Current vintage: 2004	94

Firm, drying and complex, this meaty nebbiolo should open up delightfully over time. Its wild and briary aromas of meaty, herbal and raspberry-like fruit precede a powerful palate. Its very spicy and slightly spirity expression of plum and berry flavours is framed by tight, bony tannins, finishing long and savoury.

2004	94	2009	2012+
2003	91	2008	2011+
2002	83	2010	2014
2001	92	2006	2009+
2000	92	2005	2008+

GEORGIA'S PADDOCK RIESLING   RATING **3**

Heathcote	$20–$29
Current vintage: 2006	94

Long, finely sculpted and stylish, this delicious and persistent young riesling has a floral perfume of acacia, lemon rind and mineral. Clean and tangy, with a palate of white peach and citrus-like fruit over a slatey lick of mineral, it finishes with good persistence and freshness.

2006	94	2011	2014+
2005	93	2010	2013+
2004	89	2006	2009+
2003	90	2008	2011+
2002	90	2007	2010+
2001	87	2006	2009+
2000	91	2005	2008
1998	90	2003	2006
1997	93	2005	2009

GEORGIA'S PADDOCK SHIRAZ   RATING **3**

Heathcote	$50–$99
Current vintage: 2005	93

Pleasingly elegant, fine-grained and leaner in style, this rather wild and funky shiraz delivers a smoky, earthy and floral bouquet whose aromas of raspberries, liqueur cherries and dark plums are handsomely backed by polished oak and char-cuterie-like influences. Full to medium in weight, it's fine-grained and bony, with a pleasing depth of red and black berry fruit, chocolate/vanilla oak and drying, powdery tannin finishing long and savoury, with nuances of licorice and fennel.

2005	93	2013	2017
2004	89	2009	2012+
2003	95	2015	2023
2002	90	2014	2022
2001	95	2009	2013+
2000	90	2008	2012+
1999	87	2004	2007
1998	88	2006	2010+
1997	93	2009	2017
1996	94	2008	2016
1995	96	2007	2015
1994	95	2002	2006+
1993	96	2005	2013
1992	95	2004	2012
1991	89	1999	2003
1990	94	2002	2010

Jim Barry

Craigs Hill Road (off Main North Road), Clare SA 5453. Tel: (08) 8842 2261. Fax: (08) 8842 3752.
Email: jbwines@jimbarry.com

Region: **Clare Valley** Winemaker: **Mark Barry** Viticulturist: **John Barry** Chief Executive: **Peter Barry**

Jim Barry is a well-established and traditional maker of Clare Valley reds, although it has recently developed a vineyard on the former Penola cricket ground in the southern sector of Coonawarra. Its 2004 red releases include a redoubtable and sumptuous The Armagh and a long, elegant and rather stylish McRae Wood. The 2006 Watervale Riesling is the finest for some years, while the 2005 vintage (the second) of The Florita Riesling (91/100, drink 2013–2017) is intense, mineral and very focused.

THE ARMAGH (Shiraz)

RATING **2**

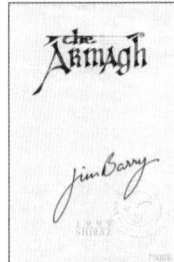

Clare Valley $50–$99
Current vintage: 2004 94

Sumptuous, ripe and spirity, this powerful but smooth and pliant shiraz is a fine example of its kind. Densely packed with black, briary flavours of plums, cassis and currants, it's meaty and briary, with an assertive underswell of dark chocolate oak and a massive, but balanced extract of assertive tannin. Laced with suggestions of cracked pepper, cinnamon and cloves, mint and menthol, it's slightly overcooked but not at the expensive of its considerable longevity.

2004	94	2016	2024
2002	95	2014	2022
2001	89	2009	2013
2000	91	2005	2008+
1999	95	2011	2019
1998	92	2006	2010
1997	95	2005	2009+
1996	93	2004	2008
1995	95	2003	2007+
1994	93	2006	2014
1993	88	1998	2001+
1992	94	2004	2012
1991	93	2003	2011
1990	95	2010	2020
1989	94	2009	2019
1988	93	2000	2005
1987	93	2007	2017

THE LODGE HILL SHIRAZ

RATING **5**

Clare Valley $12–$19
Current vintage: 2005 89

A short to medium term and slightly jammy red whose pleasingly fresh, briary flavours of blackberries, cassis and dark plums are backed by mocha/coconut oak, suggestions of choc-mint, cloves and cinnamon. Full to medium weight, it's smooth, supple and rather polished, with an intense, approachable palate underpinned by fine, supple and loose-knit tannin.

2005	89	2010	2013
2004	89	2006	2009
2003	89	2005	2008+
2002	90	2004	2007+
2001	92	2006	2009+

THE McRAE WOOD SHIRAZ

RATING **5**

Clare Valley $30–$49
Current vintage: 2004 93

Very ripe and oaky, long and vibrant, with concentrated and slightly minty cassis, raspberry, blackberry and dark plum-like fruit tightly knit with handsome smoky vanilla/chocolate oak and fine, firmish and cultivated tannins. Scented with cloves, white pepper, dried herbs and a hint of cherry, it's surprisingly elegant and stylish, finishing with a pleasing length of juicy flavour.

2004	93	2016	2024
2003	86	2005	2008
2002	88	2007	2010+
2001	82	2003	2006+
2000	87	2002	2005+
1999	88	2004	2007
1998	89	2003	2006
1997	84	2002	2005
1996	93	2004	2008
1995	91	2000	2003
1994	94	2002	2006
1993	87	1995	1998
1992	93	2000	2004+

RATING **3**

	Clare Valley	$12–$19
	Current vintage: 2006	**93**

A vibrant, floral and schisty perfume of penetrative citrusy aroma precedes a round, juicy and generous palate of genuine length and freshness. It's long and refreshing, with slightly confectionary fruit, a lemon sherbet texture and a crisp, crunchy finish that reveals just a hint of sweetness.

2006	93	2011	2014
2005	91	2010	2013
2004	91	2009	2012+
2003	89	2005	2008
2002	94	2007	2010+
2001	92	2009	2013
2000	89	2005	2008
1999	95	2004	2007
1998	93	2003	2006+
1997	93	2005	2009
1996	89	2004	2008
1995	91	2003	2007+
1994	88	1999	2002
1993	91	2001	2005

John Duval

9 Park Street, Tanunda SA 5352. Tel: (08) 8563 2591. Fax: (08) 8563 0372.
Website: www.johnduvalwines.com Email: john@johnduvalwines.com
Region: **Barossa Valley** Winemaker: **John Duval** Viticulturist: **John Duval** Chief Executive: **John Duval**
Former Penfolds chief winemaker John Duval has wasted little time since his departure from Australia's largest maker of classic red wine. He is involved as the Australian winemaker for the international Oriel project, and has already released three vintages of his own label. In addition to the Entity (Barossa) Shiraz, his sumptuous and spicy Plexus blend of Barossa shiraz, grenache and mourvèdre has become one of the best of its kind.

PLEXUS (Shiraz Grenache Mourvèdre)

RATING **3**

	Barossa Valley	$30–$49
	Current vintage: 2005	**90**

Pleasingly generous, firm and harmonious, this smooth and polished red blend is presently rather closed and withdrawn. It steadily unfolds bright and spicy aromas of plums, cassis, dark chocolate and white pepper. Framed by firm, fine-grained tannins, its intense, confiture-like palate of blueberries, cassis and plums reveals earthy undertones, finishing with persistent and vibrant fruit qualities.

2005	90	2010	2013
2004	94	2009	2012
2003	93	2008	2011+

Katnook Estate

Riddoch Highway, Coonawarra SA 5263. Tel: (08) 8737 2394. Fax: (08) 8737 2397.
Website: www.katnookestate.com.au Email: katnook@wingara.com.au
Region: **Coonawarra** Winemakers: **Wayne Stehbens, Michael Marcus** Viticulturist: **Chris Brodie**
Chief Executive: **David Yunghanns**
While Katnook Estate has access to some Coonawarra vineyards of genuine maturity, most of its fruit is now sourced from comparatively recent plantings from different sites to those whose fruit helped create its reputation. Its wines continue to be made with high levels of skill and care by Wayne Stehbens, and the company takes great trouble to ensure that the fruit used for its premier wines is of the highest possible standard. It is showing a healthy return to form with its 2004 Cabernet Sauvignon, 2003 Prodigy and 2006 Sauvignon Blanc.

CABERNET SAUVIGNON

RATING **3**

	Coonawarra	$30–$49
	Current vintage: 2004	**91**

An elegant, focused and fine-grained cabernet whose intense cassis, mulberry, plum and blackberry flavours are carefully integrated with cedar/vanilla/dark chocolate oak and supported by fine, tight-knit tannins. Scented with violets, it's smooth, seamless and briary, with a suggestion of lightly herbal complexity.

2004	91	2012	2016+
2003	90	2011	2015
2002	86	2007	2010+
2001	92	2009	2013+
2000	86	2002	2005
1999	95	2007	2011
1998	95	2010	2018
1997	95	2009	2017
1996	95	2008	2016
1995	88	2000	2003
1994	94	2002	2006
1993	94	2005	2013
1992	87	2004	2012
1991	94	2003	2011
1990	92	2002	2010

CHARDONNAY

RATING 4

Coonawarra $30–$49
Current vintage: 2004 86

Rather flabby, awkward and out of shape. Pungent melon skin-like aromas of green olives and wheatmeal appear to reflect dried-out fruit. Backed by rich, buttery and slightly cardboard-like oak, its ripe melon and stonefruit flavours become quite flabby down the palate, lacking length and definition.

2004	86	2006	2009
2003	90	2005	2008+
2002	92	2004	2007+
2001	88	2003	2006+
2000	86	2002	2005
1999	87	2001	2004
1998	90	2000	2003
1997	89	1999	2002
1996	93	2001	2004
1995	94	2000	2003
1994	94	1999	2002
1993	94	1998	2001

CHARDONNAY BRUT

RATING 5

Coonawarra $30–$49
Current vintage: 2005 88

Fresh and vibrant, with flavours of peach, melon, nectarine and pineapple backed by lightly toasty, creamy nuances, this long and tangy sparkling chardonnay finishes long and clean, with lingering juicy flavours and refreshing acids.

2005	88	2007	2010
2004	86	2006	2009
2002	87	2004	2007
2001	85	2003	2006
1996	93	2001	2004
1995	90	2000	2003
1994	82	1996	1999
1993	90	1995	1998
1990	94	1995	1998

MERLOT

RATING 5

Coonawarra $30–$49
Current vintage: 2004 88

An early-drinking, sweet and juicy merlot with a browning appearance and a smoky, tobaccoey aspect. Backed by sweet cedar/vanilla oak, juicy, forward and confiture-like flavours of dark cherries, mulberries and dark plums are framed by smooth, fine-grained tannins. It's showing plenty of age, and finishes with slightly cooked and herbal notes.

2004	88	2006	2009
2002	88	2007	2010
2001	82	2003	2006
2000	87	2002	2005
1999	82	2001	2004
1998	96	2006	2010+
1997	93	2002	2005+
1996	94	2004	2008
1995	87	1997	2000
1994	94	1999	2002
1993	94	1998	2001
1992	93	1997	2000

ODYSSEY CABERNET SAUVIGNON

RATING 4

Coonawarra $50–$99
Current vintage: 2002 88

Earthy and minty, with under and over-ripe influences of cooked meaty notes of stewed, currant-like fruit with herbaceous undertones. Sumptuously oaked, it's rather dehydrated and beginning to dry out. Minty and meaty, the palate is framed by rather hard-edged tannins and appears to have been overworked given its lack of mid-palate intensity, evenness of ripeness and fruit sweetness.

2002	88	2007	2010+
2001	91	2009	2013
2000	87	2008	2012
1999	95	2011	2019
1998	90	2006	2010
1997	90	2005	2009+
1996	97	2008	2016+
1994	95	2006	2014
1992	94	2004	2012
1991	96	2003	2011+

PRODIGY SHIRAZ

RATING 4

Coonawarra $50–$99
Current vintage: 2003 91

A rustic, leathery shiraz with plenty of meaty evolution. Rather old-fashioned, its spicy and developed bouquet reveals tarry and cedary complexity. Smooth and unctuous, its plump and richly fruited palate is smooth and firm, but lacks just a little intensity and brightness. It finishes long and savoury, with persistent flavours or dark fruits and currants.

2003	91	2008	2011
2002	92	2010	2014
2001	89	2006	2009
2000	88	2002	2005+
1999	89	2004	2007
1998	97	2006	2010
1997	91	2005	2009

RIESLING

RATING 5

Coonawarra	$12–$19
Current vintage: 2005	**88**

A lean, taut, high-acid expression of young riesling with a floral perfume of lime juice and lemon rind. It's clean and refreshing, penetrative and citrusy, with a tangy, lemony finish and a lightly chalky texture.

2005	88	2010	2013
2004	86	2006	2009
2003	89	2005	2008+
2002	90	2004	2007+
2001	87	2003	2006+
2000	89	2005	2008
1999	82	2001	2004
1998	91	2003	2006+
1997	86	1999	2002
1996	87	2001	2004
1995	82	2000	2003

SAUVIGNON BLANC

RATING 4

Coonawarra	$20–$29
Current vintage: 2006	**91**

Almost an exaggerated wine, whose lightly herbal and floral perfume of intense passionfruit, gooseberries and blackcurrant fruit is just a fraction estery and spicy. It's round and generously flavoured, with mouthfilling but not overblown varietal flavour cleanly wrapped in refreshingly tight acids. Long and lingering, it finishes with a persistent core of fruit.

2006	91	2007	2008+
2005	86	2005	2006
2004	90	2005	2006
2003	90	2004	2005+
2002	90	2003	2004
2001	88	2001	2002
2000	82	2001	2002
1999	82	1999	2000
1998	88	1998	1999

SHIRAZ

RATING 5

Coonawarra	$30–$49
Current vintage: 2004	**89**

Musky, spicy and gamey, this slightly meaty and peppery shiraz marries its sweet flavours of raspberries, blackberries and cherries with fresh cedar/vanilla oak and earthy, leathery undertones. Just lacking a genuine core of intensity, it's moderately generous but fractionally cooked and raw, finishing marginally hollow and dried out. Might have been better if blended with some of the Founder Block component.

2004	89	2009	2012
2003	88	2005	2008+
2002	87	2004	2007+
2001	89	2003	2006+
2000	88	2002	2005+
1999	88	2001	2004+
1998	86	2006	2010

Keith Tulloch

Hunter Ridge, Hermitage Road, Pokolbin NSW 2321. Tel: (02) 4998 7500. Fax: (02) 4998 7211.
Website: www.keithtullochwine.com.au Email: carol@keithtullochwine.com.au

Region: **Hunter Valley** Winemaker: **Keith Tulloch** Chief Executives: **Keith and Amanda Tulloch**

Keith Tulloch produces the usual range of Hunter Valley varieties with a few variations of his own, such as a blend of Coonawarra cabernet with Hunter shiraz. The best is his flagship, the rustic and meaty Kester Shiraz.

KESTER SHIRAZ

RATING 4

Lower Hunter Valley	$30–$49
Current vintage: 2003	**87**

Rustic leathery and spicy aromas with nuances of dark pepper, sweet new pencil shavings oak and smoked meats. Medium to full in weight, it's evolved and leathery, with suggestions of roast lamb, rosemary and sweet cedary oak. Moderately long and drying at the finish with some herbal undertones, it just lacks real fruit depth and sweetness.

2003	87	2008	2011+
2002	90	2007	2010+
2001	87	2003	2006+
2000	81	2005	2008
1999	84	2001	2004
1998	90	2006	2010

Kilikanoon

Penna Lane, Penwortham SA 5451. Tel: (08) 8843 4377. Fax: (08) 8843 4377.
Website: www.kilikanoon.com.au Email: admin@kilikanoon.com.au

Region: **Clare Valley** Winemaker: **Kevin Mitchell** Viticulturist: **Kevin Mitchell** Chief Executive: **Kevin Mitchell**

Based in the Clare Valley, Kilikanoon creates a wide range that include a number of carefully chosen individual vineyard combinations of region and variety. Several of these, such as the rieslings covered below, come from the Clare Valley, while others are sourced from the Barossa, McLaren Vale and Adelaide Hills. I admire Kevin Mitchell's rieslings, but I find the red Kilikanoon wines present fruit and oak of rather exaggerated sweetness.

MORT'S BLOCK RIESLING

RATING 4

Clare Valley $30–$49
Current vintage: 2005 90

Lightly spicy and oxidative, with dusty scents of apple, pear and lime juice prior to an elegant and restrained palate of delicacy and fragility. Finishing with lingering fruit and soft acids, it's shapely and stylish, unobtrusive and balanced.

2005	90	2010	2013+
2004	90	2009	2012+
2003	89	2008	2011
2002	84	2004	2007

MORT'S RESERVE RIESLING

RATING 2

Clare Valley $30–$49
Current vintage: 2005 93

A smooth, restrained and elegant cellar style of riesling with a lightly toasty and oxidative bouquet of dried flowers and a long, supple palate that steadily builds in its intensity and richness of lime juice and pear-like fruit. Finely layered and balanced, with a lingering finish punctuated by fresh lemony acids.

2005	93	2013	2017
2004	95	2012	2016+
2003	95	2011	2015

Killerby

Caves Road, Willyabrup WA 6285. Tel: 1-800 655 722. Fax: 1-800 679 578.
Website: www.killerby.com.au Email: grapevine@killerby.com.au

Regions: **Geographe, Margaret River** Winemaker: **Simon Ding** Viticulturist: **Michael Brocksopp**
Chief Executive: **Ben Killerby**

A very stylish, long-term Cabernet Sauvignon from 2004, a sumptuous Shiraz from 2003 and a lightly toasty Semillon 2006 are the new highlights from Killerby, a small winery that mixes and matches between its complementary vineyards in Capel (Geographe) and Margaret River from vintage to vintage.

CABERNET SAUVIGNON

RATING 5

Geographe, Margaret River $20–$29
Current vintage: 2004 93

Shapely and balanced, this elegant and cultivated cabernet combines intense flavours of cassis and raspberries with lightly minty undertones of chocolate and dried herbs. Scented with violets and backed by sweet vanilla and cedary oak, it's long and seamless, with a dusty, powdery under-carriage of loose-knit tannin.

2004	93	2016	2024
2003	80	2005	2008+
2002	89	2007	2010
2001	89	2009	2013
2000	93	2008	2012+
1999	87	2004	2007
1998	86	2003	2006+
1997	86	2002	2005
1996	83	2004	2008
1995	87	2003	2007
1994	82	1999	2002
1993	93	2005	2013
1992	94	2000	2004
1991	87	2003	2011

CHARDONNAY

RATING 4

Margaret River, Geographe, $20–$29
Current vintage: 2004   84

Delicate, herbal and dusty, with aromas of lightly candied fruit and vanilla oak so restrained they almost lack intensity. Its soft and richly textured palate of peachy, tropical fruit and nutty vanilla oak thins out towards the finish, becoming rather dilute. Needs more intensity and brightness.

2004	84	2006	2009
2003	87	2005	2008
2002	92	2007	2010
2001	89	2003	2006
2000	92	2005	2008
1999	80	2000	2000
1998	86	2000	2003+
1997	84	1999	2002
1996	93	2001	2004
1995	93	2000	2003

SAUVIGNON BLANC

RATING 4

Margaret River $20–$29
Current vintage: 2006   90

Rather herbaceous, this complex, distinctive and oak-matured sauvignon blanc has a dusty, herbal bouquet of freshly cut grass, capsicum, gooseberries and honeydew melon backed by very lightly toasty French oak. Long and smooth, with a lively expression of grassy melon/gooseberry fruit backed by restrained vanilla oak, it finishes tight and focused, with pleasing length of gooseberries, a hint of cassis, but slightly green-edged acids.

2006	90	2007	2008+
2005	83	2005	2006+
2004	88	2005	2006+
2003	92	2004	2005+
2002	93	2004	2007
2001	88	2003	2006

SEMILLON

RATING 4

Geographe $20–$29
Current vintage: 2006   93

Sumptuously flavoured but shapely and elegant, this carefully oak-matured semillon opens with ripe aromas of honeydew melon and lemon backed by herbal, tobaccoey undertones and scents of nutty vanilla oak. Its mouthfilling palate of tightly focused melon-like fruit and lightly toasty oak retains plenty of zest and freshness, finishing long and dry with lingering fruit and smooth, soft acids.

2006	93	2011	2014
2005	91	2010	2013+
2004	90	2006	2009+
2003	90	2005	2008+
2002	91	2004	2007+
2001	90	2003	2006
1999	93	2004	2007
1998	84	2000	2003
1997	90	2002	2005
1996	93	2001	2004
1995	94	2000	2003
1994	91	2002	2006
1993	90	1998	2001
1992	91	1997	2000
1991	91	1999	2003
1990	87	1995	1998

SHIRAZ

RATING 4

Geographe $20–$29
Current vintage: 2003   91

A sumptuous but neatly balanced combination of meaty shiraz fruit and chocolate-like, almost gamey oak. With a sweet fragrance of small black and red berries, spices and vanilla oak plus a juicy ripe and slightly tarry palate of deep plum currant-like flavour, it's smoothly framed by velvet tannins.

2003	91	2011	2015
2001	89	2009	2013
2000	89	2005	2008+
1999	95	2007	2011
1998	93	2006	2010
1997	86	2002	2005
1996	89	2001	2004
1995	94	2003	2007
1994	94	2002	2006
1993	93	2001	2005
1992	82	1997	2000
1991	94	1999	2003
1989	89	1997	2001

A B C D E F G H I J K L M N O P Q R S T U V W X Y Z

Knappstein

2 Pioneer Avenue, Clare SA 5453. Tel: (08) 8842 2600. Fax: (08) 8842 3831.
Website: www.knappsteinwines.com.au Email: knappsteinwines@knappstein.com.au
Region: **Clare Valley** Winemaker: **Paul T. Smith** Viticulturist: **Kate Strachan** Chief Executive: **Anthony Roberts**
While the single vineyard Ackland Riesling maintains its high standard, the other Knappstein wines lack their customary focus and conviction. The 2004 reds are meatier and more cooked than most from the Clare Valley.

ACKLAND VINEYARD RIESLING

RATING 2

Clare Valley	$20–$29
Current vintage: 2006	**92**

A perfumed, musky and intensely flavoured riesling in the typically tangy, juicy house Knappstein style. Its floral and limey aromas are backed by suggestions of mineral. Long and shapely, it's also quite round and juicy, with an intense core of rich, tangy citrus fruit that extends well down the palate towards a lingering finish of refreshing lime juice acidity

2006	92	2011	2014
2005	96	2013	2017
2004	95	2012	2016+

CABERNET MERLOT

Clare Valley	$20–$29
Current vintage: 2004	**80**

Meaty, menthol-like aromas of fruitcake and raisins, chocolate and spice precede a forward palate that becomes harder and leaner towards its finish, lacking brightness and charm.

2004	80	2006	2009
2003	86	2008	2011
2002	88	2004	2007+
2001	86	2003	2006+
2000	82	2002	2005
1999	88	2004	2007
1998	90	2003	2006
1997	89	2002	2005
1996	91	2001	2004
1995	89	2000	2003
1994	89	2002	2006
1993	87	1998	2001
1992	88	1997	2000
1991	91	1999	2003
1990	90	1992	1995

SINGLE VINEYARD CABERNET SAUVIGNON
(formerly Enterprise)

RATING 4

Clare Valley	$30–$49
Current vintage: 2004	**86**

Meaty, rather overcooked aromas of currants, plums and raisins precede rather a dried-out palate offering some fruitiness in mid-palate, but essentially lacking brightness and vitality. It's supported by firm tannins and fresh oak, with a regional touch of menthol and mint.

2004	86	2006	2009+
2003	89	2011	2015+
2002	93	2014	2022
2000	86	2002	2005+
1999	89	2004	2007+
1998	90	2010	2018+
1997	93	2005	2009+
1996	95	2008	2016+
1995	90	2003	2007+
1994	89	2006	2014

HAND PICKED RIESLING

RATING 3

Clare Valley	$12–$19
Current vintage: 2006	**86**

Toasty, oily and fast-developing, this musky and rather cooked riesling delivers fresh lime and lemon flavour, but tends to lack shape and focus. It's broad and quite phenolic, with a minerality that its candied fruit struggles to match.

2006	86	2008	2011
2005	88	2007	2010
2004	91	2009	2012
2003	94	2008	2011
2002	93	2007	2010+
2001	94	2009	2013+
2000	95	2008	2012
1999	93	2004	2007
1998	95	2006	2010
1997	94	2005	2009
1996	93	2004	2008+
1995	90	2003	2007
1994	94	2006	2014
1993	95	2001	2005
1992	91	1997	2000
1991	90	1996	1999

SHIRAZ

RATING **5**

KNAPPSTEIN	Clare Valley	$20–$29	2004	80	2006	2009
	Current vintage: 2004	**80**	2003	85	2008	2011
			2002	90	2007	2010+
CLARE VALLEY	A stressed, meaty shiraz whose currant and raisin-like aromas are backed by sweet oak. Forward, cooked and porty, it lacks mid-palate sweetness, drying out to a hard-edged finish.		2001	89	2006	2009+
			2000	86	2002	2005
			1999	90	2004	2007
			1998	92	2003	2006+
			1997	88	2002	2005
			1996	83	1998	2001

Kooyong

110 Hunts Road, Tuerong Vic 3933. Tel: (03) 5989 7355. Fax: (03) 5989 7677.
Website: www.kooyong.com Email: wines@kooyong.com

Region: **Mornington Peninsula** Winemaker: **Sandro Mosele** Viticulturist: **Sandro Mosele**
Chief Executive: **Giorgio Gjergja**

Kooyong is a significant maker of complex, savoury Chardonnay and brightly lit, deeply fruited and perfumed Pinot Noir. Quite surprisingly for such a young operation, it has already evolved an upper tier of labels that uncannily reflect the specific differences between various vineyard blocks on the diverse site. Kooyong also releases a very respectable earlier-drinking duo of Massale Pinot Noir and Clonale Chardonnay.

CHARDONNAY

RATING **3**

KOOYONG 2005	Mornington Peninsula	$30–$49	2005	93	2007	2010+
	Current vintage: 2005	**93**	2004	93	2006	2009
			2003	93	2005	2008+
ESTATE	Presently lean, stylish and finely balanced, this generously fruited and savoury chardonnay should develop more weight and richness over time. Backed by funky suggestions of charcuterie, bakery yeasts and lanolin, its floral and lifted aromas of white peach and melon precede a smooth and juicy expression of melon, grapefruit and tightly knit vanilla oak. It finishes with tangy lemony acids and a hint of soapiness.		2001	95	2006	2009
			2000	94	2002	2005+
			1999	92	2001	2004

FAULTLINE CHARDONNAY

RATING **2**

FAULTLINE	Mornington Peninsula	$50–$99	2004	95	2009	2012
	Current vintage: 2004	**95**	2003	95	2008	2011
			2001	95	2006	2009

Polished and pristine, this elegant and tightly focused wine underpins its fresh citrus, melon and floral aromas with dusty nuances of hessian, matchstick and wheatmeal. Its fine, supple palate steadily reveals layers of juicy grapefruit and melon-like flavour backed by fresh new oak and bound by citrusy acids. Already quite complex, it has the potential to develop further.

HAVEN PINOT NOIR

RATING **2**

HAVEN	Mornington Peninsula	$50–$99	2004	95	2009	2012
	Current vintage: 2004	**95**	2003	91	2008	2011
			2001	96	2006	2009+

A measured and balanced pinot of considerable breeding. Its deep, complex and floral perfume of fresh cherries, berries and plums reveals slightly spicy undertones of charcuterie and mocha. Long, smooth and silky, it opens layers of lingering and vibrant cherry, plum and berry-like fruit backed by suggestions of undergrowth. Very fine, tightly focused and measured; likely to take some time to truly flourish.

PINOT NOIR

		Mornington Peninsula	$30–$49
		Current vintage: 2005	94

A robust but measured pinot, with intense, penetrative aromas of dark cherries, dark plums and red berries revealing undertones of briar, smoked meats and currants. Smooth and sumptuous, medium to full in weight, its rich, dark-fruited palate is underpinned by a firm and bony chassis before finishing savoury, with meaty complexity. Long, complete and finely balanced.

2005	94	2010	2013+
2004	94	2009	2012+
2003	93	2008	2011
2001	95	2006	2009+
2000	90	2005	2008
1999	92	2001	2004+

Labyrinth

PO Box 7372, Shepparton Vic 3622 (postal only). Tel: (03) 5831 2793. Fax: (03) 5831 2982.
Website: www.labyrinthwine.com Email: ajhill@labyrinthwine.com
Region: **Yarra Valley** Winemaker: **Ariki Hill** Chief Executive: **Ariki Hill**

Operated by American winemaker Ricki Hill, Labyrinth is a small but international pinot noir brand that produces another wine from the Bien Nacido vineyard in California's Santa Maria Valley. The Yarra Valley sites comprise the coolish Viggers Vineyard and the higher elevated but warmer Valley Farm Vineyard. In each of the three vintages bottled to date, I believe that the Viggers site has ripened its fruit more evenly and successfully.

VIGGERS VINEYARD PINOT NOIR

	Yarra Valley	$30–$49
	Current vintage: 2004	93

Supple, fine and delicate, this tightly focused pinot is simply waiting to flower. Its delicate perfume of raspberries, cherries and restrained cedar/vanilla oak suggests a dustiness, while its sweet, round and seamless palate of juicy red cherry and raspberry fruit finishes with nuances of spice and cedar. Moderately firm, with velvet-like tannins, it should acquire more depth and richness.

2004	93	2009	2012
2003	88	2008	2011
2002	91	2005	2008+

Lake Breeze

Step Road, Langhorne Creek SA 5255. Tel: (08) 8537 3017. Fax: (08) 8537 3267.
Website: www.lakebreeze.com.au Email: wines@lakebreeze.com.au
Region: **Langhorne Creek** Winemaker: **Greg Follett** Viticulturist: **Tim Follett**
Chief Executives: **Ken and Marlene Follett**

Lake Breeze is a long-established and highly respected wine producer in South Australia's Langhorne Creek, where it regularly makes some of the region's finest wines. I am most impressed with its elegant, handsome and deeply fruited reds, which are usually sold on the market for a fraction of their true worth. Take a look at either of the 2004 reds below and you will see exactly what I mean.

BERNOOTA SHIRAZ CABERNET

	Langhorne Creek	$12–$19
	Current vintage: 2004	94

Beautifully structured, long and stylish with intense, pristine and peppery blackberry and cassis-like fruit handsomely backed by dark chocolate/vanilla oak. It's lifted with a heady whiff of exotic spice, and its juicy palate is underpinned by smooth, smoky vanilla/coconut oak and firm, pliant tannin. Wonderfully long, bright and evenly balanced.

2004	94	2016	2024
2003	89	2008	2011
2002	90	2010	2014+
2001	87	2006	2009
2000	89	2008	2012
1998	92	2006	2010

CABERNET SAUVIGNON

RATING **4**

Langhorne Creek		**$12–$19**	2004	93	2016	2024
Current vintage: 2004		**93**	2003	82	2005	2008+

Elegant, stylish and finely balanced, with deep flavours of cassis, mulberries, dark plums and blackberries supported by retrained dusty, cedary oak and minty undertones of dried herbs. Its violet-like perfume is fragrant and heady, while its long, smooth palate is framed by fine, powdery tannin. Destined to cellar superbly.

2002	90	2007	2010+
2001	88	2006	2009
2000	82	2002	2005+
1998	93	2006	2010+

Lake's Folly

Broke Road, Pokolbin NSW 2320. Tel: (02) 4998 7507. Fax: (02) 4998 7322.
Website: www.lakesfolly.com.au Email: wine@lakesfolly.com.au

Region: **Lower Hunter Valley** Winemaker: **Rodney Kempe** Viticulturist: **Jason Locke**
Chief Executive: **Peter Fogarty**

Lake's Folly is a small and iconic Hunter winery and vineyard whose followers are doubtless rejoicing in the remarkable consistency and quality being achieved by the team headed by Rodney Kempe. Its silky, fine and superbly balanced Chardonnay is among the finest now made in Australia, while the Cabernets blend sensitively marries an unusual set of varieties by Hunter standards with the region's inherent elegance and ability to encourage complexity with time in the bottle.

LAKE'S FOLLY (Cabernet blend)

RATING **2**

Lower Hunter Valley		**$50–$99**	2005	95	2013	2017+
Current vintage: 2005		**95**	2004	92	2006	2024

Stylish, complete and finely crafted, with an intense perfume of cassis, mulberries, dark plums and morello cherries backed by neatly entwined oak, pepper, spice and minerals. Long and supple, its sweet-fruited and silky palate is framed by dusty tannins, leaving a lingering core of vibrant, peppery fruit and minerals with a healthy suggestion of petit verdot.

2003	93	2011	2015
2002	95	2014	2022
2001	96	2013	2021+
2000	96	2012	2020+
1999	93	2011	2019
1998	95	2010	2018
1997	89	2005	2009+
1996	82	2001	2004
1995	88	2003	2007
1994	95	2002	2006+
1993	94	2001	2005
1992	87	1997	2000
1991	90	2003	2011
1990	87	1998	2002+
1989	92	2001	2009

CHARDONNAY

RATING **2**

Lower Hunter Valley		**$30–$49**	2005	93	2010	2013
Current vintage: 2005		**93**	2004	96	2012	2016

A smooth, generous and slightly earlier-maturing Lakes Folly style whose delicate aromas of lemon rind, peach, grapefruit and melon overlie suggestions of tobacco and lavender. Silky-smooth and unctuous, its long and seamless palate delivers vibrant stonefruit and melon flavour neatly bound by refreshing citrusy acids.

2003	96	2008	2011+
2002	95	2007	2010+
2001	96	2009	2013
2000	95	2005	2008
1999	89	2001	2004
1998	94	2003	2006+
1997	89	1999	2002
1996	95	2001	2004+
1995	89	2000	2003
1994	90	1999	2002
1993	89	1998	2001+
1992	92	2000	2004

Langmeil

Corner Langmeil & Para Roads, Tanunda SA 5352. Tel: (08) 8563 2595. Fax: (08) 8563 3622.
Website: www.langmeilwinery.com.au Email: info@langmeilwinery.com.au
Region: **Barossa Valley** Winemaker: **Paul Lindner** Viticulturist: **Carl Lindner** Chief Executive: **Chris Bitter**
Langmeil's ancient Freedom vineyard — which is one of the oldest in the Barossa and also one of the oldest vineyards on this planet still producing great wine — moved into top gear in 2004, making its best wine since 1999 and one of the finest Barossa reds from what might be the region's best-ever vintage since 1966. It's silky and seamless, a classic expression of what used to be known as the Australian 'burgundy' style.

THE BLACKSMITH CABERNET SAUVIGNON

RATING **5**

Barossa Valley	$20–$29
Current vintage: 2005	86

Straightforward, jammy and early-drinking cabernet, whose herbal, minty, rather cooked and stewy aromas of plums, cranberries and rhubarb are backed by sweet chocolate/vanilla oak. Lacking great length, it thins out towards the finish, leaving an impression of slightly raw and under-ripe tannin.

2005	86	2007	2010+
2004	90	2012	2016+
2003	87	2008	2011
2002	87	2004	2007
2001	86	2003	2006+
2000	88	2005	2008
1999	91	2007	2011+
1998	90	2006	2010

THE FIFTH WAVE GRENACHE

RATING **4**

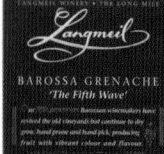

Barossa Valley	$20–$29
Current vintage: 2004	86

Slightly hot and angular, with musky, spicy grenache, it has a wild and briary aroma of blueberries, blackberries and dark plums. Tending more towards prune and currant-like fruit, its smooth but stewy palate shows some brambly complexity, but finishes spirity and cooked.

2004	86	2006	2009
2003	90	2005	2008+
2001	90	2006	2009
1999	91	2004	2007

THE FREEDOM SHIRAZ

RATING **3**

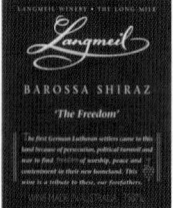

Barossa Valley	$100–$199
Current vintage: 2004	96

A brilliant modern expression of the old-fashioned red Australian burgundy style that delivers a silky, pristine and seamless expression of perfectly ripened and focused fruit tightly knit with lightly smoky and gamey oak and framed by the finest of velvet tannin. It's brambly and briary, with a peppery and spicy perfume of ripe cherries and smoked bacon plus a finely crafted and deeply layered palate that opens layer after layer of extremely persistent blackberry, plum and blackcurrant fruit, finishing long and savoury.

2004	96	2012	2016+
2003	94	2015	2023
2002	93	2010	2014+
2001	91	2006	2009+
2000	91	2005	2008+
1999	96	2011	2019
1998	93	2006	2010+
1997	90	2002	2005+

THREE GARDENS (Shiraz Grenache Mourvèdre)

RATING **5**

Barossa Valley	$20–$29
Current vintage: 2005	86

Cooked and spirity, with jammy flavours of blackberries, redcurrants and plums backed by more dehydrated currant-like fruit and spirity undertones. It's lifted by some sweet vanilla/chocolate oak, but falls rather short and flat.

2005	86	2007	2010
2004	89	2006	2009
2003	89	2005	2008
2002	90	2004	2007
2001	91	2006	2009
2000	90	2005	2008

VALLEY FLOOR SHIRAZ

RATING **5**

Barossa Valley — $20–$29
Current vintage: 2005 — 86

Simple and jammy, with funky, reductive and earthy aromas of raspberries, red plums and sweet vanilla oak. Its juicy palate lacks genuine richness, but continues smooth and supple, backed by fine, slippery tannins and sweet oak.

2005	86	2007	2010
2004	90	2009	2012
2003	86	2005	2008
2002	88	2004	2007
2001	89	2003	2006+
2000	88	2002	2005
1999	93	2011	2019
1998	89	2003	2006+

Leasingham

7 Dominic Street, Clare SA 5453. Tel: (08) 8842 2555. Fax: (08) 8842 3293.
Website: www.leasingham-wines.com.au Email: cellardoor@leasingham-wines.com.au

Region: **Clare Valley** Winemakers: **Kerri Thompson, Simon Cole, Simon Osicka, Stephen Hall**
Viticulturist: **Marcus Woods** Chief Executive: **John Grant**

Part of The Hardy Wine Company, Leasingham is a major Clare Valley producer with long traditions of fine riesling and shiraz, plus its popular Bin 56 Cabernet Malbec blend. Its team have done a fine job with the 2005 vintage, producing some well constructed and flavoursome Bin wines. The Magnus label has replaced the Bastion brand.

BIN 7 RIESLING

RATING **3**

Clare Valley — $12–$19
Current vintage: 2006 — 90

Long, stylish and bone-dry, this flavoursome and finely phenolic riesling has a forward, honeysuckle-like scent of toast, lime and mineral. Tangy citrus fruit is tightly focused along its taut, clean and stylish palate. Good freshness and balance.

2006	90	2011	2014+
2005	94	2010	2013+
2004	89	2009	2012
2003	95	2008	2011
2002	88	2004	2007
2001	91	2003	2006
2000	94	2008	2012
1999	89	2004	2007
1998	92	2006	2010
1997	85	2002	2005
1996	90	2001	2004+

BIN 56 CABERNET MALBEC

RATING **4**

Clare Valley — $20–$29
Current vintage: 2005 — 90

Constructed atop a robust spine of grainy tannin, this assertive, punchy and briary shiraz combines its minty flavours of cassis, black cherries and dark plums with cedar/vanilla oak and undertones of menthol, cloves and cinnamon. It's long and complete, with some youthful rawness, and should build well in the bottle.

2005	90	2013	2017
2002	91	2010	2014+
2001	87	2006	2009+
2000	84	2002	2005
1999	90	2004	2007+
1998	92	2006	2010
1997	86	2002	2005+
1996	90	2004	2008
1995	90	2000	2003
1994	90	1999	2002
1993	89	2001	2005

BIN 61 SHIRAZ

RATING **4**

Clare Valley — $20–$29
Current vintage: 2005 — 90

A fine result from a tough vintage, with layers of deep, minty cassis, blackberries, mulberries and dark plums harmoniously knit with well-mannered oak and a firm, drying astringency that should settle down with time. Scented with violets, musk and menthol, it finishes earthy and savoury, with length, richness and brightness.

2005	90	2013	2017
2004	91	2012	2016
2003	89	2008	2011+
2002	83	2007	2010
2001	90	2006	2009
2000	88	2005	2008
1999	93	2004	2007+
1998	94	2003	2006+
1997	91	2005	2009
1996	90	2001	2004
1995	93	2003	2007
1994	93	1999	2002
1993	89	2001	2005

A
B
C
D
E
F
G
H
I
J
K
L
M
N
O
P
Q
R
S
T
U
V
W
X
Y
Z

CLASSIC CLARE CABERNET SAUVIGNON

RATING 4

| Clare Valley | $30–$49 |
| Current vintage: 2003 | 89 |

An old-fashioned, dark, ripe and brooding cabernet whose slightly meaty aromas of cassis, dark plums and violets overlie fresh cedar/vanilla oak. Very closed, its deep-fisted core of black and red berry fruits and dark chocolate/cedar oak is framed by firm, powdery tannins. It finishes long and persistent, with lingering meaty and jammy fruit.

2003	89	2015	2023
2002	83	2004	2007+
2001	89	2009	2013
1999	94	2011	2019
1998	92	2006	2010+
1997	86	2002	2005
1996	91	2004	2008
1995	87	2000	2003
1994	91	2002	2006
1993	93	2001	2005

CLASSIC CLARE RIESLING

RATING 2

| Clare Valley | $20–$29 |
| Current vintage: 2006 | 89 |

Faster maturing and a little simple, this is quite a phenolic riesling whose toasty aromas of honeysuckle and lime juice precede an assertive but less complex palate. With slightly candied lime marmalade flavours, it lacks its customary tightness, length and focus.

2006	89	2011	2014
2005	96	2013	2017+
2004	90	2009	2012
2002	96	2010	2014+
2000	93	2008	2012
1998	88	2000	2003
1996	93	2004	2008
1995	94	2003	2007
1994	95	2002	2006+

CLASSIC CLARE SHIRAZ

RATING 3

| Clare Valley | $30–$49 |
| Current vintage: 2002 | 93 |

This big, oaky shiraz is bursting with intense cassis, raspberry flavours and deeply scented with exotic spices. There are some earthy, meaty and slightly reductive notes beneath its voluminous fragrance, while the palate reveals a similar aspect that might also be linked to some unusually assertive oak. That aside, the wine is sumptuous and smooth, with a profoundly juicy presence of dark, peppery fruit framed by a fine-grained but almost creamy extract.

2002	93	2010	2014+
2001	91	2006	2009+
1999	90	2004	2007
1998	95	2006	2010+
1997	93	2005	2009
1996	95	2001	2004+
1995	92	2003	2007
1994	95	2006	2014
1993	94	2001	2005
1992	88	1997	2000
1991	94	2003	2011

CLASSIC CLARE SPARKLING SHIRAZ

RATING 3

| Clare Valley | $30–$49 |
| Current vintage: 1997 | 93 |

Smooth and sumptuous, evolved and meaty, this rustic and savoury shiraz combines intense, confiture-like flavours of blackberries and dark plums with suggestions of boot polish, old furniture, cinnamon and cloves. Backed by nuances of dark chocolate, it's generous and invigorating, with a fine effervescence and a lingering notes of blackberry and licorice.

1997	93	2005	2009+
1996	92	2004	2008
1995	93	2007	2015
1994	95	2006	2012+
1992	93	2000	2004+
1991	88	1999	2003

MAGNUS RIESLING

RATING 4

| Clare Valley | $12–$19 |
| Current vintage: 2006 | 92 |

Deliciously tangy, citrusy and chalky, this flavoursome and stylish young riesling has a floral, limey perfume backed by hints of bathpowder and toastiness. Its long, penetrative palate is tightly focused around its powdery structure and refreshing lemony acidity. It's just a fraction candied for a higher score.

2006	92	2011	2014+
2004	90	2012	2016
2003	85	2005	2008

Leconfield

Riddoch Highway, Coonawarra SA 5263. Tel: (08) 8737 2326. Fax: (08) 8737 2285.
Website: www.leconfieldwines.com Email: coonawarra@leconfieldwines.com

Regions: **Coonawarra, McLaren Vale** Winemaker: **Paul Gordon** Viticulturist: **Bendt Rasmussen**
Chief Executive: **Richard Hamilton**

Leconfield is a Coonawarra winery linked by common ownership to the McLaren Vale-based brand of Richard Hamilton. Its Shiraz actually comes from McLaren Vale these days, which from my personal perspective is something of a shame, since Coonawarra can produce exceptional, savoury and elegant shiraz which would be more closely aligned to Leconfield's other red wines from merlot and cabernet sauvignon.

CABERNET SAUVIGNON   RATING 5

Coonawarra	$20–$29
Current vintage: 2005	**89**

A ripe, forward and meaty cabernet whose deep and rather closed fragrance of slightly meaty dark plums, cassis and mulberries is backed by dark chocolate, mocha and cedar-like influences. It's firm, thick and dark-fruited, offering length and structure, but finishes fractionally sappy and metallic. Rich and balanced, without a shred of greenness.

2005	89	2010	2013+
2004	93	2012	2016+
2003	82	2008	2011
2002	83	2007	2010
2001	91	2009	2013+
2000	84	2002	2005
1999	84	2001	2004+
1998	83	2003	2006
1997	86	2009	2011
1996	87	2001	2004
1995	82	2000	2003
1994	89	1999	2002

CHARDONNAY

Coonawarra	$20–$29
Current vintage: 2006	**82**

Oaky and likely to dry out quickly, this simple, dull and forward expression of stonefruit, citrus and wheatmeal thins out towards the finish, where it is excessively reliant on buttery vanilla oak for palate sweetness.

2006	82	2007	2008
2003	82	2003	2004
2002	88	2003	2004+
2000	86	2002	2005
1999	84	2000	2001
1998	90	2000	2003

MERLOT RATING 5

Coonawarra	$30–$49
Current vintage: 2005	**85**

An early-drinking merlot whose meaty dark plum and berry-like fruit depends on some well-handled cedar/vanilla/mocha oak for length and palate sweetness. Initially rich and sumptuous, its overcooked palate becomes quite thin and raw, lacking brightness and elegance. It finishes rather dried-out, with metallic edges and an impression of dead fruit.

2005	85	2007	2010
2004	90	2009	2012+
2003	89	2008	2011+
2002	81	2004	2007
2001	87	2006	2009
2000	88	2002	2005
1998	90	2003	2006
1997	92	2005	2009
1996	95	2004	2008

OLD VINES RIESLING RATING 5

Coonawarra	$20–$29
Current vintage: 2006	**83**

Bracingly acidic and angular, with a lightly floral perfume of lemon sherbet and bathpowder. The palate is a little dull and leesy, with some rather raw acidity beneath its juicy lemon and lime flavours. It finishes rather raw and unpolished.

2006	83	2008	2011
2005	87	2007	2010
2004	88	2006	2009
2003	90	2008	2011
2002	93	2004	2007+
2001	88	2003	2006
1999	77	2000	2001
1998	89	2003	2006+
1997	90	2002	2005
1996	87	2001	2004
1995	91	2000	2003

McLaren Vale			
(formerly Coonawarra)	**$20–$29**		
Current vintage: 2005	**88**		

Meaty, spicy and lifted by sweet, fine-grained oak, this is a well-handled shiraz made from rather over-cooked fruit. Backed by firmish, pliant tannin, its peppery flavours of prunes, currants, raisins, blackberries and plums are rather baked, finishing with nuances of menthol and mocha oak.

2005	88	2010	2013+
2004	92	2012	2016+
2003	89	2008	2011+
2002	83	2003	2006
2001	82	2003	2006
2000	87	2002	2005
1999	81	2001	2004
1998	85	2003	2006
1997	92	2002	2005
1996	92	1998	2001
1995	93	2003	2007
1994	92	1999	2002
1993	93	2001	2005

Leeuwin Estate

Stevens Road, Witchcliffe WA 6285. Tel: (08) 9759 0000. Fax: (08) 9750 0001.
Website: www.leeuwinestate.com.au Email: info@leeuwinestate.com.au
Region: **Margaret River** Winemakers: **Paul Atwood, Damien North** Viticulturist: **David Winstanley**
Chief Executive: **Tricia Horgan**

Leeuwin Estate is a long-established elite maker of Margaret River wine that is best known for its iconic Art Series Chardonnay. This is an exemplary wine that has performed at very high levels on each and every vintage since its first in 1980. I can't think of another table wine in the world that could match its consistent brilliance. The 2004 wine is excellent, but lacks the tightness and length of the two preceding years. 2006 was an excellent white vintage for Leeuwin, with a delightful Sauvignon Blanc and Siblings blend.

ART SERIES CABERNET SAUVIGNON
RATING **5**

Margaret River	**$30–$49**		
Current vintage: 2002	**83**		

Rimmed by greenish, under-ripe influences, this assertive and hard-edged cabernet combines deep, meaty berry, cherry and plummy fruit with an awkward, sappy extract and an overly enthusiastic measure of smoky mocha/vanilla oak which attempts without success to compensate for the fruit's lack of mid-palate sweetness. Its herbal, tomatoey aromas of cassis, violets and raspberries tend towards capsicum and green beans, while its thinning palate is excessively reliant on coffee ground-like oak.

2002	83	2007	2010+
2001	87	2009	2013+
2000	85	2005	2008+
1999	87	2004	2007+
1998	89	2006	2010+
1997	82	2005	2009
1996	83	2001	2004
1995	80	2003	2007
1994	89	2006	2014
1993	88	2001	2005
1992	95	2000	2004
1991	95	2003	2011+
1990	95	2002	2010
1989	95	2001	2009
1988	86	2000	2008

ART SERIES CHARDONNAY
RATING **1**

Margaret River	**$50–$99**		
Current vintage: 2004	**95**		

A stylish, elegant and seamless chardonnay whose floral aromas of grapefruit, lemon, mango and sweet vanilla oak overlie nuances of mineral, pineapple and honeysuckle. Initially round and juicy, it's long and mouthfilling, with a core of explosively intense fruit. It finishes with clean acids and a hint of minerality, and while it's a first class wine, it remains a little less defined and is likely to mature earlier than the top vintages.

2004	95	2009	2012+
2003	97	2011	2015+
2002	97	2010	2014+
2001	96	2009	2013+
2000	95	2008	2012
1999	95	2007	2011
1998	95	2006	2010
1997	95	2005	2009
1996	95	2004	2008
1995	97	2003	2007
1994	94	2002	2006
1993	93	1998	2001
1992	93	1997	2000
1991	93	1999	2003
1990	95	2002	2010
1989	94	1997	2001
1988	93	1996	2000
1987	97	1999	2007
1986	97	1998	2006
1985	94	1993	1997+
1984	91	1992	1996+

ART SERIES RIESLING

Margaret River $20–$29
Current vintage: 2006 89

Tight, and zesty, this spicy, floral riesling presents an intense array of pear, peach, apple and lime flavours with lifted floral qualities. Its long, refreshing palate is round and mouthfilling before a bracingly clear, slightly mineral and phenolic finish of bright, chalky acids.

2006	89	2008	2011+
2005	88	2007	2010+
2004	89	2006	2009+
2003	89	2008	2011
2002	88	2004	2007+
2001	89	2006	2009
2000	87	2002	2005
1999	87	2001	2004
1998	83	1999	2000
1997	87	2002	2005
1996	90	2001	2004
1995	89	2000	2003
1994	87	1999	2002

ART SERIES SAUVIGNON BLANC

Margaret River $20–$29
Current vintage: 2006 93

Punchy aromas of gooseberries, passionfruit and melon with lightly herbaceous and lemony undertones precede a juicy, unctuous palate whose brightly lit fruit has a lifted tropical aspect. Long, clean and refreshing, it's a classic example of this maker's style.

2006	93	2008	2011
2005	92	2006	2007
2004	86	2005	2006
2003	88	2004	2005
2002	91	2003	2004
2001	93	2002	2003+
2000	87	2001	2002
1999	91	2000	2001+
1998	93	1999	2000
1997	94	1999	2002
1996	95	1998	2001
1995	94	1997	2000

ART SERIES SHIRAZ

Margaret River $30–$49
Current vintage: 2004 87

Evolved and smoky, this slightly hard and angular shiraz has a Bovril-like meatiness about its musky aroma of dark plums, cherries and undergrowth. Full to medium weight, its sumptuously ripened flavours of blackberries, dark plums and redcurrants are framed by smooth, pliant tannins that finish with just a herbal hint of menthol and metallic greenness. It should settle down and integrate with a little age.

2004	87	2009	2012+
2003	87	2008	2011
2002	91	2007	2010+
2001	90	2006	2009
2000	83	2002	2005
1999	90	2007	2011

PRELUDE CHARDONNAY

Margaret River $20–$29
Current vintage: 2005 89

A juicy, spicy and lightly tropical chardonnay whose intense melon, lemon and grapefruit flavours are backed by nutty vanilla oak and a sherbet-like texture of powdery phenolics. Round and juicy, it's kept in shape by refreshing acidity, but lacks top-level style and focus.

2005	89	2007	2010
2004	87	2006	2009
2003	89	2005	2008
2002	87	2004	2007
2001	93	2003	2006+
2000	90	2002	2005
1999	90	2001	2004+
1998	92	2000	2003+
1997	87	1999	2002
1996	82	1997	1998
1994	92	1999	2002
1993	93	1998	2001
1992	89	1997	2000

Margaret River	$12–$19
Current vintage: 2006	**93**

Long and shapely, this distinctively floral and mineral white blend has a perfume of passionfruit, lychees and gooseberries with fresh grassy undertones. Its intense, pristine and generous palate overlies mineral and powdery phenolics. Extended by the length and acidity of its semillon component, it culminates in a fresh and racy finish.

2006	93	2007	2008+
2005	88	2005	2006
2004	92	2004	2005+
2003	88	2003	2004+
2002	92	2002	2003+
2001	89	2001	2002

Lenton Brae

Caves Road, Willyabrup Valley, Margaret River WA 6295. Tel: (08) 9755 6255. Fax: (08) 9755 6268.
Website: www.lentonbrae.com Email: info@lentonbrae.com

Region: **Margaret River** Winemaker: **Edward Tomlinson** Chief Executive: **Jeanette Tomlinson**

Lenton Brae is a small family-owned operation that has proven capable of making outstanding wine from the typical Margaret River mix of varieties. Aside from a finely crafted, tight and mineral Chardonnay, its current releases are below the standard usually set by this very typically competent winery.

CABERNET MERLOT
RATING 5

Margaret River	$20–$29
Current vintage: 2005	**80**

Raw and angular, with a simple overcooked, soupy and currant-like aroma. Neither fruit nor oak are particularly fresh, and the wine finishes with greenish acids.

2005	80	2007	2010
2004	90	2009	2012
2003	88	2005	2008
2002	87	2004	2007
2001	87	2003	2006
2000	90	2002	2005+
1999	89	2004	2007
1998	87	2000	2003
1997	82	1998	1999
1996	87	2001	2004
1995	89	2000	2003
1993	82	1995	1998

CABERNET SAUVIGNON
RATING 5

Margaret River	$30–$49
Current vintage: 2004	**82**

Tough and chewy, this rather raw and hard-edged cabernet has a simple, dusty and herbal aroma whose dark berry/plum fruit appears rather jammy, cooked and meaty. Initially forward and juicy, it then thins out, lacking polish and smoothness, falling away to a finish that could use more fruit and charm.

2004	82	2009	2012
2002	82	2007	2010
2001	87	2006	2009+
2000	89	2008	2012
1999	94	2007	2011+
1998	88	2006	2010
1997	87	2002	2005
1996	95	2004	2008+
1995	93	2003	2007
1994	92	2006	2014

CHARDONNAY
RATING 3

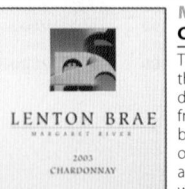

Margaret River	$30–$49
Current vintage: 2005	**92**

Tightly focused, lean, mineral and refreshing, this contemporary young chardonnay has a delicate and lightly meaty bouquet whose grapefruit, tropical and lime juice aromas are backed by nuances of minerals and sweet, creamy vanilla oak. It's long and elegant, delivering a succulent and fine-grained expression of spicy grapefruit, white peach and tropical flavour, finishing taut and refreshing.

2005	92	2010	2013
2004	88	2006	2009
2003	92	2005	2008+
2002	88	2004	2007+
2001	94	2003	2006+
2000	91	2002	2005+
1999	93	2001	2004+
1998	92	2000	2003
1997	89	1999	2002+
1996	89	2001	2004

SEMILLON SAUVIGNON BLANC

Margaret River $20–$29
Current vintage: 2006   77

A slightly candied and under-ripe wine with a lightly fruited, leesy, cheesy aroma and a rather short, angular palate that lacks depth and punchiness.

2006	77	2006	2007
2005	86	2006	2009
2004	89	2005	2006
2003	89	2004	2005+
2002	90	2003	2004+
2001	90	2001	2002+
2000	91	2001	2002
1999	89	1999	2000
1998	86	2000	2003
1997	88	1999	2002
1996	93	2001	2004

Leo Buring

Tanunda Road, Nuriootpa SA 5355. Tel: (08) 8568 9389. Fax: (08) 8562 1669.
Website: www.leoburing.com.au
Regions: **Eden Valley, Clare Valley** Winemaker: **Matthew Pick** Viticulturist: **Greg Pearce**
Chief Executive: **Jamie Odell**

Leo Buring is a benchmark riesling brand noted for the excellence and longevity of its wines from the Eden and Clare valleys of South Australia. Recent years have seen Eden Valley take centre stage, since it is the source of a more regular release of top-level Leonay wine. Despite the challenges presented by the 2006 and 2007 vintages, Matthew Pick and his team continue to produce wines of style and regional identity.

CLARE VALLEY RIESLING

Clare Valley $12–$19
Current vintage: 2007   88

Fleshy, forward and juicy, lacking its customary intensity and perfume, this open, lightly floral and mildly fragrant riesling has a moderate length of confectionary lime juice and lemon rind flavour. Initially round and generous, it finishes a little lean.

2007	88	2012	2015
2006	88	2008	2011+
2005	91	2013	2017
2004	94	2009	2012+
2003	94	2011	2015+
2002	93	2010	2014
2000	87	2005	2008
1999	93	2007	2011
1998	89	2000	2003
1997	91	2005	2009
1996	91	2004	2008
1995	86	2000	2003
1994	93	2002	2006
1993	94	2001	2005

EDEN VALLEY RIESLING

Clare Valley $12–$19
Current vintage: 2007   88

Lean, tight and austere, with an oily, slightly waxy expression of spicy and rather candied lime juice flavour. It's scented with floral aromas and lemon rind, while its steely palate delivers pleasing length and definition over a fine and lingering chalkiness. Slightly too cooked and candied.

2007	88	2012	2015
2006	90	2011	2014
2005	95	2013	2017
2004	95	2012	2016+
2003	95	2011	2015
2002	90	2010	2014

LEONAY EDEN VALLEY RIESLING

Eden Valley $30–$49
Current vintage: 2007   93

An intense floral perfume with limey and chalky undertones precedes a long, fine and racy palate whose concentrated citrusy fruit and powdery undercarriage culminate in a taut and mineral finish of excellent persistence. It's lean, taut and stylish, and needs time to flesh out.

2007	93	2015	2019+
2006	91	2011	2014
2005	95	2017	2025
2004	96	2012	2016+
2003	97	2015	2023
1999	95	2007	2011+
1998	92	2006	2010
1997	93	2005	2009
1995	96	2003	2007
1994	96	2006	2014+
1993	93	2001	2005
1991	96	2003	2011
1990	94	2002	2010

Lillydale Estate

Lot 10 Davross Court, Seville Vic 3139. Tel: (03) 5964 2016. Fax: (03) 5964 3009.
Website: www.mcwilliams.com.au Email: liloffice@mcwilliams.com.au
Region: **Yarra Valley** Winemakers: **Max McWilliam, Jim Brayne** Viticulturist: **Alex Van Driel**
Chief Executive: **George Wahby**

One of the larger operations in the Yarra Valley, Lillydale is owned by the McWilliam family. While its wines are typically elegant, flavoursome and ready to drink at or shortly after release, it would be interesting to see what this highly capable wine producer could achieve if it decided to take the brand up-market. It has followed up its racy 2005 Chardonnay with a refreshing and tangy edition from 2006.

CHARDONNAY

RATING 5

Lillydale Estate
Yarra Valley
Chardonnay

Yarra Valley $12–$19
Current vintage: 2006   90

Very well handled, this fine, taut and powdery chardonnay has a slightly candied spectrum of melon, grapefruit and tropical flavour over restrained buttery vanilla oak and a fine, chalkiness. Initially juicy, it's fractionally funky, with suggestions of oatmeal and a trim, refreshing finish of tangy acidity.

2006	90	2008	2011
2005	90	2007	2010
2004	88	2006	2009
2003	87	2004	2005+
2002	89	2004	2007
2001	84	2002	2003+
2000	87	2002	2005
1999	87	2001	2004
1998	88	1999	2000
1997	90	1999	2002
1996	87	1998	2001
1995	86	1997	2000
1994	82	1996	1999

GEWÜRZTRAMINER

RATING 4

Lillydale Estate
Yarra Valley
Gewürztraminer

Yarra Valley $12–$19
Current vintage: 2005   93

A delightful traminer that presents deliciously spicy and intensely aromatic varietal qualities without the excessive fatness or oiliness usually found in wines of such intensity. A musky, floral perfume of lychees and rose oil precedes a juicy, bright and crunchy palate whose pristine fruit is tightly bound by crackly acids. Excellent shape and future.

2005	93	2010	2013
2004	82	2004	2005
2003	90	2005	2008+
2002	83	2002	2003
2000	92	2002	2005
1998	89	2000	2003
1996	90	2001	2004
1995	94	2000	2003
1993	85	1995	1996

PINOT NOIR

RATING 5

Lillydale Estate
Yarra Valley
Pinot Noir

Yarra Valley $20–$29
Current vintage: 2006   87

Simple, honest and flavoursome, this rather jammy young pinot has a juicy expression of red cherries and plums backed by cedar/vanilla oak and undertones of cloves and cinnamon. Supported by a fine-grained spine of powdery, almost crunchy tannin, it's chewy and generous, but falls a fraction short.

2006	87	2008	2011
2005	89	2007	2010
2004	86	2006	2009
2003	87	2008	2011
2002	89	2004	2007
2001	86	2003	2006
2000	83	2002	2005
1999	89	2001	2004
1998	85	1999	2000
1997	89	1999	2002
1996	90	1998	2001
1995	87	1997	2000
1994	88	1996	1999

Lindemans

Karadoc Winery, Edey Road, Karadoc via Red Cliffs Vic 3496. Tel: (03) 5051 3285. Fax: (03) 5051 3390.
Website: www.lindemans.com.au

Regions: **Coonawarra, Padthaway, South Australia, Victoria** Winemaker: **Wayne Falkenberg**
Viticulturist: **Marcus Everett** Chief Executive: **Jamie Odell**

It seems the fate of Lindemans Coonawarra is forever to be a brand in limbo. A previous ownership and management slashed its price and its profile in the mid 1990s after which, thanks in large measure to its extraordinary 1998 vintage, it managed to recover its profile in full. It has since been affected by a combination of poor vintages and another change in ownership and appears to have fallen through some corporate cracks. Other than the Pyrus, the 2004 reds are well below the standard traditionally expected under this label.

BIN 65 CHARDONNAY

Southern Australia		**$5–$11**
Current vintage: 2006		**86**

Citrusy, mango-like fruit with a dusty background of vanilla, buttery and cashew-like oak precedes a juicy and forward palate whose mouthfilling peach, melon and nectarine-like fruit finishes with soft, but refreshing acids. Fruit-driven, with good intensity and brightness.

2006	86	2006	2007+
2005	80	2005	2006
2004	83	2004	2005
2003	83	2003	2004+
2002	86	2002	2003
2001	81	2001	2002

LIMESTONE RIDGE (Shiraz Cabernet Sauvignon)   RATING ❷

Coonawarra		**$50–$99**
Current vintage: 2004		**88**

Advanced, forward and lacking genuine structure, with slightly baked and varnishy aromas of blackberries, cassis and dark cherries above nuances of menthol and mint. Its smooth, polished and oaky palate marries spicy, blackberry-like flavour with chocolate, cedar and vanilla, but finishes with a cooked, currant-like aspect.

2004	88	2006	2009+
2001	93	2013	2021
2000	86	2005	2008
1999	95	2011	2011+
1998	96	2006	2010+
1997	90	2005	2009+
1996	94	2004	2008+
1994	95	2014	2024
1993	91	2001	2005
1992	88	1997	2000
1991	94	2003	2011

PYRUS   RATING ❸

Coonawarra		**$50–$99**
Current vintage: 2004		**90**

This piercingly flavoured, fine-grained and firmish young cabernet blend has a minty expression of blackberries, mulberries and dark plums, with an underswell of fresh vanilla and dark chocolate oak. Supported by powdery tannin, it's long, elegant and finely balanced, but lacks genuine distinction.

2004	90	2009	2012+
2000	90	2005	2008
1999	93	2007	2011+
1998	95	2006	2010+
1997	89	2002	2005+
1996	89	2004	2008
1995	88	2000	2003+
1994	90	2002	2006+
1993	89	1998	2001
1992	88	1997	2000

ST GEORGE CABERNET SAUVIGNON   RATING ❸

Coonawarra		**$50–$99**
Current vintage: 2004		**86**

Dull, plastic-like and menthol aromas of stressed berries and plums precede a modest, confectionary palate supported by smooth and creamy tannin that is already ageing and tiring. Lacking fruit brightness, it finishes herbal and flat, falling short and disappointing.

2004	86	2009	2012
2001	88	2006	2009
2000	88	2005	2008
1999	94	2007	2019
1998	95	2010	2018
1997	90	2002	2005+
1996	94	2008	2016
1995	94	2003	2007+
1994	94	2006	2014
1993	87	1998	2001
1992	89	2000	2004
1991	95	2003	2011
1990	92	2002	2010
1989	87	1994	1997
1988	93	1993	1996
1987	82	1989	1992
1986	94	1998	2006

Madew

Lake George via Collector NSW 2581. Tel: (02) 4848 0165. Fax: (02) 4848 0164.
Website: www.madewwines.com.au Email: cellardoor@madewwines.com.au

Region: **Canberra** Winemaker: **David Madew** Chief Executive: **David Madew**

Madew is forging a fine reputation for its very European-styled rieslings, most of which ably carry some residual sweetness as part of their style. It's also a very capable maker of some first-rate Pinot Gris and some smoky, savoury Shiraz.

BELLE LATE PICKED RIESLING

RATING **3**

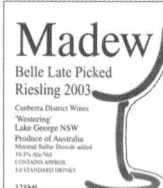

Canberra	$30–$49
Current vintage: 2006	**94**

A delightfully racy, juicy and crisp young riesling of halbtrocken-like 'off-dry'-ness whose vibrant and slightly sweet expression of stonefruit, lime juice, pear and apple flavours finishes with crunchy acidity. It's floral and perfumed, long and smooth, with delightful palate weight and texture supported by a fine, chalky spine of powdery phenolics.

2006	94	2008	2011+
2004	95	2006	2009
2003	91	2008	2011
2002	95	2007	2010

RIESLING

RATING **4**

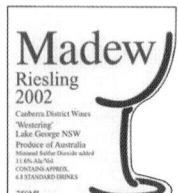

Canberra	$20–$29
Current vintage: 2005	**90**

Pungent, youthful and estery floral aromas of apple and pear precede a juicy and fleshy palate bursting with vibrant flavour. Its intense core of apple, pear and lemon zest culminates in a marginally sweet and refreshing finish of slightly mineral acids. Excellent shape and balance. Quite Alsatian.

2005	90	2010	2013
2003	88	2005	2008
2002	94	2010	2014
2001	86	2002	2003
2000	90	2002	2005

Maglieri

Sturt Highway, Nuriootpa SA 5355. Tel: (08) 8383 2211. Fax: (08) 8383 0735.
Website: www.fosters.com.au

Region: **McLaren Vale** Winemaker: **Alex Mackenzie** Viticulturist: **Chris Dundon** Chief Executive: **Jamie Odell**

After what will hopefully not prove to be a false start with some very promising wines from red Italian varieties, Maglieri has released a juicy and concentrated Cabernet Sauvignon plus a slightly dried-out Shiraz from 2005. Its future, in the exceptionally large and diverse Foster's wine portfolio, perhaps remains uncertain. When bought by Mildara Blass, Maglieri was one of the hottest wine brands in McLaren Vale.

CABERNET SAUVIGNON

RATING **5**

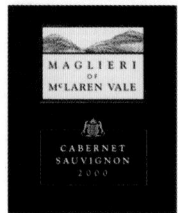

McLaren Vale	$12–$19
Current vintage: 2005	**88**

An honest, dark-fruited cabernet whose fresh aromas of dark berries, plums and blackcurrants are backed by toasty vanilla oak. Generous and juicy, it's initially ripe and concentrated and while it's underpinned by firm, drying tannins, its fruit does thin out a fraction.

2005	88	2007	2010+
2004	81	2006	2009
2003	88	2005	2008+
2002	88	2004	2007+
2001	81	2003	2006
2000	82	2002	2005
1999	83	2001	2004
1997	90	2002	2005
1995	91	2003	2007

SHIRAZ

RATING **5**

McLaren Vale	$12–$19
Current vintage: 2005	**86**

Sumptuous, flavoursome and early-drinking, this meaty and slightly dehydrated shiraz has a menthol-like aroma of dark plums with undertones of currants and toasty vanilla oak. Very ripe, rich plum and blackberry-like flavours begin with plenty of intensity but break up a little, finishing short and lacking focus.

2005	86	2007	2010
2004	89	2009	2012+
2003	90	2008	2011
2002	77	2003	2004
2001	88	2003	2006
2000	82	2002	2005
1999	83	2001	2004
1998	87	2000	2003
1997	90	2002	2005
1996	89	2004	2008
1995	91	2003	2007

Main Ridge Estate

80 William Road, Red Hill Vic 3937. Tel: (03) 5989 2686. Fax: (03) 5931 0000.
Website: www.mre.com.au Email: mrestate@mre.com.au
Region: **Mornington Peninsula** Winemaker: **Nat White** Viticulturist: **Nat White**
Chief Executives: **Rosalie & Nat White**

Main Ridge Estate was one of the first vineyards on Victoria's Mornington Peninsula, but through thick and thin, this tiny estate has justified all the accolades it has collected. From 2005 comes a luxuriant and sumptuous Chardonnay, a perfumed and smoky The Acre Pinot Noir and a powerful, deeply layered Half Acre Pinot Noir. This story just gets better and better...

CHARDONNAY

RATING **3**

Mornington Peninsula	$50–$99
Current vintage: 2005	**95**

A luxuriant and deeply flavoured chardonnay whose concentrated fragrance of pristine melon, citrus and tropical aromas are tightly knit with sweet, buttery and vanilla oak, which is also the source of some underlying clove and cinnamon-like complexity. It's voluptuous without a hint of over-ripeness, with lingering melon and pineapple flavour culminating in a tight and refreshing finish of citrusy acids. Wonderful balance and integration.

2005	95	2010	2013
2004	94	2009	2012+
2003	93	2008	2011
2002	86	2004	2007
2001	89	2003	2006+
2000	93	2005	2008
1999	93	2004	2007
1998	95	2006	2010
1997	88	1999	2002+

HALF ACRE PINOT NOIR

RATING **2**

Mornington Peninsula	$50–$99
Current vintage: 2005	**96**

Perhaps the most powerful Main Ridge pinot yet, this ripe and assertive young pinot has a sweet and intensely perfumed aroma of dark cherries, beetroot, plums and redcurrant backed by assertive new oak. Steeped in powerful berry, plum and cherry-like flavour, its unctuous palate is backed by sweet, fine-grained oak and framed by firm, tightly knit tannin. Finely balanced, it finishes long and savoury with a lingering core of persistent fruit and pleasing gamey qualities.

2005	96	2013	2017
2004	97	2009	2012+
2003	96	2008	2011+
2002	90	2004	2007+
2001	95	2006	2009+
2000	95	2008	2012
1999	94	2007	2011
1998	93	2003	2006
1997	95	2002	2005+
1996	87	2001	2004
1995	88	1997	2000
1994	93	2002	2006
1993	90	2001	2005

THE ACRE PINOT NOIR

RATING **3**

Mornington Peninsula	$30–$49
Current vintage: 2005	**93**

Perfumed and floral, laced with rose petals, red cherries, cinnamon and raspberries, this savoury and lightly smoky pinot is stylish and elegant, with a pleasing structure of fine, underlying tannin. It's forward and juicy, with underlying suggestions of molasses before a lingering, slightly meaty finish.

2005	93	2010	2013+
2004	91	2006	2009+
2003	93	2005	2008+
2002	87	2004	2007
2001	93	2003	2006

Majella

Lynn Road, Coonawarra SA 5263. Tel: (08) 8736 3055. Fax: (08) 8736 3057.
Website: www.majellawines.com.au Email: prof@majellawines.com.au
Region: **Coonawarra** Winemaker: **Bruce Gregory** Viticulturist: **Anthony Lynn** Chief Executive: **Brian Lynn**

Majella is an expanding family owned and operated wine business in the heart of Coonawarra. It's a red specialist, with significant holdings of mature red vineyards, although it still releases a Riesling. Its affordable blend of cabernet sauvignon and shiraz labelled 'The Musician' has recently won international acclaim. The current releases include the 2004 Malleea blend, the winery's finest effort since 1998.

CABERNET SAUVIGNON

 RATING 3

Coonawarra	$20–$29
Current vintage: 2005	93

Powerful, closed and brooding, with heady and deeply layered aromas of blackcurrant, blackberries, dark plums and polished cedar/vanilla oak over dusty nuances of dried herbs. Coated by creamy, fine-grained tannins, its vibrant and concentrated expression of dark cherries, dark plums and cassis is long and youthful, firm and refined.

2005	93	2013	2017
2004	93	2012	2016+
2003	86	2005	2008
2002	88	2010	2014
2001	95	2009	2013+
2000	93	2005	2008
1999	90	2004	2007
1998	95	2006	2010+
1997	93	2005	2009
1996	93	2001	2004
1995	86	1997	2000
1994	82	1996	1999

SHIRAZ

 RATING 3

Coonawarra	$30–$49
Current vintage: 2005	91

An attractive and flavoursome shiraz whose ripe, slightly jammy and meaty aromas of blackberries, currants and cassis are backed by sweet chocolate/vanilla oak and lifted by a whiff of white pepper. Intense and forward, its juicy palate of dark berry flavours and sweet toasty oak is supported by a fine, powdery spine of firmish tannin, finishing with lingering savoury notes of pencil shavings and meaty fruit. Just a fraction cooked for an even higher rating.

2005	91	2010	2013+
2004	90	2012	2016
2003	92	2008	2011+
2002	87	2004	2007
2001	95	2009	2013
2000	89	2005	2008
1999	90	2004	2007
1998	95	2003	2006+
1997	94	2002	2005+
1996	94	2001	2004
1995	87	1997	2000
1994	93	2002	2006
1993	86	1995	1998
1992	84	1994	1997
1991	86	1993	1996

THE MALLEEA

RATING 3

Coonawarra	$50–$99
Current vintage: 2004	95

An oaky but finely crafted cabernet shiraz blend whose deep, dark, iodide-like aromas of cassis, blackberries and cedar reveal spicy, slightly meaty and leathery undertones. Its spicy, peppery palate is full to medium in weight, delivering an assertively oaked but intensely fruited expression of searingly intense and juicy flavour. It culminates in a restrained and finely crafted finish.

2004	95	2016	2024
2003	89	2011	2015
2002	90	2010	2012
2001	91	2009	2013+
2000	87	2005	2008
1999	92	2004	2007
1998	95	2006	2010+
1997	92	2002	2005+
1996	94	2001	2004

Margan

1238 Milbrodale Road, Ceres Hill, Broke NSW 2330. Tel: (02) 6579 1317. Fax: (02) 6579 1267.
Website: www.margan.com.au Email: di@margan.com.au

Region: **Lower Hunter Valley** Winemaker: **Andrew Margan** Viticulturist: **Andrew Margan**
Chief Executive: **Andrew Margan**

Margan is a family-owned wine business in the Hunter Valley. Its wines are made by Andrew Margan to be enjoyed without a requisite period of cellaring. The most interesting Margan wine tasted recently was the 2005 Limited Release Shiraz (92/100, drink 2013–2017+), a firm wine of medium to full body with delightful smoky and meaty complexity beneath its penetrative small berry flavours.

BOTRYTIS SEMILLON

RATING **4**

Lower Hunter Valley $12–$19 (375 ml)
Current vintage: 2006   **82**

Candied and smoky, possibly thanks to the nearby presence of bushfires, this modestly luscious and meaty dessert wine delivers simple flavours of apricot brandy and barley sugar with a smoky, bitter and lemony finish that lacks great freshness.

2006	82	2007	2008
2005	91	2006	2007
2004	90	2005	2006+
2003	93	2005	2008
2002	89	2004	2007
2001	86	2003	2006+

CABERNET SAUVIGNON

RATING **5**

Lower Hunter Valley   **$20–$29**
Current vintage: 2004   **89**

Quite an elegant, stylish cabernet whose dusty and rather floral aromas of ripe cassis, raspberries and fresh cedar/vanilla oak reveal undertones of mulberries and dried herbs. Its vibrant, lightly chalky palate of pristine raspberry and blackcurrant flavour marries neatly with restrained oak and fine, grippy tannins, finishing with length and freshness.

2004	89	2009	2012
2003	90	2008	2011+
2002	87	2004	2007+
2001	87	2003	2006
2000	90	2005	2008
1999	87	2001	2004+
1997	84	2002	2005

CHARDONNAY

RATING **5**

Lower Hunter Valley   **$12–$19**
Current vintage: 2006   **81**

Buttery, candied and slightly herbal, with moderately bright lemon sherbet-like fruit and nutty vanilla oak finishing savoury, with cashew-like nuances. Medium weight, it lacks genuine fruit brightness and intensity.

2006	81	2007	2008
2005	88	2006	2007
2004	86	2005	2006
2003	88	2004	2005+
2002	86	2003	2004+
2001	82	2002	2003+
2000	86	2001	2002
1998	91	1999	2000

SEMILLON

RATING **5**

Lower Hunter Valley   **$12–$19**
Current vintage: 2006   **88**

Lightly herbal, lemony and tobaccoey, with a slightly confectionary and reductive aspect. Smooth, juicy and mouthfilling, it's generously flavoured with melon, pear and apple, finishing with refreshing acids but also a hint of sweetness.

2006	88	2008	2011
2005	88	2007	2010
2004	88	2005	2006
2003	90	2008	2011+
2002	90	2004	2007
2001	85	2001	2002+
2000	89	2002	2005
1998	87	2003	2006

SHIRAZ

RATING **4**

Lower Hunter Valley   **$20–$29**
Current vintage: 2005   **89**

Likely to settle into a typically fine and rustic regional style, this earthy and meaty shiraz has a briary bouquet of dark plums and berries backed by reductive and leathery undertones. Medium to full in weight, it presents a pleasing depth of ripe and almost jujube-like fruit over a firm and grainy chassis of powdery tannins.

2005	89	2010	2013+
2004	89	2009	2012
2003	90	2008	2011
2002	90	2004	2007
2001	89	2003	2006
2000	92	2005	2008+
1999	90	2004	2007
1998	85	2000	2003
1997	89	2002	2005

McAlister Vineyards

RMB 6810 Golden Beach Road, Longford South-East Gippsland Vic 3851. Tel: (03) 5149 7229.
Fax: (03) 5149 7229

Region: **Gippsland** Winemaker: **Peter Edwards** Viticulturist: **Peter Edwards** Chief Executive: **Peter Edwards**

The McAlister is a single-vineyard blend of red Bordeaux varieties that typically exhibits vibrant, complex flavours delivered in a refined and elegant package. The 2001 is a classic example, now looking very much like a fine Margaux. The dramatic climatic variations of recent vintages have certainly made it challenging for Peter Edwards to maintain the style he is seeking. The rather plush 2004 release is possibly his ripest and most powerful yet.

THE McALISTER
RATING **4**

Gippsland	$50–$99
Current vintage: 2004	**90**

One of the riper wines from this vineyard, with a perfume of raspberries, cherries and cassis backed by a hint of currants, nuances of undergrowth and a minty, floral aspect. It's smooth, seamless and evenly fruited, with a plush mouthfeel of briary black and red berry flavour and restrained cedar/vanilla oak framed by fine, drying and dusty tannin. Retains its customary elegance.

2004	90	2012	2016
2003	88	2008	2011+
2002	87	2007	2010+
2001	94	2009	2013
2000	91	2005	2008
1999	87	2004	2007
1998	85	2003	2006+
1997	87	2005	2009
1996	84	1998	2001
1995	87	2000	2003
1994	95	2002	2006
1993	90	1998	2001
1992	93	2000	2004
1991	93	1999	2003
1990	94	2002	2010
1989	87	1997	2001
1988	93	2000	2005
1987	92	1999	2004

McWilliam's

Doug McWilliam Road, Yenda NSW 2681. Tel: (02) 6968 1001. Fax: (02) 6968 1312.
Website: www.mcwilliams.com.au Email: mcwines@mcwilliams.com.au

Regions: **Various SA, WA & NSW** Winemakers: **Jim Brayne, Russell Cody**
Viticulturists: **Terry McLeary, Jeoff McCorkelle** Chief Executive: **George Wahby**

McWilliams is one of the larger family-owned Australian wine companies that, like several others, is based near Griffith in NSW. It's responsible for a huge array of wine, the best of which includes the excellent Hanwood range, the Regional Series and a couple of unattached premier wines like the 1877 Cabernet Sauvignon Shiraz and the modern Riverina benchmark, the Botrytis Semillon. It has a successful export relationship with Gallo.

1877 CABERNET SAUVIGNON SHIRAZ
RATING **3**

Coonawarra, Hilltops	$50–$99
Current vintage: 2003	**90**

Rich and powerful, this finely crafted, flavoursome and old-fashioned red blend does need some time. Closed and earthy, its meaty bouquet of red berries and sweet cedar/vanilla oak reveals slightly cooked, leathery and spicy aspects with a whiff of iodide. Firm and full-bodied, it's dark, spicy and savoury, with deep and slightly baked flavours of blackberries and plums backed by cedar/vanilla oak and framed a slightly raw and drying astringency.

2003	90	2011	2015+
2002	93	2014	2022
2001	93	2009	2013
2000	87	2005	2008
1999	87	2004	2007
1998	95	2006	2010+

CLARE VALLEY RIESLING
RATING **4**

Clare Valley	$12–$19
Current vintage: 2005	**92**

A very stylish, taut and limey riesling whose punchy floral perfume of citrus, musk and mineral precedes a long and pristine palate with a slightly chalky undercarriage. Its tangy fruit and rose oil undertones culminate in a clean, refreshing and sculpted finish with a lingering core of intense fruit.

2005	92	2010	2013+
2004	91	2009	2012+
2003	82	2004	2005+
2002	87	2004	2007+
2001	90	2006	2009+

EDEN VALLEY RIESLING

RATING 5

Eden Valley $12–$19
Current vintage: 2006 86

A delicate, floral riesling whose simple lemon candy fruit lacks great intensity and focus. Finished by thin and slightly green-edged acids, its palate could use more shape and ripeness.

2006	86	2008	2011
2005	82	2007	2010
2004	89	2006	2009+
2003	91	2008	2011+
2002	86	2004	2007
2001	89	2006	2009
1996	89	2001	2004

MARGARET RIVER SEMILLON SAUVIGNON BLANC

RATING 5

Margaret River $12–$19
Current vintage: 2005 88

A slightly angular young blend whose lightly herbal, capsicum-like scents underpin aromas of fresh melon/lemon fruit and vanilla oak. Backed by restrained oak, its generous, juicy flavours of tangy lemon fruit extend towards some presently hard-edged acids that should become better balanced with time.

2005	88	2010	2013
2004	84	2006	2009
2003	89	2004	2005
2002	88	2003	2004
2001	86	2002	2003

RIVERINA BOTRYTIS SEMILLON

RATING 2

Riverina $20–$29 (375 ml)
Current vintage: 2005 86

Simple, cooked and candied, with a bouquet of marmalade and crème caramel over vanilla oak and light mineral notes. Its initially luscious pineapple/cumquat fruit thins out, lacking much length of flavour, finishing moderately sweet but lean and hollow.

2005	86	2007	2010
2004	95	2009	2012
2003	90	2005	2008
2001	95	2003	2006
2000	94	2005	2008
1999	96	2004	2007
1998	95	2003	2006
1997	92	2002	2005
1996	88	1998	2001

Meadowbank Estate

699 Richmond Road, Cambridge Tas 7170. Tel: (03) 6248 4484. Fax: (03) 6248 4485.
Website: www.meadowbankwines.com.au Email: bookings@meadowbankwines.com.au
Region: **Derwent Valley** Winemaker: **Andrew Hood** Viticulturist: **Adrian Hallam** Chief Executive: **Gerald Ellis**
2005 was always tipped to be a fine vintage in Tasmania, and has helped Meadowbank to produce its best chardonnays for several years. Like many other cool-climate Australian wineries, Meadowbank lost around 80% of its expected yield in 2007 thanks to October frosts in late 2006.

CHARDONNAY

Derwent Valley $20–$29
Current vintage: 2005 90

A very good unwooded chardonnay whose aromas of peach, melon, pineapple, passionfruit and guava precede a creamy and vibrant palate of genuine length and freshness. Punctuated by refreshingly soft and tingly acids, it's very clean and persistent.

2005	90	2006	2007+
2004	84	2005	2006
2003	86	2004	2005
2002	77	2002	2003
2001	88	2002	2003
1999	87	2001	2004
1998	86	2000	2003

GRACE ELIZABETH CHARDONNAY

RATING 5

Derwent Valley	$30–$49
Current vintage: 2005	**90**

Fresh, lightly oaked aromas of nectarine and peach are backed by hints of cashew, clove, cinnamon and toast. Long and supple, its fresh, tangy palate has a light creamy fattiness, wrapping clean flavours of stonefruit and melon around tangy, lemony acids.

2005	90	2007	2010
2004	81	2005	2006+
2003	87	2005	2008
2002	89	2004	2007
2000	87	2002	2005
1998	82	2000	2003
1997	83	1998	1999
1995	95	2003	2007

HENRY JAMES PINOT NOIR

RATING 5

Derwent Valley	$30–$49
Current vintage: 2005	**88**

Lightly minty aromas of berries, cherries and rather raw and dusty, cardboard-like oak precede a long, forward and juicy palate of pleasingly vibrant, intense and sour-edged flavours of red and black berries, cherries and plums. Quite attractive and focused, but could have used some better oak.

2005	88	2010	2013
2003	77	2004	2005+
2001	88	2003	2006
2000	91	2002	2005
1999	89	2001	2004+
1998	82	2000	2003+
1997	84	1999	2002

mesh

Tel: (08) 8561 3200. Fax: (08) 8561 3465
Website: www.meshwine.com Email: marketing@meshwine.com
Region: **Eden Valley** Winemakers: **Jeff Grosset, Robert Hill Smith**
Viticulturists: **Jeff Grosset, Robert Hill Smith** Chief Executives: **Jeff Grosset, Robert Hill Smith**
mesh is the joint venture between an unlikely couple of riesling devotees in Jeff Grosset and Robert Hill Smith. The fruit is equally divided between the two parties but then, after vintage, the finished components are compared to define the final blend. mesh is heady and perfumed, remarkably floral and citrusy, with the classic lime juice qualities and chalky tightness expected of Eden Valley riesling.

RIESLING

RATING 2

Eden Valley	$30–$49
Current vintage: 2005	**97**

An incredible riesling in the classically stylish and powdery Eden Valley style, with a purity of accent and simply exceptional delivery. There's something about the wild, mineral and exotic about its heady perfume of floral, citrus and stonefruit aromas. Long, tight and tangy, its clear lime juice palate builds towards a crescendo of flavour prior to a taut and mineral finish of wonderful length. Grand Cru stuff.

2005	97	2017	2025+
2004	95	2009	2012
2003	95	2011	2015
2002	97	2014	2022+

Metala

Nuriootpa Road, Angaston SA 5353. Tel: (08) 8564 3355. Fax: (08) 8564 2209. Website: www.fosters.com.au
Region: **Langhorne Creek** Winemaker: **Nigel Dolan** Viticulturists: **Tom & Guy Adams** Chief Executive: **Jamie Odell**
Metala is an historic Australian brand made by Nigel Dolan and sourced from a very old vineyard in Langhorne Creek. In better vintages its oldest vines contribute to the Black Label Shiraz, which shows the effects of extreme heat in the 2001 release. The rather charming 'standard' white label blend of shiraz with cabernet sauvignon from 2004 is typically supple, minty and packed with intense berry flavour.

BLACK LABEL SHIRAZ

RATING 3

Langhorne Creek	$30–$49
Current vintage: 2001	**88**

Firm, grippy and flavoursome, this early-drinking shiraz dries out a shade at the back of the palate. Its slightly cooked aromas of cherries, raspberries and sweet vanilla/coconut American oak reveal violet-like and meaty undertones, while its fullish and forward palate lacks its customary length and brightness. Its rather stewed expression of dark berry fruit is backed by sweet oak and suggestions of mint and eucalypt.

2001	88	2006	2009
2000	94	2008	2012
1998	90	2003	2006
1996	95	2004	2008
1995	90	2003	2007
1994	95	2002	2006

SHIRAZ CABERNET

Langhorne Creek	**$12–$19**	2004	90	2012	2016
Current vintage: 2004	**90**	2002	82	2004	2007
		2001	89	2006	2009

Elegant and supple, with a spicy and minty fragrance of cassis, redcurrants, slightly stewed plums and vanilla oak over nuances of cloves, cinnamon and violets. Vibrant flavours of cassis, raspberries, redcurrants and plums knit tightly with cedary oak and fine tannins, culminating in a long, firm finish. Charmingly balanced.

2000	90	2005	2008
1999	86	2001	2004
1998	93	2006	2010
1997	89	2002	2005
1996	91	2001	2004
1995	90	2000	2003
1994	91	2002	2006
1993	92	2001	2005
1992	91	2000	2004

Mildara Coonawarra

Riddoch Highway, Coonawarra SA 5263. Tel: (08) 8736 3380. Fax: (08) 8736 3307.
Website: www.fosters.com.au
Region: **Coonawarra** Winemaker: **Andrew Hales** Viticulturist: **Brendan Provis** Chief Executive: **Jamie Odell**

In what seems half a lifetime ago, Mildara's Coonawarra Cabernet Sauvignon occupied a similar place and prestige in the market to Wynns' Coonawarra Estate (black label) Cabernet Sauvignon. After a period in the marketing wilderness, during which its makers never let go of their game, the wine is again subject to attention and interest. In other words, one of wine's best-kept secrets is out, and becoming more expensive! Keep an eye out for this wine, and for its re-emerging stablemates of Shiraz, Cabernet Merlot and Cabernet Shiraz.

CABERNET SAUVIGNON

Coonawarra	**$20–$29**	2005	89	2010	2013+
Current vintage: 2005	**89**	2004	94	2016	2024
		2003	92	2011	2015+

A bright, floral and cassis-like fragrance backed by cedar/vanilla reveals undertones of gamey oak. Long and fine-grained, it's elegant but slightly spirity, delivering intense, minty, but marginally overcooked flavours of blackcurrants and dark plums backed by dark chocolate and cedary oak. It finishes with intense fruit flavour, but just a hint of spirit.

2002	92	2010	2014
2000	87	2005	2008
1999	88	2004	2007+
1998	93	2006	2010+
1997	83	1999	2002
1996	88	2004	2008
1995	87	2000	2003
1994	93	2002	2006
1993	95	2001	2005
1992	94	2000	2004

Mitchell

Hughes Park Road, Sevenhill via Clare SA 5453. Tel: (08) 8843 4258. Fax: (08) 8843 4340.
Website: www.mitchellwines.com.au Email: amitchell@mitchellwines.com
Region: **Clare Valley** Winemaker: **Simon Pringle** Viticulturist: **Leon Schramm**
Chief Executives: **Andrew Mitchell & Jane Mitchell**

A small producer of compelling and individual Clare Valley wines, Mitchell is one of the leading makers of the region's white speciality, riesling. The 2005 release has a powdery texture and sculpted tightness akin to the Eden Valley's finest, while the 2006 combines quite youthful complexity with genuine elegance. The second release of the deliciously rustic and savoury McNicol Shiraz should find a welcome home on restaurant lists.

GSM GRENACHE SANGIOVESE MOURVÈDRE
(formerly The Growers Grenache)

Clare Valley	**$20–$29**	2003	90	2008	2011+
Current vintage: 2003	**90**	2002	90	2007	2010
		2001	86	2003	2009

Scented with five spice and delicate earthy, floral aromas, it's confiture-like bouquet of dark plums, red cherries and raspberries precedes a juicy and a rather jammy palate underpinned by sandpapery, fine-grained tannins. It's stony and bony, with warmth and richness of flavour, but only medium to full in palate weight, being elegant and fine-grained for its style.

2000	87	2002	2005
1999	86	2001	2004
1998	88	2000	2003
1997	90	1999	2002
1996	86	1998	2001

McNICOL SHIRAZ

RATING 3

Clare Valley	$50–$99
Current vintage: 1999	**93**

A meaty, rustic, briary and leathery shiraz of great complexity and interest. It's smoky and seductive, with scents of plums and cassis, polished furniture and earthy nuances. Round and generous, with a firm but approachable spine of fine tannins, it's smooth and polished, with a fine length of complex, evolved character, reductive undertones and a hint of mint.

2002	94	2014	2022+
1999	93	2007	2011+
1998	93	2010	2018+
1997	90	2005	2009+

PEPPERTREE VINEYARD SHIRAZ

RATING 4

Clare Valley	$20–$29
Current vintage: 2004	**93**

A very well handled wine that opens slowly to reveal brightness and length. Its meaty, spicy aromas of red berries and plums are backed by peppery undertones of cinnamon and nutmeg, with charcuterie-like notes. Long and vibrant, its deeply ripened palate of black and red berry flavours and minty, menthol-like regional qualities is wound around a firmish but fine-grained and powdery spine of pliant tannin. Just marginally too cooked and stressed for a higher rating.

2004	93	2012	2016+
2003	90	2011	2015
2002	87	2007	2010+
2001	85	2003	2006
2000	81	2005	2008
1999	90	2007	2011
1998	92	2010	2018
1997	82	2002	2005
1996	93	2001	2004
1995	82	2000	2003
1994	90	1999	2003
1993	93	2001	2005
1992	92	2000	2004
1991	91	1996	1999

SEMILLON

RATING 5

Clare Valley	$12–$19
Current vintage: 2005	**88**

Juicy and generous, with slightly brassy green melon and apple-like flavour with undertones of smoky vanilla oak, wheatmeal, minerality and a light funkiness. Finished with refreshing acids, it's broad but well balanced, and lacks great length and genuine finesse.

2005	88	2010	2013
2004	88	2006	2009
2002	90	2004	2007+
2001	89	2003	2006
2000	88	2002	2005
1999	89	2001	2004+
1998	88	2000	2003
1997	89	2002	2005
1996	90	2001	2004
1995	88	2000	2003
1994	93	2002	2006
1993	95	2001	2005

SEVENHILL VINEYARD CABERNET SAUVIGNON

RATING 3

Clare Valley	$20–$29
Current vintage: 2003	**91**

A measured and polished cabernet showing some elegance and maturity. Minty cassis, mulberry, blackberry, dark plum-like fruit and cedar/vanilla oak overlie nuances of dried herbs, dark chocolate and briar. It's floral bouquet precedes a layered palate of deep, brooding dark-fruited aspects, smooth creamy oak and supple, grainy tannins.

2003	91	2011	2015
2002	89	2010	2014
2001	93	2013	2021+
2000	87	2008	2012
1999	94	2011	2019
1998	94	2010	2018+
1997	87	2005	2009
1996	92	2008	2016
1995	82	2000	2003
1994	91	2002	2006
1992	91	2004	2012
1991	93	2003	2011
1990	94	2002	2010
1988	88	1996	2000

WATERVALE RIESLING

Clare Valley $12–$19
Current vintage: 2006   **90**

Delicate and floral, with lightly toasty, buttery aromas of lemon rind, beeswax and honey. Its moderately long palate of fresh lime juice and lemon reveals waxy undertones, finishing dry and savoury with reductive and mineral nuances. Elegant and restrained, lacking its ususal focus and length, it's possibly experiencing the classic riesling adolescence.

2006	90	2008	2011+
2005	95	2013	2017+
2004	95	2012	2016+
2003	92	2011	2015
2002	86	2004	2007+
2001	94	2009	2013+
2000	91	2005	2008+
1999	80	2001	2004
1998	94	2006	2010+
1997	92	2005	2009
1996	87	2001	2004
1995	94	2003	2007
1994	88	1999	2003
1993	93	2001	2005
1992	91	1997	2000

Mitchelton

Mitcheltstown Road, Nagambie Vic 3608. Tel: (03) 5736 2222. Fax: (03) 5736 2266.
Website: www.mitchelton.com.au Email: mitchelton@mitchelton.com.au

Region: **Nagambie Lakes** Winemaker: **Ben Haines** Viticulturist: **John Beresford** Chief Executive: **Robert Auld**

A monumental Victorian winery that has struggled to cement a place in the hearts of Australian wine drinkers, Mitchelton is moving towards a Rhône Valley set of varieties and blends with some success, although it needs to release the white Airstrip blend as well as back vintages of Marsanne at a significantly younger age than it is presently doing. The Print Shiraz returned to form in 2004 with a smooth and deeply flavoured wine.

AIRSTRIP (Marsanne Roussanne Viognier blend)

Nagambie Lakes $20–$29
Current vintage: 2004   **88**

Very restrained and elegant, this rather evolved and savoury white blend has a delicate bouquet of honeysuckle and lemon rind, dried flowers and grilled nuts backed by vanilla oak and buttery, toasty bottle-aged aspects. Dusty and spicy, its surprisingly viscous palate is underpinned by a powdery cut of fine tannin, culminating in a lingering finish of secondary flavours and soft acids.

2004	88	2006	2009
2003	89	2005	2008
2002	93	2004	2007
2001	93	2003	2006
2000	89	2002	2005+
1999	90	2001	2005+
1998	85	2000	2003
1994	92	1999	2002+

BLACKWOOD PARK RIESLING

Nagambie Lakes $12–$19
Current vintage: 2006   **87**

Candied, citrusy and sherbet-like aromas of moderate intensity overlie a lightly floral suggestion of talcum powder. Rather broad and phenolic, its rather confectionary palate of moderate intensity lacks genuine length and persistence.

2006	87	2008	2011+
2005	89	2010	2013+
2004	93	2009	2012+
2003	90	2008	2011
2002	90	2007	2010+
2001	88	2003	2006+
2000	93	2008	2012
1999	87	2001	2004
1998	93	2006	2010
1997	90	2002	2005+
1996	93	2004	2008
1995	93	2000	2003
1994	93	1999	2002
1993	91	1998	2001

CLASSIC RELEASE MARSANNE

Nagambie Lakes $20–$29
Current vintage: 2000   **90**

Smoky hints of honeysuckle still pervade the toasty, buttery and honeyed development of this mature and elegant white wine. It's slightly candied, smooth and savoury, finishing with refreshing acids and lingering influences from well-handled oak.

2000	90	2005	2008+
1999	86	2004	2007
1998	89	2003	2006
1997	89	1999	2002+
1996	90	2000	2003
1995	88	1997	2000+
1994	82	1995	1998
1993	95	1998	2001
1992	94	2000	2004

CRESCENT (Shiraz Mourvèdre Grenache blend)

Nagambie Lakes $20–$29
Current vintage: 2003   86

Developing some meaty bottle-aged complexity, this firmish but cooked and stewy red blend reveals both under and over-ripe characters. Beneath vibrant scents of dark plums and cherries lie earthy, dusty influences, while its generous but slightly hollow palate of redcurrant-like flavour shows the presence both of raisined fruit and green-edged tannin.

2003	86	2008	2011
2002	87	2010	2014
2001	91	2006	2009
2000	93	2005	2008
1999	89	2004	2007+
1998	89	2003	2006+
1997	84	1999	2002

PRINT SHIRAZ

Nagambie Lakes $50–$99
Current vintage: 2004   93

Smooth, firm and concentrated, this long and spicy shiraz marries blackberries, blueberries, plums and cassis with creamy, chocolate-like oak and a drying, loose-knit extract. It reveals a confiture-like quality, with underlying nuances of cloves, cinnamon, eucalypt and menthol, finishing complex and savoury with a lingering core of slightly jammy fruit.

2004	93	2012	2016
2003	83	2008	2011
2002	95	2010	2014+
2001	93	2009	2013+
2000	90	2005	2008+
1999	92	2007	2011
1998	93	2010	2018
1997	91	2005	2009
1996	89	2001	2004
1995	92	2003	2007
1994	88	2002	2006
1993	94	2005	2013
1992	88	2000	2004+
1991	94	2003	2011
1990	90	1998	2002

SHIRAZ

Nagambie Lakes $20–29
Current vintage: 2005   83

Closed, meaty and already browning, this smoky, cooked and over-oaked shiraz offers jammy, currant-like flavours of plums and prunes that dry out towards a musky finish of stale fruit and suede leather.

2005	83	2007	2010
2004	87	2009	2012
2003	92	2005	2008+
2002	93	2007	2010+
2001	90	2006	2009+
2000	92	2005	2008
1999	89	2004	2007
1997	85	1999	2002
1996	83	1998	2001
1995	87	2000	2003
1994	85	1996	2001

VIOGNIER

Nagambie Lakes $20–$29
Current vintage: 2005   83

Candied aromas of nectarines, apricots and tropical fruits with undertones of cloves and cinnamon precede a forward, juicy and rather broad palate that delivers sumptuous fruit but lacks brightness and penetration of flavour. Honeyed, buttery and toasty, it needs a more convincing presence of bright, varietal fruit and finishes a little hard-edged. Caricature-like.

2005	83	2005	2006+
2003	90	2004	2005+
2002	89	2003	2004+
2001	88	2002	2003+
2000	79	2000	2001
1998	84	1999	2000

Mitolo

34 Barossa Valley Way, Tanunda SA 5352. Tel: (08) 8292 9012. Fax: (08) 8282 9062.
Website: www.mitolowines.com.au Email: enquiries@mitolowines.com.au
Regions: **Barossa Valley, McLaren Vale** Winemaker: **Ben Glaetzer** Chief Executive: **Frank Mitolo**

With its deep and unctuous Savitar Shiraz, Mitolo has produced one of McLaren Vale's highlights from 2005. The G.A.M. is smoother, more pliant and nearly as good, while the rather more cooked and meaty Reiver reflects the heat of the Barossa vintage. As ever, I am unconvinced about the Serpico cabernet, but rejoice in the fact that it's just as well we are not all turned on by precisely the same wines. Life is competitive enough already!

G.A.M. SHIRAZ

RATING **5**

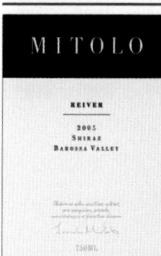

McLaren Vale	$50–$99
Current vintage: 2005	93

Smooth, luscious and deeply fruited, this artfully made shiraz opens with a dark, smoky and meaty bouquet of dark plums and berries, with reductive, charcuterie-like undertones as well as a cinnamon/nutmeg-like spiciness. Its warm and deeply layered palate of sour-edged plums and blackberries, licorice and mint knits tightly with fine-grained cedary oak and a firmish, but pliant undercarriage.

2005	93	2010	2013+
2004	89	2009	2012+
2003	87	2005	2008
2002	89	2004	2007+
2001	88	2006	2009+

REIVER SHIRAZ

RATING **3**

Barossa Valley	$50–$99
Current vintage: 2005	90

Smoky, meaty aromas of sweet and slightly jammy red and black berries are backed by nuances of white pepper, caramel, raisins and spicecake. Plump and juicy, its slightly cooked and dehydrated expression of meaty fruit is enhanced by some high-end sweet vanilla oak and framed by very fine tannins. It just lacks the genuine palate length and brightness for a higher rating.

2005	90	2007	2010+
2004	89	2009	2012
2003	92	2008	2011+
2002	92	2007	2010
2001	90	2006	2009

SAVITAR SHIRAZ

RATING **3**

McLaren Vale	$50–$99
Current vintage: 2005	94

Deep, complex and slightly jammy aromas of black-berries, plums, red berries and nutty, meaty oak have a gamey edge. Smoothly knit with luxuriant oak and finely powdered tannin, its plush and generous palate is sufficiently rich and unctuous to almost hide its underlying grip and firmness.

2005	94	2010	2013+
2004	93	2009	2012+
2003	94	2008	2011+
2002	91	2004	2007+
2001	89	2006	2009

Montalto

33 Shoreham Road, Red Hill South Vic 3937. Tel: (03) 5989 8412. Fax: (03) 5989 8417.
Website: www.montalto.com.au Email: info@montalto.com.au
Region: **Mornington Peninsula** Winemaker: **Robin Brockett** Viticulturist: **Geoff Clarke**
Chief Executive: **John Mitchell**
Montalto is a very diverse business, with a high-level restaurant, an olive grove and wetland development.
Its winemaking takes place at Scotchman's Hill on the Bellarine Peninsula. In my view there is perhaps more
potential latent in the vineyard than we are presently seeing as quality in the bottle.

CHARDONNAY

RATING **3**

Mornington Peninsula	$30–$49
Current vintage: 2005	**86**

A rather funky but also formulaic-tasting chardonnay whose aromas of pineapple, nectarine, melon and peach overlie dusty, toasty oak influences. The palate is generous and juicy, almost flabby, presenting ripe tropical and peachy fruit before an awkward, disjointed and slightly sweet finish of sappy, edgy acids.

2005	86	2007	2010
2004	89	2006	2009
2003	94	2008	2011
2001	93	2003	2006+
2000	92	2002	2005
1999	91	2001	2004

PINOT NOIR

RATING **4**

Mornington Peninsula	$30–$49
Current vintage: 2005	**89**

A plush and rather cultivated young pinot whose smoky, floral perfume of cherries, dark plums and dark chocolate/mocha oak overlie a herbal aspect. Its smooth, fleshy palate of vibrant fruit and well-mannered oak are backed by smooth, polished tannin, finishing with a lingering core of cherry/berry fruit, meaty complexity, fractionally sour acids and some greenish, vegetal notes around the edges.

2005	89	2007	2010+
2004	86	2005	2006+
2003	93	2005	2008+
2001	93	2003	2006+
2000	90	2002	2005
1999	80	2001	2004

Moondah Brook

Dale Road, Middle Swan WA 6056. Tel: (08) 9274 9547. Fax: (08) 9274 8949.
Website: www.moondahbrook.com.au
Region: **Western Australia** Winemaker: **Ross Pamment** Viticulturist: **Diane Stewart**
Chief Executive: **John Grant**
Moondah Brook is a Hardy Wine Company brand has been slowly downgraded to a generic Western Australian
source of cheap, cheerful and well-made wines of lively varietal flavours and short-term appeal.

CABERNET SAUVIGNON

RATING **5**

Western Australia	$12–$19
Current vintage: 2005	**87**

Juicy, jammy and slightly herbal, with rather sumptuous berry and plum-like fruit, cedar/vanilla oak and robust, powdery tannin combining with pleasing balance and structure. It's earthy and uncomplicated, with lingering herbal undertones.

2005	87	2007	2010+
2002	83	2007	2010
2001	77	2003	2006
2000	86	2002	2005+
1999	88	2004	2007
1998	88	2003	2006+
1997	82	1999	2002
1996	90	2004	2008
1995	87	2000	2003
1993	84	1995	1998

SHIRAZ

RATING **5**

Western Australia $12–$19
Current vintage: 2004 87

A flavoursome, slightly jammy and herbal shiraz with a violet-like perfume. Lightly toasty mocha/chocolate oak backs its perfume of violets and cassis, plums and blackberries, while its palate is almost confectionary, with sweet berry-like fruit and cedar/mocha oak framed by somewhat sappy, but pliant tannins. It finishes with pleasing length and a light herbal sappiness.

2004	87	2006	2009+
2002	81	2004	2007
2001	83	2003	2006
2000	86	2002	2005+
1999	88	2004	2007
1998	87	2003	2006
1997	86	1999	2002
1996	88	2001	2004

Moondarra

Browns Road, Moondarra via Erica Vic 3825. Tel: (03) 9598 3049. Fax: (03) 9598 0766.
Region: **Gippsland** Winemakers: **Sandro Mosele, Neil Prentice** Viticulturist: **Neil Prentice**
Chief Executive: **Neil Prentice**

Moondarra is a tiny Gippsland pinot noir specialist whose wines are made at Kooyong on the Mornington Peninsula. Difficult seasons have prevented me from including the wonderful Samba Side until now, for it has taken several years to clock up the minimum required number of vintages. The wait is worth it.

CONCEPTION PINOT NOIR

RATING **4**

Gippsland $50–$99
Current vintage: 2005 89

Dusty, slightly menthol-like scents of maraschino cherries and raspberries, sweet cedar/vanilla oak, cloves and cinnamon precede a fine and silky palate that becomes a little green-edged and sappy. A firmish extract supports its flavours of redcurrants, cherries and raspberries, with a neatly interwoven contribution from savoury oak. Well made, but a little greenish.

2005	89	2010	2013
2003	93	2008	2011+
2001	90	2006	2009
2000	90	2005	2008
1999	88	2004	2007

SAMBA SIDE PINOT NOIR

RATING **3**

Gippsland $50–$99
Current vintage: 2005 95

A beautifully elegant and complex pinot. Its alluring, lightly smoky and musky perfume of rose petals, dark red cherries and vanilla oak overlies earthy, slightly meaty nuances of forest floor. Pliant, drying and powdery, its sumptuously flavoured palate bursts with vibrant flavours of berries and cherries. It has excellent weight and texture, finishing with brambly fruit and meaty undertones.

2005	95	2010	2013+
2001	89	2003	2006+
2000	95	2005	2008

Moorilla Estate

655 Main Road, Berriedale Tas 7011. Tel: (03) 6277 9900. Fax: (03) 6249 4093.
Website: www.moorilla.com.au Email: cellardoor@moorilla.com.au
Region: **Southern Tasmania** Winemaker: **Alan Ferry** Viticulturist: **Alan Ferry**

Based at Berriedale, close to central Hobart, Moorilla Estate is a serious maker of cool-climate table wines. It regularly achieves success with its spicy, dusty pinot noir and often perfumed and musky expressions of riesling and gewürztraminer. The Claudio's Reserve Pinot Noir 2005 was tasted just after bottling and has every chance of developing beyond my initial expectations.

CABERNET SAUVIGNON

RATING

Southern Tasmania	**$20–$29**		
Current vintage: 2003	**90**		

A complex, fine-grained and tightly knit cabernet whose sweet, slightly varnishy aromas of small berries and vanilla oak gradually open to reveal brightness and freshness. Moderately rich and firm, its intensely juicy palate of red berries, blackberries, plums and cedary oak has a drying spine of fine tannins, finishing with dusty, herbal undertones beneath its vibrant fruit.

2003	90	2011	2015
2002	77	2004	2007+
2001	86	2003	2006
2000	91	2008	2012
1999	88	2004	2007
1998	88	2003	2006
1997	86	2002	2005+
1995	81	2000	2003
1994	93	2002	2006
1993	82	2001	2005

CLAUDIO'S RESERVE PINOT NOIR

RATING

Southern Tasmania	**$30–$49**		
Current vintage: 2005	**91**		

A very minty and powerfully fruited young pinot that needs time to settle in the bottle and for its aromas and flavours to build further. Its briary, concentrated aromas of sweet raspberries, cherries and plums overlies nuances of cedar/vanilla oak. Silky-fine and sumptuous, its minty, brambly and intensely fruited palate is backed by a slightly raw extract of cedary oak, but should smooth out and become more luxuriant as it ages.

2005	91	2013	2017
2002	90	2004	2007+
2001	93	2006	2009
2000	91	2002	2005+
1999	91	2004	2007
1998	83	2000	2003
1997	88	2002	2005
1996	87	1998	2001

RIESLING

RATING

Southern Tasmania	**$20–$29**		
Current vintage: 2006	**87**		

Slightly sweet, simple and confectionary, this clean and lightly herbal riesling has a floral aroma of fresh pear and apple with greenish, cashew-like undertones. Its juicy palate finishes a little short and quite chalky, with a lingering note of lemon sherbet.

2006	87	2007	2008+
2005	92	2010	2013+
2004	88	2006	2009
2003	84	2005	2008+
2002	80	2003	2004+
2001	93	2006	2009+
2000	87	2008	2012
1999	87	2004	2007
1998	90	2003	2006
1997	87	1999	2002
1996	91	2001	2004
1995	88	1997	2000
1994	95	2006	2014

Moodrooduc Estate

501 Derril Road, Moorooduc Vic 3933. Tel: (03) 5971 8506. Fax: (03) 5971 8550.
Website: www.moorooduc-estate.com.au Email: us@moorooduc-estate.com.au
Region: **Mornington Peninsula** Winemaker: **Richard McIntyre** Chief Executive: **Richard McIntyre**

Moorooduc Estate was one of the first makers from the Mornington Peninsula to fashion table wines of genuine class. After some years of struggling to regain its early form, it is edging its way back from 2004 onwards with some very flavoursome and adventurous wines, of which the 2005 chardonnays are complex and interesting examples. There's no doubt about the potential of this site, which has a spectacular history.

CHARDONNAY

RATING 5

Mornington Peninsula	$30–$49
Current vintage: 2005	**91**

A handsome, well handled chardonnay whose lightly dusty aromas of lemon, stonefruit and melon overlie restrained vanilla oak and suggestions of wheatmeal. Its vibrant, shapely palate of intense peach, pineapple and grapefruit flavour culminates in a lingering and tightly focused finish of crisp acidity. It is mouthfilling and generous, with a youthful baby-fatness which should not become too pronounced over time.

2005	91	2007	2010
2004	84	2006	2009
2003	89	2005	2008
2002	83	2003	2004
2001	77	2002	2003
2000	77	2002	2005
1999	87	2001	2004
1998	92	2000	2003
1997	88	2002	2005
1996	93	2001	2004
1995	93	2000	2003
1994	95	1999	2002

PINOT NOIR

RATING 4

Mornington Peninsula	$30–$49
Current vintage: 2005	**88**

Rather old-fashioned, this rustic, lightly browning pinot has a slightly cooked presence of cherries and plums with rather vegetal, earthy undertones and some greenish, sappy edges. It opens up on the palate with genuine fruit sweetness and spice, finishing savoury and meaty with dusty tannins and persistent flavour. A charming country style.

2005	88	2007	2010
2004	89	2006	2009+
2003	91	2005	2008+
2002	91	2004	2007+
2001	84	2003	2006
2000	84	2002	2005
1998	88	2003	2006
1997	93	2002	2005
1996	87	2001	2004
1995	93	2000	2003
1994	92	1999	2002
1993	93	1998	2001
1992	95	2000	2004
1991	84	1996	1999

THE MOOROODUC CHARDONNAY

RATING 4

Mornington Peninsula	$50–$99
Current vintage: 2005	**92**

A complex and polished chardonnay with delicate, rather closed aromas of citrus, melon and dusty, vanilla and faintly nutty undertones from some classy oak. Its pristine palate of fresh nectarine and grapefruit flavour has a creamy texture of yeast-derived complexity, with undertones of fresh vanilla oak and butterscotch. It finishes with lingering stonefruit flavours, soft acids and just a slightly overdone level of malolactic influence.

2005	92	2007	2010+
2004	92	2006	2009+
2002	84	2004	2007+
2001	86	2003	2006
2000	76	2002	2005
1999	84	2001	2004
1998	91	2003	2006

THE MOOROODUC PINOT NOIR

RATING 5

Mornington Peninsula	$50–$99
Current vintage: 2004	**90**

Distinctly varietal but a little edgy all the same, this smooth and richly textured pinot benefits from a very funky complexity. There's a meaty, charcuterie aspect beneath its spicy, assertively floral and slightly candied aromas of raspberries, red cherries, plums, cinnamon and cloves. Long and even, it presents tightly focused but ripe fruit over white pepper-like influences, dusty fine tannins and restrained oak.

2004	90	2009	2012
2003	87	2005	2008
2001	87	2003	2006
2000	81	2002	2005
1998	77	2000	2003
1997	94	2005	2009

Morris

Mia Mia Road, Rutherglen Vic 3685. Tel: (02) 6026 7303. Fax: (02) 6026 7445.
Website: www.morriswines.com.au Email: morriswines@orlando-wyndham.com
Region: **Rutherglen** Winemakers: **David Morris, Mick Morris** Chief Executive: **Laurent Lacassgne**

Morris is one of the traditional makers of red wines in Victoria's warm-to-hot and northeasterly Rutherglen region. The 2004 Shiraz is a classically uncompromising Rutherglen style that achieves its richness and depth without excessive alcohol or portiness. Other makers in the region might take note. Morris is also one of the elite makers of Rutherglen's unique tokay and muscat.

BLUE IMPERIAL

Rutherglen	$20–$29
Current vintage: 2002	**88**

An honest, but lighter wine whose meaty, spicy aromas of plums and blueberries, prunes and currants have sweet vanilla oak and floral undertones. Ripe and forward, then slightly hollow, its sweet, rather cooked and meaty prune/currant fruit qualities overlie nuances of blueberries and blackberries, before finishing soft and smooth.

2002	88	2010	2014+
2001	89	2006	2009
1999	88	2007	2011
1998	86	2003	2006

CABERNET SAUVIGNON

Rutherglen	$12–$19
Current vintage: 2002	**89**

A rustic, old-fashioned and largely over-ripe cabernet that has the depth and structure to last for some time. Its meaty, earthy and gamey aromas of plums, prunes and currants suggests plenty of time hanging to develop sugar sweetness, while its chewy and astringent palate offers sufficient vibrant plum and berry flavour to complement its firm extract.

2002	89	2010	2014+
2001	89	2009	2013
2000	86	2008	2012
1999	89	2007	2011+
1998	89	2006	2010
1997	82	1999	2002+
1996	88	2004	2008+
1995	87	2003	2007
1994	89	2006	2014
1993	87	2005	2013
1992	88	2000	2004
1990	91	2002	2010
1989	91	2001	2009
1988	91	2000	2005

CHARDONNAY

Rutherglen	$12–$19
Current vintage: 2005	**89**

A big, generous and juicy chardonnay whose uncompromisingly ripe flavour of juicy, peachy fruit is handsomely backed by creamy vanilla oak before a lingering and tangy finish of lively acids and a hint of minerality. Clean and refreshing despite its ripeness, this is a very fine effort from this warmer region.

2005	89	2007	2010+
2003	88	2005	2008
2002	89	2004	2007
2001	87	2003	2006
2000	88	2002	2005
1999	87	2000	2001
1998	86	2000	2003
1997	83	1999	2002

DURIF

Rutherglen	$20–$29
Current vintage: 2003	**90**

Extracted and powerful, this firm, fruit-driven and rustic cellar style delivers meaty, licorice-like flavours of baked blackberries, currants and chocolate, with undertones of old oak, spices and bitumen. Its palate is closed, dark and brooding, while there's a floral aspect to its restrained perfume. Cloaked in powerful, chalky tannin, it needs time to become less of a bruiser.

2003	90	2015	2023
2002	90	2014	2022
2001	90	2013	2021
2000	90	2012	2020
1999	87	2007	2011
1998	93	2010	2018+
1997	91	2009	2017
1996	88	2004	2008+
1995	93	2007	2015
1994	93	2002	2006
1993	87	2001	2005
1992	90	2004	2012
1991	93	2003	2011
1990	93	2002	2010
1989	88	2001	2009

SHIRAZ

Ratherglen	$12–$19
Current vintage: 2004	**91**

Ripe and meaty, this rich, juicy and substantial Rutherglen red delivers plenty of plump, juicy dark plum and berry flavour backed by gamey, currant and raisin-like notes, plus a hint of treacle. It's thick and succulent, leaving little to the imagination. Framed by firm, rather assertive tannins, it's a classic regional style that finishes with fresh acidity. Drink now or keep…

2004	91	2016	2024+
2002	90	2014	2022
2001	90	2009	2013
2000	85	2005	2008
1999	88	2004	2007+
1998	89	2003	2006+
1997	85	2005	2009
1996	89	2004	2008+
1995	87	2000	2003
1994	87	2002	2006
1993	82	1998	2001
1992	91	2004	2012
1991	90	2003	2011

Moss Wood

926 Metricup Road, Willyabrup WA 6284. Tel: (08) 9755 6266. Fax: (08) 9755 6303.
Website: www.mosswood.com.au Email: mosswood@mosswood.com.au

Regions: **Margaret River, Pemberton** Winemakers: **Keith Mugford, Josh Bahen, Amanda Shepherdson**
Viticulturist: **Steve Clarke** Chief Executives: **Keith & Clare Mugford**

One of the iconic Margaret River producers, Moss Wood is firing on its traditional cylinders of estate Cabernet Sauvignon, Chardonnay and Semillon, as well as steadily upgrading the style and quality of the wines from the nearby Ribbon Vale Vineyard. Keith Mugford's ambition is to achieve opulent, densely concentrated fruit in his flagship Cabernet Sauvignon, and the price he pays for this is an alcoholic strength that is marginally higher than ideal. That said, these wines are invariably delicious and thoroughly deserve their reputation.

AMY'S CABERNET SAUVIGNON
(formerly Glenmore Vineyard)

Margaret River	$30–$49
Current vintage: 2005	**92**

Smooth and supple, with floral aromas and lightly toasty cedar/vanilla oak lifting intense flavours of small black and red berries, regional earthy undertones and lingering suggestions of dark olives. Supported by a chassis of fine tannins, it's finely balanced, long and savoury, building its flavours towards a pleasing intense crescendo at the finish.

2005	92	2010	2013+
2004	89	2006	2009+
2003	89	2008	2011
2002	86	2004	2007+
2001	89	2003	2006+
2000	93	2008	2012
1999	93	2004	2007+

CABERNET SAUVIGNON

Margaret River	$50–$99
Current vintage: 2004	**95**

Typically ripe and sumptuous, with a confiture-like array of blackberry, cassis, dark cherry, mulberry and dark plum flavour handsomely cloaked in cedar/vanilla oak and coated by exceptionally fine, dusty and powdery tannin. It's heady and perfumed, smooth and silky, finishing with exemplary length and depth of fruit, plus a hint of warmth. Its very modern depth of ripeness perhaps comes at the cost of a small measure of finesse.

2004	95	2016	2024
2003	96	2015	2023+
2002	95	2014	2022
2001	97	2013	2021+
2000	93	2008	2012+
1999	93	2011	2021
1998	90	2006	2010+
1997	89	2005	2009
1996	96	2008	2016
1995	96	2015	2025
1994	95	2014	2024
1993	87	2001	2005
1992	89	2000	2004
1991	96	2003	2011+
1990	95	2002	2010+
1989	91	2001	2009
1988	89	2000	2008
1987	89	1999	2007
1986	95	2006	2016
1985	97	2005	2015

CHARDONNAY

RATING 2

Margaret River $50–$99
Current vintage: 2006   **95**

Stylish and citrusy, this sumptuous marriage between peach, melon, nectarine and grapefruit flavour and dusty, toasty, clove-like vanilla oak has a floral, lemony perfume with undertones of butter. Long, smooth and seamless, it's richly fruited but artfully elegant and refined. Underpinned by a powdery chalkiness, it finishes fresh and savoury, with suggestions of grilled nuts and pecan pie.

2006	95	2011	2014+
2005	96	2007	2010+
2004	96	2009	2012
2003	95	2008	2011
2002	95	2007	2010+
2001	95	2006	2009
2000	91	2005	2008
1999	96	2007	2011
1998	90	2003	2006+
1997	95	2002	2005
1996	93	1998	2001
1995	93	2003	2007
1994	95	2002	2006
1993	92	1998	2001
1992	94	2000	2004
1991	91	2003	2011
1990	94	2002	2010

LEFROY BROOK VINEYARD CHARDONNAY

RATING 4

Pemberton $30–$49
Current vintage: 2005   **81**

A very herbaceous chardonnay whose restrained aromas of dried flowers, chardonnay and melon are overshadowed by assertively herbal, sweaty and silage-like nuances, with creamy, butterscotch undertones. Vegetal and forward, it lacks length and mid-palate brightness and freshness.

2005	81	2006	2007
2004	89	2006	2009
2003	93	2005	2008+
2002	89	2004	2007+
2001	91	2003	2006
1997	92	1999	2002

PINOT NOIR

RATING 5

Margaret River $30–$49
Current vintage: 2004   **88**

A smooth, polished dry red with a supple, fine and elegant expression of meaty, earthy flavours of tomato, cherry, cedar and five spice, before a lingering plummy finish. It's framed by firmish and drying tannins and backed by nuances of dried herbs. Attractive, but not incredibly pinot-like.

2004	88	2009	2012
2003	88	2008	2011
2002	89	2004	2007+
2001	87	2006	2009
2000	81	2002	2005
1999	81	2004	2007
1998	88	2003	2006
1997	86	2002	2005
1996	89	2001	2004
1995	93	2003	2007
1994	87	1999	2002
1993	83	1998	2001

RIBBON VALE VINEYARD CABERNET BLEND

RATING 3

Margaret River $30–$49
Current vintage: 2005   **92**

A firm, grippy and finely balanced blend whose juicy flavours of blackberries, dark plums, mulberries and raspberries are tightly knit with smoky mocha, dark chocolate and vanilla oak. Slightly cooked, it's backed by a hint of mint and menthol with undertones of dried herbs. Supported by smooth, polished tannin, it finishes with length, emphasis and fine-grained astringency.

2005	92	2013	2017
2004	90	2012	2016
2003	93	2011	2015+
2002	91	2010	2014+
2001	92	2009	2013
2000	93	2008	2012
1999	90	2011	2019
1998	77	2000	2003
1997	93	2005	2009
1996	90	2004	2008+
1995	87	2003	2007+
1994	87	2002	2006
1993	84	1995	1998

RIBBON VALE VINEYARD MERLOT

RATING 4

Margaret River	$30–$49
Current vintage: 2005	94

A willowy and stylish merlot underpinned by firm, fine and slightly drying tannins. It's laced with pristine flavours of black cherries and dark plums tightly knit with cedar/vanilla/dark chocolate oak and lightly herbal, briary undertones. Long and finely balanced, it shows a suppleness and focus rare in Australian expressions of this variety.

2005	94	2010	2013+
2004	87	2006	2009+
2003	88	2008	2011
2002	88	2007	2010+
2001	90	2006	2009+
2000	91	2005	2008
1999	92	2007	2011
1998	77	2000	2003
1997	91	2002	2005
1996	90	2004	2008
1995	90	2000	2003
1994	80	1999	2002
1993	89	2001	2005
1992	92	2000	2004
1991	93	1999	2003

SEMILLON

RATING 3

Margaret River	$30–$49
Current vintage: 2006	94

Stylish and finely crafted, this generous and juicy semillon has a lightly herbal but punchy expression of melon and lemon fruit that becomes long, smooth and creamy before finishing with a focused, wet slate-like cut of powdery minerality. It's tightly balanced and refreshing, with a lingering note of reductive complexity.

2006	94	2011	2014+
2005	86	2007	2010
2004	89	2006	2009
2003	93	2005	2008+
2001	95	2006	2009
2000	92	2002	2005+
1999	91	2001	2004
1998	87	2000	2003
1997	84	1998	1999
1994	86	1996	1999
1993	87	1998	2001

Mount Horrocks

The Old Railway, Station Curling Street, Auburn SA 5451. Tel: (08) 8849 2202. Fax: (08) 8849 2265.
Website: www.mounthorrocks.com Email: sales@mounthorrocks.com

Region: **Clare Valley** Winemaker: **Stephanie Toole** Chief Executive: **Stephanie Toole**

Mount Horrocks is an energetic Clare Valley wine producer whose proprietor and maker, Stephanie Toole, is relentlessly working to refine her wines towards classic status. It's impossible for me not to conclude that the vineyards are better suited to white varieties than reds, although the reds still meet a good standard. The 2006 Riesling is an exceptional result from this challenging vintage, with immense cellaring potential.

CABERNET MERLOT (Cabernet Sauvignon in 2004)

RATING 4

Clare Valley	$30–$49
Current vintage: 2004	88

Moderately rich, with slightly meaty and herbaceous expression of violets, cassis, dark plum and blackberries suggesting some under and overripe influences. Intense, but lacking a genuine core of brightness, it's framed by firm, but slightly raw edged tannins. Give it a little time.

2004	88	2009	2012+
2002	90	2010	2014+
2001	90	2009	2013
2000	89	2005	2008
1999	91	2007	2011
1998	90	2003	2006+
1996	94	2004	2008+
1995	90	2000	2003
1994	91	1999	2002
1993	87	1998	2001
1992	89	1997	2000

CHARDONNAY

RATING 4

Clare Valley	$20–$29
Current vintage: 2004	89

Floral and lightly spicy, with a peachy fragrance of orange blossom and creamy, nutty undertones. Smooth and elegant, it's an early-drinking wine with pristine stonefruit flavours wrapped in citrusy acids, with a lingering note of reductive complexity.

2004	89	2005	2006+
2003	85	2003	2004+
2002	90	2004	2007
2000	90	2002	2005+
1999	90	2001	2004
1998	80	1999	2000

CORDON CUT

RATING

Clare Valley $20–$29 (375 ml)
Current vintage: 2006   **89**

Slightly candied, with citrus and apricot-like fruit backed by smoky, barley sugar-like undertones, it's forward and cloying, but dries out a little towards the finish. It's generous and luscious, but lacks its typical length and exceptional freshness.

2006	89	2008	2011
2005	95	2010	2013
2004	93	2006	2009
2003	90	2004	2005+
2002	96	2002	2007
2001	94	2003	2006
2000	95	2002	2005
1999	91	2001	2004
1998	90	1999	2000
1997	87	1999	2002
1996	93	2001	2004

RIESLING

RATING

Clare Valley $20–$29
Current vintage: 2006   **93**

A slatey, bone-dry and austere young riesling whose limey, mineral and floral, honeysuckle-like aromas precede a long, fine and tightly sculpted palate. There's plenty of juicy lime and lemon flavour over a finely textured backbone. Long and refreshing, it's likely to age very well

2006	93	2014	2026
2005	93	2013	2017
2004	96	2012	2016+
2003	95	2011	2015
2002	95	2010	2014+
2001	92	2006	2009+
2000	87	2002	2005
1999	93	2004	2007
1998	93	2003	2006
1997	90	2002	2005
1996	90	1998	2001
1995	90	1997	2000
1994	93	1999	2002
1993	94	2001	2005
1992	91	2000	2004

SEMILLON (formerly blended with Sauvignon Blanc)

RATING

Clare Valley $20–$29
Current vintage: 2006   **88**

Lightly grassy aromas of melon, lemon rind and restrained vanilla oak precede a soft and refreshing palate. Tangy, juicy fruit flavours are backed by hints of bathpowder and finished with lemony acids. It's moderately long, finishing slightly nutty, with clean, lemony acids. Reflects its region and variety.

2006	88	2007	2008+
2005	95	2010	2013+
2004	94	2006	2009+
2003	94	2005	2008+
2002	91	2004	2007
2001	95	2006	2009
2000	90	2002	2005
1999	92	2004	2007+
1998	90	2000	2003

SHIRAZ

RATING 5

Clare Valley $30–$49
Current vintage: 2005   **81**

Ripe, jammy aromas of plums and berries with herbal undertones of mint and menthol are lifted by sweet cedar/vanilla oak, spicy notes of clove, cinnamon and white pepper, plus a lifted floral aspect. Initially forward and minty, its confiture-like expression of blackberries and redcurrants becomes more raisined and currant-like down the palate, tasting more hollow and thin before a green-edged and sappy finish.

2005	81	2007	2010
2004	80	2006	2009
2003	83	2005	2008
2002	87	2004	2007
2001	88	2006	2009
2000	92	2005	2008+
1999	91	2004	2007
1998	93	2003	2006+
1997	82	1999	2002
1996	86	1998	2001

Mount Langi Ghiran

80 Vine Road, Bayindeen Vic 3375. Tel: (03) 5354 3207. Fax: (03) 5354 3277.
Website: www.langi.com.au Email: sales@langi.com.au

Region: **Grampians** Winemakers: **Trevor Mast, Dan Buckle** Viticulturist: **Damien Sheehan**
Chief Executive: **Gordon Gebbie**

Mount Langi Ghiran is best known for its peppery expression of western Victorian shiraz, and was right there when the American market discovered top-notch Australian wine. While I am aware of the huge effort being undertaken with the company's shiraz vineyard and the others with which it has contracts, I still feel that the flagship Langi Shiraz is not being given its best chance to excel. While it's a good wine, there are clear signs of shrivel and fruit breakdown with the 2004 edition, a wine I expected to reach a higher standard.

BILLI BILLI (Shiraz & Grenache)

Victoria $12–$19
Current vintage: 2005   **87**

Spicy, peppery aromas of moderately intense dark fruits precede a restrained, elegant and fine-grained palate. Finishing rather savoury and meaty, it's lively and quite stylish, while its flavours of dark fruits, white pepper, cloves and cinnamon are just fractionally hollow.

2005	87	2007	2010
2004	84	2005	2006+
2003	87	2005	2008
2002	82	2004	2007
2001	83	2003	2006+
2000	92	2005	2008
1999	86	2001	2004
1998	82	2000	2003

CLIFF EDGE SHIRAZ

RATING 5

Grampians $20–$29
Current vintage: 2004   **88**

Just a little lean and green-edged, this spicy, smoky and savoury young shiraz presents peppery and slightly meaty flavours of blackberries and plums underpinned by a fine and bony chassis of drying powdery tannin. It's supported by dark chocolate oak, with suggestions of cola. Just lacks the ripeness and follow-through for a higher score.

2004	88	2009	2012+
2003	77	2004	2005
2002	87	2004	2007+
2001	88	2003	2006
2000	92	2002	2005
1999	86	2001	2004

LANGI CABERNET SAUVIGNON MERLOT

RATING 5

Grampians $30–$49
Current vintage: 2001   **82**

Rather awkward and drying, this lean and hard-edged cabernet blend has a lightly floral and stewy bouquet of cooked plums, prunes and currants, with meaty, cherry kernel-like nuances beneath. Long, firm and grainy, its initial attack of dark fruit thin out towards a dusty, savoury finish that lacks brightness and freshness.

2001	82	2006	2009+
2000	81	2005	2008
1999	93	2007	2011+
1998	88	2006	2010
1997	91	2005	2009+
1996	90	2004	2008+
1994	95	2006	2014
1993	94	2001	2005
1992	95	2000	2004
1991	93	1999	2003
1990	92	1995	1998

LANGI SHIRAZ

RATING 4

Grampians $50–$99
Current vintage: 2004   **90**

Ripe juicy aromas of blackberries, cassis and plums are backed by cedar/vanilla oak, nuances of white pepper, cloves and nutmeg, with a hint of spirit. Sumptuous and forward, its slightly meaty palate of plums, redcurrants and blackberries breaks up fractionally at the finish, but culminates with lingering savoury, spicy and licorice-like qualities. It's supported by a firmish, rod-like spine of chalky tannin. A good wine, but perhaps would have been even better if harvested earlier.

2004	90	2009	2012
2003	87	2008	2011
2000	94	2008	2020
1999	88	2001	2004+
1998	90	2003	2006
1997	86	2002	2005
1996	94	2004	2008
1995	94	2003	2007
1994	97	2006	2014
1993	80	2001	2005
1992	93	2004	2012
1991	90	1999	2003
1990	93	2002	2010
1989	95	2001	2009
1988	91	1996	2000

2008   **THE AUSTRALIAN WINE ANNUAL**   **187**
www.jeremyoliver.com

PINOT GRIS

Grampians	$20–$29
Current vintage: 2006	**86**

Rather evolved and buttery, this broad and generous pinot gris has a restrained bouquet of citrus fruit, wheatmeal and grilled nuts, plus a dry and savoury palate of toasty, honeysuckle-like flavour.

2006	86	2006	2007
2005	90	2006	2007
2004	90	2005	2006+
2003	90	2004	2005+
2002	86	2003	2004+
2001	89	2001	2002+

RIESLING

Grampians	$20–$29
Current vintage: 2006	**92**

Delicate floral aromas of honeysuckle and orange blossom precede a fine and silky palate whose tightly focused citrusy fruit culminates in a long and austere finish. Pleasingly lean, taut and sculpted.

2006	92	2011	2014+
2005	93	2010	2013+
2004	90	2009	2012
2003	93	2008	2011
2002	93	2007	2010
2000	92	2005	2008
1999	80	2000	2001
1998	83	2000	2003
1997	82	1999	2002
1996	94	2004	2008
1995	94	2003	2007

Mount Mary

Coldstream West Road, Lilydale Vic 3140. Tel: (03) 9739 1761. Fax: (03) 9739 0137.

Region: **Yarra Valley** Winemaker: **Rob Hall** Viticulturist: **Jamie McGlade** Chief Executive: **David Middleton**

David Middleton has embarked upon a remarkable period of development at Mount Mary. He purchased the property opposite the bottom of the vineyard, with the sole intention of turning part of it into vineyard, but most of it into lake and natural wetlands. New vineyards will be developed on the site and old vineyards will be regenerated, while he and his team in the vineyard and cellar have underlined their commitment to the wine styles that have seen this small estate become one of the most influential in wine's New World.

CABERNET 'QUINTET'

Yarra Valley	$100–$199
Current vintage: 2005	**96**

Supremely elegant, stylish and focused, this aristocratic red has a heady, floral perfume of dark cherries, plums, cassis and blackberries backed by scents of violets and dried herbs, dark chocolate/vanilla oak and suggestions of mocha. Sumptuously flavoured but silky-smooth, it's dark-fruited, dusty and savoury, with an intensity that builds steadily towards its palate-staining finish. Framed by fine and beautifully ripened tannins, it flaunts its considerable influence from merlot.

2005	96	2017	2025
2004	97	2016	2024+
2003	96	2015	2023
2002	94	2014	2022
2001	97	2013	2021
2000	97	2012	2020+
1999	97	2011	2019
1998	97	2010	2018
1997	91	2002	2005+
1996	95	2004	2008+
1995	91	2007	2015
1994	96	2006	2014
1993	90	2001	2005
1992	95	2000	2004
1991	95	1999	2003
1990	97	2002	2010
1989	85	1994	1997
1988	97	2000	2008
1987	90	1995	1999
1986	95	1998	2006

CHARDONNAY

Yarra Valley	$50–$99
Current vintage: 2006	**95**

Elegant, supple and shapely, with fresh flavours of white peach, melon and citrus backed by nutty, creamy and vanilla-like undertones, it's long, taut and vibrant, with a refreshing finish of tightly integrated and lightly mineral acids. There's a hint of toast and butter beneath its bouquet, while beneath its juicy palate lies a fine chalkiness. It becomes more powdery and austere, with lingering fruit and faint cashew-like undertones. A keeper.

2006	95	2011	2014
2005	95	2010	2013+
2004	97	2009	2012
2003	96	2008	2011+
2002	95	2007	2010+
2001	96	2006	2009+
2000	95	2008	2012
1999	94	2004	2007
1998	92	2003	2006+
1997	90	2002	2005
1996	93	2004	2008
1995	92	2003	2007

PINOT NOIR

RATING 2

Yarra Valley	$50–$99
Current vintage: 2005	**94**

Elegant, smooth and supple with a spicy, floral perfume of raspberries, redcurrants, cloves and cinnamon, over suggestions of sweet vanilla/cedary oak and a hint of raisins. It opens slowly, becoming more juicy, fleshy and silky, presenting a restrained array of sweet cherry/berry fruit knit tightly with fine, bony tannins.

Year	Rating	Drink	
2005	94	2010	2013
2004	96	2012	2016
2003	95	2008	2011+
2002	92	2004	2007+
2001	93	2006	2009
2000	97	2008	2012
1999	95	2007	2011
1998	89	2003	2006
1997	89	2002	2005+
1996	89	1998	2001
1995	88	2000	2003
1994	94	2002	2006
1993	88	1998	2001
1992	94	2000	2004
1991	93	1999	2003
1990	92	1995	1998

TRIOLET

RATING 2

Yarra Valley	$50–$99
Current vintage: 2006	**95**

Savoury, taut and mineral, this elegant and shapely white blend underpins its juicy flavours of gooseberries, melon and lemon rind with a finely powered chalkiness. Backed by dusty suggestions of herbs, cloves and cinnamon, with a hint of fresh lychees and vanilla oak, it's long and briny, finishing with texture, shape and focus.

Year	Rating	Drink	
2006	95	2011	2014
2005	96	2010	2013+
2004	96	2009	2012
2003	95	2005	2008+
2002	95	2007	2010
2001	95	2006	2009
2000	95	2005	2008
1999	94	2004	2007
1998	95	2003	2006+
1997	92	2002	2005
1996	95	2001	2004
1995	95	2000	2003
1994	93	1999	2002
1993	95	1995	1998
1992	95	1997	2000+
1991	94	1996	1999
1990	94	1998	2002

Mount Pleasant

Marrowbone Road, Pokolbin NSW 2321. Tel: (02) 4998 7505. Fax: (02) 4998 7761.
Website: www.mcwilliams.com.au Email: mcwines@mcwilliams.com.au

Region: **Lower Hunter Valley** Winemaker: **Phillip Ryan** Viticulturist: **Peter Rohr** Chief Executive: **George Wahby**

Mount Pleasant is the McWilliams family's beachhead in the Hunter Valley, and home to classic, traditional wines made from ancient and historic vineyards. Its efforts with semillon under the Elizabeth and Lovedale labels are the stuff of legend, while the rustic, earthy and typically regional reds from the 'OP & OH' and Rosehill Vineyards can be spectacular. Somehow, the O'Shea Shiraz fell short of expectations in 2004.

CLASSIC CHARDONNAY
(formerly Hunter Valley Chardonnay)

RATING 5

Lower Hunter Valley	$12–$19
Current vintage: 2005	**87**

Juicy, exuberant and overtly oaky, this flavoursome and refreshing young chardonnay matches its ripe, vibrant flavours of peach, nectarine, quince and grapefruit with toasty vanilla oak. Wrapped in clean and refreshing acids, it's overt, showy and right in your face, but makes delightful, if uncompli-cated drinking.

Year	Rating	Drink	
2005	87	2006	2007
2004	90	2005	2006+
2003	88	2005	2008
2002	87	2002	2003
2001	89	2003	2006
2000	87	2002	2005
1999	89	2001	2004
1997	88	1999	2002
1996	90	2001	2004
1995	87	2000	2003
1994	85	1996	1999

ELIZABETH (Semillon)

RATING 4

Lower Hunter Valley $12–$19
Current vintage: 2003   89

A toasty, smoky and forward Elizabeth from a hot vintage. Its evolving melon and citrusy aromas are backed by rather a funky, meaty and reductive quality, while its unusually robust palate has more texture and ripeness than usual. There's a rich core of sumptuous fruit, plenty of developed complexity and a persistent and tangy finish.

2003	89	2008	2011+
2002	95	2010	2014+
2001	89	2006	2009
2000	90	2005	2008+
1999	88	2001	2004+
1998	93	2006	2010+
1997	93	2005	2009
1996	95	2008	2016
1995	93	2003	2007+
1994	95	2006	2014
1993	93	2001	2005
1992	87	2000	2004
1991	88	1993	1996
1990	87	1995	1998
1989	93	2001	2009
1988	88	1990	1993
1987	91	1995	1999+
1986	95	1998	2006+

LOVEDALE SEMILLON

RATING 2

Lower Hunter Valley $50–$99
Current vintage: 2002   94

A classically smooth and silky Lovedale semillon with some toasty development. Its delicate floral and wheatmeal aromas of lemon rind and melon precede a long, almost fluffy palate whose vibrant but restrained honeydew melon flavours are neatly bound by lemony acids. Very good indeed, but not for the super-long term.

2006	93	2014	2018
2002	94	2010	2014
2001	91	2009	2013
2000	93	2008	2012
1998	95	2010	2018
1997	91	2005	2009+
1996	96	2008	2016
1995	90	2007	2015
1986	95	1998	2006+
1984	96	1996	2004

MAURICE O'SHEA SHIRAZ

RATING 3

Lower Hunter Valley $50–$99
Current vintage: 2004   82

Porty, meaty and over-ripened, this sumptuous and leathery shiraz backs its forward and hollow expression of chocolatey plum and raspberry fruit with some ordinary, ashtray-like oak. It lacks life and brightness.

2004	82	2006	2009+
2003	88	2011	2015
2000	94	2012	2020
1999	92	2007	2011
1998	93	2006	2010+
1997	91	2005	2009
1996	88	2001	2004+
1994	88	2002	2006
1993	91	1998	2001

OLD PADDOCK & OLD HILL SHIRAZ

RATING 4

Lower Hunter Valley $30–$49
Current vintage: 2003   94

Charmingly old-fashioned and balanced, this is powerfully ripened, slightly meaty Hunter shiraz of unusual concentration and richness. Its smoky, leathery and rustic bouquet of blackberries, plums and red berries precedes a sumptuous and sweet-fruited palate whose deliciously rich fruit is unobtrusively supported by oak and framed by firm but velvet-smooth tannins.

2003	94	2015	2023
2002	90	2010	2014
2001	89	2009	2013+
1999	89	2004	2007
1998	94	2006	2010+
1997	88	2002	2005
1996	92	2004	2008+
1995	90	2003	2007

PHILIP (Shiraz)

RATING 5

Lower Hunter Valley $12–$19
Current vintage: 2004   87

A typically earthy, leathery Philip of medium weight whose light plum and berry notes are backed by older oak characters and supported by supple, almost fragile tannins. It's meaty and rustic, with a modest depth of flavour but some pleasing length and elegance.

2004	87	2009	2012+
2003	89	2008	2012
2002	88	2007	2010+
2000	85	2005	2008
1999	88	2004	2007
1998	83	2003	2006
1997	82	1999	2002
1996	84	1998	2001
1995	88	2000	2003
1994	83	1999	2002
1993	77	1995	1998

ROSEHILL SHIRAZ

RATING **4**

Lower Hunter Valley		$20–$29		
Current vintage: 2003		90		

Spicy, rather spirity aromas of fresh sweet berries, plums, menthol and mint overlie mocha-like nuances of prunes and currants. Firm and meaty, its sumptuous and treacle-like palate of fresh plum and rather more dehydrated prune and currant-like characters is framed by firm and slightly blocky tannin. Clearly reflective of a hot vintage, it's very awkward right now, but should settle down and age well over the medium term.

2003	90	2011	2015+
2001	85	2006	2009
2000	84	2005	2008
1999	91	2004	2007+
1998	93	2006	2010+
1997	93	2002	2005
1996	93	2004	2008
1995	84	1997	2000
1991	91	1996	1999
1990	80	1992	1995

Mountadam

High Eden Road, Eden Valley SA 5235. Tel: (08) 8564 1900. Fax: (08) 8564 1999.
Website: www.mountadam.com Email: office@mountadam.com.au

Region: **Eden Valley** Winemaker: **Con Moshos** Viticulturist: **Con Moshos** Chief Executive: **David Brown**

To listen to Con Moshos talk about his ambitions for Mountadam, a frankly rather run-down vineyard of immense innate potential, is just the same thing as listening to a car enthusiast discussing his latest restoration. Moshos has been able to start from the bottom up — the dirt — to fine-tune his mix of varieties and sites, and to renovate existing vineyard plots that have been neglected. His early wines are very encouraging, and he harbours justifiably high expectations for Riesling, Chardonnay and Shiraz. As I have suggested before, watch this space!

CHARDONNAY

RATING **5**

Eden Valley		$30–$49	
Current vintage: 2006		87	

A slightly flat and awkward chardonnay whose delicate aromas of peach, lemon and grilled nuts overlie dusty suggestions of vanilla and clove-like oak. It's smooth and soapy, delivering a viscous and sappy expression of peach, nectarine and pineapple fruit finishing with slightly sour-edged lemony acids. Lacks genuine freshness and brightness.

2006	87	2008	2011
2004	89	2006	2009+
2002	89	2004	2007+
2001	77	2002	2003
2000	86	2002	2005
1999	87	2001	2004
1998	87	2000	2003+
1997	80	1999	2002
1996	86	1998	2001

RIESLING

RATING **4**

Eden Valley		$20–$29	
Current vintage: 2006		95	

Delicate floral aromas of fresh lime juice and lemon rind precede a sumptuous, penetratively flavoured palate of profound length and concentration. Punctuated by a steely acid finish, it's a long term wine whose rich, almost luscious depth of fruit finishes with sculpted focus.

2006	95	2014	2018+
2004	87	2006	2009+
2003	87	2005	2008+
2001	84	2003	2006
1995	91	2003	2007

Mr Riggs

McLaren Vale SA 5171. Tel: (08) 8556 4460. Fax: (08) 8556 4462.
Website: www.mrriggs.com.au Email: mrriggs@pennyshill.com.au

Region: **McLaren Vale** Winemaker: **Ben Riggs** Viticulturist: **Toby Bekkers** Chief Executive: **Ben Riggs**

Former Wirra Wirra winemaker-turned-consultant Ben Riggs now has his own brand, making a delightfully Germanic and slightly sweet Riesling, a spicy and fragrant Shiraz Viognier, a very rustic Tempranillo, a juicy Viognier and a voluptuous and fine-grained Shiraz that is steadily growing in stature. The 2005 Shiraz appears to have been given a little too much hang time, an easy mistake when grapes are ripening all at once!

SHIRAZ

RATING **3**

McLaren Vale		$30–$49	
Current vintage: 2005		87	

Supported by high-toned chocolate/cedar oak, its sour-edged cherry, plum and currant-like fruit is coated by smooth but firmish tannin and backed by a hint of varnish. It's generous and juicy, but finishes a little cooked and soupy.

2005	87	2010	2013
2004	93	2009	2012
2003	94	2011	2015+
2002	92	2007	2010+
2001	92	2006	2009+

Nepenthe

Jones Road, Balhannah SA 5242. Tel: (08) 8388 4439. Fax: (08) 8398 0488.
Website: www.nepenthe.com.au Email: cellardoor@nepenthe.com.au
Region: **Adelaide Hills** Winemakers: **Peter Leske, Michael Paxton** Viticulturist: **Murray Leake**
Chief Executive: **James Tweddell**

James Tweddell has engineered the purchase by McGuigan Simeon of Nepenthe, which for most observers, would be as unlikely a marriage as you could get. However, it does give McGuigan Simeon a much-needed dip of a toe into the premium wine market, and it does give Tweddell the chance to impart a premium wine culture on a company that could do with an upgrade in this department. I assume that Nepenthe will continue to make its eclectic array of wines, some of which, like the 2004 Ithaca Chardonnay, can be absolutely delightful.

CHARLESTON PINOT NOIR

RATING 5

Adelaide Hills $20–$29
Current vintage: 2005 86

Rather under and over-ripe, with a stewed, minty expression of cherries, plums and currants with undertones of menthol and lanolin. It's lightly floral, smooth and generous, finishing with a moderate length of green-edged fruit and fresh acids.

2005	86	2007	2010
2004	88	2006	2009
2003	85	2004	2005+
2002	89	2004	2007
2001	86	2003	2006
2000	86	2002	2005
1999	87	2001	2004+
1998	88	2000	2003+
1997	81	1998	1999

ITHACA CHARDONNAY

RATING 4

Adelaide Hills $30–$49
Current vintage: 2004 95

A superbly balanced, top-class chardonnay of great brightness and intensity with a complex, smoky bouquet of grapefruit, melon, butterscotch, minerals and funky, matchstick-like undertones. Punctuated by tightly focused acids and backed by bacony, nutty complexity, its succulent, sumptuous palate of melon, grapefruit and nectarine flavours finishes taut and refreshing, with a lingering minerality.

2004	95	2006	2009+
2003	91	2008	2011
2002	87	2003	2004
2000	86	2002	2005
1999	88	2001	2004+
1998	90	2000	2003
1997	87	1998	1999

LENSWOOD ZINFANDEL

RATING 5

Adelaide Hills $30–$49
Current vintage: 2004 81

Briary, autumnal and herbal, with a moderately intense expression of redcurrants, blackberries, cherries and plums backed by nuances of snow peas, dried herbs, cloves and cinnamon. With a moderately firm structure of slightly sappy tannin, it's meaty but lacking true ripeness, finishing with green edges.

2004	81	2006	2009
2003	87	2008	2011
2001	89	2003	2006+
2000	76	2002	2005
1999	91	2004	2007
1998	81	2000	2003
1997	87	1999	2002+

PINOT GRIS

RATING 5

Adelaide Hills $20–$29
Current vintage: 2006 84

Rather overworked, which has compromised the integrity and freshness of its melon and citrusy flavours, this wild, spicy and oxidative pinot gris has a floral bouquet and a rich, broad palate that finishes with savoury suggestions of grilled nuts.

2006	84	2006	2007+
2005	86	2005	2006+
2004	89	2005	2006
2003	88	2004	2005+
2002	92	2003	2004+
2001	77	2001	2002
2000	82	2000	2001

SAUVIGNON BLANC

Adelaide Hills $20–$29
Current vintage: 2006   91

Long, fine and sculpted, with a restrained and lightly grassy aroma of fresh gooseberries and lychees backed by a hint of citrus. Ripe and succulent, but clean and refreshing, it's not overly concentrated or cloying, finishing with persistent fruit, shape and racy acidity.

2006	91	2006	2007+
2005	88	2005	2006+
2004	91	2004	2005+
2003	91	2004	2005
2002	91	2002	2003+
2001	91	2002	2003
2000	87	2001	2002
1999	94	2000	2001
1998	92	1999	2000+
1997	92	1997	1998

THE FUGUE (Cabernet Sauvignon Merlot Cabernet Franc)

RATING 4

Adelaide Hills $20–$29
Current vintage: 2003   86

Powerful and extracted but ageing and tiring, this meaty and rather vegetal cabernet blend just lacks the density and ripeness to counter its slightly raw astringency. Backed by cedar/chocolate oak and suggestions of capsicum, there's some plum and blackberry fruit, but it finishes slightly short, with an edgy, metallic aspect.

2003	86	2008	2011
2002	90	2010	2014
2000	85	2005	2008
1999	90	2007	2011
1998	89	2003	2006
1997	93	2005	2009

THE ROGUE (Cabernet Sauvignon Merlot Shiraz)

RATING 5

Adelaide Hills $20–$29
Current vintage: 2004   89

Spicy, peppery and dusty, with meaty, slightly dehydrated flavours of plums and mulberries, currants and raisins backed by dark chocolate, coconut and vanilla-like oak. Lightly herbal and green-edged to finish, it slowly opens to show some elegance and finesse, finishing long and savoury, with drying, fine-grained tannins but a lingering hint of sappiness.

2004	89	2009	2012+
2003	88	2008	2011
2002	82	2004	2007
2001	90	2006	2009+
2000	88	2002	2005+

Ninth Island

1216 Pipers Brook Road, Pipers Brook Tas 7252. Tel: (03) 6382 7527. Fax: (03) 6382 7226.
Website: www.pipersbrook.com Email: enquiries@pipersbrook.com
Region: **Tamar River, Pipers River** Winemaker: **Rene Bezemer** Viticulturist: **Bruce McCormack**
Managing Director: **Paul de Moor**

Ninth Island is Pipers Brook's second label. It typically offers a range of fresh and flavoursome early-drinking table wines of brightness and vitality of which the Pinot Noir is usually the most interesting.

PINOT NOIR

RATING 5

Tasmania $20–$29
Current vintage: 2006   80

Under and over-ripened, with meaty, greenish aspects beneath its jammy, almost treacle-like expression of red cherry and plum-like fruit. It finishes raw and powdery, with a bitter-edged extract.

2006	80	2007	2008
2005	87	2007	2010
2004	87	2005	2006+
2003	87	2004	2005+
2001	89	2002	2003
2000	89	2001	2002
1999	87	2000	2001+
1998	88	2000	2003

Oakridge

864 Maroondah Highway, Coldstream Vic 3770. Tel: (03) 9739 1920. Fax: (03) 9739 1923.
Website: www.oakridgeestate.com.au Email: info@oakridgeestate.com.au

Region: **Yarra Valley** Winemaker: **David Bicknell** Viticulturist: **Daniel Dujic** Chief Executive: **Martin Johnson**

David Bicknell continues to make wine of character, style and consistency at Oakridge. His flair is to capture depth of fruit to which he adds winemaking artefact and complexity without compromising either freshness or flavour. He understands structure and finish, especially with cabernet sauvignon, shiraz and the grape that is quite possibly his pet favourite, chardonnay.

CABERNET MERLOT

RATING 5

Yarra Valley	$20–$29
Current vintage: 2004	89

A pretty, fruit-driven wine with some sappy and unfinished aspects. Its slightly minty, floral aromas of violets, cranberries, cassis, cherries and mulberries reveal oaky undertones of cedar and vanilla. Medium to full in weight, its fine and supple palate of slightly confection-like red berries, cherries and blackberries overlies a firmish, fine-grained backbone.

2004	89	2009	2012
2003	88	2008	2011
2001	86	2003	2006
2000	89	2005	2008
1999	87	2001	2004
1998	87	2000	2003
1997	84	2002	2005
1995	87	1997	2000
1994	82	1996	1999
1993	87	1998	2001
1992	93	2000	2004

CABERNET SAUVIGNON (formerly Reserve)

RATING 3

Yarra Valley	$30–$49
Current vintage: 2005	91

Firm and astringent, with pleasing intensity, balance and tightness. A floral, violet-like perfume precedes a juicy expression of mulberries, plums and dark cherries, tightly knit with cedar/vanilla oak and its grainy tannin. Genuinely elegant, it finishes with plenty of length and brightness of flavour.

2005	91	2013	2017
2004	92	2012	2016
2003	93	2015	2023
2001	86	2003	2006
2000	90	2008	2012+
1999	93	2007	2011+
1997	88	2005	2009+
1995	89	2000	2003+
1994	93	2002	2006
1991	96	2003	2011
1990	94	2002	2010
1987	82	1992	1995
1986	94	1994	1998

CHARDONNAY

RATING 4

Yarra Valley	$20–$29
Current vintage: 2006	92

Tightly focused and crystal-clear, with some appealingly smoky, funky complexity, this tangy, brightly flavoured and refreshing young chardonnay has a meaty bouquet whose grapefruit-like fruit overlies floral, matchstick and lanolin-like suggestions. It's long and taut, with plenty of juicy flavour and well-handled artefact, before a taut and slightly austere finish.

2006	92	2008	2011+
2005	89	2007	2010
2004	86	2006	2009+
2003	93	2005	2008+
2002	92	2007	2010
1999	82	2001	2004
1998	89	2003	2006
1997	93	2002	2005
1996	94	2001	2004
1995	85	1997	2000

PINOT NOIR

RATING 5

Yarra Valley	$20–$29
Current vintage: 2006	89

Tasted just after bottling, this pretty, slightly candied young pinot supports its slightly simple but charmingly sour-edged expression of cherry and raspberry flavours with carefully handled oak and fine, dusty tannins. Likely to flesh out well.

2006	89	2008	2011
2005	91	2010	2013
2004	81	2005	2006
2003	89	2005	2008
2002	80	2004	2007
2000	87	2002	2005
1999	81	2000	2001
1998	82	1999	2000
1997	89	1999	2002+

SHIRAZ

Yarra Valley	$20–$29
Current vintage: 2005	**90**

Meaty, smoky and savoury, this rather spicy Rhône-ish shiraz marries with cherry, cassis, blackberry and plum-like fruit with dusty, vanilla and smoked bacon-like oak. Floral and perfumed, with briary undertones, it's framed by firmish, slightly gritty tannins, finishing with pleasing balance and tightness. It should evolve with interest.

2005	90	2010	2013+
2004	92	2006	2009+
2003	90	2008	2011
2002	86	2004	2007
2000	81	2002	2005
1999	83	2001	2004
1998	89	2003	2006

Oliver's Taranga

Olivers Road, McLaren Vale SA 5171. Tel: (08) 8323 8498. Fax: (08) 8323 7498.
Website: www.oliverstaranga.com Email: admin@oliverstaranga.com

Region: **McLaren Vale** Winemaker: **Corrina Rayment** Viticulturist: **Don Oliver** Chief Executive: **Don Oliver**

A specialist red wine maker in McLaren Vale, Oliver's Taranga crafts small releases of high-class shiraz and shiraz-cabernet blend that reflect Corrina Rayment's determination to deliver exceptional regional flavour and intensity without sacrificing an ounce of elegance, harmony or longevity. Its spectacular releases from 2002 and 2004 make her point more eloquently than words are able to.

HJ RESERVE SHIRAZ

McLaren Vale	$30–$49
Current vintage: 2003	**88**

Dark-fruited, chocolatey and slightly herbaceous, this is a solid but unexceptional shiraz from a hot year. It opens up a little more on the palate, revealing a pleasing lusciousness and plumpness of slightly cooked and meaty fruit, although it lacks genuine length. Backed by sweet caramel-like oak, it might yet evolve out of its faintly vegetal nature.

2003	88	2008	2011
2002	97	2022	2032
2001	86	2006	2009
2000	93	2008	2012+

SHIRAZ

McLaren Vale	$20–$29
Current vintage: 2004	**96**

A finely crafted and superbly structured shiraz whose slightly closed and withdrawn bouquet gradually unfolds layers of brooding, briary fruit and tightly balanced oak. Long, evenly balanced and sumptuously fruited, its deliciously spicy and focused palate delivers mouthfilling small berry flavour and dusty French oak undertones framed by fine-grained tannins. With a terrific structure and surprising elegance, it should cellar superbly over the medium to long term.

2004	96	2016	2024
2003	86	2008	2011
2002	95	2010	2014+
2001	85	2006	2009
2000	88	2005	2008+
1999	93	2007	2011
1998	91	2006	2010
1997	88	2002	2005
1996	94	2008	2016+
1994	87	2002	2006+

Omrah

Albany Highway, Mount Barker WA 6324. Tel: (08) 9851 3111. Fax: (08) 9851 1839.
Website: www.plantagenetwines.com Email: sales@plantagenetwines.com
Region: **Great Southern** Winemaker: **John Durham** Viticulturist: **Jaysen Gladish** Chairman: **Tony Smith**
Omrah is the highly rated second label of Plantagenet, one of the Great Southern's leading wineries. Its wines
are approachable and often quite delicious. The 2005 Shiraz is a great example, and easily beats a number
of much more expensive wines of a similar style.

SAUVIGNON BLANC

RATING **5**

Western Australia	$12–$19				
Current vintage: 2006	**88**	2006	88	2007	2008
		2005	90	2005	2006+
Pleasingly varietal, lean and focused, with a		2004	87	2005	2006+
lightly herbaceous bouquet of tropical fruits, pas-		2003	91	2003	2004+
sionfruit and lychees backed by green pea-like		2002	88	2003	2004
aromas. Tight and trim, its intensely flavoured, juicy		2000	86	2001	2002
and lightly chalky palate has a mineral edge and		1999	77	1999	2000
a refreshingly crisp finish.					

SHIRAZ

RATING **5**

Western Australia	$12–$19				
Current vintage: 2005	**90**	2005	90	2007	2010+
		2004	86	2006	2009
A deliciously savoury and spicy shiraz whose fresh,		2003	86	2004	2005
juicy and slightly gamey aromas of small black		2002	89	2004	2007+
berries, cracked pepper and fresh vanilla oak precede		2001	87	2003	2006
a generous, juicy, smooth and succulent palate		2000	89	2001	2002+
framed by fine-grained, moderately firm and		1999	90	2001	2004
powdery tannin. It bursts with intense small		1998	82	2000	2003
berry flavours, finishes with length of fruit and delivers					
exceptional value.					

UNOAKED CHARDONNAY

RATING **5**

Western Australia	$12–$19				
Current vintage: 2006	**87**	2006	87	2007	2008
		2005	83	2005	2006
Spicy, estery and tropical aromas of citrus, banana		2004	86	2005	2006
and green olives precede a juicy, round and		2003	88	2004	2005
generous palate that presents an even length of		2002	88	2003	2004
fruit punctuated by clean, soft acids. It finishes quite		2001	84	2001	2002
refreshing, with faint mineral undertones.		2000	87	2001	2002

Orlando

Barossa Valley Way, Rowland Flat SA 5352. Tel: (08) 8521 3111. Fax: (08) 8521 3100.
Website: www.pernod-ricard-pacific.com Email: contact_us@orlando-wyndham.com
Region: **South Australia** Winemakers: **Don Young, Hylton McLean, Nick Bruer** Viticulturist: **Joy Dick**
Chief Executive: **Laurent Lacassgne**
With several wines transferred to its stablemate Jacob's Creek brand, the Orlando collection is diminished in
diversity and cohesion, perhaps, but certainly not quality. The wines represented here include one of Coonawarra's
finest cabernets, Padthaway's best (minty) red, an exceptional and very affordable Riesling and a smooth, measured
Chardonnay. Look for the value in the 2005 St Hilary — it's long, and vibrant, crystal-clear and refreshing.

JACARANDA RIDGE CABERNET SAUVIGNON

RATING **2**

Coonawarra	$50–$99				
Current vintage: 2003	**91**	2003	91	2011	2015+
		1999	94	2011	2019+
Old-fashioned, firm and grippy, with a powerfully		1998	97	2010	2018+
oaked array of plum, blackberry and cassis-like		1997	92	2009	2017
flavour backed by nuances of mint and dried herbs.		1996	97	2008	2016
Slightly varnishy and deeply ripened, its jammy,		1994	95	2006	2014
almost overcooked palate of black and red fruit,		1992	89	2000	2004
dark chocolate, cedar and vanilla undertones finishes		1991	94	2003	2011
robust and slightly blocky.		1990	94	2002	2010
		1989	93	1997	2001

LAWSON'S SHIRAZ

RATING 3

Padthaway	$50–$99		
Current vintage: 2002	**88**		

Impressively concentrated and oaky, this rather over-ripened, cooked and meaty shiraz presents a very minty and rather baked expression of blackberry and currant-like fruit, mocha and dark chocolate. Lacking genuine fruit brightness, it dries out towards the finish, leaving a raw impression of drying tannins and menthol.

2002	88	2010	2014
2000	89	2008	2012
1999	93	2007	2011+
1998	94	2010	2018
1997	93	2005	2009+
1996	95	2004	2008+
1995	90	2003	2007
1994	96	2006	2014+
1993	90	2001	2005
1992	86	2004	2012
1991	95	2003	2011
1990	93	2002	2010

ST HELGA RIESLING

RATING 2

Eden Valley	$12–$19		
Current vintage: 2006	**89**		

Delicately scented, generous and juicy, with intense flavours of pear, apple and lime juice finishing long and lemony, with soft, open acidity. Vibrant and ready to drink.

2006	89	2011	2014
2005	95	2013	2017
2004	95	2012	2016
2003	90	2011	2015
2002	95	2010	2014+
2001	94	2006	2009+
2000	88	2002	2005+
1999	95	2007	2011
1998	94	2006	2010
1997	89	2002	2005
1996	95	2004	2010
1995	89	2003	2007
1994	95	2002	2006+
1993	87	1995	1998

ST HILARY CHARDONNAY

RATING 5

Padthaway	$12–$19		
Current vintage: 2005	**90**		

A lightly toasty chardonnay whose delicate aromas of lemon, melon and grapefruit are backed by restrained vanilla and clove-like oak. Smooth and polished, long and even, its vibrant, crystal-clear palate of melon, citrus and peachy fruit knits tightly with fresh acids and creamy, leesy undertones, finishing long and refreshing.

2005	90	2007	2010+
2003	88	2005	2008
2002	89	2004	2007
2001	86	2002	2003+
2000	90	2002	2005+
1999	88	2001	2004
1998	90	2003	2006
1997	90	1999	2002
1996	90	2001	2004
1995	85	1996	1997

Oxford Landing

PMB 31 Waikerie SA 5330. Tel: (08) 8561 3200. Fax: (08) 8561 3393.
Website: www.oxfordlanding.com Email: info@oxfordlanding.com

Region: **Riverlands** Winemaker: **Teresa Heuzenroeder** Viticulturist: **Bill Wilksch** Chief Executive: **Robert Hill Smith**
I have long rated Oxford Landing highly among the more competitively priced Australian brands and there's nothing in the current releases to lessen my faith. There's plenty of vibrant, juicy flavour in the 2006 Cabernet Sauvignon Shiraz, which also has a surprising depth of structure.

CABERNET SAUVIGNON & SHIRAZ

RATING 5

South Australia	$12–$19		
Current vintage: 2006	**87**		

A ripe, plump, juicy and flavoursome blend whose deep but slightly stewy expression of plums, blueberries and blackberries is tightly knit with chocolate/vanilla oak, with undertones of spice and pepper. It's long, vibrant and generous, with a genuine structure of ripe, dry tannins, finishing with pleasing length and brightness. Just a fraction cooked.

2006	87	2008	2011
2005	87	2007	2010
2003	85	2005	2008
2002	89	2004	2007
2001	86	2003	2006
2000	84	2002	2005
1999	84	2000	2001
1998	81	1999	2000
1997	89	1998	1999
1996	87	1998	2001
1995	80	1996	1997

CHARDONNAY

RATING

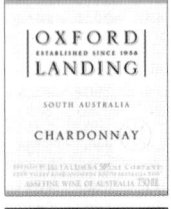

Riverlands	$12–$19
Current vintage: 2006	**86**

Punchy, ripe and flavoursome, with a slightly candied aroma of banana and melon over a hint of sweetcorn. Finishing with bright acids, its juicy, generous palate is intense to begin, but lacks great length.

2006	86	2006	2007+
2005	88	2006	2007
2004	88	2005	2006
2003	80	2003	2004

Panorama

1848 Cygnet Coast Road, Cradoc Tas 7109. Tel: (03) 6266 3409. Fax: (03) 6266 3482.
Website: www.panoramavineyard.com.au Email: panoramavineyard@bigpond.com
Region: **Huon Valley** Winemaker: **Michael Vishacki** Viticulturist: **Michael Vishacki**
Chief Executives: **Michael & Sharon Vishacki**

Panorama has emerged as one of the most sought-after makers of Tasmanian pinot noir. The richly flavoured, soundly structured and meaty 2001 Reserve Pinot Noir has won a number of accolades, while I found more brightness and less herbal influence in the very worthy 'standard' release of that year. There's no doubt in my mind that this vineyard is worth keeping an eye out for.

PINOT NOIR

RATING

Huon Valley	$50–$99
Current vintage: 2005	**87**

Rich and plummy, with undertones of cherries and dried herbs, this rather weighty and textured young pinot has an oxidative, slightly aldehydic aspect but might freshen up with time in the bottle.

2005	87	2007	2010
2004	89	2006	2009+
2003	92	2008	2011+
2001	90	2006	2009
2000	88	2002	2005+

Paringa Estate

44 Paringa Road, Red Hill South Vic 3937. Tel: (03) 5989 2669. Fax: (03) 5931 0135.
Website: www.paringaestate.com.au Email: paringa@cdi.com.au
Region: **Mornington Peninsula** Winemaker: **Lindsay McCall** Viticulturists: **Lindsay McCall, Nick Power**
Chief Executives: **Lindsay & Margaret McCall**

Paringa Estate has made a name for its deeply ripened, coloured, dark-fruited and spicy Pinot Noir, and its fragrant and peppery Shiraz, both of which are typically given generous treatment in new oak, qualities that are regularly appreciated on the Australian wine show circuit.

CHARDONNAY

RATING

Mornington Peninsula	$30–$49
Current vintage: 2005	**88**

Juicy aromas of lemon rind, pineapple and grapefruit with slightly herbal undertones precede a smooth, elegant palate whose tropical and citrusy fruit finishes just a little sweet and cloying.

2005	88	2007	2010+
2003	86	2004	2005+
2002	85	2004	2007
2001	90	2003	2006
2000	89	2002	2005
1999	89	2001	2004
1998	91	2000	2003
1997	93	2002	2005
1996	84	1997	1998
1995	92	2000	2003
1994	93	1996	1999
1993	92	1998	2001
1992	89	1997	2000

PINOT NOIR

RATING **5**

Mornington Peninsula	$50–$99
Current vintage: 2005	**88**

Intense aromas of polished, smoky, bacony oak and rather simple, confectionary red cherry/berry fruit precede a ripe and rather thickly set palate that lacks genuine charm and elegance. Rather too ripe and oaky for a higher rating.

2005	88	2007	2010
2004	89	2006	2009+
2003	83	2005	2008
2002	88	2004	2007
2001	89	2003	2006
2000	93	2002	2005+
1999	89	2004	2007
1998	95	2003	2006+
1997	95	2002	2005
1996	87	1998	2001
1995	93	2000	2003
1994	87	1996	1999

SHIRAZ

RATING **4**

Mornington Peninsula	$50–$99
Current vintage: 2004	**91**

Scented with violets, white pepper and spices, this firmish and oaky shiraz has a bouquet of ripe red and black berries and dark chocolate. Fine, smooth and elegant, its moderately rich expression of plum and berry flavour is quite restrained and meaty, but should flesh out with time. Framed by fine-grained tannins, it finishes long and savoury.

2004	91	2009	2012+
2003	87	2005	2008+
2001	88	2003	2006+
2000	90	2005	2008
1999	88	2001	2004+
1998	88	2003	2006
1997	95	2005	2009
1996	88	2001	2004
1995	88	2000	2003
1994	94	1999	2002
1993	93	2001	2005
1992	86	2000	2004
1991	91	1999	2003

Parker Coonawarra Estate

Riddoch Highway, Coonawarra SA 5263. Tel: (08) 8737 3525. Fax: (08) 8737 3527.
Website: www.parkercoonawarraestate.com.au Email: cellardoor@parkercoonawarraestate.com.au

Region: **Coonawarra** Winemaker: **Peter Bissell** Viticulturist: **Doug Balnaves** Chief Executive: **Gordon Gebbie**
Parker Coonawarra Estate is the brainchild of the late John Parker. It was Parker's aim to create a definitive marque of Coonawarra red wines, offering the depth of fruit and longevity for which the region is famous. The business was then acquired by the Rathbone family, owners of Yering Station and Mount Langi Ghiran. It's encouraging to see such good 2004 reds under this brand, which suggest a full resurgence is imminent.

TERRA ROSSA CABERNET SAUVIGNON

RATING **5**

Coonawarra	$20–$29
Current vintage: 2004	**90**

Minty and floral, its fragrance of cassis, violets, dark chocolate and cedar/vanilla oak precedes a fine, elegant and slightly one-dimensional palate. Framed by firmish but pliant tannins, its intense blackberry, plum and cassis-like fruit is handsomely backed by fine-grained oak, finishing with tightness and focus.

2004	90	2012	2016
2003	86	2005	2008
2002	83	2004	2007+
2001	89	2006	2009
1999	90	2001	2004+
1998	87	2003	2006
1997	86	1999	2002+
1996	84	1998	2001
1995	87	2000	2003
1994	84	1999	2002
1992	82	1997	2000
1991	88	1999	2003

TERRA ROSSA FIRST GROWTH

RATING **2**

Coonawarra	$50–$99
Current vintage: 2004	**90**

Deep, dense and slightly meaty aromas of dark plums, cassis and sweet oak are backed by suggestions of violets and vanilla. Sumptuously ripened, its palate-staining and slightly jammy expression of cassis, blackberries and plums is framed by mouth-coating tannin and backed by assertive new cedar/vanilla oak. There's just a hint of over-ripeness, with a spirity presence, a trace of over-cooked fruit and a slightly blocky aspect.

2004	90	2012	2016
2001	93	2013	2021
2000	95	2008	2012+
1999	88	2004	2007
1998	95	2018	2028
1996	97	2008	2016+
1994	84	1999	2002
1993	90	2001	2005
1991	95	2003	2011+
1990	97	2002	2010
1989	92	1997	1991
1988	95	2000	2008

TERRA ROSSA MERLOT

RATING **4**

		Coonawarra	$30–$49
		Current vintage: 2004	92

2004	92	2012	2016
2001	83	2006	2009
2000	91	2002	2005+
1999	89	2004	2007
1998	93	2006	2010

Firm and concentrated, but rather brooding all the same, this handsomely structured merlot has a brightly lit perfume of dark cherries and plums dusted with hints of tobacco and backed by sweet newish vanilla/mocha oak. Its lingering core of intense fruit is supported by dark chocolate/mocha oak, framed by a firm and fine-grained astringency. It finishes long and savoury.

Passing Clouds

Kurting Road, Kingower Vic 3517. Tel: (03) 5438 8257. Fax: (03) 5438 8246.
Email: passingclouds@bordernet.com.au
Region: **Bendigo** Winemaker: **Graeme Leith** Viticulturist: **Graeme Leith**
Chief Executives: **Graeme Leith, Sue Mackinnon**
Passing Clouds has long been an important and consistent maker of central Victorian red wines of immense depth and longevity. There's barely a concession to modernity, as the style has hardly altered since I was first attracted by them more than two decades ago. These wines simply demand time in the cellar.

ANGEL BLEND (Cabernet Sauvignon Merlot)

RATING **4**

		Bendigo	$30–$49
		Current vintage: 2004	89

2004	89	2012	2016+
2003	90	2015	2023
2002	89	2010	2014+
2001	86	2006	2009+
2000	87	2005	2008
1999	91	2007	2011
1998	90	2010	2018
1997	93	2005	2009+
1996	90	2008	2016
1995	94	2007	2015
1994	91	2006	2014
1992	93	2000	2004
1991	90	1999	2003
1990	89	2002	2010
1987	87	1995	1999
1985	93	1993	1997
1984	87	1989	1992

Minty, dusty aromas of cassis, plums, fine-grained oak and dried herbs precede a long and lively palate whose bright small black and red berry/cherry fruit is framed by a firm and fine-grained cut of sandpapery tannin. It builds solidly towards the end of the palate, leaving a lingering core of intense, if slightly simple fruit. Just lacks genuine cut and polish.

GRAEME'S BLEND (Shiraz Cabernet Sauvignon)

RATING **5**

		Bendigo	$20–$29
		Current vintage: 2004	89

2004	89	2012	2016
2003	88	2008	2011
2002	92	2014	2022
2001	87	2006	2009
2000	83	2002	2005+
1999	89	2011	2019
1998	91	2006	2010+
1997	90	2005	2009
1996	89	2004	2008+
1995	94	2003	2007
1994	88	2006	2014
1992	94	2004	2012
1991	91	1996	1999
1990	88	2002	2010
1989	85	1994	1997

A natural, balanced and moderately firm red with a heady, briary summer pudding-like fragrance of small red and black berries with minty, spicy undertones. Long and even, smooth and supple, its slightly meaty palate of berry-like fruit reveals dusty undertones of dried herbs, finishing firm and drying. Would have done credit to some better oak.

RESERVE SHIRAZ

RATING **3**

Bendigo	$50–$99	2005	88	2013	2017	
Current vintage: 2005	88	2004	96	2016	2024+	
		2003	93	2011	2015+	
		2002	93	2014	2022	
		2001	91	2013	2021	

Slightly minty red berry and plum-like aromas are backed by cedar/vanilla oak and a hint of menthol. A little angular and forward, it delivers a sweet expression of lightly cooked berry/currant, fruit before a rather hollow mid palate and dilute finish. Its heavily worked, robust and blocky tannin compensates for some stressed fruit characters, but it's raw enough to need a lengthy time in the cellar.

SHIRAZ

RATING **4**

Bendigo	$30–$49	2004	90	2012	2016+
Current vintage: 2004	90	2002	90	2010	2014+
		2001	93	2009	2013+
		1998	87	2010	2018
		1997	87	2005	2009
		1996	89	2004	2008
		1994	93	2002	2006+

Richly flavoured, balanced and likely to build in the bottle, this honest and minty shiraz has a slightly herbal and meaty bouquet of dark plums and cherries backed by older cedary oak. Firm, long and astringent, its drying, chalky palate of bright minty small berry/plum fruit has a lingering finish with menthol-like undertones. Give it time.

Pauletts

Polish Hill Road, Polish Hill River SA 5453. Tel: (08) 8843 4328. Fax: (08) 8843 4202.
Website: www.paulettwines.com.au Email: info@paulettwines.com.au
Region: **Clare Valley** Winemaker: **Neil Paulett** Viticulturist: **Matthew Paulett** Chief Executive: **Neil Paulett**

Pauletts is a small maker of a typically regional selection of rustic Clare Valley reds and Riesling. Its best current release is the reserve level Andreas Shiraz 2003 (90/100, drink 2011–2015+), a ripe, forward and generous wine with delightful leathery and meaty complexity that will continue to age well.

CABERNET MERLOT

RATING **5**

Clare Valley	$20–$29	2004	86	2009	2012+
Current vintage: 2004	86	2003	81	2005	2008+
		2002	90	2010	2014
		2001	88	2006	2009+
		2000	89	2008	2012
		1999	88	2004	2007
		1998	81	2000	2003
		1997	88	2002	2005
		1996	93	2004	2008
		1995	89	2000	2003
		1994	90	1996	1999
		1993	84	1995	1998

Simple, rather jammy and meaty flavours of cassis and dark plums overlie slightly raw and mocha-like oak, with undertones of mint and dried herbs. There's plenty of forward intensity, but it finishes with a powerful extract of hard-edged tannin as well as herbal and metallic influences. A rustic style — it needs time to flesh out.

RIESLING

RATING **5**

Clare Valley	$12–$19	2006	85	2008	2011
Current vintage: 2006	85	2005	93	2013	2017
		2004	87	2009	2012
		2003	88	2008	2011+
		2001	85	2003	2006
		2000	87	2005	2008
		1999	89	2004	2007
		1998	89	2000	2003+
		1997	82	2002	2005
		1996	88	2001	2004
		1995	93	2003	2007
		1994	93	2002	2006
		1993	90	1995	1998

Slightly hollow and lacking in brightness, this lemony young riesling is austere and dry, but could use more intensity and impact.

SHIRAZ

Clare Valley	$20–$29
Current vintage: 2004	82

Rustic and meaty, with flavours of plums, berries and currants backed by earthy, leathery complexity and vanilla oak. Beginning to tire, with simple, evolved fruit lacking much freshness and brightness, finishing dull and eucalypt-like.

2004	82	2006	2009+
2003	83	2005	2008+
2002	86	2007	2010
2001	89	2009	2013+
2000	90	2005	2008
1999	90	2004	2007
1998	86	2000	2003+
1997	86	2002	2005
1996	88	2001	2004
1995	89	2000	2003
1994	91	1999	2002
1993	94	2001	2005
1992	91	2000	2004
1991	91	1996	1999

Paxton

Landcross Farm, Lot 100, Wheaton Road, McLaren Vale SA 5171. Tel: (08) 8323 8645. Fax: (08) 8323 8903.
Website: www.paxtonvineyards.com Email: paxton@paxtonvineyards.com

Region: **McLaren Vale** Winemaker: **Michael Paxton** Viticulturist: **Toby Bekkers** Chief Executive: **David Paxton**

Paxton is a McLaren Vale label developed by one of Australia's leading viticulturists. While its 2004 Shiraz is rather more treacle-like and ripe than usual, its AAA Shiraz Grenache blend from 2006 is delicious, vibrant and great value.

AAA SHIRAZ GRENACHE   RATING **4**

McLaren Vale	$20–$29
Current vintage: 2006	93

Deep, dark and briary, with meaty, licorice-like aromas of blueberries and plums backed by dark chocolate and mocha-like oak. Smooth and sumptuous, forward and juicy, its vibrant palate of blackberries, dark plums, blueberries and dark cherries sits comfortably with smooth, smart vanilla oak and meaty undertones. Very balanced and stylish; a huge improvement in this wine.

2006	93	2008	2011
2005	90	2007	2010
2004	86	2005	2006+

JONES BLOCK SHIRAZ   RATING **4**

McLaren Vale	$30–$49
Current vintage: 2005	86

Reliant on its oak treatment for sweetness, this oaky, rather dull and treacle-like shiraz has a raisined aroma strongly backed by suggestions of vanilla and molasses. Like a rich Christmas cake, its over-ripened and currant-like palate is steeped in sweet mocha-like oak, but finishes rather thin and stewed.

2005	86	2007	2010
2004	90	2009	2012
2003	90	2011	2015
2002	92	2010	2014
2001	86	2003	2006
2000	87	2002	2005+
1999	88	2001	2004+
1998	90	2000	2003+

Penfolds

Magill Estate Winery, 78 Penfold Road, Magill SA 5072. Tel: (08) 8301 5569. Fax: (08) 8364 3961.
Website: www.penfolds.com.au Email: penfolds.bv@cellar-door.com.au

Region: **South Australia** Winemaker: **Peter Gago** Viticulturist: **Tim Brooks** Chief Executive: **Jamie Odell**

Penfolds' premier collection of table wines has never, ever looked better than today. From the supremely elegant 2002 Grange to the finely crafted and mineral Yattarna 2004 (which is beginning to justify its expectation, to the magnificent 2004 Bin 707 and the savoury Magill Estate, the top drawer has never been richer. The 2004 Bin releases, from a fine vintage, are also excellent, despite the fact they were virtually given away on the retail market. Penfolds now needs to rationalise its crowded lower end, which sees brands like Rawson's Retreat, Koonunga Hill and Thomas Hyland slugging it out against each other from retailer to retailer.

BIN 05A CHARDONNAY
RATING 3

Adelaide Hills			$50–$99
Current vintage: 2005			**94**

Floral and slightly funky aromas of melon, grapefruit and pineapple are backed by sweet vanilla, buttery and bubblegum-like oak, with underlying suggestions of lime juice and minerals. Succulent and chewy, its long, complex and savoury palate marries fresh melon and quince-like fruit with nuances of smoked meats, finishing with refreshing acidity.

2005 05A	94	2010	2013
2004 04A	93	2006	2009+
2003 03A	92	2005	2008+
2000 00A	94	2005	2008
1998 98A	92	2003	2006
1995 95A	93	2000	2003
1994 94A	93	1999	2002

BIN 128 COONAWARRA SHIRAZ
RATING 4

Coonawarra			$20–$29
Current vintage: 2004			**91**

Something of a sleeper, this fine, well-integrated and structured wine presents delicate, dusty and peppery aromas of blackberries, dark plums and older oak with a distinctly meaty aspect. There's also a background of earthiness and a briary fruit quality suggestive of brandied cherries. Smooth and polished, long and savoury, its presently rather simple palate of vibrant berry/blackcurrant/plum-like fruit is backed by a pleasingly firm undercarriage of drying tannin. It needs five years.

2004	91	2012	2016
2003	89	2015	2023
2002	88	2007	2010
2001	93	2009	2013+
2000	83	2002	2005
1999	90	2004	2007
1998	93	2010	2018
1997	87	2002	2005
1996	94	2008	2016
1995	86	2000	2003
1994	93	2002	2006
1993	88	2001	2005
1992	93	2000	2004
1991	89	1999	2003
1990	92	1998	2002
1989	86	1994	1997
1988	90	2000	2005
1987	82	1992	1995
1986	93	1994	1998

BIN 138 OLD VINE RHÔNE BLEND
RATING 4

Barossa Valley			$20–$29
Current vintage: 2005			**87**

Slightly jammy and confectionary aromas of red plums, redcurrants and violets are backed by dusty, spicy notes of cloves and cinnamon, light mocha oak plus a distinctly tarry aspect. Forward and juicy, it's vibrant and intense enough, but lacks great palate length, finishing with a savoury and slightly salty aspect and a lingering note of licorice. Backed by fine, restrained tannins, it's an early drinker.

2005	87	2007	2010
2004	90	2009	2012
2003	87	2005	2008
2002	91	2004	2007+
2001	88	2003	2006+
1999	89	2004	2007
1998	92	2006	2010
1997	90	2005	2009
1996	92	2004	2008
1995	86	1997	2000
1994	92	2002	2006
1993	89	2001	2005

BIN 389 CABERNET SHIRAZ

RATING **3**

South Australia		**$30–$49**
Current vintage: 2004		**95**

A tightly focused, firm and sassy 389 of structure and sophistication. Deeply scented with alluring and lightly spicy aromas of crushed dark berries and cedary oak, this slightly meaty red blend reveals undertones of briar, white pepper, mint and a hint of game. Long and smooth, its intense and dark-fruited palate of cassis, mulberries, cherries and plums is underpinned by a chalky chassis of firm tannin. It slowly reveals nuances of dried herbs and underlying meatiness, while its generous complement of vanilla oak shows some classy integration. It's a lot more contemporary than the traditional 389, but very impressive, all the same.

2004	95	2016	2024+
2003	94	2015	2023+
2002	93	2014	2022
2001	91	2009	2013
2000	89	2005	2008+
1999	92	2007	2011
1998	96	2010	2018+
1997	93	2005	2009+
1996	97	2008	2016
1995	92	2004	2008
1994	95	2006	2014+
1993	93	2005	2013
1992	92	2004	2012
1991	94	2003	2011
1990	95	2002	2010
1989	87	1994	1997
1988	93	1996	2000
1987	91	1995	1999
1986	95	1998	2006

BIN 407 CABERNET SAUVIGNON

RATING **4**

South Australia		**$30–$49**
Current vintage: 2004		**94**

Stylish, structured and finely crafted, this impressive young cabernet reveals a minty aroma of cassis, violets, dark cherries and small red berry fruits neatly interwoven with cedar/dark chocolate oak. Its slightly vegetal undertones of dried herbs should become more tobacco-like with time in the bottle. Smooth and silky, its spotless and pristine palate of vibrant, juicy small berry fruits and fine-grained oak is framed by a fine cut of firm tannin. A very correct cabernet indeed, even with the presence of some genuinely valid cooler characters.

2004	94	2012	2016+
2003	93	2011	2015+
2002	89	2010	2014
2001	87	2006	2009
2000	87	2005	2008
1999	90	2004	2007+
1998	91	2006	2010
1997	89	2005	2009
1996	95	2004	2008
1995	90	2003	2007+
1994	94	2002	2006
1993	93	2001	2005
1992	88	1997	2000
1991	94	2003	2011
1990	93	2002	2010

BIN 707 CABERNET SAUVIGNON

RATING **1**

South Australia		**$100–$199**
Current vintage: 2004		**97**

A long, seamless and very sophisticated cabernet despite its significant dimensions, structure and power. It opens with an intense violet-like perfume of aromatic cassis, blackberries and dark plums over dark chocolate and mocha-like oak, with meaty, briary undertones. Simultaneously very firm and cultivated, it's steeped in piercing flavours of blackberries, dark plums and cassis, and backed by very smart oak and robust, pliant tannins. It's long and savoury, with a lingering core of explosive dark fruit and dusty, dried herb-like nuances. A genuine Bin 707.

2004	97	2024	2034+
2002	96	2022	2032
2001	93	2013	2021+
1999	95	2007	2011+
1998	97	2010	2018+
1997	93	2005	2009+
1996	96	2008	2016+
1994	94	2006	2014
1993	95	2005	2013
1992	94	2004	2012
1991	97	2003	2011+
1990	95	2010	2018
1989	91	1997	2001
1988	95	2000	2008
1987	93	1999	2007
1986	95	2006	2016
1985	91	1997	2005
1984	93	1996	2004

GRANGE

RATING **1**

Barossa Valley
(predominantly) $200+
Current vintage: 2002   **97**

Deep, closed and brooding, with perfectly ripened aromas of dark berries, plums and typical smoky cedar/vanilla/dark chocolate Penfolds oak that become more fragrant with aeration, revealing scents of violets, cloves and cinnamon. Smooth, unctuous and exceptionally elegant for Grange, its voluptuous palate of black cherries, plums, black olives and smoky dark oak finishes with exceptional length of vibrant fruit over suggestions of minerals and vanilla. The longer it's opened, the silkier and more ethereal it becomes, as the quality of its fine-grained tannin becomes apparent. A classic reflection of a great cool vintage.

2002	97	2022	2032+
2001	95	2021	2031
2000	87	2008	2012
1999	96	2019	2029+
1998	97	2018	2028+
1997	95	2017	2027+
1996	98	2026	2036+
1995	95	2025	2035+
1994	95	2014	2024+
1993	89	2005	2013
1992	94	2012	2022
1991	97	2021	2031
1990	97	2020	2030
1989	95	2001	2009+
1988	91	2000	2008+
1987	91	1999	2007
1986	95	2016	2026
1985	92	2005	2015
1984	90	2004	2014
1983	96	2023	2033
1982	93	2002	2012
1981	88	2001	2011
1980	90	2000	2010
1979	87	1991	1999
1978	94	1998	2008+
1977	92	1997	2007
1976	94	1986	1996+
1975	89	1987	1995
1974	89	1986	1994+
1973	83	1981	1985
1972	90	1984	1992
1971	97	2001	2011
1970	93	1980	1990
1969	91	1989	1994
1968	94	1988	1998
1967	92	1987	1997
1966	97	1996	2006
1965	95	1995	2005+
1964	96	1984	1994+
1963	95	1983	1993+
1962	97	1992	2002+
1961	95	1991	2001

KALIMNA BIN 28 SHIRAZ

RATING **4**

South Australia   **$20–$29**
Current vintage: 2004   **93**

This richly fruited, smooth and sumptuous shiraz has a deeply layered aroma of fresh blackberries, raspberries and blueberries, without so much as a hint of overcooked fruit. It's backed by fragrant new oak, with slightly meaty — almost gamey — and floral undertones. Framed by moderately firm, fine-grained and pliant tannins, its plush, sweet-oaked palate of juicy and almost confectionary dark berry/plum fruit finishes with a suggestion of briar and a hint of gamey development. Already very approachable, but destined to improve for some time.

2004	93	2012	2016+
2003	93	2011	2015+
2002	88	2010	2014
2001	87	2006	2009
2000	88	2005	2008
1999	86	2004	2007+
1998	95	2010	2018+
1997	91	2005	2009
1996	94	2008	2016
1995	90	2003	2007
1994	92	2002	2006
1993	84	1998	2001
1992	92	2000	2004
1991	93	1999	2003
1990	93	1998	2002
1989	87	1994	1997
1988	89	1996	2000
1987	88	1995	1999
1986	93	1998	2003
1985	87	1993	1997
1984	85	1989	1992
1983	82	1995	2000
1982	88	1990	1994

A B C D E F G H I J K L M N O P Q R S T U V W X Y Z

KOONUNGA HILL SHIRAZ CABERNET SAUVIGNON

South-Eastern Australia $12–$19
Current vintage: 2005 82

Briary, meaty aromas of dark plums, berries and currants precede a forward and rather stewy palate whose hollow middle extends to a thin and drying finish of inadequately ripened tannin. Lacks fruit and stuffing.

2005	82	2007	2010
2004	81	2006	2009
2003	87	2005	2008
2002	82	2004	2007
2001	81	2003	2006
2000	86	2002	2005+
1999	87	2004	2007
1998	87	2003	2006+
1997	86	2002	2005
1996	90	2004	2008
1995	87	2000	2003
1994	87	1999	2002
1993	88	2001	2005
1992	88	2000	2004
1991	92	1999	2003
1990	90	1998	2002
1989	88	1997	2001
1988	90	1996	2000
1987	82	1995	1999
1986	93	1998	2006
1985	84	1993	1997
1984	90	1996	2004
1983	89	1995	2003
1982	90	1994	2002
1981	88	1993	2001
1980	89	1992	2000+
1979	87	1987	1991
1978	93	1990	1998
1977	91	1989	1997
1976	88	1988	1996

MAGILL ESTATE SHIRAZ

RATING **3**

Adelaide Metropolitan $50–$99
Current vintage: 2004 95

An old-fashioned shiraz of charm and personality, with a rather meaty, spicy and evolving bouquet of brandied plums, brambly small red berries, creamy dark chocolate/vanilla oak and blackberries. Its long, linear palate of piercing and pristine blackberry, redcurrant and dark cherry flavours is still closed and very tight, with undertones of dried herbs and spices. Framed by firm, bony tannins, it is beginning to smooth out, and easily soaks up some sweet newish oak. Give it time.

2004	95	2016	2024+
2003	89	2011	2015
2002	88	2007	2010
2001	93	2013	2021
2000	90	2005	2008+
1999	95	2011	2019
1998	93	2010	2018
1997	92	2005	2009+
1996	95	2008	2016
1995	93	2003	2007
1994	91	2002	2012
1993	93	2005	2013
1992	90	2000	2004
1991	95	2011	2021
1990	94	2002	2010
1989	93	1997	2001
1988	91	2000	2005
1987	93	1995	1999
1986	94	1998	2003
1985	93	1993	1997
1984	90	1989	1992

RESERVE BIN EDEN VALLEY RIESLING

RATING **3**

Eden Valley $20–$29
Current vintage: 2005 91

Intense, penetrative lime juice and lemon rind aromas with a floral, mineral and bath powder-like background precede a long, tangy and tightly focused palate punctuated by refreshing acidity. There's a slightly candied and over-ripe aspect about the fruit, but it's still a delightful wine that finishes long, lean and stylishly taut.

2005	91	2010	2013+
2004	93	2009	2012+
2003	93	2008	2011
2002	92	2007	2010
2001	92	2003	2006+
2000	93	2002	2005+
1999	94	2004	2007+

RWT SHIRAZ

RATING **3**

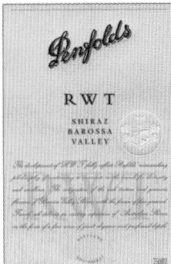

Barossa Valley $100–$199
Current vintage: 2004   **96**

A classic 2004 Australian red of superb, effortless natural balance and elegance. Its deep, heady aromas of liqueur-like cassis, dark plums and berries overlie lightly smoky aromas of smallgoods, dark chocolates and vanilla, with undertones of violets, red berries and currants. Deep, juicy and concentrated, its jujube-like fruit is tightly harnessed with smooth, newish oak and supported by a firm but pliant undercarriage of drying tannins. Long and lavish, it finishes with deep, meaty fruit and lingering suggestions of licorice, spices and dried herbs.

2004	96	2024	2034+
2003	90	2011	2015
2002	93	2010	2014+
2001	88	2009	2013+
2000	91	2005	2008+
1999	96	2011	2019
1998	97	2010	2018+
1997	95	2005	2009

ST HENRI SHIRAZ

RATING **2**

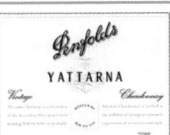

South Australia $50–$99
Current vintage: 2003   **92**

Well-mannered, smooth and savoury, this rich and sumptuous shiraz delivers plenty of ripe and just very slightly baked fruit framed by typically smooth and velvet-like tannin. There's a meaty, pungent aspect about its slightly spirity aromas of blackberries, dark plums, raspberries and prunes. Its rich, thick and smoky palate of meaty dark fruits, raisins and currants finishes savoury but surprisingly fresh and vibrant, with a lingering core of persistent flavour.

2003	92	2011	2015+
2002	97	2022	2032+
2001	90	2009	2013
2000	89	2008	2012
1999	95	2011	2019
1998	94	2018	2028
1997	93	2005	2009
1996	95	2008	2016
1995	91	2003	2007+
1994	94	2006	2014
1993	92	2003	2007
1992	90	2000	2004
1991	94	2003	2011
1990	96	2002	2010
1989	94	2001	2009
1988	93	2000	2005
1987	93	1999	2004
1986	96	1998	2008+
1985	91	1997	2002
1984	80	1992	1996
1983	90	1995	2003
1982	90	1990	1994
1981	82	1993	1998
1980	90	1992	1997
1979	77	1987	1991
1978	80	1990	1995
1977	82	1989	1994
1976	93	1996	2006+

YATTARNA CHARDONNAY

RATING **2**

Henty $100–$199
Current vintage: 2004   **96**

Pristine aromas of tangerine, melon and grapefruit overlie slightly dusty, nutty, waxy and mineral nuances, with subliminal suggestions of wheatmeal and vanilla. Round and smooth, its juicy core of citrus and melon flavour is neatly trimmed by an underlying powdery minerality and a tangy, lemony acidity. Long, austere and shapely, finishing taut and stylish, it finishes with a lingering lemon sherbet-like aspect. Very classy, and made without a single barrel of new oak.

2004	96	2009	2012+
2003	95	2008	2011
2002	90	2007	2010
2001	96	2006	2009+
2000	95	2005	2008
1999	95	2004	2007+
1998	97	2006	2010
1997	95	2002	2005+
1996	95	2001	2004+
1995	94	2000	2003

Penley Estate

McLeans Road, Coonawarra SA 5263. Tel: (08) 8736 3211. Fax: (08) 8736 3124.
Website: www.penley.com.au Email: penley@penley.com.au

Region: **Coonawarra** Winemaker: **Kym Tolley** Viticulturist: **Michael Wetherall** Chief Executive: **Kym Tolley**

Penley Estate is a small and serious maker of Coonawarra wines, principally rich and briary reds from cabernet sauvignon, merlot and shiraz. The 2004 vintage reds released to date present lively, bright and pristine varietal flavours and luxuriantly smooth textures, with just a hint of the meatiness and richness for which Penley is well known. Like many others from the region, the 2005s are generally rather riper and slightly overcooked.

CHARDONNAY

RATING **5**

Coonawarra	$20–$29
Current vintage: 2005	**83**

Simple candied aromas of lemon butter and sweetcorn precede a juicy, round and forward palate that is already very buttery and creamy. Lacking a little tightness and freshness, it's rather broad, oily and evolved.

2005	83	2007	2010
2004	88	2006	2009
2003	86	2004	2005
2002	88	2004	2007
2001	90	2003	2006
2000	81	2001	2002
1999	82	2001	2004

GRYPHON MERLOT

RATING **5**

Coonawarra	$20–$29
Current vintage: 2005	**87**

Meaty, currant-like and lightly browning, with a rather cooked expression of plums, currants and raisins with mocha and ground coffee-like oak beneath. Oak also lends a sweetness and a creamy vanilla influence, helping the wine's smoothness and generosity, but it does lack intensity and brightness, finishing a little warm and spirity.

2005	87	2007	2010
2004	89	2006	2009+
2002	87	2004	2007+
1999	87	2001	2004
1998	83	2000	2003
1997	86	1999	2002
1996	80	1997	1998

HYLAND SHIRAZ

RATING **4**

Coonawarra	$20–$29
Current vintage: 2005	**90**

A brightly flavoured, intense and confiture-like early-drinking shiraz with notes of violets, menthol, cloves and cinnamon beneath its vibrant, jujube-like flavours of blackcurrants, dark plums and raspberries. It's quite peppery, with some tight-knit cedar/vanilla oak and smooth, approachable tannins. It even holds its 15% alcohol well, for the short term at least.

2005	90	2007	2010+
2004	90	2009	2012
2003	86	2005	2008
2002	87	2004	2007
2001	91	2006	2009
2000	88	2002	2005+
1999	91	2004	2007
1998	87	2003	2006
1997	89	1999	2002+
1996	89	2001	2004
1994	82	1996	1999

PHOENIX CABERNET SAUVIGNON

RATING **5**

Coonawarra	$20–$29
Current vintage: 2005	**80**

Lifted to some extent by fresh vanilla and chocolate-like oak, this young cabernet can't conceal its stressed, stewy dark fruit. Fruit pie-like aromas of blackberries and dark plums precede a palate that quickly fades towards a short, flat and dried-out finish that simply cries out for some fruit ripeness.

2005	80	2007	2010
2004	90	2012	2016
2003	87	2005	2008+
2002	89	2007	2010
2001	93	2006	2009+
2000	82	2002	2005
1999	82	2001	2004
1998	89	2003	2006
1997	89	1999	2002+
1996	90	1998	2001+

RESERVE CABERNET SAUVIGNON

RATING

Coonawarra		$50–$99		
Current vintage: 2004		89		

Sumptuously ripened, this rather jammy, smooth and spirity cabernet delivers some very pretty forward and mid-palate fruit, but at 15% by volume is perhaps slightly overcooked. Confiture-like aromas of blackberries and plums are backed by dark chocolate/mocha-like oak, with under-tones of dark olives and a light meatiness. Warm and spirity, the slightly sweet palate of juicy, ripe fruit falls away marginally, lacking some intensity at the finish.

2004	89	2009	2012+
2002	89	2007	2010
2000	88	2005	2008
1999	93	2007	2011
1998	91	2006	2010
1997	90	2002	2005+
1996	91	2004	2008
1995	87	2000	2003
1994	90	1998	2002
1993	93	2005	2013
1992	93	2000	2004
1991	95	2003	2011
1990	94	1998	2002

SPECIAL SELECT SHIRAZ

RATING 5

Coonawarra		$30–$49		
Current vintage: 2004		90		

Ripe, juicy and intensely flavoured, this firm and pliant shiraz marries concentrated blackberry, black-currant and mulberry flavour with sweet vanilla/dark chocolate oak and nuances of spice, licorice, mint and menthol. It finishes with lingering and slightly meaty flavours of dark berries, and without any overcooked influences.

2004	90	2009	2012+
2002	87	2007	2010
2000	88	2005	2008+

Penny's Hill

Ingleburne, Main Road, McLaren Vale SA 5171. Tel: (08) 8556 4460. Fax: (08) 8556 4462.
Website: www.pennyshill.com.au Email: info@pennyshill.com.au
Region: **McLaren Vale** Winemaker: **Ben Riggs** Viticulturists: **Toby Bekkers, David Paxton**
Chief Executive: **Tony Parkinson**

Penny's Hill is a newcomer to McLaren Vale that has deployed the experienced duo of David Paxton and Ben Riggs to create its wine. All the fruit used for its wines is estate-grown, and the range includes a typical McLaren Vale mix of shiraz, grenache, semillon plus a 'Specialized' release of shiraz, cabernet and merlot.

SHIRAZ

RATING 4

McLaren Vale		$30–$49		
Current vintage: 2005		89		

There's just a hint of stressed fruit beneath this otherwise pleasingly flavoursome and concen-trated wine. Its heady, spicy aromas of pro-foundly ripened dark plums, cassis and blackberries are handsomely backed by sweet and slightly smoky mocha/vanilla oak. Intense, long and juicy, its full-bodied palate has a silkiness enhanced by its smooth, lightly smoky/vanilla oak.

2005	89	2010	2013
2004	90	2009	2012
2003	90	2008	2011
2002	90	2007	2010
2000	81	2002	2005

Pepperjack

Saltram Estates, Nuriootpa-Angaston Road, Angaston SA 5353. Tel: (08) 8564 3355. Fax: (08) 8564 2209.

Region: **Barossa** Winemaker: **Nigel Dolan** Chief Executive: **Jamie Odell**

Pepperjack is a Beringer Blass-owned brand spawned out of the Saltram business. Its very approachable, soft and flavoursome Barossa Valley reds are richly flavoured, generously oaked and usually ready to drink by release. The pick of the current crop is the floral, smoky and spicy Shiraz Viognier from 2005.

CABERNET SAUVIGNON
RATING **5**

			2005	88	2010	2013
Barossa Valley		$20–$29	2004	87	2006	2009+
Current vintage: 2005		88	2003	87	2005	2008
			2000	81	2001	2002
			1999	87	2001	2004+
			1998	81	2000	2003

Honest and generous, but slightly raw and uncultivated, with a minty cut of cassis, plum and blackberry flavour backed by toasty vanilla oak. With a violet-like perfume, it's richly ripened, slightly meaty and raisined, but still delivers a good length of fruit backed by firm, drying tannin.

SHIRAZ
RATING **5**

			2005	86	2007	2010
Barossa Valley		$12–$19	2004	89	2009	2012+
Current vintage: 2005		86	2002	88	2005	2008
			2001	86	2003	2006
			2000	86	2002	2005
			1999	86	2001	2004
			1998	89	2003	2006
			1997	82	1999	2002
			1996	89	2001	2004+

An honest, juicy and slightly meaty shiraz whose musky, meaty dark berry and plum-like fruit tends to rely on its coconut/vanilla oak for sweetness and smoothness. Moderately vibrant, it lacks great length and cellaring potential.

Pertaringa

Corner Hunt & Rifle Range roads, McLaren Vale SA 5171. Tel: (08) 8323 8125. Fax: (08) 8323 7766.
Website: www.pertaringa.com.au Email: wine@pertaringa.com.au

Region: **McLaren Vale** Winemakers: **Geoff Hardy, Ben Riggs** Viticulturist: **Ian Leask**
Chief Executives: **Ian Leask & Geoff Hardy**

Geoff Hardy and Ian Leask are major grape growers whose fruit is largely used for the Pertaringa and K1 wine brands. Their Pertaringa label comprises a range of usually ripe, meaty and generous McLaren Vale wines. The 2005 releases are typically sumptuous and raisined, and rather reliant on oak for palate sweetness.

OVER THE TOP SHIRAZ
RATING **5**

			2005	88	2010	2013
McLaren Vale		$30–$49	2004	90	2012	2016
Current vintage: 2005		88	2002	87	2007	2010+
			2001	89	2006	2009
			2000	83	2002	2005
			1999	90	2004	2007
			1998	88	2003	2006+

Silky-smooth and sumptuous, this deeply flavoured shiraz is steeped in juicy and slightly cooked flavours of blackberries, dark plums and redcurrants, with a meaty, mocha-like background of dark chocolate oak. Its thick, luscious and sour-edged palate is supported by robust, velvet tannins, and finishes with suggestions of mint and menthol.

RIFLE AND HUNT CABERNET SAUVIGNON
RATING **5**

			2005	87	2007	2010
Adelaide		$30–$49	2004	89	2012	2016
Current vintage: 2005		87	2002	87	2007	2010
			2001	88	2003	2006
			2000	82	2002	2005
			1999	87	2001	2004

Very concentrated and sumptuous but dehydrated and raisined, this substantially oaked and gamey shiraz is reliant on its oak for palate sweetness. It's firm and fine-grained, with lingering prune, currant and chocolate-like flavours.

Petaluma

Spring Gully Road, Piccadilly SA 5151. Tel: (08) 8339 9300. Fax: (08) 8339 9301.
Website: www.petaluma.com.au Email: petaluma@petaluma.com.au

Regions: **Adelaide Hills, Clare Valley, Coonawarra** Winemaker: **Andrew Hardy** Viticulturist: **Mike Harms**
Chief Executive: **Anthony Roberts**

Petaluma is a benchmark Australian winery initially established by Brian Croser. While several of the white label wines are still finding their feet, those which carry the traditional yellow label reflect high-quality marriages between varieties and regions. An extensive vertical tasting in 2006 which enabled me to fully update all the Petaluma ratings confirmed the longevity of the company's best vintages, very few of which looked any better than the simply brilliant 2004 Coonawarra blend of cabernet sauvignon and merlot.

CHARDONNAY

RATING **2**

Adelaide Hills $30–$49
Current vintage: 2005   95

Supple and stylish, this tangy, dry and Macon-like chardonnay has a lightly floral and banana-like aroma of grapefruit and melon fruit with underlying nuances of toasty vanilla oak and creamy, charcuterie-like lees-derived complexity. Initially vibrant and juicy, with neatly integrated nutty vanilla oak, it extends towards a long, crisp and savoury finish of refreshing acidity.

2005	95	2010	2013+
2004	95	2012	2016
2003	91	2008	2011
2002	88	2007	2010
2001	89	2006	2009
2000	93	2005	2008
1999	95	2004	2007
1998	94	2006	2010
1997	95	2005	2009
1996	95	2004	2008
1995	95	2003	2007
1994	94	2002	2006
1993	93	1995	1998
1992	93	2000	2004
1991	91	1996	1999
1990	93	1998	2002
1989	90	1991	1994

COONAWARRA (Cabernet Sauvignon & Merlot)

RATING **2**

Coonawarra $50–$99
Current vintage: 2004   97

Typical of many of Australia's leading 2004 red wines, this is a very finely balanced, natural and effortless long-term cabernet blend very reminiscent of its stylish and beautifully harmonious predecessor from 1991. Its heady perfume of violets, cassis and dark plums, lightly toasty mocha/cedar/vanilla oak precedes a classically tight and finely integrated palate whose deep fruit qualities are perfectly married with oak and firm tannins.

2004	97	2024	2034
2003	89	2011	2015
2002	91	2010	2014+
2001	93	2013	2021
2000	93	2008	2012+
1999	97	2019	2029+
1998	96	2018	2028
1997	94	2009	2017+
1996	95	2016	2026
1995	91	2007	2015
1994	93	2006	2014
1993	86	2001	2005
1992	95	2012	2022
1991	97	2011	2021+
1990	96	2010	2020+
1988	92	1996	2000+
1987	89	1999	2007
1986	87	1994	1998+
1985	82	1990	1993
1984	81	1986	1989
1982	87	1987	1990

CROSER (Sparkling Wine)

RATING **3**

Adelaide Hills $30–$49
Current vintage: 2004   93

Vibrant and refreshing, this shapely and elegant aperitif style has a creamy, floral and lightly musky nose of pear, apple and peach backed by delicate, creamy leesy influences. Its tangy palate of citrus, melon and grapefruit is fresh and fluffy, finely focused and creamy, finishing with tight acidity.

2004	93	2006	2009
2003	91	2005	2008
2002	89	2004	2007+
2001	93	2003	2006+
2000	89	2005	2008
1999	93	2001	2004+
1998	91	2000	2003+

HANLIN HILL RIESLING

RATING 2

Clare Valley $20–$29
Current vintage: 2006   **88**

A yeasty, estery and rather pungent aroma with lime, lemon sherbet and confectionary notes reveals some spiky aspects suggestive of a stressed ferment. Fine and smooth but lacking genuine length, it's slightly candied and oily, finishing with tangy notes of lime and lemon. Just a little angular and clunky.

2006	88	2011	2014
2005	93	2013	2017+
2004	90	2009	2012+
2003	96	2011	2015+
2002	95	2010	2014+
2001	89	2009	2013
2000	90	2005	2008+
1999	88	2004	2007+
1998	90	2006	2010
1997	94	2009	2017
1996	95	2008	2016
1995	96	2007	2015
1994	93	2006	2014
1993	87	1998	2001
1992	88	2000	2004
1991	93	2003	2011
1990	90	2005	2008+
1989	90	1997	2001+
1988	90	1996	2000

MERLOT

RATING 2

Coonawarra $50–$99
Current vintage: 2004   **87**

A pretty but essentially hollow wine whose lack of genuine density and palate weight suggests an element of overcropping. Its minty, violet-like perfume of raspberries, cherries and plums is sweetly oaked, while some hotness remains evident on its smooth but sappy palate. It's well enough handled in the cellar.

2004	87	2009	2012
2003	92	2011	2015
2001	95	2009	2013+
2000	87	2005	2008
1999	95	2007	2011+
1998	96	2010	2018
1997	88	2002	2005+
1996	87	2001	2004
1995	90	2003	2007
1994	93	2006	2014+
1993	86	1998	2001
1992	96	2004	2012+
1991	93	2003	2011
1990	92	1998	2002

SHIRAZ

RATING 4

Adelaide Hills $30–$49
Current vintage: 2005   **89**

Briary and meaty aromas of dark plums, currants and blackberries overlie smoky undertones of vanilla oak, cloves and cinnamon. Forward and sumptuous, its ripe and slightly baked palate of blackberry and plum-like flavour lacks genuine mid-palate sweetness, but is supported by a firm, fine and drying extract. While it should flesh out somewhat, it remains slightly deficient in fruit brightness.

2005	89	2010	2013
2004	89	2009	2012
2003	87	2005	2008+
2002	93	2010	2014
2001	95	2009	2013
2000	91	2005	2008
1999	89	2004	2007
1998	91	2003	2006

SUMMERTOWN CHARDONNAY

RATING 3

Piccadilly Valley $50–$99
Current vintage: 2002   **90**

Herbal and confectionary aromas of tropical fruits and peach overlie herbal, estery nuances. Juicy and generous, with intense forward flavours of melon and grapefruit, it becomes greener, more cloying and herbaceous down the palate, finishing with pleasing nutty and savoury qualities but also a hint of tinned fruit.

2004	91	2009	2012
2003	96	2008	2011
2002	90	2004	2007+
2001	93	2009	2013

TIERS CHARDONNAY

Piccadilly Valley	$100–$199		
Current vintage: 2003	**91**		

Spicy aromas of white peach and grapefruit with a toasty background of vanilla and bubblegum-like oak precede a grainy, forward and buttery palate that lacks the length and depth of fruit expected of this label. It's elegant and handsomely oaked, finishing with a hint of sweetcorn and a chalky texture.

2005	96	2010	2013+
2004	95	2009	2012+
2003	91	2008	2011
2002	90	2004	2007+
2001	94	2006	2009+
2000	96	2005	2008+
1999	93	2004	2007
1998	97	2005	2008
1997	97	2002	2005+
1996	93	2004	2008

VIOGNIER

Adelaide Hills	$30–$49		
Current vintage: 2005	**83**		

Simple, estery aromas of pineapples, lemon detergent and sherbet-like confection are backed by floral and spicy nuances. Juicy, sweet and tropical, its rather candied fruit lacks length and intensity, finishing simple and sweet. Possibly a stuck ferment?

2005	83	2006	2007
2003	89	2005	2008
2002	91	2004	2007
2001	89	2003	2006
2000	90	2001	2002+
1999	90	2001	2004
1998	90	2000	2003+

Peter Lehmann

Off Para Road, Tanunda SA 5352. Tel: (08) 8563 2100. Fax: (08) 8563 3402.
Website: www.peterlehmannwines.com Email: plw@peterlehmannwines.com
Region: **Barossa Valley** Winemakers: **Andrew Wigan, Kerry Morrison, Leonie Lange & Ian Hongell**
Viticulturist: **Peter Nash** Chief Executive: **Douglas Lehmann**

Peter Lehmann is a large Barossa-based brand whose wines are typically very faithful to variety and region. Its inexpensive Barossa brand delivers generous flavour and occasionally genuine excellence, while its Eden Valley Riesling, Reserve Riesling and Reserve Semillon offer more finesse and age-worthiness. 2002 was an excellent vintage for its premier red wines, especially for the flagship Stonewell Shiraz, the best since 1996.

BAROSSA CABERNET SAUVIGNON

Barossa Valley	$12–$19		
Current vintage: 2004	**92**		

Dusted with nuances of dried herbs, this richly flavoured and finely balanced young cabernet has a violet-like fragrance of intense black and red berries backed by fresh cedar/vanilla oak. Its supple, polished palate of vibrant plum, berry and dark cherry flavour is framed by firmish, pliant and loose-knit tannin, finishing with length and persistence. Great value.

2004	92	2012	2016+
2003	84	2005	2008
2002	91	2007	2010
2001	83	2003	2006
2000	88	2002	2005+
1999	87	2001	2004+
1998	93	2006	2010
1997	93	2002	2005+
1996	90	2001	2004
1995	88	2000	2003
1994	93	1999	2002
1993	93	2001	2005
1992	94	2000	2004
1991	89	1999	2003
1990	93	2002	2010
1989	91	1997	2001
1988	93	2000	2008

BAROSSA CHARDONNAY

Barossa Valley	$12–$19		
Current vintage: 2005	**87**		

Creamy, peachy aromas of nectarine, cashew and sweet vanilla oak precede a juicy and vibrant palate whose smooth expression of stonefruit flavours is deftly balanced with restrained and lightly toasty vanilla oak. It finishes long and fresh.

2005	87	2006	2007+
2004	89	2006	2009
2002	87	2004	2007
2001	84	2002	2003
2000	81	2001	2002

A B C D E F G H I J K L M N O **P** Q R S T U V W X Y Z

BAROSSA RIESLING (formerly Eden Valley Riesling)

Barossa Valley $12–$19
Current vintage: 2006 88

Delicate and floral, with a bathpowder-like perfume of lime zest and lemon sherbet before a round, generous and juicy palate whose forward flavours of apple, lemon and lime finish clean and tangy, with suggestions of talcum powder. Fresh and varietal, with plenty of personality.

2006	88	2008	2011+
2005	89	2007	2010+
2004	92	2009	2012
2003	90	2005	2008+
2002	90	2004	2007+
2001	88	2003	2006
2000	86	2001	2005
1999	85	2000	2001
1998	90	2003	2006
1997	87	1999	2002
1996	90	2001	2004
1995	82	1997	2000
1994	88	1999	2002
1993	93	1998	2001
1992	92	1997	2000

BAROSSA SEMILLON

Barossa Valley $5–$11
Current vintage: 2005 88

A vibrant and varietal semillon whose fresh aromas of green melon and lemon juice precede a refreshing and lively palate whose bright, tangy fruit finishes with clean and zesty acidity.

2005	88	2007	2010
2004	89	2006	2009+
2003	92	2008	2011
2002	91	2004	2007+
2001	89	2001	2002+
2000	92	2002	2005
1999	89	2001	2004
1998	89	2000	2003
1997	90	1999	2002
1996	89	1998	2001

BAROSSA SHIRAZ

Barossa Valley $12–$19
Current vintage: 2004 90

Vibrant aromas of fresh blackberries, redcurrant, cassis and raspberries overlie fresh coconut/vanilla oak and undertones of violets and white pepper. Medium to full in weight, it's smooth but firmish, with pleasingly long and juicy flavours of spicy small berry and redcurrant fruit backed by cedar/vanilla oak and framed by fine, powdery tannins.

2004	90	2009	2012
2003	86	2005	2008
2002	90	2007	2010
2001	90	2003	2006
2000	89	2002	2005+
1999	88	2001	2004+
1998	92	2003	2006
1997	93	2002	2005+
1996	91	1998	2001
1995	87	1997	2000
1994	91	1999	2002
1993	90	2001	2005
1992	93	2000	2004
1991	91	1996	1999

BOTRYTIS SEMILLON (formerly Noble Semillon)

Barossa Valley $12–$19 (375 ml)
Current vintage: 2006 87

Sweet, juicy and moderately luscious, with lightly toasty flavours of melon, peach and lemon over suggestions of nutty vanilla oak and fresh, citrusy acids. It's fresh, clean and flavoursome, but lacks an identifiable presence of botrytis.

2006	87	2007	2011
2005	86	2007	2010
2002	91	2004	2007+
2001	87	2003	2006+
2000	90	2002	2005+
1999	82	2001	2004
1998	84	2003	2006
1997	86	1999	2002
1996	81	1997	1998
1995	87	2000	2003
1994	91	1999	2002
1992	84	1997	2000

CLANCY'S (Shiraz Cabernet Sauvignon Merlot)

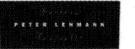

Barossa Valley $12–$19
Current vintage: 2004   86

Rather simple, earthy and slightly thin, with lightly floral and peppery aromas of fresh small black and red berries and violets over restrained cedar/vanilla oak. Smooth and supple, with an initially vibrant expression of blueberries and dark plums, it thins out towards a dusty, chalky finish with earthy undertones.

2004	86	2006	2009
2003	87	2005	2008
2002	89	2004	2007
2000	80	2002	2005
1999	81	2000	2001
1998	85	2000	2003
1997	92	2002	2005
1996	89	1998	2001
1995	89	1997	2000
1994	90	1996	1999

EDEN VALLEY RIESLING (formerly Blue Eden Riesling)   RATING 3

Eden Valley $12–$19
Current vintage: 2006   90

A generous and intensely flavoured riesling with lightly floral and spicy varietal qualities of lime juice, apple and lemon rind enhanced by undertones of chalk and minerality. Even if it hasn't quite the focus for the long term, it's long, fine and shapely, with a lingering lemony finish.

2006	90	2011	2014
2005	93	2013	2017+
2004	90	2006	2009+
2003	95	2008	2011+
2002	95	2007	2010
2001	95	2009	2013
2000	89	2005	2008

EIGHT SONGS SHIRAZ   RATING 4

Barossa Valley $30–$49
Current vintage: 2002   90

A substantial, ripe and meaty medium to long-term Barossa shiraz. Its deep, gamey aromas of blackberries and plums are handsomely backed by sweet, smoky oak and black pepper, with nuances of cinnamon and cloves. Deeply spiced, its sumptuous, smooth and slightly overcooked palate of earthy shiraz fruit is thickly coated with firm, grippy tannin before finishing long, persistent and savoury.

2002	90	2010	2014
2001	88	2006	2009
2000	89	2005	2008
1999	92	2004	2007+
1998	94	2006	2010+
1997	88	2002	2005+
1996	96	2004	2008+

MENTOR   RATING 3

Barossa Valley $30–$49
Current vintage: 2002   93

An elegant, smooth and silky cabernet blend whose dusty, floral perfume of violets, cassis, cedar and vanilla oak reveals undertones of dried herbs, mint and menthol. Full to medium weight, it's long and vibrant, with intense flavours of mulberries, plums and blackberries backed by creamy oak and framed by powdery, bony tannins. It finishes with lingering minty dark fruits and nuances of menthol.

2002	93	2014	2022
2001	88	2009	2013
2000	88	2005	2008+
1999	91	2004	2007
1998	93	2010	2018
1997	91	2005	2009
1996	95	2008	2016
1995	87	2007	2015
1994	93	2006	2014
1993	87	2001	2005+
1992	93	2000	2004+
1991	93	1999	2003
1990	94	2002	2010
1989	94	2001	2006
1986	95	1998	2003

RESERVE RIESLING   RATING 3

Eden Valley $20–$29
Current vintage: 2002   93

Surprisingly intense and youthful, with a lightly honeyed and waxy perfume of crystal-clear lime juice and lemon rind, with a hint of oiliness. Generous and juicy, its pristine expression of piercing lemon sherbet, lime juice, pear and lemon tart-like flavour is backed by a fine-grained and chalky backbone. It builds flavour and density on the palate, and needs more time in the bottle.

2002	93	2010	2014+
2001	92	2009	2013+
2000	90	2005	2008+
1998	95	2006	2010+
1997	90	2005	2009
1996	90	2001	2004
1995	92	2000	2003
1994	93	2002	2006
1993	96	2005	2013
1992	93	2000	2004
1991	93	1996	1999

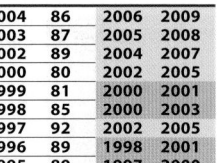

STONEWELL (Shiraz)

RATING **2**

Barossa Valley $50–$99
Current vintage: 2002 96

A classic Barossa shiraz that effortlessly marries remarkable intensity and concentration with elegance and finesse. Deeply concentrated, its vibrant, minty and briary aromas of blackcurrants and red berries are backed by cedar/dark chocolate oak. Rather closed, it slowly unfolds layers of dark berry and plum-like flavour knit tightly with dusty, fine-grained oak, culminating in a long, lingering finish of meaty, wild berry flavour, dark olives and robust, but pliant tannin.

2002	96	2014	2022+
2001	85	2006	2009
2000	89	2008	2012
1999	95	2007	2011+
1998	89	2006	2010
1997	93	2005	2008+
1996	96	2008	2016+
1995	91	2003	2007+
1994	96	2002	2006+
1993	95	2005	2013
1992	93	2000	2004
1991	95	2011	2021
1990	89	1998	2002+
1989	95	2001	2006+
1988	95	2000	2008
1987	94	1999	2004

Pewsey Vale

Browns Road, Pewsey Vale SA 5235. Tel: (08) 8561 3200. Fax: (08) 8561 3393.
Website: www.pewseyvale.com Email: info@pewseyvale.com
Region: **Eden Valley** Winemaker: **Louisa Rose** Viticulturist: **Robin Nettelbeck** Chief Executive: **Robert Hill Smith**
Pewsey Vale is best known for its two Rieslings, each of which is consistently reliable, true to type and long-living. The 2001 The Contours confirms yet again what a classic vintage this was across the Eden Valley for its deeply perfumed, tightly sculpted and chalky expression of riesling. The vineyard is also responsible for a deeply scented and citrusy Pinot Gris.

RIESLING

RATING **4**

Eden Valley $12–$19
Current vintage: 2006 91

Delicate, slightly candied aromas of apple, peach and lime juice precede forward and juicy lime, lemon and apple-like flavours that extend well down the palate over a fine, chalky chassis. It's long, generous and stylish, with plenty of regional elegance.

2006	91	2011	2014+
2005	93	2013	2017
2004	87	2006	2009
2003	93	2008	2011+
2002	91	2007	2010+
2001	90	2006	2009
2000	91	2005	2008+
1999	95	2007	2011+
1998	88	2003	2006
1997	94	2005	2009
1996	94	2008	2016
1995	92	2003	2007
1994	93	2006	2014
1993	94	1998	2001
1992	93	1997	2000
1991	93	1999	2003
1990	94	1998	2002
1989	89	1997	2001
1988	90	1993	1996

THE CONTOURS RIESLING

RATING **2**

Eden Valley $20–$29
Current vintage: 2001 95

Funny how people still doubt the ability of wines to age under a screwcap seal. Here is a delightfully youthful expression of riesling whose brightness and raciness belie its five years of age, yet it has also started to reveal some very pleasing complexity. There's a pungent and slightly meaty aspect beneath its floral fragrance of slightly candied lime juice and lemon, while it's also unfolding suggestions of toast and butter. Round and generous, its smooth and very finely shaped palate of lemon and lime is underpinned by a slatey, almost schisty cut of bathpowder-like minerality. It finishes long and austere, with a lingering presence of fruit.

2001	95	2009	2013+
2000	91	2008	2012
1999	94	2007	2011+
1998	95	2006	2010+
1997	89	2002	2005
1996	95	2008	2016
1995	92	2003	2007+

Pierro

Caves Road, Willyabrup via Cowaramup WA 6284. Tel: (08) 9755 6220. Fax: (08) 9755 6308.
Website: www.pierro.com.au Email: pierro@iinet.net.au

Region: **Margaret River** Winemaker: **Mike Peterkin** Viticulturist: **Mike Peterkin** Chief Executive: **Mike Peterkin**

Mike Peterkin is a leader among Australian makers of chardonnay. Pierro's has traditionally been one of the country's more opulent and powerful chardonnays, but since 2002 it has acquired additional dimensions of tightness and silkiness. The 2005 release shows perhaps further refinement, with an extraordinary backbone of powdery mineral texture beneath its tightly controlled but unctuous fruit.

CABERNET SAUVIGNON MERLOT (LTCf)

RATING 4

Margaret River	$50–$99
Current vintage: 2004	88

Backed by herbal, earthy and light meaty notes, this is a smooth and fine-grained cabernet blend of medium to full weight. Its heady perfume reveals layers of dark berries and redcurrants with floral and leathery undertones. Its briary palate of lively plum and small berry flavour finishes fine and savoury, but with slightly green-edged tannins.

2004	88	2012	2016
2003	88	2008	2011+
2001	92	2009	2013+
2000	87	2002	2005+
1999	93	2007	2011+
1998	90	2006	2010+
1997	86	2002	2005
1996	93	2004	2008+
1995	87	2000	2003

CHARDONNAY

RATING 1

Margaret River	$50–$99
Current vintage: 2005	97

A very stylish, powdery and mineral chardonnay whose sumptuously ripened flavours of honeydew melon, grapefruit and pineapple are tightly knit with sweet, spicy vanilla oak. It's heady and perfumed, with an unctuous, silky-smooth but explosively flavoured palate whose intense tropical and citrusy fruit is carefully backed by creamy oak. It finishes long and chalky, with a wet slate-like backbone of fine phenolics and minerality.

2005	97	2010	2013+
2004	90	2006	2009
2003	97	2008	2011+
2002	96	2005	2008
2001	89	2003	2006
2000	95	2005	2008+
1999	96	2007	2011
1998	93	2000	2003+
1997	95	2002	2005+
1996	97	2001	2004
1995	93	2000	2003
1994	95	2002	2006
1993	95	2001	2005
1992	96	2000	2004
1991	94	1996	1999
1990	94	1998	2002

SEMILLON SAUVIGNON BLANC (LTC)

RATING 4

Margaret River	$20–$29
Current vintage: 2006	90

Very restrained, dusty and delicate aromas of melon and lemon backed by a light grassiness. Fine and austere, it's moderately intense, with lively melon and citrus flavours tightly wound around refreshingly austere acidity. Pleasing length and shape.

2006	90	2007	2008+
2005	91	2007	2010+
2004	94	2006	2009+
2003	91	2005	2008+
2002	91	2004	2007
2001	92	2003	2006+
2000	94	2002	2005
1999	89	2001	2004
1998	91	2000	2003
1997	93	2002	2005
1996	94	2001	2004
1995	93	1997	2000
1994	93	1999	2002
1993	93	1998	2001

Pike & Joyce

Polish Hill River Road, Sevenhill via Clare SA 5453. Tel: (08) 8843 4370. Fax: (08) 8843 4353.
Website: www.pikeswines.com.au/pikeandjoyce Email: pikeandjoyce@pikeswines.com.au
Region: **Lenswood** Winemakers: **Neil Pike, John Trotter** Viticulturists: **Andrew Pike, Sam Luke, Mark Joyce**
Chief Executives: **Neil Pike, Andrew Pike & Mark Joyce**

This joint venture between Pikes Wines (Clare Valley) and Joyson Orchards (Lenswood) produced another deliciously wild, savoury and funky Chardonnay in 2005 but rather an overcooked Sauvignon Blanc in 2006. Neither the Pinot Noir or Pinot Gris enjoyed the heat of the early 2006 season.

CHARDONNAY

RATING

Lenswood	$20–$29	2005	92	2007	2010+
Current vintage: 2005	**92**	2004	93	2006	2009+
		2003	92	2005	2008
		2002	82	2003	2004+
		2001	87	2003	2006

Juicy aromas of nectarine and melon with funky, floral and meaty undertones, minerals and suggestions of creamy oak precede a long and juicy palate tied together with taut, tight-fitting mineral acids. Its generous peach, lime and grapefruit flavours knit tightly with fine oak, finishing with attractive crispness, brightness and shape. Fine balance and harmony.

SAUVIGNON BLANC

RATING 4

Lenswood	$20–$29	2006	83	2006	2007+
Current vintage: 2006	**83**	2005	90	2006	2007
		2004	83	2004	2005+
		2003	89	2003	2004+
		2002	93	2003	2004

A broad, slightly sweaty and oily white whose candied gooseberry flavours are overshadowed by green, herby, capsicum and nettle-like influences. Lacks length of fruit and freshness.

Pikes

Polish Hill River Road, Sevenhill SA 5453. Tel: (08) 8843 4370. Fax: (08) 8843 4353.
Website: www.pikeswines.com.au Email: info@pikeswines.com.au
Region: **Clare Valley** Winemakers: **Neil Pike, John Trotter** Viticulturist: **Andrew Pike**
Chief Executives: **Neil Pike & Andrew Pike**

Pikes is an energetic family-owned and operated winery in Clare. Its 2005 reds lack the polish and natural elegance of the 2004 releases; a common phenomenon across South Australia. The pick of the current wines is the bracingly lean and austere 2006 Riesling, which for reasons about which I am not qualified to remark, has been called 'Traditionale'.

EASTSIDE SHIRAZ

RATING 5

Clare Valley	$20–$29	2005	87	2007	2010+
Current vintage: 2005	**87**	2004	94	2012	2016+
		2003	89	2008	2011
		2002	86	2007	2010
		2001	89	2006	2009
		2000	87	2005	2008
		1999	89	2004	2007
		1998	88	2006	2010+
		1997	90	2005	2009
		1996	87	2001	2004
		1995	93	2000	2003
		1994	91	1999	2002
		1993	90	2001	2005
		1992	94	2000	2004
		1991	94	2003	2011
		1990	94	2002	2010

Very spicy and fragrant, this ripe, slightly candied and meaty shiraz delivers juicy flavours of blackberries, blueberries and dark plums backed by suggestions of currants, mint and menthol. It's a fraction thin but finishes smooth and savoury.

THE HILL BLOCK CABERNET RATING 5

Clare Valley $20–$29
Current vintage: 2005 89

A polished wine from a difficult season, with a slightly herbal fragrance of violets, spearmint and cassis backed by sweet vanilla/cedar oak and nuances of menthol. Forward and juicy, its intense, minty flavours of blackberries, dark plums and menthol are backed by fresh cedar/vanilla oak. Framed by fine-grained, powdery tannins, it finishes with vibrant flavour. It just lacks the genuine depth of fruit for the long term.

2005	89	2010	2013
2004	87	2009	2012
2002	86	2007	2010
2001	87	2006	2009
2000	86	2002	2005+
1999	89	2004	2007
1998	91	2006	2010+
1997	89	2005	2009
1996	91	2004	2008+
1995	87	1997	2000
1994	94	2002	2006
1993	93	1998	2001
1992	94	2000	2004
1991	93	1999	2003
1990	93	1998	2002

THE MERLE RESERVE RIESLING RATING 2

Clare Valley $20–$29
Current vintage: 2005 95

A very classy and long-term riesling whose musky, floral perfume of rose petal and lime aromas reveals undertones of minerals. Fine, long and chalky, the palate is deliciously concentrated and presents an open, almost juicy expression of pristine, essential varietal flavour before an austere but refreshing finish.

2005	95	2017	2025
2004	96	2016	2024
2002	96	2010	2014+
2001	94	2009	2013+
1997	95	2005	2009

TRADITIONALE RIESLING RATING 3

Clare Valley $12–$19
Current vintage: 2006 90

A bracingly lean and austere riesling whose pungent, floral and musky aromas of lime juice and lemon are dusted with chalky undertones. The palate is long, finely crafted and taut, and while it should flesh out in the medium term, it just lacks its typical intensity of fruit.

2006	90	2011	2014
2005	92	2010	2013+
2004	92	2009	2012
2003	94	2008	2011+
2002	94	2007	2010
2001	92	2006	2009
2000	94	2008	2012
1999	95	2007	2011
1998	93	2003	2006+
1997	89	2002	2005
1996	90	2001	2004
1995	81	1997	2000
1992	87	1997	2000
1990	93	1998	2002
1988	93	1993	1996

Pipers Brook

1216 Pipers Brook Road, Pipers Brook Tas 7254. Tel: (03) 6382 7527. Fax: (03) 6382 7226.
Website: www.pipersbrook.com Email: enquiries@pipersbrook.com

Region: **Pipers River** Winemaker: **Rene Bezemer** Viticulturist: **Bruce McCormack** Chief Executive: **Paul de Moor**

Over the decades, its various owners have matched European grape varieties with the wide range of different sites and soils within the various Pipers Brook vineyards. This attention to detail has led this company to produce some of Australia's most Alsace-like wines from riesling, pinot gris and gewürztraminer. Furthermore, but perhaps a little less consistently, it can create some deliciously savoury, complex expressions of chardonnay and pinot.

CUVÉE CLARK RIESLING (Late Harvest) RATING 3

Pipers River $30–$49 (375 ml)
Current vintage: 2003 93

Nutty, pastry-like scents of fresh flowers, melon and mango, pear and apple, backed by confection-like baby powder undertones. Pure, bright and lively, it offers a sweet and luscious palate whose concentrated flavours of apricots, lime and pear finish savoury and clean, with racy and refreshing acidity.

2003	93	2005	2008+
2001	95	2006	2009+
2000	96	2005	2008+

ESTATE PINOT GRIS

PIPERS BROOK VINEYARD
2001 PINOT GRIS
TASMANIA

| Pipers River | $20–$29 |
| Current vintage: 2006 | 87 |

Dusty, herbal and floral aromas of spicy pear and melon precede a long, brightly lit palate whose intense fruit conceal a slightly stale flatness and what appears to be oakiness. It finishes clean and vibrant, with refreshing acids.

2006	87	2007	2008
2005	95	2007	2010+
2004	84	2005	2006
2003	82	2003	2004
2001	77	2002	2003
2000	90	2002	2005
1999	94	2001	2004
1998	87	1999	2000

ESTATE PINOT NOIR (formerly Pellion)

RATING 5

PIPERS BROOK VINEYARD
2000 PINOT NOIR
TASMANIA

ESTATE

| Pipers River | $30–$49 |
| Current vintage: 2005 | 88 |

An assertive young pinot with flavour and structure. Backed by spicy suggestions of cloves and cinnamon, its leathery, floral and slightly reductive perfume of cherries, plums and dark berries precedes a firmish, meaty and Volnay-like palate supported by firm, drying and powdery tannin. A savoury style that could use a little more stuffing, it finishes with slightly green-edged acids.

2005	88	2010	2013
2004	88	2006	2009
2003	90	2008	2011
2002	87	2004	2007
2001	81	2002	2003
2000	90	2002	2005
1999	90	2004	2007
1998	86	2000	2003+
1997	89	2002	2005
1996	82	2001	2004
1995	91	1997	2000
1994	90	1999	2002
1993	89	1995	1998
1992	91	1997	2000

RESERVE PINOT NOIR

RATING 3

PIPERS BROOK VINEYARD
1998 PINOT NOIR RESERVE
Tasmania

| Pipers River | $50–$99 |
| Current vintage: 2004 | 86 |

A herbal, green-edged pinot that also reveals some slightly cooked notes. Its dusty and slightly meaty aromas of rose petals, red cherries and berries overlie fresh cedar/vanilla oak. Firmish and rather robust, the palate delivers currant-like fruit over greenish, under-ripe influences, culminating in a raw, rather hard-edged finish.

2004	86	2006	2009
2003	96	2008	2011
2002	93	2007	2010+
1998	79	2000	2003

Pirramimma

Johnston Road, McLaren Vale SA 5171. Tel: (08) 8323 8205. Fax: (08) 8323 9224.
Website: www.pirramimma.com.au Email: enquiries@pirramimma.com.au
Region: **McLaren Vale** Winemaker: **Geoff Johnston** Chief Executive: **Alexander Johnston**

A long-established maker of luscious McLaren Vale reds of typically high ripeness but balanced levels of alcohol, Pirramimma was one of the first Australian wineries to release a 100% Petit Verdot. The intensity and exuberance of that wine exemplifies the uncomplicated and approachable style that has become Pirramimma's hallmark.

PETIT VERDOT

RATING 5

PIRRAMIMMA
2001
McLAREN VALE
Petit Verdot
750ML

| McLaren Vale | $20–$29 |
| Current vintage: 2004 | 88 |

Deep, dark and concentrated, this relatively uncomplicated but richly fruited red delivers intense flavours of blackberries and plums with sweet chocolate/vanilla oak and modest tannins in support. It's up-front and very intense, with marginally over-ripe flavours and a hint of baked fruit that robs it of a little length.

2004	88	2006	2009
2003	86	2005	2008
2002	89	2007	2010
2001	82	2003	2006
2000	90	2005	2008

SHIRAZ

RATING **4**

McLaren Vale	$20–$29
Current vintage: 2004	**92**

A luscious, smooth and sour-edged shiraz whose deeply spiced and peppery flavours of blackberries, cassis and dark plums are carefully matched with sweet vanilla/dark chocolate oak and supported by velvet tannins. Long and sumptuous, it's rich and juicy — just what McLaren Vale does better with shiraz than almost anywhere else.

2004	92	2009	2012+
2003	90	2008	2011+
2002	82	2004	2007
2001	90	2009	2013
2000	83	2002	2005

Pizzini

175 King Valley Road, Whitfield Vic 3678. Tel: (03) 5729 8278. Fax: (03) 5279 8495.
Website: www.pizzini.com.au Email: pizzini@bigpond.com

Region: **King Valley** Winemakers: **Joel & Alfred Pizzini** Chief Executives: **Alfred & Katrina Pizzini**

Pizzini is just the sort of winery Australia needs more of. It's working hard to develop authentic expressions of Italian varieties in Australia, sells what it makes at a very fair price, and is prepared to cellar its reds until they're ready for sale. These wines emphatically demand to be enjoyed around the dining table.

IL BARONE CABERNET BLEND

RATING **5**

King Valley	$30–$49
Current vintage: 2003	**89**

Spicy, meaty and browning, this firm, rustic and powerfully structured blend has a slightly raisined expression of deep, dark plum-like fruit backed by meaty suggestions of prunes, dried herbs, polished leather and dark chocolate. Drying and powdery, it has plenty of personality and richness. Give it some time.

2003	89	2011	2015
2002	91	2014	2022
2001	89	2009	2013

NEBBIOLO

RATING **4**

King Valley	$50–$99
Current vintage: 2002	**93**

A firm, drying and sinewy nebbiolo with a browning appearance and an aged, raisined expression of meaty, gamey, currant and raisin-like fruit lifted by floral qualities and tarry, chocolatey complexity. It's powerful and layered, with excellent length and a fine-grained undercarriage of tightly integrated firmness. It finishes savoury, with persistent fruit and refreshing acids.

2002	93	2010	2014+
2001	92	2009	2013+
2000	91	2005	2008+
1999	90	2007	2011+
1998	92	2010	2018

RIESLING

RATING **4**

King Valley	$12–$19
Current vintage: 2006	**77**

Oily, spicy and toasty, with slightly sour-edged and candied fruit backed by unusually caramel-like undertones, it's angular and spiky, lacking genuine freshness and focus.

2006	77	2007	2008
2005	84	2007	2010
2004	90	2009	2012
2003	90	2008	2011
2002	87	2007	2010+

SANGIOVESE

RATING **5**

King Valley	$20–$29
Current vintage: 2005	**89**

A rustic, meaty sangiovese whose sweet, slightly confectionary flavours of red cherries and plums are backed by dusty, herbal nuances of under-brush and tomato stalk. It's moderately long, with a slightly raw and drying backbone of cherry kernel tannins and green-edged acidity, but should build weight in the bottle.

2005	89	2010	2013
2004	93	2009	2012+
2003	82	2005	2008
2002	89	2004	2007+

Plantagenet

Albany Highway, Mount Barker WA 6324. Tel: (08) 9851 3111. Fax: (08) 9851 1839.
Website: www.plantagenetwines.com Email: sales@plantagenetwines.com
Region: **Mount Barker** Winemaker: **John Durham** Viticulturist: **Jaysen Gladish** Chairman: **Tony Smith**

Plantagenet is a well-established small winery with good access to mature vineyards. Over the years it has proven capable of exceptional Riesling, Shiraz and Cabernet Sauvignon. I am delighted with the news that former Cape Mentelle winemaker John Durham has taken up the post at Plantagenet, for I believe that his talents and fondness for complex, natural wine fit very neatly with the latent potential within Plantagenet's vineyards.

CABERNET SAUVIGNON

RATING **5**

Mount Barker	$30–$49
Current vintage: 2003	**87**

A cooler year cabernet whose slightly leafy and cedary aromas of red and black berries overlie meaty nuances of blue cheese and leather. Its moderate length of plum and berry flavour is supported by quite a firm grip of slightly sappy tannin and sweet underlying oak. It finishes with a hint of capsicum, but not too green.

2003	87	2008	2011+
2002	90	2007	2010+
2001	89	2009	2013
1999	89	2004	2007+
1998	88	2003	2006+
1997	88	2005	2009
1996	87	2001	2004
1995	88	2003	2007
1994	95	2006	2014
1993	93	2005	2013+
1992	94	2000	2004+
1991	91	1999	2003+
1990	89	1998	2002
1989	95	2001	2009+

CHARDONNAY

RATING **3**

Mount Barker	$20–$29
Current vintage: 2005	**93**

A finely weighted, balanced and tightly integrated chardonnay that marries its fresh citrusy and tropical fruit with restrained creamy, leesy complexity, dusty vanilla oak and refreshing acidity. It opens with a fresh and lightly toasty nose of quince, cumquat, grapefruit and pineapple, while its palate is long, supple and elegant, delivering juicy, slightly meaty and creamy fruit plus matchstick-like oak before a warm, savoury and wheatmeal-like finish.

2005	93	2010	2013
2004	86	2006	2009
2003	94	2008	2011
2001	85	2003	2006
2000	93	2005	2008
1999	94	2004	2007+
1998	89	2003	2006
1997	91	2002	2005
1996	87	2001	2004
1995	93	2000	2003

RIESLING

Great Southern $20–$29
Current vintage: 2006 91

A delicate, musky and lightly floral perfume of fresh fresh lemony fruit precedes a taut and austere palate whose penetrative citrus and apple-like flavours overlie a chalky undercarriage that extends its length and mouthfeel. It finishes lean and stylish, tight and refreshing.

PLANTAGENET
RIESLING
GREAT SOUTHERN
750ML   WINE OF AUSTRALIA   13.0% vol

Year	Score		
2006	91	2011	2014+
2005	95	2013	2017
2004	95	2009	2013+
2003	92	2011	2015
2002	90	2007	2010
2001	94	2009	2013
2000	95	2005	2008
1999	94	2007	2011
1998	95	2006	2010
1997	93	2005	2009
1996	95	2004	2008
1995	94	2003	2007
1994	94	2006	2014
1993	94	1998	2001

SHIRAZ

Mount Barker $30–$49
Current vintage: 2004 88

Minty and slightly overcooked, this meaty and fruitcake-like shiraz marries sweet flavours of red berries and plums with polished, chocolate-like oak and spicy nuances of cloves and cinnamon. Its slightly syrupy and spirity palate would benefit from more structure.

PLANTAGENET
SHIRAZ
GREAT SOUTHERN
750ML   WINE OF AUSTRALIA   13.0% vol

Year	Score		
2004	88	2006	2009+
2003	89	2008	2011+
2002	93	2014	2022
2001	93	2000	2013+
2000	90	2005	2008
1999	91	2007	2011
1998	90	2006	2010+
1997	86	1999	2002
1996	87	2002	2008
1995	90	2003	2007+
1994	96	2002	2006
1993	93	2005	2013
1991	89	1996	1999+
1990	92	2002	2010
1989	90	2001	2009
1988	90	2000	2008
1987	90	1999	2007
1986	88	1994	1998+

Poole's Rock

DeBeyers Road, Pokolbin NSW 2320. Tel: (02) 4998 7389. Fax: (02) 4998 7682.
Website: www.poolesrock.com.au Email: info@poolesrock.com.au

Region: **Lower Hunter Valley** Winemaker: **Patrick Auld** Viticulturist: **Evan Powell** Chief Executive: **Peter Russell**

With the purchase of the Tulloch winery from Southcorp in 2002, Poole's Rock acquired a base in the heart of the Hunter Valley. Then, with the appointment of former Tulloch winemaker Patrick Auld, it bought itself an inestimable resource of Hunter Valley experience and talent. Poole's Rock is owned by investment banker David Clarke, who has recently become Chairman of the Winemakers Federation of Australia.

CHARDONNAY

Lower Hunter Valley $20–$29
Current vintage: 2005 87

Slightly developed and candied, this intensely flavoured and lightly chalky chardonnay combines lightly buttery flavours of lemon, melon, peach and quince with restrained oak and undertones of mineral and tobacco. It's tied together by a zesty cut of lemony acidity.

POOLE'S ROCK
CHARDONNAY
HUNTER VALLEY
750 ML

Year	Score		
2005	87	2007	2010
2003	72	2004	2005
2002	86	2004	2007
2001	89	2003	2006
1999	89	2001	2004
1998	90	2003	2006
1997	90	2002	2005
1996	92	1998	2001
1995	87	1997	2000

Port Phillip Estate

261 Red Hill Road, Red Hill South Vic 3937. Tel: (03) 5989 2708. Fax: (03) 5989 3017.
Website: www.portphillip.net Email: sales@portphillip.net
Region: **Mornington Peninsula** Winemaker: **Sandro Mosele** Viticulturist: **Doug Wood**
Chief Executive: **Giorgio Gjergja**
Port Phillip Estate is a tiny Mornington Peninsula producer now part of the same stable as the Kooyong winery.
The 2005 season produced richer, meatier reds than typical from this vineyard, while the 2006 Sauvignon Blanc
struggled in some tough, early conditions.

PINOT NOIR

 RATING **4**

Mornington Peninsula $30–$49
Current vintage: 2005 92

A dark and powerful pinot whose deep-set fruit
should settle down with its presently rather raw
tannins and hard-edged acids. Slightly jammy and
confectionary, its intense expression of blackberry
and cassis-like fruit does have a cooked and greenish
aspect, while its oak has a resiny edge. It should
develop some pleasing smoothness and complexity over time.

2005	92	2010	2013
2004	95	2009	2012+
2003	89	2005	2008
2002	87	2003	2004+
2001	89	2003	2006
2000	82	2002	2005
1999	91	2001	2004+
1998	88	1999	2000

SAUVIGNON BLANC

RATING **4**

Mornington Peninsula $20–$29
Current vintage: 2006 86

Rather chewy, chunky and reductive, this pungent
and slightly sweaty sauvignon blanc delivers herbaceous aromas and a palate that lacks genuine fruit
sweetness and freshness.

2006	86	2006	2007
2005	93	2006	2007+
2004	92	2005	2006
2003	81	2003	2003

SHIRAZ

RATING **5**

Mornington Peninsula $30–$49
Current vintage: 2005 88

Just a fraction cooked and stewy, this rather savoury
and Rhôney shiraz marries spicy flavours of redcurrants, cassis, blackberries, dark plums and
currants with creamy vanilla oak and smooth, fine-
grained powdery tannin. It's peppery and meaty,
but slightly closed. Medium to full in weight, smooth
and soft, it's likely to flesh out well.

2005	88	2010	2013
2004	88	2006	2009+
2003	90	2005	2008+
2001	79	2003	2006
2000	89	2002	2005+
1999	86	2000	2003
1998	89	2002	2005+

Primo Estate

McMurtrie Road, McLaren Vale SA 5171. Tel: (08) 8323 6800. Fax: (08) 8323 6888.
Website: www.primoestate.com.au Email: info@primoestate.com.au
Region: **Adelaide** Winemakers: **Joe Grilli, David Tait** Chief Executive: **Joe Grilli**
A bright and savoury Il Briccone 2005, a handsome and deeply layered Angel Gully Shiraz 2004 and a Joseph
Nebbiolo 2005 (95/100, drink 2013-2017) you could jump into are the highlights of Joe Grilli's latest work. As
ever, Grilli is only content when pushing styles and ideas to their sensible and deeply considered limits. Primo
Estate's wines are largely sourced from vineyards in McLaren Vale and its original home in the Adelaide Plains.

IL BRICCONE SHIRAZ SANGIOVESE

RATING **4**

Various, South Australia $20–$29
Current vintage: 2005 91

Smoky, meaty, dark and briary, this appealing young
blend packs a delicious punch of dark plum, blackberry and dark cherry-like flavour over a drying
and bony chassis of tight-fit tannin. Full in weight
but already approachable and ready to enjoy, it's
earthy, spicy and savoury, leaving a bright,
lingering core of dark fruit and refreshing acidity.

2005	91	2007	2010
2004	88	2006	2009
2003	91	2005	2008
2002	86	2004	2007
2001	92	2003	2006+
2000	89	2002	2005
1999	89	2001	2004
1998	82	1999	2000

JOSEPH ANGEL GULLY SHIRAZ

RATING **2**

McLaren Vale	$50–$99
Current vintage: 2004	96

2004	96	2016	2024+
2003	90	2008	2011
2002	95	2010	2014+
2001	93	2009	2013

Right on the style cue for this wine comes this luscious, seamless and finely integrated shiraz whose brooding, mocha-like aromas of dark plums, berries and black pepper reveal undertones of dried earth and charcuterie meats. Initially closed and introverted, it steadily opens layers and length of luscious black, briary fruit, spicy vanilla oak, all of which is framed handsomely by a drying cut of firm astringency.

JOSEPH LA MAGIA RIESLING GEWÜRZTRAMINER

RATING **2**

Eden Valley, Clare Valley, Coonawarra	$20–$29 (375 ml)
Current vintage: 2006	93

2006	93	2008	2011
2005	93	2007	2010
2003	89	2005	2006+
2002	95	2004	2007+
2001	94	2003	2006+
1998	86	2000	2003+
1996	90	2001	2004
1995	95	2000	2003
1994	94	1999	2002
1993	95	2001	2005
1991	94	1999	2003
1989	88	1994	1998

Scented with musky, spicy, traminer-driven aromas of cloves, cinnamon and lychees over suggestions of rose oil, honey and mineral, it's elegant, juicy and luscious. Sweet, concentrated layers of vibrant apricot, peach, pear and apple fruit overlie a fine chalkiness, finishing long and clean with tropical pineapple flavour and fresh acidity.

JOSEPH MODA CABERNET SAUVIGNON MERLOT

RATING **3**

McLaren Vale	$50–$99
Current vintage: 2004	93

2004	93	2016	2024
2002	90	2010	2014
2001	93	2009	2013+
2000	92	2008	2012
1999	95	2011	2019
1998	89	2003	2006
1997	88	2002	2005
1996	93	2008	2016
1995	94	2007	2015
1994	97	2006	2014
1993	95	2005	2013
1992	92	2004	2012
1991	97	2003	2011
1990	94	2002	2010
1989	94	2001	2009

A fragrant perfume of violets, cassis, raspberries and dark cherries overlies sweet vanilla/mocha oak and nuances of game meats. Firm and tightly structured, with a meaty palate of dark berries and cherries closely knit with cedar/vanilla oak, it finishes with lingering suggestions of vibrant fruit, baked earth and clean acids. It should open up and develop beautifully.

LA BIONDINA COLOMBARD BLEND

RATING **5**

South Australia	$12–$19
Current vintage: 2007	82

2007	82	2007	2008
2006	87	2006	2007
2005	88	2005	2006
2004	83	2004	2005+
2003	89	2004	2005
2002	87	2002	2003
2001	88	2002	2003
1999	83	2000	2001
1997	86	1997	1997

Rather sweet and juicy, forward and oily, with a lightly grassy presence beneath its tropical expression of melon and passionfruit. Rather candied, it finishes with slightly cloying flavours of pineapple and lemon.

Prince Albert

100 Lemins Road, Waurn Ponds Vic 3216. Tel: (03) 5241 8091. Fax: (03) 5241 8091.

Region: **Geelong** Winemaker: **Bruce Hyett** Viticulturist: **Bruce Hyett** Chief Executive: **Bruce Hyett**

Prince Albert was the first Victorian vineyard to be entirely devoted to pinot noir. It has produced some excellent wines, but remains particularly vulnerable to seasonal fluctuation. Clearly, the vineyard experienced significant stress before the 2005 and 2006 harvests. At the time of writing, there is a question mark over the future of this vineyard. One hopes it will be able to continue to fulfil its unquestioned potential.

PINOT NOIR

RATING **5**

Geelong	$30–$49
Current vintage: 2006	**81**

Cooked, meaty and menthol-like aromas of stewed plums and mocha oak lack freshness and brightness. Rich and forward, but lacking fruit sweetness on the palate, it's rather dehydrated, with stressed fruit characters of currants and raisins finishing without much brightness and freshness. Heavy-handed, but very much a product of its drought-affected vintage.

2006	81	2008	2011
2005	82	2007	2010
2004	90	2009	2012
2003	87	2005	2008
2002	84	2004	2007
2001	92	2006	2009
2000	95	2005	2008
1999	89	2007	2011
1998	91	2003	2006
1997	93	2002	2005
1996	82	1998	2001

Radenti

Freycinet, 15919 Tasman Highway, Bicheno Tas 7215. Tel: (03) 6257 8574. Fax: (03) 6257 8454.
Website: www.freycinetvineyard.com.au

Region: **East Coast Tasmania** Winemakers: **Claudio Radenti & Lindy Bull** Viticulturist: **Claudio Radenti**
Chief Executive: **Geoff Bull**

The sparkling wine from the highly rated Freycinet vineyard, Radenti is usually made in rather a wild, earthy and complex style with ultra-long maturation on lees. This was certainly the case with the very rich and chewy 1999 edition, which I have since been able to confirm with even richer, meatier and chewier later disgorgings of the same wine.

CHARDONNAY PINOT NOIR

RATING **3**

East Coast Tasmania	$30–$49
Current vintage: 1999	**91**

A complex, nutty and mineral fragrance of lime, grapefruit and apple reveals developing nuances of wheatmeal, toast, honey and butter. Slightly sweet and awkward to finish, it's chewy, rich and creamy, with a generous depth and character, but would have been better if left a little drier.

1999	91	2007	2011
1998	93	2003	2006+
1997	92	2002	2005+
1996	89	2001	2004
1995	93	2000	2003
1994	95	1999	2002
1993	88	1998	2001

Redgate

Boodjidup Road, Margaret River WA 6285. Tel: (08) 9757 6488. Fax: (08) 9757 6308.
Website: www.redgatewines.com.au Email: info@redgatewines.com.au

Region: **Margaret River** Winemaker: **Simon Keall** Viticulturist: **Paul McGrath** Chief Executive: **Paul Ullinger**

Most evident in its white wines, which are of course released earlier, Redgate's steady improvement continues apace. The delightful 2005 Chardonnay has been followed up with an even better wine from 2006, while the Sauvignon Blanc Semillon has rediscovered its raciness and brightness. There's no doubting that this vineyard has what it takes.

CHARDONNAY

RATING **4**

Margaret River	$30–$49
Current vintage: 2006	**93**

A vibrant, balanced and finely focused chardonnay whose fresh, restrained aromas of lemon, grapefruit and white peach are neatly backed by nutty vanilla oak. It's juicy, round and generous, but also long and shapely, with lightly spicy oak and refreshingly tangy acids adding depth and definition to its deliciously clean and flavoursome fruit.

2006	93	2008	2011+
2005	91	2007	2010+
2004	82	2005	2006+
2003	87	2005	2008
2002	89	2004	2007
2001	87	2003	2006
1999	82	1999	2000

SAUVIGNON BLANC RESERVE

RATING 5

Margaret River	$12–$19
Current vintage: 2005	**91**

A lifted and herbal bouquet of gooseberries, passionfruit and grassy undertones is carefully knit with lightly smoky vanilla oak. Supple and juicy, its long and elegant palate of vibrant, tangy fruit and neatly balanced toasty oak culminates in a racy finish of bright, refreshing acids. Manages to retain plenty of fruit freshness in an oaked style.

2005	91	2007	2010
2004	89	2005	2006+
2003	89	2004	2005
2002	86	2002	2003
2001	86	2002	2003+
2000	87	2002	2005
1999	82	1999	2000
1998	90	1999	2000
1997	87	1998	1999

SAUVIGNON BLANC SEMILLON

RATING 5

Margaret River	$12–$19
Current vintage: 2006	**91**

A tightly focused, flavoursome and vibrant regional blend whose lightly grassy fragrance of tropical fruit precedes a tangy, juicy palate underpinned by chalky phenolics that culminates in a refreshing finish of zesty acids. Right on the style button.

2006	91	2008	2011
2005	86	2006	2007
2004	88	2005	2006
2003	88	2004	2005+
2002	88	2004	2007
2001	83	2002	2003
2000	87	2002	2005
1999	88	1999	2000

Redman

Riddoch Highway, Coonawarra SA 5263. Tel: (08) 8736 3331. Fax: (08) 8736 3013. Website: www.redman.com.au
Region: **Coonawarra** Winemakers: **Bruce & Malcolm Redman** Viticulturists: **Bruce & Malcolm Redman**
Chief Executives: **Bruce & Malcolm Redman**

One of the oldest continually operating Coonawarra wine companies, Redman owns some of the most ancient and best vineyards in Coonawarra. While its reds are consistent and elegant, they rarely achieve the depth of fruit and polish sought after in the finest contemporary Coonawarra wine. That they do from time to time, indeed handsomely, makes its releases from 2004 a little bewildering.

CABERNET SAUVIGNON

RATING 5

Coonawarra	$20–$29
Current vintage: 2004	**88**

Framed by fine, firm and bony tannins and backed by rather restrained and cedary oak, this is a typically smooth and supple Coonawarra cabernet of medium to full weight. Its dusty, spicy and herbal aromas of violets, dark plums, blackcurrants, red berries and dark chocolate reveal a slight meatiness, while its palate is finely balanced but reveals a somewhat cooked aspect.

2004	88	2012	2016
2003	93	2015	2023
2002	88	2014	2022
2001	89	2006	2009
2000	88	2008	2012
1999	90	2007	2011
1998	89	2006	2010
1997	88	2002	2005
1996	89	2004	2008
1994	93	2002	2006
1993	93	2001	2005
1992	92	2004	2012
1991	84	2003	2011
1990	93	2002	2010
1989	82	1997	2001
1988	88	2000	2008

CABERNET SAUVIGNON MERLOT

RATING 4

Coonawarra	$20–$29
Current vintage: 2003	**81**

Under and over-ripe, with meaty, herbal undertones and a browning colour, this lightly fruited, sappy and raisined red blend simply lacks evenness of ripening.

2003	81	2005	2008
2001	95	2013	2021+
2000	89	2008	2012
1999	86	2004	2007+
1998	94	2010	2018
1997	83	1999	2002
1996	90	2004	2008+
1995	86	2000	2003
1994	93	2006	2014
1993	93	2001	2005
1992	94	2000	2004

SHIRAZ

RATING **5**

Coonawarra	$12–$19
Current vintage: 2004	**88**

There's a slightly herbal thread beneath this savoury, spicy and fine-grained shiraz. Its sweet red cherry, raspberry and currant-like perfume overlies lightly smoky vanilla oak. Medium in weight, its smooth palate of lively red berry flavours and sweet oak is framed by gentle tannins.

2004	88	2009	2012
2003	81	2005	2008
2002	89	2010	2014
2001	89	2003	2006+
2000	89	2003	2006+
1999	82	2001	2004
1998	86	2003	2006
1997	81	1998	1999
1996	84	1998	2004+
1995	86	1997	2000
1994	84	1996	1999
1993	90	2001	2005
1992	91	2000	2004
1991	88	1993	1996
1990	91	1995	1998

Reynell

Reynell Road, Reynella SA 5161. Tel: (08) 8392 2222. Fax: (08) 8392 2202.

Region: **McLaren Vale** Winemaker: **Paul Lapsley** Viticulturist: **Brenton Baker** Chief Executive: **John Grant**

The Reynell label is now home to the Basket Pressed series of traditional McLaren Vale red varieties. Recent vintages of these wines have evidently been made from extremely ripe and dehydrated fruit, and the 2004 Cabernet Sauvignon is no exception. I'm not sure its makers made the most of this very good vintage for McLaren Vale cabernet, but they certainly did with the stellar and delightfully old-fashioned Shiraz.

BASKET PRESSED CABERNET SAUVIGNON

RATING **4**

McLaren Vale	$30–$49
Current vintage: 2004	**88**

Framed by very firm and powdery tannin, this cooked and meaty cabernet lacks brightness and sweetness of fruit and charm. Its heady aromas of confiture-like blackberries, dark plums, black-currants and older vanilla/cedar oak are backed by earthy, leathery and meaty undertones. Forward and very ripe, its substantial palate of raisined, currant-like fruit tastes riper and more alcoholic than the 13.5% declared on the label. Probably made from stressed fruit.

2004	88	2009	2012
2002	88	2010	2014
1998	95	2010	2018+
1997	89	2005	2009+
1996	92	2008	2016
1995	91	2007	2015

BASKET PRESSED SHIRAZ

RATING **2**

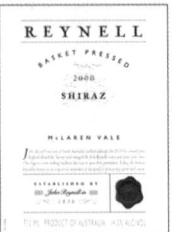

McLaren Vale	$50–$99
Current vintage: 2004	**95**

Slightly jammy and old-fashioned, with heady, ripe and briary aromas of dark plums, red and black berries backed by chocolate/vanilla oak and musky nuances of cinnamon and cloves. Coated by firm and tightly knit tannins, its palate-staining, sour-edged expression of dark berries and plums reveals a tangy and faintly mineral saltiness. Very full and rich, but also balanced and harmonious.

2004	95	2016	2024
2003	88	2008	2011
2000	90	2002	2005
1998	94	2018	2028
1997	93	2009	2017
1996	95	2008	2016
1995	94	2007	2015

Richard Hamilton

Corner Main and Johnston roads, McLaren Vale SA 5171. Tel: (08) 8323 8830. Fax: (08) 8323 8881.
Website: www.leconfieldwines.com Email: info@leconfieldwines.com

Region: **McLaren Vale** Winemaker: **Paul Gordon** Viticulturist: **Lee Harding** Chief Executive: **Richard Hamilton**

There's no avoiding the fact that the extremely hot, dry vintages of 2003 and 2005 have sadly left their mark on the present collection of Richard Hamilton red wines. Despite some significant advances in the winery by Paul Gordon, this company appears to have been at the mercy of conditions (of weather, certainly) and possibly vineyard management that were beyond its control. The Gumprs' Shiraz is the only real highlight.

BURTON'S VINEYARD (Grenache Shiraz Blend)

RATING 5

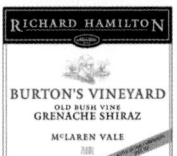

McLaren Vale	$20–$29
Current vintage: 2003	81

Meaty and varnishy, with dehydrated fruit characters of currants and prunes in addition to herbal nuances. Dried-out and lifeless, but backed by smooth polished tannin, it's a dead grape wine.

2003	81	2005	2008
2002	88	2007	2010
2001	86	2006	2009
1999	88	2004	2007
1998	93	2003	2006+
1997	86	2005	2008
1996	89	2001	2004
1995	93	2003	2007
1994	88	1999	2002
1992	86	1998	2001

CENTURION SHIRAZ

RATING 4

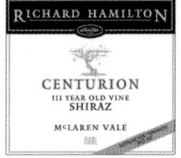

McLaren Vale	$30–$49
Current vintage: 2003	81

Briary and meaty, with a leathery expression of currants, prunes and plums backed by chocolate-like oak, it's dehydrated and overworked, drying out towards a metallic and hard-edged finish of blocky tannin.

2003	81	2005	2008
2002	93	2010	2014+
2001	91	2009	2013
2000	87	2002	2005+
1999	93	2007	2011+
1998	93	2006	2010+
1996	88	2001	2004+
1995	94	2003	2007
1994	91	2002	2006
1992	87	2000	2004

GUMPRS' SHIRAZ

RATING 4

McLaren Vale	$20–$29
Current vintage: 2005	90

Well handled, spicy and elegant, this finely crafted, long and pliant shiraz is scented with a violet-like perfume of fresh small berries, pepper, clove and cinnamon. Its vibrant flavours of cranberries and blackberries are backed by chocolate/vanilla oak, with dusty, peppery and cedary undertones. It finishes with firmness and suppleness, length and balance.

2005	90	2010	2013+
2004	92	2009	2012+
2003	90	2008	2011+
2002	89	2007	2010
2001	89	2006	2009
2000	90	2008	2012
1999	89	2001	2004+
1998	91	2006	2010
1997	89	1999	2002
1996	83	1998	2001+

HUT BLOCK CABERNET SAUVIGNON

RATING 4

McLaren Vale	$20–$29
Current vintage: 2005	80

Green-edged and meaty, with stewed dark berry and plum-like fruit that sits rather listlessly on the palate. It finishes flat and drying, green-edged and metallic.

2005	80	2007	2010
2004	91	2012	2016
2003	91	2011	2015
2002	81	2007	2010
2001	93	2009	2013+
2000	90	2005	2008+
1999	91	2004	2007+
1998	94	2006	2010
1997	88	2002	2005
1996	84	2004	2008
1995	91	2003	2007
1994	89	1999	2002
1993	87	1998	2001
1992	90	2000	2004
1991	94	1999	2003

LOT 148 MERLOT

RATING 4

| McLaren Vale | $12–$19 |
| Current vintage: 2005 | 85 |

Slightly browning, cooked and meaty with a sumptuous expression of dark plums, currants and prunes lifted by spicy, smoky oak. Very forward on the palate, it becomes leaner and quite gritty towards the finish, lacking genuine length of bright fruit. Plenty of flavour, but not much finesse.

2005	85	2007	2010
2004	90	2009	2012+
2002	86	2004	2007+
2001	89	2006	2009
2000	90	2005	2008+
1999	90	2001	2004+
1998	87	2003	2006
1997	89	2002	2005

SLATE QUARRY RIESLING

RATING 5

| McLaren Vale | $12–$19 |
| Current vintage: 2006 | 86 |

Broad and advanced, with confectionary flavours of citrusy fruit that offers little perfume but some thickness on the palate. Rich and juicy, but lacking balance and freshness.

2006	86	2008	2011
2005	89	2007	2010+
2003	89	2005	2008
2002	87	2004	2007
2001	80	2002	2003
2000	89	2002	2005
1999	87	2001	2004
1998	86	2000	2003

Richmond Grove

Para Road, Tanunda SA 5352. Tel: (08) 8563 7300. Fax: (08) 8563 7330.
Website: www.richmondgrove.com.au Email: info@richmondgrove.com.au

Region: **Various** Winemakers: **John Vickery, Steve Clarkson, Steve Meyer** Viticulturist: **Joy Dick**
Chief Executive: **Laurent Lacassgne**

Richmond Grove is a popular Pernod Ricard brand that comprises honest, well-made wines blended and sourced from a number of prominent Australian regions. By some distance, its finest and most consistent wine is its tangy, citrusy and perfumed Watervale Riesling, from South Australia's Clare Valley. The multi-regional French Cask Chardonnay from 2006 is a delicious and refreshing little quaff.

FRENCH CASK CHARDONNAY

RATING 5

| Various | $12–$19 |
| Current vintage: 2006 | 90 |

Genuinely elegant and stylish, this approachable young chardonnay has a nutty aroma of nectarine, white peach and melon backed by lightly toasty vanilla oak. Smooth and supple, its succulent but tightly restrained palate of juicy melon, grapefruit, peach and pear-like flavour is neatly partnered by toasty oak and finished with refreshing acids.

2006	90	2007	2008+
2005	82	2006	2007
2003	84	2004	2005+
2002	87	2003	2004+
2001	87	2002	2003
2000	87	2002	2005
1997	80	1998	1999

LIMITED RELEASE BAROSSA SHIRAZ

RATING 4

| Barossa Valley | $12–$19 |
| Current vintage: 2002 | 90 |

Stylish, smooth and silky, this minty expression of very modern shiraz reveals intense flavours of maraschino cherries, currants, cassis and red plums underpinned by cedar/dark chocolate oak and meaty, smoky undertones. Backed by a lingering spearmint note, it's deeply flavoured, medium to full in weight, framed by silky tannin, finishing with spicy and menthol-like undertones.

2002	90	2010	2014
2001	90	2009	2013
2000	81	2002	2005
1999	88	2001	2004+
1998	88	2000	2003+
1997	87	1999	2002
1996	90	2001	2004
1995	87	1997	2000
1994	91	1999	2002

LIMITED RELEASE CABERNET SAUVIGNON

RATING 5

Coonawarra	$12–$19
Current vintage: 2002	83

Well-handled but made from under-ripe, herbaceous and green-edged fruit that is partially smoothed over by sweet vanilla oak, this rather simple and jammy young cabernet delivers a light expression of mulberry, cassis and capsicum-like flavour.

2002	83	2007	2010
2001	88	2006	2009
2000	83	2002	2005
1999	88	2004	2007
1998	86	2003	2006
1997	82	1999	2002
1996	88	1998	2001
1995	87	2000	2003
1994	94	2002	2006
1993	88	1998	2001
1992	89	1997	2000

WATERVALE RIESLING

RATING  3

Clare Valley	$12–$19
Current vintage: 2006	91

Flavoured with lemon rind, lime juice and candy, this finely crafted, austere and tightly focused riesling is long, powdery and austere, finishing with pleasing tightness and a lingering briny aspect.

2006	91	2011	2014
2005	91	2013	2017
2004	90	2006	2009
2003	93	2008	2011
2002	95	2010	2014
2001	93	2006	2009
2000	93	2008	2012
1999	94	2004	2007+
1998	93	2006	2010
1997	89	2006	2010
1996	92	2001	2004
1995	94	2003	2007
1994	91	1999	2002

Rochford

Corner Maroondah Highway & Hill Road, Coldstream Vic 3770. Tel: (03) 5962 2119. Fax: (03) 5962 5319.
Website: www.rochfordwines.com   Email: info@rochfordwines.com

Regions: **Macedon Ranges, Yarra Valley** Winemaker: **David Creed** Chief Executive: **Helmut Konecsny**

Rochford is an energetic small wine business that acquired Eyton On Yarra in 2001 to complement its existing vineyards in the cool Macedon Ranges region. Recent vintages have revealed some genuinely positive movement towards some focused and mineral Chardonnays from both regions.

MACEDON RANGES CHARDONNAY

RATING 4

Macedon Ranges	$20–$29
Current vintage: 2005	91

Stylish, modern and shapely, this taut and mineral chardonnay has a smoky, lightly flinty bouquet and a long, dry palate finishing with refreshing citrusy acids. Its tangy flavours of grapefruit, melon, lemon and pear knit tightly with nutty vanilla oak, before a lingering finish of pleasing minerality.

2005	91	2007	2010+
2004	91	2006	2009
2002	83	2003	2004+
2000	87	2002	2005
1999	82	2001	2004

MACEDON RANGES PINOT GRIS

RATING 4

Macedon Ranges	$20–$29
Current vintage: 2007	89

Generous and quite elegant, soft and mellow, with a lightly floral, estery aroma of peach, pear and apple, backed by spicy suggestions of cloves and cinnamon. Round and juicy, with pleasing richness, length and texture, its lingering fruit finishes clean and refreshing. Pleasing varietal qualities.

2007	89	2008	2009
2005	91	2006	2007+
2004	84	2004	2005
2003	90	2004	2005
2001	88	2002	2003

MACEDON RANGES PINOT NOIR

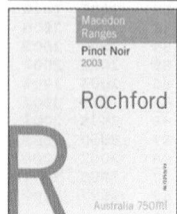

Macedon Ranges $30–$49
Current vintage: 2005 88

Dusty, spicy and herbal aromas of cool-climate pinot reveal red cherries and plums with a restrained oak background. Fine-grained, long and focused, it presents a pleasing length of fruit over a bony spine of drying tannins. With genuine length and structure, plus a taut and refreshing finish, it is just a little too herbal for a higher rating.

2005	88	2010	2013
2004	77	2005	2006
2003	88	2005	2008+
2002	78	2003	2004
2001	90	2006	2009
2000	90	2005	2008
1999	83	2001	2004
1996	86	1998	2001
1995	91	2000	2003
1994	87	2002	2006
1993	94	2001	2005
1992	94	2000	2004

YARRA VALLEY CHARDONNAY

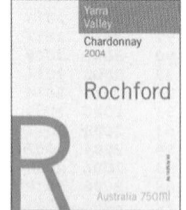

Yarra Valley $20–$29
Current vintage: 2006 90

Ripe, pungent and lightly grassy, with some slightly sweaty undertones, this very generous and almost out-sized sauvignon blanc is sumptuously packed with rich flavours of gooseberries, passionfruit and lychees. It's finished with plenty of refreshing acidity, but is a fraction over-ripe and clumsy for a higher rating.

2006	90	2008	2011
2004	90	2006	2009
2003	86	2004	2005+

YARRA VALLEY SAUVIGNON BLANC

Yarra Valley $20–$29
Current vintage: 2006 88

Ripe, pungent and lightly grassy, with some slightly sweaty undertones, this very generous and almost out-sized sauvignon blanc is sumptuously packed with rich flavours of gooseberries, passionfruit and lychees. It's finished with plenty of refreshing acidity, but is a fraction over-ripe and clumsy for a higher rating.

2006	88	2007	2008
2005	87	2005	2006
2004	90	2005	2006
2003	84	2003	2004
2002	90	2003	2004+

Rockford

Krondorf Road, Tanunda SA 5352. Tel: (08) 8563 2720. Fax: (08) 8563 3787.
Email: info.contact@rockfordwines.com.au

Region: **Barossa Valley** Winemakers: **Robert O'Callaghan, Ben Radford** Chief Executive: **David Kalleske**

Rockford is a dedicated small Barossa maker and a committed supporter of the region's small vineyards and their owners. Its wines are made with a refreshing disregard for trends and fashion and are bottled without artefact or manipulation. That is not to suggest that they are made and assembled without great care, experience and dedication, but these are essentially 'natural' wines that faithfully reflect their sites and seasons. The current releases of its icon wines, the Basket Press Shiraz and Black Shiraz, are simply wonderful.

BASKET PRESS SHIRAZ

Barossa Valley $100–$199
Current vintage: 2004 95

A classic, long-living example of why 2004 is so highly rated. Its deep, brambly aromas of dark cherries, blueberries, blackberries, sweet coconut ice/vanilla oak overlie meaty, smoky and slightly reductive complexity. Deeply and richly layered, it's ripe and juicy, delivering a warm and fractionally spirity expression of small berries and smoky undertones framed by firm but velvet-smooth and loose-knit tannins. It's natural and balanced, without a hint of overcooked fruit.

2004	95	2016	2024+
2003	93	2011	2015
2002	96	2014	2022
2001	89	2009	2013
2000	93	2005	2008+
1999	96	2007	2011+
1998	96	2008	2018
1997	93	2005	2009
1996	96	2016	2026
1995	90	2003	2007
1994	93	2002	2006+
1993	88	2005	2013
1992	89	2000	2004
1991	96	2011	2021

BLACK SHIRAZ

RATING **2**

Barossa Valley $50–$99
Current disgorging: 2006 96

An alluringly spicy fragrance of intense small black and red berries reveals faint, but distinct undertones of mushrooms, chocolate oak, ground coffee and a slight meatiness. Long, smooth and seamless, its sumptuous expression of black and red fruits finishes with notes of treacle, cassis, dark chocolate, cloves and cinnamon. Refined and creamy, with a lively, crackly bead, it's wonderfully balanced and showing delightful signs of maturing complexity.

2006 dis	96	2011	2014+
2005 dis	93	2007	2010+
2004 dis	95	2005	2009
2003 dis	90	2005	2008
2002 dis	96	2006	2010
2001 dis	95	2004	2008
2000 dis	97	2006	2010
1998 dis	91	1999	2003

HAND PICKED RIESLING

RATING **3**

Eden Valley $12–$19
Current vintage: 2004 90

A honeyed, beeswaxy and lightly toasty fragrance of lime juice, lemon rind, dried lavender and faint herbal nuances precedes an unusually juicy and rather broad palate for Eden Valley riesling. It's long and reserved, right in the middle of riesling's adolescent period, and its fresh apple, pear and limey flavours should develop more complexity and character with time in the bottle.

2004	90	2009	2012+
2003	86	2005	2008
2002	93	2007	2010+
2001	93	2009	2013
2000	95	2005	2008+
1999	93	2004	2007
1998	94	2003	2006+
1997	88	1999	2002
1996	92	2004	2008
1995	93	2000	2003+

LOCAL GROWERS SEMILLON

RATING **3**

Barossa Valley $20–$29
Current vintage: 2004 92

Round and generous, this evolving and slightly brassy semillon backs its dusty melon, apple and citrus fruit with assertive, lightly toasty vanilla oak. It's smooth and creamy, long and dry, with a measured and savoury finish of soft acidity.

2004	92	2009	2012
2003	89	2005	2008+
2002	92	2007	2010
2001	87	2003	2006
2000	92	2002	2005+
1999	92	2004	2007
1998	93	2003	2006+
1997	91	2005	2009
1996	90	2001	2004
1995	94	2000	2003+
1994	92	1999	2002

MOPPA SPRINGS (Grenache Shiraz Mataro)

RATING **5**

Barossa Valley $20–$29
Current vintage: 2003 88

Beginning to show signs of age, this meaty, spicy and floral grenache has a sweet, earthy fragrance whose aromas of raspberries, cloves and cinnamon are backed by suggestions of baked berries and currants. Of moderate length, its fine and supple palate of spicy, currant-like fruit and firm, bony tannin shows signs of breaking up and finishes just fractionally short.

2003	88	2008	2011
2002	89	2007	2010
2001	89	2003	2006+
2000	88	2002	2005
1999	90	2004	2007
1998	89	2003	2006+

RIFLE RANGE CABERNET SAUVIGNON

RATING **4**

Barossa Valley $30–$49
Current vintage: 2004 89

A sumptuous, firm and astringent cabernet whose deep, slightly stewed and jammy flavours of dark currants, plums and prunes deliver plenty of ripe juiciness in the middle of the palate, but dry out marginally towards the finish. Framed by loose-knit tannins, it's actually quite spicy, but finishes with a hint of sweetness. Slightly overcooked given the nature of this vintage.

2004	89	2012	2016
2003	92	2011	2015
2002	91	2010	2014
2001	90	2009	2013+
2000	89	2005	2008
1999	94	2007	2011+
1998	94	2010	2018
1997	89	2005	2009
1996	94	2004	2008+
1995	91	2000	2003+
1994	89	1999	2002

ROD & SPUR (Shiraz Cabernet Sauvignon)

RATING 5

Barossa Valley	$30–$49	2004	90	2012	2016
Current vintage: 2004	**90**	2003	88	2005	2008+
		2002	89	2004	2007+
		2001	87	2003	2006
		2000	91	2005	2008
		1999	87	2004	2007

A charming older style red whose spicy aromas of slightly baked small red berries, currants and vanilla oak overlie nuances of cloves and cinnamon. Smooth and restrained, its palate of reserved but lingering fruit and moderately firm tannin provides structure and substance. It just needs time to develop more complexity.

Rosemount

Rosemount Road, Denman NSW 2328. Tel: (02) 6549 6400. Fax: (02) 6549 6499.
Website: www.rosemountestate.com.au Email: rosemountestates.hv@cellardoor.com.au

Regions: **Various** Winemakers: **Charles Whish, Matthew Johnson**
Viticulturists: **Sam Hayne, Nigel Everingham** Chief Executive: **Jamie Odell**

Now that some of the higher-level Rosemount wines are beginning to appear in its new diamond bottle and diamond label, it's evident that the wines are actually quite different to those whose names they now wear. This runs quite counter to the PR spin, which states that the Rosemount makers have been researching and rediscovering their winemaking roots — something I simply can't agree with. There's absolutely nothing wrong with the modern releases, which as far as I can tell are of similar style but of higher fruit standard and winemaking polish than the basic Diamond Series varietals. I just hope the same doesn't happen to the Roxburgh, et al.

BALMORAL SYRAH

RATING 4

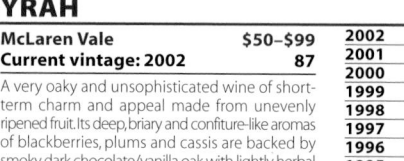

McLaren Vale	$50–$99	2002	87	2007	2010
Current vintage: 2002	**87**	2001	91	2009	2013
		2000	89	2005	2008
		1999	90	2004	2007
		1998	97	2010	2018
		1997	90	2002	2005
		1996	94	2004	2008
		1995	97	2007	2015
		1994	95	2002	2006+
		1993	88	1998	2001
		1992	96	2000	2004+
		1991	95	2003	2011
		1990	94	2002	2010
		1989	94	1997	2003+

A very oaky and unsophisticated wine of short-term charm and appeal made from unevenly ripened fruit. Its deep, briary and confiture-like aromas of blackberries, plums and cassis are backed by smoky dark chocolate/vanilla oak with lightly herbal tones. Full to medium in weight, it's jammy and forward, reliant on sweet oak and alcohol for palate intensity. It is underpinned by a greenish thread and lacks genuine definition.

CABERNET SAUVIGNON

RATING 5

Various	$12–$19	2005	86	2006	2007+
Current vintage: 2005	**86**	2003	89	2005	2008+
		2001	80	2002	2003
		2000	81	2002	2005
		1999	87	2000	2001
		1998	87	2000	2003
		1996	84	1998	2001

Ready to enjoy, with a fresh, juicy and slightly confectionary aroma of violets, cassis, dark plums, sweet oak and small berries, before a smooth, supple and generous palate whose lively varietal flavours are underpinned by fine, smooth tannins. Medium to full in weight and very approachable.

CHARDONNAY

Various	$12–$19	2006	87	2006	2007+
Current vintage: 2006	**87**	2005	86	2006	2007
		2004	86	2004	2005+
		2003	82	2004	2005+
		2002	87	2003	2004+
		2001	83	2002	2003
		2000	87	2001	2002

Spotlessly clean, vibrant and refreshing, with a ripe, juicy and tropical aroma of white peach and banana, backed by hints of cashew and sweet vanilla. Round and generous, it's very soft, smooth and focused, delivering a lingering palate of peach and melon fruit finished by soft acids. Very pretty, but nothing like the older expressions of this label.

GIANTS CREEK CHARDONNAY

RATING 4

Upper Hunter Valley $30–$49
Current vintage: 2004   87

Its wild, slightly meaty, oxidative and floral aromas reveal a pungent, leesy and funky charcuterie-like element with an underlying depth of citrus, melon and tobaccoey fruit and restrained vanilla oak. Initially round and juicy, its ripe, forward expression of cumquat, peach and nectarine fruit becomes more savoury and meaty down the palate, finishing with soft acids and suggestions of green melons. Slightly lacking in length and acidity, and possibly with some stuck ferment influences.

2004	87	2006	2009
2002	93	2007	2010
2001	90	2003	2006+
1999	93	2004	2007
1998	90	2003	2006
1997	87	2002	2005
1996	90	2001	2004
1995	89	1997	2000
1994	90	1999	2002
1993	94	1998	2001
1992	84	1994	1997

MOUNTAIN BLUE

RATING 2

Mudgee $30–$49
Current vintage: 2001   95

A welcome return to form for this important Mudgee label, delivering a firm, complete and savoury palate of depth and structure. Its spicy white pepper fragrance of blackberries and violets is backed by sweet gamey chocolate/vanilla oak and a meaty, slightly reductive and smoky suggestion of animal hide. Full to medium in weight, it's smooth and polished, delivering a plump, juicy expression of dark plums and berries framed by a drying extract and finishing with lingering meaty and sour-edged fruit qualities.

2001	95	2013	2021
2000	87	2005	2008+
1999	82	2001	2004+
1998	96	2010	2018
1997	95	2005	2009
1996	95	2008	2016
1995	95	2007	2015
1994	93	2006	2014

ORANGE VINEYARD CHARDONNAY

RATING 2

Orange $20–$29
Current vintage: 2003   93

Quite a punchy but shapely and elegant chardonnay with a deep, vibrant core of peach and citrusy flavours that culminate in a lingering savoury and wheatmeal-like finish. There's a hint of dried flowers and a smoky meatiness beneath its cumquat and stonefruit aromas, while its soft and supple palate presents finely integrated fruit and butterscotch-like malolactic qualities.

2003	93	2005	2008+
2002	89	2004	2007+
2001	95	2006	2009
2000	94	2002	2005+
1999	95	2004	2007
1998	93	2003	2006
1997	94	2005	2009
1996	93	2001	2004
1995	93	2003	2007
1994	94	1999	2002

ROXBURGH CHARDONNAY

RATING 3

Upper Hunter Valley $50–$99
Current vintage: 2003   90

Backed by slightly edgy and splintery oak, intense aromas of grapefruit and mango show some toasty development. Slightly oily, its long, creamy palate has a nougat-like quality, delivering concentrated and generous flavours of ripe juicy fruit. It finishes slightly sweet, with some raw-edged oak, but should settle down with time.

2003	90	2008	2011
2002	94	2004	2007
2001	91	2003	2006+
1999	91	2004	2007
1998	95	2003	2006+
1997	91	2002	2005
1996	94	2002	2006
1995	94	2000	2003
1994	91	1999	2001
1993	88	1998	2001
1992	88	1997	2000
1991	94	2003	2011

A B C D E F G H I J K L M N O P Q **R** S T U V W X Y Z

SHIRAZ

RATING 5

Various $5–$11
Current vintage: 2005 86

Competent, flavoursome and juicy, this early-drinking shiraz has a minty expression of jammy blackberry and dark plum-like fruit backed by fine, firmish tannins and fresh vanilla oak. Backed by minty and earthy undertones, it's quite long and generous.

2005	86	2006	2007
2004	87	2006	2009
2003	88	2005	2008
2002	86	2003	2004+
2001	86	2002	2003+
2000	86	2001	2002
1999	87	2000	2001
1998	89	2000	2003+
1997	87	1999	2002

SHOW RESERVE CHARDONNAY

Upper Hunter Valley $20–$29
Current vintage: 2006 90

A fresh, ripe and stylish chardonnay whose youthful aromas of green melon, lemon and tobacco reveal nuances of vanilla, bathpowder and lanolin. Generous and juicy, its ripe flavours of tangy lime and lemon overlie a long, fine-grained and chalky undercarriage, culminating in a refreshing and nutty finish.

2006	90	2008	2011+
2005	83	2007	2010
2004	89	2006	2009
2002	91	2004	2007
2001	87	2002	2003
2000	95	2005	2008+
1999	94	2004	2007
1998	93	2006	2010
1997	93	2002	2005+
1996	95	2004	2008+
1995	93	2003	2007
1994	90	2002	2006
1993	91	1998	2001

SHOW RESERVE GSM

McLaren Vale $20–$29
Current vintage: 2004 89

Smooth, polished and modern, it's dominated by its shiraz and mourvèdre components. Spicy suggestions of cinnamon and clove back slightly confectionary flavours of blackberries, blueberries, raspberries and plums, while sweet vanilla oak and fine tannins lend smoothness and suppleness.

2004	89	2006	2009+
2003	84	2005	2008
2002	90	2007	2010
2001	91	2006	2009
1999	93	2007	2011
1998	90	2003	2006
1997	88	1999	2002+
1996	90	2001	2004
1995	86	2003	2007
1994	88	1999	2002

SHOW RESERVE SHIRAZ

McLaren Vale, Langhorne Creek, Currency Creek $20–$29
Current vintage: 2004 92

Ripe, smooth and approachable, this finely balanced modern shiraz has a slightly meaty and peppery bouquet of dark plums and berries, musk and cinnamon and fresh cedar/vanilla oak lifted by a fragrant floral perfume. Medium to full in weight, its bright and slightly sour-edged fruit knits neatly with fresh oak and firmish, loose-knit tannin, finishing with notes of licorice and dark olives.

2004	92	2009	2012+
2001	90	2006	2009
2000	87	2002	2005+
1999	86	2004	2007
1998	88	2003	2006
1997	88	2002	2005
1996	95	2004	2008
1995	91	2003	2007

SHOW RESERVE TRADITIONAL (Cabernet blend)

McLaren Vale, Langhorne Creek $20–$29
Current vintage: 2004 88

Smooth and generous, this floral and approachable wine is brightly lit with vibrant red and black berry flavour backed by polished vanilla/cedar oak and undertones of dried herbs. Framed by pliant tannins, it has slightly greenish edges but is now ready to enjoy.

2004	88	2006	2009+
2003	82	2005	2008
2002	88	2007	2010
2001	89	2003	2006+
2000	87	2002	2005+
1999	88	2001	2004
1998	93	2006	2010
1997	90	2002	2005
1996	91	2004	2008

Rosily Vineyard

871 Yelveton Road, Willyabrup WA 6280. Tel: (08) 9755 6336. Fax: (08) 9755 6336.
Website: www.rosily.com.au Email: info@rosily.com.au
Region: **Margaret River** Winemaker: **Mike Lemmes** Chief Executives: **Mike Scott & Ken Allan**

Rosily is an emergent Margaret River vineyard whose wines are honest, flavoursome and well made, but to this time lack the intensity and structure of those from the leading players. Mind you, they're asking a fraction of the price.

CABERNET SAUVIGNON   RATING 5

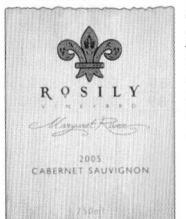

Margaret River		$20–$29
Current vintage: 2005		**87**

Smooth, juicy and flavoursome, this uncomplicated and cheery little early-drinking cabernet has a fresh aroma of raspberries, blackberries, plums and dusty cedar/vanilla oak, plus a sweetly and assertively oaked palate of modest depth and texture.

2005	87	2007	2010
2004	90	2009	2012
2003	87	2005	2008+
2002	88	2010	2014
2001	87	2003	2006
2000	81	2002	2005

CHARDONNAY   RATING 4

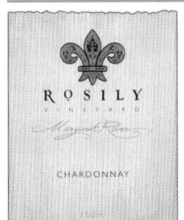

Margaret River		$20–$29
Current vintage: 2006		**89**

Fresh, flavoursome and uncomplicated, with tropical, pineapple-like aromas backed by lightly dusty vanilla oak. It's long and quite sumptuous, and retains pleasing shape and focus even if its acids are marginally herbal and metallic.

2006	89	2008	2011
2005	91	2007	2010+
2004	88	2006	2009
2001	93	2003	2006+
2000	92	2002	2005+

SAUVIGNON BLANC   RATING 5

Margaret River		$12–$19
Current vintage: 2006		**91**

A concentrated and refreshing sauvignon blanc whose pungent, lightly herbal and tropical scents of pineapple, tinned tropical fruit and nectarine precede a surprisingly rich palate with a luscious mouthfeel and a fine length of flavour. Quite overt, it's brightly lit and finishes clean, tangy and refreshing.

2006	91	2007	2008
2005	87	2005	2006+
2004	82	2004	2005
2003	91	2003	2004+
2002	88	2002	2003
2001	82	2001	2002

Ross Estate

Barossa Valley Highway, Lyndoch SA 5351. Tel: (08) 8524 4033. Fax: (08) 8524 4533.
Website: www.rossestate.com.au Email: rossestate@rossestate.com.au

Region: **Barossa Valley** Winemaker: **Rod Chapman** Chief Executive: **Darius Ross**

Ross Estate has produced some deeply flavoured and approachable wines from grenache, shiraz and cabernet. Its Shiraz is clearly its finest wine, and typically reflects the more elegant textures and red fruit flavours from the Lyndoch sub-district of the Barossa.

OLD VINE GRENACHE

RATING 5

Barossa Valley	$20–$29
Current vintage: 2004	82

Confiture-like aromas of sweet raspberries, blackberries and spice precede a simple, juicy and uninspiring palate that falls away towards a thin, sweet and confectionary finish.

2004	82	2006	2009
2003	92	2005	2008+
2002	83	2004	2007
2001	89	2003	2006+
2000	88	2002	2005
1999	81	2001	2004

SHIRAZ

RATING 4

Barossa Valley	$20–$29
Current vintage: 2005	87

A competent, if slightly cooked and jammy shiraz whose lightly spicy flavours of blackberries and dark plums reveal meaty undertones. It's carried along by sweet mocha oak, but finishes just a little flat and thin.

2005	87	2007	2010+
2004	90	2009	2012+
2002	93	2007	2010+
2001	90	2006	2009+
2000	88	2005	2008
1999	86	2001	2004+

Rothbury Estate, The

Broke Road, Pokolbin NSW 2320. Tel: (02) 4998 7555. Fax: (02) 4998 7553.
Website: www.fosters.com.au

Region: **Lower Hunter Valley** Winemaker: **Mike DeGaris** Chief Executive: **Jamie Odell**

Rothbury Estate exists only today as a brand of Hunter wine. Its only notable current release is actually perhaps the worst wine ever sold under its label, since in my view, the Brokenback Semillon described below is badly smoke-tainted. I am surprised indeed that it was ever let out for sale.

BROKENBACK SEMILLON

RATING 4

Lower Hunter Valley	$20–$29
Current vintage: 2003	72

Aged, toasty and butterscotch-like, with underlying fig, melon and lemony fruit. The wine, however, has been very adversely affected by the ashtray-like presence of what is likely to be smoke-taint from the bushfires that raged very near the vineyards responsible for this wine in 2003. In all honesty, I do not believe this wine should have been released.

2003	72	2004	2005
2002	90	2007	2010+
2001	82	2003	2006
2000	91	2008	2012
1998	92	2003	2006
1997	94	2005	2009

Rufus Stone

Tyrrell's, Broke Road, Pokolbin NSW 2320. Tel: (02) 4993 7000. Fax: (02) 4998 7723.
Website: www.tyrrells.com.au Email: tyrrells@tyrrells.com.au
Regions: **Heathcote, McLaren Vale** Winemakers: **Andrew Spinaze, Mark Richardson**
Chief Executive: **Bruce Tyrrell**

A brand owned by Tyrrell's that features red wines sourced from outside the company's native Hunter Valley, Rufus Stone is a well-priced source of medium to full-bodied reds usually made without excessive ripeness or extract, although the 2005 vintage Shirazes have suffered over-ripeness as a result of the extreme droughts and heatwaves prevalent in each region.

HEATHCOTE SHIRAZ

RATING **5**

Heathcote	$20–$29
Current vintage: 2005	84

Competently made, but rather cooked and lacking in fruit brightness, this young shiraz of full to medium weight has a spicy and lightly brandied aroma of plums, cherries and sweet chocolate/vanilla oak. It's very intense and forward, with concentrated flavours of liqueur-like blackberries, plums, blackcurrants and small red berries that thin out towards a slightly disappointing finish.

2005	84	2007	2010+
2004	86	2006	2009
2003	88	2008	2011
2002	88	2004	2007
2001	87	2003	2006
2000	92	2005	2008+
1999	91	2004	2007
1998	88	2006	2010
1997	92	2002	2005+

McLAREN VALE CABERNET SAUVIGNON MALBEC

RATING **5**

McLaren Vale	$20–$29
Current vintage: 2004	91

Vibrant aromas of black and red berries backed by dark chocolate, cedar and vanilla oak, with earthy undertones of mocha and dark olives. It's smooth, measured and deeply flavoured, bursting with intense forest berry flavours with meaty undertones offset by a mineral saltiness. Bound by fine-grained and powdery tannins, it's harmoniously structured, with length and balance, finishing dry and savoury.

2004	91	2012	2016+
2003	83	2005	2008
2002	89	2007	2010+

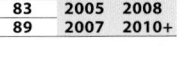

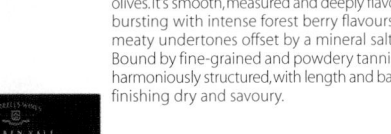

McLAREN VALE SHIRAZ

RATING **4**

McLaren Vale	$20–$29
Current vintage: 2005	88

Forward, ripe and vibrant, this flavoursome and slightly minty shiraz opens with a spicy aroma of meaty plums and currants backed by vanilla/dark chocolate oak and suggestions of menthol. Richly fruited, with a generous dollop of sweet chocolate/vanilla oak that enhances its marginally jammy palate, it lacks great length, but fits neatly with a fine-grained extract of tannin. Finishes a tad soupy, so drink it soon.

2005	88	2007	2010+
2004	88	2006	2009+
2003	90	2008	2011
2002	91	2010	2014+
2000	87	2002	2005+
1999	90	2004	2007
1998	93	2003	2006+
1997	93	2002	2005
1996	84	2001	2004

Sally's Paddock

1 Sally's Lane, Redbank Vic 3478. Tel: (03) 5467 7255. Fax: (03) 5467 7248.
Website: www.sallyspaddock.com.au Email: info@sallyspaddock.com.au

Region: **Pyrenees** Winemaker: **Neill Robb** Viticulturist: **Scott Hutton** Chief Executive: **Neill Robb**

Souls other than mine must have been confused by the recent presence of two 'Redbanks'. Neill Robb recently re-badged his wines to the 'Sally's' label, which incorporates a number of idiosyncratic reds that reflect his rather unique self. The other Redbank wines are made for a label owned by Robert Hill Smith, and they are entirely worthy in their own right. So, here is where you can find reference to the blend of cabernet sauvignon, shiraz, cabernet franc and merlot from the dryland vineyard at the front of the original Redbank property.

SALLY'S PADDOCK

RATING 3

Pyrenees		$50–$99	2005	93	2017	2025
Current vintage: 2005		93	2004	96	2016	2024+

2005	93	2017	2025
2004	96	2016	2024+
2003	89	2011	2015
2002	93	2014	2022+
2001	88	2009	2013+
2000	93	2012	2020+
1999	88	2007	2011+
1998	96	2010	2018+
1997	88	2005	2009
1996	90	2004	2008+
1995	95	2007	2015
1994	94	2006	2014
1993	94	2005	2013
1992	92	2000	2004
1991	91	2003	2011
1990	93	2020	2030
1989	87	2001	2009
1988	95	2000	2008
1987	82	1999	2004
1986	93	2006	2016
1985	88	1997	2005
1984	85	1989	1992
1983	87	2003	2013
1982	93	2002	2012
1981	94	2001	2011

Stylish, smooth and elegant, with a floral and brambly perfume of violets, cassis, redcurrants, plums and mulberries over restrained dusty cedar/vanilla oak and spicy suggestions of dried herbs and lanolin. Framed by firmish, pliant and dusty tannins, its layers of pristine small berry flavours, lightly toasty and dark chocolate oak finish with lingering nuances of herbs, vanilla and undergrowth. Fine shape and balance.

Saltram

Nuriootpa-Angaston Road, Angaston SA 5353. Tel: (08) 8564 3355. Fax: (08) 8564 2209.
Website: www.saltramwines.com.au Email: cellardoor@saltramestate.com.au

Region: **Barossa** Winemaker: **Nigel Dolan** Viticulturist: **Murray Heidenreich** Chief Executive: **Jamie Odell**

Saltram's leading wines are the exceptionally consistent reds under the Mamre Brook label, the luscious No. 1 Shiraz and a new arrival for this edition, the not inexpensive flagship The Eighth Maker Shiraz, of which the brilliant 2002 edition is a worthy highlight of Nigel Dolan's (the eighth Saltram winemaker) career to this time. Of particular merit is the sumptuously and evenly ripened 2005 Mamre Brook Cabernet Sauvignon, one of the very best from this challenging Barossa vintage.

MAMRE BROOK CABERNET SAUVIGNON

RATING 3

Barossa Valley		$20–$29
Current vintage: 2005		90

2005	90	2010	2013+
2004	95	2024	2034
2003	90	2011	2015
2002	95	2014	2022
2001	88	2006	2009
2000	88	2005	2008
1999	90	2004	2007
1998	95	2010	2018
1997	93	2005	2009
1996	93	2008	2016
1995	88	1997	2000
1994	90	2002	2006
1993	91	1998	2001
1988	85	1993	1998
1986	93	2006	2016

A ripe, voluptuous and velvet-smooth cabernet with a deep, briary expression of vibrant blackberry, cassis, dark plum and dark olive flavour whose sweet, toasty and slightly raw grade of vanilla/chocolate oak should ease back as the wine ages. Long and juicy, it's plush and creamy, with a firm, fine-grained undercarriage of drying tannins.

MAMRE BROOK CHARDONNAY

RATING **5**

South Australia $20–$29
Current vintage: 2005 85

Unusually brassy and quite funky, with cooked, meaty, buttery and barley sugar-like aromas and a broad, toasty palate. Lacking great length, the palate delivers juicy flavours of peach, melon and citrus fruit but finishes a little flat, despite some creamy and meaty complexity.

2005	85	2007	2010
2004	88	2006	2009
2003	87	2005	2008
2002	90	2004	2007
2001	89	2003	2006
2000	90	2002	2005+
1999	87	2000	2001
1998	87	2000	2003
1997	83	1998	1999
1996	89	1998	2001

MAMRE BROOK SHIRAZ

RATING **3**

Barossa Valley $20–$29
Current vintage: 2004 93

A supple, deeply flavoured and crowd-pleasing shiraz of the early-drinking Barossa style. Its heady, floral and slightly minty aromas of wild blueberries, raspberry confection and pristine blackcurrant fruit overlie nuances of plums and sweet vanilla oak. Silky-smooth and luscious, its juicy expression of blackberries, raspberries and creamy vanilla oak is supported by fine tannins and finished with bright, refreshing acids. It leaves a spicy fennel-like aftertaste.

2004	93	2009	2012+
2003	89	2008	2011
2002	93	2010	2014
2001	88	2003	2006+
2000	89	2005	2008
1999	93	2007	2011+
1998	95	2006	2010
1997	95	2005	2009+
1996	90	2001	2004

NO. 1 SHIRAZ

RATING **2**

Barossa Valley $50–$99
Current vintage: 2003 94

Super-rich and firmly structured, this deeply flavoured and powerful shiraz has a meaty and slightly pruney bouquet of jammy cassis, dark plums and currant-like undertones backed by fresh cedar/vanilla oak. Slightly tarry and dehydrated, it's brooding and luxuriant, making up in concentration what it might lack in complexity. It finishes with lingering suggestions of dark olives, licorice, cassis and meaty notes, but without any hard edges or excessive grip.

2003	94	2011	2015+
2002	95	2014	2022
2001	94	2009	2013
2000	90	2005	2008+
1999	94	2007	2011+
1998	96	2010	2018
1997	88	2005	2009
1996	94	2008	2016
1995	93	2003	2007+
1994	93	2002	2006

THE EIGHTH MAKER SHIRAZ

RATING **3**

Barossa Valley $100–$199
Current vintage: 2002 97

Pristine, elegant and stylish, this is a classically balanced, spotlessly presented and silky-fine shiraz. Its heady and brambly, with pure flavours of dark cherries, cassis and dark berries backed by smoked bacon-like oak, suggestions of licorice and musky spices. Long and harmonious, its super-plush palate finishes with a hint of savoury saltiness.

2002	97	2014	2022+
2001	92	2009	2013
2000	90	2008	2012

Sandalford

3210 West Swan Road, Caversham WA 6055. Tel: (08) 9374 9374. Fax: (08) 9274 2154.
Website: www.sandalford.com Email: sandalford@sandalford.com
Region: **Margaret River** Winemaker: **Paul Boulden** Viticulturist: **Peter Traeger** Chief Executive: **Grant Brinklow**
Sandalford is a moderately large Margaret River-based producer whose wines have traditionally been very
affordably priced. Its reds have fared a little better than whites over recent vintages.

CABERNET SAUVIGNON
RATING 4

Margaret River $30–$49
Current vintage: 2005 93

A serious, dark-fruited cabernet with the depth
of fruit and structure for the long haul. Its concentrated flavours of cassis, mulberries, dark
cherries and plums are balanced by assertive, lightly
smoky and cedary oak and framed by firm,
drying tannins. Its violet-like bouquet reveals a
trace of mint and dark chocolate, while its long
and measured palate drips with intense dark fruit,
finishing with length of flavour and a hint of menthol.

2005	93	2017	2025
2004	90	2012	2026
2003	90	2008	2011
2002	90	2007	2010+
2001	90	2009	2013
2000	88	2005	2008
1999	87	2004	2007
1998	84	2000	2003
1997	84	1999	2002+
1996	81	1998	2001
1995	92	2000	2003
1994	92	2002	2006
1993	81	1998	2001
1992	87	1994	1997
1991	87	1999	2003
1990	90	2002	2010
1989	85	2001	2009

RIESLING
RATING 5

Margaret River $20–$29
Current vintage: 2006 86

An honest, simple, but slightly coarse riesling with
intense but slightly candied lemon rind and green
apple aromas. Forward, juicy and confection-like,
it then thins out towards lean, drying and lemon
sherbet-like finish. Lacks genuine length of fruit.

2006	86	2008	2011
2005	88	2007	2010+
2004	89	2006	2009+
2003	89	2005	2008
2002	90	2007	2010
2001	83	2002	2003
2000	93	2005	2008+
1998	90	2006	2010

SHIRAZ
RATING 5

Margaret River $30–$49
Current vintage: 2004 90

Smooth and stylish, this rather polished shiraz has
a slightly jammy expression of cherries, plums, blackberries and raspberries, with undertones of
licorice, game meats and a faint tomato-like
regional influence. Its juicy palate is supported
by fresh vanilla oak and firmish but pliant tannin,
finishing with lingering notes of black pepper and
menthol.

2004	90	2009	2012+
2003	88	2005	2008+
2002	84	2003	2004+
2001	89	2006	2009
1999	81	2001	2004
1998	83	2000	2003
1997	82	1999	2002+
1996	87	2001	2004
1995	89	2003	2007
1994	90	2002	2006

VERDELHO
RATING 4

Margaret River $20–$29
Current vintage: 2006 87

Lightly herbal and saltbush-like, with delicate floral
and melon aromas backed by mineral undertones.
Forward and generous, with plenty of up-front
simple melon and tropical fruit, it finishes thin and
lacking length, but with refreshing acidity.

2006	87	2007	2008
2005	86	2006	2007
2004	90	2006	2009
2003	90	2005	2008
2002	90	2004	2007
2001	84	2006	2009
2000	77	2001	2002
1999	89	2001	2004
1998	88	2003	2006
1997	83	1998	1999

Sandstone

PO Box 346, Cowaramup WA 6284. Tel: (08) 9755 6271. Fax: (08) 9755 6292.
Email: info@sandstonewines.com.au

Region: **Margaret River** Winemaker: **Jan McIntosh** Chief Executive: **Jan McIntosh**

Jan McIntosh is an immensely talented winemaker whose two Margaret River wines are varietal expressions of Semillon and Cabernet Sauvignon. Typically, these are generously flavoured, smooth and seamlessly oaked and integrated. Both these wines have established long track records in the cellar.

SEMILLON

RATING 4

Margaret River	$20–$29
Current vintage: 2004	**93**

A luscious, smooth and carefully honed oak-fermented semillon whose dusty, lightly herbal and grassy aromas of melon and gooseberry are tightly knit with smoky vanilla oak. Its long, creamy palate of sumptuous melon and honeysuckle-like fruit and beautifully crafted, lightly charry oak extends towards a clean, soft and persistent silky finish.

2004	93	2009	2012
2003	95	2008	2011
2002	87	2007	2010
2001	91	2006	2009
2000	84	2002	2005+
1999	90	2004	2007
1998	94	2003	2006
1997	94	2002	2005
1995	94	2003	2007
1994	93	1999	2002
1993	93	2001	2005

Scotchmans Hill

190 Scotchmans Road, Drysdale Vic 3222. Tel: (03) 5251 3176. Fax: (03) 5253 1743.
Website: www.scotchmanshill.com.au Email: info@scotchmans.com.au

Region: **Geelong** Winemaker: **Robin Brockett** Viticulturist: **Robin Brockett**
Chief Executives: **David & Vivienne Browne**

Scotchmans Hill is a successful small winery business located near Geelong, on Melbourne's Port Phillip Bay. The drought hasn't made viticulture easy for the last few years yet its wines are typically very true to variety, honest and generous. Pick of the current releases is its smoky and savoury 2005 Shiraz.

PINOT NOIR

RATING 5

Geelong	$20–$29
Current vintage: 2005	**80**

Meaty, smoky and almost acrid aromas whose evolved, earthy, leathery and gamey aspects almost entirely lack primary fruit. Cooked and stressed, the palate similarly lacks fruit, finishing raw and forward with under-ripened tannins. Simply the result of the season.

2005	80	2007	2010
2004	88	2006	2009
2003	88	2005	2008
2002	88	2004	2007
2001	89	2002	2006
2000	84	2001	2002
1999	87	2000	2001+
1998	86	1999	2000
1997	93	2002	2005

SAUVIGNON BLANC

RATING 5

Geelong	$20–$29
Current vintage: 2006	**83**

Slightly meaty, candied aromas of gooseberries and melon lack real freshness and penetration. Forward, then rather cooked, dull and flat, it's held up to a degree by some fresh acidity, but lacks genuine length and brightness of fruit.

2006	83	2006	2007
2005	89	2006	2007
2004	85	2005	2006
2003	89	2003	2004+
2002	89	2003	2004
2001	90	2002	2003+
2000	88	2001	2002

SHIRAZ

RATING 4

Geelong	$20–$29
Current vintage: 2005	**89**

Lifted with a spicy floral perfume, this smoky and savoury shiraz has a musky and slightly baked bouquet of dark plums, redcurrants and blackberries with nuances of older chocolate/vanilla oak. Rich and juicy, its slightly meaty expression of dark blueberry-like fruit borders on ultra-ripeness, with toasty vanilla oak influences helping to smooth over some green-edged acids.

2005	89	2007	2010+
2004	81	2006	2009
2003	90	2005	2008+
2000	91	2002	2005+
1999	89	2001	2004+

Seppelt

Moyston Road, Great Western Vic 3377. Tel: (03) 5361 2239. Fax: (03) 5361 2328.
Website: www.seppelt.com.au Email: greatwestern.cellardoor@seppelt.com.au
Seppeltsfield Road, Seppeltsfield via Nuriootpa SA 5355. Tel: (08) 8568 6217. Fax: (08) 8562 8333.
Website: www.seppelt.com.au Email: seppeltsfield.cellardoor@seppelt.com.au

Regions: **Great Western, Drumborg, Barooga, Barossa**
Winemakers: **Emma Wood, James Godfrey** Viticulturist: **Paul Dakis** Chief Executive: **Jamie Odell**

While it's natural that Seppelt found harder going with its shirazes from Bendigo and Heathcote from 2005, it has produced another excellent St Peters from Great Western. It's eminently sensible that the Mount Ida Shiraz, from a small individual vineyard in the best part of the Heathcote region, become a part of Seppelt's expanding collection of Victorian shiraz. The white highlight of the current releases is another tight, textured and mineral Drumborg Riesling, from the same vineyard, incidentally, that has produced all the fruit for the 2004 Yattarna Chardonnay.

BELLFIELD MARSANNE ROUSSANNE

RATING 4

Pyrenees	$20–$29
Current vintage: 2005	**90**

Lightly candied aromas of honeysuckle, cinnamon and dusty oak reveal nutty and herbal undertones. Long and elegant, the palate is supple, honeyed, nutty and savoury, pleasingly rich, quite viscous and soft before a tangy finish of citrusy acids. Given some very restrained oak treatment, it's tightly focused, with a lingering hint of mineral.

2005	90	2007	2010+
2004	93	2009	2012+
2003	93	2005	2008+

BENNO SHIRAZ

RATING 2

Bendigo	$30–$49
Current vintage: 2005	**93**

Rather closed, firm and fractionally raw, this is a very fine shiraz from such a hot vintage. Its meaty, slightly jammy expression of dark plums, currants and blackberries overlies suggestions of iodide and a ferrous, fine-grained extract of astringent tannin. It retains layers of clear, bright fruit, and is likely to evolve and open up in future.

2005	93	2013	2017+
2004	96	2016	2024+
2003	96	2015	2023+

CHALAMBAR SHIRAZ

RATING 2

Great Western, Bendigo	$20–$29
Current vintage: 2005	**88**

A competent, but slightly raw and awkward shiraz whose spicy, lightly smoky, musky and minty aromas of dark plums and cherries overlie a whiff of cedar/vanilla oak. Full to medium in weight, it presents a long and meaty palate whose dark flavours of blackberries, plums and blueberries are smoothed out by creamy oak, before finishing savoury, rather firmish but currant-like.

2005	88	2010	2013+
2004	96	2016	2024+
2003	95	2015	2023
2002	96	2014	2022
2001	93	2009	2013+
2000	93	2008	2012+
1999	86	2001	2004+
1998	93	2006	2010+
1997	89	2002	2005+
1996	83	1998	2001
1995	91	2003	2007
1994	88	1999	2002
1993	84	1995	1998

DRUMBORG RIESLING

RATING 2

Drumborg		$20–$29	
Current vintage: 2006			**95**

Slightly awkward and gangly in its youth, this tightly defined, long and schisty young riesling will settle down into a wine of superb definition and focus. Its lightly spicy and musky aromas of apple and pear, lemon and lime reveal undertones of minerals and lanolin. Long, dry and succulent, its juicy palate of pristine fruit is punctuated by a cut of crunchy acids that will help to ensure its considerable cellaring potential.

2006	95	2014	2018
2005	97	2017	2025
2004	96	2016	2024
2003	95	2011	2015+
2000	94	2008	2012
1999	94	2011	2019
1998	89	2003	2006+
1997	87	2002	2005
1996	90	2001	2004
1993	94	2001	2005
1991	89	1999	2003
1988	88	1996	2000

JALUKA CHARDONNAY

RATING 4

Henty		$20–$29	
Current vintage: 2006			**87**

Delicate, floral and mineral, with aromas of white peach, mango and lightly creamy vanilla oak preceding an elegant palate whose initial attack of fresh citrus, melon and mango-like flavour becomes a little thin in the middle. It could yet flesh out with more buttery richness, but its edges are presently a little greenish, sappy and awkward, and its finish slightly metallic.

2006	87	2007	2008+
2005	94	2007	2010+
2004	93	2006	2009+
2003	90	2005	2008+
2002	88	2003	2004+

MOUNT IDA SHIRAZ (formerly a stand-alone brand)

RATING 3

Heathcote		$30–$59	
Current vintage: 2005			**88**

Firm and drying, with some under and over-ripe aspects, this minty shiraz has a peppery bouquet whose blackberry and cassis aromas are backed by nuances of dried herbs, meaty currant-like suggestions and chocolate oak. Long and smooth, its sour-edged expression of dark berries and plums finishes faintly sappy. Framed by fine, astringent tannin, it's quite approachable.

2005	88	2010	2013+
2004	93	2012	2016
2003	93	2015	2023
2002	93	2010	2014+
2001	84	2003	2006
1999	92	2004	2007
1998	96	2003	2006+
1997	91	2002	2005
1996	93	2001	2004
1995	96	2003	2007
1994	94	1999	2002
1992	95	1997	2000
1991	94	1999	2003
1990	93	1995	1998

ORIGINAL SPARKLING SHIRAZ

RATING 3

Victoria		$12–$19	
Current vintage: 2005			**89**

A flavoursome, vibrant early-drinking shiraz that might surprise if given time in the bottle. Punchy summer pudding aromas of small berries and plums are backed by suggestions of violets, white pepper and spice, plus a hint of vanilla oak. Black and briary, it's mouthfilling berry and plum flavours and lively effervescence overlie a moderately firm and powdery extract, finishing with lingering blueberry-like fruit.

2005	89	2010	2013
2002	89	2004	2007+
1998	90	2006	2010
1996	93	2004	2008
1995	94	2003	2007
1994	93	2002	2006+
1993	92	2001	2005
1992	87	1997	2000
1991	93	2003	2011
1990	91	1998	2002
1989	85	1997	2001
1988	88	1996	2000

SALINGER

RATING 4

Victoria, Southern Australia		$30–$49	
Current vintage: 2002			**89**

Smooth and easy-drinking with fresh apple, pear, white peach and melon-like flavour backed by toasty, lightly creamy complexity suggestive of bakery yeasts and dried flowers, this tangy, vibrant and fruit-driven wine finishes soft and slightly angular, with herbal undertones.

2002	89	2007	2010
2001	90	2006	2009
2000	91	2005	2008
1999	94	2004	2007
1998	94	2003	2006
1997	93	2002	2005+
1996	91	2001	2004
1995	91	2003	2007
1994	92	1999	2002+

SHOW SPARKLING SHIRAZ

RATING **3**

Great Western	$50–$99
Current vintage: 1994	92

Earthy, rather rustic sparkling shiraz with attractive fruit sweetness, undergrowth-like complexity and firmness, but a suggestion of under-ripened fruit. There's a greenish, sweetcorn-like note beneath its peppery, spicy perfume of earthy cassis, plums and cigarboxy influences. Smooth and elegant, its sweet, chewy palate reveals meaty, forest floor and savoury complexity beneath its lingering jujube-like expression of black and red berries.

1994	92	2006	2014
1993	93	2005	2013
1990	95	2002	2010+
1987	90	1995	1999+
1986	95	1998	2006
1985	91	1993	1997
1984	94	1999	2001

ST PETERS SHIRAZ (formerly Great Western Shiraz)

RATING **1**

Grampians	$50–$99
Current vintage: 2005	95

Very stylish, elegant and savoury, with a heady, spicy and ethereal bouquet of smoked meats, blackberries, dark plums, briar and white pepper, backed by tightly integrated oak. Medium to full in weight, it's underpinned by finely powdered, dusty tannins, delivering a long, silky expression of dark and slightly meaty fruit culminating in a long and persistent finish. Evenly ripened and very regional.

2005	95	2013	2017+
2004	97	2024	2034
2003	96	2015	2023
2002	98	2014	2022+
2001	96	2013	2021+
2000	95	2012	2020+
1999	90	2004	2007+
1998	95	2010	2018+
1997	92	2009	2017
1996	95	2008	2016
1995	95	2007	2015
1993	95	2005	2013
1992	90	2000	2004
1991	96	2003	2011+
1988	88	1996	2000

VICTORIAN CABERNET SAUVIGNON MERLOT
(formerly Harpers Range)

RATING **4**

Victoria	$12–$19
Current vintage: 2004	87

An honest, varietal quaffer whose minty, meaty aromas of black berries, plums and vanilla oak precede a smooth, generous and juicy palate of moderate length. Framed by simple but robust tannin, it's quite long and evenly ripened, with fresh, vibrant flavours of berries, cherries and dark plums, finishing with lingering earthy and meaty undertones.

2004	87	2009	2012
2003	87	2005	2008+
2000	91	2008	2012
1998	90	2006	2010
1997	91	2002	2005+
1996	87	2001	2004
1995	89	2003	2007
1994	88	1999	2002
1993	82	1995	1998
1992	90	1997	2000

VICTORIA SHIRAZ

RATING **4**

Victoria	$12–$19
Current vintage: 2005	88

A savoury, fruit-driven shiraz whose minty, menthol-like aromas of blackberry confiture and fresh oak reveal a light spiciness, and whose smooth, moderately rich palate frames its dark berry and plummy fruit with slightly awkward tannins that just lack a little definition.

2005	88	2010	2013
2004	90	2009	2012
2003	90	2008	2011
2002	92	2010	2014
2001	87	2003	2006+

Sevenhill

College Road, Sevenhill via Clare SA 5453. Tel: (08) 8843 4222. Fax: (08) 8843 4382.
Website: www.sevenhillcellars.com.au Email: sales@sevenhillcellars.com.au

Region: **Clare Valley** Winemakers: **Liz Heidenreich & Brother John May** Viticulturist: **Craig Richards**
Chief Executive: **Paul McClure**

Clare's oldest winery, Sevenhill, is still operated by the same order of Jesuit priests who bought the land it occupies in 1851. Recent years have seen the emergence of more cut and polish about its wines, which today, more than ever, provide a lively and vibrant reflection of their vineyards and seasons. The pick of its current releases is the rather sumptuous and meaty 2004 Cabernet Sauvignon.

CABERNET SAUVIGNON
RATING 5

| Clare Valley | $20–$29 |
| Current vintage: 2004 | 90 |

A pliant, layered and firmly structured cabernet with intense, slightly meaty flavours of dark plums, cassis, dark cherries and blackberries framed by tightly knit, powdery tannins. It has a floral lift, with faintly herbal undertones and a polished measure of gamey vanilla oak. Long and sumptuous, it's stylish and finely balanced.

2004	90	2016	2024
2003	86	2008	2011
2002	87	2007	2010+
2001	87	2006	2009
2000	83	2002	2005
1999	88	2007	2011
1998	86	2003	2006
1997	86	2002	2005+
1996	88	2004	2008
1995	84	1997	2000
1994	90	2006	2014
1993	90	2005	2013
1992	90	2000	2004

ST ALOYSIUS RIESLING
RATING 4

| Clare Valley | $12–$19 |
| Current vintage: 2006 | 88 |

A long, lean and focused medium-term riesling with some austerity. Its zesty, floral perfume of apple and lemon reveals undertones of mineral, while its taut, restrained and elegant palate delivers a very reserved expression of lime and lemony fruit. Very dry and balanced, with a phenolic undercarriage.

2006	88	2011	2014
2005	92	2013	2017+
2004	91	2009	2012+
2003	89	2008	2011
2002	87	2004	2007
2001	90	2006	2009
2000	91	2005	2008+
1999	88	2004	2007
1998	91	2003	2006
1997	93	2002	2005
1996	93	2004	2008
1995	94	2000	2003
1994	93	2002	2006

SEMILLON
RATING 5

| Clare Valley | $12–$19 |
| Current vintage: 2005 | 87 |

Rather spirity and alcoholic, this clean and mineral semillon does, however, reveal a lifted, floral and apple-like aroma with undertones of lemon detergent and wet slate. Round and generous, its rich, melon-like palate is flavoursome and varietal, finishing with powdery mineral nuances.

2005	87	2007	2010+
2004	89	2006	2009
2003	87	2005	2008
1999	90	2005	2007+
1998	89	2003	2006
1996	87	1998	2001
1995	82	1997	2000
1994	87	1999	2002

SHIRAZ
RATING 5

| Clare Valley | $20–$29 |
| Current vintage: 2004 | 87 |

Extended on the palate by sweet chocolate and vanilla oak, this rather cooked shiraz has an earthy, currant-like spectrum of plum, cherry kernel and raisin-like fruit. With a spicy scent of roast lamb and cloves, it's firm and full-bodied, underpinned by regional suggestions of mint and menthol, but lacks true length of bright fruit.

2004	87	2009	2012
2003	86	2008	2011
2002	89	2010	2014
2001	89	2009	2013
1999	87	2004	2007
1998	90	2003	2006
1997	89	2002	2005+
1996	91	2001	2004
1995	91	2003	2007
1994	91	2002	2006
1993	93	2005	2013
1992	90	2000	2004

Seville Estate

Linwood Road, Seville Vic 3139. Tel: 1300 880 561. Fax: (03) 5964 2633.
Website: www.sevilleestate.com.au Email: wine@sevilleestate.com.au
Region: **Yarra Valley** Winemaker: **Dylan McMahon** Viticulturist: **Margaret van der Muelen**
Chief Executives: **Graham & Margaret van der Muelen**
Seville Estate is a mature vineyard with one of the cooler sites in the Yarra Valley. Its original plantings of nearly 30-year-old vines provide a rare and valuable resource. The present wines are not of the same standard as those which established the reputation of this property.

CHARDONNAY   RATING 4

Yarra Valley	$20–$29
Current vintage: 2005	**87**

Uncomplicated, fresh and juicy, with flavours of peach, grapefruit and melon given a light dusting of nutty oak. Lacking genuine shape and structure, its creamy palate finishes with soft acids and lingering nuances of peach, butter and vanilla.

2005	87	2007	2010
2004	91	2009	2012
2003	90	2005	2008
2002	87	2004	2007
2001	88	2003	2006
2000	87	2002	2005
1999	89	2001	2004
1998	89	2003	2006
1997	94	2002	2005+
1996	91	2001	2004
1995	92	2000	2003

PINOT NOIR   RATING 5

Yarra Valley	$20–$29
Current vintage: 2005	**87**

An angular, up-front, early-drinking pinot whose slightly baked flavours of maraschino cherries, red-currants and plums reveal raisined and spicy under-tones. It's up-front, but lacks real freshness and follow-through, finishing hot and spirity, with firm, fine tannins that are just too clunky for its weight of fruit.

2005	87	2007	2010
2003	88	2005	2008
2002	86	2004	2007
2001	88	2003	2006+
2000	89	2002	2005
1999	87	2001	2004
1998	87	2000	2003+
1995	87	2000	2003
1993	93	1998	2001
1992	88	2000	2004

RESERVE CABERNET SAUVIGNON   RATING 3

Yarra Valley	$30–$49
Current vintage: 2003	**86**

Meaty, greenish and rather flat, lacking genuine brightness of fruit, with minty, earthy aromas supported by assertive chocolate/mocha oak. Framed by firm, but sappy tannins, its meaty expression of rather simple and confection-like red and black berries and mocha/vanilla oak is rather overwhelmed by its extract and greenness.

2003	86	2008	2011
2001	92	2009	2013+
2000	93	2012	2020
1999	90	2001	2004
1998	84	2000	2003+
1997	89	2005	2009
1995	86	2002	2006
1994	89	2002	2006
1992	94	2004	2012

RESERVE SHIRAZ   RATING 3

Yarra Valley	$50–$99
Current vintage: 2004	**87**

Very oaky, spicy and savoury; medium in weight and slightly overcooked. Backed by toasty/vanilla new oak, its peppery, briary flavours of mulberries, blackberries, dark cherries and plums are framed by fine but slightly edgy tannins, but lack genuine depth and intensity. Backed by herbal nuances, it finishes musky and savoury, but without much length.

2004	87	2009	2012
2003	87	2005	2008+
2001	95	2013	2021
2000	95	2008	2012+

SHIRAZ

RATING 3

Yarra Valley	$20–$29
Current vintage: 2004	**77**

Flat, cooked and browning, with dried out flavours of prunes and currants framed by weedy tannins and green-edged acids. Quite hollow, lacking intensity and presence of fruit.

2004	77	2006	2009
2003	89	2008	2011
2002	93	2010	2014+
2001	93	2006	2009
2000	86	2002	2005
1999	92	2004	2007
1997	93	2005	2009
1996	93	2004	2008
1995	93	2003	2007
1994	90	2002	2006
1993	95	2001	2005
1992	94	2004	2012+

Shadowfax

K Road, Werribee Vic 3030. Tel: (03) 9731 4420. Fax: (03) 9731 4421.
Website: www.shadowfax.com.au Email: cellardoor@shadowfax.com.au
Regions: **Various** Winemaker: **Matt Harrop** Viticulturist: **Andrew Tedder**

Located on the grounds of Werribee Park, Shadowfax is steadily acquiring vineyard sites and long-term relationships with growers all over Australia to provide its diverse range of regional specialty wines. They're all very competently made by Matt Harrop; typically spotlessly clean and very true to variety and region. Another terrific Pink Cliffs Shiraz from Heathcote is the highlight of the current Shadowfax releases; a firm and brooding regional classic.

CHARDONNAY

RATING 4

Various, Victoria	$20–$29
Current vintage: 2005	**87**

Buttery, toasty and lightly varnishy aromas of assertive oak and citrus, melon and banana-like fruit precede a round, generous and juicy palate whose slightly candied melon-like fruit reflects some under- and over-ripe influences. Finished by clean acids, it lacks genuine brightness and focus.

2005	87	2006	2007+
2004	93	2006	2009+
2003	89	2005	2008
2002	90	2004	2007
2001	87	2003	2006
2000	89	2002	2005
1999	93	2001	2004

ONE EYE SHIRAZ

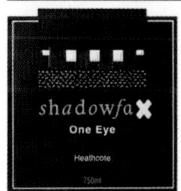

RATING 4

Heathcote	$50–$99
Current vintage: 2004	**90**

Firm, dry and unyielding, this closed and sinewy shiraz has a meaty, leathery bouquet whose rather sweet and jammy aromas of red and black berries are backed by earthy and peppery complexity. Its powerful, ferrous and leathery palate of deep, minty fruit finishes rather hard and drying, and should flesh out with time in the bottle.

2004	90	2012	2016
2003	87	2005	2008+
2002	92	2010	2014
2001	91	2009	2013

PINK CLIFFS SHIRAZ

RATING 2

Heathcote	$50–$99
Current vintage: 2004	**94**

Firm, linear and substantial, this deeply fruited and powerful shiraz will flesh out over time. Its musky perfume of dark plums, berries and meaty undertones is lifted by heady aromas of pepper and spice. Steeped in sumptuous flavours of black berries, plums and dark chocolate, its brooding and deeply layered palate is framed by a drying cut of powdery astringency, finishing long and savoury.

2004	94	2016	2024
2003	80	2005	2008
2002	95	2010	2014+
2001	95	2009	2013

PINOT GRIS

RATING 4

Adelaide Hills $20–$29
Current vintage: 2006 **90**

Lively, crisp and crunchy, with a floral, lightly spicy and nutty fragrance of dusty pear, apple and cloves. Long and refreshing, its clean, tangy palate of bright varietal flavour finishes with lemony acids.

2006	90	2007	2008+
2005	86	2006	2007
2004	88	2005	2006
2003	91	2003	2004+
2002	83	2003	2004
2001	84	2002	2003
2000	91	2002	2005

PINOT NOIR

RATING 4

Geelong, Gippsland, Yarra Valley $30–$49
Current vintage: 2004 **87**

A minty and rather candied pinot whose menthol-like aromas of red cherries, raspberries and plums are backed by a lightly herbal, undergrowth-like complexity and vanilla oak. Moderately rich and ripe, with rather stewed and forward fruit framed by slightly sappy and metallic tannins, it's firm and drying, lacking real brightness and silkiness.

2004	87	2006	2009+
2003	90	2005	2008
2002	86	2004	2007
2001	89	2003	2006
2000	93	2002	2005

SAUVIGNON BLANC

RATING 3

Adelaide Hills $12–$19
Current vintage: 2006 **87**

Clean and well made, but slightly out of focus, its herbal and rather sweaty aroma of skinsy gooseberry and melon fruit is backed by meaty, herbal nuances. Broad and generous, it remains a little cloying and syrupy, lacking genuine freshness and tightness.

2006	87	2007	2008
2005	88	2006	2007
2004	92	2005	2006
2003	92	2003	2004+
2002	84	2003	2004
2001	90	2002	2003+

SHIRAZ

RATING 4

Victoria $20–$29
Current vintage: 2004 **89**

A minty and eucalypt-like fragrance of dark cherries, blackberries and plums is backed by smoky cedar/vanilla oak. Just a fraction blocky, its ripe and juicy palate has length and structure, finishing with a shade more oak than ideal. In all, a competent and varietal shiraz.

2004	89	2006	2009
2003	87	2005	2008
2002	90	2007	2010+
2000	84	2001	2002+
1999	91	2004	2007

Shaw and Smith

Lot 4 Jones Road, Balhannah SA 5242. Tel: (08) 8398 0500. Fax: (08) 8398 0600.
Website: www.shawandsmith.com Email: info@shawandsmith.com
Region: **Adelaide Hills** Winemaker: **Martin Shaw** Viticulturist: **Wayne Pittaway**
Chief Executives: **Martin Shaw, Michael Hill Smith**

Shaw and Smith now focuses on just three wines — its Sauvignon Blanc, Shiraz and M3 Vineyard Chardonnay. Its M3 is made with special effort to retain brightness of flavour and its fluffy, fine and vibrant texture, qualities that certainly contribute to longevity, which its makers view as an essential component in chardonnay quality. I agree all the way. The Sauvignon Blanc is the winery's popular standard, an intensely fruited and typically austere style that remains one of the region's finest.

M3 VINEYARD CHARDONNAY

RATING 2

Adelaide Hills $30–$49
Current vintage: 2005 **93**

An unctuous, stylish and very showy chardonnay whose sweet, oaky aromas of peach, nectarine and citrusy fruit reveal undertones of vanilla, cloves, and cinnamon. Long and smooth, its seamless palate of melon, grapefruit, lemon and apple flavour is tightly knit with assertive butter/vanilla oak, finishing long and creamy, with soft acids. Very focused and tightly integrated, but lacks wow factor.

2005	93	2010	2013
2004	95	2009	2012
2003	94	2008	2011
2002	95	2007	2010
2001	93	2003	2006+
2000	94	2002	2005+

SAUVIGNON BLANC

RATING **4**

Adelaide Hills	$20–$29
Current vintage: 2006	**90**

A round, juicy, smooth and generous sauvignon blanc whose heady aromas of fresh gooseberries, passionfruit and lychees reveal just a hint of grassiness. Very ripe, round and mouthfilling, its essence-like palate of intense, pure fruit finishes with lingering soft acids. Just lacks the shape and bite for a higher score.

2006	90	2006	2007+
2005	93	2006	2007
2004	91	2004	2005
2003	88	2003	2004
2002	95	2003	2004+
2001	91	2002	2003+
2000	87	2000	2001
1999	88	2000	2001
1998	91	1998	1999

SHIRAZ

RATING **4**

Adelaide Hills	$30–$49
Current vintage: 2005	**88**

A finely crafted shiraz with a slightly overcooked expression of meaty, currant-like plum and dark berry fruit tightly knit with smooth, fine-grained oak and tannin. It's briary and musky, with a confection-like aspect, some spirity warmth and a savoury finish. It would rate more highly with more mid-palate intensity and richness.

2005	88	2007	2010+
2004	91	2009	2012+
2003	91	2005	2008+
2002	95	2007	2010+

Shottesbrooke

Bagshaw Road, McLaren Flat SA 5171. Tel: (08) 8383 0002. Fax: (08) 8383 0222.
Website: www.shottesbrooke.com.au Email: admin@shottesbrooke.com.au
Region: **McLaren Vale** Winemaker: **Hamish Maguire** Viticulturist: **Hamish Maguire**
Chief Executive: **Nick Holmes**

Shottesbrooke is a well-established winery whose smoothly structured reds have traditionally been finer and more elegant than most in McLaren Vale. Its Sauvignon Blanc is usually pungent and arrestingly varietal.

MERLOT

RATING **5**

McLaren Vale	$20–$29
Current vintage: 2005	**89**

Smooth and savoury, this plump, generous and rather smoky young merlot has an earthy bouquet of dark, spicy plums, smoked meats and leather over nuances of currants and dark cherries. Its juicy palate is backed by assertive, chocolate-like oak and framed by a fine and dusty cut of pliant tannin.

2005	89	2007	2010+
2004	88	2009	2012
2003	82	2005	2008
2002	83	2004	2007+
2001	86	2006	2009
2000	89	2008	2012
1999	89	2004	2007
1998	90	2003	2006
1997	92	2002	2005
1996	90	2001	2004
1995	90	2000	2003

SAUVIGNON BLANC

RATING **5**

Fleurieu, Adelaide Hills	$12–$19
Current vintage: 2006	**89**

Pungent, slightly meaty and reductive, with herbal aromas of lychees, gooseberries and citrus, revealing mineral undertones. Richly textured and generous, it's long and lightly phenolic, with a pleasing length of fruit finishing savoury, smoky and briney.

2006	89	2007	2008+
2005	84	2006	2007
2004	77	2004	2004
2003	87	2004	2005
2002	89	2003	2004
2001	91	2002	2003+
2000	88	2002	2005
1999	86	2000	2001

Skillogalee

Trevarrick Road, Sevenhill via Clare SA 5453. Tel: (08) 8843 4311. Fax: (08) 8843 4343.
Email: admin@skillogalee.com Website: www.skillogalee.com

Region: **Clare Valley** Winemaker: **Dan Palmer** Viticulturist: **Craig McLean** Chief Executive: **Dave Palmer**

Skillogalee is one of the Clare Valley's small family-run vineyards. While its rustic, earthy reds are typically less ripe and assertive than others of the region, its best wines are its typically juicy and intense regional expression of Riesling, plus its spicy, savoury and slightly meaty Gewürztraminer, of which the 2005 is a fine example.

GEWÜRZTRAMINER

RATING 5

Clare Valley	$12–$19
Current vintage: 2005	**90**

A generous, clean and savoury wine whose slowly evolving but rather pungent and bath powdery aromas of musky, spicy and floral traminer characters of lychees and rose oil reveal faint hints of toastiness. Rather round, broad and generous, with a hint of meatiness, its juicy palate of pronounced varietal fruit culminates in a fractionally sweet but clean and savoury finish of some length.

2005	90	2007	2010
2004	86	2005	2006+
2003	84	2004	2005
2002	93	2004	2007
1999	87	2004	2007

RIESLING

RATING 5

Clare Valley	$12–$19
Current vintage: 2006	**87**

A juicy and confectionary riesling whose candied fragrance of white peach and lemon meringue precedes a juicy, forward palate of tinned peach flavour. Moderately long, it's broad and generous, finishing with soft, lemon sherbet-like acids.

2006	87	2008	2011
2005	90	2010	2013+
2004	88	2006	2009+
2003	87	2005	2008
2002	89	2007	2010
2001	93	2006	2008+
2000	89	2002	2005+
1999	90	2004	2007
1998	90	2003	2006
1997	92	2005	2009
1996	91	2001	2004
1995	93	2003	2007
1994	94	2006	2014
1993	90	2001	2005
1992	93	1997	2000

Smithbrook

Smithbrook Road, Pemberton WA 6260. Tel: (08) 9772 3557. Fax: (08) 9772 3579.
Website: www.smithbrook.com.au Email: smithbrk@karriweb.com.au

Region: **Pemberton** Winemakers: **Mike Symons, Ashley Lewkowski** Viticulturists: **Mike Symons, Ashley Lewkowski** Chief Executive: **Anthony Roberts**

Lion Nathan's Western Australian outpost is a large vineyard in Pemberton that delivers one of Australia's finest Sauvignon Blancs, as well as an earthy, leathery Merlot of some charm. Its flagship wines are labelled 'The Yilgarn'. The red is a merlot-dominant blend with cabernet sauvignon and petit verdot, while the white is principally oak-matured sauvignon blanc, often with a dash of semillon.

MERLOT

RATING 5

Pemberton	$20–$29
Current vintage: 2004	**91**

Firm, savoury and slightly gamey, this is a well structured and finely balanced merlot with plenty of sour-edged plum and dark cherry flavour backed by restrained cedar/chocolate oak. It has a pleasing willowy quality and a vibrant finish of persistent fruit and refreshing acids.

2004	91	2009	2012+
2003	87	2008	2011
2002	88	2007	2010
2001	87	2003	2006+
2000	89	2005	2008
1999	89	2001	2004

SAUVIGNON BLANC

RATING 3

Pemberton	$12–$19	2006	92	2007	2008+
Current vintage: 2006	**92**	2005	86	2005	2006
		2004	93	2004	2005+
		2003	93	2004	2005+
		2002	90	2003	2004
		2001	87	2002	2003
		2000	91	2000	2001

Tight and focused, with a pleasing lemon-edged shape and freshness, its bright and juicy flavours of gooseberry, cassis, passionfruit and melon are backed by lightly herbal and mineral nuances. It's long, racy and sculpted, finishing fresh and briny.

THE YILGARN (Merlot blend)

RATING 4

Pemberton	$30–$49	2005	84	2010	2013
Current vintage: 2005	**84**	2004	90	2012	2016
		2001	93	2006	2009+
		2000	87	2005	2008

Firm and drying, this sinewy red blend shows some under and over-ripe influences. Its slightly cooked and herbal aromas of currants and plums are reliant on sweet cedar/vanilla oak, while its relatively simple palate lacks mid-palate substance and ripeness. Lacks genuine balance and freshness.

THE YILGARN (Sauvignon Blanc blend)

RATING 4

Pemberton	$20–$29	2006	90	2007	2008+
Current vintage: 2006	**90**	2005	86	2007	2010
		2004	90	2006	2009

A delicate fragrance of lemon, grapefruit and minerals reveals lightly herbaceous and goose-berry-like undertones. Fresh and moderately juicy, its flavoursome and generous palate marries vibrant fruit with restrained buttery/vanilla oak, a long lick of slate and tightly focused lemony acids. Complex and refreshing, with genuine style and definition.

Sorrenberg

Alma Road, Beechworth Vic 3747. Tel: (03) 5728 2278. Fax: (03) 5728 2278. Website: www.sorrenberg.com

Region: **Beechworth** Winemaker: **Barry Morey** Viticulturist: **Barry Morey** Chief Executive: **Barry Morey**

Sorrenberg is a small and highly rated maker of distinctive and complex wines in the Beechworth hills of north-east Victoria. Its finest wine is usually its savoury, mineral Sauvignon Blanc Semillon blend, while in certain years — such as 2005 — its Chardonnay can be sumptuous and savoury, and the Gamay rather wild and briary.

CABERNET BLEND

RATING 4

Beechworth	$30–$49	2005	89	2013	2017
Current vintage: 2005	**89**	2004	89	2009	2012+
		2002	93	2014	2022
		2001	87	2006	2009
		2000	90	2005	2008+
		1999	88	2004	2007
		1998	87	2003	2006
		1997	83	1999	2002
		1994	88	1998	2003

Herbal, slightly leafy and menthol-like, with juicy small red and black berry flavours backed by cedar/mocha oak and suggestions of undergrowth. Smooth and polished, its palate is long, pleasingly balanced and supported by a good structure of fine-grained, powdery tannin.

CHARDONNAY

RATING 3

Beechworth	$30–$49
Current vintage: 2005	92

Slightly candied, this charmingly complex and vibrant chardonnay has a delicate bouquet and a long, creamy and shapely palate that finishes with lively, refreshing acidity. Its melon, grapefruit and nectarine fruit reveals lightly funky, buttery nuances and undertones of smoky vanilla oak. Quite stylish, with a lingering core of intense flavour.

2005	92	2007	2010+
2004	89	2006	2009
2003	84	2005	2008
2002	90	2004	2007
2001	95	2003	2006+
2000	94	2005	2008
1999	90	2004	2007
1998	86	2000	2003
1997	93	2002	2005

GAMAY

RATING 5

Beechworth	$30–$49
Current vintage: 2006	88

A pretty, lightly minty and early-drinking gamay whose smooth and slightly candied expression of cherries, raspberries, blueberries and plums is fine and restrained, framed by supple, fine tannins. While there's a hint of meatiness and a light floral perfume, the palate could use a little more length.

2006	88	2007	2008
2004	91	2005	2006+
2002	87	2004	2007
2001	88	2003	2006
2000	91	2002	2005
1999	84	2000	2001
1998	87	1999	2000

SAUVIGNON BLANC SEMILLON

RATING 3

Beechworth	$20–$29
Current vintage: 2006	87

Lightly candied and early drinking, this lively and generous white marries lightly herbal gooseberry/melon fruit with nutty, dusty vanilla oak. It's supple and elegant, with a reasonably long palate that finishes soft and savoury with lemony acids and a slight tinned fruit-like aspect. Could perhaps use more brightness and acidity.

2006	87	2007	2008+
2005	86	2006	2007
2004	95	2006	2009+
2003	91	2005	2008
2002	95	2007	2010
2001	93	2006	2009
2000	90	2002	2005
1999	87	2001	2004
1998	88	2000	2003

St Hallett

St Hallett's Road, Hallet Valley, Tanunda SA 5352. Tel: (08) 8563 7000. Fax: (08) 8563 7001.
Website: www.sthallett.com.au Email: sthallett@sthallett.com.au

Region: **Barossa Valley** Winemakers: **Stuart Blackwell, Toby Barlow** Viticulturist: **Chris Rogers**

St Hallett is a Barossa shiraz specialist. Its Faith is typically vibrant, spicy and silky-smooth, while the Blackwell has more richness, structure and expression. The sumptuous, deeply layered and velvet-smooth Old Block justifies its reputation as a Barossa benchmark. Of the current releases, the 2005 Blackwell is unusually cooked and meaty, the 2003 Old Block very rustic and horsey, while the supple, spicy 2005 Faith is a terrific quaff.

BLACKWELL SHIRAZ

RATING 3

Barossa Valley	$20–$29
Current vintage: 2005	86

Like many 2005 shirazes, it's firm, well structured and elegant, but has a rather overcooked, meaty and currant-like nature. With plenty of smoky, meaty artefact and charry oak, its jammy expression of plums and small berries overlies spicecake-like notes of cloves and cinnamon. It's well-handled tannins are polished and pliant.

2005	86	2007	2010+
2004	94	2012	2016+
2003	93	2008	2011
2002	93	2007	2010+
2001	92	2006	2009+
1999	92	2004	2007+
1998	95	2006	2010+
1997	88	2002	2005
1996	91	2004	2008
1995	87	2000	2003
1994	92	1999	2002+

EDEN VALLEY RIESLING

RATING 4

Eden Valley	$12–$19
Current vintage: 2006	**89**

A long, rather chalky and mineral riesling with delicate floral aromas of pear juice, white peach and citrus. There's intensity, brightness and freshness, with a lingering finish of tangy fruit.

2006	89	2011	2019
2005	89	2010	2013
2004	87	2006	2009
2003	92	2008	2011+
2002	93	2007	2010
2001	89	2006	2009
2000	90	2005	2008
1999	90	2004	2007
1998	90	2003	2006+
1997	93	2002	2005+
1996	88	2001	2004

FAITH SHIRAZ

RATING 5

Barossa Valley	$12–$19
Current vintage: 2005	**90**

Silky and approachable, this juicy, easy-drinking shiraz has a lightly toasty and peppery aroma of blackberries, cassis, dark plums, coconut and vanilla. Supported by fine, supple and slightly bony tannin, it finishes with length of vibrant fruit and clean acids. A great quaff.

2005	90	2007	2010
2004	87	2006	2009
2003	90	2005	2008
2002	89	2004	2007
2001	86	2003	2006
2000	82	2002	2005
1999	92	2004	2009
1998	90	2003	2006
1997	88	1998	1999
1996	86	1998	2001
1995	88	2000	2003
1994	89	1996	1999+

OLD BLOCK SHIRAZ

RATING 3

Barossa Valley	$50–$99
Current vintage: 2003	**88**

Rather meaty, rustic and horsey aromas of spicy, leathery fruit precede a generous and dark-fruited palate whose berry and plum-like flavours culminate with lingering meaty and savoury characters. Medium to full in weight, quite smooth and silky, but finishes with some meaty, hard-edged and drying influences suggestive of microbial instability.

2003	88	2008	2011
2002	93	2014	2022
2001	89	2009	2013
2000	84	2002	2005+
1999	94	2007	2011
1998	95	2010	2018
1997	82	1999	2002
1996	89	2001	2004
1995	89	2000	2003+
1994	94	2002	2006
1993	91	1998	2001
1992	92	1997	2000
1991	95	2003	2011
1990	95	2002	2010
1989	91	1997	2001
1988	95	2000	2008

SEMILLON (formerly Semillon Select and Blackwell Semillon)

RATING 4

Barossa Valley	$12–$19
Current vintage: 2004	**90**

This powdery, slightly phenolic and handsomely oaked Barossa semillon marries fresh, nutty melon and banana-like fruit with toast, vanilla and some herbal undertones. It retains plenty of juicy freshness, and its palate extends towards a lingering finish of clean, soft acidity. A little more cellaring time will pay dividends.

2004	90	2009	2012
2003	92	2008	2011+
2002	86	2004	2007+
2001	87	2003	2006
1999	84	2001	2004
1998	88	2000	2003
1997	90	1999	2002
1996	88	1998	2001
1995	83	1996	1997

St Huberts

St Huberts Road, Coldstream Vic 3770. Tel: (03) 9739 1118. Fax: (03) 9739 1096.
Website: www.fosters.com.au

Region: **Yarra Valley** Winemaker: **Shavaughn Wells** Viticulturist: **Damien de Castella**
Chief Executive: **Jamie Odell**

St Huberts was redeveloped in the late 1970s. It shares its name and much of its identification with one of the three grand properties that dominated Yarra viticulture in the 1800s, even though its vineyards are planted next to, and not on the original St Huberts site. Its wines are typically very elegant, finely crafted and very true to their regional origins. The vine louse phylloxera was discovered on a St Huberts vineyard in late 2006.

CABERNET SAUVIGNON

RATING **3**

Yarra Valley	$20–$29
Current vintage: 2005	**90**

Firm and ripe, this long, grainy and slightly meaty cabernet has a heady, but slightly dusty bouquet of crushed violets, cassis, blackberries, cedar and dark chocolates. Long and robust, its drying and slightly minty palate reveals undertones of menthol and forest floor. It needs some cellaring to open up.

2005	90	2010	2013+
2003	93	2011	2015
2001	90	2009	2013+
2000	90	2008	2012+
1999	90	2004	2007
1998	93	2006	2010
1997	92	2005	2009+
1996	87	1998	2001
1995	92	2000	2003
1994	94	2002	2006
1993	90	1998	2003
1992	93	2000	2004

CHARDONNAY

RATING **4**

Yarra Valley	$20–$29
Current vintage: 2006	**90**

Quite a stylish and elegant young chardonnay whose fresh, lightly toasty aromas of melon and grapefruit are backed by suggestions of cloves and cinnamon. Smooth and generous, with some underlying leesy and meaty complexity, its forward and brightly lit peach, melon and citrus fruit marries neatly with fresh vanilla oak, finishing soft and refreshing.

2006	90	2008	2011
2005	89	2007	2010+
2004	91	2006	2009+
2003	91	2005	2008+
2002	86	2003	2004
2001	87	2002	2003
2000	90	2002	2005+
1999	92	2004	2007
1998	87	2000	2003
1997	84	1999	2002
1996	87	1998	2001

PINOT NOIR

RATING **5**

Yarra Valley	$20–$29
Current vintage: 2005	**86**

A firmish, faster-maturing and rather meaty young pinot whose slightly brandied aromas of cherries, plums and berries are backed by sweet vanilla and slightly charry oak. Its assertive, but mono-dimensional palate of simple berry/cherry flavour does reveal some herbal edges, finishing with under and over-ripe gamey influences.

2005	86	2007	2010+
2004	89	2006	2009
2003	89	2005	2008
2002	90	2007	2010
2001	89	2003	2006
2000	86	2002	2005
1999	89	2001	2004
1998	87	2000	2003
1997	87	2002	2005
1996	87	1998	2001

ROUSSANNE

RATING **4**

Yarra Valley	$20–$29
Current vintage: 2005	**90**

Funky, evolved and meaty and mineral, with a smoky, rather reductive bouquet of honeysuckle, lavender, cloves and cinnamon backed by earthy, lanolin-like complexity. Supple and restrained, its dusty and finely phenolic palate delivers juicy citrus and melon-like flavour with underlying honeysuckle influences, finishing long and savoury.

2005	90	2007	2010+
2004	91	2006	2009+
2003	90	2005	2008+
2002	90	2003	2004+
2000	86	2002	2005
1999	89	2001	2004
1998	87	1999	2000+

Stanton & Killeen

Murray Valley Highway, Rutherglen Vic 3685. Tel: (02) 6032 9457. Fax: (02) 6032 8018.
Website: www.stantonandkilleenwines.com.au Email: skwines@bigpond.net.au

Region: **Rutherglen** Winemaker: **Chris Killeen** Viticulturist: **Paul Geddes** Chief Executive: **Chris Killeen**

Stanton & Killeen is a long-established maker of the traditionally rich and smooth Rutherglen dry reds and luscious fortified wines. It was with immense regret that the wine industry and his many friends learned of the passing of Chris Killeen just a few weeks prior to the printing of this book. I join my name to the long list of those who wish the very best for his family. Australian vintage port has lost its champion.

CABERNET SHIRAZ

RATING **4**

Rutherglen	$20–$29	2004	90	2012	2016+
Current vintage: 2004	**90**	2003	89	2008	2011
		2001	88	2006	2009+
		1998	88	2006	2010
		1997	90	2005	2009+
		1996	90	2004	2008+
		1995	88	2007	2015
		1994	88	2006	2014
		1992	91	2004	2012

A richly flavoured but finely balanced Rutherglen red whose deeply spiced and alluring aromas of blackberries, dark plums, chocolate, cedar and vanilla are backed by peppery nuances of cloves and cinnamon. Fully but not over-ripened, its sumptuous and well-integrated palate of intense black and red berries, cedar/vanilla oak and firm but pliant tannin finishes long, spicy and slightly meaty.

JACK'S BLOCK SHIRAZ

RATING **3**

Rutherglen	$30–$49	2004	87	2009	2012
Current vintage: 2004	**87**	2000	93	2012	2020
		1998	94	2006	2010+
		1997	93	2009	2017
		1993	88	2001	2005+

Deep, spicy, earthy and leathery aromas of slightly cooked and juicy small berries reveal musky undertones of cloves and cinnamon, with underlying cedar/vanilla oak and meaty, rather horsey and herbal undertones. Framed by firm, fine tannins, its rich, meaty palate of dark plums, cherries and licorice is supported by fine oak but finishes raw and bitter, with a metallic hardness and Bandaid-like notes.

MOODEMERE SHIRAZ

RATING **5**

Rutherglen	$20–$29	2005	86	2007	2010
Current vintage: 2005	**86**	2004	89	2009	2012+
		2003	88	2008	2011
		2002	87	2004	2007+
		2001	82	2003	2006+
		2000	86	2005	2008
		1999	87	2004	2007
		1996	90	2004	2008
		1995	89	2007	2015
		1993	91	2005	2013
		1992	94	2004	2012
		1991	88	1999	2003
		1990	92	2002	2010

Rather cooked, meaty and currant-like, with flavours of sweet raspberries, blackberries and mulberries over suggestions of molasses, vanilla oak and herbal undertones. Initially intense and jammy, it falls away down the palate to a less ripe and slightly green-edged finish.

VINTAGE PORT

RATING **2**

Rutherglen	$20–$29	2002	93	2010	2014
Current vintage: 2002	**93**	2001	92	2009	2013+
		2000	95	2008	2012+
		1999	93	2007	2011+
		1998	96	2010	2018+
		1997	95	2009	2017
		1996	95	2008	2016+
		1995	95	2015	2025
		1994	93	2006	2014
		1993	94	2005	2013
		1992	95	2004	2012
		1991	94	2003	2011
		1990	93	1998	2002
		1989	90	1997	2001
		1988	94	2000	2005

Supple, elegant and harmonious, this silky-fine port has a restrained but delightfully perfumed bouquet of brandied morello cherries, dark chocolate, cinnamon and cloves backed by notes of fresh spirit and floral aromas. It opens slowly, with intense flavours of dark cherries, plums, briar and spices lifted by warm, fresh spirit and a modest sweetness. Underpinned by smooth, fine tannins, it finishes with a delightful length of flavour, refreshing spirit and acidity.

Starvedog Lane

Ravenswood Lane, Hahndorf SA 5245. Tel: (08) 8388 1250. Fax: (08) 8388 7233.
Website: www.thelane.com.au Email: john@thelane.com.au

Region: **Adelaide Hills** Winemaker: **Genevieve Stols** Viticulturist: **Alex Sas** Chief Executive: **John Grant**

Starvedog Lane is a Hardy Wine Company brand based in the Adelaide Hills that delivers a thoroughly contemporary collection of cooler climate wines. The tight, citrusy and often quite mineral Chardonnay, which often punches well above its weight (especially in terms of price) consistently rates well in my tastings and is also something of a darling of the wine show circuit. The 2004 Shiraz Viognier is handsomely the finest yet.

CABERNET MERLOT (formerly Cabernet Sauvignon)

RATING **4**

Adelaide Hills $20–$29
Current vintage: 2005   90

Stylish and elegant, with pleasing brightly lit flavours of plums, blackberries and cherries over minty, meaty nuances of dark olives, briar and tea leaves. Partnered by smoky, almost gamey and cedary oak, it's smooth and supple, providing a long, fine and sumptuous palate of evenly ripened fruit.

2005	90	2010	2013+
2004	91	2012	2016
2003	83	2005	2008
2001	93	2009	2013+
2000	89	2008	2012
1999	87	2004	2007
1998	89	2010	2018

CHARDONNAY

RATING **3**

Adelaide Hills $20–$29
Current vintage: 2004   92

A fine and polished chardonnay with appealing reductive and toasty complexity beneath its juicy presence of citrus, melon and apple-like flavour. Floral, nutty, matchstick and wheatmeal-like influences underpin its citrusy bouquet. Its smooth, silky and creamy palate of melon, peach and apple reveals some buttery malolactic influences before finishing with tangy, citrusy acids and lingering sweet toasty oak.

2004	92	2006	2009+
2003	93	2005	2008+
2002	95	2004	2007+
2001	90	2003	2006+
2000	91	2002	2005+
1999	93	2001	2004+
1998	87	2000	2003

SAUVIGNON BLANC

RATING **3**

Adelaide Hills $12–$19
Current vintage: 2006   87

Lightly grassy, this generous, broad and slightly phenolic sauvignon blanc delivers clean, if slightly confectionary flavours of lychees and gooseberries.

2006	87	2006	2007
2005	94	2006	2007+
2004	93	2005	2006+
2003	93	2003	2004+
2002	95	2003	2004+
2001	91	2002	2003
1999	90	2000	2001
1998	90	2000	2003

SHIRAZ VIOGNIER (formerly Shiraz)

RATING **5**

Adelaide Hills $20–$29
Current vintage: 2004   94

Smooth and elegant, this perfumed young blend has a fresh and spicy bouquet of sweet, juicy black-berries, cassis and chocolate-like oak backed by suggestions of apricot, cloves and white pepper. Its silky, fine-grained palate presents a vibrant but thoroughly restrained expression of intense small berry fruit married to an assertive but measured expression of creamy chocolate/vanilla oak.

2004	94	2012	2016
2003	84	2005	2008
2002	88	2007	2010
2001	87	2006	2009
2000	80	2002	2005
1999	82	2001	2004+
1998	84	2003	2006
1997	87	2002	2005

Stefano Lubiana

60 Rowbottoms Road, Granton Tas 7030. Tel: (03) 6263 7457. Fax: (03) 6263 7430.
Website: www.slw.com.au Email: wine@slw.com.au

Region: **Southern Tasmania** Winemaker: **Steve Lubiana** Chief Executive: **Steve Lubiana**

Stefano Lubiana is a small and highly committed producer of cool-climate Tasmanian wine, and its efforts
are becoming more consistent from vintage to vintage. The Pinot Noir reveals layers of flavour and texture,
while the Riesling is tightly sculpted and refreshing, with a lingering minerality. The aromatic Primavera continues
its very impressive recent form, while Lubiana's sparkling wines are becoming some of Australia's finest.

CHARDONNAY

RATING 3

Southern Tasmania	$30–$49
Current vintage: 2004	**92**

Already significantly mature and complex, this floral,
funky and meaty chardonnay reveals a honeyed,
toasty and slightly mineral bouquet of honeysuckle,
melon and cinnamon over powerful suggestions
of butterscotch and cheesy, leesy undertones. Juicy,
round and generous, it's long and meaty, delivering a wild and savoury expression of evolved
chardonnay character held together by tight and
refreshing acidity.

2004	92	2006	2009+
2003	92	2005	2008
2002	85	2004	2007
2001	94	2006	2009
2000	93	2005	2008
1999	91	2004	2007
1998	91	2000	2003

PINOT GRIGIO

RATING 5

Tasmania	$20–$29
Current vintage: 2006	**86**

Rather broad and heavy-handed, with an estery,
spicy and almost spiky aroma of mango, melon
and lemon rind. Broad, generous and richly
fruited, its round and juicy palate of melon and
citrusy fruit is just a little spirity and warm,
lacking genuine shape and definition.

2006	86	2007	2008
2005	89	2006	2007
2004	89	2006	2007
2003	90	2005	2008
2002	83	2002	2003+
2001	87	2002	2003+

PINOT NOIR

RATING 3

Southern Tasmania	$30–$49
Current vintage: 2005	**93**

Backed by suggestions of undergrowth and
lightly smoky vanilla oak, this generously proportioned pinot has a bright and ethereal aroma
of maraschino cherries, redcurrants, cloves and
cinnamon. Smooth and sumptuous, bursting
with ripe cherry/berry fruit over meaty, smoky and
funky undertones, it's supported by a firmish
structure of drying tannin and finished by refreshing acidity.

2005	93	2010	2013+
2004	95	2009	2012+
2003	88	2005	2008
2002	87	2004	2007+
2001	92	2003	2006+
2000	87	2002	2005
1999	86	2001	2004
1998	88	2000	2003

PRIMAVERA PINOT NOIR

RATING 3

Southern Tasmania	$20–$29
Current vintage: 2006	**92**

Wild, heady and floral, with fresh, penetrative aromas
of dark cherries, plums and berries backed by spicy
vanilla/bubblegum oak. Its slightly minty palate
of juicy summer pudding-like berry fruit is deliciously penetrative and stylish. With more structure
and depth than previous vintages, it is supported
by firmish, fine-grained tannin.

2006	92	2008	2011+
2005	92	2007	2010+
2004	89	2005	2006+
2003	94	2005	2008+
2002	93	2007	2010
2001	89	2003	2006+

RATING  4

Tasmania $20–$29
Current vintage: 2006 89

Lean, taut and tightly focused, this fragrant and estery young riesling is a racy young cellar style with a spicy, lemon detergent-like aroma. Long and linear, its brightly flavoured palate of apple and citrusy fruit culminates in a sculpted, high acid finish.

2006	89	2011	2014+
2005	94	2010	2013+
2003	90	2008	2011
2002	77	2002	2003+
2001	93	2006	2009+

Stoney Vineyard

105 Tea Tree Road, Campania Tas 7026. Tel: (03) 6260 4174. Fax: (03) 6260 4390.
Website: www.domaine-a.com.au Email: althaus@domaine-a.com.au
Region: **Coal River Valley** Winemaker: **Peter Althaus** Viticulturist: **Peter Althaus** Chief Executive: **Peter Althaus**
Stoney Vineyard is the recently expanded Coal River Valley vineyard whose best fruit is carefully apportioned into the Domaine A label, with the Stoney Vineyard name used as a pretty solid and interesting second brand. The Sauvignon Blanc can be racy and vivacious, the Cabernet Sauvignon elegant and structured, and the Pinot Noir complex and textured. Like other Tasmanian vineyards, it tends to produce its best wine in warmer seasons.

PINOT NOIR

RATING 4

Coal River Valley $20–$29
Current vintage: 2004 89

Likely to become quite meaty and savoury with age, this fragrant and fine-grained pinot has a charmingly smooth palate supported by fine-grained, bony tannins. Scented with kernel-like aromas of red cherries, dark plums and marzipan over spicy nuances of cinnamon, it steadily builds on the palate, finishing long and dusty and leaving a lingering core of vibrant fruit.

2004	89	2006	2009+
2003	90	2005	2008
2001	90	2006	2009
1996	90	1998	2001+

SAUVIGNON BLANC

RATING 5

Coal River Valley $12–$19
Current vintage: 2005 89

A very herbaceous sauvignon blanc whose lightly sweaty aromas of gooseberries and melon reveal chalky undertones. Round and generous, with a tangy, slippery and full-flavoured palate of gooseberry and passionfruit flavour, it finishes very dry and mineral, with clean acids.

2005	89	2006	2007+
2003	90	2004	2005+
2002	89	2003	2004+
2001	87	2002	2003+
2000	87	2002	2005+
1999	86	1998	1999+
1998	93	1999	2000+

Stonier

2 Thompsons Lane, Merricks Vic 3916. Tel: (03) 5989 8300. Fax: (03) 5989 8709.
Website: www.stoniers.com.au Email: stoniers@stoniers.com.au
Region: **Mornington Peninsula** Winemaker: **Geraldine McFaul** Viticulturist: **Stuart Marshall**
Chief Executive: **Anthony Roberts**

Aided by several fine maturing vineyards, Geraldine McFaul has taken the Pinot Noirs of Stonier to a new level. She has steadily introduced elements of elegance, perfume and finesse, heading the Reserve wines and the individual vineyard KBS and Windmill pinots in a more ethereal and savoury direction.

CHARDONNAY

RATING 5

Mornington Peninsula	$20–$29
Current vintage: 2005	**86**

Pungent and smoky, with assertive aromas of butterscotch, melon and honeysuckle backed by cheesy undertones, this young chardonnay lacks the depth of fruit for its powerful presence of malolactic influences. Finishing a little dull and shallow in fruit, with some fine oak and refreshing acidity, it's just a little forward and simple.

2005	86	2006	2007
2004	90	2006	2009
2003	87	2003	2004
2002	82	2003	2004
2001	87	2003	2006
2000	89	2002	2005
1999	89	2001	2004
1998	88	1999	2000
1997	88	1998	2001

PINOT NOIR

RATING 5

Mornington Peninsula	$30–$49
Current vintage: 2006	**87**

A fine, forward and rather fragile young pinot whose sweet raspberry, cherry and candy floss-like fruit lacks genuine length and focus. Supported by fresh vanilla oak, it's sweet-fruited and forward, but thins out towards a slightly simple finish.

2006	87	2007	2008+
2005	83	2005	2006+
2004	87	2006	2009
2003	90	2004	2005+
2002	88	2003	2004+
2001	88	2002	2003+
2000	91	2002	2005
1999	89	2001	2004
1998	88	1999	2000
1997	88	1999	2002
1996	91	2001	2004
1995	87	1997	2000

RESERVE CHARDONNAY

RATING 3

Mornington Peninsula	$30–$49
Current vintage: 2005	**91**

Tight and focused, this alluringly elegant, brightly flavoured and supple chardonnay has a fresh bouquet of white peach, nectarine, sweet vanilla oak and undertones of cloves. Backed by suggestions of vanilla and cashew, its fleshy palate of concentrated grapefruit, pineapple and melon fruit is tied around a finish of fresh, citrusy acids.

2005	91	2007	2010+
2004	93	2009	2012
2003	93	2005	2008+
2002	93	2007	2010
2001	95	2006	2009
2000	95	2005	2008
1999	92	2001	2004
1998	95	2003	2006
1997	95	2002	2005
1996	92	1998	2001
1995	92	2003	2007
1994	93	1996	1999

RESERVE PINOT NOIR

RATING 3

Mornington Peninsula	$30–$49
Current vintage: 2005	**92**

Long and savoury, this slowly developing pinot has a lightly meaty, musky fragrance of ripe plum and cherries over slightly minty nuances of menthol, forest floor and capsicum. Finely crafted, its generous, luscious expression of slightly herbal berry, cherry and plum-like fruit is supported by sweet new oak and framed by smooth, polished tannin. It finishes with a hint of meatiness, lingering flavours of raspberries and cherries, and should acquire more length and richness of fruit.

2005	92	2007	2010+
2004	93	2009	2012
2003	94	2008	2011+
2001	84	2003	2006
2000	91	2002	2005
1999	93	2004	2007
1998	94	2003	2006
1997	95	2002	2005
1995	77	1997	2000
1994	93	1996	1999
1993	95	1998	2001
1992	93	1997	2000
1991	88	1993	1996

Stringy Brae

Sawmill Road, Sevenhill SA 5453. Tel: (08) 8843 4313. Fax: (08) 8843 4319.
Website: www.stringybrae.com.au Email: sales@stringybrae.com.au
Region: **Clare Valley** Winemaker: **Contract** Viticulturist: **Hannah Rantanen** Chief Executive: **Donald Willson**
Stringy Brae is a small Clare Valley maker whose Rieslings are slightly broader, more candied and fractionally sweeter than those typical of the region, while its reds are usually minty, robust and briary.

RIESLING

RATING 4

Clare Valley	$20–$29
Current vintage: 2006	89

Rather closed, with a toasty and honeyed bouquet but a generous, dry palate whose intense lime juice and lemon fruit overlies a pleasing mineral austerity, culminating in a tight, steely and well-defined finish of length and austerity.

2006	89	2011	2014
2005	91	2010	2013+
2004	90	2009	2012+
2003	89	2008	2011
2002	91	2007	2010+
2001	90	2009	2013
2000	87	2002	2005+

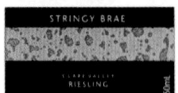

SHIRAZ

RATING 5

Clare Valley	$20–$29
Current vintage: 2004	88

Slightly raw and rustic, this firm and minty Clare shiraz delivers bright fruit flavours of mulberries, plums and blackberries backed by meaty, earthy, charcuterie-like complexity and cedar/vanilla oak. It's initially sweet-fruited and juicy, but becomes slightly metallic towards the finish. Give it time to develop further.

2004	88	2009	2012+
2002	89	2007	2010+
2001	88	2003	2006+
2000	87	2002	2005+
1999	86	2001	2004+

Suckfizzle

Lot 4 Gnaraway Road, Margaret River WA 6290. Tel: (08) 9757 6377. Fax: (08) 9757 6022.
Website: www.stellabella.com.au Email: wines@stellabella.com.au
Region: **Margaret River** Winemaker: **Janice McDonald** Viticulturist: **Travis Linaker** Chief Executive: **John Britton**
Suckfizzle is a brand associated with a significant planting near Augusta, in the cooler, southerly reaches of the Margaret River region. Its white blend of Bordeaux varieties counters its significant oak-derived creaminess with wonderful length and racy austerity, while its Cabernet Sauvignon is rather herbaceous.

SAUVIGNON BLANC SEMILLON

RATING 3

Margaret River	$30–$49
Current vintage: 2005	94

Vibrant and shapely, this long, powdery and tightly sculpted white blend has a dusty, herbal bouquet of lively gooseberry and passionfruit aromas backed by fresh toasty vanilla oak and herbal, nettle-like nuances. Punctuated by crisp acids, it's beautifully focused and elegant, finishing with lemony acids and chalky undertones.

2005	94	2007	2010+
2004	93	2006	2009
2003	94	2005	2008
2002	91	2004	2007
2001	89	2002	2003+
1998	93	2000	2003
1997	95	1999	2002

Summerfield

5967 Stawell-Avoca Road, Moonambel Vic 3478. Tel: (03) 5467 2264. Fax: (03) 5467 2380.
Website: www.summerfieldwines.com Email: info@summerfieldwines.com

Region: **Pyrenees** Winemakers: **Ian & Mark Summerfield** Viticulturist: **Ian Summerfield**
Chief Executive: **Ian Summerfield**

Summerfield is a small, mature and family-owned vineyard in the Pyrenees area whose popular red wines have taken a powerful forward stride with the 2004 and 2005 vintages. As a group, its wines reveal more polish, focus and freshness, and are certainly benefiting from newer and better oak than in previous years. In particular, the 2004 Reserve Shiraz, Summerfield's finest wine yet, convinces me that this vineyard has more to show.

RESERVE CABERNET SAUVIGNON (Cab. Shiraz in 2003) RATING 5

Pyrenees	$50–$99
Current vintage: 2005	**92**

Uncomplicated but deliciously generous, plush and smooth, this dark and luscious cabernet has an intense perfume of violets, cassis, blackberries and plums knit with fresh cedar/vanilla oak. Its luxuriant, finely textured and minty palate of vibrant dark fruits and creamy oak finishes just a fraction warm, but the wine should hold its alcohol well for the short to medium term.

2005	92	2010	2013+
2004	89	2009	2012
2003	87	2008	2011+
2002	86	2007	2010
2001	86	2003	2006
2000	89	2005	2008+
1999	86	2004	2007

RESERVE SHIRAZ RATING 4

Pyrenees	$50–$99
Current vintage: 2005	**90**

Sumptuous and layered, it's concentrated, youthful but presently rather disjointed. Backed by nuances of mint and eucalypt, its intense and slightly sour-edged flavours of cherries, plums and blackberries are matched with assertive creamy and cedary oak, revealing just a hint of currants. It's long and concentrated, underpinned by supple tannins and finishes slightly warm and spirity with a trace of saltiness. It just needs time.

2005	90	2010	2013+
2004	94	2012	2016
2003	89	2008	2011
2002	87	2004	2007+
2001	88	2003	2006
2000	88	2002	2005
1999	89	2004	2007

Tahbilk

254 O'Niels Road, Tahbilk Vic 3608. Tel: (03) 5794 2555. Fax: (03) 5794 2360.
Website: www.tahbilk.com.au Email: admin@tahbilk.com.au

Region: **Nagambie Lakes** Winemakers: **Alister Purbrick, Neil Larson, Alan George** Viticulturist: **Ian Hendy**
Chief Executive: **Alister Purbrick**

Tahbilk is an historic vineyard and winery on the banks of the Goulburn River in central Victoria. The winery is blessed with large old cellars replete with very large old cooperage, which Alister Purbrick feels is essential to the make-up and identity of Tahbilk red wine. The current 2002 Reserve Shiraz is a classic example of Tahbilk's idiosyncratic house style, and it's absolutely delicious. Another fine current release is the 2004 Cabernet Sauvignon, which is a little more forward and juicy than usual, but will also last the distance.

1860 VINES SHIRAZ (formerly Claret) RATING 4

Nagambie Lakes	$100–$199
Current vintage: 2002	**90**

A heady, earthy perfume of fresh spices, white pepper, fennel and cedar precedes a long, fine, smooth and supple palate that builds strength and firmness in the mouth. There's an ethereal aspect about its intense palate of small red berries, plums and dusty spices, and it finishes with a lingering core of red currant-like fruit. Finely balanced and very persistent, it's an old-fashioned style whose fruit is likely to fade as it ages, becoming quite complex and secondary fairly quickly.

2002	90	2014	2022
2001	90	2013	2021+
2000	86	2008	2012+
1999	91	2011	2019
1998	95	2010	2018+
1997	90	2009	2017+
1996	93	2008	2016+
1995	91	2007	2015
1994	90	2002	2006
1992	93	2012	2022
1991	90	2011	2021
1990	90	2010	2020
1989	82	2001	2011
1988	88	2000	2010
1987	92	2007	2017

CABERNET SAUVIGNON

RATING  **4**

Nagambie Lakes		**$20–$29**	
Current vintage: 2004		**91**	

Charming, juicy and approachable, this carefully structured, finely balanced and potentially long-term cabernet has a minty scent of violets, red berries, menthol and cassis backed by restrained mocha/vanilla oak. Its smooth, loose-knit palate of blackberry-like fruit has a powdery undercarriage with a firmness that creeps up on you.

2004	91	2016	2024+
2003	89	2015	2023
2002	91	2014	2022
2001	83	2003	2006+
2000	90	2008	2012+
1999	88	2007	2011
1998	86	2006	2010
1997	86	2005	2009
1996	83	2001	2004
1995	92	2015	2025
1994	90	2006	2014
1993	91	2005	2013
1992	93	2004	2012
1991	93	2011	2021
1990	93	2010	2020

MARSANNE

RATING **4**

Nagambie Lakes		**$12–19**	
Current vintage: 2006		**88**	

Packed with melon and stonefruit flavour, this generous, juicy and slightly confectionary young white is long, clean and evenly fruited, finishing clean, dry and savoury with refreshing lemony acids.

2006	88	2011	2014
2005	89	2010	2013
2004	92	2012	2016
2003	92	2011	2015
2002	91	2007	2010+
2001	87	2006	2009
2000	88	2005	2008
1999	90	2004	2007
1998	87	2003	2006+
1997	90	2005	2009
1996	93	2004	2008
1995	90	2007	2015
1994	92	2006	2014

RESERVE CABERNET SAUVIGNON

RATING **3**

TAHBILK

RESERVE
CABERNET SAUVIGNON

Nagambie Lakes		**$50–$99**	
Current vintage: 2002		**91**	

Earthy and slightly meaty, with deep aromas of cassis, blackberries and cedar/vanilla oak backed by suggestions of mint and menthol. Firm and fine-grained, it's long and sinewy, with intense, rather primary and minty flavours of blackberries and plums coated with a drying astringency. It's very complete, and has all the fruit and structure for the long journey.

2002	91	2014	2022+
2001	89	2013	2021
2000	93	2012	2020+
1998	93	2010	2018+
1997	93	2009	2017+
1996	90	2008	2016+
1994	89	2014	2024
1993	88	2005	2013
1992	91	2012	2022

RESERVE SHIRAZ

RATING **3**

TAHBILK

RESERVE
SHIRAZ

Nagambie Lakes		**$50–$99**	
Current vintage: 2002		**95**	

Here is a classic Tahbilk wine, that shows what the house style is all about. It's fragrant and earthy, scented with flowers and fresh plums, confidently backed by older cedar/vanilla oak. Framed by firmish, chalky tannins, its brooding, powerful palate of slightly minty dark berry/plum fruit culminates in lingering nuances of smoky, leathery and chocolate-like complexity.

2002	95	2022	2032
2001	92	2013	2021
2000	89	2012	2020
1999	92	2011	2019+
1998	95	2018	2028
1997	92	2009	2017
1996	90	2004	2008+
1994	90	2002	2006+

RIESLING

Nagambie Lakes	$12–$19
Current vintage: 2006	**88**

Lightly floral, this limey, bathpowdery and chalky young riesling presents slightly candied but vibrant riesling qualities, finishing clean and refreshing. It's tight and dry, but fractionally hollow.

2006	88	2011	2014
2005	87	2007	2010
2004	92	2009	2012+
2003	88	2005	2008
2001	83	2003	2006
2000	90	2005	2008
1999	87	2001	2004
1998	82	2003	2006+
1997	93	2005	2009
1996	92	2004	2008
1995	90	2003	2007
1994	91	2002	2006

SHIRAZ

Nagambie Lakes	$20–$29
Current vintage: 2004	**88**

A typical older-styled Tahbilk with a meaty, leathery expression of relatively simple, cooked and minty plum and berry flavours. With a firm, fine and dusty undercarriage, it's slightly hollow and dilute, finishing rather lean and dull. It should hang together for some time.

2004	88	2012	2016
2003	91	2015	2023+
2002	88	2014	2022
2001	88	2009	2013
2000	89	2008	2012+
1999	87	2004	2007
1998	87	2006	2010+
1997	87	2005	2009
1996	82	2001	2004
1995	89	2007	2015
1994	90	2014	2024
1993	86	1998	2001
1992	93	2004	2012
1991	92	2011	2021
1990	89	2002	2010

Tallarook

2 Delaney's Road, Warranwood Vic 3134. Tel: (03) 9876 7022. Fax: (03) 9876 7044.
Website: www.tallarook.com Email: info@tallarook.com
Region: **Upper Goulburn** Winemaker: **Trina Smith** Viticulturist: **Daniel Ebert** General Manager: **Anthony Woollams**
Tallarook makes interesting and complex Chardonnay and Marsanne, each of which is given full Burgundian treatment in the cellar. The best releases are those with the depth of fruit to handle the significant level of artefact they acquire along the way. The reds I have tasted are greenish, minty and medicinal.

CHARDONNAY

Upper Goulburn	$20–$29
Current vintage: 2004	**84**

Rich, juicy and heavily worked, but lacking the intensity and length of fruit to handle the amount of winemaker-derived complexity it has acquired. Very oaky and slightly varnishy, its buttery and toffee-like aromas of quince, cumquat, peaches and varnishy vanilla oak are backed by meaty, leesy undertones. Forward and unctuous, its fruit struggles for attention throughout its cloying and caramel-like palate.

2004	84	2006	2009
2002	88	2004	2007
2001	87	2003	2006
2000	93	2002	2005+
1999	87	2001	2004
1998	89	2000	2003

MARSANNE

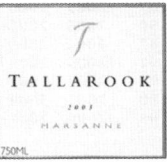

Upper Goulburn	$20–$29
Current vintage: 2004	**87**

A powerfully winemaker-influenced wine whose interesting complexity somewhat overshadows its varietal identity. Meaty, mineral and lanolin-like aromas of lime juice, musky spices and match-stick/vanilla oak precede a richly textured and reductive palate. Long and smooth, it dries out a little quickly, and was perhaps bottled with too high a level of reduction for a screwcap seal.

2004	87	2006	2009
2003	88	2005	2008
2002	88	2004	2007
2001	91	2003	2006+
2000	82	2002	2005

Taltarni

Taltarni Road, Moonambel Vic 3478. Tel: (03) 5459 7900. Fax: (03) 5467 2306.
Website: www.taltarni.com.au Email: info@taltarni.com.au

Region: **Pyrenees** Winemakers: **Leigh Clarnette, Loïc Le Calvez, Louella McPhan**
Viticulturist: **Kym Ludvigsen** Chief Executive: **Adam Torpy**

Taltarni's re-mergence as a maker of fine, long-living red wines is gathering momentum. This edition welcomes its Cephas blend of shiraz and cabernet sauvignon, a profoundly structured and brooding long-term prospect if ever there was one. The 2004 Cabernet Sauvignon is a more classically styled wine, the kind that rarely gets noticed in wine shows, but which will mature gracefully for many years.

BRUT

RATING 4

Victoria, Tasmania	$20–$29
Current vintage: 2005	**90**

Fresh, long, fine and creamy, with a lively, nutty bouquet of peach, melon and citrus fruit. Long and lightly toasty, its smooth and elegant palate has a long, persistent core of lively citrus and melon flavour. It's very fruit-driven, with a fine, creamy bead. While there's not much yeast-derived complexity, it's clean, tangy and refreshing.

2005	90	2007	2010
2004	90	2006	2009
2003	92	2005	2008
2002	88	2004	2007
2001	87	2003	2006
2000	88	2003	2006
1999	89	2001	2004+

CABERNET SAUVIGNON

RATING 3

Pyrenees	$30–$49
Current vintage: 2004	**93**

A complex, classically structured and stylish cabernet whose deep, layered flavours of blackberries, cassis and dark plums are tightly knit with sweet cedar/vanilla oak and firm, powdery tannins. With a smoky, violet-like perfume and dark chocolate undertones, it's long, smooth and charming, finishing with lingering fruit and a savoury aspect.

2004	93	2016	2024
2002	88	2010	2014
2001	93	2013	2021
2000	84	2008	2012
1998	94	2006	2010+
1997	86	2002	2005+
1996	88	2004	2008
1995	89	2003	2007
1994	93	2006	2014+
1993	91	2005	2013
1992	93	2004	2012+
1991	91	2011	2021
1990	93	2002	2010+
1989	87	1997	2001
1988	94	2000	2008
1987	89	1999	2007
1986	89	1998	2006

CEPHAS SHIRAZ CABERNET

RATING 4

Pyrenees	$30–$49
Current vintage: 2002	**93**

Powerful, firm and chalky, it needs extended cellaring to look its best. Intense, almost jujube-like raspberry, cassis, plum and blackberry fruit is backed by assertive, but tightly knit new oak, with cedar, chocolate and vanilla characters. Its powerful, youthful and rather primary palate shows balance and integration, and despite its outsized structure, some elegance and finesse.

2002	93	2022	2032
2001	89	2013	2021
2000	91	2008	2012

SAUVIGNON BLANC

RATING 4

Victoria, Tasmania	$12–$19
Current vintage: 2006	**88**

Fragrant, slightly herbal and powdery, with fresh, forward flavours of gooseberries, melon and lime juice, it's moderately long and tangy, finishing with a pleasing suggestion of wet slate. Not a bad effort, but could use more brightness.

2006	88	2007	2008
2005	87	2005	2006
2004	90	2005	2006+
2003	87	2004	2005
2002	91	2003	2004
2001	90	2001	2002
2000	90	2001	2002
1999	93	2000	2001+

SHIRAZ (formerly French Syrah)

RATING 3

Pyrenees	$30–$49
Current vintage: 2003	89

Likely to develop charming rustic and leathery complexity, this powerful, dark and meaty shiraz has a sweetly oaked and gamey bouquet of plums, blackberries and currants backed by vanilla, cloves and white pepper. Its rich, slightly baked palate of ripe fruit and aggressive tannin reveals a hint of red chilli, and finishes with a drying astringency.

2003	89	2017	2023
2002	91	2010	2014+
2001	90	2009	2013
2000	93	2008	2012+
1999	93	2007	2011
1998	95	2006	2010
1997	95	2005	2009+
1996	95	2004	2008
1995	87	2000	2003
1994	92	1999	2002
1993	94	2001	2005
1992	94	2004	2012
1991	93	2003	2011
1990	89	1998	2002+

THREE MONKS CABERNET MERLOT

RATING 4

Victoria	$12–$19
Current vintage: 2005	89

Charmingly intense and almost jujube-like, with deep, minty flavours of cassis, blackberries and dark plums framed by genuinely firm and chalky astringency. It's backed by suggestions of cedar, dark chocolate and is very much a more serious prospect than its price might suggest.

2005	89	2013	2017
2004	90	2012	2016
2003	90	2011	2015
2002	88	2007	2010+
2001	89	2006	2009
2000	91	2005	2008
1999	82	2001	2004
1998	84	2000	2003
1997	82	2002	2005

TarraWarra Estate

Healesville Road, Yarra Glen Vic 3775. Tel: (03) 5962 3311. Fax: (03) 5962 3887.
Website: www.tarrawarra.com.au Email: enq@tarrawarra.com.au
Region: **Yarra Valley** Winemaker: **Clare Halloran** Viticulturist: **Stuart Sissins** General Manager: **Simon Napthine**
This dedicated and ambitious small winery operation in the Yarra Valley is owned by the Besen family, who set it up in the early 1980s with the help of David Wollan, today one of the world's foremost wine technologists. The richness, complexity and elegance of the 2005 Chardonnay is totally faithful to Wollan's original ambitions for the style, as was the similarly proportioned 2004 vintage.

PINOT NOIR

RATING 5

Yarra Valley	$50–$99
Current vintage: 2004	89

A pretty, sappy and autumnal pinot whose leafy aromas of red cherries, raspberries, plums and forest floor reveal gamey undertones. Medium to full in weight, it's forward and juicy, with a good length of vibrant fruit framed by greenish tannins. Already showing some development, and likely to age quickly.

2004	89	2006	2009
2003	93	2008	2011
2002	89	2004	2007
2001	89	2003	2006+
2000	83	2002	2005
1999	88	2001	2004
1998	95	2006	2010
1997	90	2002	2005
1996	95	2001	2004+

RESERVE CHARDONNAY

RATING 2

Yarra Valley	$30–$49
Current vintage: 2005	95

Big, beautiful and sumptuous; here is a wine that shows we weren't all wrong about the attractions of chardonnay at its more statuesque. Powerful and brooding, its aromas of melon, grapefruit and white peach reveal nutty, funky undertones of smoked bacon, cumquat and quince, with a lifted floral aspect. Smooth and creamy, its succulent expression of plush, vibrant fruit effortlessly glides down the palate, finishing long and savoury, with lingering fruit and spice

2005	95	2010	2013
2004	96	2012	2016
2003	94	2008	2011
2002	94	2007	2010
2001	92	2005	2008
2000	90	2002	2005
1999	90	2004	2007
1998	94	2006	2010
1997	95	2005	2009
1996	91	2001	2004
1995	91	2000	2003+

Tatachilla

151 Main Road, McLaren Vale SA 5171. Tel: (08) 8323 8656. Fax: (08) 8323 9096.
Website: www.tatachillawines.com.au Email: enquiries@tatachillawines.com.au
Region: **McLaren Vale** Winemaker: **Fanchon Ferrandi** Chief Executive: **Anthony Roberts**

Tatachilla has been a successful Lion Nathan brand, but there are indications that it is experiencing difficulty selling its wine. There has not been a huge and obvious quality difference between its more expensive wines and those considerably cheaper. While the older vintages of expensive labels are now showing signs of tiredness, the more youthful cheaper labels, like the 2004 McLaren Vale Shiraz, are simply bursting with fruit and vitality.

McLAREN VALE CABERNET SAUVIGNON
RATING 5

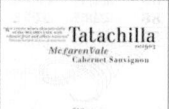

McLaren Vale	$20–$29
Current vintage: 2004	89

An elegant and generously flavoured cabernet with a floral, cassis-like aroma backed by blackberries, plums, dark olives and cedar/vanilla oak. Overlying dusty herbal nuances, its fine, supple palate of juicy, dark plum and berry fruit is neatly married with smooth cedary oak. There's a suggestion of under and over-ripeness, and the wine just lacks the follow-through for a higher rating.

2004	89	2009	2012+
2003	87	2005	2008+
2002	90	2007	2010
2001	87	2003	2006
2000	89	2002	2005+
1999	82	2001	2004
1998	91	2003	2006+
1997	89	1999	2002
1996	87	2001	2004
1995	87	2000	2003
1994	82	1996	1999

McLAREN VALE SHIRAZ
RATING 5

McLaren Vale	$20–$29
Current vintage: 2004	90

A delicious young shiraz whose spicy, peppery fragrance of blackberries, cassis and dark plums overlies sweet coconut ice-like oak and scents of violets. Sumptuous, smooth and silky, its long and lively palate is packed with juicy berry and plum flavours. Framed by smooth, creamy tannin and backed by rather smart and lightly smoky oak, it finishes with length and brightness of fruit, and a refreshing acidity. Terrific value.

2004	90	2006	2009+
2002	89	2007	2010+
2001	88	2003	2006
2000	81	2002	2005
1999	82	2001	2004
1998	90	2006	2010
1997	89	2002	2005
1996	90	2004	2008

Taylors

Taylors Road, Auburn SA 5451. Tel: (08) 8849 1100. Fax: (08) 8849 1199.
Website: www.taylorswines.com.au Email: cdoor@taylorswines.com.au
Region: **Clare Valley** Winemakers: **Adam Eggins, Helen McCarthy** Viticulturists: **Ken Noack, Colin Hinze**
Chief Executive: **Mitchell Taylor**

Having enjoyed some very good recent seasons, this comparatively large Clare Valley maker has stepped back a peg with its current release wines. The St Andrews label is the company's most expensive, but its wines appear to be sold once they're tired and flat. Other than its delicious 2005 Riesling, the multi-regional wines under the Jaraman label are similarly disappointing.

CABERNET SAUVIGNON
RATING 5

Clare Valley	$12–$19
Current vintage: 2005	82

Minty, meaty, dark and smoky, this jammy, pruney and rather cooked cabernet has plenty of depth and richness, but insufficient life and brightness. It finishes short and dull, with meaty suggestions of plums and currants.

2005	82	2007	2010
2004	89	2009	2012+
2003	88	2008	2011+
2002	88	2007	2010
2001	90	2009	2013
2000	88	2008	2012
1999	93	2004	2007+
1998	90	2003	2006
1997	81	1999	2002
1996	82	1998	2001
1995	86	1997	2000
1994	87	1999	2002
1993	81	2001	2005
1992	83	2000	2004

JARAMAN RIESLING

Clare Valley, Eden Valley	$20–$29
Current vintage: 2005	**94**

2005	94	2013	2017
2004	88	2006	2009
2992	82	2004	2007

Supple, smooth and silky, this powdery and elegant riesling has a fresh perfume of lime, lemon juice and musky rose petal. Its long and vibrant palate reveals a pleasingly juicy core of flavour, finishing with clean, refreshing acidity.

RIESLING

Clare Valley	$12–$19
Current vintage: 2006	**88**

2006	88	2011	2014
2005	88	2005	2013
2004	89	2006	2009
2003	88	2005	2008
2002	83	2003	2004
2001	93	2006	2009
2000	92	2005	2008
1999	86	2001	2004
1998	85	2000	2003
1997	85	1999	2002
1996	92	2004	2008
1994	93	2002	2006
1993	89	1995	1998

Floral, lightly musky aromas of lime juice, cinnamon and tea leaves precede a juicy, forward and slightly candied expression of tangy and well-focused fruit and citrusy acids. It's long, honest, persistent and well punctuated.

SHIRAZ

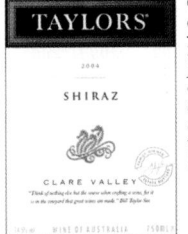

Clare Valley	$12–$19
Current vintage: 2005	**86**

2005	86	2007	2010
2004	88	2006	2009+
2003	88	2005	2008
2002	89	2004	2007
2001	91	2003	2006+
2000	89	2002	2005+
1999	88	2001	2004
1998	90	2003	2006
1997	88	2002	2005
1996	87	2001	2004
1995	88	2000	2003
1994	87	1996	1999
1993	87	1998	2001

Slightly cooked and dehydrated, with meaty, jammy flavours of blackberries, dark plums, currants and berries made more sumptuous, sweet and mouthfilling courtesy of some generously applied sweet and smoky American oak. It finishes slightly syrupy and treacle-like, with lingering suggestions of menthol and licorice.

ST ANDREWS CABERNET SAUVIGNON

Clare Valley	$50–$99
Current vintage: 2002	**90**

2002	90	2004	2007
2000	91	2012	2020
1999	90	2007	2011
1998	87	2003	2006
1997	84	2002	2005

An old-fashioned Australian red whose deep aromas of dark, jammy plums, olives and currants reveal minty undertones and some herbal, under-ripe qualities. Now tiring and losing freshness, its palate retains some forward plum and berry fruit, but is clearly drying out, exposing some strong, firm tannins beneath.

ST ANDREWS RIESLING

Clare Valley	$30–$49
Current vintage: 2002	**82**

2002	82	2007	2010
2001	90	2009	2013
2000	92	2008	2012
1998	91	2003	2006
1996	92	2004	2008

Varnishy, oxidised and slightly volatile, this toasty, evolved and floral expression of lemon rind and buttery fruit is smooth and juicy, but finishes with a toasty, volatile rawness.

ST ANDREWS SHIRAZ

RATING 5

Clare Valley	$50–$99
Current vintage: 2002	**88**

Sumptuous and smoky, this extracted and over-cooked shiraz supports its meaty, currant-like fruit with ground coffee and chocolate oak influences. It's slightly varnishy, with some drying out from the back of the palate. As it breathes in the glass it does reveal more of a presence of vibrant and lively fruit, but it remains rather too heavy and oaky.

2002	88	2007	2010+
2001	88	2009	2013
2000	87	2005	2008+
1999	93	2007	2011
1998	90	2003	2006+
1997	89	2002	2005

The Lane Vineyard

Ravenswood Lane, Hahndorf SA 5245. Tel: (08) 8388 1250. Fax: (08) 8388 7233.
Website: www.thelane.com.au Email: cellar@thelane.com.au

Region: **Adelaide Hills** Viticulturist: **John Edwards** Chief Executive: **John Edwards**

This brand has changed its name from Ravenswood Lane to The Lane. It should perhaps be given more credit than it receives for its consistently classy and racy Sauvignon Blanc, of which the 2005 vintage is typically tight and mineral. The company releases a very herbal and dark-fruited 19th Meeting Cabernet Sauvignon.

BEGINNING CHARDONNAY

RATING 4

Adelaide Hills	$30–$49
Current vintage: 2004	**87**

A supple and citrusy chardonnay with a delicate lemony, grapefruit-like aroma of tropical fruit and nutty/vanilla oak and a smooth, restrained palate that just lacks genuine length and intensity. It's soft and creamy, with stonefruit and citrus flavours before a savoury finish.

2004	87	2006	2009+
2002	84	2004	2007
2001	90	2006	2009
2000	93	2002	2005
1999	88	2000	2001
1998	82	1999	2000

GATHERING SAUVIGNON SEMILLON

RATING 3

Adelaide Hills	$30–$49
Current vintage: 2005	**93**

A complex, flavoursome and tightly crafted but oak-enhanced blend of some class. Its pungent aromas of gooseberries, passionfruit and cassis overlie floral, mineral and lightly herbal complexity, with restrained undertones of vanilla oak. There's also a hint of oak beneath its soft and generously flavoured palate, whose vibrant fruit and mineral, baby powder-like complexity finishes with excellent length and refreshing acidity.

2005	93	2007	2010+
2002	93	2003	2004+
2001	94	2003	2006
2000	75	2000	2001

REUNION SHIRAZ

RATING 5

Adelaide Hills	$30–$49
Current vintage: 2003	**86**

Tightly crafted but cooked and meaty, this smooth and fine-grained shiraz just lacks the fruit brightness and intensity to counter its oak and extract. Pungent mocha and dark chocolate-like aromas of blackberries, currants, plums and raisins with undertones of pepper and musk precede a moderately rich palate whose currant and raisin-like fruit are framed by fine-grained but drying tannins.

2003	86	2008	2011
2001	90	2006	2009+
2000	80	2002	2005
1999	87	2007	2011
1998	86	2000	2003+
1997	84	1999	2002
1996	88	1998	2001

Thompson Estate

Lot 10 Harmans Road South, Willyabrup WA 6280. Tel: (08) 9755 6406. Fax: (08) 9386 1708.
Website: www.thompsonestate.com.au Email: peterlthompson@bigpond.com

Region: **Margaret River** Winemakers: **Michael Peterkin, Mark Messenger, Mark Lane & Harold Osborne**
Viticulturist: **Ian Bell** Chief Executive: **Peter Thompson**

Thompson Estate is a very different wine business whose owner, Peter Thompson, has been able to persuade some of the best winemakers around to assist with the making of their own speciality varieties. The Chardonnay, is made by Pierro's Michael Peterkin. The SSB blend is a typically grassy, racy and tropical Margaret River style.

CHARDONNAY

RATING 3

Margaret River	$30–$49
Current vintage: 2005	**91**

Smoky, lightly mineral aromas of grapefruit, lime and tangerine overlie buttery, creamy oak and hints of tropical fruit. Tangy and forward, its taut, lean and finely sculpted palate of pineapple, grapefruit, lemon and peach overlies a drying and slightly powdery texture of fine, mineral phenolics. Long, refreshing and finely sculpted.

2005	91	2007	2010+
2004	94	2006	2009+
2003	89	2005	2008
2002	87	2004	2007
2001	93	2003	2006

SSB SEMILLON SAUVIGNON BLANC

RATING 4

Margaret River	$20–$29
Current vintage: 2006	**90**

Zesty and herbal, with a lightly grassy and lemony expression of tropical and passionfruit qualities backed by mineral undertones, this generous, flavoursome and finely crafted blend finishes tight and focused. With plenty of depth of generous, tangy fruit, it's crisp, clean and delicious.

2006	90	2007	2008+
2005	90	2007	2010
2004	88	2006	2009

Thorn-Clarke

PO Box 402, Angaston SA 5353. Tel: (08) 8564 3036. Fax: (08) 8564 3255.
Website: www.thornclarkewines.com.au Email: thornclarke@thornclarke.com.au

Region: **Barossa Valley** Winemaker: **Derek Fitzgerald** Viticulturist: **Peter Wild**
Chief Executives: **David and Cheryl Clarke**

Thorn-Clarke is an emerging family-operated Barossa maker whose vineyards are spread from the northern Barossa (St Kitts and Truro), the Barossa floor (Kabininge) to Mt Crawford and Milton Park in the Eden Valley. It has established three tiers of labels, starting with the lively and early-drinking Sandpiper range of Shiraz, Cabernet Sauvignon and 'The Blend', plus three Eden Valley white wines. The principal range of high-quality wines is given the Shotfire Ridge label, while the company's flagship is its William Randell Shiraz.

SHOTFIRE RIDGE QUARTAGE (Cabernet Blend)

RATING 4

Barossa Valley	$20–$29
Current vintage: 2004	**90**

Fine and harmonious, with plenty of flavour, but elegance and refinement. Its slightly meaty aroma of vibrant dark berry, plum and black olive-like fruit is backed by dark chocolate/mocha oak, cloves, cinnamon and faint undertones of marzipan. Sumptuously flavoured yet smooth and silky, its deeply ripened dark berry and plum flavours reveal hints of treacle and a slightly herbal aspect. Framed by fine-grained tannins, it finishes with a touch of salty minerality.

2004	90	2009	2012+
2003	82	2005	2008
2002	91	2010	2014

WILLIAM RANDELL SHIRAZ

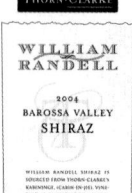

Barossa Valley	$50–$99
Current vintage: 2004	**95**

Smooth, sumptuous and genuinely elegant, this finely crafted shiraz is effortlessly balanced and stable. There's a minty note behind its perfume of fresh red and black fruits, white pepper and sweet cedar/vanilla/coconut oak. Long, supple and very refined, it delivers pristine, measured and slightly minty cassis/plum-like fruit backed by nuances of dark olives and licorice. Finishing with a pleasing meatiness, it's supported by a firm spine of slightly gritty tannin that should soften out.

2004	95	2012	2016
2002	90	2007	2010+
2001	84	2003	2006

Tim Adams

Warenda Road, Clare SA 5453. Tel: (08) 8842 2429. Fax: (08) 8842 3550.
Website: **www.timadamswines.com.au** Email: sales@timadamswines.com.au
Region: **Clare Valley** Winemaker: **Tim Adams** Viticulturist: **Mick Plumridge**
Chief Executives: **Tim Adams, Pam Goldsack**

One might argue right now that Tim Adams does indeed possess an oenological equivalent of the Midas Touch. Not only does he choose to create a Reserve label for his reputed Riesling, but he does it in a difficult year (2006) and then releases a superlative wine (95/100, drink 2014–2018+) out of it. Not to rest on his laurels, he gets excited by his first crop of Tempranillo and releases a Reserve wine out of it as well. The 2005 vintage (94/100, drink 2010–2013+) is terrific, one of this country's best. And yes, the 'standard' wines look good too.

CABERNET

Clare Valley	$20–$29
Current vintage: 2004	**89**

Finely astringent and drying, this moderately rich but uncomplicated cabernet presents sweet flavours of blackberries, dark plums and vanilla oak with slightly vegetal undertones of dried herbs. It has a supple, fine-grained presence and should develop quite well.

2004	89	2016	2024
2003	89	2008	2011+
2002	94	2010	2014+
2001	93	2013	2021
2000	88	2005	2008
1999	87	2004	2007+
1998	90	2010	2018
1997	89	2002	2005
1996	89	2004	2008
1995	89	2003	2007
1994	88	2002	2006
1993	90	2001	2005
1992	92	2000	2004
1991	90	2003	2011

PINOT GRIS

Clare Valley	$20–$29
Current vintage: 2007	**88**

Scented with lemon blossom, apple and pear, this unctuous, round and juicy white delivers plenty of tangy and slightly confectionary fruit. It lacks a little definition at the finish, which is perhaps a fraction sweet.

2007	88	2007	2008+
2006	91	2007	2008+
2005	89	2006	2007+
2004	89	2004	2005+

RIESLING

RATING 2

Clare Valley $20–$29
Current vintage: 2006   94

A first-rate wine from this vintage. Its intense, tangy aromas of lime juice and lemon sherbet reveal suggestions of mineral and a fractionally candied fruit aspect. Long, fine and austere, its shapely palate delivers fine length and persistence over a fine-grained powdery phenolic undercarriage. It finishes with crunchy acids.

2006	94	2011	2014+
2005	95	2013	2017
2004	92	2009	2012
2003	95	2011	2015
2002	96	2010	2014+
2001	90	2006	2009
2000	93	2008	2012
1999	93	2007	2011
1998	92	2006	2010
1997	93	2005	2009
1996	91	2004	2008
1995	84	1997	2000
1994	93	2002	2006

SEMILLON

RATING 3

Clare Valley $20–$29
Current vintage: 2006   91

A very good, vibrant and lightly herbal semillon whose lively flavours of pear, melon and apple are tightly knit with toasty vanilla oak and refreshing acidity. It's long, smooth and fleshy, with a pleasing juiciness before a crisp and vibrant finish.

2006	91	2011	2014
2005	93	2010	2013
2004	92	2009	2012
2003	93	2005	2008
2002	94	2007	2010
2001	86	2003	2006
2000	88	2002	2005
1999	90	2004	2007
1998	88	2003	2006
1997	94	2002	2005+
1996	92	2004	2008
1995	84	1997	2000
1994	94	2006	2014

SHIRAZ

RATING 3

Clare Valley $20–$29
Current vintage: 2005   93

While there's a shade of currant-like flavour about this wine, which simply reflects the heat of the vintage, this is a finely crafted and effortlessly balanced shiraz that delivers genuine regional character and identity. There's a hint of pepper and a spicy suggestion of clove and cinnamon beneath its vibrant aromas of redcurrants, raspberries and cassis, backed by lightly toasty vanilla oak. Long and lingering, firm and smooth, its palate of pristine blueberry and cassis-like flavour reveals undertones of meaty and slightly menthol/mint influences. Backed by polished oak, it finishes with lingering nuances of licorice and cloves.

2005	93	2010	2013+
2004	91	2012	2016
2003	90	2008	2011
2002	94	2010	2014+
2001	94	2009	2013
2000	91	2002	2005+
1999	91	2007	2011
1998	93	2003	2006+
1997	92	2002	2005
1996	86	2001	2004
1995	91	2003	2007
1994	92	1999	2002
1993	90	1995	1998
1992	92	2000	2004

THE ABERFELDY

RATING 2

Clare Valley $50–$99
Current vintage: 2004   95

Deeply ripened and luscious, this spicy and powerfully concentrated shiraz reveals a heady perfume of jujube-like blackberries, dark plums and cassis backed by clove, cinnamon, white pepper and assertive dark chocolate/vanilla oak. Its luscious palate of searingly intense dark berry fruit and polished, creamy vanilla oak is framed by firm but smooth tannins, finishing long and briary, with suggestions of mint and mineral.

2004	95	2016	2024
2003	95	2015	2023+
2002	97	2014	2022
2001	95	2013	2021
2000	92	2008	2012+
1999	95	2007	2011+
1998	97	2010	2018+
1997	91	2005	2009+
1996	94	2008	2016
1995	90	2007	2015
1994	95	2006	2014+
1993	87	1998	2001+
1992	90	2004	2012
1991	94	2003	2011+
1990	91	2002	2010
1988	90	2000	2008

THE FERGUS (Grenache blended with cabernet varieties) RATING 3

Clare Valley	$20–$29
Current vintage: 2005	**86**

An honest, grenache-driven red whose jammy, meaty and minty flavours of plums, prunes, blueberries and currants reveal undertones of cloves, nutmeg and menthol. Smooth and spicy, it lacks great length, finishing warm and savoury, with a slight rawness and a lingering suggestion of choc-mint.

2005	86	2007	2010+
2004	91	2009	2012
2003	92	2008	2011
2002	93	2004	2007+
2001	85	2003	2006
2000	87	2002	2005+
1999	90	2004	2007
1998	93	2003	2006+
1997	92	2002	2005
1996	91	2001	2004
1995	93	2000	2003
1994	92	2002	2006
1993	93	1998	2001

Tin Cows

Healesville Road, Yarra Glen Vic 3775. Tel: (03) 5962 3311. Fax: (03) 5962 3887.
Website: www.tincows.com.au Email: enq@tincows.com.au
Region: **Yarra Valley** Winemaker: **Clare Halloran** Viticulturist: **Stuart Sissins** General Manager: **Simon Napthine**
Tim Cows is TarraWarra's second label, which once was known rather ingloriously as Tunnel Hill. Its juicy and early-drinking Chardonnay remains its best wine, while its Pinot Noir made a significant improvement in 2005.

CHARDONNAY RATING 5

2005 Tin Cows
chardonnay
Yarra Valley 750ML

Yarra Valley	$12–$19
Current vintage: 2005	**87**

A tangy, citrusy young chardonnay for the shorter term. Its estery, spicy aromas of pineapple, grapefruit and melon overlie creamy, nutty nuances, with suggestions of butter and vanilla. Ripe and juicy, its spicy and slightly herbal expression of peach, melon and grapefruit flavour is backed by assertive and slightly varnishy oak. It should flesh out.

2005	87	2006	2007+
2003	88	2004	2005+
2002	86	2004	2007
2001	87	2003	2006
2000	83	2001	2002

Toolangi

?, Dixon's Creek Vic 3775. Tel: (03) 9822 9488. Fax: (03) 9804 3365.
Website: www.toolangi.com Email: toolangivineyards@bigpond.com
Region: **Yarra Valley** Winemakers: **Tom Carson, Rick Kinzbrunner, Matt Harrop**
Chief Executives: **Garry and Julie Hounsell**
Toolangi is an ambitious project established by Garry Hounsell, a Melbourne-based businessman. He chose the Yarra Valley as his base, but contracts a number of leading winemakers in different regions to fashion the Toolangi wines. The Estate Chardonnay, made by Tom Carson at Yering Station, is typically seamless and savoury, while the more adventurous and overt Reserve Chardonnay is crafted by Rick Kinzbrunner at Giaconda.

ESTATE CHARDONNAY RATING 3

Yarra Valley	$30–$49
Current vintage: 2005	**93**

An elegant, polished and measured chardonnay whose delicate citrusy fragrance of melon, grapefruit and fresh vanilla and nutty oak reveals faint smoky, bacony undertones. Finely crafted and neatly balanced, it's fine and measured, delivering a lingering and lightly creamy expression of limey, cumquat-like flavour and slightly dusty, nutty oak that culminates in a fresh, lemony finish.

2005	93	2007	2010+
2004	95	2009	2012
2003	90	2005	2008+
2002	88	2004	2007

RESERVE CHARDONNAY

RATING **3**

Yarra Valley $50–$99
Current vintage: 2005 92

Quite a developed colour, this chewy and sumptuously textured chardonnay sports a heavily worked, slightly cooked and grainy perfume of quince, grapefruit, sweet oak and honeysuckle. It's round and generous, with deep citrus and melon skin-like flavour almost over-awed by the extent of smoky, creamy and matchstick-like winemaking artefact. It finishes with good, if not exceptional length, but retains plenty of freshness.

2005	92	2007	2010+
2004	92	2009	2012
2003	93	2008	2011+
2002	88	2004	2007+
2001	91	2006	2009

Torbreck

Roennfeldt Road, Marananga SA 5356. Tel: (08) 8562 4155. Fax: (08) 8562 4195.
Website: www.torbreck.com Email: dave@torbreck.com
Region: **Barossa Valley** Winemakers: **David Powell, Craig Isbel** Viticulturist: **Michael Wilson**
Chief Executive: **David Powell**

While I greatly respect the innovative and energetic wines of Torbreck, I am a little critical that several — including the latest edition of RunRig — are lacking the brightness and flavour ripeness of their earlier vintages. I love the wild, smoky aspects of these wines, but would prefer to see more of them — like the 2005 Descendant (from a hotter and much more difficult vintage that the 2004 RunRig) — deliver brightness, poise and harmony.

CUVÉE JUVENILES (Grenache Mataro Shiraz)

RATING **5**

Barossa Valley $20–$29
Current vintage: 2006 87

Typically meaty, briary, with a brambly, licorice-like expression of cassis, raspberry and cranberry-like fruit, this smooth, grenache-driven blend has plenty of charcuterie-like complexity, but lacks genuine palate length and substance, finishing a little dilute.

2006	87	2007	2008+
2005	87	2006	2007
2004	89	2005	2006+
2003	89	2004	2005+
2002	90	2003	2004
2001	89	2001	2002
2000	90	2001	2002
1999	90	2001	2004+

DESCENDANT (Shiraz Viognier)

RATING **2**

Barossa Valley $100–$199
Current vintage: 2005 95

An exceptionally balanced wine from this hot vintage, with a briary, spicy fragrance of raspberries, cherries and blackberries backed by nuances of blueberries and redcurrants, fresh cedar/vanilla oak, white pepper, cloves and aniseed. Full to medium weight, its smooth, polished palate of vibrant, lingering berry fruits, bacony, charcuterie-like undertones and licorice overlies a fine spine of powdery tannin. Excellent poise and harmony.

2005	95	2017	2025
2004	95	2012	2016+
2003	93	2011	2015
2002	96	2010	2014+
2001	94	2006	2009
2000	91	2002	2005
1999	95	2004	2007+
1998	92	2003	2006+

RUNRIG (Shiraz Viognier)

RATING **2**

Barossa Valley $200+
Current vintage: 2004 88

Rather a cooked and herbal expression of this wine that fails to meet the expectations of this stellar Barossa vintage. Heady and briary, its spicy aromas of dark plums, licorice, cassis and violets are assertively backed by smoked meats, raisins and almost herbaceous undertones. Forward and sumptuous, it's richly concentrated with baked Christmas cake-like flavours, but becomes rather thin and hollow by mid-palate, lacking drive and direction. Framed and finished by firm, drying tannins, it's given some sweetness by dark chocolate/vanilla oak.

2004	88	2009	2012
2003	93	2008	2011+
2002	92	2007	2010
2001	94	2009	2013
1999	96	2007	2011
1998	97	2010	2018+
1997	93	2005	2009+
1996	95	2008	2016+

THE FACTOR (Shiraz)

Barossa Valley	$100–$199
Current vintage: 2004	89

A heady, spicy and meaty bouquet of pungent viognier-like aromatics reveals dark, licorice and cassis-like undertones. Sumptuous and juicy, it's warm, spirity and very spicy — very mouthfilling and opulent but slightly overcooked and just lacking a little tightness, shape and focus. Its impressively concentrated but slightly raisined expression of plums, prunes and cassis is backed by suggestions of cloves, licorice and nutmeg.

2004	89	2009	2012
2003	90	2008	2011+
2002	96	2010	2014+
2001	91	2003	2006
2000	95	2005	2008+
1999	97	2007	2011+
1998	93	2006	2010+

THE STEADING (Grenache Mataro Shiraz)

Barossa Valley	$30–$49
Current vintage: 2004	90

Fragrant, spicy and slightly meaty, its grenache-driven aromas of redcurrants, cassis, dark plums and raisins have a floral and almost citrusy aspect. Ripe and juicy, its sumptuous, assertive and mouth-coating palate of concentrated, briary fruits is framed by a moderately firm cut of smooth tannins. A powerful wine with loads of presence, it just lacks the genuine shape and definition for a higher score.

2004	90	2006	2009+
2003	93	2008	2011+
2002	95	2007	2010+
2001	90	2003	2006
2000	93	2005	2008
1999	95	2004	2007+
1998	87	2003	2006
1997	94	2002	2005+

THE STRUIE (Shiraz)

Barossa Valley, Eden Valley	$50–$99
Current vintage: 2005	91

Spicy and brambly, with intense floral and blueberry-like aromas, there's something reminiscent of grenache about this vibrant and juicy shiraz. Its wild, confiture-like aromas of ripe berry fruits reveal a hint of currant and raisin, with a sweet creamy backing of vanilla oak. Long and sumptuous, its plump and juicy palate of vibrant black, red and blueberry flavours is smooth and pliant, finishing with just a hint of hotness.

2005	91	2010	2013
2004	93	2009	2012+
2003	90	2008	2011+
2002	95	2004	2007+
2001	93	2003	2006+

Tuck's Ridge

37 Shoreham Road, Red Hill South Vic 3937. Tel: (03) 5989 8660. Fax: (03) 5989 8579.
Website: www.tucksridge.com.au Email: cellardoor@tucksridge.com.au

Region: **Mornington Peninsula** Winemaker: **Michael Kyberd** Viticulturist: **Tyson Lewis**
Chief Executive: **Peter Hollick**

Tuck's Ridge reliably and consistently makes honest, affordable and uncomplicated expressions of Mornington Peninsula pinot noir and chardonnay. The 2006 Chardonnay is fleshing out well, and is the vineyard's best for several years. Cellar door and mailing list buyers can select from a wider range of individual vineyard wines.

CHARDONNAY

Mornington Peninsula	$20–$29
Current vintage: 2006	90

Brightly lit with fresh white peach, lemon and pineapple flavour, this very slightly candied and crunchy chardonnay reveals undertones of wheatmeal and fresh vanilla oak. It's rather floral and fragrant, and delivers a fresh, tangy and very generous and creamy palate that finishes with lingering suggestions of ripe fruit, green olives and undertones of funky smokiness.

2006	90	2008	2011
2005	86	2006	2007
2004	89	2006	2009
2003	89	2005	2008
2002	92	2004	2007
2001	92	2003	2006
2000	89	2002	2005
1999	85	2000	2001
1998	86	2000	2003
1997	90	1999	2002

PINOT NOIR

Mornington Peninsula	$20–$29	2005	86	2007	2010+

Current vintage: 2005   86

Slightly stewed and awkward, this firm and assertive young pinot reveals deep aromas of dark berries, cherries and plums with a sweaty reductive background. Succulent and juicy, its palate presents a jammy spectrum of cooked plums, tomatoes and cherries before finishing thin and slightly bitter. It should flesh out, but lacks finesse.

2005	86	2007	2010+
2004	86	2005	2006
2003	88	2005	2008
2002	89	2004	2007
2001	90	2003	2006+
2000	90	2002	2005
1999	88	2001	2004
1998	87	2000	2003
1997	91	1999	2002
1996	87	1998	2001

Turkey Flat

Bethany Road, Tanunda SA 5352. Tel: (08) 8563 2851. Fax: (08) 8563 3610.
Website: www.turkeyflat.com.au Email: turkeyflat@bigpond.com
Region: **Barossa Valley** Winemaker: **Peter Schulz** Viticulturist: **Peter Schulz** Chief Executive: **Christie Schulz**
Turkey Flat boasts some of the oldest vineyards still in commercial production in Australia, which means about as old as any still being used for serious wine anywhere in the world. By contrast, its winery is the oenological equivalent of a new Maserati. Its current red wines are fairly true to form, other than the rather thin 2005 Cabernet Sauvignon and the deliciously vibrant 2006 Grenache, which is a cut above the usual in terms of freshness.

BUTCHERS BLOCK (Shiraz Grenache Mourvèdre)

Barossa Valley $30–$49
Current vintage: 2005   88

A spicy meaty fragrance of small black and red berries and dark plums precedes a vibrant, forward and juicy palate of medium weight. Fresh and forward, its blueberry, cassis and plum-like flavour thins out marginally towards the finish, where lively acids provide some refreshing punctuation.

2005	88	2007	2010
2004	87	2006	2009
2003	88	2005	2008
2002	90	2004	2007
2001	89	2003	2006
2000	89	2002	2005+
1999	90	2001	2004+
1998	88	2000	2003
1997	85	1998	1999

CABERNET SAUVIGNON

Barossa Valley $30–$49
Current vintage: 2005   81

Rather thin and sour-edged, this herbal and rather cooked cabernet supports its meaty flavours of dark berries, currants and raisins with dark chocolate/vanilla oak and undertones of cloves and nutmeg. It finishes rather thin and sour-edged, lacking genuine fruit sweetness.

2005	81	2007	2010
2004	89	2012	2016+
2003	83	2005	2008
2002	91	2010	2014+
2001	85	2003	2006+
2000	89	2008	2012
1999	92	2004	2007
1998	90	2003	2006
1997	91	2002	2005
1996	88	2001	2004+

GRENACHE

Barossa Valley $20–$29
Current vintage: 2006   90

A delightfully floral, briary and spicy young grenache whose intense blueberry, raspberry and plum-like fruit is lifted by nuances of cloves and cinnamon and backed by an appealing meaty edge. Long, fresh and vibrant, with just a hint of currant, it's underpinned by firmish powdery tannins, before finishing with lingering sour fruit and refreshing acidity.

2006	90	2008	2011+
2005	81	2007	2010
2004	85	2006	2009
2003	87	2005	2008
2002	89	2007	2010+
2001	88	2003	2006
2000	81	2002	2005
1999	90	2001	2004+
1998	87	2000	2003
1997	84	1998	1999
1996	89	2001	2004
1994	89	2002	2006

SHIRAZ

RATING 4

Barossa Valley	$30–$49
Current vintage: 2005	88

Earthy, musky and pepper, with a slightly cooked and meaty expression of dark plums and black-berries; it's slightly raw-edged, but does deliver a pleasing length of sweet fruit backed by dark chocolate oak and supported by an assertive firmness. A little too meaty for a higher score.

2005	88	2010	2013
2004	90	2012	2016
2003	91	2008	2011
2002	94	2010	2014
2001	90	2006	2009
2000	90	2005	2008
1999	93	2007	2011
1998	95	2006	2010
1997	89	2002	2005
1996	94	2004	2008+
1993	89	2001	2005

Tyrrell's

Broke Road, Pokolbin NSW 2320. Tel: (02) 4993 7000. Fax: (02) 4998 7723.
Website: www.tyrrells.com.au Email: info@tyrrells.com.au
Region: **Lower Hunter Valley** Winemakers: **Andrew Spinaze, Mark Richardson**
Viticulturists: **Cliff Currie, Andrew Pengilly** Chief Executive: **Bruce Tyrrell**

Tyrrell's is a custodian of the traditional Hunter Valley wine styles of early-harvested, unwooded semillon and meaty, leathery shiraz of medium to full weight. In this it succeeds admirably, with a stable full of semillons, and shirazes, each with different terroirs and stories to tell. This year it is the turn of the Vat 9 Shiraz to excel. Its 2004 vintage is a barely modern expression of the old-fashioned Hunter 'burgundy', and can be expected to develop remarkable layers of depth and savoury complexity over the years.

BROKENBACK SHIRAZ

RATING 5

Lower Hunter Valley	$20–$29
Current vintage: 2004	90

Rustic and meaty, this fragrant, slightly jammy and spotlessly clean shiraz is smooth, supple and medium weight, with a juicy, vibrant core of fresh berry and plum-like flavour. Framed by fine, supple tannin, it's long and tightly focused, with pleasing earthy regional influences, elegance and balance. For the short to medium term.

2004	90	2006	2009+
2003	89	2008	2011+
2002	89	2007	2010+
2001	87	2003	2006
2000	86	2002	2005
1999	89	2004	2007
1998	90	2006	2010
1997	85	1999	2002
1996	83	1998	2001
1995	89	2000	2003
1994	90	2002	2006

LOST BLOCK SEMILLON

RATING 5

Lower Hunter Valley	$12–$19
Current vintage: 2006	85

Candied and herbal, with a lightly grassy, almost sweaty expression of melon and lemon sherbet-like fruit that become rather broad and generous for this style. Finishing with perhaps a trace of sweetness, it's early-drinking and has rather more in common with sauvignon blanc.

2006	85	2007	2008+
2005	88	2006	2007
2004	87	2006	2009+
2003	88	2005	2008+
2002	92	2007	2010+
2001	90	2003	2006
1999	89	2001	2004
1998	94	2003	2006+
1997	90	2002	2005+
1996	92	2004	2008
1995	89	2000	2003+

'QUINTUS' MOON MOUNTAIN CHARDONNAY

RATING 4

Lower Hunter Valley	$20–$29
Current vintage: 2006	83

Sweet, fruity, simple and confectionary, this rather citrusy and marmalade-like chardonnay delivers juicy, barley sugar-like chardonnay flavour backed by sweet, toasty oak. It's a little angular and syrupy, and finishes with green-edged acids.

2006	83	2007	2008
2005	86	2006	2007+
2004	90	2005	2006+
2003	75	2003	2004
2002	90	2004	2007
2000	90	2002	2005
1998	85	1999	2000
1997	82	1998	1999
1996	90	1998	2001

RESERVE STEVENS SEMILLON

RATING 3

	Lower Hunter Valley	$20–$29
	Current vintage: 2002	**89**

Slightly green-edged and angular, this developing semillon has a honeyed, toasty and buttery bouquet of slightly cooked melon and lemon, with undertones of dried straw and dukka. It's forward and juicy, with intense, toasty lemon rind flavours over a hint of sweetcorn. Close to peaking.

2002	89	2007	2010+
2001	87	2006	2009
2000	95	2012	2020
1999	93	2007	2011+
1998	94	2006	2010+
1997	94	2005	2009
1996	86	2001	2004
1995	90	2003	2007+

RESERVE STEVENS SHIRAZ

RATING 3

	Lower Hunter Valley	$20–$29
	Current vintage: 2003	**93**

Rustic, meaty and leathery, this older-style Australian 'burgundy' marries the warmth and richness of a warmer season with delightfully fine-grained tannins, fresh acids and pristine plum and berry flavours. It's soft, medium weight and spicy, with undertones of cloves, cinnamon, licorice and white pepper, but perhaps rather more of a juicy ripeness than typical of a Tyrrell.

2003	93	2011	2015+
2002	92	2007	2010+
2000	89	2005	2008+
1999	87	2001	2004+
1998	92	2006	2010+
1997	88	2002	2005
1996	84	1998	2001
1995	87	2000	2003

VAT 1 SEMILLON

RATING 2

	Lower Hunter Valley	$30–$49
	Current vintage: 2000	**90**

A more forward, sumptuous and slightly candied Vat 1 from a warmer season. Its restrained and still rather closed and dusty bouquet of lemon rind and sage has a spicy and slightly toasty element. Long and earthy, its elegant palate is smooth and restrained, with lemon drop-like fruit finishing tangy and refreshing, with a rather chalky, sherbet-like impression. Quite phenolic and textured.

2000	90	2008	2012+
1999	97	2007	2011+
1998	95	2010	2018
1997	96	2009	2017
1996	95	2004	2008
1995	95	2007	2015
1994	96	2002	2006+
1993	95	2001	2005+
1992	95	2004	2012
1991	92	1999	2003
1990	88	1998	2002
1989	86	1991	1994
1988	88	1993	1996
1987	93	1995	1999
1986	95	1998	2008
1985	88	1993	1997
1984	93	1996	2004

VAT 8 SHIRAZ CABERNET

RATING 5

	Lower Hunter Valley, Mudgee	
		$30–$49
	Current vintage: 2004	**88**

Meaty, leathery and rustic, with a smoky presence of red berry and plum-like fruit backed by rather equine complexity, it's soft, smooth and early-maturing. Initially quite rich, it shows signs of drying out from the back of the palate, with a faintly metallic edge to its tannins. Old-fashioned and perhaps with a small presence of brettanomyces, which would make it mature even faster.

2004	88	2009	2012
2003	90	2011	2015
2002	87	2007	2010
2000	87	2005	2008
1999	89	2004	2007+
1998	95	2006	2010
1997	92	2005	2009+
1996	91	2001	2004
1995	93	2003	2007
1994	92	2002	2006

VAT 9 SHIRAZ

RATING 4

	Lower Hunter Valley	$30–$49
	Current vintage: 2004	**95**

Old-fashioned Hunter style and elegance personified, this charmingly smooth, soft and deeply flavoured shiraz is meaty and medium-bodied, with a floral, spicy red-fruited perfume backed by white pepper and spice. Its long, vibrant palate of intense berry, cherry and dark plum flavour overlies lightly creamy cedar/vanilla oak and a fine-grained, dusty backbone. It finishes with tightness, focus and refreshing acids. Measured and classy.

2004	95	2012	2016+
2002	88	2007	2010+
2001	87	2006	2009
1999	88	2007	2011+
1998	94	2010	2018
1997	89	2002	2005+
1996	88	2004	2008
1995	80	1997	2000
1994	91	2002	2006+
1993	87	1998	2001
1992	93	1997	2000
1991	95	2003	2011

A B C D E F G H I J K L M N O P Q R S T U V W X Y Z

VAT 47 CHARDONNAY

Lower Hunter Valley	$50–$99
Current vintage: 2005	**92**

A richer, more assertive and earlier-maturing Vat 47 with a fragrant aroma of melon and lemon, knit with a hint of toasty oak and backed by hints of dried flowers and a slightly buttery and candied aspect. Juicy and forward for this style, it's richly fruited, smooth and unctuous, finishing slightly drying with ripe and almost candied fruit flavours.

2005	92	2010	2013+
2004	96	2012	2016
2003	88	2005	2008+
2002	96	2010	2014
2001	95	2009	2013
2000	96	2008	2012
1999	94	2001	2004+
1998	95	2006	2010+
1997	90	1999	2002+
1996	94	2001	2004+
1995	93	2003	2007+
1994	94	2002	2006+
1993	94	2001	2005

Vasse Felix

Corner Caves Road, and Harmans Road South, Cowaramup WA 6284. Tel: (08) 9756 5000.
Fax: (08) 9755 5425. Website: www.vassefelix.com.au Email: info@vassefelix.com.au

Region: **Margaret River** Winemaker: **Virginia Willcock** Viticulturist: **Bart Maloney**
Chief Executive: **Paul Holmes à Court**

Vasse Felix is one of the Margaret River region's oldest and leading wine makers. Despite the fact that some releases under its varietal range have been very erratic, its Cabernet Sauvignon and Heytesbury labels in particular are showing some recent consistency. Respected winemaker Virginia Willcock has taken over the reins, which will give her the chance to perform on a bigger stage, with sound vineyards and excellent winemaking resources.

CABERNET MERLOT

Margaret River	$20–$29
Current vintage: 2005	**79**

Rather varnishy and volatile, with cooked, stewy fruit and ordinary oak backed by a firm, drying extract of raw tannin. Lacks length and focus.

2005	79	2007	2010
2004	88	2009	2012
2003	88	2005	2008+
2002	80	2004	2007
2001	89	2003	2006
2000	88	2002	2005+
1999	82	2001	2004
1998	83	2000	2003
1997	88	2002	2005
1996	88	2001	2004
1995	87	2000	2003
1994	88	1996	1999

CABERNET SAUVIGNON

Margaret River	$20–$29
Current vintage: 2005	**93**

Pleasingly elegant, balanced, restrained and charming, this tightly focused and varietal cabernet has a dusty, violet-like fragrance whose fresh blackberry and cassis-like fruit are neatly backed by sweet cedar/vanilla oak. Smooth and polished, it's long and supple, with dark berry/cherry/plum-like flavours framed by firm, loose-knit tannins and backed by suggestions of dried herbs and evenly measured, cedary oak.

2005	93	2013	2017+
2004	93	2016	2024
2003	89	2008	2011+
2002	83	2004	2007
2001	90	2006	2009
2000	93	2008	2012
1999	93	2007	2011+
1998	96	2010	2018
1997	89	2002	2005+
1996	86	2001	2004+
1995	87	2003	2007
1994	93	2006	2014
1993	88	1995	1998
1991	93	2003	2011

CHARDONNAY

Margaret River	$20–$29
Current vintage: 2006	**81**

Light aromas of peachy, tropical, cashew and sweetcorn-like fruit with dusty vanilla oak in support precedes a rather clunky and unpolished palate whose broad, almost flabby fruit qualities are backed by raw oak, and finish without much brightness or freshness.

2006	81	2007	2008
2005	87	2007	2010
2004	89	2006	2009
2003	89	2005	2008
2002	87	2004	2007
2001	92	2006	2009
2000	90	2002	2005+
1999	89	2001	2004
1998	80	1999	2000
1997	87	1999	2002

HEYTESBURY (Cabernet blend)

RATING 3

Margaret River		$50–$99		
Current vintage: 2004		**95**		

Stylish, measured and very elegant, this rather classy and showy cabernet has an intense violet-like perfume of cassis, liqueur cherries and dried herbs supported by sweet cedar/vanilla oak. Smooth and silky, its palate supports its intense and spotlessly presented core of deep and lingering fruit with a slightly powdery undercarriage of firm, fine tannins. Finishing with suggestions of mint and dark olives, it's already very approachable and balanced.

2004	95	2012	2016
2003	95	2015	2023
2002	87	2004	2007+
2001	91	2006	2009+
2000	90	2005	2008
1999	91	2004	2007
1998	89	2003	2006
1997	93	2005	2009
1996	89	2002	2008
1995	94	2003	2007+

HEYTESBURY CHARDONNAY

RATING 2

Margaret River		$30–$49		
Current vintage: 2005		**95**		

Meaty, funky aromas of citrusy fruit, dried flowers and grilled nuts precede a bright, mouthfilling and tangy palate wrapped in refreshing and mineral acids. It's citrusy and tropical, with plenty of lemony oak and length of fruit. Already deliciously flavoursome, complex and savoury, and able to soak up its smart new French oak, it's perhaps not for the long term.

2005	95	2007	2010+
2004	94	2009	2012
2003	95	2008	2011
2002	89	2004	2007
2001	95	2006	2009
2000	90	2002	2005
1999	90	2001	2004
1998	88	2000	2003+
1996	86	1997	1998

SEMILLON

RATING 4

Margaret River		$20–$29		
Current vintage: 2005		**81**		

Estery, spicy and varnishy, with herbal, melon-like aromas and a slightly sweet, oily and forward palate that lacks depth, balance and freshness. Possibly the result of a stuck ferment.

2005	81	2005	2005
2004	86	2005	2006
2002	93	2004	2007
2001	89	2003	2006+
2000	90	2005	2008
1999	91	2004	2007
1998	86	2000	2003

SHIRAZ

RATING 3

Margaret River		$20–$29		
Current vintage: 2005		**86**		

Ripe and meaty, with bright red cherry, blackberry and tomato-like fruit backed by sweet smoky oak, suggestions of menthol and spice, plus leafy, herbal nuances. Full to medium in weight, it's oaky and dark-fruited, but lacks genuine length and focus.

2005	86	2010	2013
2004	92	2012	2016
2003	88	2008	2011
2002	93	2010	2014+
2001	93	2006	2009
2000	93	2008	2012
1999	93	2004	2007+
1998	82	2000	2003
1997	93	2005	2009
1996	90	2001	2004
1995	94	2000	2003
1994	93	2002	2006

Voyager Estate

Stevens Road, Margaret River WA 6285. Tel: (08) 9757 6354. Fax: (08) 9757 6494.
Website: www.voyagerestate.com.au Email: wine@voyagerestate.com.au
Region: **Margaret River** Winemaker: **Cliff Royle** Viticulturist: **Steve James** Chief Executive: **Michael Wright**

A spectacular Margaret River winery development, Voyager Estate has become one of the region's leading makers. Its Cabernet Sauvignon Merlot has joined the region's elite wines, and with high expectations from the fine 2004 season and excellent 2005, it could shortly join the tiny number of 'Perfect 1s' in this guide. Meanwhile, the Shiraz is showing some genuine class, and the Chardonnay is steadily becoming finer and tighter.

CABERNET SAUVIGNON MERLOT

RATING

Margaret River		$30–$49	2003	96	2015	2023
Current vintage: 2003		**96**	2002	95	2014	2022
			2001	97	2013	2021

A deeper hue with more ruby colour than the same wine sealed with cork, this is a classy, seamless Margaret River cabernet of immense potential. Scented with a heady, smoky and slightly meaty and perfume of dark plums, cherries and cassis, it's backed by nuances of forest floor, mocha and spearmint with undertones of pencil shavings oak. Long and sumptuous, it's vibrant, deeply fruited and finely crafted, presenting a rare marriage of impact and structure with elegance and balance. Tasted under Stelvin.

2000	91	2008	2012
1999	92	2011	2019
1998	96	2010	2018
1997	91	2005	2009
1996	95	2004	2008+
1995	95	2003	2007+
1994	94	2006	2014

CHARDONNAY

RATING

Margaret River		$30–$49	2005	93	2010	2013
Current vintage: 2005		**93**	2004	96	2009	2012
			2003	93	2005	2008+

Tangy aromas of lime, grapefruit and minerals overlie lightly spicy and dusty oak. Lean and focused, its tight and somewhat reserved expression of melon, grapefruit, lemon and lime unfold layers of depth and flavour. Bound by a refreshing cut of mineral acidity, it's long, stylish and finely balanced, with just a slight question mark against some slightly drying oak.

2002	95	2007	2010
2001	93	2006	2009
2000	93	2005	2008
1999	94	2001	2004
1998	88	2000	2003
1997	90	1999	2002
1996	91	1998	2001

SAUVIGNON BLANC SEMILLON

RATING

Margaret River		$12–$19	2006	93	2008	2011+
Current vintage: 2006		**93**	2005	91	2007	2010+
			2004	92	2004	2005+

Tangy and refreshing, this uncomplicated but intensely flavoured blend is spotlessly clean, tightly focused and very contemporary. Its punchy tropical flavours of gooseberries, passionfruit and melon overlie nuances of citrus and pineapple, as well as a dusty, grassy aspect. It's long and lively, finishing with an attractive austerity.

2003	93	2004	2005+
2002	90	2004	2007
2001	87	2002	2003
2000	94	2005	2008
1999	95	2001	2004+
1996	95	2001	2004

SHIRAZ

RATING

Margaret River		$30–$49	2005	95	2013	2017
Current vintage: 2005		**95**	2004	90	2009	2012
			2003	94	2008	2011+

A sumptuous, smooth and polished Margaret River shiraz that avoids the excessively tomato-like and greenish elements not uncommon with shirazes from this region. Its slightly meaty and gamey aromas of cassis, violets, dark chocolates and cedar are lifted by a viognier-enhanced floral perfume. Framed by firm, pliant tannins, it is long and lavishly oaked, expressing a luscious, meaty and power-fully accentuated shade of dark berry/plum flavour. Finishing with a lingering core of fruit and licorice-like spices, it's very balanced and savoury.

2002	82	2007	2010
2001	94	2006	2009
2000	88	2005	2008
1999	92	2004	2007

Wandin Valley Estate

Wilderness Road, Lovedale, NSW 2320. Tel: (02) 4930 7317. Fax: (02) 4930 7814.
Website: www.wandinvalley.com.au Email: sales@wandinvalley.com.au
Region: **Lower Hunter Valley** Winemaker: **Matthew Burton** Viticulturist: **Scott Ling**
Chief Executives: **James & Philippa Davern**

A small Hunter vineyard and winery, Wandin Valley Estate's leading two wines are its regional specials of Bridie's Shiraz and Reserve Semillon. These wines are typically true to the Hunter traditions of leathery and elegant shirazes and long-living, taut and refreshing but low-alcohol semillons. Wandin Valley Estate also boasts a very attractive private cricket ground that is available for social fixtures.

BRIDIE'S RESERVE SHIRAZ

RATING 4

Lower Hunter Valley	$20–$29	2004	92	2012	2016
Current vintage: 2004	92	2003	90	2008	2011+
		2001	83	2003	2006
		2000	90	2008	2012
		1998	93	2006	2010+

A typical older-style Hunter shiraz whose meaty, leathery and earthy expression of dark berry and plum-like shiraz is tightly crafted into a fine, supple and silky wine with very restrained vanilla oak and a delightful lingering sour edge to the fruit. It's very perfumed and spicy, long and supple, with plenty of rustic character.

RESERVE SEMILLON

RATING 4

Lower Hunter Valley	$20–$29	2007	90	2012	2015
Current vintage: 2007	90	2006	90	2011	2014+
		2005	91	2010	2013+
		2002	91	2010	2014

Very intensely aromatic and concentrated, with pristine, very slightly confectionary flavours of lemon and lime juice, nectarine and melon backed by nuances of minerals. Very long and persistent, it's surprisingly juicy and piercingly fresh. It finishes with suggestions of bath salts and clean, slatey acids.

Wantirna Estate

10 Bushy Park Lane, Wantirna South Vic 3152. Tel: (03) 9801 2367. Fax: (03) 9887 0225.
Website: www.wantirnaestate.com.au Email: wantirnaestate@bigpond.com.au
Region: **Yarra Valley** Winemakers: **Maryann Egan, Reg Egan** Viticulturist: **Reg Egan** Chief Executive: **Reg Egan**

Wantirna Estate's spotlessly crafted, elegant and fine-grained table wines typically reveal deeply scented perfumes of pristine fruit and fine-grained oak, before poised, supple and seamless palates of intensity and integration. The latest releases are typically spotless, profoundly fruited and superbly crafted. Again, my only concern is that because they are so immediately drinkable, little will live to see their full maturity and potential.

AMELIA CABERNET SAUVIGNON MERLOT

RATING 2

Yarra Valley	$50–$99	2005	95	2013	2017+
Current vintage: 2005	95	2004	97	2016	2024
		2003	91	2008	2011+
		2002	93	2010	2014+
		2001	95	2009	2013
		2000	95	2008	2012+
		1999	94	2007	2011+
		1998	96	2006	2010
		1997	96	2009	2017
		1996	92	2004	2008
		1995	94	2003	2007+

Classic Yarra cabernet, very floral and perfumed, with intense violet, cassis, dark cherry and cedar/vanilla oak over nuances of undergrowth. Smooth, finely crafted and velvet-like, it's long, pliant and deeply flavoured, with black fruit, dark chocolate and cedar oak culminating in a pleasing and grippy astringency.

HANNAH CABERNET FRANC MERLOT

RATING 2

Yarra Valley	$100–$199
Current vintage: 2005	**96**

Australian cabernet franc doesn't often reach these levels. Perfumed and spicy, with pristine cherry/berry/plum fruit and sweet cedar/vanilla oak framed by loose-knit and silky tannin, it's long, smooth and seamless, building towards a crescendo of intensity and richness towards its tightly focused and savoury finish. Backed by nuances of cloves and cinnamon, it's likely to build in weight and structure as it ages.

2005	96	2013	2017+
2004	96	2012	2016+
2003	91	2008	2011
2002	93	2007	2010+
2001	95	2009	2013+
2000	95	2008	2012+
1999	95	2007	2011

ISABELLA CHARDONNAY

RATING 2

Yarra Valley	$30–$49
Current vintage: 2006	**95**

A smooth, seamless and smoky chardonnay whose succulent expression of grapefruit, quince, melon and white peach flavour is tightly knit with meaty, lightly cheesy reductive notes, sweet bubblegum/vanilla oak and a restrained hint of minerality. Scented with dried flowers and meaty undertones, it becomes quite sumptuous and succulent before finishing with soft and tightly integrated lemony acids.

2006	95	2011	2014
2005	97	2010	2013
2004	95	2009	2012+
2003	95	2008	2011
2002	96	2007	2010
2000	93	2005	2008
1999	90	2001	2004+
1998	95	2003	2006+
1997	93	2002	2005+
1996	96	2004	2008
1994	94	2002	2006

LILY PINOT NOIR

RATING 2

Yarra Valley	$50–$99
Current vintage: 2006	**93**

Smooth and supple, this perfumed and heady young pinot has a youthful and slightly confectionary aroma of raspberries, cherries and sweet vanilla/bubblegum oak. Its ripe, polished palate of deep, juicy pinot fruit is supported by a fine cut of tannin and finished with fresh acidity. It finishes with just a hint of riper, currant-like flavour.

2006	93	2011	2014
2005	96	2010	2013+
2004	94	2009	2012+
2003	94	2008	2011
2002	95	2007	2010
2001	94	2006	2009
2000	95	2005	2008
1999	97	2004	2007+
1998	94	2003	2006
1997	95	2002	2005
1996	92	2001	2004+
1995	92	2000	2003

Warrenmang

Mountain Creek Road, Moonambel Vic 3478. Tel: (03) 5467 2233. Fax: (03) 5467 2309.
Website: www.warrenmang.com.au Email: mail@warrenmang.com.au

Region: **Pyrenees** Winemaker: **Sear Schwager** Viticulturist: **Luigi Bazzani** Chief Executive: **Luigi Bazzani**

Warrenmang is a mature vineyard at Moonambel, in Victoria's picturesque Pyrenees region. It enjoyed a superb vintage in 2004, creating reds of finely controlled power and intensity. 2005 was hotter and more difficult, but again the vineyard delivered two typically firm shirazes, of which the Black Puma is the more concentrated.

BLACK PUMA SHIRAZ

RATING 4

Pyrenees	$50–$99
Current vintage: 2005	**90**

Assertively backed by smoky, almost soupy oak, are deep, rather closed and brooding aromas of meaty dark fruits, white pepper, cloves and cinnamon. Framed by firm, powdery tannins, its intense, briary palate of cassis, blackberries, plums and briar also receives sweet, coconut ice-like oak, finishing long, dark-fruited and mineral. Very sumptuous and concentrated, with regional nuances of mint and menthol.

2005	90	2017	2025
2004	95	2016	2024+
2001	87	2006	2009
2000	90	2012	2020
1998	90	2006	2010+

ESTATE SHIRAZ

RATING **4**

Pyrenees	$50–$99
Current vintage: 2005	**88**

Smoky, vanilla and ashtray-like oak sits alongside deep, spicy aromas of blackberries, plums and currants, with a musky background of clove and cinnamon-like spiciness. Powerful, dark and chocolatey, its sumptuous, ultra-ripe and meaty palate of blackberries and plums is slightly overwhelmed by its rather charry and raw-edged complement of smoky oak, which tends to detract a little from the fruit's lusciousness and depth of flavour.

2005	88	2013	2017
2004	93	2016	2024
2002	81	2007	2010+
2001	89	2006	2009
2000	93	2012	2020
1999	92	2004	2007+
1998	81	2003	2006
1997	90	2002	2005+
1996	89	2004	2008
1995	80	2000	2003
1994	88	1999	2002
1993	90	2001	2005
1992	93	2004	2012

Water Wheel

Raywood Road, Bridgewater-on-Loddon Vic 3516. Tel: (03) 5437 3060. Fax: (03) 5437 3082.
Website: www.waterwheelwine.com Email: info@waterwheelwine.com

Region: **Bendigo** Winemakers: **Peter Cumming, Bill Trevaskis** Viticulturist: **Peter Cumming**
Chief Executive: **Peter Cumming**

Water Wheel is an operation of surprising scale given its relatively modest winemaking facility. Its typically ripe and forward varietal table wines are usually well-made, fresh and fruity, with a generous length of palate flavour. Furthermore, the reds are typically made with the structure to live well beyond the mean for wines of their price. The 2005 red releases are both of the deeply ripened style.

CABERNET SAUVIGNON

RATING **5**

Bendigo	$12–$19
Current vintage: 2005	**88**

Slightly spirity and just a fraction dehydrated, this sumptuously flavoured and full-bodied cabernet is built around a deep, ultra-ripe and concentrated core of plum, raspberry and currant-like fruit, with a restrained background of cedar/vanilla oak. Very intense and generous, it's just bordering on over-ripe.

2005	88	2007	2010+
2004	90	2012	2016
2003	89	2013	2017
2002	87	2007	2010
2001	88	2009	2013
2000	89	2008	2012
1999	87	2004	2007+
1998	91	2006	2010
1997	92	2002	2005+
1996	91	2001	2004
1995	90	2000	2003

SHIRAZ

RATING **4**

Bendigo	$12–$19
Current vintage: 2005	**89**

Deep, dark and vibrant, its intense blackcurrant, blackberry and dark plum fruit soaks up its sweet vanilla/cedar American oak influences, but leaves a lingering suggestion of slightly dehydrated raisin and currant-like flavour. Backed by peppery, spicy suggestions of cloves and cinnamon, it's thick, rich and meaty, with a firm undercarriage of pliant tannin.

2005	89	2010	2013
2004	90	2009	2012+
2003	90	2008	2011+
2002	92	2007	2010
2001	87	2006	2009
2000	89	2005	2008+
1999	88	2004	2007
1998	94	2007	2010
1997	90	2005	2009+
1996	93	2004	2008
1995	89	2003	2007
1994	93	1999	2002+

Wedgetail Estate

40 Hildebrand Road, Cottles Bridge Vic 3099. Tel: (03) 9714 8661. Fax: (03) 9714 8676.
Website: www.wedgetailestate.com.au Email: info@wedgetailestate.com.au
Region: **Yarra Valley** Winemaker: **Guy Lamothe** Viticulturist: **Guy Lamothe**
Chief Executives: **Dena Ashbolt & Guy Lamothe**

Guy Lamothe, who previously worked in wineries in France and on the Mornington Peninsula, produces small volumes of handcrafted table wine at Cottles Bridge, just 40 kilometres north-east of Melbourne. His best wine is his Pinot Noir, whose easterly aspect enables it to capture the early morning sunshine.

PINOT NOIR

RATING **5**

Yarra Valley	$30–$49
Current vintage: 2006	82

Spicy, slightly meaty aromas of cooked currants and raisins reveal some lively cherry-like qualities and spicy, herbal undertones of cloves, nutmeg and menthol. Its initial impression of black and red cherry flavour thins out towards a thin, minty finish supported by fine, bony tannin, but the fruit lacks length and presence.

2006	82	2008	2011
2005	86	2007	2010
2003	92	2005	2008
2002	88	2007	2010
2001	86	2003	2006

Wellington

208 Denholms Road, Cambridge Tas 7170. Tel: (03) 6248 5844. Fax: (03) 6248 5855.
Website: www.hoodwines.com Email: wellington@hoodwines.com
Region: **Southern Tasmania** Winemaker: **Andrew Hood** Chief Executive: **Graeme Allen**

Made by one of Tasmania's finest winemakers in Andrew Hood, Wellington's wines are long and intensely flavoured, but fine and restrained. Its current releases include a sweet but refreshing Iced Riesling, while the 2005 vintage of Hood's rather technically named FGR Riesling (Five Grams of Residual sugar) is floral, spicy, musky and rather Germanic — whose people, incidentally would probably delight in the wine's nomenclature.

CHARDONNAY

RATING **5**

Southern Tasmania	$20–$29
Current vintage: 2005	89

Long, tangy and austere, this slightly mineral chardonnay has a sweet-fruited and slightly candied expression of tangerine, melon and marmalade-like flavour, with undertones of wheatmeal, toast and butter. It finishes with a pleasingly long and persistent core of fruit, but could perhaps have used some more sympathetic oak.

2005	89	2010	2013
2004	79	2005	2006+
2003	90	2005	2008+
2002	88	2004	2007
2001	87	2003	2006
2000	91	2005	2008
1999	90	2004	2007
1998	90	2003	2006+
1997	87	2002	2005

ICED RIESLING

RATING **3**

Southern Tasmania $20–$29 (375 ml)	
Current vintage: 2006	92

Luscious, long and concentrated, with a piercing expression of pristine white peach, pear and apple-like flavour balanced by refreshing acidity, this very fragrant and slightly mineral riesling has a floral and lemony perfume. It's very stylish and persistent, with plenty of sweetness but no hint of cloying or fatness.

2006	92	2008	2011
2005	93	2007	2010
2004	82	2006	2009
2003	83	2004	2005+
2000	93	2005	2008
1999	92	2004	2007
1998	83	1999	2000
1997	89	1999	2002

PINOT NOIR

RATING **5**

Southern Tasmania	$20–$29
Current vintage: 2004	92

Charming and satiny, this long, slightly minty and vibrant young pinot should gain flesh and structure as it ages. With a genuine depth of fine tannin, it's perfumed and floral, with intense red and black berry/cherry fruit tightly knit with quality oak. Long and smooth, its finishes with a lingering fruit and a hint of candied sugar.

2004	92	2009	2012+
2003	80	2005	2008
2002	90	2004	2007
2001	88	2003	2006
2000	89	2002	2005
1999	89	2001	2004
1998	92	2000	2003
1997	89	2002	2005
1994	90	1999	2002

RIESLING

Southern Tasmania $20–$29
Current vintage: 2006 92

Just a little raw and reductive in its youth, this slightly hard-edged, mineral and citrusy riesling has all the right things in the right places to develop nicely. It's both floral and meaty, with a long, dry and austere palate with a latent depth of fruit that is waiting to explode.

2006	92	2011	2014
2004	92	2006	2009
2003	92	2008	2011
2000	91	2005	2008
1999	95	2007	2011
1998	89	2000	2003+
1997	89	2002	2005

Wendouree

Wendouree Road, Clare SA 5453. Tel: (08) 8842 2896.

Region: **Clare Valley** Winemakers: **Tony & Lita Brady** Viticulturist: **I Cerchi** Chief Executive: **Tony Brady**

Wendouree is an iconic maker of small volumes of deeply flavoured, firmly structured and finely crafted red wine from its historic dryland Clare Valley vineyard. The 2005 Shiraz is a perfect illustration of how very mature, deeply-rooted vines are best-equipped to deal with significant variations in climatic conditions.

SHIRAZ

Clare Valley $100–$199
Current vintage: 2005 95

A superlative and evenly ripened wine from this hot vintage, with a deep, dark and brooding bouquet whose deep blackberry and dark plum aromas overlie dusty vanilla oak and suggestions of mint, menthol and cloves. Richly textured and sumptuously flavoured, it's concentrated and brooding, revealing layers of black and red berry fruit, dark plums and firm, loose-knit tannin culminating in a long, persistent and licorice-like finish.

2005	95	2017	2025+
2004	97	2024	2023+
2003	95	2015	2023
2002	97	2022	2032
2001	89	2009	2013+
2000	88	2008	2012
1999	96	2019	2029
1998	97	2018	2028+
1997	89	2009	2017+
1996	95	2008	2016+
1995	94	2015	2025
1994	91	2006	2014+
1993	86	2001	2005+
1992	91	2012	2022
1991	96	2021	2031
1990	90	2010	2020+
1989	93	2009	2019
1988	93	2008	2018
1987	88	1999	2007
1985	95	2005	2015
1983	89	2003	2013+

SHIRAZ MATARO

Clare Valley $50–$99
Current vintage: 2004 95

Profoundly true to its terroir, this rustic, meaty, black-fruited blend marries intense, minty fruit with sweet oak and powerful, but pliant tannins. There's a hint of menthol beneath its juicy aromas of blackberries, redcurrants and dark plums, while its open, loose-knit palate is both vibrant and concentrated. It's long, finely balanced and integrated, with charming earthy undertones.

2004	95	2016	2024+
2003	92	2011	2015+
2002	95	2014	2022+
2001	90	2021	2031
2000	87	2008	2012+
1999	95	2019	2029
1998	96	2018	2028+
1997	88	2009	2017
1996	94	2016	2026
1995	94	2005	2015+
1994	87	2004	2014
1991	95	2011	2021
1988	93	2000	2008+
1987	89	1999	2007

Westend

1283 Brayne Road, Griffith NSW 2680. Tel: (02) 6969 0800. Fax: (02) 6962 1673.
Website: www.westendestate.com.au Email: westend@webfront.net.au
Region: **Riverina** Winemakers: **William Calabria, Bryan Currie** Viticulturist: **Anthony Trimboli**
Chief Executive: **William Calabria**

Bill Calabria's family business continues to make Griffith's finest range of wine. The 3 Bridges range reflects his desire to put Riverina wines on the same stage as the finest from the more fashionable regions. The current releases include his best-ever Chardonnay, a wine whose richness and finesse could easily eclipse many significantly dearer wines. The reds do reflect the heat of recent vintages.

3 BRIDGES CABERNET SAUVIGNON

RATING **4**

Riverina $20–$29
Current vintage: 2004 87

Meaty, slightly pruney and green-edged, with a deep and almost stewy core of cassis and dark plum fruit coated by robust, slightly raw tannins. Sweet cedar/vanilla oak smooths out the palate, before finishing savoury, earthy and quite grippy. It still needs time to settle.

2004	87	2009	2012+
2002	88	2004	2007+
2001	91	2006	2009+
2000	87	2002	2005+
1999	89	2004	2007
1998	90	2003	2006+
1997	90	1999	2002+

3 BRIDGES CHARDONNAY

RATING **5**

Riverina $12–$19
Current vintage: 2004 90

Big, broad but balanced, this smooth and harmonious chardonnay reveals a delicate perfume of peach and melon over nutty, dusty and lightly toasty nuances of vanilla oak. Smooth and buttery, its generous, juicy expression of peaches, cream and grapefruit-like flavour, sweet vanilla oak and buttery malolactic undertones finishes with a soft but tightly knit acidity.

2004	90	2006	2009
2003	87	2004	2005+
2002	87	2003	2004
2001	84	2002	2002
2000	88	2001	2002+
1999	87	2000	2001
1998	87	1999	2000

3 BRIDGES DURIF

RATING **5**

Riverina $20–$29
Current vintage: 2005 87

Charry, oaky and meaty, this very forward, juicy and in-your-face durif offers a meaty dollop of dark plums, blackberries and briar backed by some pretty toasty, caramel and vanilla-like American oak. It finishes with sweet fruit and smoky oak, with a hint of spice.

2005	87	2007	2010
2004	88	2006	2009
2003	89	2005	2008
2002	93	2007	2010
2001	87	2003	2006+
2000	91	2005	2008+

3 BRIDGES GOLDEN MIST BOTRYTIS SEMILLON

RATING **5**

Riverina $20–$29 (375 ml)
Current vintage: 2005 89

Buttery, luscious and very concentrated, this toasty, honeyed late-harvest semillon delivers an oily and candied expression of melon, cumquat and apricot-like fruit with undertones of burned butter. It's rich and oaky, and while it lacks the vinosity for the longer term, it offers plenty of flavour for early drinking.

2005	89	2007	2010
2004	88	2006	2009
2003	87	2005	2008
2002	89	2003	2004+
2001	88	2002	2003
1999	91	2001	2004+
1998	87	1999	2000
1997	94	1999	2002+
1996	90	1998	2001
1995	84	1996	1997

3 BRIDGES RESERVE SHIRAZ

RATING 4

| | | Riverina | $20–$29 |
| | | **Current vintage: 2005** | **86** |

Very ripe, slightly cooked and awkward, with jammy flavours of blueberries, blackberries and dark plums backed by sweet, rather smoky vanilla/coconut oak and slightly muddy, menthol-like undertones. It's rich and very intense, but finishes a little short, with lingering notes of currants and menthol.

2005	86	2007	2010+
2004	86	2006	2009
2003	90	2005	2008+
2002	91	2007	2010+
2001	90	2006	2009
2000	91	2005	2008+
1999	86	2001	2004

Willow Creek

166 Balnarring Road, Merricks North Vic 3926. Tel: (03) 5989 7448. Fax: (03) 5989 7584.
Website: www.willow-creek.com.au Email: admin@willow-creek.com.au
Region: **Mornington Peninsula** Winemaker: **Phil Kerney** Viticulturist: **Robert O'Leary**
Chief Executive: **Phil Kerney**

Willow Creek has been part of the Mornington Peninsula scene for some time. It is making sound, well-structured and handsomely crafted wines that reflect some fine work in the cellar. Willow Creek is also doing something that many of us have considered impossible, but they have indeed been helped by global warming. That feat is to fashion some pretty smart Peninsula cabernet sauvignon, which appears under the Tulum label.

TULUM CHARDONNAY

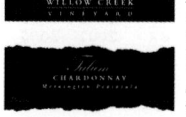

RATING 4

| | | Mornington Peninsula | $30–$49 |
| | | **Current vintage: 2006** | **90** |

A pure, tangy and juicy chardonnay whose delicate, nutty aromas of lemon, pineapple and white peach overlie some funky undertones. Pleasingly balanced, with a smooth, juicy palate of brightly lit fruit wrapped in clean, soft acids, it finishes with lingering lemony flavours.

2006	90	2008	2011+
2005	90	2007	2010+
2004	90	2006	2009
2003	87	2005	2008
2002	89	2004	2007

TULUM PINOT NOIR

RATING 5

| | | Mornington Peninsula | $30–$49 |
| | | **Current vintage: 2005** | **87** |

Slightly meaty and over-ripened, this sumptuous, flavoursome and confectionary pinot marries stewy, spicy flavours of cherries, redcurrants, cloves and cinnamon with a moderately firm undercarriage of loose-knit tannin. It finishes with pleasing length and freshness, but with some evidence of stressed fruit.

2005	87	2007	2010
2004	88	2006	2009+
2003	88	2005	2008
2002	88	2004	2007

WCV PINOT NOIR

RATING 5

| | | Mornington Peninsula | $20–$29 |
| | | **Current vintage: 2005** | **87** |

A neat little quaff, this slightly herbal and meaty young pinot has a ripe, floral and slightly confectionary aroma of cherries and raspberries, with a smooth, supple and generous palate of lively cherry/berry fruit, pleasing length and freshness.

2005	87	2007	2010
2004	86	2006	2009
2003	87	2005	2008
2002	88	2004	2007

A B C D E F G H I J K L M N O P Q R S T U V **W** X Y Z

Wilson Vineyard, The

Polish Hill Road, Sevenhill via Clare SA 5453. Tel: (08) 8843 4310. Website: www.wilsonvineyard.com.au

Region: **Clare Valley** Winemakers: **Daniel Wilson, John Wilson** Viticulturist: **John Wilson**
Chief Executive: **John Wilson**

The Wilson Vineyard is one of the Clare Valley's long-established producers of classic Australian riesling, typically making a richer and more generous style that cellars slowly. The DJW Riesling is made by the second generation of winemaking Wilsons, Daniel, who made a contrastingly tight, shapely and racy wine in 2006.

DJW RIESLING

RATING **5**

Clare Valley		$12–$19
Current vintage: 2006		**94**

Aromatic and perfumed, finely shaped and defined, this very floral and citrusy riesling presents intense varietal fruit along a supple and gentle, but tightly sculpted palate that finishes long and austere, with a lingering focus of persistent fruit and refreshing acids.

2006	94	2011	2014+
2005	89	2010	2013
2004	88	2006	2009+
2003	93	2011	2015
2002	82	2004	2007
2001	89	2005	2008

RIESLING (formerly Gallery Series)

RATING **4**

Clare Valley		$12–$19
Current vintage: 2006		**88**

Ripe and generous, this slightly confectionary wine has a fresh lemon butter fragrance and a juicy, almost broad palate that extends towards a dry, citrusy finish. It leaves a lingering impression of lemon tart.

2006	88	2011	2014
2005	83	2007	2010+
2004	90	2009	2012+
2003	91	2011	2015+
2002	89	2007	2010
2001	88	2006	2009
2000	91	2005	2008+
1999	94	2007	2011+
1998	95	2006	2010+
1997	87	2002	2005
1996	93	2004	2008
1995	94	2003	2007

Wirra Wirra

McMurtrie Road, McLaren Vale SA 5171. Tel: (08) 8323 8414. Fax: (08) 8323 8596.
Website: www.wirra.com.au Email: info@wirra.com.au

Regions: **McLaren Vale, Various SA** Winemaker: **Samantha Connew** Viticulturist: **Luke Wormald**
Chief Executive: **Andrew Kay**

Wirra Wirra is part of the McLaren Vale establishment. It produces a wide range of regional wine, although some of its larger run Scrubby Rise wines are made from fruit sourced outside the area. Its wines are typically generous and artfully made, and while the 2005 and 2006 vintages were far from easy, it appears at this time at least, that Wirra Wirra didn't handle them as well as they might have expected.

CHURCH BLOCK

McLaren Vale		$20–$29
Current vintage: 2005		**83**

Rather meaty, cooked and browning, with prune and Bovril-like aromas before a rich, smooth and currant-like palate that dries out towards an oaky finish of firmish tannins. Quite polished despite its robust nature, it is however lacking in fruit brightness and freshness.

2005	83	2007	2010
2004	89	2009	2012+
2003	81	2005	2008
2002	86	2003	2004+
2001	81	2002	2003+
2000	83	2002	2005
1999	92	2004	2007
1998	93	2003	2006+
1997	93	2002	2005+
1996	87	1998	2001
1995	88	2000	2003

HAND PICKED RIESLING

RATING 5

Adelaide Hills $12–$19
Current vintage: 2006 88

Long and limey, this fresh and brightly fruited young riesling has a floral aroma of pear and apple. Its tangy palate of intense flavour finishes crisp and clean, with persistent citrusy fruit and acidity.

2006	88	2011	2014
2005	90	2010	2013
2004	88	2006	2009
2003	86	2004	2005
2002	82	2003	2004+
2001	87	2003	2006+
2000	82	2002	2005
1999	88	2001	2004+
1998	85	2003	2006
1997	86	1999	2002

RSW SHIRAZ

RATING 3

McLaren Vale $50–$99
Current vintage: 2005 88

Handsomely oaked, with assertive mocha, dark chocolate and vanilla influences beneath its slightly currant-like expression of dark, plummy fruit, it's initially very smooth and approachable. Ripe and minty, with dark berry flavours framed by powdery tannins, it finishes with some overt oak, a hint of spirity hotness and a slightly gritty extract.

2005	88	2010	2013+
2004	94	2012	2016+
2003	93	2011	2015+
2002	94	2010	2014+
2001	91	2006	2009
2000	87	2002	2005+
1999	87	2004	2007
1998	94	2003	2006+
1997	90	2002	2005
1996	96	2004	2008
1995	92	2000	2003
1994	94	1999	2002
1993	91	1998	2001
1992	93	2000	2004

SCRUBBY RISE (Sauvignon Blanc Semillon Viognier)

Various SA $12–$19
Current vintage: 2006 82

Slightly sweet, perhaps lacking some length and freshness, this rather disjointed, herbal and viognier-dominant blend has a spicy spectrum of flavour suggestive of gooseberries, apricots and passionfruit.

2006	82	2007	2008
2005	87	2005	2006
2004	86	2004	2005
2003	86	2004	2005
2002	87	2003	2004
2001	86	2001	2002
2000	80	2000	2001
1999	80	1999	2000
1998	87	2000	2003

THE 12TH MAN CHARDONNAY

RATING 4

Adelaide Hills $20–$29
Current vintage: 2006 88

A fresh, forward and generous chardonnay whose youthful and brassy expression of peach and nectarine flavours are backed by slightly awkward, smoky and meaty oak, with undertones of sweetcorn, barley sugar and butter. Smooth and savoury, it's moderately generous, and despite some lively acidity, tends to lack brightness towards the finish.

2006	88	2008	2011
2005	91	2007	2010+
2004	91	2006	2009
2002	86	2004	2007
2000	81	2001	2002
1999	87	2001	2004
1998	88	2000	2003
1997	89	1999	2002

THE ANGELUS CABERNET SAUVIGNON

RATING 3

McLaren Vale $50–$99
Current vintage: 2005 86

Rather oaky and simple, with a confectionary expression of red berries and plums whose creamy texture thins out towards the finish. Backed by suggestions of mint and menthol, it lacks the richness of fruit typically delivered by this label.

2005	86	2007	2010+
2004	94	2016	2024
2003	90	2011	2015
2002	93	2014	2022
2001	87	2006	2009
2000	90	2005	2008
1999	88	2004	2007
1998	95	2006	2010+
1997	86	2002	2005
1996	95	2004	2008+
1995	91	2003	2007
1994	88	1999	2002
1993	93	2001	2005
1992	93	2000	2004

WOODHENGE SHIRAZ

RATING **5**

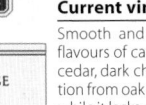

McLaren Vale	$20–$29
Current vintage: 2005	**88**

Smooth and easy-drinking, with sweet, juicy flavours of cassis, blackberries and plums and a cedar, dark chocolate and vanilla-like contribution from oak cooperage. It's spicy and lively, and while it lacks great length, it's relatively seamless and approachable.

2005	88	2007	2010
2004	91	2009	2012
2003	88	2008	2011+
2002	88	2007	2010
2001	87	2003	2006
2000	82	2002	2005
1999	85	2001	2004+

Wolf Blass

Sturt Highway, Nuriootpa SA 5355. Tel: (08) 8568 7303. Fax: (08) 8568 7380.
Website: www.wolfblass.com.au Email: cellardoor@wolfblass.com.au
Regions: **Langhorne Creek, Barossa Valley, Various SA** Winemakers: **Caroline Dunn, Chris Hatcher, Kirsten Glaetzer, Wendy Stuckey** Viticulturist: **Stuart McNab** Chief Executive: **Jamie Odell**

The modern Wolf Blass brand is a well-ordered hierarchy of labels, atop of which are perched the Black Label and Platinum Label Shirazes. The current releases of these wines are from 2003 and 2004 respectively, and even while the Black Label has for this vintage returned in a large way to its traditional hunting ground of Langhorne Creek, their quality does not quite equate with their recent vintages. In fact, the recent unusually hot and dry seasons have taken their toll across this entire range.

BLACK LABEL

RATING **3**

Various, SA	$100–$199
Current vintage: 2003	**89**

Dark and meaty, with concentrated flavours of dark plums, cassis and blueberries, it's rather hammered by very assertive and slightly soupy vanilla, smoked oyster, chocolate and mocha-like oak. Backed by nuances of eucalypt, mint and menthol, it's an old-fashioned blockbuster style whose fruit tends to be rather too dehydrated, raisined and currant-like for genuine brightness and intensity. It finishes a little hard and angular, with a hint of saltiness.

2003	89	2011	2015
2002	97	2022	2032+
2001	92	2009	2013
2000	88	2005	2008+
1999	89	2007	2011
1998	94	2010	2018+
1997	86	2002	2005
1996	92	2008	2016
1995	93	2007	2015+
1994	89	2000	2003
1993	81	1998	2001
1992	90	2000	2004+
1991	93	2003	2011+
1990	93	2002	2010+
1989	88	1997	2001+
1988	90	1993	1996+
1987	87	1995	1999+
1986	93	1999	2006+

GOLD LABEL CHARDONNAY

RATING **3**

Adelaide Hills	$20–$29
Current vintage: 2006	**87**

Heavily worked for its depth of fruit, with funky, slightly candied aromas of grapefruit, peach and melon backed by greenish undertones. Generous and sweet fruited, its handsomely oaked palate of juicy melon, peach and grapefruit flavours lacks a little length and focus, drying out fractionally dusty and raw, with nutty, creamy artefact-like notes.

2006	87	2007	2008
2005	91	2007	2010
2004	94	2006	2009
2003	93	2005	2008
2002	94	2004	2007+

GOLD LABEL RIESLING

RATING 3

Clare Valley, Eden Valley			$12–$19
Current vintage: 2006			**89**

Vibrant musky aromas of lavender and lime juice with earthy undertones of wet slate precede a moderately long, generous and juicy palate that is rather finer and less structured than most vintages of this wine. Drink it soon, while it retains its brightness and refreshing acidity.

2006	89	2007	2008+
2005	87	2007	2010
2004	93	2006	2009
2003	92	2005	2006
2002	94	2007	2010
2001	95	2006	2009+
2000	90	2002	2005
1999	90	2001	2004
1998	94	2003	2006
1997	91	2002	2005
1996	94	2004	2008

GOLD LABEL SHIRAZ VIOGNIER

RATING 4

Adelaide Hills			$20–$29
Current vintage: 2005			**85**

A firm, gritty red with meaty, evolved and rather baked aromas of currants, raisins and cedar/dark chocolate oak. Very savoury and meaty, its initial expression of punchy fruit dries out towards a lean and rather blocky finish that lacks charm and fruitiness.

2005	85	2007	2010
2004	93	2009	2012+
2003	88	2005	2008+
2002	90	2004	2007

GREY LABEL CABERNET SAUVIGNON

RATING 3

Langhorne Creek			$30–$49
Current vintage: 2005			**88**

Stylish, finely crafted, but very steeped in regional peppermint character, this smooth, elegant and intensely flavoured cabernet bursts with fresh cassis, dark plum and dark berry flavour. Handsomely backed by dark chocolate/mocha oak, its juicy palate is framed by firm, powdery tannin, finishing with tightness and length of bright fruit.

2005	88	2010	2013
2004	93	2016	2024+
2003	93	2011	2015+
2002	88	2010	2014
2001	90	2006	2009
1999	87	2004	2007
1997	84	1999	2002
1996	90	2001	2004+
1995	93	2002	2007
1994	94	2002	2006
1993	89	2001	2005
1992	93	2000	2004
1991	94	1999	2003
1990	91	1995	1998

GREY LABEL SHIRAZ (formerly Brown Label)

RATING 3

McLaren Vale			$30–$49
Current vintage: 2005			**88**

Some classy winemaking has married sweet, toasty vanilla oak and smooth tannin with well-ripened, generous and juicy dark-fruited shiraz, whose flavours of plums, blackberries and cassis just lack genuine impact and presence on the palate. Like so many 2005 reds, it lacks the essential fruit quality for a higher rating.

2005	88	2007	2010
2004	93	2016	2024
2003	92	2008	2011+
2002	94	2010	2014+
2001	88	2003	2006
2000	86	2002	2005
1999	88	2001	2004
1998	89	2006	2010
1997	88	2002	2005
1996	91	2004	2008
1995	87	2000	2003
1994	92	2002	2006
1993	89	1998	2001
1992	90	2000	2004
1990	92	1998	2002

PLATINUM LABEL SHIRAZ

Various, SA $100–$199
Current vintage: 2004   89

Smoky, ground coffee aromas of cassis, prunes and plums reveal spirity undertones of smoked oyster oak and suggestions of tea tin. Densely laden with thick, dripping, meaty plum-like fruit, its sumptuously concentrated palate dries out towards the finish, exposing some raw tannins and alcohol. Unlikely to cellar well, it's more of an exaggerated and awkward caricature-like shiraz that despite plenty of depth and richness, simply lacks finesse and balance.

2004	89	2009	2012+
2003	95	2015	2023
2002	96	2009	2013+
2001	97	2013	2021+
2000	95	2008	2012
1999	95	2011	2019+
1998	96	2010	2018+

RED LABEL SHIRAZ CABERNET SAUVIGNON

Various $5–$11
Current vintage: 2005   81

The hot vintage also caught up with this little red, delivering a jammy and rather soupy blend of sweet red berries, plums and vanilla oak. Lacking length and genuine brightness, its cooked fruit is supported by rather slippery and awkward oak.

2005	81	2006	2007+
2004	86	2006	2009
2003	80	2004	2005+
2002	89	2004	2007
2001	86	2003	2006
1999	82	2000	2001
1998	81	2002	2003
1997	87	1999	2002
1996	82	1997	1998

YELLOW LABEL CABERNET SAUVIGNON

South Australia $12–$19
Current vintage: 2005   82

Meaty, rather simple and cooked flavours of earthy red plums and currants provide some initial impact and smoothness, but dry out towards the finish. Lacks real presence of fruit.

2005	82	2006	2007+
2004	82	2006	2009
2003	88	2005	2008
2002	88	2005	2008+
2001	87	2003	2006
2000	88	2002	2005+
1998	89	2003	2006
1997	81	1999	2002
1996	88	1998	2001
1995	87	2000	2003

YELLOW LABEL RIESLING

Various, SA $5–$11
Current vintage: 2006   87

Crisp, fresh and early-maturing, with lightly toasty and floral qualities over juicy lime, apple and lemon-like fruit. There's a bathpowder and confection-like aspect, but there's also pleasing length, shape and dryness. A pleasant little early-drinking quaff.

2006	87	2008	2011
2005	82	2006	2007+
2004	87	2004	2005
2003	82	2003	2004
2002	83	2003	2004
2001	92	2005	2008
2000	87	2001	2002
1999	86	2000	2001
1998	92	2000	2003
1997	87	1999	2002

Woodlands

Lot 1 Caves Road, Willyabrup WA 6280. Tel: (08) 9755 6226. Fax: (08) 9755 6236.
Website: www.woodlandswines.com Email: mail@woodlandswines.com

Region: **Margaret River** Winemaker: **Stuart Watson** Viticulturist: **Nick Clark** Chief Executive: **David Watson**

Established in 1973, Woodlands might not be terribly well known, but it was among the first wave of plantings in Margaret River. Developed by David and Heather Watson, it is undergoing a renaissance in the hands of their son Stuart, whose first vintage at the winery was 2002. While the 2006 reds lack their customary intensity thanks to the cool and cloudy vintage, the 2005s are simply breathtaking.

BARREL RESERVE CABERNET FRANC

RATING 3

| Margaret River | $50–$99 |
| Current vintage: 2006 | 86 |

Supple and sappy, this rather herbaceous and green-edged cabernet franc packs plenty of varietal raspberry, redcurrant fruit and clove/cinnamon spiciness, but falls a little short and sour-edged for a higher rating. Some well-handled oak contributes sweetness and smoothness.

2006	86	2008	2011+
2005	95	2013	2017
2004	90	2009	2012
2003	93	2011	2015+
2002	87	2007	2010+

BARREL RESERVE MALBEC

RATING 3

| Margaret River | $50–$99 |
| Current vintage: 2006 | 93 |

Elegant and refined, smooth and supple, this rather lean and lightly herbal malbec should build in the bottle. Its estery aromas of fresh cherries, cranberries and sweet vanilla oak precede a brightly lit but fractionally sappy and hollow palate whose flavours of black and red cherries are tightly knit with dusty vanilla oak. Could develop great shape and character.

2006	93	2011	2014+
2005	95	2017	2025
2004	95	2016	2024
2003	91	2008	2011+
2002	90	2007	2010+

CABERNET MERLOT

RATING 3

| Margaret River | $12–$19 |
| Current vintage: 2005 | 91 |

A brambly fragrance of sweet blackberries and plums reveals slightly gamey undertones of ripe cherry-like merlot and cedary oak. Full to medium in weight, it's supple and silky, with a deeply flavoured palate of juicy, briary berry and plum flavours backed by cedar/vanilla oak and framed by smooth and dusty tannins.

2005	91	2010	2013
2004	93	2009	2012+
2003	92	2011	2015+
2002	82	2007	2010+

CABERNET SAUVIGNON

RATING 2

| Margaret River | $50–$99 |
| Current vintage: 2005 | 96 |

Perched somewhere between Worlds Old and New, this is a pristine, stylish and profoundly structured cabernet. Scented with violets, dried herbs and undergrowth, its deep presence of cassis, dark cherry, blackberry and dark plum flavour is tightly knit with polished dark and lightly smoky chocolate/cedar oak and framed by gravelly, firm and loose-knit tannin. Long and seamless, it's an exercise in restrained power, finishing with a lingering core of vibrant fruit.

2005	96	2017	2025+
2004	97	2016	2024+
2003	96	2015	2023
2002	95	2014	2022
2001	87	2006	2009

MARGARET RESERVE CABERNET MERLOT

RATING **3**

Margaret River	$30–$49
Current vintage: 2005	97

A brilliantly elegant, fine and stylish cabernet blend with a structure and texture more akin to a fine Pauillac. Its slightly meaty aromas of liqueur cherries, cassis, earthy minerals and cedar/vanilla oak have almost a pinot-like musky, heady quality. Smooth and seamless, it's long and luscious, with a lavish array of dark berries, plums and cherries backed by lightly smoky cedar/dark chocolate oak and framed by fine-grained and chalky tannins. Long, plump and savoury, with wonderful smoked meat-like complexity, it's simply a cracker.

2005	97	2017	2025+
2004	97	2016	2024
2003	90	2011	2015
2002	87	2007	2010+
2001	88	2009	2012

Woodside Valley Estate

Abbey Farm Road, Yallingup WA 6282. Tel: (08) 9345 4065. Fax: (08) 9345 4541.
Website: www.woodsidevalleyestate.com.au Email: mail@woodsidevalleyestate.com.au
Region: **Margaret River** Winemaker: **Kevin McKay** Viticulturist: **Jim Campbell-Claues**
Chief Executive: **Peter Woods**

Woodside Valley Estate is a relatively new Margaret River development that is very serious about the making of high-quality varietal wines from cabernet sauvignon, shiraz, merlot and chardonnay. To date, its best wine is the Baudin Cabernet Sauvignon. Releases of the Bissy Merlot and the Bonnefoy Shiraz have tended to be excessively herbaceous.

BAUDIN CABERNET SAUVIGNON

RATING **3**

Margaret River	$50–$99
Current vintage: 2004	91

A leathery and slightly rustic cabernet whose complex, slightly herbal and dusty bouquet of small black and red berries overlies new cedar/mocha oak and suggestions of tobacco. Fine, smooth and supple, its long and elegant palate reveals tightly focused varietal fruit and fresh new oak, even if it's just a fraction warm and spirity. There's a measure of herbal influence, plus a very minor suggestion of barnyard and horse hair.

2004	91	2012	2016
2003	95	2015	2023
2002	89	2007	2010
2001	95	2009	2013

LE BAS CHARDONNAY

RATING **5**

Margaret River	$30–$49
Current vintage: 2005	88

Oaky aromas of vanilla, lemon, cloves and cinnamon slightly obscure an underlying bouquet of grapefruit and light grilled nuts. Restrained and reserved, with a pleasing length of fruit given obvious extended sur-lie contact, it's long, nutty and savoury, finishing with pleasing acidity but rather a surfeit of oak.

2005	88	2007	2010
2004	94	2006	2009+
2003	84	2005	2008+

Woodstock

Douglas Gully Road, McLaren Flat SA 5171. Tel: (08) 8383 0156. Fax: (08) 8383 0437.
Website: www.woodstockwine.com.au Email: woodstock@woodstockwine.com.au
Regions: **McLaren Vale, Limestone Coast, Langhorne Creek** Winemaker: **Ben Glaetzer**
Viticulturist: **Scott Collett** Chief Executive: **Scott Collett**

Woodstock's wines are mainly but not exclusively based in McLaren Vale and are made by one of South Australia's busiest contract winemakers, Ben Glaetzer. Its ripe and juicy styles of red tended towards the meaty and treacle-like in 2005, which was largely a function of the vintage heat. With the help of some pretty smart oak, the flagship The Stocks has still managed to deliver a handsomely crafted, smooth and pliant Shiraz.

BOTRYTIS SWEET WHITE

RATING **3**

Various	$20–$29 (375 ml)	2005	88	2007	2010
Current vintage: 2005	**88**	2004	94	2006	2009+
		2003	94	2005	2008+
Slightly cooked and candied, this generous,		1999	87	2001	2004
luscious and early-drinking dessert wine doesn't		97/98	81	2000	2003
complement its juicy citrus fruit with much in the		1996	92	2001	2004
way of genuine botrytis influence. Backed by plenty		1995	93	2000	2003
of sweet toasty/vanilla oak, it's uncomplicated, sweet		1994	91	2002	2006
and flavoursome, with a clean finish of soft		1993	90	1995	1998
acidity.					

CABERNET SAUVIGNON

RATING **4**

McLaren Vale	$20–$29	2005	89	2010	2013
Current vintage: 2005	**89**	2004	90	2009	2012+
		2002	91	2010	2014+
Ripe, luscious and slightly treacle-like, with juicy		2001	86	2006	2009
flavours of blackcurrant, dark plums and raspberries		2000	81	2002	2005
knit with sweet, rather toasty chocolate oak.		1999	84	2001	2004+
Backed by suggestions of mint and menthol, it's		1998	86	2003	2006
smooth and luscious, finishing with lingering choc-		1997	89	2005	2009
mint flavours and pliant, fine-grained tannin.		1996	87	2001	2004
		1995	87	2000	2003
		1994	93	2002	2006
		1993	91	2001	2005
		1992	93	2004	2012
		1991	95	2003	2011

SHIRAZ

RATING **4**

Limestone Coast, Langhorne Creek,		2005	87	2007	2010
McLaren Vale	$20–$29	2004	91	2012	2016
Current vintage: 2005	**87**	2002	91	2007	2010+
		2001	86	2003	2006+
Smoothed over by sweet, lightly toasty vanilla oak,		2000	90	2005	2008
this polished and well made shiraz does however		1999	83	2001	2004
reveal both under and over-ripe influences in the		1998	92	2006	2010
form of meatiness and some herbal, greenish under-		1997	90	2002	2005+
tones. It's framed by fine, polished tannins and		1996	92	2004	2008
is great for the short term.		1995	86	2000	2003
		1994	88	1999	2002
		1993	93	2001	2005

THE STOCKS

RATING **3**

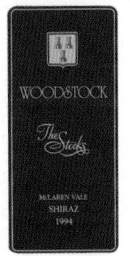

McLaren Vale	$30–$49	2005	91	2010	2013+
Current vintage: 2005	**91**	2004	96	2016	2024
		2002	93	2010	2014
Modern, oaky and opulent, with deep, dark plum,		2001	90	2003	2006+
blackberry, mulberry and cassis-like fruit hand-		2000	89	2002	2005+
somely backed by suggestions of dark olives and		1999	89	2001	2004+
roasted, barrel-matured elements of mocha,		1998	96	2010	2018
chocolate and vanilla. It's long and firm, with a		1997	87	1999	2002
smooth, creamy palate of slightly subdued fruit		1996	95	2004	2008
framed by fine, drying tannins and finished with		1995	92	2003	2007
a fresh cut of acidity.		1994	95	2002	2006
		1993	93	2001	2005
		1991	89	1999	2003

Wyndham Estate

Dalwood Road, Dalwood NSW 2335. Tel: (02) 4938 3444. Fax: (02) 4938 3555.
Website: www.wyndhamestate.com.au

Regions: **Various, Lower Hunter Valley** Winemakers: **Sam Kurtz, Tony Hooper, Andrew Miller**
Viticulturist: **Stephen Guilbaud-Oulton** Chief Executive: **Laurent Lacassgne**

While its popular Bin series wines remains unchanged, Wyndham Estate was recently reinvented with the release of the George Wyndham range, which features a collection of shiraz-based wines blended across a number of regions. As a group, they represent easy drinking and excellent value. I'm saddened by the loss of the wines under the Show Reserve label.

BIN 222 CHARDONNAY

RATING **5**

Various	$12–$19	2005	87	2005	2006+
Current vintage: 2005	**87**	2004	88	2005	2006
		2003	88	2004	2005+
A clean, crisp and shapely chardonnay whose		2002	89	2003	2004+
peachy, lightly tropical and buttery fruit and fresh		2001	88	2003	2006
cashew/vanilla oak combine in a juicy and mod-		2000	79	2001	2002
erately intense palate that finishes refreshingly long and creamy.					

BIN 555 SHIRAZ

Various	$12–$19	2004	85	2006	2009
Current vintage: 2004	**85**	2003	87	2005	2008+
		2002	86	2004	2007
Medium to full in weight, with vibrant flavours		2001	87	2003	2006
of blackcurrant, raspberries, blackberries and		2000	82	2001	2002
sweet but slightly sawdusty vanilla/coconut oak		1999	86	2001	2004+
framed by supple tannin, this lightly peppery young		1998	82	2000	2003
shiraz reveals a hint of dried herb and earthiness		1997	88	1999	2002
before finishing with fresh acids.		1996	86	1998	2001
		1995	86	2000	2003

Wynns Coonawarra Estate

Memorial Drive, Coonawarra SA 5263. Tel: (08) 8736 3266. Fax: (08) 8736 3202.
Website: www.wynns.com.au

Region: **Coonawarra** Winemaker: **Sue Hodder** Viticulturist: **Suzanne McLoughlin** Chief Executive: **Jamie Odell**

The renaissance continues. Without a shard of doubt in my mind, Wynns has returned to the winning circle. Years of effort in the vineyard are now being translated to the wines themselves, as Sue Hodder's team is able to work with better fruit, seemingly vintage by vintage. The flagship John Riddoch and Michael reds from 2004 are both close to their all-time high water marks, while the under-sold black label Cabernet Sauvignon could justify twice or more the price being asked by its proprietors.

CABERNET SAUVIGNON

RATING **3**

Coonawarra	$20–$29	2005	95	2017	2025+
Current vintage: 2005	**95**	2004	93	2016	2024
		2003	92	2015	2023
A fine, elegant Coonawarra cabernet whose ripe,		2002	93	2014	2022+
floral perfume of cassis, blackberries, dark choco-		2001	90	2013	2021
lates and cedar/vanilla oak has a faintly confiture-		2000	87	2008	2012
like aspect. Fully ripened but smooth and supple,		1999	94	2011	2019+
its long, fleshy and spotlessly presented palate of		1998	91	2010	2018+
vibrant small black berries, mulberries and plums		1997	90	2005	2009+
knits tightly with vanilla/cedar oak. Full to medium		1996	96	2016	2026+
in weight, framed by firm, pliant tannins, it's a wine		1995	91	2007	2015
of style and stature.		1994	95	2014	2024+
		1993	87	2001	2005
		1992	82	2000	2004
		1991	96	2011	2021
		1990	94	2010	2020
		1989	87	1994	1997
		1988	88	1996	2000
		1987	86	1996	1999+
		1986	90	1998	2006

CABERNET SHIRAZ MERLOT

Coonawarra	$12–$19
Current vintage: 2005	**90**

Complete, elegant and fine-grained, this is a stylish and well-priced wine with pleasing balance and integrity. Restrained aromas of dark berries, plums and cherries overlie dusty scents of cloves and white pepper and a restrained background of cedar/vanilla oak. Long and neatly balanced, its smooth, polished palate of juicy dark plum and blackberry and blueberry fruit is sweet-centred and knit with fine grainy tannins.

2005	90	2013	2017
2003	86	2008	2011
2002	87	2004	2007
2000	82	2002	2005
1999	82	2001	2004
1998	85	2000	2003
1997	83	1999	2002
1996	88	2004	2010
1995	90	2000	2003
1994	89	1999	2002

CHARDONNAY

Coonawarra	$12–$19
Current vintage: 2006	**87**

Soft, fresh and fruit-driven, this lively young chardonnay marries delicate citrus, peach, cashew and melon flavour with restrained butter/vanilla oak, before a soft and refreshing finish.

2006	87	2008	2011
2005	90	2007	2010
2004	88	2005	2006+
2003	88	2005	2008
2002	84	2002	2004+
2001	88	2003	2006
2000	82	2001	2002
1999	87	2001	2004
1998	89	2000	2003
1997	88	1999	2002

JOHN RIDDOCH CABERNET SAUVIGNON

Coonawarra	$50–$99
Current vintage: 2004	**96**

A traditional Coonawarra classic. Its heady perfume of fresh cassis, violets, mulberries and cedar/vanilla oak reveals a suggestion of undergrowth. Smooth, polished and seamless, its supremely elegant and deeply layered palate of pristine small berry flavour and tightly knit oak builds on the palate, in harmony with its effortlessly restrained but finely crafted undercarriage of fine, powdery tannin. Beneath its fruit lies some slightly minty and dusty herbal varietal cabernet complexity. Superb focus and balance; set for the long term.

2004	96	2016	2024
2003	94	2015	2023+
1999	95	2019	2029
1998	95	2010	2018+
1997	89	2005	2009
1996	95	2016	2026
1994	95	2006	2014
1993	94	2001	2005
1992	93	2004	2012
1991	94	2003	2011
1990	96	2010	2020
1988	91	2000	2005
1987	93	1999	2004
1986	94	1998	2006
1985	90	1993	1997
1984	89	1992	1996
1982	96	1994	2002+

MICHAEL SHIRAZ

Coonawarra	$50–$99
Current vintage: 2004	**96**

A superbly measured, beautifully integrated and stylish shiraz steeped in intense and perfectly focused fruit. Delicate, ethereal and musky, its dusty and peppery bouquet of spicy small black and red berries is tightly knit with fine-grained cedar/vanilla oak. There's a meaty varietal quality about its exceptionally long palate of intense sweet berry and plum fruit, which is framed by a firm but pliant spine of polished tannin. It builds weight and power along the palate, finishing with wonderful restraint and savoury qualities.

2004	96	2016	2024+
2003	95	2015	2023
1999	89	2007	2011
1998	95	2010	2018
1997	87	2002	2005
1996	94	2008	2016
1994	96	2006	2014
1993	95	2005	2013
1991	95	2003	2011
1990	94	2002	2010
1955	97	1975	1985

RIESLING

Coonawarra	$12–$19
Current vintage: 2006	**88**

Every now and again, Coonawarra spins out a eye-catching riesling that develops well in the bottle. Wynns has achieved this with its refreshing and uncomplicated 2006 release. Its fresh aromas of lime juice and green apple are lifted by a floral aspect, while its long, lean and shapely palate of apple, pear and limey fruit finishes crisp and lively. It's underpinned by an appealing chalkiness and will develop for around five years.

2006	88	2011	2014
2005	87	2010	2013+
2004	90	2006	2009+
2002	90	2007	2010
2001	90	2006	2009
2000	90	2005	2008
1999	86	2001	2004
1998	90	2003	2006
1997	86	2002	2005
1996	90	2001	2004
1995	85	1997	2000
1994	91	1999	2002

SHIRAZ

Coonawarra	$12–$19
Current vintage: 2005	**90**

A typically vibrant young Coonawarra shiraz of elegance and charm. Scented with violets and white pepper, its vibrant aromas of spicy redcurrant, musky and sweet cedar/vanilla oak overlie some gamey complexity. Smooth and polished, it bursts with intense berry and plum flavour, with a pleasing underswell of lightly toasty and creamy oak. Framed by pliant, loose-knit tannin, it finishes with plenty of length and freshness.

2005	90	2010	2013+
2004	89	2009	2012
2003	88	2008	2011
2002	91	2004	2007+
2001	86	2003	2006
2000	87	2002	2005
1999	89	2004	2007
1998	89	2003	2006
1997	88	2002	2005
1996	84	1998	2001
1995	89	2000	2003
1994	87	1996	1999
1993	88	1998	2001
1992	91	2000	2004
1991	89	1996	1999

Yabby Lake

112 Tuerong Road, Tuerong Vic 3933. Tel: (03) 9251 5375. Fax: (03) 9639 1540.
Website: www.yabbylake.com Email: info@yabbylake.com
Region: **Mornington Peninsula** Winemakers: **Tod Dexter, Larry McKenna**
Viticulturist: **Keith Harris** Chief Executives: **Robert & Mem Kirby**

Yabby Lake is a new and highly feted entrant to the Mornington Peninsula's crowded wine industry. The early wines were made by Larry McKenna, while Tod Dexter recently joined the business (which also cooperates closely with Heathcote Estate) as Group Winemaker. While the Pinot Noirs have shown promise, the Chardonnay is settling into an earlier-maturing but sumptuously flavoured and complex style.

CHARDONNAY

Mornington Peninsula	$30–$49
Current vintage: 2005	**93**

A stylish, winemaker-driven chardonnay whose controlled measure of artefact does complement its fruit and depth. It's complex, funky and nutty, with restrained peach/melon fruit over sweet clove-like vanilla oak, lanolin and suggestions of dried flowers. Smooth and savoury, it marries a sumptuous expression of peach/melon flavour with creamy vanilla oak. It's already quite buttery, which suggests a relatively short cellaring life.

2005	93	2007	2010+
2004	93	2006	2009
2003	89	2005	2008
2002	82	2003	2004+

PINOT NOIR

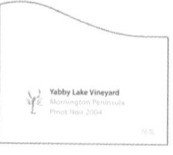

Mornington Peninsula	$30–$49
Current vintage: 2005	**89**

Musky, rather spicy and meaty aromas of plums, kirsch and marzipan overlie suggestions of cloves and animal hide. Smooth, sumptuous and velvet-like, its lingering, mouthfilling palate of dark cherry, plum and blackberry flavours are supported by firmish, fine and powdery tannins, but finishes with a distinctly cooked aspect. Very well handled in the cellar, but made from slightly stewy fruit.

2005	89	2007	2010
2004	87	2006	2009
2003	90	2005	2008+
2002	89	2004	2007

Yalumba

Eden Valley Road, Angaston SA 5353. Tel: (08) 8561 3200. Fax: (08) 8561 3393.
Website: www.yalumba.com Email: info@yalumba.com

Regions: **Barossa, Coonawarra, Eden Valley, Adelaide Hills** Winemakers: **Louisa Rose, Peter Gambetta, Kevin Glastonbury, Phillip Lehmann, Andrew LaNauze** Viticulturist: **Robin Nettelbeck**
Chief Executive: **Robert Hill Smith**

The historic Yalumba winery is the centrepiece of a series of vineyard holdings which extends across several States and regions. Within all this sits the Yalumba label, a Barossa brand (which incorporates the Eden Valley sub-region), with the exception of The Menzies, from Coonawarra and the multi-regional D sparkling wine. Today Yalumba represents some first-class riesling and viognier, some excellent quaffing reds and whites under a regional banner, some eclectic Hand-Picked red wines and the elegant and oaky extremes of Barossa red. Its best current wine has the deep and meaningful name of FDW7C Chardonnay (?!), vintage 2005.

BAROSSA SHIRAZ

RATING **5**

Barossa Valley	$12–$19
Current vintage: 2004	87

A sumptuous and slightly soupy shiraz with slightly dehydrated and menthol-like aromas of baked, currant-like fruits, blackberries, plums and mocha-like oak. Thick and heavy, its dark, plummy palate is framed by a raw extract of firm tannin. While it lacks a little cut and polish today, it should improve significantly over the next few years..

2004	87	2006	2009+
2002	88	2004	2007+
2001	87	2003	2006
2000	87	2002	2005
1999	87	2001	2004+
1998	87	2000	2003
1997	90	2002	2005
1996	86	1998	2001
1995	89	1997	2000

BAROSSA SHIRAZ VIOGNIER

RATING **4**

Barossa Valley, Eden Valley	$30–$49
Current vintage: 2004	89

A vibrant and savoury quaffer whose spicy, rather peppery and meaty bouquet of dark plums, blackberries and apricot blossom reveals gamey, cinnamon-like undertones. Smooth and juicy, long and even, its brightly lit small berry fruit and firmish, pliant tannin extend well down the palate, finishing with refreshing acidity.

2004	89	2006	2009+
2003	93	2008	2011
2002	91	2007	2010
2000	88	2002	2005
1999	88	2004	2007
1998	87	2000	2003+

BUSH VINE GRENACHE

RATING **5**

Barossa Valley	$12–$19
Current vintage: 2006	83

An honest, simple and early-drinking grenache whose stewy, rather meaty bouquet of dark plums and blackberries reveals undertones of currants. Framed by modest tannins, forward and juicy, its smooth, soft expression of redcurrants, plums and currants then finishes rather thin.

2006	83	2007	2008
2005	90	2007	2010+
2002	89	2004	2007+
2001	89	2003	2006+
2000	88	2002	2005
1999	86	2001	2004+
1998	89	2003	2006
1997	90	2002	2005
1996	87	1998	2001

'D' CUVÉE

RATING **4**

Tasmania, Victoria, South Australia	$30–$49
Current vintage: 2002	91

Attractive and refreshing, with a creamy fragrance of citrus fruit, dried flowers and lemon sherbet over nutty and bakery-like undertones. Long and tangy, it's fine and elegant, with a clean, creamy and citrusy palate finishing with bread-like nuances and a hint of greenish and tropical fruit.

2002	91	2004	2007+
2001	90	2003	2006+
1999	95	2004	2007
1998	89	2003	2006
1997	90	1999	2002
1996	93	2001	2004
1995	90	2000	2003
1994	94	1999	2002

EDEN VALLEY VIOGNIER

Eden Valley $12–$19
Current vintage: 2006 87

Spicy aromas of apricot blossom, cloves, cinnamon and nutmeg reveal a faint spikiness, but also a fine mineral quality. Juicy and generous, rich and forward, it's slightly candied but becomes more savoury down the palate. Underpinned by chalky phenolics and finished with soft acids, it's a faithful expression of this variety.

Year	Score	Drink	Drink
2006	87	2007	2008+
2005	88	2006	2007
2004	90	2005	2006
2003	90	2004	2005+
2002	89	2003	2004+
2001	88	2003	2006
2000	88	2001	2002
1999	86	2000	2001
1998	90	1999	2000

HAND PICKED EDEN VALLEY RIESLING

Eden Valley $20–$29
Current vintage: 2004 95

A supple, fine and beautifully presented young riesling scented with a delicate, lightly toasty and honeyed perfume of dried flowers, blossom, rosewater, honeysuckle and lime juice. Pristine, smooth and supple, its long and effortless palate is utterly charming, with ripe, restrained and juicy fruit wrapped in clean, bright acids and finishing with seamless length.

Year	Score	Drink	Drink
2004	95	2009	2012+
2003	83	2005	2006+
2002	94	2007	2010
2001	95	2009	2013+
2000	94	2008	2012

THE MENZIES CABERNET SAUVIGNON

Coonawarra $20–$29
Current vintage: 2003 87

Lacking complete ripeness, this well-handled cabernet matches its jammy aromas of cassis, mulberries and herbaceous undertones with sweet vanilla oak. Initially forward and juicy, its vibrant flavours of raspberries and blackcurrants become more green-edged towards its slightly sappy finish.

Year	Score	Drink	Drink
2003	87	2008	2011
2002	87	2010	2014
2001	87	2009	2013
2000	86	2005	2008
1999	89	2004	2007+
1998	88	2003	2006
1997	87	2002	2005
1996	94	2004	2008+
1995	87	2000	2003
1994	87	2006	2014
1993	89	2001	2005
1992	93	2002	2004

THE OCTAVIUS SHIRAZ

Barossa Valley $50–$99
Current vintage: 2003 87

A very ripe, treacle-like and rather cooked shiraz whose baked and slightly dehydrated expression of currants, prunes and blackberries delivers plenty of concentration but insufficient genuine fruit sweetness. While oak is integral to the Octavius style, here it becomes excessively assertive and exaggerated, delivering powerful, smoky, mocha and ashtray-like character to nose and palate. The wine finishes very firm but slightly soupy.

Year	Score	Drink	Drink
2003	87	2008	2011+
2002	96	2014	2022
2001	92	2009	2013+
2000	89	2008	2012
1999	93	2011	2019
1998	95	2006	2010
1997	87	2002	2005
1996	89	2004	2008
1995	93	2003	2007
1994	95	2002	2006+
1993	91	1998	2001
1992	95	2000	2004
1990	95	2002	2010

THE RESERVE (Cabernet Sauvignon & Shiraz) RATING 5

YALUMBA

Barossa Valley, Eden Valley   **$50–$99**
Current vintage: 2001   **90**

Still a little raw and sinewy, this firm and slightly gritty red blend should evolve considerably further. A floral, meaty and cassis-like bouquet reveals undertones of currants, prunes and baked earth, while its palate already has plenty of leathery development, finishing with suggestions of baked plums, cherry kernels, mint and menthol.

2001	90	2013	2021
1998	86	2003	2006+
1996	87	2001	2004+
1992	87	2000	2004
1990	94	2002	2010+

THE SIGNATURE (Cabernet Sauvignon & Shiraz)   RATING 2

YALUMBA

Barossa Valley   **$30–$49**
Current vintage: 2003   **91**

Ripe and juicy, sumptuous and assertive, this richly fruited, handsomely oaked but carefully balanced red blend is constructed around slightly baked but not overcooked fruit. Its meaty, mocha-like bouquet of cassis, blackberries, blueberries, plums and cedar/vanilla oak precedes a smoky, firm and powdery palate packed with flavours of dark fruits and dark olives. It's long, grippy and needs time.

2003	91	2015	2023
2002	95	2014	2022
2001	86	2006	2009
2000	89	2008	2012
1999	94	2011	2019
1998	95	2010	2018+
1997	89	2005	2009
1996	95	2008	2016
1995	90	2003	2007
1994	94	2006	2014
1993	93	2001	2005
1992	95	2004	2012
1991	94	2003	2011
1990	94	2002	2010
1989	93	1994	1997

THE VIRGILIUS VIOGNIER   RATING 3

YALUMBA

Eden Valley   **$30–$49**
Current vintage: 2005   **93**

Pungent, wild, very reductive and rubbery aromas blow away to reveal spicy, honeysuckle-like scents of apricot-like fruit with undertones of wheatmeal. It's long, smooth and unctuous, delivering a seamless and almost silky expression of juicy flavour that culminates in a savoury, smoky finish. Likely to flesh out nicely.

2005	93	2007	2010+
2004	95	2006	2009+
2003	93	2005	2008
2002	90	2003	2004+
2001	91	2003	2006+
2000	87	2002	2005

TRICENTENARY VINES GRENACHE   RATING 5

Barossa Valley   **$30–$49**
Current vintage: 2003   **92**

Firm and savoury, with pleasingly deep red fruit flavours, this spicy, perfumed and floral grenache avoids the exaggerated varietal characters of so many from this region. Scented with flowers, cloves and cinnamon, red plums and cherries, it's fresh and juicy, with a generous but medium-bodied palate of vibrant spicy fruit framed by firmish tannins.

2003	92	2008	2011
2002	88	2004	2007
2001	87	2003	2006+
2000	89	2005	2008
1999	86	2001	2004

2008   **THE AUSTRALIAN WINE ANNUAL**   **303**
www.jeremyoliver.com

Yarra Burn

60 Settlement Road, Yarra Junction Vic 3797. Tel: (03) 5967 1428. Fax: (03) 5967 1146.
Website: www.yarraburn.com.au Email: cellardoor@yarraburn.com.au
Region: **Yarra Valley** Winemakers: **Mark O'Callaghan, Ed Carr** (sparkling) Viticulturist: **Ray Guerin**
Chief Executive: **John Grant**

Yarra Burn is The Hardy Wine Company's Yarra Valley brand, and it has access to some of the region's largest vineyards. Why, then, it needs to incorporate fruit from Heathcote and the Pyrenees in its Shiraz is totally beyond me. Furthermore, Hardy's has launched a mid-priced multi-regional brand under the Yarra Burn name called Third Light, whose wines will be sourced from the Heathcote and the Pyrenees. And the Yarra Valley as well! I remain convinced that if a wine brand includes a region's name, it should come exclusively from that region.

BASTARD HILL CHARDONNAY   RATING 2

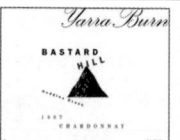

Yarra Valley $30–$49
Current vintage: 2004   95

An intense, smooth and mineral chardonnay of considerable class. Bright aromas of melon and grapefruit are backed by smoky, toasty undertones of grilled nuts plus creamy leesy nuances. Its long, vibrant palate bursts with juicy, crystalline melon and citrus flavour over a wet slate-like texture and reductive complexity. It's clean, crisp, delightfully balanced and precisely honed.

2004	95	2009	2012+
2000	93	2005	2008+
1999	95	2004	2007
1998	96	2003	2006
1997	90	2002	2004
1996	87	1997	1998
1994	91	1996	1999

CABERNET SAUVIGNON   RATING 3

Yarra Valley $20–$29
Current vintage: 2003   87

Both meaty and herbal, this plummy and cedary cabernet has an earthy, leathery bouquet of small dark berries with greenish undertones. Simple, forward and sappy to finish, it's an honest but uncomplicated wine whose plum and blackberry fruit reveal under-and over-ripe characters.

2003	87	2008	2011
2002	89	2007	2010+
2001	92	2009	2013+
2000	90	2008	2012
1999	95	2011	2019
1998	93	2006	2010
1997	89	2002	2005
1995	94	2003	2007
1994	89	1999	2002
1993	89	1998	2001
1992	94	2000	2004

CHARDONNAY   RATING 4

Yarra Valley $20–$29
Current vintage: 2006   89

Scented with orange blossom, lemon rind and sweet matchstick-like oak, this fresh, early-drinking chardonnay marries flavours of peach, melon and cumquat with restrained creamy vanilla barrel-matured influences. It's forward and juicy, finishing with zesty acids.

2006	89	2007	2008+
2005	88	2007	2010
2003	92	2005	2008+
2002	87	2003	2004+
2001	90	2003	2006+
2000	91	2005	2008
1999	91	2001	2004
1998	87	1999	2000
1997	93	2002	2005
1996	90	2001	2004

PINOT NOIR   RATING 5

Yarra Valley $20–$29
Current vintage: 2006   92

A charming, pristine young pinot whose vibrant flavours of red cherries and dark plums are lifted by a scent of rose petals and toasty vanilla oak. Supple and sappy, it's smooth and polished, with a velvet-like spine of genuine structure beneath its lingering palate of bright fruit and meaty undertones. It needs time to flesh out and for its oak to ease back.

2006	92	2008	2011+
2005	86	2006	2007+
2004	86	2006	2009
2002	82	2004	2007
2001	89	2003	2006
2000	87	2002	2005
1999	82	2001	2004
1998	87	2003	2006
1997	92	2002	2005
1994	75	1999	2002

Yarra Valley	$20–$29
Current vintage: 2004	90

A crisp, pretty young wine whose lightly mineral aromas of lemon, pineapple and banana reveal a light yeast-derived creaminess. Fine and elegant, it's long, clean and refreshing, with tangy flavours of melon, grapefruit and peach over a light, meaty background. It finishes crisp and quite dry.

2004	90	2006	2009
2002	85	2004	2007
2001	92	2006	2009
2000	88	2002	2005
1999	88	2001	2004
1998	93	2000	2003
1997	95	1999	2002+
1996	85	1998	2001

Yarra Ridge

Racecourse Vineyard, Yarra Glen Vic 3775. Tel: 1800 186 456. Website: www.yarraridge.com.au
Region: **Yarra Valley** Winemaker: **Shavaughn Wells** Viticulturist: **Damien de Castella**
Chief Executive: **Jamie Odell**

Yarra Ridge is intended as an early-drinking range of Yarra Valley wine obtainable for a relatively light investment. Its wines, to be frank, are under-performing in a big way right now. And, for a few extra cents, you could be drinking much better wine under the St Huberts or Coldstream Hills labels (from the same Foster's stable), which have been better grown, made and are likely to have a little more age. Yarra Ridge needs to improve.

CHARDONNAY RATING 5

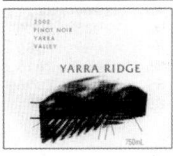

Yarra Valley	$12–$19
Current vintage: 2004	89

Fresh aromas of peaches and grilled nuts, with a background of wheatmeal, precede a soft, elegant and restrained palate whose generous stonefruit and melon flavours finish with some assertive vanilla oak. Should flesh out over the short term.

2004	89	2005	2006+
2003	87	2004	2005+
2001	90	2002	2003+
2000	87	2001	2002
1999	86	1999	2000
1998	87	1999	2000
1997	89	1998	1999

PINOT NOIR RATING 5

Yarra Valley	$12–$19
Current vintage: 2005	81

Rather dull, with faintly meaty, earthy and floral aromas lacking in freshness and perfume. Simple and confectionary, skinny and hollow, the palate needs more depth and fruit.

2005	81	2006	2007
2004	89	2006	2009
2003	87	2005	2008
2002	88	2004	2007
2001	82	2003	2006
2000	89	2002	2005
1999	85	2000	2001
1998	84	2000	2003

Yarra Yarra

239 Hunts Lane, Steels Creek Vic 3775. Tel: (03) 5965 2380. Fax: (03) 5965 2086.
Website: www.yarrayarravineyard.com.au Email: wine@yarrayarravineyard.com.au
Region: **Yarra Valley** Winemaker: **Ian Maclean** Viticulturist: **Ian Maclean** Chief Executives: **Ian & Anne Maclean**

Yarra Yarra is a small and dedicated maker of finely crafted Yarra Valley table wines from the Bordeaux varieties in particular. Its forte is at present its various wines based on cabernet sauvignon, especially the reserve level Yarra Yarra blend, but the 2005 Syrah Viognier might suggest otherwise in future. Ian Maclean also fashions one of Australia's finest oak-matured blends of sauvignon blanc and semillon.

CABERNETS RATING 3

Yarra Valley	$50–$99
Current vintage: 2004	89

Moderately firm and astringent, this rather meaty and herbal Yarra Valley cabernet combines intense flavours of plums, black and red berries with smooth, creamy and cedary oak. It's full to medium in weight, with plenty of juiciness and generosity, but it becomes rather raw and slightly metallic towards the green-edged finish. There's some delightful intensity and forest floor-like complexity, but it is angular and unbalanced enough to be slightly nervous about.

2004	89	2009	2012
2003	93	2011	2015
2002	88	2007	2010
2000	93	2012	2020
1999	93	2007	2011
1998	90	2003	2006
1997	91	2005	2009+
1996	87	1998	2001+
1995	92	2003	2007+
1994	93	2002	2006+
1993	90	2003	2007
1992	91	2003	2007
1991	95	1999	2003+
1990	95	2002	2010+

SAUVIGNON BLANC SEMILLON

Yarra Valley	$30–$49
Current vintage: 2004	**94**

Long and seamless, this carefully oaked white Bordeaux blend has a lightly herbal fragrance of fresh lemon, gooseberries and melon with a floral, mineral and lightly toasted, dusty vanilla oak background. Its generous, creamy palate of mouth-filling lemon/melon fruit is tightly knit with oak, finishing long and seamless, with lemony acids. Significantly more fruit-driven than herbaceous, it just lacks the acid definition for an even higher score.

2004	94	2006	2009+
2003	88	2005	2008
2002	94	2004	2007
2001	88	2003	2006
2000	83	2002	2005
1999	95	2004	2007+
1998	88	2003	2006
1997	94	2002	2005
1996	92	2001	2004
1995	95	2003	2007
1994	87	1999	2002

SYRAH VIOGNIER (with Viognier since 2003)

Yarra Valley	$30–$49
Current vintage: 2005	**96**

Clonakilla has some genuine competition! This ripe, complex and spicy red has a musky, meaty bouquet of wild, briary dark fruits over pungent hints of polished leather, heady spices and deep scents of apricot blossom. Steeped in dark cherries and plums, it's powerful and assertive but smooth and pliant, with undertones of minerals and briar. Framed by pliant, but powdery tannins, it finishes long and savoury, with just a hint of ultra-ripeness.

2005	96	2013	2017
2004	88	2009	2012+
2003	90	2008	2011+
2002	87	2007	2010
2001	92	2009	2013

THE YARRA YARRA (formerly Reserve Cabernet Sauvignon)

Yarra Valley	$50–$99
Current vintage: 2004	**96**

A plush, polished and luxuriant cabernet blend of excellent structure and seamless length. Its penetrative, deeply layered perfume of brambly blackberry, plum and blackcurrant-like fruit knits tightly with scents of cedar, violets, dark chocolate and a lightly herbal, undergrowth-like background. Sumptuous and aristocratic, its powerful and handsomely oaked palate of dark plum and berry fruit is framed by firm, pliant and powdery tannin.

2004	96	2016	2024+
2003	97	2015	2023+
2002	93	2014	2022
2001	88	2013	2021
2000	96	2012	2020
1999	95	2007	2011+
1998	92	2003	2006
1997	96	2002	2005+
1995	95	2007	2015
1994	89	2002	2006+
1993	89	1998	2001

Yarra Yering

Briarty Road, Gruyere via Coldstream, Vic 3770. Tel: (03) 5964 9267. Fax: (03) 5964 9239.
Website: www.yarrayering.com Email: info@yarrayering.com
Region: **Yarra Valley** Winemaker: **Mark Haisma** Chief Executives: **Dr Bailey Carrodus, Mark Haisma**
Yarra Yering is one of the wineries that began the rebirth of the Yarra Valley as a wine region in the early 1970s. Under the guidance of its founder, Dr Bailey Carrodus, Mark Haisma has excelled as a winemaker, simultaneously and dramatically working to increase the size of the vineyard holdings and improve the standard of its wine, two tasks that certainly do not necessarily go hand in hand. Yarra Yering is again an international benchmark, across a wide range of wines. Incidentally, I am totally captivated by the 2005 Portsorts, a genuinely Portuguese-fashioned vintage port style made with the full spectrum of genuine port varieties.

DRY RED NO. 1 (Cabernet Blend)

Yarra Valley	$50–$99
Current vintage: 2005	**96**

A very fine, elegant and tightly focused cabernet blend whose floral perfume reveals heady scents of small black berries backed by fresh vanilla/cedary oak and undertones of dried herbs. Long and finely crafted, its very refined palate of vibrant cassis, mulberry and plum-like fruit overlies a finely ground and almost chalky extract. Carefully balanced, with lingering dark fruit and nuances of dried herbs.

2005	96	2017	2025
2004	91	2012	2016
2003	89	2008	2011+
2002	86	2004	2007
2001	96	2013	2021
1998	91	2006	2010
1997	92	2009	2017
1996	87	2001	2004
1995	80	2000	2003
1994	93	2006	2014
1993	94	2001	2005
1992	91	2000	2004
1991	95	1999	2003
1990	97	2010	2020+

DRY RED NO. 2 (Shiraz Viognier blend)

RATING 2

Yarra Valley $50–$99
Current vintage: 2005 95

An opulent and hedonistic shiraz-viognier blend whose slightly gamey bouquet of fully-ripened blackberries, dark plums and sweet chocolate/vanilla oak is lifted by a spicy, floral perfume. Smooth and silky, it's richly endowed with sumptuous, succulent fruit, extending long towards a drying finish. Reflecting the meaty, spicy flavours of a warm year, it's also underpinned by fine, dusty, powdery tannins.

2005	95	2013	2017+
2004	97	2016	2024
2003	95	2011	2015
2001	96	2013	2021
1996	81	2001	2004
1994	89	1999	2002+
1993	93	1998	2001
1992	94	1997	2000
1991	93	1996	1999
1990	95	2010	2020+
1989	90	2011	2019
1988	88	1990	1993
1987	85	1992	1995
1986	95	2006	2016

MERLOT

RATING 3

Yarra Valley $100–$199
Current vintage: 2005 94

A ripe, generous and deeply fruited merlot whose delicate, floral and dark-fruited aromas of mulberries, dark cherries and plums knit neatly with sweet cedar/vanilla oak. Framed by rather kernel-like tannin, its sumptuous expression of dark berry/cherry flavour and dusty, newish oak culminates in a persistent, meaty finish of refreshing acidity. It's all about restrained power.

2005	94	2013	2017
2004	93	2009	2012
2003	89	2005	2008+
2001	94	2009	2013
1994	95	2002	2006
1993	94	1998	2001
1992	91	1997	2000
1990	90	1996	1998

PINOT NOIR

RATING 2

Yarra Valley $50–$99
Current vintage: 2005 95

Very measured and polished, this floral and faintly peppery young pinot has a spicy bouquet of sweet red cherries and rose petals over a light stalkiness and a whiff of spearmint. Fine and supple, it bursts with bright, pristine flavours of small berries, cherries and dark plums, finishing long and slightly meaty. Its juicy palate is neatly offset by a well-integrated chassis of fine, sandpapery tannin and gamey oak.

2005	95	2010	2013+
2004	95	2009	2012
2003	93	2008	2011+
2001	95	2006	2009
1996	86	2001	2004
1995	87	2000	2003
1994	90	1999	2002
1993	82	1998	2001
1992	95	2000	2004
1991	95	1999	2003

UNDERHILL SHIRAZ

RATING 2

Yarra Valley $50–$99
Current vintage: 2005 94

Long, trim and elegant, this typically fine, supple and peppery shiraz delivers an intense, almost opulent perfume of juicy mulberry and blackcurrant fruit backed by nuances of crushed leaves, white pepper and herbal, forest floor-like suggestions. Its plump, ripe and rather succulent palate is backed by an almost fragile extract of fine tannin, finishing long and dry with lingering flavours of dark fruits, licorice and spice.

2005	94	2013	2017
2004	90	2009	2012
2003	96	2011	2015
2001	97	2013	2021
1999	96	2007	2011
1997	94	2005	2009+
1996	87	2001	2004
1995	90	2000	2003+
1994	89	1999	2002
1993	89	1998	2001
1992	96	1997	2000

Yarrabank

38 Melba Highway, Yering Vic 3775. Tel: (03) 9730 1107. Fax: (03) 9739 0135. Website: www.yering.com
Regions: **Various, Victoria** Winemakers: **Michael Parisot, Tom Carson** Viticulturist: **John Evans**
Chief Executives: **Doug Rathbone, Laurent Gillet**
From the small house of Devaux, Champagne winemaker Michael Parisot collaborates with Tom Carson of Yering Station in the making of this blend from different Victorian cool-climate regions. Typically, the wines are elegant and creamy, with genuine evolution of complexity, richness and texture.

YARRABANK CUVÉE

RATING

Various, Victoria	$30–$49
Current vintage: 2003	**92**

Fine and stylish, this long and tightly focused sparkling wine has a toasty, buttery bouquet of floral, slightly meaty, nutty and lanolin-like character. Long and dry, its meaty, slightly earthy and austere palate of slightly candied fruit is likely to develop more power and richness with age. Very much a Devaux-like style.

2003	92	2008	2011+
2002	89	2007	2010
2000	91	2005	2008
1999	95	2004	2007
1998	89	2000	2003+
1997	88	2002	2005
1996	89	2001	2004
1995	96	2003	2007
1994	89	1996	1999+
1993	94	1998	2001+

Yering Station

38 Melba Highway, Yering Vic 3775. Tel: (03) 9730 0100. Fax: (03) 9739 0135.
Website: www.yering.com Email: info@yering.com
Region: **Yarra Valley** Winemaker: **Tom Carson** Viticulturist: **John Evans** Chief Executive: **Gordon Gebbie**
Yering Station is one of the most impressive new facilities in the Yarra Valley and it has set its sights unquestionably high. As time goes on, it's becoming more clear that the company's best wine, and by some margin, is its Reserve Chardonnay, a typically seamless, savoury and generously proportioned wine that ages very slowly indeed. The other Reserve level wines are invariable of good quality, while the 'standard' label does tend to struggle from time to time, especially with Cabernet Sauvignon and Pinot Noir.

CHARDONNAY

RATING

Yarra Valley	$20–$29
Current vintage: 2006	**90**

Long, vibrant and rather polished, this supple, elegant and fruit-driven chardonnay backs its lively flavours or white peach and melon skin with lightly smoky vanilla oak and creamy complexity. Delightfully intense, it finishes with refreshing acidity and a lingering core of fruit.

2006	90	2008	2011
2005	90	2007	2010
2004	89	2006	2009
2002	87	2003	2004
2001	87	2003	2006
2000	84	2001	2002
1999	87	2000	2001
1998	93	2000	2003+
1997	90	1999	2002
1996	80	1997	1998

PINOT NOIR

RATING

Yarra Valley	$20–$29
Current vintage: 2005	**87**

Rather advanced and meaty, this smoky, rather rustic and horsey pinot's aromas of cherries and plums are lifted by sweet vanilla/mocha oak. Forward and leathery, with generous but developed earthy, leathery qualities, its smooth palate is rimmed by slightly hard-edged tannins.

2005	87	2007	2010
2004	88	2006	2009
2003	86	2004	2005
2002	86	2004	2007
2001	88	2002	2003
2000	80	2002	2005
1999	83	2000	2001
1998	89	2000	2003
1997	87	1998	1999

RESERVE CHARDONNAY

RATING 2

Yarra Valley $50–$99
Current vintage: 2003   95

Perfumed and fragrant, with scents of lemon zest, dried flowers, white peach and creamy, nutty leesy influences backed by fresh, toasty matchstick-like oak. Concentrated and tangy, its intense flavours of grapefruit, lime, melon and mango knit tightly with sweet buttery, vanilla oak, finishing long and clean, with refreshing citrusy acids and suggestions of oatmeal. Should be excellent once the oak eases back.

2003	95	2010	2013+
2002	95	2007	2010+
2001	95	2006	2009
1999	95	2004	2007+
1997	95	2002	2005

RESERVE PINOT NOIR

RATING 4

Yarra Valley $50–$99
Current vintage: 2005   92

A relatively delicate and fine-grained young pinot whose presently restrained expression of raspberry, cherry and plum-like fruit is slightly overawed by its assertive, rather sweet and gluey new oak influences and firm tannins. Fragrant and floral, with a lingering core of vibrant fruit, it is likely to build weight and depth in the bottle, becoming quite powerful as it does.

2005	92	2010	2013
2003	89	2005	2008+
2002	88	2004	2007+
2000	90	2002	2005+
1998	87	2000	2003+
1997	93	2002	2005

RESERVE SHIRAZ VIOGNIER

RATING 3

Yarra Valley $50–$99
Current vintage: 2005   92

Scented with ethereal, musky suggestions of violets and white pepper backed by blueberries and cassis, blackberries and polished cedar/vanilla oak, this restrained and cultivated blend of medium to full weight is framed by dusty, drying tannins. Its layers of intense dark berry/plum fruit show just a hit of jamminess and spirity warmth, before finishing long and slightly mineral. Fractionally over-ripe.

2005	92	2010	2013+
2003	93	2008	2011
2002	96	2007	2010+
2001	93	2006	2009+
1998	90	2003	2006+
1997	95	2005	2009

SHIRAZ VIOGNIER

RATING 3

Yarra Valley $20–$29
Current vintage: 2005   89

Earthy, floral and apricot-like viognier-driven aromas lift scents of fresh blackberries, cassis and raspberries, with a sweet background of vanilla/mocha oak. Medium to full in weight, its plump, juicy palate is underpinned by a powdery chassis of pliant tannins, finishing savoury and Rhôney, with measured oak and brightness. It's well enough balanced, but perhaps the viognier was fractionally overdone.

2005	89	2007	2010+
2004	91	2009	2012
2003	92	2005	2008+
2002	94	2007	2010
2001	92	2003	2006+
2000	86	2002	2005
1999	81	2000	2001

Yeringberg

Maroondah Highway, Yeringberg, Coldstream Vic 3770. Tel: (03) 9739 1453. Fax: (03) 9739 0048.
Region: **Yarra Valley** Winemakers: **Guill & Sandra De Pury** Viticulturist: **David De Pury**
Chief Executive: **Guill De Pury**

Yeringberg makes small volumes of fastidiously grown wine in the cellars beneath its historic 19th century winery. This year the estate Yeringberg cabernet blend has reached what I believe to be an all-time high for this wine of 14.5% alcohol by volume. While it carries it easily enough in its bounteous youth, a concern does lurk in the corner of my mind over whether or not this will still be the case in twenty-plus years time, the age at which most fine expressions of this wine are coming into their peak. Other than this, the current releases are basically flawless.

CHARDONNAY

RATING 2

Yarra Valley　　　　　　　$30–$49
Current vintage: 2006　　　　　　95

Beautifully measured and controlled, this elegant young chardonnay exudes finesse and balance. Backed by faint undertones of butter and sweet vanilla oak, it reveals nutty, floral perfume of white peach and pear before a smooth and fluffy but surprisingly sumptuous and substantial palate. Pristine flavours of pear and citrus fruits knit tightly with fresh oak, undertones of cashew, neatly punctuated by fresh acidity.

2006	95	2011	2014+
2005	96	2010	2013+
2004	94	2009	2012
2003	93	2008	2011
2002	94	2007	2010
2001	93	2006	2009+
2000	95	2005	2008+
1999	89	2004	2007
1998	95	2003	2006
1997	94	2005	2009
1996	94	2004	2008
1995	92	2003	2007

MARSANNE ROUSSANNE

RATING 2

Yarra Valley　　　　　　　$30–$49
Current vintage: 2006　　　　　　93

Brightly focused, long and mineral, this juicy, crystalline white blend has a floral, lemony aroma of nectarine-like fruit and a generous palate of tangy, vibrant fruit. It finishes smooth and generous, with tight acids and definition.

2006	93	2011	2014
2005	94	2010	2013+
2004	94	2009	2012
2003	94	2008	2011+
2002	90	2007	2010+
2001	93	2009	2013
2000	93	2008	2012
1999	93	2007	2011
1998	93	2003	2006
1997	94	2005	2009
1996	91	2004	2008
1995	88	2003	2007
1994	94	2002	2006

PINOT NOIR

RATING 2

Yarra Valley　　　　　　　$50–$99
Current vintage: 2005　　　　　　95

Supremely smooth and elegant, this beautifully focused, charmingly crafted and willowy pinot has a musky, heady perfume of rose petals, sweet red cherries, raspberries and fresh vanilla oak backed by spicy nuances of cloves and cinnamon. Beneath its supple and almost fragile but entirely mouthfilling palate of cherry/berry flavour lies a genuine spine of silky suppleness. It should build quite dramatically with time in the bottle.

2005	95	2010	2013+
2004	95	2009	2012+
2003	92	2008	2011
2002	94	2007	2010+
2001	90	2003	2006
2000	92	2005	2008
1999	89	2004	2007
1998	82	2000	2003
1997	96	2005	2009
1996	94	2004	2008
1995	90	2000	2003
1994	92	2002	2006
1993	91	1995	1998

YERINGBERG (Cabernet Blend)

RATING 2

Yarra Valley $50–$99
Current vintage: 2005 94

A smooth, sumptuous and seamless Yarra Valley cabernet blend that appears to handle with ease its comparatively high level of 14.5% alcohol. With a sweet, pristine fragrance of violets and small berries, it's firm and finely balanced. Deep, dark berry/cherry and plum-like fruit knits tightly with sweet vanilla, cedary and dark chocolate oak, while it's underpinned by fine-grained and supple tannins.

2005	94	2017	2025
2004	93	2012	2016
2003	90	2011	2015
2002	89	2010	2014
2001	96	2013	2021
2000	94	2012	2020+
1999	92	2007	2011
1998	95	2010	2018
1997	95	2005	2009+
1996	93	2004	2008
1995	88	2003	2007
1994	94	2006	2014
1993	91	2001	2005
1992	95	2012	2022
1991	93	2003	2011
1990	95	2002	2010+
1989	86	1994	1997
1988	95	2000	2008+

Zema Estate

Riddoch Highway, Coonawarra SA 5263. Tel: (08) 8736 3219. Fax: (08) 8736 3280.
Website: www.zema.com.au Email: zemaestate@zema.com.au

Region: **Coonawarra** Winemaker: **Greg Clayfield** Viticulturist: **Nick Zema** Chief Executive: **Demetrio Zema**

Zema Estate is a small, family-owned winery whose growth in size and stature has been measured and even, despite a slight and hopefully temporary drop in the quality of its 'standard' reds thanks to some challenging vintages. Zema recently appointed well-known Coonawarra winemaker Greg Clayfield to look after production, and have also opened a dramatic extension of their winery complex. The Zema story is one of hard work and deserved success by an unassuming family.

CABERNET SAUVIGNON

RATING 5

Coonawarra $20–$29
Current vintage: 2005 88

Slightly awkward and disjointed, with sweet blackberry, plum and berry fruit backed by lightly smoky vanilla oak, this medium to full-bodied cabernet should find more harmony with a little time. Its meaty and herbaceous undertones suggest slightly uneven ripening, while its tannins are presently slightly raw-edged.

2005	88	2010	2013+
2004	93	2016	2024
2003	89	2011	2015+
2002	84	2010	2014
2001	86	2009	2013
2000	87	2008	2012
1999	87	2007	2011
1998	89	2006	2010+
1997	84	2005	2009
1996	80	2001	2004
1995	81	2000	2003
1994	84	2002	2006+
1993	83	2001	2005
1992	87	2004	2012+
1991	89	2003	2011
1990	86	1995	1998

CLUNY (blend of red Bordeaux varieties)

RATING 5

Coonawarra $20–$29
Current vintage: 2004 94

A supple, finely balanced and elegant blend whose violet-like fragrance of fresh black and red berries and restrained cedar/vanilla oak are lifted by a light mintiness. Smooth and fine-grained, its surprisingly plush palate of pristine fresh berries, cherries and dark plums knits tightly with fine oak. It finishes long and smooth, with a lingering reminder of its fine texture and structure.

2004	94	2016	2024
2003	89	2011	2015
2002	82	2004	2007+
2001	82	2003	2006+
2000	87	2005	2008
1999	89	2007	2011+
1998	93	2010	2018
1997	80	1999	2002
1996	89	2004	2008+
1995	83	2000	2003+
1994	90	2002	2006+

FAMILY SELECTION CABERNET SAUVIGNON

RATING **3**

Coonawarra		$30–$49	
Current vintage: 2004		95	

Measured, elegant and stylish, with deeply layered flavours of cassis, blackberries, dark cherries and mulberries tightly knit with polished cedar/vanilla oak and fine, silky tannin. Full to medium in weight, with a dusty, cedary and violet-like perfume backed by suggestions of dried herbs, it builds surprising strength on the palate, finishing long and persistent.

2004	95	2016	2024+
2002	87	2010	2014
2001	93	2013	2021+
2000	88	2005	2008+
1999	91	2011	2019
1998	93	2010	2018
1996	90	2006	2016
1994	86	1999	2002
1993	81	1998	2001
1992	82	2000	2004
1991	92	2003	2011+
1988	88	2000	2008

FAMILY SELECTION SHIRAZ

RATING **5**

Coonawarra		$30–$49	
Current vintage: 2004		87	

Slightly porty and raisined, this meaty, musky and dark-flavoured shiraz marries deep, but rather cooked, raisin-like and dehydrated fruit with assertive oak and firmish, moderately structured tannins. It's well made, thick and generous, but lacks great length and richness of fruit.

2004	87	2009	2012+
2002	89	2010	2014
2001	87	2009	2013
2000	88	2008	2012+

MERLOT

RATING **5**

Coonawarra		$20–$29	
Current vintage: 2004		91	

An elegant and fine-grained merlot with richness and plumpness of sweet berry, cherry and plum-like fruit. Its fresh, floral aromas of dark cherries, mulberries and cassis overlie restrained and lightly toasty cedar/vanilla oak. Medium to full in weight, it's supple and juicy, with a lingering choco-latey finish. It should develop well.

2004	91	2009	2012+
2001	87	2009	2013
2000	88	2005	2008+

SHIRAZ

RATING **4**

Coonawarra		$20–$29	
Current vintage: 2005		87	

Full to medium weight, with meaty, dark-fruited aromas of blackberries, currants and raisins with a spicy, Christmas cake-like quality. Forward and smooth, backed by polished oak, its moderately luscious palate of blackberry and plum-like fruit just lacks a little freshness and brightness.

2005	87	2010	2013
2004	95	2016	2024
2003	86	2005	2008+
2002	88	2007	2010
2001	91	2013	2021
2000	87	2005	2008
1999	90	2011	2019
1998	96	2010	2018+
1997	86	2002	2005
1996	90	2008	2016
1995	80	1997	2000+
1994	88	2002	2006+
1993	90	2005	2013
1992	89	2004	2012
1991	87	1999	2003+
1990	89	2002	2010
1989	81	1994	1997
1988	88	1996	2000+
1987	94	1992	1997+
1986	90	1998	2006

Index